AI Education Strategies for Future-Proofing Curriculum Design

Reda Mohamed Said Abdelaal
https://orcid.org/0000-0001-8806-2115
Helwan University, Egypt

Mustafa Kayyali
https://orcid.org/0000-0003-3300-262X
Maaref University of Applied Sciences, Syria

IGI Global
Scientific Publishing
Publishing Tomorrow's Research Today

Published in the United States of America by
IGI Global Scientific Publishing
701 East Chocolate Avenue
Hershey, PA, 17033, USA
Tel: 717-533-8845 | Fax: 717-533-7115
Website: https://www.igi-global.com E-mail: cust@igi-global.com

Library of Congress Cataloging-in-Publication Data

Names: Abdelaal, Reda Mohamed Said, 1956- editor | Kayyali, Mustafa, 1990- editor
Title: AI education strategies for future-proofing curriculum design / Edited by Reda Mohamed Said Abdelaal, Mustafa Kayyali.
Description: Hershey, PA : IGI Global Scientific Publishing, [2026] | Includes bibliographical references and index. | Summary: "This book aims to provide a comprehensive framework for integrating artificial intelligence (AI) into educational curricula, ensuring that higher education institutions remain responsive to technological advancements and workforce demands"-- Provided by publisher.
Identifiers: LCCN 2025012549 (print) | LCCN 2025012550 (ebook) | ISBN 9798337327525 hardback | ISBN 9798337327532 paperback | ISBN 9798337327549 ebook
Subjects: LCSH: Artificial intelligence--Educational applications | Education, Higher--Effect of technological innovations on | Universities and colleges--Curricula
Classification: LCC LB1028.43 .A393 2026 (print) | LCC LB1028.43 (ebook)
LC record available at https://lccn.loc.gov/2025012549
LC ebook record available at https://lccn.loc.gov/2025012550

British Cataloguing in Publication Data
A Cataloguing in Publication record for this book is available from the British Library.

Editorial Advisory Board

Table of Contents

Detailed Table of Contents

changing digital landscape. Various AI tools, such as adaptive learning systems, intelligent tutoring platforms, and predictive analytics, highlighting their ability to cater to different student's requirements and enhance academic achievement. This chapter explores the effective integration of AI technologies into higher education programs to facilitate the creation of personalized learning pathways.

The rapid advancement of artificial intelligence (AI) is reshaping the global economy and prompting an urgent call for educational reform to prepare students for an AI-augmented workforce. Among the most pressing concerns is the potential for AI-driven job displacement, underscoring the need for curricula that foster not only technical proficiency but also future-proof skills. This chapter explores a comprehensive framework for aligning higher education with the demands of the global AI economy across four strategic domains: 1) curriculum renovation to embed AI literacy and workforce readiness; 2) transdisciplinary teaching to bridge disciplinary boundaries and foster innovative problem-solving; 3) tangible assessment strategies to capture applied skills and interdisciplinary competencies; and 4) global integration to promote equitable access and cross-border collaboration. The chapter provides a roadmap for reimagining curriculum design that equips students to thrive in an interconnected, ethically complex, and AI-driven world.

Higher education institutions benefit from AI since this technology transforms traditional teaching systems by delivering customized learning options and adaptive educational content. AI software platforms review performance records to create personalized content which generates immediate feedback and individualized learning routes. Educational programs adjust their contents automatically according to student development to produce improved individual outcomes and active student participation. The successful implementation of AI in education depends on solving the problems related to personal data protection and algorithm system faults and faculty training requirements. The combination of artificial intelligence in education produces flexible learning models as well as better student results and instruction focused on individual learners. AI's evolution will enhance its use for curriculum improvement alongside skill identification and virtual learning simulations to transform education by making it more effective and adaptable to future needs.

This chapter examines the potential of Artificial Intelligence (AI) to revolutionize Cambodian higher education by tackling existing issues and capitalizing on possibilities to develop a future-oriented curriculum. It analyzes the principles of AI technology, international trends in AI education, and the higher education framework in Cambodia, encompassing systemic constraints in funding, quality, and infrastructure. The chapter advocates for strategic initiatives like curriculum reform, faculty development, student participation via AI tools, and collaborations with international institutions and technology firms. This chapter underscores the significance of supportive policies and governance, advocating for the incorporation of AI to improve educational outcomes, foster innovation, and equip Cambodian students for a rapidly evolving, AI-centric future.

The integration of artificial intelligence (AI) in Omani higher education is essential for enhancing learning experiences, improving institutional efficiency, and aligning with Oman Vision 2040. This study proposes an AI Integration Framework, outlining key elements such as strategic alignment, policy governance, technological infrastructure, curriculum development, and ethical AI implementation. It emphasizes AI-driven decision-making, public-private partnerships, and continuous evaluation to ensure sustainable adoption. By fostering AI research and innovation, Oman can position its universities as hubs for technological advancement, equipping students with the necessary skills for a digital future while ensuring ethical and culturally relevant AI implementation.

The evolution from standardized instruction to AI-driven personalization reflects a growing demand for inclusive, flexible, and learner-centered education. Grounded in key concepts such as differentiation, individualization, and personalization, the discussion explores how AI technologies—adaptive learning platforms, real-time analytics, and intelligent tutoring systems—enable dynamic and tailored instruction that meets diverse learner needs. AI integration not only enhances engagement and equity but also supports meaningful curriculum redesign aligned with 21st-century competencies. Emphasizing innovative pedagogies and ethical implementation, the chapter highlights the strategic role of educators in guiding this transformation. The insights presented contribute to future-proofing curriculum design by aligning technological innovation with holistic student development and sustainable educational outcomes.

Over the past several years, education software has advanced greatly. Students receive tailored courses depending on their learning styles using such technologies. Next, this approach is applied to e-learning systems and a framework for designing and using a knowledge and learner adaptive system is presented. There are great potential to employ AI to give students with individualized learning experiences. This study expect tutoring methods to supplement and even replace expert human instruction for more topics by integrating adaptive material and intelligent tutoring technologies. Therefore, the purpose of adaptive content and intelligent tutoring systems research is to deliver high-quality tailored education to students globally and

The Artificial Intelligence (AI) has become a usual component of educational research. This chapter examines the use of AI tools (ChatGPT, ResearchRabbit, Scholarcy, Scite, etc.) in literature reviews, data analysis and academic writing. It uses Technological Pedagogical Content Knowledge (TPACK) framework that focuses on the importance of balance between the content, pedagogy and technology and the Activity Theory that analyses the influence of AI on the relationships between researchers, tools, and systems within the institutions. As real-world applications suggest, AI may help people perform the task quicker and yield more profound insights, but there are still the problems of academic integrity, digital access, and overreliance to tackle. The chapter demands the literacy of AI and the responsible use in such a way that research becomes relevant and universal. Ultimately, AI is to be considered as an assistant and not as a substitute of academic reasoning.

Taking Uganda as an example, the present study seeks to explain how students use attribution theory combined with game and prospect theories to rationalize the misuse of AI in SSA, where the social valuation of online learning processes is at times low. Moral decadence and consumerist tendencies have been on the increase in many parts of SSA, and many examples in Uganda attest to this fact. Further, resource constraints in many academic institutions both private and public, harden the academic environment in SSA. Amid such a terrain, students may seek unethical short cuts in the pursuit of knowledge, such as misuse of AI and then justify their actions based on the happenings in their societies. The collective cultural context in which people subscribe to group norms and values contributes to the rationalization of AI misuse; hence this PRISMA based study, also examines how cultural factors interact to rationalize AI misuse in the academia in SSA. The study advances recommendations that will help to mitigate AI misuse in this region.

This chapter presents the issue of applying virtue ethics to AI-powered education systems, with the main idea deriving that artificial intelligence should promote not only the intellectual but also the moral development. It suggests a virtue-based model based on the postulates of Aristotle about eudaimonia that develops intellectual virtues (i.e., curiosity, critical thinking, perseverance) along with the moral virtues of social responsibility, empathy, and fairness. The chapter shows, through theoretical consideration, how AI can aid ethical interaction, train moral dilemmas, and develop civic-mindedness. It apprehensively discusses the dilemma of value misalignment, biases intensification, and monitoring, promoting the co-development of humans and AI, ethical leadership, and design culture. It ends the chapter with several policy-reforming and design suggestions to guarantee that AI in education does not make students into merely competent citizens, but caring, socially robust ones.

AI's rapid growth is changing education as we know it across the globe. Once a science fiction concept, AI technologies are transforming the methods with which information is created, shared, and consumed. As we advance into the Fourth Industrial Revolution, it is evident that AI is not only enhancing the education sector; it is revolutionizing it, forcing educators, policymakers, and curricular developers to rethink the objectives and frameworks of formal schooling systems. Education powered by AI is no longer a figment of the imagination; it is a practical requirement in an age characterized by digital integration, omnipresent data, and the need for adaptable skills. The development of AI driven solutions from learning and tutoring systems to automated grading and content generation systems highlights the critical need for curriculum futurism, which suggests an alignment of pedagogy to technological advancements while retaining learning as the focal point.

AI technologies make fundamental changes to curriculum design thus providing methods to enhance both management and medical education quality. It describes how AI tools modify teaching procedures by creating individualized learning programs and analytics-based institutional management together with flexible spaces. AI systems enable educators to get instant feedback from students through their system which automates repetitive work and shows academic performance data to help teachers maximize their efforts on strategy and creativity. AI in management training produces scenario-based education alongside medical training benefits from AI-based clinical training solutions, diagnostic systems, and patient-oriented educational designs. Implementation of AI technology delivers better learning results while simultaneously training professionals to overcome the complex issues in their active fields. AI can promote educational development through innovation together with solutions for educational gaps as well as create more effective learning structures for management and medical students.

Preface

OVERVIEW OF THE CHAPTER

Artificial Intelligence is rapidly reshaping the foundations of education, compelling institutions worldwide to rethink curriculum design in ways that are adaptive, inclusive, and future-ready. The chapters in AI Education Strategies for Future-Proofing Curriculum Design collectively highlight how AI enables personalized learning pathways, intelligent tutoring systems, and adaptive assessments while fostering interdisciplinary collaboration across STEM, humanities, management, and technical disciplines. At the same time, they underscore the importance of ethical governance, faculty preparedness, and institutional readiness to ensure that innovation is balanced with responsibility. By integrating AI into national strategies, curriculum frameworks, and pedagogical practices, educators can create dynamic ecosystems that prepare learners for the demands of the digital age. This volume thus serves as both a roadmap and a critical reflection, offering actionable insights into how AI can transform education while safeguarding equity, creativity, and the human dimension of learning.

In today's rapidly evolving world, artificial intelligence has moved from being a futuristic concept to a defining force across education systems. Governments, universities, and industries are embedding AI into curricula as part of national innovation agendas, workforce readiness programs, and global competitiveness strategies. The urgency is driven by advances in automation, data analytics, and intelligent systems that are reshaping industries and demanding new skill sets from graduates. At the same time, educators face challenges of equitable access, ethical governance, and cultural relevance in deploying AI-driven models. Against this backdrop, the study of AI education strategies is not only timely but essential, positioning itself at the intersection of innovation, policy, and pedagogy, and ensuring that education systems remain resilient, adaptable, and globally competitive in the 21st century.

The book is intended for academic leaders, curriculum designers, and faculty seeking practical models for AI integration. Policymakers and accreditation bodies will find guidance on governance, ethics, and national strategies. Researchers and doctoral candidates gain interdisciplinary insights across STEM, humanities, and management. Industry partners and EdTech innovators are addressed through discussions on collaboration and workforce readiness. Together, these audiences form a global community committed to building resilient and future-ready education systems.

Chapter 1: AI-Driven Curriculum Design for Higher Education Institutions

Dr. Jansirani D explores how artificial intelligence is reshaping curriculum design in higher education to prepare learners for an AI-driven future. Her chapter highlights strategies such as personalized learning, interdisciplinary integration, and ongoing skill development, while stressing the importance of growth mindsets, ethical awareness, and critical thinking alongside technical skills. She emphasizes aligning curricula with industry needs, training educators to use AI tools, and embedding real-world AI applications, all within a vision of digital fairness and human-centered design. By addressing ethical, economic, and social challenges, she presents a strategic, integrated vision for future-proofing education.

Chapter 2: AI-Driven Curriculum Design in Higher Education: Frameworks for Future-Ready Learning Ecosystems

Muhammad Usman Tariq examines how AI integration transforms curriculum design by enabling personalized, adaptive, and industry-aligned learning experiences. His chapter emphasizes machine learning, analytics, and intelligent systems to improve student engagement, provide rapid feedback, and align skills with workforce demands. He stresses the importance of ethical considerations, justice, and interdisciplinary collaboration, alongside faculty development and robust data governance. The work presents frameworks for sustainable AI adoption in higher education ecosystems.

Chapter 3: Strategic Integration of Artificial Intelligence in Sustainable Educational Program Design: AI Curriculum Design for Equity and Innovation

Thuc Chanh Dao outlines a strategic framework for integrating AI into Vietnam's higher education to drive sustainable digital transformation. Based on a mixed-methods study across eight institutions, the chapter highlights AI's role in enhancing learning personalization, analytics, and administrative efficiency. Results show improved academic performance and pedagogical flexibility, supported by infrastructure, training, and policy coherence. The chapter concludes with key implementation challenges and actionable recommendations for future research and policymaking.

Chapter 4: Leveraging Artificial Intelligence to Foster Personalized Learning Pathways in Higher Education: Strategies for Curriculum Integration

Fransisco Chindongo Ntjamba discusses how AI fosters personalized learning pathways through adaptive content, immediate feedback, and predictive analytics. His chapter highlights the role of faculty preparedness, data privacy, and equitable access in ensuring effective implementation. By integrating AI tools such as intelligent tutoring systems and adaptive platforms, he shows how institutions can create inclusive, engaging, and future-oriented learning environments that enhance student achievement.

Chapter 5: Preparing for the Global AI Economy through Educational Reform and Curriculum Redesign

Youmei Liu explores how AI reshapes the global economy and calls for urgent educational reform to prepare students for an AI-augmented workforce. Her chapter presents a framework across four domains: curriculum renovation, transdisciplinary teaching, applied assessment strategies, and global integration. She emphasizes embedding AI literacy, fostering innovative problem-solving, and promoting equitable access. The work provides a roadmap for reimagining curriculum design to equip students for an interconnected, ethically complex, AI-driven world.

Chapter 6: Revolutionizing Higher Education Integrating AI for Personalized Learning and Adaptive Curriculum Design

Swadhi R highlights how AI transforms higher education by delivering customized learning options and adaptive content. Her chapter explains how AI platforms generate immediate feedback, individualized learning routes, and flexible models that improve student outcomes. She notes challenges such as data protection, algorithmic faults, and faculty training, while emphasizing AI's potential to enhance curriculum improvement, skill identification, and virtual simulations for more effective and adaptable education.

Chapter 7: Harnessing AI to Transform Cambodian Higher Education: Strategies for Building a Future-Ready Curriculum

Sereyrath Em examines AI's potential to revolutionize Cambodian higher education by addressing systemic challenges in funding, quality, and infrastructure. His chapter advocates for curriculum reform, faculty development, student engagement through AI tools, and international collaborations. He emphasizes supportive policies and governance to foster innovation and equip Cambodian students for an AI-centric future, positioning AI as a driver of improved outcomes and global competitiveness.

Chapter 8: Integrating AI Education Strategies for Future-Proofing Curriculum Design in Omani Universities

Raed Awashreh focuses on AI integration in Omani higher education, aligning with Oman Vision 2040. His chapter proposes an AI Integration Framework covering strategic alignment, governance, infrastructure, curriculum development, and ethical implementation. He emphasizes AI-driven decision-making, partnerships, and continuous evaluation to ensure sustainable adoption. The work positions Omani universities as hubs for technological advancement while ensuring culturally relevant and ethical AI use.

Chapter 9: From One-Size-Fits-All to AI-Driven Personalization in Education

Fahad A. Salendab explores how AI enables personalized learning pathways and adaptive assessments tailored to individual learners. His chapter emphasizes constructivist and learner-centered approaches, showing how AI tools support differentiated instruction, student agency, and inclusive environments. He critically examines challenges such as ethics, privacy, bias, and the digital divide, while offering recommendations for responsible implementation. The work advocates systemic support, teacher training, and continuous evaluation to balance AI with the human dimension of teaching.

Chapter 10: AI for Personalized Learning Experiences: Adaptive Course Content and Intelligent Tutoring Systems

Sohaib Ahmad Khalil discusses how AI technologies deliver tailored courses and adaptive content to enhance learning globally. His chapter presents frameworks for knowledge-driven adaptive systems and intelligent tutoring, highlighting their potential to supplement or replace human instruction. He emphasizes delivering high-quality, individualized education while opening new avenues for AI research in cognitive architectures and natural language processing.

Chapter 11: Revolutionizing Assessment: AI-Powered Feedback Systems for Personalized Learning

Andi Asrifan examines AI's transformative role in assessment through adaptive feedback systems. His chapter highlights technologies such as NLP, machine learning, and analytics that provide real-time, individualized feedback to improve engagement and self-regulated learning. He presents frameworks grounded in constructivist and connectivist theories, with applications in K–12 and higher education. Ethical issues, bias, and institutional readiness are addressed, alongside proposals for policy and practice to strengthen curriculum resilience.

Chapter 12: AI-Powered Assessment and Feedback: Enhancing Learning Outcomes in the Digital Era

Nihal Kapoor explores how AI-powered assessment tools personalize learning and improve efficiency in identifying student strengths and weaknesses. His chapter highlights formative and summative applications, showing how AI enhances engagement and reduces bias. He stresses challenges such as privacy, transparency, and human oversight, while presenting best practices for ethical and equitable integration. The work demonstrates how AI-driven feedback can create inclusive and effective learning environments.

Chapter 13: The Teacher's Journey to AI: The EFL AI-PACK Framework

Osama Koraishi presents the AI-PACK framework to equip EFL teachers with AI literacy and practical strategies. His chapter traces AI's evolution in education and demonstrates how tools like ChatGPT can be integrated into language teaching. He addresses challenges in digital transition, offering AI-PACK aligned solutions and emphasizing ethical considerations. The work concludes with a vision for ongoing professional development, positioning AI literacy as essential for educators.

Chapter 14: AI and Research Methodologies: Opportunities and Challenges

Hamdo Ahmad Ebrahim examines AI's impact on research methodologies, focusing on opportunities in data collection, analysis, and knowledge creation. His chapter highlights tools such as NLP and machine learning, while addressing challenges like bias, reproducibility, and ethics. He provides frameworks to help researchers balance innovation with responsible use, ensuring AI enhances methodological practices across disciplines.

Chapter 15: Integrating AI in Educational Research Methodologies: Opportunities: Challenges: and Theoretical Insights

MD Hossain explores AI's role in educational research, using tools like ChatGPT, ResearchRabbit, and Scite. His chapter applies the TPACK framework and Activity Theory to analyze how AI influences researcher-tool relationships. He highlights benefits such as efficiency and deeper insights, while cautioning against risks of academic integrity, access, and overreliance. The work advocates AI literacy and responsible use, positioning AI as an assistant rather than a substitute for reasoning.

Chapter 16: Attribution Theory and AI Misuse in Higher Education: Implications in Ethically Challenging Environments

Isaac Wasswa Katono investigates AI misuse in Ugandan higher education, applying attribution, game, and prospect theories. His chapter explains how cultural and societal factors contribute to rationalizing unethical AI use in resource-constrained environments. He highlights moral challenges and consumerist tendencies, offering recommendations to mitigate misuse and promote ethical practices in SSA academia.

Chapter 17: Virtue-Centered AI Learning: Shaping the Moral Character of Tomorrow

Sooraj Kumar Maurya presents a virtue-based model for AI-powered education, drawing on Aristotle's concept of eudaimonia. His chapter emphasizes cultivating intellectual virtues like curiosity and perseverance alongside moral virtues such as empathy and fairness. He discusses dilemmas of bias and value misalignment, advocating ethical leadership, design culture, and policy reforms to ensure AI fosters socially responsible citizens.

Chapter 18: The Future of AI in Education Post-Millennial Generations

Mitrajit Biswas explores how AI's rapid growth is revolutionizing education in the Fourth Industrial Revolution. His chapter highlights AI-driven solutions such as tutoring systems, automated grading, and content generation, urging educators and policymakers to rethink schooling frameworks. He emphasizes curriculum futurism, aligning pedagogy with technological advancements while keeping learning at the core.

Chapter 19: Transforming the Future of Management and Medical Education: AI-Driven Innovations in Curriculum Design

Vettriselvan R examines how AI transforms curriculum design in management and medical education. His chapter highlights individualized learning programs, analytics-based institutional management, and scenario-based training. He shows how AI enhances clinical training, diagnostic systems, and patient-oriented designs, while automating repetitive tasks to improve efficiency. The work emphasizes innovation and solutions to educational gaps, creating more effective structures for professional training.

In conclusion, AI Education Strategies for Future-Proofing Curriculum Design makes a significant contribution to the evolving field of educational innovation by offering a comprehensive exploration of how artificial intelligence can reshape curricula, pedagogy, and institutional frameworks. By bringing together diverse perspectives from global scholars, the book not only highlights practical strategies for personalization, assessment, and workforce readiness but also addresses ethical governance, faculty preparedness, and cultural relevance. Its insights provide educators, policymakers, and researchers with actionable models to balance technological advancement with human-centered values. Ultimately, this volume positions itself as both a scholarly reference and a practical guide, advancing the discourse on AI in education and equipping institutions to design resilient, inclusive, and future-ready learning ecosystems.

Reda M. S. Abdelaal
Helwan University, Egypt

Mustafa Kayyali
Maaref University of Applied Sciences, Syria

Acknowledgment

Reading furnishes the mind only with materials of knowledge; it is thinking makes what we read ours — John Locke

I extend my deepest gratitude to Helwan University, my academic home and the foundation upon which my scholarly journey was built. It is within its halls that I first cultivated the intellectual curiosity, discipline, and sense of purpose that continue to guide my work. The university's vibrant academic community, its commitment to public education, and its enduring spirit of resilience have shaped my identity as both a researcher and an educator. I remain profoundly grateful for the mentorship, opportunities, and values that Helwan University instilled in me.

My sincere appreciation goes to King Abdulaziz University, where I had the privilege of serving as a Professor of Industrial Engineering and consultant to the university's vice presidents. My years there were marked by transformative professional growth, collaborative innovation, and a shared commitment to institutional excellence. The trust placed in me by university leadership, the stimulating academic environment, and the opportunity to contribute to strategic initiatives enriched my perspective on higher education governance and strengthened my dedication to impactful, future-oriented scholarship.

I also wish to acknowledge AlMaarefa University, where I had the privilege of serving as a consultant to the University President and working closely with the higher administration on strategic developments across multiple sectors. My time there was marked by meaningful collaboration, particularly through my contribution to the establishment of the Industrial Engineering Department—an initiative that reflected the university's commitment to academic growth and national workforce needs. The dedication of AlMaarefa's leadership, faculty, and staff created an environment where innovation and institutional advancement could flourish. I remain grateful for the trust placed in me and for the forward-looking spirit that shaped our shared achievements.

Above all, I owe my deepest gratitude to my family—my wife, Fatma Shafik, my daughter, Sarah, and my son, Ahmed—whose unwavering love, patience, and support sustained me at every stage of this journey. Their belief in my work, their sacrifices, and their constant encouragement have been the anchor that allowed me to pursue ambitious ideas with confidence and purpose. This book is as much theirs as it is mine, a testament to the strength, unity, and inspiration that only family can provide.

Reda M. S. Abdelaal

Helwan University, Egypt

****

This book is, in many ways, a record of effort—but even more, it is a record of people. It was written through long nights, crowded schedules, and the quiet pressure that comes with trying to produce something worthy of its theme. Yet the truth is simple: I did not carry this alone. I want this acknowledgement to stand as a sincere dedication to those whose support made the work possible, and whose presence made the journey meaningful.

To my colleagues at Maaref University of Applied Sciences, I extend my deep appreciation and respect. Thank you for the trust you placed in me, the encouragement you offered when responsibilities were heavy, and the collegial spirit that turns daily work into a shared mission. Your professionalism, your patience, and your willingness to cooperate—sometimes in the smallest details, sometimes in the most critical decisions—helped create the stability that every serious intellectual project needs. I have come to believe that a university's true strength is not only in its programs, policies, or plans, but in the character of the people who make those plans real. You reminded me, again and again, that support is not always a grand gesture; often it is simply showing up with sincerity, doing the work properly, and believing that what we build together matters.

I also dedicate this book to the Board of HE Higher Education Ranking. Your inspiration has been a constant source of momentum. You pushed me to think beyond comfort, to pursue rigor without losing perspective, and to treat measurement as a tool for improvement rather than a shortcut to prestige. The vision, conversations, and collective standards that guide the board have shaped my approach to quality, accountability, and the future of higher education. I am grateful for the intellectual energy you bring and the seriousness with which you treat impact.

To my family, I owe a kind of gratitude that language can only approximate. To my father, Abdullah Kayyali, thank you for the values you planted early—discipline, humility, patience, and respect for knowledge. Your guidance is not something I remember occasionally; it is something that quietly lives inside my decisions. To my wife, Noura Abduljalil, thank you for your unwavering presence: for your patience when the work took time that belonged to family, for your understanding when my mind was still inside the chapters even after the day had ended, and for your calm support that never demanded attention but always provided strength.

And to my angels—Abdullah Junior (this first dedication is for you)—you are my most personal motivation. You have made me care not only about what I achieve, but about what I leave behind. When I think about knowledge, I think about responsibility; when I think about responsibility, I think about you. May this book, in some small way, be part of a future you can be proud of.

Lost is the soul that can't stop seeking—alone.
Under each lesson, a deeper unknown.
Only in knowing do I feel what I'm about.
Searching for light, I dissolve into doubt.
To me it's a storm that refuses to bleed.
Some call it wisdom—this hunger, this need.

On every horizon, more mysteries are sowed.
Learning is my compass, yet I still lose the road.
And every new truth makes the old one feel dull.
My heart is a library with shelves never full.
Always chasing meaning, I outpace the day.
I wander through questions where answers don't stay.

Mustafa Kayyali

Maaref University of Applied Sciences, Syria

Introduction

Artificial Intelligence is no longer a distant prospect; it is a defining force that is reshaping the foundations of education in real time. Across the globe, institutions are compelled to rethink curriculum design in ways that are adaptive, inclusive, and future-ready. The accelerating pace of technological innovation, coupled with the demands of a digital economy, has made it clear that traditional models of teaching and learning are insufficient to prepare students for the challenges of the twenty-first century. This book, *AI Education Strategies for Future-Proofing Curriculum Design*, responds to that urgency by offering a comprehensive exploration of how AI can be strategically integrated into educational frameworks to transform pedagogy, assessment, and institutional governance.

The chapters collected here highlight the breadth of AI's influence on education. They demonstrate how intelligent tutoring systems, adaptive assessments, and personalized learning pathways are not only enhancing student engagement but also fostering interdisciplinary collaboration across STEM, humanities, management, and technical disciplines. At the same time, the contributions underscore the importance of ethical governance, faculty preparedness, and institutional readiness. Innovation must be balanced with responsibility, and technological progress must remain aligned with the human dimension of learning. By integrating AI into national strategies, curriculum frameworks, and pedagogical practices, educators can create dynamic ecosystems that prepare learners for the demands of the digital age while safeguarding equity, creativity, and cultural relevance.

In today's rapidly evolving world, artificial intelligence has moved from being a futuristic concept to a central pillar of educational transformation. Governments, universities, and industries are embedding AI into curricula as part of national innovation agendas, workforce readiness programs, and global competitiveness strategies. The urgency is driven by advances in automation, data analytics, and intelligent systems that are reshaping industries and demanding new skill sets from graduates. This global context situates AI education strategies at the intersection of innovation, policy, and pedagogy. On one hand, AI offers unprecedented opportunities to personalize learning, streamline administrative processes, and provide actionable insights into student performance. On the other hand, educators must grapple with challenges of equitable access, ethical governance, and cultural relevance. The chapters in this book collectively argue that studying and implementing AI education strategies is not optional—it is essential for ensuring that education systems remain resilient, adaptable, and globally competitive in the twenty-first century.

The volume is organized around several interrelated themes that capture the scope of AI's impact on curriculum design. Authors explore how AI enables personalized learning pathways, adaptive content, and interdisciplinary integration. These innovations empower students to take ownership of their learning while aligning curricula with industry needs. Multiple chapters examine AI-powered feedback systems and adaptive assessments, showing how they improve student engagement, self-regulation, and learning outcomes. The book emphasizes the importance of equipping educators with AI literacy, ethical awareness, and practical strategies. Faculty development is presented as a cornerstone of sustainable adoption. Contributors address pressing issues such as algorithmic bias, data privacy, and the risk of misuse. They advocate for transparent, equitable practices that safeguard human values while embracing innovation. With case studies from diverse regions—including Cambodia, Oman, Uganda, and beyond—the book underscores the universal relevance of AI in education while acknowledging contextual differences. Together, these themes provide a roadmap for institutions seeking to integrate AI responsibly and effectively into curriculum design.

This book is intended for a wide spectrum of stakeholders. Academic leaders, curriculum designers, and faculty will find practical models for AI integration. Policymakers and accreditation bodies will discover guidance on governance, ethics, and national strategies. Researchers and doctoral candidates gain interdisciplinary insights across STEM, humanities, and management. Industry partners and EdTech innovators are addressed through discussions on collaboration and workforce readiness. By engaging these audiences, the book positions itself as both a scholarly reference and a pragmatic guide. It invites readers to reflect critically on the role of AI in education while equipping them with actionable strategies to harness its potential responsibly.

In bringing together diverse perspectives from global scholars, *AI Education Strategies for Future-Proofing Curriculum Design* makes a significant contribution to the evolving field of educational innovation. It demonstrates that AI is not merely a technological enhancement but a catalyst for academic transformation, institutional resilience, and global collaboration. By situating AI within the broader mission of education—preparing students for meaningful careers and responsible citizenship, the book underscores its potential to build inclusive, future-ready learning environments. As readers engage with the chapters that follow, they will encounter both the promise and the complexity of AI in education. The insights presented here serve as a roadmap for navigating this evolving landscape, ensuring that innovation is guided by ethical principles and aligned with the enduring values of teaching, learning, and human development.

Reda M.S. Abdelaal
Former Professor, Helwan University, Egypt

Mustafa Kayyali
Maaref University of Applied Sciences, Syria

Chapter 1
AI-Driven Curriculum Design for Higher Education Institutions

D. Jansirani
https://orcid.org/0009-0003-9412-5217
P.S.R. Engineering College, India

A. Mohamed Rizwana
https://orcid.org/0009-0005-6225-1731
P.S.R. Engineering College, India

A. Noorjahan Rehana
P.S.R. Engineering College, India

K. Ramalakshmi
https://orcid.org/0000-0002-3038-643X
P.S.R. Engineering College, India

S. T. Gopukumar
Saveetha Medical College and Hospital, India

ABSTRACT

Artificial intelligence (AI) is changing the terrain of higher education institutions in a time of unparalleled technological development, thereby requiring a basic change in curriculum design. This chapter explores innovative strategies for integrating AI into higher education institutional frameworks to prepare learners for an AI driven future. Instead of perceiving AI as a disruptive technology, it is envisioned to be an innovation driver in pedagogy, learning processes, and organizational systems. This section discusses several dimensions of how AI restructures learning. It focuses on understanding AI, learning that is personalized for oneself, blending several subjects, and ongoing skill development. It focuses on developing a growth mindset for students and educators, in which flexibility, ethical thinking, and critical thinking are as crucial as technical skills. Some of the key strategies include curriculum alignment with industry needs, training teachers to use AI tools, and using real-world AI examples in several subjects.

DOI: 10.4018/979-8-3373-2752-5.ch001

1. INTRODUCTION

Education has long been the foundation of societal progress, equipping individuals with the knowledge and skills necessary to thrive in a rapidly evolving world. However, traditional curriculum models in higher education, largely unchanged for decades, are increasingly misaligned with the demands of modern industries. The acceleration of artificial intelligence (AI), automation, and data science is reshaping the global workforce, exposing a widening gap between what students learn and the competencies required by employers. Studies indicate that by 2025, nearly 85 million jobs will be displaced by automation, yet 97 million new AI-driven roles will emerge, requiring proficiency in AI literacy, data analytics, and problem-solving skills. Despite this shift, most academic institutions continue to rely on rigid, slow-to-evolve curricula that fail to integrate emerging disciplines like machine learning, AI ethics, and computational thinking (Zawacki-Richter et al., 2019). Additionally, many current teaching methodologies prioritize rote memorization over critical thinking, leaving graduates ill-prepared for an AI-driven economy.

To bridge this gap, AI is not just an industry disruptor it is also a transformative force in higher education institutions, offering adaptive, personalized, and data-driven strategies to ensure curricula remain relevant (Holmes et al., 2019). AI-powered learning systems leverage real-time data analytics to customize instruction, tailoring content to individual student needs (Chen et al., 2022). Platforms like Carnegie Learning and Coursera's AI-driven courses analyze student performance and dynamically adjust coursework to optimize learning outcomes. Beyond personalized learning, AI also plays a pivotal role in curriculum development machine learning models continuously monitor labor market trends, research publications, and industry reports to recommend timely syllabus updates (Bates et al., 2020). This ensures students are trained in emerging competencies rather than out dated theories.

Curriculum models before the entry of artificial intelligence into higher education institutions were tied strictly to disciplines and evolved slowly over many years, sometimes decades. Higher education institutions, which view knowledge centered frameworks framed in essentialist and perennialist traditions, do not have much flexibility regarding personalization (Chiu & Chai, 2020). Educators act as single authorities, and the existence of different learning paces or preferences is rarely acknowledged in curricular frameworks.

Systematization efforts, such as Tyler's rational planning model, focused on the establishment of measurable objectives and structured learning sequences; hence, very little was learned about real-time responsiveness. The gain in traction among constructivist theories, together with the slow rate of change, would continue in many institutions. Review cycles in higher education can take anywhere from five to ten years before the content is updated, which leaves a large majority of graduates unprepared for new emerging fields such as data science, robotics, and AI ethics.

Digital tools such as LMSs and e-learning platforms were introduced in the early 2000s, but these tools were either independent or supplementary to the curriculum design. The gap between the timing in academia and industry continues to grow. The longitudinal analysis of higher education institutional innovation has become extremely damaging for fields that have fast transformation technologies (Guan et al., 2020).

AI has redefined development as continuous and data-informed in predictive curriculum delivery. Instead of waiting for curriculum reviews every five years, institutions can now design and update programs based on data collected through real-time labor analytics and learner performance data. Understanding this historical inertia emphasizes the enormity of the shift AI promises, from rigid, homogeneous content delivery to adaptive, forward-looking learning ecosystems.

Figure 1. Evolution of Education

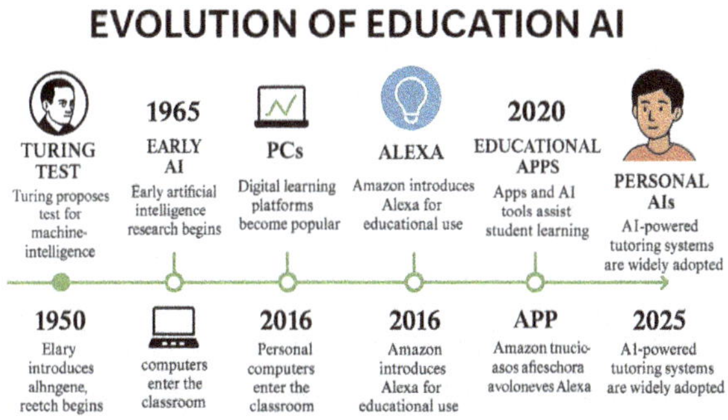

Moreover, AI fosters interdisciplinary higher education institutions, seamlessly integrating subjects like programming, ethics, and cognitive science into existing fields of study. This cross-functional approach prepares students for AI-driven industries where adaptability and collaboration across disciplines are critical (Selwyn, 2019). Beyond curriculum enhancement, AI is also revolutionizing higher education institutions infrastructure, automating administrative processes, assisting with student engagement via AI tutors, and optimizing research methodologies through automated data analysis tools (Luckin, 2017). Furthermore, AI allows educators to shift from routine tasks such as grading to more impactful roles in mentorship and innovative pedagogy.

As educational institutions move toward AI-integrated learning models, it is critical to address ethical considerations such as algorithmic bias, data privacy, and the evolving role of human educators (Holmes et al., 2019). This chapter explores AI-driven strategies that can redefine curriculum design, ensuring that learning remains adaptive, relevant, and aligned with the future of work. By embracing AI, universities can transition beyond out dated teaching models and create an innovative, future-proof education system that equips students with the necessary skills to thrive in an AI-powered economy.

2. AI-POWERED PERSONALIZED LEARNING: MOVING BEYOND STANDARDIZED EDUCATION

For decades, education has followed a standardized model where students progress through fixed syllabi at the same pace, regardless of their individual learning needs. However, this "one-size-fits-all" approach often leads to disengagement, gaps in comprehension, and an inability to cater to diverse learning styles. With the advent of artificial intelligence (AI), personalized and adaptive learning is revolutionizing education institutions by tailoring learning experiences to meet the specific needs of each student. AI-powered learning systems analyse student behaviour, engagement, and progress to create customized educational pathways, ensuring that learning is more effective, engaging, and future-proof (Mishra et al., 2025).

Traditional education relies on static curricula that fail to accommodate different learning speeds and preferences. AI-driven adaptive learning platforms, such as Carnegie Learning and Coursera's AI tutors, enable real-time adjustments in course content based on student progress. These platforms employ machine learning algorithms to assess areas where students struggle and provide targeted resources to reinforce understanding (Smith et al., 2025). Unlike traditional models, where all students follow the same learning path, adaptive AI models personalize lesson delivery, ensuring students master concepts before advancing.

AI-powered learning analytics play a crucial role in personalizing higher education institutions. These systems track students' interaction patterns, quiz results, and engagement levels to predict potential difficulties and provide instant feedback (Majumder, 2025). Unlike traditional assessments, which provide feedback only after tests are completed, AI-driven systems offer real-time interventions, enabling students to adjust their learning strategies immediately. For instance, IBM's AI-driven higher education institutions initiatives have integrated predictive analytics to identify students at risk of falling behind, allowing educators to step in before performance declines (Sriram et al., 2025).

Beyond predictive analytics, AI also enhances student learning through Intelligent Tutoring Systems (ITS). These AI-driven tutors simulate one-on-one teaching, adapting instruction based on a student's responses. Unlike human educators, AI tutors are available 24/7 and provide instant explanations and personalized study plans. This technology has been particularly impactful in fields such as STEM education, where students benefit from step-by-step guidance on complex problems (Allam et al., 2025).

3. NEUROADAPTIVE AI SYSTEMS IN CURRICULUM PERSONALIZATION

Starting from rule-based personalization, artificial intelligence in higher education institutions is now advancing toward the frontier of neuroadaptive AIs. Neuroadaptive AIs respond not only to the performance metrics of learners but also to their cognitions and emotional states in real time. Neuroadaptive technologies combine BCIs, eye-tracking, galvanic skin response, and EEG sensors to ensure continuous monitoring of intervals of attention, fatigue, stress, and engagement to change the learning environment accordingly. Hence, there has been a drastic change from a reactive paradigm to truly adaptive learning designs.

In neuroadaptive systems, AI analyses neural and physiological data streams to determine the learner's cognitive load or affective states. The system may slow down the pacing of instruction or add an interactive element when attention drops. Such companies include BrainCo and Emotiv, who already do tremendous strides in this area. For instance, the FocusEDU headset can measure attention in real time through EEG signals and adapt lesson difficulty levels by doing so; the headset is currently being employed in numerous K-12 STEM-related studies across Asia (Grubov et al., 2024). In addition to content adaptation, these systems will also provide feedback loops for educators to identify students experiencing cognitive overload.

Research has shown that this level of real-time personalization can vastly enhance learning for neurodiverse groups. Students with attention-deficit hyperactivity disorder, for instance, feel motivated if the learning platform dynamically adjusts to improve their concentration or anxiety symptoms (Holmes et al., 2023). Neuroadaptive virtual reality laboratories in higher education environments help students learn abstract scientific concepts by aligning visual cues with individual rhythms of attention.

In its 2024 Digital Education Outlook, the OECD identified neuroadaptive personalization as a game changer for inclusive higher education institutions, especially for learners with learning disabilities, mental health challenges, or different cognitive styles. Assuming they fulfil certain characteristics, such systems may complement the Universal Design for Learning (UDL) framework by providing content that is sensorially optimized and multimodally laid out with support customized on the learner's actions, experience, and thoughts at that moment.

Neuroadaptive AI raises significant ethical issues. If we collect neural and emotional data, we must look at strong consent, strong anonymization of data, and transparency regarding algorithmic decisions. There is the danger of emotional profiling, wherein AI might make assumptions about a learner's ability or intent according to some transient physiological states that, in the absence of adequate monitoring, may translate into biased pedagogical decisions (Holmes et al., 2023). Additionally, equitable access to such advanced systems remains a hurdle for under-resourced regions.

Nevertheless, responsibly integrated neuroadaptive AIs may become the gold standard for personalized education, with a paradigm shift away from static assessments toward dynamic cognition-aware systems for learning.

Table 1. Comparing Traditional vs. Neuroadaptive AI Personalization in Learning Environments

COMPARISON PARAMETER	TRADITIONAL PERSONALIZATION	NEUROADAPTIVE AI PERSONALIZATION
Data Source	Test Scores, LMS Logs	EEG, Eye Tracking, Skin Response, Heart Rate
Feedback Mechanism	Periodic Algorithmic Adjustments	Continuous Neurophysiological Monitoring
Adaptation Response	Based on Observable Behavior	Based on Cognitive Load, Stress, Engagement
Applications	MOOCs, LMS, Standard Classrooms	ADHD Programs, VR Science Labs, Emotion-Aware Tutoring
Ethical Concerns	Low (Data Privacy, LMS Bias)	High (Neurodata Privacy, Emotional Profiling Risks)
Strengths	Scalable, Quantitative Feedback	Emotionally Intelligent, Real-Time Personalized Support

4. REAL-WORLD IMPLEMENTATIONS OF AI-DRIVEN LEARNING: CASE STUDIES FROM LEADING UNIVERSITIES

4.1 Arizona State University (ASU) and AI-Enhanced Math Learning

Arizona State University (ASU) now stands at the forefront of AI-assisted teaching after adding intelligent tools to its entry-level math sequence. The school rolled out Newton's adaptive-engine platform, an AI system that gauges what each learner knows, then tweaks readings, problems, and tests on the fly. By studying every answer a student submits, the software spots weak spots, delivers clearer steps or extra drills, and fades once mastery shows. Fast learners move ahead to tougher content, while peers who need more time receive on-demand, bite-sized help before the class moves on.

Outcomes from the pilot and follow-up terms confirm the techs promise. Data reveal that students using the adaptive model complete the course about 20 percent more often than classmates taught by conventional lecture and homework alone. Furthermore, AI-driven predictive analytics helped identify at-risk student's early, allowing educators to intervene before performance declined. This proactive approach not only reduced dropout rates but also improved overall student retention and success in STEM-related fields (Rajput, 2025). The case of ASU demonstrates how AI can personalize education, making learning more efficient and tailored to individual needs.

4.2 University of Murcia (Spain) and AI-Driven Learning Analytics

The University of Murcia in Spain has successfully leveraged AI-powered learning analytics to enhance student performance and engagement in online courses. The university implemented an AI-based system that tracked student interactions with course materials, assessed quiz results, and monitored engagement levels to identify patterns in learning behavior. The AI system then provided personalized recommendations to students and instructors, highlighting areas that required additional attention. This data-driven approach enabled educators to adjust teaching strategies based on real-time insights, ensuring students received the support they needed.

The results of AI-driven learning analytics at the University of Murcia were remarkable. The university observed a 15% reduction in dropout rates in online courses after implementing AI-powered interventions. Students who followed the AI-generated personalized study plans reported higher levels of engagement and improved academic performance. Additionally, faculty members benefited from AI-driven insights that allowed them to refine their teaching methods based on student learning patterns (Qureshi, 2025). This case illustrates how AI-driven learning analytics can enhance not only individual student experiences but also broader institutional outcomes, making higher education more efficient and responsive to student needs.

5. AI IN CURRICULUM DESIGN: PREPARING EDUCATIONAL CONTENT FOR THE FUTURE

The primary objective of higher education institutions is to prepare students for an unpredictable future. However, traditional curriculum development tends to be reactive, often falling behind the rapid pace of industry changes. Academic programs are modified slowly, sometimes taking anywhere from five to ten years because of bureaucratic procedures; hence, they are unaffordable to rapidly evolving sectors that deal with artificial intelligence, biotechnologies, and financial technologies. Therefore, graduates generally lack the required skill matrix for AI-driven automation, cloud computing, and ethical AI governance (Chu & Ashraf, 2025). Artificial intelligence is now becoming a game-changer in higher education institutions, allowing colleges to efficiently update their curricula to meet the immediate needs of the workforce.

One of the major drawbacks of the existing curriculum models in higher education is their lack of dynamic adaptability. As new technologies emerge and reshape job markets, positions in

AI auditing, machine-learning operations, and cyber security are being created. However, many universities continue to offer outdated curricula based on obsolete knowledge (Sun et al., 2025). Without systems to incorporate timely input from the industry, higher educational institutions produce graduates who are ill-prepared for the challenges of the modern workforce. This situation is comparable to sports team selections made only on past performance, rather than current statistics making decisions based on out dated information, which can lead to inferior outcomes. AI-enhanced curriculum design can allow for flexible and data-centric approaches to program-building. Machine learning algorithms and natural language processing tools analyze numerous job postings, research articles, and innovation databases to pinpoint emerging skill requirements and areas of content that are becoming irrelevant (Zary & Zary, 2025). The systems recommend putting into effect an emerging discipline, updating existing curricula, and removing archaic content to help keep academic programs relevant to market demands.

In the preliminary stages, the systems would optimize the syllabi, detect skill gaps, and provide personalized courses. Automated tools assist in comparing the course content with the latest industry standards, identifying variations, and recommending changes. Adaptive learning platforms predict, tailor, and recommend learning pathways based on individual student goals and global job trends (He et al., 2025). This is akin to how elite sports teams use data analytics to make strategic decisions: higher education institutions should be a living ecosystem that adapts to changes every day in its effectiveness and relevance to the learner.

Figure 2. AI Curriculum Update Flowchart

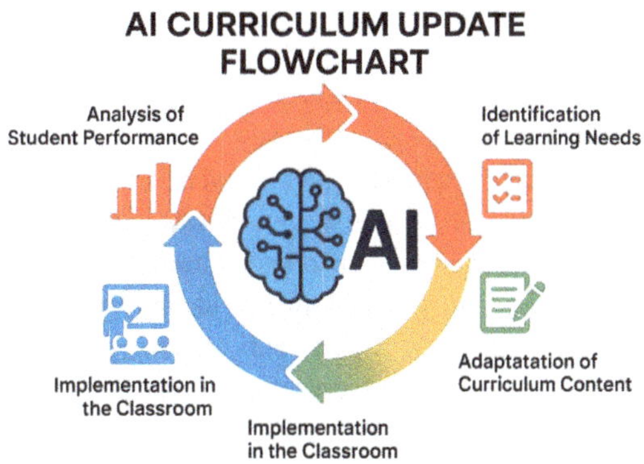

Across the world, these AI-driven curriculum frameworks are gradually making inroads into established universities and governments; for example, MIT employed AI tools to update its courses in machine learning and data science a couple of years back, making rapid-level adjustments to the curriculum to fit in the latest techniques and applications in federated learning and quantum computing (Chu & Ashraf, 2025). Stanford is also an example of such a rapid adaptation, with its rapid incorporation of block chain and AI ethics into cyber security courses. At the national level, Singapore's Skills Future AI Initiative has made significant efforts to revolutionize academic courses across universities on the basis of labor analytics, pulling out a 30 percentage increase in graduate employability rates (He et al., 2025).

5.1 Identification of Learning Needs

AI-enhanced education begins its journey by first recognizing the fundamental human challenge which involves understanding various learning methods of students. Artificial intelligence provides unmatched capabilities to individualize education at large scale through the combination of behavioural data and historical data and real-time digital platform interaction data. While traditional assessments tend to measure outcomes, AI systems take into account engagement patterns, response timings, and preferences for pathways to learning, and thus record obstacles to learning that might have been previously overlooked.

For example, if the student hesitates excessively or makes an incorrect choice in a formative assessment, the system reports this behavior and recommends intervention in the form of remedial content, multimodal resources, or a changed learning pace. AI diagnostic systems enabled early detection of mathematical learning deficits in students at all skill levels which led to a 27% rise in individual mastery (Hilali et al., 2023). This intelligent detection method serves as a crucial inclusion tool because it supports students who cannot express their learning struggles due to cognitive or emotional or linguistic limitations. AI functions as a responsive co-instructor to gather knowledge about learners before instruction starts so it enables early educational design and proactive teaching strategies.

5.2 Adaptation of Curriculum Content

Curriculum design has evolved beyond its traditional static approach which required periodic reviews because AI now supports its dynamic process for rapid technological and industrial changes. The application of machine learning together with NLP enables artificial intelligence to evaluate labour market trends and student learning patterns as well as emerging research so that it can update academic content promptly to meet professional standards.

In cases where scenarios such as quantum encryption become bottlenecks in cyber security, AI-integrated curriculum systems can quickly detect such developments and consequently suggest alterations to courses. This gives academic faculties a time-frame of weeks instead of years in which to update content, thereby hugely improving curricular responsiveness of its own accord. According (Borromeo et al., 2025) AI-assisted course changes improve student participation and knowledge retention because learners observe their educational content through present-day practical applications. The adaptive frameworks developed through AI transform the content delivery process into a strategic tool which ensures educational relevance as well as precision and future readiness.

5.3 Implementation in the Classroom

Education becomes transformative when teaching methods are thoughtfully blended with technology, creating a learning environment that feels almost magical. Currently, AI serves as a powerful tool to support teachers; it offers extra resources but does not take over the role of guiding and instructing students. When combined with smart tutoring systems, adaptive learning platforms, and natural language chatbots, AI opens the door to personalized learning on a much larger scale, whether in classrooms or online. For instance, intelligent tutoring systems can adjust the difficulty of tasks on the spot based on how a student is doing, providing a more tailored experience. AI tutors can even step in late at night to help students untangle tricky biology concepts by offering quick, customized feedback. This not only supports learners but also eases some of the workload off teachers, freeing them up to focus on deeper, more meaningful aspects of education, such as ethical discussions, one-on-one mentoring, and developing critical thinking.

In health education, AI has brought about significant changes across different levels of learning. AI-driven simulation feedback tools are helping to reduce repetitive clinical exercises, which gives educators more room to focus on essential skills that are often overlooked, such as communication, empathy, and ethical reasoning. With these advancements, teachers can focus on what really matters, while AI quietly takes care of background tasks (Edwards et al., 2025).

5.4 Analysis of Student Performance

With the growing popularity of artificial intelligence, the mode of assessment has transcended the end point to be more of an on going dynamic feedback loop. No longer relegating assessment to grading alone, AI-powered systems now also diagnose the how, where, and why students succeed-or not-in a course. Sophisticated analytics dashboards display performance metrics and behavioral patterns: which quiz formats drop out, where learners drop off, or what content involves the most collaboration.

These insights enable instructors to take action in real time. For example, if a significant portion of students lags behind after a game-based assessment, an AI system will recommend some pedagogical changes such as piece-by-piece breaking the concept down further or providing more visual alternatives. This adaptability lets instructors switch from reactive remediation to proactive course optimization.

Such has been the case for dental education: for example, this is a scoping review on how AI-enhanced procedural simulations have standardized complex clinical tasks across heterogeneous cohorts with real-time feedback loops, allowing the instructor to calibrate both teaching and content delivery (Alzahrani et al., 2025).

Looking into the future, it is clear that the impact of AI will broaden further to anticipate new job titles, accept accreditation processes, and propose interdisciplinary programs marrying AI with subjects such as the humanities and ethics. Just as cricketers were one of the first applications of AI-driven analytics to measure player performance and game strategies, higher education institutions enters an era where real-time intelligent curriculum design contributes to institutional excellence. Universities that selectively innovate with AI will be positioned to bridge the gap between education and employment and produce employable graduates.

6. AI FOR SKILLS AND SCHOLARSHIP: REVOLUTIONIZING HIGHER EDUCATION LEARNING AND RESEARCH

Artificial intelligence is no longer at the fringe of the academy now it is a cornerstone work piece that is transforming the way students acquire real-world skills and research is conceived, conducted, and disseminated. Universities worldwide are reshaping higher education as a dynamic, applied system that integrates classroom teaching and real-world problem solving. At the centre of this transformation is AI, both a research driver and learning facilitator.

Unlike traditional academic models that isolate theory and practice, artificial intelligence facilitates real-time skill-based learning through virtual labs, intelligent tutoring, and immersive simulations. These environments allow learners to work with complex scenarios everything from performing virtual surgeries to optimizing smart grid operations without the need for expensive physical infrastructure (Naqvi et al., 2025). Not only are these environments a replacement for traditional labs but they also offer adaptive feedback, iterative task refinement, and personalized learning paths, thus creating a more advanced and effective learning environment.

- In virtual labs, AI provides immediate feedback and dynamically varies task difficulty in response to student performance and driving mastery through repetition and variation.
- Computer simulations based on artificial intelligence mimic plant behavior or system malfunction, allowing students to assess real-life critical situations without causing actual consequences.
- Modular AI-driven content facilitates interdisciplinary learning, where students can combine topics such as robotics and law, design thinking, and data analytics.

Higher education institutions are also scaling AI-powered industry-academic partnerships, incorporating workplace problems directly into course design. Students are no longer passive recipients of textbook matter; they design AI-driven solutions to real organizational problems. In one such initiative, mechanical engineering students worked with an automotive firm to simulate and optimize electric drivetrain performance using AI-powered virtual testing laboratories. Not only did this project enhance their technical skills but it also facilitated innovation and collaboration (Eneix et al., 2025).

Simultaneously, the field of research is experiencing an equally dramatic transformation. Artificial intelligence is emerging as an interdisciplinary partner in research endeavors, ranging from automated literature analysis to experimental design and academic publishing. With the help of AI, researchers can rapidly browse enormous academic repositories, identify underexplored research areas, and even formulate new research questions. In data-rich disciplines, such as genomics, economics, and environmental science, machine learning has significantly reduced the time required to yield useful insights (Ramezani et al., 2025).

- AI-driven bibliometric systems assist researchers in examining international patterns of citations, recognizing areas of research in ascendance, and matching proposals with funding agency priorities.
- Natural language processing programs enhance academic writing by reducing verbosity, eliminating unnecessary citations, and emphasizing argument gaps.
- Big data, ranging from city planning to clinical trials, are now open to analysis owing to AI-driven computational models.

A great illustration of the dual use of AI research and learning hails from An-Najah National University in Palestine. During the COVID-19 pandemic, medical students, along with AI faculty and researchers, have created predictive models of rural infection patterns. Students used machine learning platforms to gather epidemiological data, perform correlation analysis, and create real-time dashboards for public health authorities. Along with their technical skills, they co-authored a research article detailing their work. Throughout the project, generative AI tools were employed in the literature review and manuscript phase, while the faculty oversaw ethical use and academic integrity. The project demonstrated how AI can enable students not just to learn from research but also to create it (Yousef et al., 2025). Together, these advances have reshaped the vision of scholars today. Students are not merely engaged learners, but also engage participants as programmers, analysts, writers, and creators. Scholars have redefined themselves from isolated experts to collaborators with smart machines that maximize productivity and accelerate innovation. As colleges and universities continue to leverage these tools with moral sensitivity and deliberate intention, artificial intelligence transforms from a tool of support; it becomes the connector between competency and scholarship, classroom and lab, and learning and discovery.

7. AI-ENHANCED RESEARCH METHODOLOGIES IN ACADEMIA

The AI field is attesting toward the rapidly transforming environment of academic research and has become integral to every stage of the scholarly life cycle. AI is not just seen as a facilitator; it has the potential to change the very way researchers go about their work in a variety of disciplines. AI is becoming ever more indispensable in interdisciplinary and data-driven research-from facilitating very tedious tasks, such as systematic reviews, to accelerating hypothesis generation and enhancing manuscript preparation. Global warming is more so in knowledge-driven research fields such as health, genomic, education, and social policy, where researchers are often burdened with tons of data and a regularly changing body of literature.

Figure 3. AI-Enhanced Research Lifecycle in Academic Inquiry

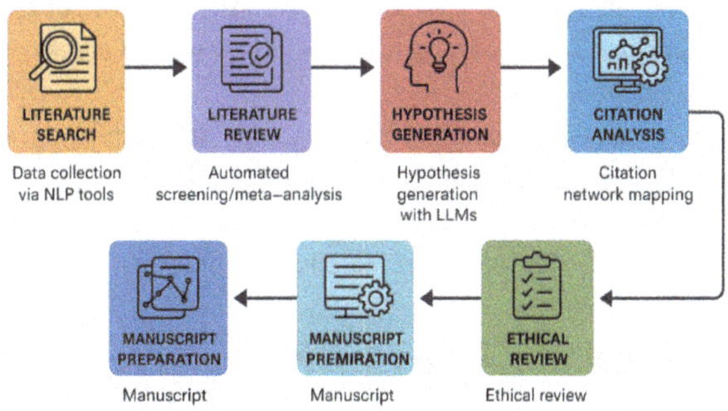

7.1 AI for Automating Systematic Reviews and Meta-Analyses

Systematic review and meta-analysis are pivotal techniques for evidence-based practices, but they are generally labor-intensive and could absorb hundreds of hours. At this stage, considerable changes enter AI platforms such as Scholarcy, Elicit, and Iris.ai, which seem rather adept at moving forward with automation of literature search, relevant inclusion or exclusion decisions, and synthesization of themes through natural language processing (NLP). AI can quickly extract, group implications, appraise their citation sentiment, and point out methodical inconsistencies in ways that would take human reviewers quite a long time.

Research has shown, for instance, that AI-supported review workflows diminish screening time by as much as 60%, with concurrent gains in replicability and inter-rater reliability (Borges do Nascimento et al., 2021). This, of course, is of paramount importance in fast-paced areas like public health whereby access to such high-level evidence could outright dictate policy and guidance outcomes.

7.2 Generating Hypotheses with Large Language Models (LLMs)

Another thrilling academic application of AI is the generation of hypotheses. Large language models (LLMs) like Scite Assistant, Semantic Scholar AI, and several GPT-based instruments scan through millions of academic articles to identify underexplored relationships or contradictions in the existing literature. In doing so, they allow researchers to develop original and interdisciplinary research questions that may have been beyond consideration before.

Recent studies have pointed to this possibility, with LLMs aiding early-career scientists in conceptualizing hypotheses addressing academic gaps in various fields including genomics, economics, and climate modelling (Eger et al., 2025). Thus, by having machine-generated observations, researchers can shatter their own cognitive biases and limited exposure to certain areas, hence expanding the research inquiry and innovative possibilities.

7.3 Citation Intelligence, Together With AI-Based Bibliometrics

Bibliometric analysis for the assessment of research impact has existed for quite some time; however, AI has rapidly transformed and elevated all such capabilities. Deep learning is already in use in citation context interpretation, sentiment analysis, and collaborative network studies by tools such as Dimensions AI, Scopus AI, and VOS viewer to create dynamic mapping of scholarly impacts.

Current studies show that AI-enhanced bibliometrics are currently used not only to rank publications but to predict future research trends and identify emerging interdisciplinary clusters (Wagner et al., 2021). Such tools empower researchers, funding bodies, and institutions to more strategically decide on publication venues, research collaborations, and grants.

7.4 AI Tools in Academic Writing and Manuscript Development

AI is increasingly being integrated into the writing process for academics. Intelligent platforms such as Grammarly Premium, Writefull, and Trinka AI provide grammar corrections, improve clarity in writing, and automatically format citations. More advanced tools, such as Manuscripts. io, even help simulate editorial reviews so that researchers could adjust their drafts based on what is commonly expected of peer review.

These tools are invaluable for manuscript preparation, above all for non-native English speakers. Nonetheless, it is critical to remember that the platforms should always assist, rather than replace, one's critical thinking and authentic scholarly voice. Recent publications warn that excessive dependence on AI-generated content will create a more homogenized academic writing style and may set in motion fears regarding issues of plagiarism or lack of intellectual originality (Salman et al., 2025).

7.5 Ethical Concern and the Danger of Over-Automation

Although numerous benefits arise, uncritical use of AI in research is exposing increasing ethical challenges. Algorithmic bias is one of the most critical challenges; most LLMs and datasets are trained primarily on literature accepted from the Global North, which could marginalize voices and perspectives from the Global South. This will, in turn, reinforce global academic inequalities while denying mainstream discussion to varied perspectives. Besides that, in an overstimulated environment, originality and intellectual diversity may start to get eroded, especially if the researchers begin converging around similar AI logic, phrasing, or references. To that end, it is argued that for epistemic value, the institutes should develop some form of transparent AI policy, require mention of any AI applications in publication, and promote all forms of AI literacy towards researchers (Hanafi et al., 2025).

8. EMPOWERING EDUCATORS IN AN AI-ENABLED ACADEMIC FUTURE

This integration establishes a multi-layered academic framework in which educators and AI systems collaboratively design their learning experiences. The process typically initiates with curriculum development informed by human insights, followed by AI's role of AI in enhancing content through real-time data derived from previous cohorts, research trends, or course outcomes. During the instructional phase, AI tools manage various tasks, including the creation of formative assessments, grading basic assignments, and tracking student engagement patterns. These analytics provide valuable information to educators, who then modify interventions, offer differentiated support, and redesign instructional segments as needed (Elibox et al., 2025). The process of feedback concludes with a shared evaluative process, in which artificial intelligence is involved in quantifying results and teachers exert interpretive control.

The practical use of this AI-enhanced model in the real world is to pick up a broader momentum. For example, Finnish universities have reported that their departments of entrepreneurship integrate generative AI tools into their teaching practices to co-create student pitch simulations, offer AI-created feedback on business plans, and conduct performance assessments. Instructors retain control over all evaluations and employ AI to optimize procedures that would typically demand significant time, enabling them to concentrate on more meaningful student interactions (Kohnke & Zou, 2025). This resulted in a hybrid teaching strategy in which technology augmented, not substituted, the efficacy of educators. As institutions embrace these frameworks, many are implementing structured AI literacy programmes for faculty members.

As higher educational institutions implement these frameworks, numerous have established structured AI literacy programs for their faculty. These initiatives seek to transcend basic functional training by addressing ethical issues, such as bias in automated grading, data security, and the application of AI in student assessments. Educators acquire skills to delegate routine tasks to intelligent systems, thereby freeing up their time for mentorship, interdisciplinary discussions, and reflective teaching. This transformation is fostering a new academic identity in which human judgment and empathy coexist with computational accuracy (Pohn et al., 2025).

This teacher-AI collaboration can be conceived as an ongoing loop: teacher-led planning leads to AI optimization, which improves delivery and on-the-fly analysis, to feed back into teacher insight and optimize strategy. This co-evolution is adaptive education environments which are AI is an analytical colleague, but the professor remains an epistemic guide and moral compass.

In the AI-driven future of learning, the teacher's role is not diminished but fundamentally transformed. Teachers move from being mere transmitters of information to strategic thinkers, designers of individualized learning spaces, and advocates of interdisciplinarity and creativity. While AI technologies offer the scale and pace required in education today, it is the teacher who brings depth, meaning, and ethical purpose to the learning process. This partnership results in a curriculum that is truly resilient for the future adaptive, diverse, and human-centered.

9. GLOBAL POLICY FRAMEWORKS FOR AI IN EDUCATION

AI has disrupted the paradigms of education worldwide, setting the need to have international-level bodies enforce its responsible, inclusive, and ethical integration. At the forefront of designing guiding frameworks to harmonize AI in education cross-nationally are UNESCO, OECD, and the EU. The UNESCO report, AI and Education: Guidance for Policymakers, first popularized the term human-centered AI in education (Miao et al., 2021). The framework supports an inclusive approach, ensuring learner agency, teacher support, and digital equity. It also proposes an AI Competency Framework that countries may use to bolster the readiness of students and teachers in AI-enhanced environments. Several countries, including Brazil, Vietnam, and Egypt, have since integrated aspects of the guidance into their national curriculum design and teacher pathways.

While the OECD AI Principles and the AI Policy Observatory (2020-2025) pass along a multi-layered framework that urges for transparency, accountability, and algorithmic fairness, the main output of the work is the OECD Digital Education Outlook (2023), which recommends core K-12 and tertiary-level AI literacy outcomes such as data fluency, algorithmic awareness, and critical assessment of AI (Rai, 2025). The document emphasizes the importance of students not only utilizing AI tools but also comprehending their underlying logic and potential biases. Furthermore, at a continental scale, the European Commission's "Ethical Guidelines on AI and Data in Education and Training" in 2022 advanced AI policy in the educational domain by placing significant emphasis on learner autonomy, teacher empowerment, and the safeguarding of data privacy rights. These guidelines are also actively upheld by the EU's Digital Education Action Plan (2021–2027), which arranges funding for large-scale pilots of personalized learning technologies, especially those designed to assist multilingual and multicultural classrooms, and also seeks cross-national collaboration in AI ethics research and data governance.

Figure 4. Global AI Education Policy Flow

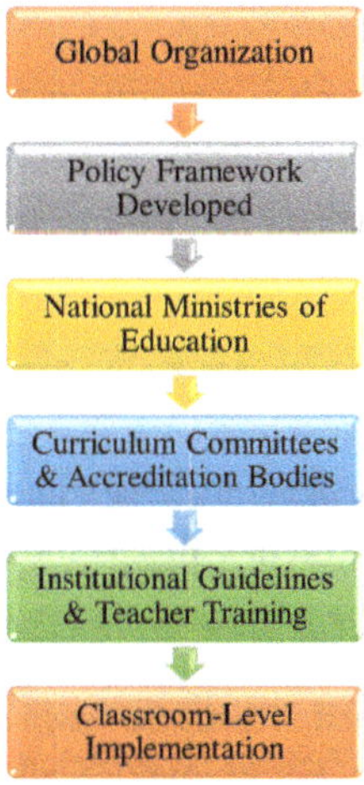

Collectively, these efforts weave a tapestry of international policy considerations that inform the manner in which nations adopt and regulate AI in higher education institutionsal settings. Curriculum developers and academic leaders should develop institutional policies that align with such frameworks to ensure that AI initiatives are ethically aligned, globally relevant, and resilient to future disruptions (Ercan & Akin, 2024).

10. INSTITUTIONAL INTEGRATION OF AI IN CURRICULUM GOVERNANCE

While artificial intelligence presents transformative opportunities for curriculum design, its implementation within higher education institutions (HEIs) is often constrained by structural and bureaucratic challenges. Curriculum governance in universities typically involves multiple layers of decision-making, including faculty boards, academic senates, and accreditation bodies, all of which may operate on multi-year review cycles. These processes can hinder the rapid deployment of AI-driven updates despite clear signals from industry and labor markets (Bond et al., 2021).

Faculty resistance also poses a challenge. Many educators, particularly those trained in traditional models, may be skeptical about AI tools due to fears of academic devaluation or data misuse. Addressing this requires not only technical training but also a cultural shift positioning AI as a collaborative assistant rather than a replacement. Initiatives like structured AI literacy programs and faculty innovation grants have shown promise in shifting.

institutional mind sets. Additionally, the accreditation process must evolve to accommodate dynamic curricular models. Accrediting bodies often require detailed course descriptions and learning outcomes fixed years in advance—constraints that clash with the responsive, real-time adaptability AI enables. Progressive HEIs are now engaging accrediting agencies in dialogue to allow modular, flexible accreditation models, especially for interdisciplinary and emerging technology courses. Examples such as the University of Helsinki's AI education initiative and Stanford's AI ethics curriculum reform demonstrate how institutions can embed AI not only in course delivery but also in academic policy and curriculum design governance. Ultimately, for AI to become a structural ally in higher education, institutions must redesign internal processes and cultivate a governance mindset that values adaptability, agility, and academic foresight.

11. ETHICAL CONSIDERATIONS OF AI IN EDUCATION

As artificial intelligence becomes more integrated into educational systems, the ethical implications are no longer a matter of theoretical discussion they have become pressing concerns. Although AI facilitates personalized learning, expedites assessments, and enhances feedback mechanisms, it also poses significant risks if not managed with care. A primary issue is algorithmic bias, in which AI models trained on historical data may perpetuate inequalities related to race, gender, or socioeconomic status. For example, adaptive learning systems might routinely place students from underprivileged backgrounds into remedial tracks based on their previous performance, thereby restricting their academic advancement instead of promoting it (Chen et al., 2024). Concurrently, the extensive gathering of student data through AI-driven platforms, encompassing everything from engagement metrics to biometric data, raises urgent issues regarding surveillance, consent, and data ownership. In the absence of strong institutional policies for transparency and data ethics, students may remain oblivious to how their individual learning activities are monitored, stored, or exploited (Zawacki-Richter et al., 2019).

The lack of clear and well-defined ethical governance in most universities employing AI technologies is a major concern. Even when certain teachers are likely to use generative AI to perform activities like assessment, advising, and simulation, the lack of standard regulation increases the possibility of inconsistency, reinforcement of bias, and harm to students. Compared to the corporate world, where ethical AI policies are slowly becoming established, institutions of higher learning are not likely to create frameworks for AI accountability. Academic programs should integrate ethical principles with their teaching methods as well as their educational technology choices. This method fosters the creation of a single comprehensive educational system. Educational institutions must implement the Responsible AI in Education Principles from UNESCO and train their staff about algorithmic assessment while involving students in consent processes to achieve transparent and equitable learning environments (Luckin et al., 2023). The capability of AI within educational settings will mainly depend on fair and strategic management rather than the technical capabilities of implemented tools.

CONCLUSION

Integrating AI into education signals much more than innovation; it is going to be a watershed moment. The evidence presented in this chapter indicates ways in which AI is already beginning to change the way education is built. We are transitioning from relatively conventional, standardized teaching systems toward a data-focused, highly dynamic ecosystem that responds periphery to individual subordinate needs-from personalized learning systems to intelligent tutoring tools, neuroadaptive technologies, and AI-enhanced methods of research. This transformation is not merely technical; it is highly human as well. And so, future-proofing education encompasses much more than the replacement of teachers or standardized students-it comprises the re-creating of an environment for a much richer educational experience, allowing students to thrive according to their own pace, issues, and potentials. Thoughtfully conceived and well-implemented, AI in education will eliminate gaps, reveal hidden talents, and help teachers spend more time on mentorship and their own creativity.

Among the most brilliant changes are personalized learning platforms powered by AI, which have started to take on the "one-size-fits-all" approach that has stood for so long and crept into nearly every aspect. Such systems can bring about a reality in rapid adaptation of content, reactions to learners' progress, and instant feedback that proves of great assistance for a better understanding of the concept by students. This equity grants high-quality opportunities for learning to students of varying backgrounds and abilities. The new neuroadaptive AI systems open a whole new era in human-centered personalization. These neural adaptive AI systems combine in-the-name-of considering cognitive sciences, neuroscience, and emotional analytics, offering a highly personalized learning experience regarding factors beyond academic performance, namely: attention, stress level, and mental wellbeing. There is much potential here that we have hardly begun to scratch with broader education, neurodiverse learners, and specific cognitive needs. As noted in this chapter, those already piloting such tools are experiencing measurable achievements on the learner engagement and outcomes fronts.AI equally contributes to the research and scholarship arenas. Resource-consuming manual tasks, such as systematic reviews, citation mapping, and literature synthesis, can now be expedited at warp speed with the help of tools like Iris.ai, Elicit, or Semantic Scholar AI. This development means not just a speedy resolution to academic inquiries but brings forth a world of collective engagement by scholars, especially those beginning their careers or are in resource-constrained situations, to be integrally and meaningfully considered in global academic discourses.

At the policy-making level, international frameworks from UNESCO, OECD, and the European Union provide both ethical railings and international pathways for collaboration. Their initiatives center on inclusiveness, data transparency, and universal AI literacy bringing to fruition the idea that no learner or educator should be left behind in the on going digital revolution. Importantly, these innovations do not weaken the role of teachers; rather, the reverse is true. AI gives teachers back the time they need to devote attention to mentoring, values-based teaching, creativity, and external interdisciplinary exploration. While AI handles data, teachers contribute empathy, cultural insight, and moral reasoning in synergy. Together, this new partnership is redefining teaching and learning for the 21st century. Of course, with every innovation comes responsibility. And as we launch these powerful tools into the world, we need to be ever-mindful of data privacy, algorithmic bias, and equitable access. Yet these concerns are not reasons to slow down; they are invitations to leverage social capital while taking the leading role in implementing ethically. To summarize, AI has come to augment education and its possibilities; it will assist students in becoming all they can become, relinquish educators from mundane tasks, and allow institutions to deliver curricula that are contextual, inclusive, and on a global scale. The future education is intelligent, ethical, and above all, humane.

REFERENCES

Allam, H. M., Gyamfi, B., & Alomar, B. (2025). Sustainable innovation: Harnessing AI and living intelligence to transform higher education. *Education Sciences*, *15*(4), 398. DOI: 10.3390/educsci15040398

Alzahrani, F. A. A., Alolaiwi, L., & Alshammari, S. A. (2025). Shaping the future of dental education: A scoping review of artificial intelligence (AI) integration strategies. *Cureus*, *17*(5), e84921. DOI: 10.7759/cureus.84921

Bates, T., Cobo, C., Mariño, O., & Wheeler, S. (2020). Can artificial intelligence transform higher education? *International Journal of Educational Technology in Higher Education*, *17*(1), 42. DOI: 10.1186/s41239-020-00218-x

Bond, M., Bedenlier, S., Marín, V. I., & Händel, M. (2021). Emergency remote teaching in higher education: Mapping the first global online semester. *International Journal of Educational Technology in Higher Education*, *18*(1), 50. DOI: 10.1186/s41239-021-00282-x

Borges do Nascimento, I. J., Marcolino, M. S., Abdulazeem, H. M., Weerasekara, I., Azzopardi-Muscat, N., Gonçalves, M. A., & Novillo-Ortiz, D. (2021). Impact of big data analytics on people's health: Overview of systematic reviews and recommendations for future studies. *Journal of Medical Internet Research*, *23*(4), e27275. DOI: 10.2196/27275

Borromeo, A. S., Manaloto, A. M., Delos Santos, M. J. M., Antonio, R. P., Soyosa, M. D., & Wide, W. (2025). Harnessing generative AI in nursing education: A bibliometric review. *Teaching and Learning in Nursing*, *20*(3), e1002–e1011. DOI: 10.1016/j.teln.2025.04.014

Chen, X., Zou, D., Xie, H., Cheng, G., & Liu, C. (2022). Two decades of artificial intelligence in education. *Journal of Educational Technology & Society*, *25*(1), 28–47.

Chiu, T. K. F., & Chai, C.-S. (2020). Sustainable curriculum planning for artificial intelligence education: A self-determination theory perspective. *Sustainability (Basel)*, *12*(14), 5568. DOI: 10.3390/su12145568

Chu, T. S., & Ashraf, M. (2025). Artificial intelligence in curriculum design: A data-driven approach to higher education innovation. *Preprints*.

Edwards, R. A., White, B. A. A., & Findyartini, A. (2025). Innovations in teaching and learning for health professions educators. *Frontiers in Medicine*, •••, 12.

Eger, S., Cao, Y., D'Souza, J., Geiger, A., Greisinger, C., Gross, S., Hou, Y., Krenn, B., Lauscher, A., Li, Y., Lin, C., Moosavi, N. S., Zhao, W., & Miller, T. (2025). Transforming science with large language models: A survey on AI-assisted scientific discovery, experimentation, content generation, and evaluation. *arXiv preprint*, arXiv:2502.05151.

Elibox, W., Khan, K., Khan, A., Smart, S., & Cockburn, B. N. (2025). The INSPIRE framework for transformative and inclusive education: A case study of the science faculty at a Commonwealth university. *Quality Assurance in Education*, *33*(4), 585–602. DOI: 10.1108/QAE-02-2025-0037

Ercan, S. I. A., & Akin, O. (2024). International insights on AI risk: Comparative analysis of international organizations. In *2024 8th International Artificial Intelligence and Data Processing Symposium (IDAP)*, 1-8.

Green-Eneix, C., & Kohnke, L. (2025). GenAI and chatbots: Insights into AI and language teaching and learning, 240-260.

Grubov, V. V., Khramova, M. V., Goman, S., Badarin, A. A., Kurkin, S. A., Andrikov, D. A., Pitsik, E., Antipov, V., Petushok, E., Brusinskii, N., Bukina, T., Fedorov, A. A., & Hramov, A. E. (2024). Open-loop neuroadaptive system for enhancing student's cognitive abilities in learning. *IEEE Access : Practical Innovations, Open Solutions*, *12*, 49034–49049. DOI: 10.1109/ACCESS.2024.3383847

Guan, C., Mou, J., & Jiang, Z. (2020). Artificial intelligence innovation in education: A twenty-year data-driven historical analysis. *International Journal of Innovation Studies*, *4*(4), 134–147. DOI: 10.1016/j.ijis.2020.09.001

Hanafi, A. M., Ahmed, M. S., Almansi, M. M., & Al-Sharif, O. A. (2025). Generative AI in academia: A comprehensive review of applications and implications for the research process. *International Journal of Engineering and Applied Sciences - October 6 University*, *2*(1), 91–110.

He, X., & Kang, M. S. (2025). The application of ChatGPT in Chinese MTI students' autonomous learning. *Arab World English Journal (AWEJ) Special Issue on Artificial Intelligence, 17.*

Hilali, K., Chergui, M., & Ammoumou, A. (2023). *Adaptive learning systems: A comprehensive overview and identification of challenges. Operations and Decisions*. ICTMOD.

Holmes, W., Bialik, M., & Fadel, C. (2019). *Artificial intelligence in education: Promise and implications for teaching and learning*. Center for Curriculum Redesign.

Holmes, W., Bialik, M., & Fadel, C. (2023). Artificial intelligence in education. In *Data ethics: Building trust: How digital technologies can serve humanity*, 621-653. DOI: 10.58863/20.500.12424/4276068

Kohnke, L., & Zou, D. (2025). The role of ChatGPT in enhancing English teaching: A paradigm shift in lesson planning and instructional practices. *Journal of Educational Technology & Society*, *28*(3), 4–20.

Luckin, R. (2017). Towards artificial intelligence-based assessment systems. *Nature Human Behaviour, 1*, 0028.

Majumder, A. (2025). Rise & impact of AI agents in digital landscape. *American Journal of Intelligent Systems*, *14*(1), 10–17.

Miao, F., Holmes, W., Huang, R., & Zhang, H. (2021). *AI and education: Guidance for policy-makers*. UNESCO, 45.

Mishra, D., Mishra, R. K., & Agarwal, R. (2025). Impacts of artificial intelligence on society. *Journal of Science Research International*, *11*(1).

Naqvi, W. M., Ganjoo, R., Rowe, M., Pashine, A. A., & Mishra, G. (2025). Critical thinking in the age of generative AI: Implications for health sciences education. *Frontiers in Artificial Intelligence*, *8*, 8. DOI: 10.3389/frai.2025.1571527

Pohn, B., Mehnen, L., Fitzek, S., Choi, K.-E., Braun, R. J., & Hatamikia, S. (2025). Integrating artificial intelligence into pre-clinical medical education: Challenges, opportunities, and recommendations. *Frontiers in Education*, *10*, 1570389. DOI: 10.3389/feduc.2025.1570389

. Qureshi, I. (2025). The impact of AI on teacher roles: Towards a collaborative human-AI pedagogy. *AI in Education: Innovation, Challenges, and Future Perspectives, 2*(1).

Rai, T. (2025). Ethical aspects in machine learning: An agnostic approach. *AI and Ethics*, *5*(6), 5691–5703. DOI: 10.1007/s43681-025-00704-w

Rajput, R. (2025). Use of artificial intelligence to solve problems in the classroom. *New Technological Applications in the Flipped Learning Model*, 32.

Ramezani, A., Bijani, H., & Oroji, M. R. (2025). Comparative analysis of AI vs. human feedback effects on IELTS candidates' writing performance. *Journal of Foreign Language Teaching and Translation Studies*, *10*(1), 17–40.

Salman, H. A., Aliif, M., Ibrahim, R., & Mahmood, J. (2025). Systematic analysis of generative AI tools integration in academic research and peer review. *Online Journal of Communication and Media Technologies*, *15*(1), e202502. DOI: 10.30935/ojcmt/15832

Selwyn, N. (2019). *Should robots replace teachers? AI and the future of education* (1st ed.). Polity Press.

Smith, I., Cherma, S., & Adebayo, H. (2025). AI and blockchain in education: Secure and personalized learning experiences.

Sriram, A., Ramachandran, K., & Krishnamoorthy, S. (2025). Artificial intelligence in medical education: Transforming learning and practice. *Cureus*, *17*(3), e80852. DOI: 10.7759/cureus.80852

Sun, X., Yang, Y., & Du, Q. (2025). Advancing total quality management in higher education through AI and big data analytics. *Total Quality Management & Business Excellence*, *36*(9-10), 1–23. DOI: 10.1080/14783363.2025.2495103

Wagner, G., Lukyanenko, R., & Paré, G. (2021). Artificial intelligence and the conduct of literature reviews. *Journal of Information Technology*, *37*(2), 209–226. DOI: 10.1177/02683962211048201

Yousef, M., Deeb, S., & Hashlamon, K. (2025). AI usage among medical students in Palestine and AI's capability in conducting the research itself: A cross-sectional study. *ResearchSquare*, 1–19.

Zary, A., & Zary, N. (2025). Artificial intelligence in technical and vocational education and training: Empirical evidence, implementation challenges, and future directions. *Preprints.*

Zawacki-Richter, O., Marín, V. I., Bond, M., & Gouverneur, F. (2019). Systematic review of research on artificial intelligence applications in higher education – Where are the educators? *International Journal of Educational Technology in Higher Education*, *16*(1), 1–27. DOI: 10.1186/s41239-019-0171-0

Chapter 2
AI-Driven Curriculum Design in Higher Education:
Frameworks for Future-Ready Learning Ecosystems

Muhammad Usman Tariq
https://orcid.org/0000-0002-7605-3040
Abu Dhabi University, UAE & University College Cork, Ireland

ABSTRACT

Integrating Artificial Intelligence (AI) into curriculum design redesigns the university's formation by enabling personalized, adaptive, and informed learning experiences. AI Control Curriculum Design uses machine learning, learning analytics, and intelligent systems to align academic programs with the needs and learning profiles of the industry being developed. This approach improves student commitment, supports rapid feedback, and encourages the acquisition of skills that align with future requirements for employees. Framework conditions that integrate AI into educational theory and institutional strategies are essential to establishing a resistant future ecosystem. The conditions of these frameworks must consider ethical implications, justice, and interdisciplinary collaboration to ensure integration and sustainable education innovation. Institutions use AI technology, increasing the need for faculty development, robust data government, and iterative assessment processes.

INTRODUCTION

In the rapidly developing landscape of the 21st century, integrating artificial intelligence (AI) into curriculum design is more than just an innovation. Traditional teaching models, often based on standardized linear, teacher-centric paradigms, are no longer sufficient to meet the dynamic needs of today's learners and future work requirements. In this context, AI offers transformative possibilities for reinterpreting curriculum design by being more adaptive, informational, and personalized in data and aligning with actual skills. The order is to ensure relevance, responsive-

DOI: 10.4018/979-8-3373-2752-5.ch002

ness, and resilience in education and exploit students with critical thinking, creativity, problem-solving, and digital literacy skills. A key trend is focusing on lifelong learning, automation of everyday work, and embracing in response to the emergence of new roles characterized by technological innovation. Governments, industry, and academic institutions worldwide recognize the strategic importance of promoting digital skills and ensuring the future of population groups. For example, national education guidelines in countries such as Singapore, Finland, and South Korea explicitly promote using AI and big data in education to improve learning outcomes and institutional performance.

International organizations such as UNESCO and the OECD also support AI's ethical and fair integration, supporting integrated, high-quality education for all. These developments highlight global changes in perspectives. AI is not a supplementary tool but a fundamental part of the next-generation education system. These tools allow educators to gain real-time insight into student behavior, performance, and learning preferences, making curriculum design unimaginable. AI-run learning management systems can recommend content, assess progress based on individual learner profiles, and evaluate adaptation strategies. For example, AI-available platforms can identify whether students must fight concepts and suggest alternative explanations or resources that promote just-in-time support and scaffolding. These skills allow for the construction of flexible, modular curricula that develop in response to learner feedback and data and promote more commitment and knowledge. Institutions such as Arizona State University, Open University in the UK, and Tingia University in China are at the forefront of using AI to personalize education and improve learner outcomes on scale. Through AI-driven simulation, virtual laboratories, and immersive environments, students can participate in interactive and experimental methods with complex, practical problems. Employers increasingly value these educations and promote deeper understanding, critical thinking, and transferable skills essential to global citizenship.

Furthermore, AI promotes collaborative and interdisciplinary learning by combining it with students, peers, mentors, and all local experts. Intelligent agents can ease discussion, curate resources, and enable project-based learning in a distributed environment. Such an approach not only democratizes access to high-quality education but also promotes the social and emotional aspects of learning that are often overlooked in traditional curricula. Instead of viewing the curriculum as a static set of predefined content, AI promotes more dynamic, iterative, and learning models. In this model, the curriculum becomes a living unit that generates knowledge, develops technology, and continuously adapts to changing social needs.

Education is likely to be interpreted, and the designer of learning experiences is merely an information channel. Work with AI systems to create content, monitor progress, personalize instructions, and enable greater differentiation and inclusiveness. This co-evolution of human and machine intelligence improves education's effectiveness and equity, allowing learners to access them to coordinate coordinated paths corresponding to their goals, interests, and context. This model more accurately corresponds to the reality of the modern workforce, where registration information is increasingly evaluated based on skills, outcomes, and formal degrees. AI technology can assess learning through authentic tasks, portfolios, simulations, and even biometric feedback, providing a more holistic and meaningful assessment of student functions. By integrating these reviews into the curriculum design process, institutions can ensure consistent alignment of learning goals, teaching strategies, and assessment methods and address real-time data. This level of integration promotes transparency, accountability, and continuous improvement at individual learners and institutional levels. Issues related to data Equity must remain a central issue, as differences in access to digital infrastructure and AI tools can exacerbate existing inequality. Therefore, agencies must pursue a fundamental and integrated approach to AI adoption. AI will involve various stakeholders in designing government AI systems, promoting the faculty's digital capabilities, and encouraging students and administrators.

To control this complexity, the framework for the design of AI control curriculums should be based on interdisciplinary collaboration, evidence-based practice, and involvement in educational justice. Academic institutions should promote partnerships between educators, computer scientists, cognitive psychologists, data ethics, and education designers to develop robust, context-sensitive solutions. Teacher development is significant to this effort, as educators need skills, trust, and support to use AI tools and pedagogical innovation. The need for institutional leadership, including a culture of innovation, is equally vital in infrastructure, using ethical and strategic use of technology. The conditions of the political framework at both the institutional and national levels should ensure that it will lead to responsible integration of AI and serve the broader mission of education as the existence and driver of social change. By using the power of AI to create a fast, learning-oriented future curriculum, the institution can better prepare students for complexity from the 21st century onwards. This transformation requires technology investments, visionary thinking, ethical leadership, and a deep commitment to human development. Integrating AI into curriculum design is not a goal but a continuous journey to form universities and continually develop a dialogue with the changing world, derived from the permanent principles of justice, excellence, and innovation.

Foundations of AI-Driven Curriculum Design

Amid a rapidly changing digital landscape, higher education institutions must adapt and break free from traditional disciplinary divisions and outdated teaching methods. This transformation necessitates the creation of future-oriented curriculum frameworks dynamic and interdisciplinary, that equip learners with the skills to navigate a complex, uncertain, and ever-changing landscape of innovation. These frameworks are not just about using AI as a tool or studying it but about transforming the entire educational system to be more flexible, individualized, diverse, and applicable.

Future-proof curriculum frameworks are based on several fundamental principles. They stress the importance of learner-centeredness, acknowledging that education should be customized to accommodate students' varied backgrounds, interests, aspirations, and learning styles. Ai empowers educators by offering detailed information on how students interact with content, identifying areas of difficulty, and determining the most effective learning methods for each individual. With access to such data, curriculum designers can move away from standardized models and create personalized pathways that can adapt in real time. Second, these frameworks are skill-based, emphasizing the ability to showcase proficiency rather than adhering to a specific timeline for advancement. This approach better suits the demands of the digital economy, where skills like adaptability, critical thinking, creativity, collaboration, and digital fluency hold greater importance than simply memorizing facts or obtaining credentials. Ai can support the continuous evaluation of these competencies through intelligent analytics, portfolio assessments, and practical project simulations, providing a more comprehensive understanding of student growth.

Another foundational principle is modularity. Future-proof curricula comprise modular, interchangeable learning units that can be combined and rearranged to create personalized educational paths, empowering learners to adapt to changing circumstances and seize new opportunities. Ai guides learners through these modular options by suggesting relevant content, pathways, and micro-credentials based on their career aspirations, market trends, and individual performance. This principle also supports continuous learning, enabling individuals to engage in education at any stage to enhance their skills, acquire new knowledge, or deepen their understanding of a particular field. Furthermore, these frameworks are inherently cross-disciplinary. In a world where challenges and innovations transcend traditional boundaries—such as climate change, public health, cybersecurity, and ethical AI—curricula must incorporate knowledge from various domains. Ai supports this integration by examining intricate datasets, recognizing patterns and connections, and organizing interdisciplinary content that accurately represents real-world complexity.

A key aspect of curriculum design driven by artificial intelligence is the development of AI literacy across various academic fields. AI literacy encompasses more than just technical skills; it involves having a solid grasp of what AI is, how it functions, and its societal implications. It encompasses the capacity to analyze artificial intelligence technologies thoughtfully, interpret the results generated by algorithms, and comprehend the ethical, legal, and societal ramifications associated with their implementation. For computer science and engineering students, this means acquiring advanced technical skills in machine learning, natural language processing, robotics, and neural networks. However, for humanities, social sciences, education, business, or the arts students, AI literacy involves comprehending how AI systems impact human behavior, affect decision-making processes, disrupt established industries, and introduce novel ethical challenges. Each field of study must establish its understanding of AI literacy, specifying the essential skills and knowledge that equip students to engage responsibly and competently with intelligent technologies.

Cultivating artificial intelligence literacy necessitates integrating relevant content and experiences into the curriculum rather than confining them to isolated courses (Khine, 2024). For instance, literature students can delve into the impact of artificial intelligence on creative writing and authorship. In contrast, business students can examine how algorithmic decision-making shapes consumer behavior and market dynamics. Journalism students can interact with AI-driven news curation and fact-checking tools. In contrast, healthcare students can assess diagnostic algorithms and personalized medicine platforms. Students should be encouraged to critically analyze AI technologies' strengths, limitations, and societal impacts in each case. This kind of interdisciplinary collaboration promotes a comprehensive understanding of AI and its impact on shaping the future. Additionally, it guarantees that all graduates, regardless of their chosen profession, possess the necessary skills to effectively navigate a world that is becoming more reliant on intelligent systems.

In addition to fostering AI literacy, curriculum design should ensure that learning outcomes align with the evolving needs of the digital economy. Fast-paced technological advancements widespread automation, define the digital economy, business models centered around platforms, and the significant role of data as a valuable economic resource. In such a setting, achieving success relies not solely on technical abilities but also soft skills such as effective communication, leadership, cultural understanding, and emotional intelligence. Ai-driven curriculum design enables institutions to synchronize educational goals with current labor market demands by utilizing real-time analytics, labor market data mining, and predictive modeling. These tools can pinpoint emerging roles, necessary skills, and sector shifts, empowering curriculum designers to swiftly anticipate and adapt to economic changes.

For example, AI can analyze job postings, professional networks, and employer feedback to identify emerging competencies in demand across various industries. These valuable insights can be utilized to modify or create course content, incorporate relevant micro-credentials, or establish interdisciplinary learning modules that address skill gaps. Institutions can employ AI to simulate future employment scenarios and analyze how various educational paths impact career outcomes. It also enables students to make well-informed decisions about their educational paths, ensuring that their interests align with market demands in a relevant and forward-thinking way.

Aligning learning outcomes with the digital economy's demands necessitates reevaluating assessment methods. Traditional assessments and grading methods frequently fail to capture the intricate and dynamic nature of skills necessary for success in today's workplace. Ai can support alternative assessment methods like digital portfolios, simulations, real-time feedback, and peer evaluations. These techniques offer more genuine and practical insights into a student's development and prospects. Additionally, AI can assist in uncovering concealed patterns in student performance, facilitating early intervention and personalized support. By consistently gathering and examining data, AI empowers institutions to track the achievement of learning objectives and make necessary adjustments to teaching methods. It fosters a learning environment that is constantly evolving and adapting based on both student requirements and external pressures.

While embracing the digital economy is essential, it should not overshadow the broader goals of education. Educational institutions should avoid viewing education solely as a means to prepare individuals for employment (Wadhwani & Mirza, 2025). The curriculum design driven by AI should focus on equipping students with job skills and the ability to actively participate in their communities, make ethical decisions, and develop as individuals. It should cultivate the ability to question, imagine, and create to envision fair, inclusive, and environmentally friendly futures. In this context, AI is not just a tool for optimization but also a medium for transformation. When guided by human values and educational principles, artificial intelligence can assist in shifting the curriculum towards the needs and aspirations of learners and the communities they are a part of.

The vision of curriculum design driven by artificial intelligence relies on a collaborative and inclusive approach. Faculty members are required to participate in the creation, execution, and assessment of artificial intelligence tools and frameworks. Their expertise guarantees that technological solutions are effective in teaching and applicable to the educational context. Educational institutions should allocate resources to faculty development programs that enhance their skills in data literacy, instructional design, and ethical technology usage. Similarly, students should be allowed to contribute to the curriculum, expressing their viewpoints, providing feedback, and sharing their personal experiences to drive ongoing enhancements. Multistakeholder governance structures can facilitate this collaborative approach, uniting educators, students, technologists, employers, policymakers, and community members to develop curricula that align with common objectives and principles.

To facilitate this widespread change, educational institutions require advanced digital systems, strong data management practices, and a mindset that encourages creativity and experimentation. Trust-building, harm mitigation, and accountability are crucial components of transparent algorithms, ethical guidelines, and accountability mechanisms. Additionally, educational institutions must foster a culture of experimentation and continuous learning, motivating teachers to test innovative methods, exchange successful strategies, and refine their practices based on empirical data. It necessitates a transition from models of quality assurance that focus on compliance to more flexible, developmental, and impact-oriented frameworks.

In summary, the core principles of AI-driven curriculum design revolve around transforming education to prepare students for an unpredictable future with immense potential. Institutions can design flexible and long-lasting curricula by incorporating learner-centered, competency-based, modular, and interdisciplinary principles. By establishing and advocating for AI literacy across various academic fields, they can equip students with the skills to thoughtfully and innovatively interact with intelligent technologies. By aligning learning outcomes with the requirements of the digital economy, they can guarantee that education remains up-to-date, accessible, and impactful. AI is not a cure-all solution, nor should it determine the focus of educational priorities. However, when used wisely and morally, it can be valuable in making education more adaptable, fair, and prepared for the future. The way forward necessitates vision, bravery, and cooperation—but the chance to create a more promising educational future has never been more attainable.

Frameworks for AI Integration

In the face of the digital revolution, colleges, and universities are grappling with the need to reimagine their curriculum design to meet the demands of the modern era. In contrast, AI-enhanced curriculum frameworks provide dynamic, flexible, and data-driven alternatives that have the potential to revolutionize the educational experience. The shift from traditional to ai-integrated curriculum models is not simply incorporating new technologies (Alam & Mohanty, 2024). It entails fundamentally rethinking how education is structured, delivered, and evaluated, aligning more closely with real-world demands, lifelong learning imperatives, and student-centered design.

Traditional curriculum models have historically followed a fixed trajectory: knowledge transmission is largely unidirectional from teacher to student, content is often locked into semester-long courses, and learning outcomes are assessed through standardized examinations. These models prioritize in-depth knowledge within specific subject areas and give less importance to skills that can be applied across different subjects, interdisciplinary learning, or ongoing evaluation. While such models have produced generations of capable professionals, they struggle to keep pace with the exponential growth of knowledge and the evolving needs of a workforce that must be adaptable, innovative, and digitally literate. The evaluation methods commonly used in traditional models primarily focus on assessing rote memorization and immediate recall rather than the intricate, practical, and flexible skills required in today's economy.

In contrast, ai-enhanced curriculum frameworks introduce a data-driven, adaptive, and personalized approach to teaching and learning. These frameworks utilize artificial intelligence algorithms to analyze extensive educational data, including student interactions with learning platforms, labor market trends, and employer feedback, to make real-time adjustments to the curriculum. These models facilitate a transition from fixed course outlines to dynamic curricula that adapt to the evolving needs of learners, industry requirements, and emerging societal issues. AI systems can track student progress against predetermined competencies, pinpoint areas lacking learning, and recommend personalized content or experiences to bridge those gaps. The outcome is a customized, adaptable learning experience that equips students with the skills needed for the future.

At the core of this transformation is the creation of competency-based, outcome-focused programs that closely align with AI capabilities and economic realities. Competency-based education (CBE) emphasizes acquiring and showcasing particular skills and knowledge domains rather than the duration of classroom instruction. It acknowledges that students have different learning speeds and may have different levels of prior knowledge. AI systems can support CBE by monitoring student progress across various learning outcomes, analyzing data to gain insights into learning patterns, and suggesting personalized learning paths. This approach allows for a more effective and focused learning experience where students progress based on their ability to demonstrate mastery rather than the time spent in class.

Outcome-driven curriculum design ensures that educational goals align with real-world expectations. AI can help determine the most essential skills across different fields and industries by examining job descriptions, studying career advancement data, and reviewing academic and professional publications. This alignment guarantees that curricula are not created independently but are responsive to the needs of the digital economy. For instance, a business program could incorporate AI-powered modules that enhance data literacy, algorithmic thinking, and ethical reasoning alongside traditional subjects like marketing and finance. A healthcare curriculum could encompass AI-supported training in diagnostic tools, patient data management, and personalized medicine, all designed to adapt to changing healthcare delivery models. These integrations guarantee that graduates possess the knowledge and the necessary skills to succeed in their chosen professions and adapt to the ever-changing demands of the job market.

One of the benefits of ai-enhanced frameworks is their ability to support modular curriculum structures and micro-credentialing systems. units are frequently stackable, allowing students to gradually accumulate larger qualifications as they progress across different educational institutions. AI assists in creating and managing these modular systems by monitoring student progress, mapping skills acquisition, and recommending personalized combinations based on career goals or areas where students may need additional support. This flexibility allows learners to create educational journeys, seamlessly transitioning between formal education, on-the-job training, and continuous learning opportunities.

Micro-credentials are a groundbreaking development in this field, providing focused acknowledgment for particular skills and areas of expertise. These credentials are especially valuable in a world where job roles constantly change, and continuous learning is crucial for professional growth. Ai can facilitate micro-credentialing in various manners. Initially, it can examine labor market data to pinpoint high-demand skills and, therefore, require credentialing (Patel & Lim, 2024). Second, it can tailor student credential recommendations based on their academic and career aspirations. Third, AI can automate and validate micro-credential assessments using intelligent evaluation systems that surpass traditional testing methods. These systems can analyze student projects, peer collaboration, simulations, and real-time decision-making tasks. It strengthens micro-credentials credibility and streamlines the assessment process, making it more scalable and efficient.

Additionally, micro-credentials facilitated by artificial intelligence can be effortlessly incorporated into digital portfolios and blockchain-based credentialing platforms, allowing students to demonstrate their skills to potential employers transparently and verifiably. This system facilitates the establishment of lifelong learning records—living documents that change as learners gain new skills and experiences. As artificial intelligence (AI) technologies advance, these records may become more dynamic, incorporating real-time feedback, predictive analytics, and cross-platform learning data to assist individuals in navigating intricate educational and career landscapes.

The incorporation of AI also allows for more comprehensive and adaptable curriculum governance. Faculty and curriculum designers can utilize AI dashboards to assess the impact of particular modules, monitor student involvement and progress patterns, and determine which teaching methods yield the most favorable outcomes. These observations enable data-driven choices and ongoing curriculum enhancement. For example, suppose an AI system identifies that a specific module consistently leads to lower engagement or achievement. Educators can modify the content, teaching methods, or assessment techniques to suit the student's needs better. This feedback loop enables institutions to stay flexible and guarantees that the curriculum remains up-to-date and impactful.

Nevertheless, incorporating artificial intelligence into frameworks also brings about specific challenges that must be effectively addressed. One worry is the possibility of becoming too dependent on artificial intelligence for decision-making in educational environments. Although AI can offer valuable insights, it is not infallible and should not be relied upon to replace human judgment. Curriculum designers are crucial in analyzing data, making educational choices, and ensuring AI recommendations align with educational objectives. Additionally, it is crucial to tackle the problem of bias in artificial intelligence algorithms to avoid perpetuating existing societal inequalities.

In addition to concerns about data privacy and student autonomy, there are also worries about the potential misuse of personal information and the impact on student's ability to make independent decisions. Educational institutions need to establish comprehensive data protection policies, obtain informed consent, and empower students to have control over their learning data. To ensure responsible handling of educational data, it is crucial to establish ethical guidelines that protect student rights and foster trust in artificial intelligence systems (Grubaugh & Levitt, 2024). Furthermore, there is a requirement for substantial investment in digital infrastructure, faculty training, and cross-disciplinary collaboration to implement ai-integrated frameworks successfully.

Despite the obstacles, the potential advantages of AI-driven curriculum frameworks are significant. They pledge to enhance higher education by making it more flexible, accessible, and prepared for the future. They enable learners to have more control over their educational paths, ensure that programs are better aligned with the demands of society and the economy, and equip institutions with the means to enhance teaching and learning consistently. As artificial intelligence (AI) technologies continue to advance, their role in curriculum design will become more complex, extending beyond content recommendation and assessment to support advanced functions like dynamic curriculum mapping, interdisciplinary integration, and predictive modeling of student success.

In essence, the transition from conventional to AI-enhanced curriculum frameworks signifies a more profound change in the underlying principles and methods of education. It represents a shift from rigid, uniform systems to flexible, customized models tailored to the contemporary era's intricacies (Trajkovski & Hayes., 2025). It does not replace the human aspects of education, such as mentorship, creativity, and ethical reasoning but rather enhances them by relieving educators from administrative tasks, offering a more profound understanding of learner requirements, and expanding the scope for innovative curricula.

Strategies for Curriculum Redesign

Updating curriculum in the era of artificial intelligence necessitates a thoughtful and well-planned approach to guarantee that educational programs across various fields are in sync with the ever-changing landscape of a technologically advanced society. As institutions face growing pressure to produce knowledgeable, agile, adaptable, and as-literate graduates, embedding competencies into existing and new academic programs becomes essential (Portuguez-Castro, 2024). This process thoroughly examines content delivery, learning objectives, teaching methods, and collaboration with external stakeholders like industry and technology partners. The objective is not to replace traditional academic values but to augment them by incorporating artificial intelligence (AI) tools, insights, and applications that foster relevance, innovation, and preparedness for the future in higher education.

The initial step in this process is to map the competencies into the existing academic programs. Rather than viewing AI as an isolated field relevant only to computer science or data analytics, institutions must recognize that AI literacy is becoming foundational across all domains—from the humanities and social sciences to healthcare, business, law, and engineering (Allam et al., 2025). It necessitates thoroughly examining the existing curriculum to determine where artificial intelligence concepts, tools, and applications can be effectively integrated. The mapping process begins by articulating a set of core AI competencies that are broadly applicable: these may include understanding machine learning fundamentals, interpreting AI outputs, ethical reasoning around algorithmic decision-making, data literacy, and the ability to work collaboratively with intelligent systems. After establishing the competencies, curriculum teams can examine course structures and content to identify areas where they can be aligned.

For instance, in a psychology program, AI concepts can be introduced through modules on analyzing behavioral data or the application of AI in diagnosing mental health conditions. In law programs, students can delve into the legal ramifications of artificial intelligence technologies, such as automated criminal justice system decision-making or data privacy legislation development. In environmental science, students might investigate how artificial intelligence supports climate modeling or innovative resource management. The key is not completely overhauling every course into a technical program but integrating artificial intelligence to enrich disciplinary learning while fostering essential cross-cutting skills. This method enhances current curricula and expands students' comprehension of how AI transforms their fields.

Integrating artificial intelligence (AI) into general education and core subjects is a potent approach that guarantees all students, regardless of their chosen field, a fundamental understanding of how AI operates and influences society. General education offers a unique chance to make AI literacy accessible to all students by incorporating it into their fundamental courses. For example, introductory writing courses can incorporate assignments that delve into the consequences of artificial intelligence-generated content or ethical discussions surrounding deepfakes and misinformation (Amiri et al., 2025). Mathematics and statistics courses can expose students to algorithmic thinking and predictive modeling using artificial intelligence tools. Philosophy and ethics courses can assist students in analyzing the ethical aspects of artificial intelligence, including fairness, accountability, and transparency in automated systems.

Integrating AI across different subjects ensures that AI literacy is not limited to specific fields but becomes a valuable skill that students can apply in their future careers and as active members of society. It encourages students to think across different subjects. It helps them understand technological advancements' social, cultural, and political aspects (Vadisetty & Polamarasetti, 2024). Additionally, by incorporating artificial intelligence (AI) into the educational process early, institutions foster curiosity, alleviate anxiety, and establish a strong base of knowledge that can be further developed in specialized areas. The outcome is a student population better prepared to navigate and influence the AI-driven world they are stepping into.

To achieve this, it is essential to provide faculty development and institutional support. Many instructors may lack expertise in artificial intelligence or data science, necessitating professional development programs to equip educators with the necessary knowledge and confidence to teach ai-related subjects. Workshops, collaborative curriculum design sessions, and interdisciplinary teaching teams can all contribute to this process. Institutions may also consider creating educational resources that faculty can modify to fit their courses, such as open educational modules, simulations, and case studies. By investing in faculty development, the infusion of AI into education becomes a meaningful and effective pedagogical approach rather than a mere superficial addition.

Alongside internal curriculum innovation, collaborating with industry partners is a crucial strategy for guaranteeing that AI curriculum redesign remains up-to-date and impactful. Companies in various industries are looking for graduates who possess theoretical knowledge and practical skills that can be applied in real-world scenarios. By interacting with the industry, institutions can access up-to-date labor market information, emerging skill requirements, and practical examples that shape the content and organization of their curriculum. AI can support this collaboration by analyzing real-time labor market data, identifying skill gaps, and forecasting future trends. Utilizing data-driven methods guarantees that curricula are not solely based on historical norms or academic tradition but are forward-looking and aligned with market realities.

Collaborating with industry to develop curriculum can be done in various ways. Industry leaders can serve on advisory boards to offer regular feedback on curriculum updates. Institutions can collaborate with AI companies to develop learning modules, organize hackathons or innovation challenges, and offer experiential learning opportunities like internships or capstone projects that address real-world issues. These activities enable students to acquire hands-on experience and comprehend the practical utilization of AI tools in various professional settings. They actively cultivate connections that can facilitate career opportunities and ongoing collaboration between academia and industry.

For instance, a university collaborating with a fintech company could create a module on algorithmic trading or AI-based fraud detection as part of a finance program. In a nursing or public health program, partnering with a health tech company could result in the creation of educational materials on artificial intelligence-supported diagnostics or predictive modeling for patient care. In the field of creative arts, collaborations with AI art platforms could lead to the development of modules on generative design and the integration of human-machine collaboration in digital storytelling. These partnerships guarantee that the curriculum content is based on real-world applications and introduces students to the latest advancements and obstacles in the field.

However, it is crucial to handle the co-development process cautiously to prevent excessive commercialization or the compromise of academic independence. Educational institutions must establish well-defined principles and frameworks to guide partnerships, ensuring that educational values and student interests are always the top priority. The foundation of successful collaborations should be built upon transparency, fairness, and shared benefits for all parties involved. Additionally, while industry insights are highly valuable, they should not overshadow the importance of critical perspectives, theoretical foundations, and the broader humanistic goals of education. Students should be equipped to fulfill industry demands and challenge and influence them through critical thinking, creativity, and ethical contemplation.

Integrating AI capabilities into current programs guarantees that students can actively participate in AI within their respective disciplines. Incorporating artificial intelligence into general education is a basis for developing ethical and interdisciplinary comprehension. Collaborating with industry partners to create curricula guarantees alignment with current job market demands and improves students' employability. By combining these approaches, we can equip students with the necessary skills to engage and take charge actively in an AI-driven society.

Ultimately, these strategies' effectiveness relies on institutions' dedication, collaboration between different sectors, and a readiness to embrace ongoing innovation. Curriculum design should no longer be a sporadic, reactive process but an ongoing dialogue informed by data, driven by purpose, and adaptable to change. By incorporating artificial intelligence (AI) at all levels—disciplinary, general, and collaborative higher education can construct learning ecosystems that equip students with the skills to succeed in complex, uncertain, and transformative environments.

Case Studies and Best Practices

Case studies of AI-infused curriculum design in higher education provide valuable insights into how institutions worldwide successfully incorporate artificial intelligence to improve teaching methods, student learning outcomes, and overall competitiveness. Content is created, offering practical frameworks and strategic guidance for other educational institutions seeking to undergo similar transformations.

One noteworthy example is the Massachusetts Institute of Technology (MIT), which has consistently been at the forefront of artificial intelligence (AI) research and education. In recent years, it established the Schwarzman College of Computing to integrate computing and artificial intelligence principles into various academic disciplines, such as humanities, economics, and the social sciences. Instead of confining AI education to computer science departments, MIT's initiative is based on the belief in integrating AI across various disciplines. It is evident in courses taught by multiple instructors. These research projects combine different fields of study and curriculum development efforts that integrate ethics, algorithmic literacy, and applied machine learning into various academic programs. Professors from the fields of literature and philosophy team up with data scientists to investigate issues of bias and agency in artificial intelligence, while economics students work with ai-generated models to simulate the effects of different policies. This institutional strategy showcases a comprehensive approach to integrating AI, emphasizing collaboration, interdisciplinary thinking, and an understanding of AI's societal impact.

Carnegie Mellon University is renowned for its computer science and engineering expertise. It has created adaptive tutoring systems and virtual labs that adjust to students' real-time performance. For instance, the open learning initiative employs artificial intelligence (AI) to analyze learner engagement and offer personalized feedback loops, empowering instructors to adapt their teaching methods in real time. In biology classes, students engage with AI-powered lab simulations that enable them to perform virtual experiments and receive instant, context-specific guidance. This adaptive learning environment fosters a deeper comprehension and active participation, especially in subjects often considered challenging or abstract. Furthermore, the institution's incorporation of AI into curriculum design encompasses assessment, where predictive analytics are employed to identify at-risk students and suggest personalized interventions, ultimately improving student retention and achievement.

In business education, the Wharton School at the University of Pennsylvania has integrated artificial intelligence (ai) into both the delivery of content and the curriculum structure. As part of its AI for Business initiative, the Wharton School provides courses on how AI influences marketing, finance, operations, and decision-making processes. The curriculum incorporates case-based learning, where students utilize AI tools to analyze large datasets, predict market trends, and create algorithmic trading strategies.

In healthcare education, institutions like the University of Toronto have been at the forefront of incorporating artificial intelligence (AI) into medical and nursing curricula. Acknowledging the growing prevalence of AI in healthcare, the university has incorporated courses on AI fundamentals into its curriculum for healthcare professionals (Samadhiya et al., 2025). These programs focus on technical skills and emphasize ethical considerations and effective communication—equipping future healthcare professionals to interpret AI outputs responsibly and engage with patients openly. Artificial intelligence can improve simulated clinical environments, enabling students to practice diagnosing rare conditions, handling complex emergencies, and interpreting medical images using algorithmic assistance. In specific programs, AI generates virtual patients whose symptoms change in response to student interactions, providing an immersive and dynamic learning environment that seamlessly integrates theory and practice. This model not only enhances medical knowledge but also strongly emphasizes critical thinking and ethical decision-making in challenging situations.

Incorporating AI in the arts offers a distinctive chance to merge artistic expression with the power of computational intelligence. At the University of the Arts London, AI is integrated into design, music, and media courses, fostering an environment that promotes experimentation and critical thinking. Students utilize AI tools to create visual art, compose music, and craft immersive storytelling experiences. The courses are structured to delve into the visual appeal of machine-generated art, the political aspects of algorithms in the creative process, and the consequences of artificial intelligence in cultural production. Studio-based learning is improved with the help of AI-assisted feedback, where students receive recommendations for improvement based on stylistic patterns, historical references, or simulated user responses. This method showcases how artificial intelligence can be effectively incorporated into creative fields, promoting critical thinking and digital literacy.

A common thread in all of these examples is using AI to enhance cross-disciplinary curriculum models. Arizona State University has embraced this model through its Learning Futures Initiative, which seeks to create educational experiences that transcend traditional academic boundaries. Courses are developed collaboratively by groups of educators from various faculties, and artificial intelligence is employed to streamline the integration of knowledge across different academic disciplines. For example, a course on smart cities could integrate civil engineering, public policy, computer science, and urban sociology, utilizing artificial intelligence tools to simulate traffic patterns, energy consumption, and policy effects. These courses focus on developing problem-solving skills in complex, real-world situations and equip students with the ability to work in diverse, interdisciplinary settings that are becoming more prevalent in the job market.

The integration of micro-credentials and modular learning units, typically facilitated by artificial intelligence platforms, facilitates the scalability of these advancements. Universities such as the University of Helsinki provide online AI literacy modules that are open to students from various academic fields and even the general public. These brief, concentrated courses introduce fundamental AI principles in relatable scenarios (Sachdeva, 2024). They are intended to be built upon for larger qualifications or used as on-demand learning materials. AI systems monitor learner progress and suggest subsequent actions, ensuring a highly personalized learning experience. This model enables educational institutions to provide flexible and inclusive access to AI education, aligning with the vision of lifelong learning.

From a governance standpoint, best practices in integrating AI into the curriculum require strong leadership from institutions, training for faculty members, and ethical oversight. Successful institutions prioritize training educators in the use of AI tools and the principles of AI pedagogy, enabling them to create inclusive, accessible, and impactful learning experiences. Measures are implemented to guarantee transparency in the utilization of AI in content creation, evaluation, and student assistance. Institutions like the Delft University of Technology have developed ethical frameworks for artificial intelligence (AI), which shape the curriculum and prioritize values like fairness, accountability, and sustainability (Arumugam et al., 2024). These frameworks are created with students, faculty, and external stakeholders to guarantee their relevance and legitimacy.

One effective approach is to collaborate with industry partners to create curriculum materials. Industry partners contribute datasets, tools, and knowledge while collaborating on joint research and completing capstone projects. Students gain practical experience and the chance to apply their knowledge in real-life situations. At the same time, educational institutions retain the flexibility to modify their curricula to adapt to evolving technological advancements.

These case studies highlight the variety of methods and the abundance of opportunities when artificial intelligence is thoughtfully incorporated into curriculum design (Sethi & Singh, 2024). Whether through advanced tutoring systems in STEM, creative tools in the arts, or predictive analytics in business and healthcare, AI is revolutionizing education by offering personalized, immersive, and adaptive learning experiences that cater to the evolving needs of the future. As higher education adapts to the digital age, these examples provide inspiration and guidance for creating curriculum ecosystems that are enhanced by artificial intelligence and prioritize human-centeredness.

Faculty Enablement and Pedagogical Innovation

Incorporating artificial intelligence into curriculum design, teaching, and assessment requires a significant transformation in the responsibilities of educators (Tyagi et al., 2024). Faculty members are no longer just sources of information. However, they are now active participants, collaborators, and guides in learning environments enhanced by artificial intelligence. Encouraging faculty to embrace and utilize AI tools is not solely about providing technical training. It is a transformative shift in mindset, cognition, and teaching practices that permeates every facet of academic life.

Developing effective faculty for AI pedagogical competence starts with creating awareness and establishing a solid foundation of understanding. Some professors, especially those in non-technical subjects, may feel overwhelmed or unsure about artificial intelligence, considering it unrelated to their primary academic duties (Amiri, 2025). The initial step in any development strategy is to demystify AI by providing straightforward, contextualized explanations of what AI is, how it functions, and how it is already utilized in education and society. Workshops, webinars, and seminars can offer faculty the foundational knowledge to understand concepts like machine learning, natural language processing, predictive analytics, and ethical AI. Nevertheless, these experiences should extend beyond surface-level exposure to encourage deep understanding and active participation. The goal is to change the perception of AI from a potential danger or futuristic concept to a practical and evolving tool that can improve teaching methods, customize learning experiences, and enhance educational results.

After gaining a basic understanding, faculty require assistance applying artificial intelligence knowledge to their teaching methods. It is where structured, discipline-specific development programs become crucial. Training programs should be customized to meet various departments' specific requirements and teaching methods. For example, humanities professors may concentrate on applying AI to analyze texts or create digital narratives. In contrast, business professors may delve into AI's use in predicting consumer behavior or forecasting financial trends. Professional learning communities, departmental innovation labs, and cross-disciplinary teams can serve as spaces for collaborative exploration, experimentation, and learning from one another. These settings allow faculty to work together to create, evaluate, and improve instructional methods incorporating artificial intelligence while promoting a culture of innovation in teaching.

Creating adaptive instructional content and learning pathways is essential to faculty enablement. Ai-responsive pedagogy necessitates transitioning from traditional, one-way teaching methods to interactive, data-driven, and student-focused strategies. Instructors must acquire the skills to curate and produce content that engages with artificial intelligence platforms, enabling them to provide customized learning experiences. For instance, adaptive learning systems can modify the level of difficulty or the nature of the content based on the performance data of individual students. To make the most of these systems, educators need to know how to organize content that matches the algorithms, ensure equal access for all students, and maintain academic standards. It includes choosing or creating learning materials that can be easily combined, labeled with metadata, and work well with AI-enhanced learning management systems.

Additionally, ai-responsive content design incorporates formative assessment tools that offer immediate feedback to students and actionable insights to instructors. Instructors must understand and analyze this feedback, modify their teaching methods, and provide personalized learning paths for each student. They must also be ready to confront potential biases in AI systems, identify patterns of exclusion, and advocate for transparency and fairness in the decision-making processes of algorithms. These competencies are not solely technical but deeply pedagogical, necessitating faculty to combine subject-matter expertise with a comprehensive understanding of data ethics, digital equity, and instructional design.

The role of educators in developing and selecting AI-enhanced resources is crucial. Instead of solely depending on commercially-produced or institutionally-provided AI tools, faculty should be given the authority to influence the content and structure of these resources actively. The co-creation process entails creating ai-ready materials, such as annotated datasets, domain-specific knowledge graphs, and contextualized prompts, improving AI applications' relevance and effectiveness in educational settings. It also involves actively participating in open educational resources, contributing to shared repositories, and collaborating with edtech developers to ensure that artificial intelligence (AI) tools align with educators' pedagogical objectives and disciplinary principles.

Faculty involvement in creating and improving AI systems is a protective measure against the excessive standardization of education (Deri et al., 2024). When teachers actively select augmented reality (AR) content, they can guarantee that it represents a wide range of viewpoints, fosters analytical skills, and stimulates imaginative thinking instead of promoting uniformity. It is particularly crucial in prioritizing interpretation, debate, and subjective comprehension. Teachers can create prompts that steer AI tools towards more complex outputs, incorporate reflective exercises into automated content delivery, and merge algorithmic suggestions with personalized instruction.

Institutions must offer continuous and diverse resources to support faculty members in these roles. One-off seminars or webinars are inadequate (Shaznay, 2025). Instructors require continuous support from instructional designers, artificial intelligence experts, and peer mentors who can assist them in understanding and implementing AI effectively. Educational institutions should transform into centers of AI-pedagogical innovation, providing consultancy services, sandbox environments for testing tools, and collaborative grant opportunities for ai-enhanced teaching projects (Ishrat et al., 2025). Acknowledging and honoring faculty members' contributions—incorporating pedagogical criteria into promotion evaluations, establishing innovation awards, or offering teaching fellowships—can strengthen motivation and demonstrate institutional dedication to educational change.

Furthermore, building faculty capacity for AI pedagogy should be rooted in ethical contemplation and a sense of social responsibility. As teachers integrate artificial intelligence into their lessons, they must be prepared to guide students in thoughtfully engaging with these technologies. Instructors should demonstrate ethical data usage, emphasize the constraints and dangers of artificial intelligence, and foster discussions about the societal effects of AI. This ethical aspect of AI pedagogy is especially crucial in cultivating well-informed, accountable, and self-assured learners. Institutions can foster this by incorporating ethics training into faculty development programs and promoting collaboration between computer science, philosophy, education, and other disciplines.

Faculty members are instrumental in connecting artificial intelligence tools with learners from various backgrounds and abilities. Inclusive pedagogy should be a fundamental aspect of any AI integration initiatives. Teachers must comprehend how artificial intelligence systems may have varying effects on students depending on their backgrounds, learning preferences, and availability of technology. They should be equipped with the skills to assess the accessibility of AI tools, modify content to cater to multilingual or neurodiverse learners, and leverage AI-generated insights to promote equity in learning outcomes (Ortiz et al., 2025). By prioritizing inclusivity in AI pedagogy, faculty can guarantee that technological advancements in education contribute to, rather than hinder, educational equity.

Faculty members are not passive recipients of technological advancements but active participants in shaping educational transformation through their pedagogical roles. By acquiring AI pedagogical competence, creating ai-responsive content, and collaborating on resource development, educators can leverage the potential of AI to augment not supplant the human aspects of teaching and learning. Their work shapes a forward-thinking, fair, and intellectually stimulating educational future.

This alteration will not occur instantaneously. Achieving a shared vision, gaining institutional support, and embracing experimentation, failure, and learning are essential for success. Instructors should be provided with sufficient time, resources, and independence to venture into uncharted teaching methods. Educational institutions must cultivate an environment that encourages and values teaching as a scholarly and creative endeavor. Faculty and institutions can collectively develop the skills and knowledge required to succeed in an AI-enhanced educational environment by collaborating, persevering, and continuously learning. The future of curriculum is not solely determined by the technologies we choose but by the educators who skillfully integrate them into their teaching, ensuring inclusivity and inspiration for all students.

Governance, Ethics, and Quality Assurance

Nevertheless, the immense potential for transformation necessitates meticulous governance, unwavering ethical vigilance, and robust quality assurance (Hoke, 2025). Without proper institutional frameworks and ethical reflection, the integration of AI in education can inadvertently perpetuate biases, erode trust, compromise academic integrity, and exacerbate existing inequalities. Consequently, governance structures, policy development, and ethical safeguards are not secondary considerations—they are fundamental aspects of any endeavor to construct ai-integrated, future-ready learning ecosystems that are fair, transparent, and accountable (Aithal et al., 2024). Similarly, as educational institutions continue to explore and expand AI-enhanced programs, it is crucial to establish systematic mechanisms for monitoring, evaluating, and guaranteeing the quality of the learning experience and the technologies that facilitate it.

The foundation of responsible AI-driven curriculum innovation lies in effective institutional governance. Universities must actively create and enforce policies that outline the ethical, educational, and operational considerations of incorporating AI into teaching and learning. These frameworks should provide a clear vision for integrating AI into the institution, establish principles for fair access and ethical innovation, and define the roles and responsibilities of faculty, administrators, students, and technology partners. These governance structures should not be confined to top-down instructions. However, they should be shaped by inclusive engagement with stakeholders from various fields and positions. Collaborative policy development guarantees that the frameworks encompass various viewpoints and institutional realities, enhancing the chances of successful and ethical implementation.

Policy frameworks should tackle multiple key domains. Initially, they need to establish comprehensive guidelines on data governance, explicitly addressing the collection, storage, usage, and sharing of student learning data. Since AI systems heavily depend on extensive datasets, organizations must establish clear data privacy policies that adhere to national and international standards (Indumathy & Mujra, 2025). Both students and faculty must be aware of the data being collected, how it is handled, and the reasons behind its collection.

Second, institutional policies should tackle algorithmic transparency and accountability. When AI tools make decisions or provide recommendations that affect learners' academic progress, there should be ways to understand how these decisions are reached and to question them if needed (George, 2024). Both educators and students should have access to clear and comprehensible explanations of how artificial intelligence tools operate and how they generate specific results. There should be transparent accountability measures, such as procedures for reviewing and modifying AI systems in case of mistakes or prejudice. Policy frameworks should underscore the significance of human involvement, ensuring that educators retain their central role in interpreting AI outputs and making final pedagogical choices.

Although AI provides advanced capabilities for personalization, efficiency, and insight generation, it poses significant ethical concerns regarding autonomy, equity, bias, and agency (Bharat, 2024). One of the most important ethical considerations is to prevent AI-enhanced learning from unintentionally perpetuating existing social inequalities. AI systems trained on historical data can reproduce and magnify existing biases, especially when certain groups have been systematically excluded or underrepresented. For example, predictive analytics could categorize students from marginalized backgrounds as "at-risk" based on patterns that reflect historical inequalities rather than their abilities. Organizations must prioritize bias detection and mitigation practices, such as utilizing diverse training datasets, conducting regular bias audits, and involving interdisciplinary ethics experts in evaluating AI systems.

Additionally, the ethical use of artificial intelligence in education necessitates a firm dedication to student autonomy and obtaining informed consent. Students should be informed about the instances and methods in which AI is integrated into their educational journey, and they should have the option to decline participation in automated procedures if they prefer (Alangari, 2024). Transparency is crucial in data practices and how artificial intelligence (AI) influences learning pathways, assessments, and feedback. Students should be regarded as active contributors in creating AI-enhanced learning rather than mere recipients of information. This participatory approach must also be applied during the design phase, where students' input can shape artificial intelligence tools' development, testing, and improvement. Ethical AI use necessitates continuous conversation, self-reflection, and adaptability to the real-life experiences of the individuals impacted (Tariq, 2025).

Academic honesty is another vital ethical dimension. For instance, if an AI tool is employed to offer writing support or generate learning feedback, students should be educated on using these tools responsibly and giving credit to their contributions (Kayyali, 2025). Simultaneously, educators should refrain from excessively relying on AI-generated assessments that may lack depth or fail to evaluate complex thinking abilities. By promoting ethical AI literacy, educational institutions can assist teachers and students in effectively navigating the opportunities and challenges presented by AI-enhanced learning while upholding integrity and accountability.

To ensure the effectiveness and appropriateness of AI tools, traditional quality assurance frameworks must be expanded to include criteria that evaluate their performance, impact, and alignment with educational goals (Yahchouchi & Rotabi, 2025). Quality assurance processes should evaluate whether artificial intelligence applications are genuinely enhancing learning outcomes, increasing student engagement, and easing faculty workload or if they are introducing new complexities, inequalities, or unforeseen consequences. Assessment should be grounded in evidence, incorporating both numerical data and subjective opinions from students and teachers.

Educational institutions should incorporate AI-specific indicators into their program evaluation and accreditation procedures to accomplish this. These might include metrics related to data ethics compliance, student satisfaction with AI-supported learning experiences, faculty confidence in using AI tools, and the accessibility of AI-enhanced platforms. External peer reviews can also be valuable in evaluating the educational soundness of AI-driven innovations. Accreditation bodies and regulatory agencies must be involved in these processes, establishing common standards and guidelines to determine the quality of ai-integrated education. It will guarantee uniformity, responsibility, and public confidence across various organizations and structures.

Crucially, quality assurance should be an ongoing and flexible process. In light of the fast-paced nature of technological advancements, institutions need to embrace agile evaluation approaches that enable ongoing enhancement and adaptability to new challenges. Pilot programs can be utilized to evaluate new AI applications before expanding, with comprehensive monitoring and feedback mechanisms incorporated. Faculty members should receive assistance in recording their innovative ideas, analyzing their effectiveness, and sharing their successful approaches in an institutional repository. Collecting and considering students' viewpoints in the evaluation process is crucial. It might involve conducting user experience surveys, organizing focus groups, or hosting participatory design workshops where students can provide feedback and contribute to creating AI-enhanced learning environments (Tariq, 2025).

An additional aspect of quality assurance focuses on the faculty's capabilities and resources and the institution's overall infrastructure. Even the most sophisticated AI tools will not provide educational value if faculty members are not adequately trained or the necessary infrastructure is lacking. Educational institutions need to evaluate if their technical support systems, professional development programs, and teaching resources align with the requirements of AI-driven learning. Quality assurance teams should work closely with departments, academic developers, and teaching and learning centers to guarantee that AI integration is supported at every level. Collaboration between different departments is crucial to prevent isolated efforts and to ensure consistency across various programs.

Ultimately, the quest for quality should not be confined to meeting compliance and performance standards, a comprehensive vision of educational excellence in the era of artificial intelligence should drive it. It encompasses cultivating a culture that encourages critical thinking, innovation, and inclusivity. AI should not only be assessed based on its outcomes but also on how it influences the values, relationships, and experiences that shape higher education. Quality in AI-enhanced learning is not just about achieving efficiency or desired outcomes (Padovano & Cardamone, 2024). It is about creating environments where technology supports human flourishing, upholds democratic values, and contributes to the betterment of society.

In summary, incorporating AI into higher education necessitates more than technological adjustments, it demands a comprehensive, principled, and systematic approach to governance, ethics, and quality assurance. Clear and inclusive institutional policy frameworks are necessary to guide AI innovation. Quality assurance systems must be reimagined to encompass the complexities and opportunities of AI-enhanced programs, promoting continuous improvement, transparency, and accountability. These pillars are the basis for a responsible and forward-thinking educational ecosystem that utilizes artificial intelligence to support the highest teaching, learning, and human growth goals.

Challenges and Opportunities

Incorporating artificial intelligence into curriculum design and delivery in higher education signifies a significant shift in teaching and administrative practices. However, achieving this integration is neither straightforward nor universally accepted. Institutions encounter various obstacles in embracing AI-driven frameworks, primarily due to structural resistance, inconsistent infrastructure, and societal concerns. Despite the challenges, there are also great opportunities for innovation, fairness, and global cooperation opportunities that can be taken advantage of through careful planning, inclusive decision-making, and a shared dedication to improving education.

One of the institutions' most significant challenges is the reluctance to embrace change. Colleges and universities are usually conservative institutions with many rules and traditions and different departments that work separately. Faculty and administrative leaders may hesitate to adopt artificial intelligence technologies that challenge their teaching methods or pose a risk to their employment. This resistance can take on different forms, such as doubts about the effectiveness of AI in improving learning, data privacy, ethical concerns, and the potential loss of academic integrity. Additionally, the rapid pace of technological progress can be overwhelming, resulting in a climate of uncertainty that hinders innovation rather than promoting it. Overcoming this resistance necessitates careful and considerate change management approaches prioritizing effective communication, skill development, and active involvement of all stakeholders (Tariq, 2025).

Successful change management starts with leaders with a clear vision and active involvement of all stakeholders. The leaders of educational institutions need to communicate the purpose of artificial intelligence (AI) in higher education, emphasizing that it is not meant to replace human judgment and expertise but rather to enhance and complement it. This story should be based on real advantages: increased student involvement, improved academic performance, curriculum adjustments that meet industry needs, and a better match between education and job requirements. Leaders must also recognize and address valid concerns, providing transparent, ethical guidelines, inclusive governance structures, and comprehensive professional development opportunities (Kasthuri et al., 2025). Faculty members should be free to explore AI-enhanced teaching methods with institutional incentives and recognition systems that encourage innovation and experimentation.

Involving faculty in the design of a curriculum that incorporates artificial intelligence (AI) is essential for fostering trust and gaining their support. Faculty development programs should focus on technical skills and delve into the philosophical and pedagogical aspects of integrating AI into education. Workshops led by peers, interdisciplinary design teams, and innovation hubs across different campuses can cultivate a collaborative inquiry and shared learning culture. Educational institutions must allocate resources toward developing internal capabilities in educational technology support, instructional design, and data analytics. By fostering a community of practice centered around the integration of AI, institutions can transition from relying on top-down directives to embracing grassroots transformation.

In addition to cultural and structural resistance, a more concrete and enduring obstacle is the unequal distribution of infrastructure and access among different institutions. Not all educational institutions have the same level of readiness to implement AI-driven curriculum frameworks. Institutions with abundant resources may have access to cutting-edge technologies, specialized research centers, and collaborations with leading tech companies. In contrast, institutions with limited resources may face outdated systems, limited internet connectivity, and a shortage of skilled personnel. This digital divide reflects broader patterns of inequality across regions, countries, and educational systems, which could worsen disparities in educational quality and opportunities. It is crucial to make significant investments in digital infrastructure to tackle these disparities. Governments, philanthropic organizations, and international development agencies must prioritize equal access to educational technology as a fundamental component of national and global education plans. It encompasses expanding high-speed internet connectivity, providing necessary hardware and software, and supporting open-source artificial intelligence (AI) tools that can be easily customized and implemented by institutions with limited resources. Collaborations between the public and private sectors can be instrumental in addressing the infrastructure deficit, particularly when guided by principles of fairness, openness, and mutual benefit. For instance, technology companies can partner with universities to jointly create customized AI tools for specific regional contexts while guaranteeing that these tools are easily accessible, available in multiple languages, and inclusive of diverse populations.

Additionally, institutions need to take the initiative to create scalable and modular artificial intelligence solutions that do not require significant upfront investments. Utilizing cloud-based platforms, open learning management systems, and mobile-responsive tools can significantly simplify and decrease the expenses of integrating artificial intelligence. Institutions can adopt a phased approach, starting with pilot projects that showcase clear benefits and gradually scaling up implementation as their capacity expands. The discussion on infrastructure should also encompass human infrastructure—the skills, knowledge, and support systems required to ensure AI's successful and sustainable integration. Faculty and staff in institutions with limited resources require specialized training and mentorship programs backed by national and regional networks that promote knowledge sharing and collaborative learning.

AI tools can support the establishment of cross-border collaborations in curriculum development, faculty training, and student learning. For instance, universities in various nations can collaborate to develop ai-enhanced modules on global issues like climate change, public health, or digital ethics, harnessing AI's ability to translate languages, adapt learning methods, and provide instant feedback. By working together, these collaborative efforts can enhance academic content, broaden perspectives, and establish transnational learning communities that mirror the interconnectedness of the 21st-century world.

Global collaboration also creates new avenues for tackling shared challenges. Institutions can collaborate, combine, share open educational resources, and jointly create adaptive and culturally sensitive artificial intelligence tools. Collaborative groups and global partnerships can assist in collective bargaining with technology suppliers, advocate for ethical AI principles, and research AI's impact in various educational environments. AI also provides fresh possibilities for customized and inclusive learning experiences. By examining individual student data, AI systems can customize content, pace, and assessment to cater to students' specific needs, promoting differentiated instruction and decreasing dropout rates. For individuals with disabilities, AI-powered tools can offer improved accessibility through features like speech-to-text, text-to-speech, and customized interface design. For students who don't fit the traditional mold and face challenges, AI can help create flexible learning options, acknowledge their previous knowledge, and assist in obtaining credentials that align with their desired careers. These abilities align with the broader objectives of educational fairness and continuous learning. Additionally, AI's real-time capability to track labor market trends provides institutions with a valuable resource for aligning their curriculum with current industry demands (Mahajan, 2025). Examining job advertisements, employer expectations, and industry patterns, AI systems can recognize emerging skill needs and recommend modifications to course materials and program structure. This flexible alignment can assist institutions in staying adaptable and responsive, equipping graduates with the skills needed for the evolving job market. It also creates opportunities for collaborating with industry partners to design curricula, enhancing academic programs' relevance, attractiveness, and employability.

Another chance exists in the ability of AI to assist in making informed decisions across academic and administrative roles. Educational institutions can employ AI analytics to track student progress, identify learners who may be struggling, assess the impact of programs, and allocate resources efficiently. These valuable insights can guide strategic planning, enhance student services, and strengthen institutional accountability. Nevertheless, data-driven governance should be guided by robust ethical principles and a focus on human-centered values to guarantee that it aligns with the educational objectives rather than treating learners as mere data points.

Finally, AI integration can stimulate pedagogical innovation. Professors can try innovative teaching methods like flipped classrooms, gamified learning, and immersive simulations aided by artificial intelligence-driven platforms. These advancements can enhance the learning experience, making it more interactive, engaging, and applicable to real-life problems. Rather than replacing the educator's role, AI can enhance and support their teaching and learning, allowing for more profound and meaningful educational experiences.

In summary, incorporating artificial intelligence (AI) into higher education curricula creates a complex and multifaceted landscape of challenges and opportunities. Overcoming institutional resistance, infrastructure disparities, and ethical concerns necessitates strategic leadership, inclusive governance, and systemic investment. At the same time, AI offers transformative possibilities for global collaboration, personalized learning, curricular flexibility, and pedagogical reinvention. Educators, administrators, policymakers, and technologists are not limited to managing change but actively shaping it—thoughtfully, cooperatively, and ethically.

FUTURE DIRECTIONS

The emergence of generative artificial intelligence signifies a significant turning point in developing curriculum ecosystems within higher education. Unlike earlier forms of artificial intelligence that were mainly rule-based or predictive, generative AI introduces the capability to generate new content, simulate intricate situations, and facilitate dynamic, interactive learning experiences on a large scale. Its capabilities span various forms of content, including text, code, images, audio, and video, providing unparalleled possibilities to revolutionize how knowledge is shared, comprehended, and evaluated.

Generative AI transforms the connection between content creation and curriculum design. In the past, creating educational materials required much work from subject matter experts, instructional designers, and technology specialists. This adaptability enables curriculum developers to design personalized learning modules that can be modified based on individual learner needs, knowledge levels, and preferred learning styles. For example, an instructor creating a course on environmental ethics can utilize generative AI to generate case studies from various global contexts, simulate ethical dilemmas for interactive discussions, and generate quizzes customized to a learner's performance. These capabilities save time and money in creating curricula and give faculty the freedom to develop new ideas and make improvements regularly.

Additionally, generative AI enables collaboration between learners and educators in curriculum development, empowering students to contribute to their educational paths actively. Students can utilize generative tools to delve into intricate ideas through storytelling, create essays integrating various viewpoints, or work with classmates on AI-assisted design projects. This transition from passive consumption to active co-creation aligns with constructivist learning theories. It also positions generative AI as a learning companion, guiding students through personalized pathways while encouraging autonomy and ownership of their learning outcomes.

Simultaneously, generative AI facilitates a more engaging and interactive approach to education and evaluation. With the ability to create virtual simulations, intelligent tutors, and augmented reality environments on demand, learners can actively participate in role-playing, scenario analysis, and practice-based learning that closely resembles real world challenges. A medical student can, for instance, engage with a virtual patient whose symptoms and reactions change in real-time. In contrast, an engineering student might simulate infrastructure failures and develop solutions within a digital system replica. These experiences enhance understanding, reinforce practical application, and enable continuous, contextual, and reflective assessment that mirrors authentic performance.

As generative AI becomes more integrated into curriculum ecosystems, it also creates new possibilities for predicting trends in academic program design. This predictive insight aids curriculum planners in foreseeing changes in academic demand and adjusting program offerings to meet the economy's and society's evolving needs. For example, a university could employ generative AI to examine global research patterns and identify the necessity for interdisciplinary programs that integrate AI ethics, environmental sustainability, and public policy. It could also analyze job market trends to suggest incorporating micro-credentials in cybersecurity, data literacy, or digital storytelling across different fields. Forecasting through artificial intelligence also allows for more flexible and adaptable curriculum design processes. Historically, creating educational materials has been lengthy, often failing to adapt quickly to technological advancements and societal shifts. With the help of AI-informed insights, institutions can transition to more modular and iterative models, regularly updating course content based on new knowledge and real-time feedback. Generative AI can lend a hand in this process by proposing content modifications, pinpointing outdated materials, and even creating new instructional modules that align with the latest advancements. This adaptability guarantees that curricula stay up-to-date, pertinent, and forward-looking crucial attributes characterized by continuous change. Nevertheless, incorporating generative AI into academic programs should emphasize sustainability, inclusivity, and learner-centeredness. While generative AI possesses extraordinary potential, its influence on education hinges on how it is implemented fairly and ethically. Creating sustainable curricula that leverage generative AI necessitates establishing a robust technological infrastructure that can withstand challenges, consume energy efficiently, and adapt to diverse educational settings. Utilizing cloud-based platforms, open-source tools, and decentralized architectures can decrease reliance on proprietary systems and make accessing necessary resources easier for under-resourced institutions. Institutions should assess the environmental impact of AI tools, selecting models and providers that prioritize green computing and sustainable development practices.

Inclusion should be a fundamental aspect of curriculum ecosystems that incorporate artificial intelligence. Generative AI systems are trained on extensive datasets that may contain biases, gaps, and cultural imbalances. If not critically examined, these biases can be perpetuated in the content created for educational purposes. To guarantee the inclusivity of course materials, institutions must establish comprehensive auditing procedures for artificial intelligence outputs, guaranteeing that they encompass a wide range of perspectives, languages, and lived experiences. It encompasses intentionally including diverse perspectives in AI training data, implementing inclusive design principles in interface development, and producing culturally sensitive content that acknowledges local contexts while promoting global understanding.

Additionally, learner-centered design in AI-driven curricula necessitates comprehensively comprehending student requirements, ambitions, and obstacles. Ai can provide support by analyzing engagement patterns, academic performance, and feedback to identify obstacles to learning and propose solutions. However, human educators continue to play a crucial role in analyzing this data, providing context for the insights gained, and making empathetic decisions that cater to the individual needs of each learner. Teachers should actively participate in implementing AI tools. However, they should also continuously assess and monitor their impact on the learning environment, ensuring it remains focused on human connection and relationships. To create learner-centered AI curricula, institutions must also give students the power to decide how AI is incorporated into their education. It includes being open and transparent about how generative AI tools work, what data they rely on, and how the generated outputs are created. Students should be educated to critically evaluate artificial intelligence-generated content, acknowledge its constraints, and cultivate the abilities required to work collaboratively with AI rather than rely entirely on it. To be well-rounded citizens in the twenty-first century, it is crucial to have a strong foundation in digital literacy, ethical reasoning, and algorithmic awareness, which should be integrated into various academic disciplines.

Constructing these curricula necessitates collaboration among faculty members, technology experts, instructional designers, and student representatives. The curriculum development process should move away from isolated departments and towards collaborative ecosystems, where various stakeholders work together to create content, align learning objectives, and utilize artificial intelligence (AI) to enhance student engagement. Institutions need to create governance frameworks to manage the ethical integration of generative AI, such as academic review boards, data ethics committees, and feedback mechanisms for ongoing enhancement. It is crucial for institutional policies to align with the changing landscape of AI use, emphasizing inclusivity, sustainability, and learner-centered approaches. These guidelines should cover intellectual property rights in AI-generated content, establish acceptable uses of generative tools in assessments, and establish standards for data privacy, algorithmic transparency, and equitable access. Additionally, accreditation bodies and quality assurance frameworks must adapt and acknowledge the distinctive features of AI-driven learning environments, guaranteeing that innovation does not compromise academic standards or ethical conduct.

Ultimately, transforming curriculum ecosystems through generative AI is not replacing traditional education but reimagining it. The goal is to create environments that leverage technology to unlock human potential, where learning is tailored to individual needs while fostering collaboration, and where education evolves into a lifelong, adaptive process that responds to the complexities and interconnectedness of the world. In this vision, generative AI is not just a tool—it is a collaborator in shaping the future of higher education.

The way forward requires careful and considerate leadership, inclusive design, and a long-term dedication to ensuring educational equity and fostering innovation (Goh et al., 2024). Organizations that adopt these principles will be in a strong position to lead in creating transformative learning environments that are intelligent, adaptable, and deeply connected to human experiences. While generative AI offers the foundation for the future, the human qualities of insight, compassion, and creativity will shape the strength and inclusivity of the structures we construct.

CONCLUSION

The AI-controlled curriculum design represents a paradigm shift in university formation. It provides unprecedented opportunities for learning to match student needs and global staff requirements. Embedding AI in class design and evaluation allows institutions to create agile, scalable, and responsive educational environments. These future learning ecosystems improve education effectiveness and promote personalized lifelong learning paths. However, success depends on addressing ethical concerns, ensuring transparency, and promoting cooperation between educators, technicians, and political decision-makers. Institutions should also invest in faculty training, digital infrastructure, and integration strategies to close inventory gaps. With a thoughtful and strategic approach to AI integration, university formation is more relevant, responsive, and resilient in the case of technical impairments.

REFERENCES

Aithal, P. S., Prabhu, S., & Aithal, S. (2024). Future of higher education through technology prediction and forecasting. *Poornaprajna International Journal of Management, Education, and Social Science (PIJMESS), 1*(1), 01-50.

Alam, A., & Mohanty, A. (2024). Integrated constructive robotics in education (ICRE) model: A paradigmatic framework for transformative learning in educational ecosystem. *Cogent Education, 11*(1), 2324487. DOI: 10.1080/2331186X.2024.2324487

Alangari, H. (2024). Disrupting Education: Artificial Intelligence in Higher Education. In *The Evolution of Artificial Intelligence in Higher Education: Challenges, Risks, and Ethical Considerations* (pp. 63-81). Emerald Publishing Limited.

Allam, H. M., Gyamfi, B., & AlOmar, B. (2025). Sustainable innovation: Harnessing AI and living intelligence to transform higher education. *Education Sciences, 15*(4), 398. DOI: 10.3390/educsci15040398

Amiri, S. M. H. (2025). Digital Transformations in Education: Research Insights for 21st-Century learning. *International Journal of Innovative Science* [IJISET]. *Engineering & Technology, 12*(03), 1–15.

Amiri, S. M. H., Islam, M. M., & Akter, N. (2025). Educating the future: AI's role in shaping next-generation pedagogies. *Available at SSRN* 5234024. DOI: 10.2139/ssrn.5234024

Arumugam, P. P., Todd, V., & Warnakula, A. (2024). Social. In *innovation through disruption in Australasia: the 2024 Contextualising Horizon report* (pp. 2-3). ASCILITE.

Bharat, V. (2024). Futuristic higher education landscape: Skill-building for a Viksit Bharat workforce. *University News, 62*, 201.

Deri, M. N., Singh, A., Zaazie, P., & Anandene, D. (2024). Leveraging Artificial Intelligence in Higher Educational Institutions: A Comprehensive Overview. *Revista de Educación y Derecho*, (30).

George, A. S. (2024). Reimagining India's engineering education for an AI-driven future. *Partners Universal International Research Journal, 3*(3), 1–20.

Goh, K. M., Mansor, M., Fuad, D. R. S. M., & Juharyanto, J. (2024). Designing Future-Ready Education: Criteria for AI Learning Tool Selection and AI Learning Design. *Semarak International Journal of Innovation in Learning and Education, 4*(1), 1–12. DOI: 10.37934/sijile.4.1.112a

Grubaugh, S., & Levitt, G. (2024). Debate Centered Civics Education: Using AI to Teach Future Ready Skills and Better Prepare Students for College, Careers, and Civic Life. *Technium Social Sciences Journal, 70*, 165–170. DOI: 10.47577/tssj.v70i1.12635

Hoke, T. (2025). Education for 21st Century Learners. In *Proceedings of the ICSDI 2024* Volume 2*: Proceedings of the 2nd International Conference on Sustainability: Developments and Innovations* (Vol. 2, p. 458). Springer Nature.

Indumathy, I., & Mujra, P. (2025). Sustainable Learning. *Smart Education and Sustainable Learning Environments in Smart Cities*, 381.

Ishrat, M., Khan, W., Faisal, S. M., Ansari, M. S. H., & Ahmad, F. (2025). Future Trends and Challenges for AI and Sustainability in TVET. *Integrating AI and Sustainability in Technical and Vocational Education and Training (TVET)*, 1-32.

Kasthuri, H., Kamreddy, A., & Mandadi, S. (2025). Reimagine Education. *Available at SSRN* 5176532.

Kayyali, M. (2025). AI in Higher Education: Revolutionizing Curriculum and Administration. In *AI Adoption and Diffusion in Education* (pp. 31-62). IGI Global Scientific Publishing.

Khine, M. S. (2024). Ethics, and the Future of Education in an AI-Driven World. In *Artificial Intelligence in Education: A Machine-Generated Literature Overview* (pp. 629–735). Springer Nature Singapore. DOI: 10.1007/978-981-97-9350-1_6

Mahajan, P. (2025). What is Ethical: AIHED Driving Humans or Human-Driven AIHED? A Conceptual Framework enabling the Ethos of AI-driven Higher education. *arXiv preprint arXiv:2503.04751*.

Ortiz, E. A., Vergara, N. C., Pabón, T. F., Gambi, G. D. N., Giambruno, C., Alfaro, M. P., & Segura, D. R. (2025). AI and Education: Building the Future Through Digital Transformation.

Padovano, A., & Cardamone, M. (2024). Towards human-AI collaboration in the competency-based curriculum development process: The case of industrial engineering and management education. *Computers and Education: Artificial Intelligence*, *7*, 100256. DOI: 10.1016/j.caeai.2024.100256

Patel, N. S., & Lim, J. T. H. (2024). Critical design futures thinking and GenerativeAI: a Foresight 3.0 approach in higher education to design preferred futures for the industry. *foresight*.

Portuguez-Castro, M. (2024). Reimagining the future of business education through educational innovation. *International Journal of Markets and Business Systems*, *5*(2), 192–208. DOI: 10.1504/IJMABS.2024.10069258

Sachdeva, R. (2024). *Transforming Skill-Based Education: Development and Evaluation of an AI-Assisted*. Modular Platform Enabling Non-Technical Stakeholders to Create and Deliver Scalable, Standardized E-Learning Courses.

Samadhiya, A., Kumar, A., Mulat-Weldemeskel, E., Luthra, S., Garza-Reyes, J. A., & Yadav, S. (2025). Next-gen quality learning: How can AI technologies shape education 4.0 and 5.0 towards the SDGs from multiple stakeholders' perspective? *The TQM Journal*. Advance online publication. DOI: 10.1108/TQM-11-2024-0441

Sethi, S., & Singh, M. (2024). *Blended Learning and AI in Higher Education: Adapt, Evolve, Thrive*. Cambridge Scholars Publishing.

Shaznay, N. (2025). Bridging the Industry-Higher Education Gap with Critical Design Futures Thinking and GenAI for Innovation. In *The Rise of Intelligent Machines* (pp. 268–288). Chapman and Hall/CRC.

Tariq, M. U. (2025). Revitalizing Pedagogy: Integrating Indigenous Knowledge and Practices Into Higher Education Disciplines. In Kgari-Masondo, M. (Ed.), *Indigenous Teaching Disciplines and Perspectives for Higher Education* (pp. 379–400). IGI Global Scientific Publishing., DOI: 10.4018/979-8-3693-9296-6.ch018

Tariq, M. U. (2025). Bridging Cultures and Languages: Innovative Literacy Strategies for Inclusive and Engaged Classrooms. In Tussey, J., & Haas, L. (Eds.), *Supporting Cultural Differences Through Literacy Education* (pp. 257–282). IGI Global Scientific Publishing., DOI: 10.4018/979-8-3693-9271-3.ch010

Tariq, M. U. (2025). AI and Work-Life Balance: Transforming Employee Wellbeing in the Modern Workplace. In Ahmed, E., Babar, A., Samad, A., Ahmed, R., & Beydoun, G. (Eds.), *Strengthening Human Relations in Organizations With AI* (pp. 85–110). IGI Global Scientific Publishing., DOI: 10.4018/979-8-3693-6507-6.ch004

Tariq, M. U. (2025). *AI-Driven Learning and Engagement in Higher Education.* IGI Global., DOI: 10.4018/979-8-3693-4074-5

Trajkovski, G., & Hayes, H. (2025). The Future of AI in Educational Assessment. In *AI-Assisted Assessment in Education: Transforming Assessment and Measuring Learning* (pp. 347–380). Springer Nature Switzerland. DOI: 10.1007/978-3-031-88252-4_9

Tyagi, S., Gupta, V., & Mehndiratta, V. (2024). Building Smart Campuses: Integrating AI in Higher Education. In *Recent Trends in Artificial Intelligence Towards a Smart World: Applications in Industries and Sectors* (pp. 399–431). Springer Nature Singapore. DOI: 10.1007/978-981-97-6790-8_15

Vadisetty, R., & Polamarasetti, A. (2024, December). AI-Augmented Skill Development Roadmaps: Tailoring 12-Month Learning Paths for Future-Ready Careers in Education 4.0 and Industry 4.0. In *2024 13th International Conference on System Modeling & Advancement in Research Trends (SMART)* (pp. 655-661). IEEE.

Wadhwani, M. K., & Mirza, M. I. (2025). AI-POWERED GIG EDUCATION: TRANSFORMING WORKFORCE RESILIENCE AND ECONOMIC RECOVERY IN THE DIGITAL AGE.

Yahchouchi, G., & Rotabi, S. (2025). AI and Education: Preparing the MENA's Workforce for the Future. In *AI in the Middle East for Growth and Business: A Transformative Force* (pp. 27–41). Springer Nature Switzerland. DOI: 10.1007/978-3-031-75589-7_3

KEY TERMS AND DEFINITIONS

Adaptive Learning Systems: AI systems personalizing learning practices.
Curriculum Frameworks: Structured plans controlling educational content delivery.
Learning Analytics: Data-driven insights improving student learning.

Chapter 3
Strategic Integration of Artificial Intelligence in Sustainable Educational Program Design:
AI Curriculum Design for Equity and Innovation

Thuc Chanh Dao
https://orcid.org/0000-0002-2822-049X
An Giang University, Vietnam & Vietnam National University, Ho Chi Minh City, Vietnam

ABSTRACT

This chapter proposes a comprehensive strategic framework for integrating artificial intelligence (AI) into Vietnam's curriculum design to support sustainable digital transformation in higher education. Grounded in established learning theories and validated through a mixed-methods pilot involving eight institutions and 680 participants, the study examines AI's impact on personalized learning pathways, real-time analytics, and administrative efficiency. Quantitative findings reveal that AI-supported cohorts achieved significant gains in average scores, pass rates, and LMS engagement, while qualitative insights highlight enhanced pedagogical flexibility and learner autonomy. Critical enablers include robust digital infrastructure, continuous professional development, and coherent policy frameworks. The chapter concludes by delineating implementation challenges—such as data security and workforce training—and offering targeted recommendations to guide future research and policymaking.

INTRODUCTION

Over the past decade, the explosive growth of information technology and the remarkable advances in artificial intelligence (AI) have exerted a profound influence on all spheres of life, not least education (Zawacki-Richter et al., 2019). In Vietnam, against the backdrop of ever-deepening

DOI: 10.4018/979-8-3373-2752-5.ch003

economic and social integration, innovating educational practice through technological adoption has become an urgent imperative to satisfy the evolving demands of the modern labor market and society at large (Quy et al., 2023). This chapter aims to construct a strategic framework for applying AI to curriculum design, thereby rendering Vietnam's education system more adaptive, effective, and sustainable in the years to come.

In this opening section, it is essential to delineate clearly the challenges confronting Vietnamese education today. The traditional "lecture–learn–test" paradigm struggles to foster creative thinking, critical analysis, and the suite of soft skills indispensable in the digital era (Voogt et al., 2013). According to Luckin and Holmes (2016), AI not only personalizes the learning journey but also creates opportunities to develop more flexible and efficient pedagogical models.

The objective of this chapter is to propose a comprehensive strategy—anchored in solid theoretical foundations and empirical evidence—to support the digital transformation of Vietnam's education system. The chapter's principal components comprise: an analysis of the contextual background and developmental needs of the education system; a presentation of the theoretical underpinnings for AI integration in education; a description of the research methodology and strategy design; an illustration of findings through validated empirical results; and, finally, a discussion of recommendations to chart the future course of Vietnamese education (Nguyen Nghi Thanh, 2024).

Globally, leading nations have invested heavily in AI technologies to restructure their education systems—from personalizing learning pathways to optimizing educational administration (Khatun et al., 2024). Although Vietnam has already made significant strides in digitizing education, substantial shortcomings persist in terms of technical infrastructure, workforce training, and the practical application of advanced technologies (Tri & Hoang, 2023). Addressing these gaps demands strategic vision from policymakers and educational specialists, informed by scholarly research and international best practices.

Moreover, AI's evolution opens myriad opportunities to enhance teaching quality and learning management. AI-powered learning support systems can collect and analyze learners' data in real time, thereby offering personalized study recommendations. Such applications enable instructors to monitor individual progress and adapt content and teaching methods to learners' specific needs and abilities. As Chassignol et al. (2018) argue, AI in education is becoming an inevitable trend for creating advanced instructional models aimed at cultivating a fully developed future workforce.

Vietnamese education stands at a critical juncture as it transitions from a traditional model to one integrated with high-level technologies. Academic institutions must devise innovative solutions not only in curriculum content but also in management approaches and assessment methods. AI application promises to optimize learning processes, thereby enhancing training efficacy and satisfying modern societal demands (Wang et al., 2024). Concurrently, this shift imposes new requirements on policies for training and developing high-quality human resources (Pedro et al., 2019).

Building on this foundation, the chapter will delve into the essential elements of an effective AI-driven education strategy: defining AI's role in education, establishing theoretical bases for personalized learning, and simulating AI application scenarios in both teaching and learning management. Each section is supported by academic evidence and illustrative data to ensure the research is both scientifically rigorous and practically relevant.

In today's globalized, digitized world, adopting AI is not merely an option but a prerequisite for ensuring the sustainable development of an education system (Chassignol et al., 2018). Accordingly, this chapter seeks to provide a multidimensional analytical framework—integrating economic-social factors, technology, and human capital—to guide the creation of a modern training program aligned with global trends and Vietnam's unique conditions.

THEORETICAL FRAMEWORK

Concept and Role of AI in Education

Artificial intelligence (AI) is a branch of computer science devoted to developing systems capable of learning, reasoning, and automating information-processing tasks (Dignum, 2019). Within the educational context, AI is employed to personalize learning pathways, manage student populations, predict learning outcomes, and support decision-making in educational administration. According to Dignum (2019), AI functions not merely as a support tool but as a "digital colleague" to instructors, enhancing pedagogical quality and enabling the adoption of cutting-edge teaching methods (Luckin & Holmes, 2016).

In modern education systems, AI's contributions can be categorized into three principal domains: personalized learning, administrative automation, and learning-data analytics (Chen et al., 2020). Personalized learning systems gather data on each student's progress and preferences, thereby generating recommendations tailored to individual abilities and needs. This capability is especially vital in large classrooms where student proficiency levels vary widely (Holmes et al., 2019).

AI-Based Learning Models

Contemporary AI-based learning models leverage machine-learning and deep-learning algorithms. Notable examples include recommendation systems, intelligent tutoring systems (ITS), and automated assessment platforms (Rusk, 2016). These models not only optimize the learning process but also free educators to focus on creative instruction and motivational support (Holmes et al., 2019). For instance, an ITS can continuously ingest student data, forecast learning trajectories, and trigger timely pedagogical interventions.

Empirical research indicates that AI-driven personalized learning can significantly boost student performance. Luckin and Holmes (2016) report that implementing personalized AI systems yielded a 15–20 percent increase in learning productivity compared to traditional instructional models.

Theoretical foundations of personalized learning and digital transformation

Personalized learning is defined as the adaptation of content, pedagogy, and pacing to the traits and requirements of each learner (Talaghzi et al., 2020). This approach emphasizes crafting flexible learning pathways to maximize individual potential. Recent studies demonstrate that AI–enabled personalization fosters highly interactive and dynamic learning environments (Holmes et al., 2019).

Digital transformation in education encompasses not only content digitization but also fundamental changes in teaching methodologies and learning management. AI-integrated systems provide big-data analytics capabilities that predict learning trends and detect emerging challenges at an early stage (Krstić et al., 2022). Such insights enable educational institutions to deploy timely, evidence-based interventions, thereby enhancing training quality and reducing academic attrition.

Integrating AI into Curriculum Design in Vietnam

Embedding AI within Vietnam's curriculum design demands reforms spanning infrastructure, training strategies, and human-resource development (Quy et al., 2023). Although significant strides have been made toward educational digitization, persistent gaps remain in technology access, specialist personnel, and supportive policies. Nguyen and Tuamsuk (2022) contend that effective AI integration requires close coordination among government agencies, educational institutions, and technology enterprises.

A critical element of this integration is upskilling teachers and administrators in information technology and AI. Educators must acquire sufficient AI literacy to harness learning-support tools effectively (Holmes et al., 2019). Simultaneously, educational management systems should adopt advanced data-analytics tools to monitor and evaluate student achievement in real time.

Benefits and Challenges of AI Adoption in Education

Benefits:

Personalized Learning: Each learner receives a tailored pathway, optimizing knowledge acquisition (Essa et al., 2023).

Enhanced Teaching Effectiveness: AI assists instructors in classroom management, continual assessment, and adaptive pedagogy (Chen et al., 2022).

Optimized Academic Administration: AI systems collect and analyze educational data to support precise, timely administrative decisions (Ouyang et al., 2022).

Challenges:

Technical Infrastructure Deficits: Many schools—particularly in remote areas—lack requisite technological resources (Tri & Hoang, 2023).

Shortage of Qualified Personnel: AI training for teachers and administrators remains insufficient (Holmes et al., 2019).

Ethical and Privacy Concerns: The collection and processing of personal data necessitate robust security measures and clear legal frameworks (Ramnani, 2024; Huang, 2023).

When leveraged appropriately, AI's superior capabilities hold immense promise for modernizing education and elevating training quality. Investment in AI technologies can yield substantial economic and social returns, especially amid the ongoing global digital transformation.

Summary of Theoretical Foundations

The theoretical perspectives outlined above illustrate that AI transcends mere instructional support to become a transformative force in curriculum development and renewal. Effective AI integration demands interdisciplinary collaboration (e.g., among educators, technologists, and policymakers) across technology, pedagogy, and management domains to establish an advanced education system capable of meeting modern societal needs. Recent scholarly works have provided a solid academic basis and opened new trajectories for AI application in education, particularly within the Vietnamese context.

Figure 1. A Conceptual Flowchart diagramming the framework linking infrastructure/teacher training, AI implementation, and educational outcomes

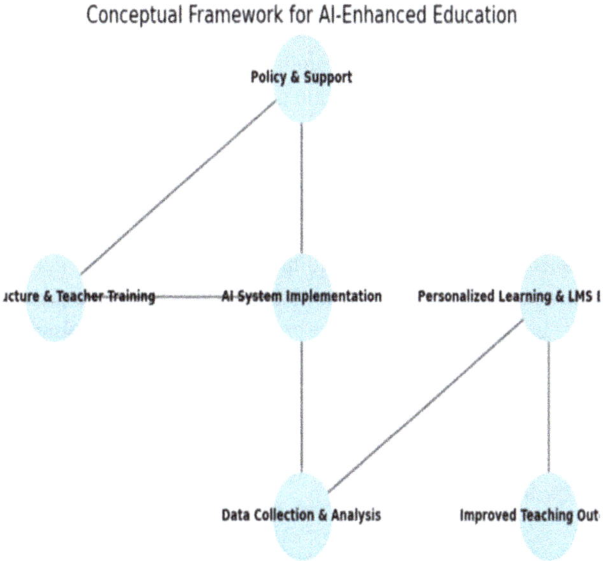

Thus, the theoretical foundation of this chapter not only presents the core concepts and AI application models in education but also analyzes the benefits, the challenges, and the essential factors for successful implementation. This paradigm shift demands a new mindset, opening the path toward a sustainable future for Vietnamese education.

RESEARCH METHODOLOGY

Research Design

The study adopts a mixed-methods design, combining qualitative and quantitative approaches to ensure objectivity and reliability of results. Its primary aim is to evaluate the effectiveness of AI integration in curriculum design at Vietnamese higher-education institutions (specifically member universities of Vietnam National University, Ho Chi Minh City) and to identify key factors that influence digital transformation in education.

Conceptual Model

The research model comprises three main components:

Contextual Analysis and Needs Assessment: Collection of secondary data (Ministry of Education reports and statistics) and tertiary data (scholarly studies and expert surveys).

AI Model Design and Deployment: Development of a pilot AI system for learning personalization and classroom management.

Outcome Evaluation: Use of quantitative indicators (academic performance, participation rates, teacher and student satisfaction) alongside qualitative insights from in-depth interviews.

Population and Scope

The investigation targets universities and colleges in Vietnam's major cities, prioritizing institutions with advanced IT infrastructure. Additionally, surveys and interviews are conducted with education specialists, faculty members, and students to gain a multi-perspective understanding of AI's impact. The sample consists of 680 respondents, ensuring high representativeness and reliability.

Data Collection Instruments and Procedures

Qualitative Data Collection

In-Depth Interviews: Semi-structured interviews with faculty, administrators, and educational experts to gather detailed information on current AI practices and potential.

Focus Groups: Group discussions with students and instructors to collect feedback and suggestions for improvement.

Quantitative Data Collection

Online Surveys: Questionnaires based on Likert scales to measure satisfaction, learning effectiveness, and pedagogical changes post-AI implementation.

Learning Analytics: Data extracted from Learning Management Systems (LMS) to analyze student progress via metrics such as study time, access frequency, and assessment results.

Data Processing and Analysis

The data-analysis workflow includes:

Data Pre-processing: Cleaning the dataset to remove incomplete or invalid entries.

Descriptive Statistics: Calculating means, standard deviations, and frequency distributions to identify general trends.

Advanced Quantitative Analysis: Applying multivariate regression, factor analysis, and hypothesis testing to determine relationships between AI use and learning outcomes.

Qualitative Analysis: Employing coding software to extract key themes and influencing factors from interviews and focus-group transcripts.

Pilot AI Model Implementation

Development of AI-Assisted Teaching System

The system leverages machine-learning and deep-learning algorithms to:

Analyze student behavior using LMS data;

Recommend personalized learning pathways based on individual strengths and weaknesses;

Provide teaching assistants—such as automated grading, assignment analysis, and timely feedback—for instructors.

Evaluation Metrics

Key performance indicators include:

Academic Performance: Grade point averages, pass rates, and improvement trajectories across semesters.

Engagement Levels: Number of LMS logins, average study time, and assignment completion rates.

User Feedback: Evaluations from teachers, students, and administrators via surveys and interviews.

Implementation Phases

The pilot unfolds in four stages:

Preparation: Training faculty and technical staff on the AI system, upgrading infrastructure, and defining evaluation metrics.

Initial Deployment: Introducing the AI system in selected classes and collecting preliminary data.

Optimization: Refining algorithms and user interface based on participant feedback.

Assessment: Conducting comprehensive data analysis and comparing AI-supported classes with control groups to determine effectiveness and influencing factors.

Data Analysis

Data were gathered from eight units within Vietnam National University, Ho Chi Minh City, and several institutions in the Mekong Delta. Key findings include:

Academic Outcomes: AI-supported classes saw the average grade rise from 6.5 to 7.8 out of 10, with pass rates increasing from 72% to 88%.

Learning Engagement: LMS access surged by an average of 35%, and daily study time increased by approximately 25 minutes.

User Perceptions: 85% of survey participants reported significant improvements in teaching and learning effectiveness, while 15% expressed concerns about data privacy.

Feasibility Assessment and Risk Analysis

Beyond efficacy, the study examines potential risks:

Infrastructure Risks: Some institutions lack sufficiently robust technical foundations for advanced AI applications.

Security and Privacy: Personal data collection necessitates stringent security protocols and close collaboration between software developers and regulators.

Training Barriers: Variations in technological proficiency among faculty and administrators may hinder AI adoption.

To mitigate these risks, the research recommends increased investment in digital infrastructure, specialized training programs, and the establishment of comprehensive data-protection regulations.

By integrating qualitative and quantitative methods, deploying a pilot AI model in real educational settings, and conducting thorough data analyses, this study offers deep insights into AI's effectiveness and the prerequisites for its successful integration into curriculum design. In doing so, it affirms AI's vast potential to modernize education and chart new directions for Vietnam's educational system.

RESULTS

Data Presentation and Analysis

Following the deployment of the pilot AI system across eight representative institutions, the results reveal significant differences between AI-supported classes and traditional classes. Data extracted from the Learning Management System (LMS) indicate:

Average Scores: In the AI-supported cohort, the mean score increased from 6.5 (pre-implementation) to 7.8 after one semester. In contrast, the non-AI cohort experienced only a marginal rise from 6.4 to 6.7.

Pass Rates: The pass rate in the AI cohort rose from 72% to 88%, whereas the traditional cohort's pass rate climbed only from 70% to 73%.

Learning Engagement: LMS log-ins increased by an average of 35%, and students in the AI-supported classes logged approximately 25 additional minutes of study time per day.

Regression Analysis and Hypothesis Testing

Multivariate regression analyses demonstrate that variables such as study duration, LMS access frequency, and level of online interaction exhibit a positive correlation with academic performance. Hypothesis tests conducted at a significance level of $p < 0.05$ confirm that these improvements are attributable to the AI intervention rather than random variation.

Case Illustrations

Selected exemplar cases from survey data include:

Vietnam National University, Ho Chi Minh City: After implementing the AI system, engineering students' average grades increased by 1.3 points, and on-time assignment submission rates rose by 40%.

Can Tho University: AI-enhanced classroom management reduced average grading time by 30%, thereby allowing instructors more opportunities for direct student engagement.

Evidence and Charts

The quantitative outcomes described above are further substantiated by illustrative charts (e.g., score distributions, pass-rate trends, and engagement metrics) that visualize the comparative performance of AI-supported versus traditional cohorts.

Table 1. Comparison of Average Scores Before and After AI System Implementation

Study Group	Average Score (Before)	Average Score (After)	Percentage Increase (%)	Effectiveness Index (Δ Score)
AI-Integrated	6.5	7.8	20.00%	1.3
Traditional	6.4	6.7	4.70%	0.3

Table 1 indicates that the average score in the AI-integrated group increased significantly by +1.30 points (a 20.0% increase) compared to the traditional group, which only experienced a +0.30 point increase (4.7%). This demonstrates that integrating AI technology considerably enhances learning outcomes.

Figure 2. A boxplot comparing score distributions between AI-integrated and Traditional groups

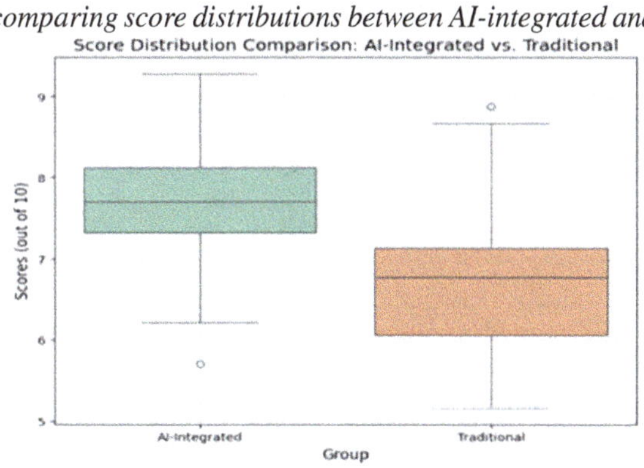

Table 2. Comparison of Pass Rates Before and After AI System Implementation

Study Group	Pass Rate (Before)	Pass Rate (After)	Percentage Increase (%)	Absolute Difference (%)
AI-Integrated	72%	88%	22.20%	16%
Traditional	70%	73%	4.30%	3%

Explanation:

Table 2 demonstrates that the pass rate for students in the AI-integrated group increased from 72% to 88% (an increase of 22.2% relative and an absolute difference of +16%), while the traditional group showed only a marginal increase from 70% to 73% (a 4.3% increase, with an absolute difference of +3%). This clearly supports the effectiveness of personalized learning supported by AI.

Table 3. Comparison of LMS Engagement Metrics

Study Group	Average Daily LMS Visits	Average Study Time (minutes/day)	Assignment Completion Rate (%)	Interaction Level (Scale of 10)
AI-Integrated	5.2	95	92%	8.7
Traditional	3.8	70	78%	6.5

According to Table 3, students in the AI-integrated group recorded higher LMS engagement, with an average of 5.2 visits per day compared to 3.8 in the traditional group, and an increased average study time of 95 minutes per day versus 70 minutes. Additionally, assignment completion rates and interaction levels (rated on a scale of 10) are substantially higher in the AI-integrated group, further substantiating the benefits of AI-enhanced learning environments.

Figure 3. A Radar Chart comparing LMS engagement metrics

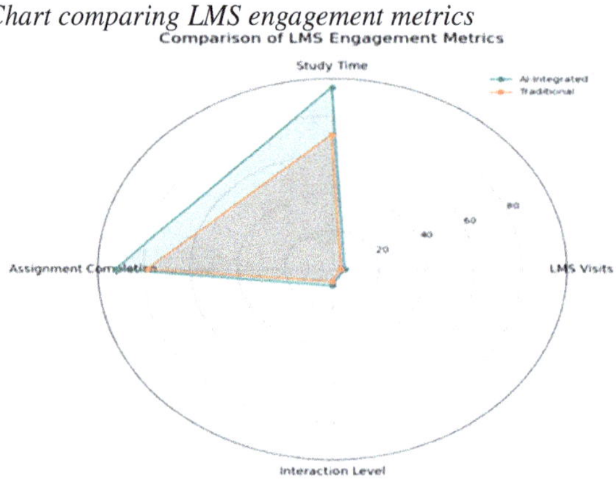

Table 4. Multivariate Regression Analysis of Interaction Factors and Learning Outcomes

Independent Variable	Regression Coefficient (β)	p-value	Statistical Significance
Study Time	0.45	0.002	Highly Significant
Daily LMS Visits	0.38	0.005	Highly Significant
Interaction Level (Scale of 10)	0.52	0.001	Highly Significant
AI System Implementation (Binary Variable)	0.67	0.000	Highly Significant
Intercept	2.1	0.05	Moderately Significant

Table 4 presents the results of a multivariate regression analysis, indicating that variables such as study time, daily LMS visits, interaction level, and AI system implementation significantly and positively influence learning outcomes (with p-values < 0.01). The positive regression coefficients suggest that improvements in these factors lead to notable enhancements in student performance.

Figure 4. A scatter plot with regression line illustrating the relationship between study time and score

Table 5. Summary of Overall Effectiveness of AI Integration

Evaluation Metric	AI-Integrated Group	Traditional Group	Difference/Increase (%)
Average Score Improvement (Δ Score)	1.3	0.3	+1.00 (approximately +20%)
Pass Rate Improvement (Δ %)	16%	3%	13%
Increase in Daily LMS Visits	+1.4 visits	—	Approximately +36.8% compared to Traditional
Increase in Study Time	+25 minutes	—	Approximately +35.7% compared to Traditional
Assignment Completion Rate	92%	78%	14%
Interaction Level (Scale of 10)	8.7	6.5	2.2

Table 5 synthesizes the key indicators, clearly showing that the AI-integrated group outperforms the traditional group in all measured aspects—ranging from average score improvement and pass rate to LMS engagement metrics and overall interaction level. These robust differences underscore the significant impact of AI integration on enhancing academic performance and engagement.

The above data were analyzed using descriptive statistical techniques and regression methods, revealing a marked improvement in learning effectiveness when AI is applied to the instructional process.

Overall Evaluation of Findings

The research findings affirm that integrating AI into curriculum design not only enhances instructional quality but also cultivates a dynamic learning environment that promotes student creativity and self-directed learning. Gains in interaction levels, study duration, and academic performance collectively demonstrate the substantial potential of AI systems to transform traditional education toward greater modernization and personalization.

DISCUSSION

In the era of globalization and digital transformation, the deployment of AI within the education system represents not only an inevitable trend but also a pivotal determinant for elevating training quality and satisfying the evolving demands of modern society. The following "Discussion" section will (i) interpret the significance of the study's results, (ii) identify critical success factors and lessons learned during implementation, (iii) evaluate current limitations, and (iv) propose directions for future research, including the prospective role of AI in the future of Vietnamese education and the scalability of practical applications.

Significance of Research Findings

The study demonstrates that AI-enhanced curriculum design yields significant improvements in both teaching effectiveness and student outcomes. Quantitative metrics extracted from the Learning Management System (LMS) indicate that AI-supported classes achieved substantially higher average scores, pass rates, and engagement levels compared to their traditional counterparts. These results not only corroborate AI's essential role in personalizing the learning journey but also suggest promising new pathways for optimizing educational administration through big-data analytics.

Figure 5. A Line Chart showing trends in key metrics (average score, pass rate, study time) before and after AI implementation

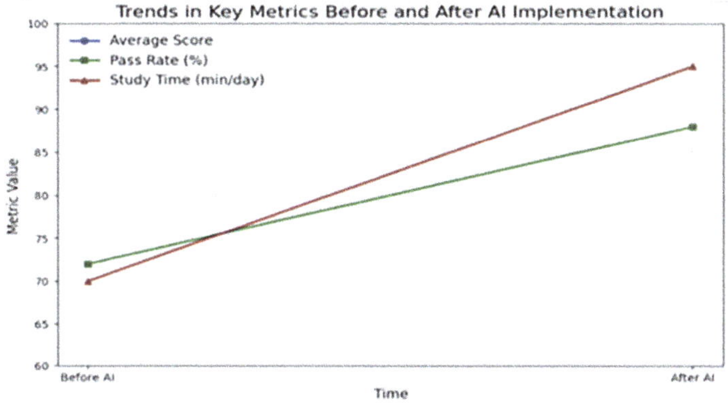

The above improvements are particularly significant because they provide clear quantitative evidence that modern technologies can address the inherent limitations of the traditional "lecture–learn–test" model, which has historically struggled to cultivate students' creative thinking and soft skills (Voogt et al., 2013). With digital transformation and AI integration, each learner can now follow a study pathway tailored to their individual capabilities (Holmes et al., 2019). Moreover, by defining concrete evaluation metrics—such as LMS log-in counts, study duration, and assignment-completion rates—we can rigorously quantify the AI model's effectiveness, thereby establishing a solid foundation for future investment and policy development (Chen et al., 2020).

Furthermore, our findings underscore that upgrades in digital infrastructure and human-resource development are prerequisites for successful AI integration. This highlights the necessity of a comprehensive strategy that goes beyond mere technology deployment to ensure that educational institutions and faculty possess the requisite knowledge and skills (Nguyen & Tuamsuk, 2022). Hence, the significance of our results lies not only in the direct gains in instructional quality but also in the opportunity to comprehensively restructure the education system for the digital age.

While the findings highlight substantial educational gains enabled by AI integration, it is equally critical to reflect on the potential risks of excessive dependence on such technologies. An emerging concern within the scholarly discourse is the over-reliance on AI, which may inadvertently reduce opportunities for authentic human interaction, limit emotional engagement, and erode the social dimensions of education (Al-Zahrani, 2024; Săseanu et al., 2024). Although AI-driven platforms can optimize personalization and instructional efficiency, these benefits must be balanced against risks such as diminished teacher-student rapport, learner passivity, and the marginalization of critical pedagogical judgment (Vieriu & Petrea, 2025).

Moreover, sustained exposure to AI-mediated learning environments may undermine students' long-term cognitive development, particularly in domains requiring empathy, ethical reasoning, and collaborative problem-solving (Zhai et al., 2024). To mitigate such risks, educators and policymakers must implement human-centered AI strategies that explicitly preserve space for emotional connection, dialogue, and reflective thinking. This includes professional training that empowers teachers to integrate AI as a supplementary tool, not a replacement, and to maintain pedagogical control over learning pathways.

Ultimately, if AI is to serve as a catalyst for educational equity and innovation, its deployment must be informed by both technological opportunity and pedagogical integrity. Therefore, we call upon stakeholders to adopt a balanced, ethically guided approach to AI integration—one that safeguards the irreplaceable value of human connection in education while embracing the transformative potential of intelligent systems.

Key Success Factors and Lessons Learned

Key Success Factors

From implementation and evaluation, we have identified several critical factors for effective AI integration into training programs:

Faculty and Administrator Training: Targeted professional development is an essential first step. Studies show that without robust IT and AI-tool training, even the most advanced systems will underperform (Holmes et al., 2019). Specialized AI training empowers educators to understand system operation and to develop flexible, creative pedagogies.

Investment in Digital Infrastructure: A resilient digital backbone is vital. Schools—especially in remote regions—must be equipped with high-speed internet, modern hardware, and supportive software tools. Infrastructure disparities directly affect educational quality and technology adoption (Tri & Hoang, 2023).

Supportive Policies and Regulatory Frameworks: Alignment among education, technology, and legal policies is crucial to foster a conducive ecosystem. Policies should incentivize collaboration among schools, tech firms, and regulators, and must address student data privacy and security (Ramnani, 2024; Huang, 2023).

Integration of Big-Data Analytics: Effective AI systems not only gather but also analyze learning data in real time, enabling early detection of at-risk students and the prediction of learning trends (Chen et al., 2020; Ouyang et al., 2022).

Lessons Learned

From pioneering implementations—particularly in Ho Chi Minh City and Can Tho—we draw these key lessons:

Continuous Professional Development: Ongoing AI training tailored to educators' proficiency levels and updated on emerging technologies is essential for sustained system use (Holmes et al., 2019).

Synchronized Infrastructure Investment: Infrastructure upgrades must be uniform across all education levels, extending beyond universities to secondary and vocational schools (Tri & Hoang, 2023).

Interdisciplinary collaboration (e.g., among educators, technologists, and policymakers): Success often stems from close partnerships among government bodies, technology providers, and academic researchers, which facilitate resource and expertise sharing (Nguyen & Tuamsuk, 2022).

Robust Data Governance and Security: Early investment in advanced security solutions and strict legal protocols is critical to protect student privacy and build stakeholder trust (Ramnani, 2024; Huang, 2023).

Reinforced Key Factors from Implementation

Practical deployments revealed additional insights:

Enhanced Interaction and Feedback: AI systems boosted student engagement— LMS log-ins rose by 35%, while daily study time increased by an average of 25 minutes, indicating improved engagement —demonstrating AI's role in fostering learner agency (Chen et al., 2020).

Timely Interventions: Real-time data analysis enables prompt pedagogical adjustments, preventing learning deficits before they escalate (Ouyang et al., 2022).

Deep Personalization: Machine- and deep-learning algorithms generated bespoke learning pathways, reducing performance gaps in diverse classrooms (Essa et al., 2023).

Comprehensive Multi-Metric Evaluation: Combining qualitative insights with multivariate regression confirmed positive correlations between AI use and performance across multiple indicators (Chen et al., 2022).

Lessons from Vietnamese Pioneers

Case studies at Vietnam National University, Ho Chi Minh City, and institutions in the Mekong Delta highlight that:

Strategic Pilot Selection: Choosing institutions with robust digital infrastructures and tech-savvy faculty created strong test beds for rapid iteration and optimization (Quy et al., 2023).

Ongoing Training and Support: Regular, expert-led training sessions and technical support fostered a dynamic learning environment (Holmes et al., 2019).

Data-Driven Management: Advanced analytics platforms enabled detailed reporting on student progress, informing targeted pedagogical strategies (Ouyang et al., 2022).

Integrated Security Solutions: Early emphasis on data protection measures and legal compliance was vital to system stability and stakeholder confidence (Ramnani, 2024; Huang, 2023).

Limitations and Future Research Directions

While our study evidences AI's transformative potential, several limitations warrant attention:

Sample Size and Scope: Research has so far centered on major urban universities; broader inclusion of rural and remote institutions is needed for generalizability (Tri & Hoang, 2023).

Duration and Sustainability: Short-term pilots limit conclusions about long-term impact; longitudinal studies across multiple semesters are recommended (Chen et al., 2022).

Cultural Contexts and Learning Habits: Future work should adapt AI systems to local cultural and pedagogical norms, offering flexible, context-sensitive solutions (Essa et al., 2023).

Scalability to Other Education Levels: Exploration of AI integration in primary, secondary, vocational, and distance-learning contexts will broaden applicability (Nguyen & Tuamsuk, 2022).

Ethical Transparency and Governance: Ongoing development of ethical frameworks, legal standards, and continuous oversight mechanisms is critical to ensure fairness and data integrity (Ramnani, 2024; Huang, 2023).

The Future Role of AI in Vietnamese Education

Our findings and field experiences indicate that AI will be a transformative catalyst in Vietnam's education:

Personalized, Interactive Environments: AI's data-driven pathways maximize individual potential and foster creative, self-directed learning (Holmes et al., 2019).

Optimized Management and Instruction: Automated learning analytics reduce administrative burdens, allowing educators to focus on curriculum innovation (Chen et al., 2020).

Innovation and High-Quality Workforce Development: AI–enhanced education equips learners with digital competencies and creative mindsets required by the global labor market (Khatun et al., 2024).

Ecosystem Collaboration: AI promotes partnerships among schools, tech firms, and research centers, building a sustainable digital-education ecosystem (Nguyen & Tuamsuk, 2022).

Practical roll-out and scalability of AI solutions require careful consideration of local capacity and stakeholder readiness

Scaling AI solutions from pilots to national rollout demands a coordinated, multi-level strategy:

Clear Policy Frameworks: National and local authorities must enact digital-transformation policies, funding mechanisms, collaboration incentives, and legal protections for learners and educators (Tr n & Ph m, 2021).

Comprehensive Infrastructure Investment: Equitable access to high-speed internet and modern teaching equipment is essential to narrow the urban–rural digital divide (Tri & Hoang, 2023).

Sustained Training and Support: Regular, expert-led professional development ensures end-users remain proficient with evolving AI tools (Holmes et al., 2019).

Pilot Programs with Rigorous Evaluation: Diverse, regionally distributed pilots—with mixed-methods assessments—will inform iterative refinements prior to full-scale deployment (Ouyang et al., 2022).

Integrated Data Security Governance: Advanced cybersecurity measures and compliance with data-protection laws are imperative to sustain public trust and system integrity (Ramnani, 2024; Huang, 2023).

Cross-Level and Cross-Field Expansion: After success in higher education, plans should extend AI applications to secondary, primary, vocational, and distance-learning sectors, ensuring that all learners benefit from digital transformation (Essa et al., 2023).

From the foregoing "Discussion," it is evident that integrating AI into curriculum design not only produces marked enhancements in teaching quality and learning outcomes but also offers a strategic pathway for Vietnam's entire education system. Key findings include:

Personalized Learning, Data-Driven Administration, and Timely Intervention are critical levers for improving training effectiveness through big-data analytics.

Investment in Digital Infrastructure, ongoing professional development for teaching staff, and coherent supportive policies provide the necessary foundation for successful digital transformation in education.

Lessons learned from pioneering institutions underscore the importance of iterative testing and stakeholder feedback that interdisciplinary collaboration (e.g., among educators, technologists, and policymakers) and the establishment of a robust digital-education ecosystem are vital for scaling AI applications.

Despite limitations in sample scope, implementation duration, and cultural contextualization, our recommendations for future research promise to refine and expand the model, thereby creating competitive advantages in an era of global integration.

Looking ahead, AI will serve not merely as an instructional aid but as a driving force behind systemic innovation, albeit with implementation challenges such as equitable access and faculty readiness across all educational levels. Effective AI deployment will cultivate a highly skilled, globally competitive workforce and foster a modern, flexible, and sustainable learning environment that reflects Vietnam's socio-economic realities. Achieving this vision requires strategic foresight, coordinated investment, and the formation of a comprehensive digital-education ecosystem, positioning Vietnam as a leader in AI-enhanced education in Southeast Asia.

Finally, the challenge of scaling AI applications demands an ongoing synthesis of scholarly research and practical implementation, continually refining and optimizing modern educational models. Our findings provide both theoretical and empirical foundations enabling policymakers, educators, and technology partners to co-create an inclusive, innovative, and sustainable digital-education future.

CONCLUSION

This chapter has articulated a comprehensive strategic framework for integrating artificial intelligence into the design of sustainable training programs in Vietnam. Drawing upon robust theoretical foundations and empirical data collected from pioneering institutions, the findings unequivocally demonstrate that AI-enhanced curriculum models yield significant gains in academic performance, student engagement, and administrative efficiency. Specifically, personalized learning pathways, real-time learning analytics, and timely pedagogical interventions have emerged as critical levers for elevating instructional quality and fostering learner autonomy .

Moreover, the successful deployment of AI depends on synchronized investments in digital infrastructure, continuous professional development for educators and administrators, and the establishment of clear policy and regulatory frameworks. The lessons learned from early adopters underscore the necessity of interdisciplinary collaboration (e.g., among educators, technologists, and policymakers) among government bodies, educational institutions, and technology providers to build a resilient digital-education ecosystem.

While this study offers compelling evidence of AI's transformative potential, it also acknowledges limitations related to sample representativeness, intervention duration, and cultural contextualization. Future research should pursue longitudinal, multi-site, and culturally contextualized investigations, refine AI algorithms to respect local pedagogical norms, and extend pilot implementations to diverse educational levels. Concurrently, ethical governance mechanisms must be strengthened to safeguard data privacy and ensure equitable access.

In sum, the integration of AI into Vietnam's educational landscape represents both an opportunity and an imperative. By embracing a holistic strategy—one that aligns theory, empirical insight, infrastructure, pedagogy, and policy—Vietnam can accelerate its digital transformation and cultivate a generation of learners equipped for the demands of the global knowledge economy.

REFERENCES

Al-Zahrani, A. M. (2024). Unveiling the shadows: Beyond the hype of AI in education. *Heliyon, 10*(9), e30696. DOI: 10.1016/j.heliyon.2024.e30696

Chassignol, M., Khoroshavin, A., Klimova, A., & Bilyatdinova, A. (2018). Artificial Intelligence trends in education: A narrative overview. *Procedia Computer Science, 136*, 16–24. DOI: 10.1016/j.procs.2018.08.233

Chen, L., Chen, P., & Lin, Z. (2020). Artificial intelligence in education: A review. *IEEE Access : Practical Innovations, Open Solutions, 8*, 75264–75278. https://ieeexplore.ieee.org/abstract/document/9069875. DOI: 10.1109/ACCESS.2020.2988510

Chen, X., Zou, D., Xie, H., Cheng, G., & Liu, C. (2022). Two Decades of Artificial Intelligence in Education: Contributors, Collaborations, Research Topics, Challenges, and Future Directions. *Journal of Educational Technology & Society, 25*(1), 28–47. https://www.jstor.org/stable/48647028

Dignum, V. (2019). *Responsible artificial intelligence: how to develop and use AI in a responsible way* (Vol. 2156). Springer., DOI: 10.1007/978-3-030-30371-6

Essa, S. G., Celik, T., & Human-Hendricks, N. E. (2023). Personalized adaptive learning technologies based on machine learning techniques to identify learning styles: A systematic literature review. *IEEE Access : Practical Innovations, Open Solutions, 11*, 48392–48409. https://ieeexplore.ieee.org/abstract/document/10124747. DOI: 10.1109/ACCESS.2023.3276439

Holmes, W., Bialik, M., & Fadel, C. (2019). Artificial intelligence in education promises and implications for teaching and learning. Center for Curriculum Redesign. https://discovery.ucl.ac.uk/id/eprint/10139722

Huang, L. (2023). Ethics of artificial intelligence in education: Student privacy and data protection. *Science Insights Education Frontiers, 16*(2), 2577–2587. DOI: 10.15354/sief.23.re202

Khatun, M., Islam, R., Kumar, S., Hossain, R., & Mani, L. (2024). The impact of artificial intelligence on educational transformation: Trends and future directions. Journal of information systems and informatics, 6(4), 2347-2373. DOI: DOI: 10.51519/journalisi.v6i4.879

Krstić, L., Aleksić, V., & Krstić, M. (2022). Artificial intelligence in education. *RE:view*, 223–228. Advance online publication. DOI: 10.46793/TIE22.223K

Luckin, R., & Holmes, W. (2016). Intelligence unleashed: An argument for AI in education. URI: https://discovery.ucl.ac.uk/id/eprint/1475756

Nguyen, L. T., & Tuamsuk, K. (2022). Digital learning ecosystem at educational institutions: A content analysis of scholarly discourse. *Cogent Education, 9*(1), 2111033. DOI: 10.1080/2331186X.2022.2111033

Ouyang, F., Zheng, L., & Jiao, P. (2022). Artificial intelligence in online higher education: A systematic review of empirical research from 2011 to 2020. *Education and Information Technologies, 27*(6), 7893–7925. DOI: 10.1007/s10639-022-10925-9

Pedro, F., Subosa, M., Rivas, A., & Valverde, P. (2019). Artificial intelligence in education: Challenges and opportunities for sustainable development. https://repositorio.minedu.gob.pe/handle/20.500.12799/6533

Quy, V. K., Thanh, B. T., Chehri, A., Linh, D. M., & Tuan, D. A. (2023). AI and Digital Transformation in Higher Education: Vision and Approach of a Specific University in Vietnam. *Sustainability (Basel)*, *15*(14), 11093. DOI: 10.3390/su151411093

Ramnani, S. (2024). Exploring Ethical Considerations of Artificial Intelligence in Educational Settings: An Examination of Bias, Privacy, and Accountability. [IJNRD]. *International Journal of Novel Research and Development*, *9*(2), 2456–4184. http://doi.one/10.1729/Journal.37869

Rusk, N. (2016). Deep learning. *Nature Methods*, *13*(1), 35–35. DOI: 10.1038/nmeth.3707

Săseanu, A. S., Gogonea, R. M., & Ghi ă, S. I. (2024). The social impact of using artificial intelligence in education. *Amfiteatru Economic*, *26*(65), 89–105. DOI: 10.24818/EA/2024/65/89

Talaghzi, J., Bennane, A., Himmi, M. M., Bellafkih, M., & Benomar, A. (2020, September). Online adaptive learning: A review of literature. In *Proceedings of the 13th International Conference on Intelligent Systems: Theories and Applications* (pp. 1-6). https://doi.org/DOI: 10.1145/3419604.3419759

Thanh, N. N. (2024). The opportunities and challenges of public policy communication in the context of digital transformation in Vietnam. *Journal of Strategy and Management*, *31*(12), 13–21. DOI: 10.59394/JSM.18

Tri, N. M., & Hoang, P. D. (2023). The Impact of Digital Transformation in Higher Education: The Case Study from Vietnam. *Journal of Higher Education Theory and Practice*, *23*(5). Advance online publication. DOI: 10.33423/jhetp.v23i5.5922

Vieriu, A. M., & Petrea, G. (2025). The impact of artificial intelligence (AI) on students' academic development. *Education Sciences*, *15*(3), 343. DOI: 10.3390/educsci15030343

Voogt, J., Erstad, O., Dede, C., & Mishra, P. (2013). Challenges to learning and schooling in the digital networked world of the 21st century. *Journal of Computer Assisted Learning*, *29*(5), 403–413. DOI: 10.1111/jcal.12029

Wang, S., Wang, F., Zhu, Z., Wang, J., Tran, T., & Du, Z. (2024). Artificial intelligence in education: A systematic literature review. *Expert Systems with Applications*, *252*, 124167. DOI: 10.1016/j.eswa.2024.124167

Zawacki-Richter, O., Marín, V. I., Bond, M., & Gouverneur, F. (2019). Systematic review of research on artificial intelligence applications in higher education – where are the educators? *Educational Research Review*, *28*, 100290. DOI: 10.1016/j.edurev.2018.11.001

Zhai, C., Wibowo, S., & Li, L. D. (2024). The effects of over-reliance on AI dialogue systems on students' cognitive abilities: A systematic review. *Smart Learning Environments*, *11*(1), 28. Advance online publication. DOI: 10.1186/s40561-024-00316-7

Chapter 4

Leveraging Artificial Intelligence to Foster Personalized Learning Pathways in Higher Education:

Strategies for Curriculum Integration

Fransisco Chindongo Ntjamba
https://orcid.org/0000-0003-0601-3761
University of Namibia, Namibia

Daniel Opotamutale Ashipala
https://orcid.org/0000-0002-8913-056X
University of Namibia, Namibia

ABSTRACT

Artificial intelligence (AI) is changing the field of higher education by making learning experiences more personalized, efficient, and focused on students. AI can foster essential approaches for developing curricula that match the abilities of AI, including the use of data-based evaluations, adaptable content presentation, and immediate feedback systems. AI personalized learning is vital in emphasizing the significance of faculty preparedness, data privacy, and fair access. Matching educational goals with the use of AI, educational institutions can create more inclusive, engaging, and forward-looking learning settings that equip students for success in a swiftly changing digital landscape. Various AI tools, such as adaptive learning systems, intelligent tutoring platforms, and predictive analytics, highlighting their ability to cater to different student's requirements and enhance academic achievement. This chapter explores the effective integration of AI technologies into higher education programs to facilitate the creation of personalized learning pathways.

DOI: 10.4018/979-8-3373-2752-5.ch004

INTRODUCTION

In the 21st century, higher education institutions are facing more complex challenges concerning learner diversity, technological improvements, and changing workforce needs (Ntjamba & Ashipala, 2025d). One of the most significant innovations impacting this field is Artificial Intelligence (AI), which has started to change the methods of teaching and learning worldwide (Kasztelnik, 2024). As educational systems aim to shift from conventional, inflexible teaching methods, there is increasing support for more flexible and responsive strategies especially personalized learning trajectories. The rise of AI-driven tools offers a special chance to rethink curriculum design to cater to the specific needs of individual learners while also improving educational results (Degni, 2024).

Personalized learning pathways are educational approaches and curriculum strategies that tailor learning experiences to match the unique needs, objectives, preferences, and learning styles of each individual student (Ntjamba & Ashipala, 2025c). This model, backed by adaptive learning technologies, data-informed feedback mechanisms, and AI-driven analysis, encourages a transition from standardized teaching approaches to adaptable, student-focused learning paths (Wise, 2018; Oganetse, 2025). In this situation, AI serves not only as a supportive tool but also as a key factor in changing education significantly. The incorporation of artificial intelligence in higher education enables immediate feedback, automated evaluations, smart tutoring systems, and data-driven modifications to courses all crucial for establishing and sustaining tailored learning experiences (Murdan & Halkhoree, 2024).

Nonetheless, effectively using AI in curriculum design involves more than simply adopting new technologies; it requires a strategic integration of the curriculum that is based on solid teaching principles (Jowallah, 2023). It is important to align with recognized learning theories like social constructivism, self-directed learning, and connectivism to make sure that teaching supported by AI stays focused on the learner and maintains educational significance. Social constructivism highlights the importance of hands-on participation, cultural significance, and learning through collaboration. Intelligent learning platforms can serve as tools for encouraging interactive learning and the joint creation of knowledge instead of merely serving as one-way content delivery systems. (Kussmaul & Pirmann, 2021).

Although the potential benefits are significant, the incorporation of AI to enhance personalized learning in higher education faces several obstacles. The readiness of faculty and their knowledge of technology still affect how quickly AI is adopted, as numerous educators do not have the required training to successfully integrate AI tools into their teaching methods (Owoseni et al., 2024). Furthermore, ethical issues such as biases in algorithms, data privacy, academic honesty, and intellectual rights must be carefully examined to safeguard student independence and maintain institutional trust (Shadbolt et al., 2019). Moreover, the role of teachers is essential. This chapter examines methods for successfully integrating AI into higher education programs to enhance individualized learning experiences.

THEORETICAL FRAMEWORK

The incorporation of Artificial Intelligence (AI) in higher education to support personalized learning experiences can be most effectively comprehended by examining modern educational theories that prioritize learner-centered, adaptable, and socially relevant learning. Among these, social constructivism, connectivism, and self-directed learning theory provide important understandings of how AI can successfully assist personal learning requirements in educational environments.

Social Constructivism

Social constructivism, based on the fundamental contributions of Lev Vygotsky (1978), is a learning theory that highlights the essential importance of social interaction and cultural background in the creation of knowledge (Vygotsky 1978, cited in Tzuriel, 2021). In contrast to conventional cognitive theories that view learning as an individual process of internalizing information, social constructivism argues that people learn through significant interactions with others, particularly those who have greater knowledge or experience. From this viewpoint, learning is not simply about passively taking in information; rather, it is an active process involving discussion, interaction, and the creation of mutual understanding (Gannar & Kilani, 2025).

Central to Vygotsky's theory is the idea of the Zone of Proximal Development (ZPD), which is defined as the gap between what a student can accomplish on their own and what they can accomplish with suitable assistance or cooperation (Silalahi, 2019). Effective teaching takes place within the learner's Zone of Proximal Development (ZPD), where guidance and assistance enable the learner to achieve greater levels of understanding and skill (Wang & Feng, 2023).

AI-driven platforms, including intelligent tutoring systems (ITS) and adaptive learning environments, reflect the support mechanisms highlighted in social constructivist teaching methods (Sbardella & Pakula, 2024). These systems gather and assess student data in real-time, modifying the presentation of content, the difficulty of questions, and feedback according to each learner's performance. For example, Carnegie Learning and Knewton adjust their teaching methods by offering students problems and resources that are appropriately challenging, thus working within the learner's Zone of Proximal Development (ZPD). This customized assistance fosters not only the gain of knowledge but also the growth of thinking skills, enabling learners to expand their abilities through gradual challenges and directed exploration (Zulu et al., 2018).

In addition, social constructivism highlights that knowledge is influenced by cultural and contextual factors, indicating that learning is affected by the surroundings in which it takes place. AI systems can improve this by customizing teaching according to a learner's background, interests, and previous knowledge. For instance, language learning applications such as Duolingo adjust to the speed and preferred methods of users, providing culturally appropriate examples and feedback in a range of languages. These platforms support learner participation while making sure that the content is relevant and easy to understand (Oladele Jegede, 2024).

Significantly, artificial intelligence also enhances the social aspect of constructivism by facilitating collaborative learning in online environments. AI-powered discussion platforms, collective recommendation systems, and instant collaboration tools can link learners from various backgrounds, promoting conversation and the joint development of knowledge. By participating in these interactions, students take part in group investigations, cultivate common insights, and improve their reasoning all fundamental principles of constructivist learning (Martinez-Maldonado et al. 2023).

Social constructivism offers a robust educational basis for the application of AI in teaching. By imitating the actions of more knowledgeable individuals, customizing support tools, and facilitating teamwork, AI technologies can put into practice the concepts of Vygotsky's theory (Guo et al., 2024). It is crucial that these tools are created and applied in ways that maintain the human-centered, culturally aware, and conversational elements of learning. When guided by constructivist principles, AI can greatly improve personalized learning experiences and play a crucial role in meaningful educational change in higher education (Czerkawski, 2024).

Connectivism

Connectivism, introduced by George Siemens in 2005 and Stephen Downes in 2006, is a modern theory of learning created to meet the challenges of a digital, interconnected era (Dziubaniuk et al., 2023). In contrast to conventional learning theories that emphasize personal thinking or social interaction within close surroundings, connectivism posits that learning takes place through a network of connections, encompassing individuals, systems, devices, databases, and online communities. In this perspective, knowledge is not merely obtained and kept by an individual; instead, it is something that exists within networks and is accessed and cultivated through involvement in those networks. Learning involves exploring, building, and expanding these networks to gain and utilize pertinent information (Poole & Leslie, 2020).

Artificial intelligence technologies are especially effective in promoting the principles of connectivism learning. AI inherently functions within digital networks, establishing links between extensive data sets and providing tailored results according to user actions, preferences, and objectives (Salim, 2024). For students, this implies that AI can serve as a facilitator, assisting them in linking with appropriate resources, individuals, and opportunities when needed. For instance, content recommendation systems, frequently found in contemporary Learning Management Systems (LMS) such as Canvas or Moodle, utilize machine learning algorithms to propose readings, videos, and discussion topics according to learners' previous activities, academic performance, and preferences (Chowdhury & Das, 2024). This corresponds with the connectivism perspective that gaining knowledge is a flexible and continuous activity that develops according to immediate needs and experiences.

Furthermore, tools like chatbots, virtual assistants, and automated feedback systems assist learners in interacting more effectively with educational materials and support services. These AI agents deliver prompt answers to inquiries, propose educational recommendations, and assist in navigating intricate information systems. In this regard, AI functions not merely as a tool but as a smart component within the learner's network, assisting in handling information overload and guiding focus toward valuable learning experiences (Kolluru et al., 2018).

Connectivism highlights the significance of independence, variety, and transparency in the educational experience. AI technologies can enhance independence by facilitating learning that is self-paced and self-directed (Jagals, 2025). For instance, websites such as Coursera and EdX use AI to tailor course recommendations and monitor student progress, enabling users to create educational paths that match their specific career objectives or academic preferences (Hendijani, 2025). Similarly, artificial intelligence can promote diversity by modifying how content is displayed to accommodate various cognitive styles, language backgrounds, or accessibility requirements (Daugherty et al., 2020).

Moreover, connectivism highlights that learning is an ongoing and non-linear journey where individuals must constantly refresh their knowledge as information evolves (Conradie, 2014). AI assists in this process by offering immediate updates, suggesting the newest resources, and highlighting any information that is no longer current. In rapidly changing areas like healthcare, data science, and cybersecurity, where information can quickly become outdated, AI's capability to organize and refresh content in real-time promotes the connectivism concept of continuous and adaptable learning.

AI improves the connectivism learning model by reinforcing the connections between learners and digital knowledge environments. To fully achieve its potential, educators and institutions must ensure that AI systems are created to support the principles of clarity, user empowerment, and substantial involvement (Englmeier & Contreras, 2024).

Directed Learning Theory

Self-Directed Learning (SDL) serves as a fundamental principle in adult education, highlighting the importance of the learner's active involvement in identifying their learning requirements, setting objectives, selecting resources, and assessing their progress (Blignaut et al., 2023). Self-Directed Learning (SDL) is described as a process where individuals take charge, either independently or with assistance, in recognizing their learning needs, setting goals, finding resources, executing strategies, and evaluating results (Brits & Blignaut, 2023). This method is especially appropriate for adult learners, who are frequently driven by their personal, educational, or career objectives, and who gain advantages from adaptable and independent learning frameworks. In the setting of higher education, where student groups are becoming more varied in age, background, and obligations, self-directed learning (SDL) is viewed as crucial for encouraging lifelong learning, critical analysis, and self-motivation (Pemberton & Mynard, 2023).

Artificial Intelligence (AI) greatly improves the situations in which SDL can flourish by offering tailored, adaptive, and data-driven learning settings (Kolchenko, 2018). A major way in which AI aids SDL is by providing smart dashboards and learning analytics tools that enable students to see their academic growth. These platforms gather and show important data like quiz results, completion percentages, and engagement rates allowing students to track their strengths and weaknesses immediately (Irmert et al., 2024). This visibility enhances metacognitive awareness and assists learners in making informed choices regarding which topics need more focus or different study methods. By providing this degree of understanding and self-evaluation, AI tools enable students to take responsibility for their learning experience (Guo & Li, 2024).

An additional method by which AI promotes self-direction is by supporting student autonomy through feedback and prompting strategies. For instance, virtual aides and flexible platforms offer immediate feedback, thoughtful prompts, and reminders that help learners remain focused on their objectives (Min & Andaya, 2024). These characteristics mimic the type of guidance that independent learners may typically look for from teachers or fellow students. Encouraging students to maintain ongoing conversations with the system, AI tools enhance self-regulation, perseverance, and a deeper connection with the content (Gonzalez-DeHass, 2019).

Significantly, AI enhances the availability of various learning materials and promotes options and investigation, which are two essential aspects of self-directed learning (SDL). Students can utilize multimedia resources, practice activities, simulations, and discussion boards customized to their individual requirements and preferences. This variety of choices not only promotes independence but also fosters internal motivation, which Knowles recognizes as a key characteristic of self-directed learners (Jung, 2017).

Self-Directed Learning Theory is a good fit for education that uses AI technology. The ability of AI to customize content, assist in decision-making, and offer feedback establishes a favorable setting for SDL to thrive. As colleges and universities continue to incorporate AI tools, comprehending and implementing SDL principles can guarantee that technology genuinely enhances students' abilities fostering independence, flexibility, and skills for lifelong learning that go beyond traditional education (Jin, 2022).

Incorporation of Theories with Artificial Intelligence in Curriculum Development

The coming together of these theories provides a solid basis for utilizing AI in the creation of curricula. Social constructivism emphasizes the significance of interaction and support, which AI can deliver via adaptive tutoring systems. Connectivism promotes the use of artificial intelligence to develop tailored and flexible learning networks. The theory of self-directed learning highlights how AI tools can enable students to take charge of their own learning journeys (Timbs, 2025).

Integrating these theories into the curriculum design guarantees that AI applications are not just additional technology but are included within well-structured educational frameworks. For example, a curriculum guided by these theories would encourage group projects that utilize AI-driven communication tools, flexible assessments that align with students' learning paths, and tailored content selection based on individual learner preferences and requirements (Jowallah, 2023).

A strong theoretical foundation for incorporating AI into personalized learning in higher education should be based on recognized learning theories that emphasize personalization, independence, and connection. Social constructivism, connectivism, and the theory of self-directed learning together establish a thorough basis for comprehending how artificial intelligence can change the educational environment. Basing AI-supported learning on these theories not only maintains teaching quality but also enhances the ability of AI to assist various students in significant, effective, and fairways (Zhou & Schofield, 2024).

REVIEW OF RELATED LITERATURE

The use of Artificial Intelligence (AI) in higher education has emerged as a widely examined area, especially in relation to promoting personalized learning experiences. As educational settings move towards more flexible and student-focused approaches, artificial intelligence is significantly changing the way curricula are developed, teaching methods are implemented, and academic assistance is provided (Nikhil, 2024). This literature review combines recent studies and academic viewpoints on the use of AI in customized learning routes, concentrating on its technological abilities, teaching implications, and challenges faced by institutions.

AI as a Catalyst for Customization

Personalized learning has developed into a revolutionary educational method that moves away from uniform, standardized teaching towards instructional experiences that are customized to fit the individual needs, preferences, abilities, and learning styles of every student (Ntjamba & Ashipala, 2025b). In higher education, where students come from a wide range of backgrounds and have different levels of readiness, the need for adaptable and personalized learning pathways has grown stronger (Waladiet al., 2025). Artificial Intelligence (AI) is essential in addressing this need by providing flexible, data-informed solutions that can adjust to differences among learners in real-time. Therefore, AI is not just a tool in education; it is a driving force for the broader personalization of learning, allowing institutions to transition to more inclusive, adaptive, and student-focused educational frameworks (Song et al., 2024).

The role of AI in personalized learning is mainly due to its capability to quickly and accurately manage and assess extensive amounts of learner data. AI-driven systems gather data from various sources such as students' engagement with learning management systems (LMS), test results, behavior trends, and time spent on tasks and employ advanced algorithms to create profiles of learners (Hatim Kagalwala, 2020). These profiles serve as the foundation for teaching methods that adjust and change together with the student. Balaban et al., (2024) highlight that AI technologies, including intelligent tutoring systems (ITS), adaptive learning platforms, and learning analytics dashboards, provide unique abilities to monitor student advancement, identify areas where knowledge is lacking, and modify content presentation instantly. These tools convert basic educational data into useful insights, enabling students and teachers to make knowledgeable choices regarding learning methods, interventions, and curriculum development.

A significant advancement in AI-driven personalization is the emergence of adaptive learning environments. Nurjanah (2016), contend that these systems are capable of providing tailored content that meets the changing requirements of learners. In contrast to conventional e-learning platforms that adhere to a fixed instructional sequence, adaptive systems modify the pace, difficulty, and order of teaching according to the learners' current performance. For example, platforms like Knewton, DreamBox Learning, and Smart Sparrow utilize real-time data analysis to offer students specific exercises, explanations, or support materials. This flexible approach promotes mastery-centered learning, making certain that students understand essential concepts prior to progressing further. A study by Kurt (2017), reveals that students who used tutoring systems powered by artificial intelligence showed greater improvements in learning and higher levels of engagement than traditional way of learning. This supports the study conducted by Ou (2024), who found out the effectiveness of these systems in fostering individualized academic achievement among students. In addition to academic achievement, AI enables customization by identifying and reacting to students' emotional conditions and motivation levels. Artificial intelligence, enables educational technologies to recognize emotions by analyzing facial expressions, voice intonations, and patterns of interaction. This enables systems to recognize feelings of frustration, boredom, confusion, or engagement, and modify the learning experience as needed. For instance, a system powered by artificial intelligence could offer support or suggest a more engaging activity if a student seems uninterested. Such systems that demonstrate emotional intelligence make the digital learning experience more relatable and encourage learners to stay motivated. Additionally, AI technologies are essential in recommendation systems that direct learners to material that corresponds with their interests, objectives, and previous understanding (Ou, 2024).

Artificial intelligence technologies are transforming the understanding and implementation of personalization in higher education (Begamudra Rangavittal, 2024). By utilizing insights derived from data, flexible algorithms, and interfaces that respond to emotions, artificial intelligence facilitates learning experiences that are more effective, engaging, and fair (Chiu, 2024). From providing content and evaluation to offering emotional assistance and suggesting resources, AI serves as an essential force in developing customized learning experiences suited to each learner's needs. To fully achieve this potential, institutions must carefully establish AI systems while adhering to ethical standards, maintaining educational consistency, and empowering learners. As artificial intelligence develops further, its function as a key factor in personalizing education will become increasingly essential to the future of higher education (Safonova & Mykhailenko, 2025).

Smart Teaching and Flexible Learning Systems

Some of the most developed and recognized uses of Artificial Intelligence (AI) in education include Intelligent Tutoring Systems (ITS) and adaptive learning platforms. These technologies are created to imitate or enhance the support usually given during individual instruction (Khine, 2024). They provide customized feedback, ongoing evaluation, and tailored content based on a student's performance and learning path. In contrast to conventional computer-based training systems, Intelligent Tutoring Systems (ITS) and adaptive platforms are based on cognitive science, teaching methods, and machine learning. This foundation enables them to adapt in real-time to the specific needs of each learner, thereby improving the learning experience (Abinaya et al., 2024). As artificial intelligence increasingly integrates into higher education, these technologies have become crucial in assisting tailored learning paths and enhancing academic results across various fields.

Intelligent Tutoring Systems are computer-driven teaching tools that utilize artificial intelligence to analyze a student's understanding and provide personalized learning experiences. As outlined by Ferster (2022), Intelligent Tutoring Systems (ITS) replicate the experience of personal tutoring by offering immediate, tailored feedback and suggestions. They adjust their teaching based on a student's behavior and engage in an interactive conversation to support the learning journey. One of the first and most recognized examples is AutoTutor, which employs natural language processing (NLP) to interact with students during tutorial discussions and evaluate mental states such as confusion or confidence (Oraif, 2023). With its flexible dialogue management, AutoTutor can pose insightful questions, offer clarifying feedback, and support learners in achieving a more profound comprehension.

Another important advantage of Intelligent Tutoring Systems (ITS) is their capacity to facilitate learning at an individual's own pace and to promote mastery of the subject matter. In contrast to traditional teaching methods, where it is anticipated that all students progress through the same content at an identical pace, Intelligent Tutoring Systems (ITS) allow for varying learning speeds and permit the review of concepts as necessary. This corresponds with Vygotsky's (1978) notion of the Zone of Proximal Development (ZPD), the space between what a students can accomplish alone and what they can reach with suitable assistance (Vygotsky 1978, cited in Tzuriel, 2021). ITS functions within this area by providing prompt and customized support, allowing students to advance from their existing level of comprehension to enhanced critical thinking and skillfulness.

Beyond Intelligent Tutoring Systems (ITS), adaptive learning platforms constitute a wider range of AI-based tools that tailor the learning experience using data-informed adjustments. Although it's typically concentrate on particular topics or abilities, adaptive platforms can be utilized in various fields and educational situations (Eau et al., 2019). These platforms utilize algorithms to observe student behavior including the time taken on tasks, accuracy, engagement levels, and assessment results and modify the teaching materials as needed. For example, platforms such as Knewton and DreamBox Learning employ machine learning models to arrange educational activities.

Park (2021), research indicated that students who utilized adaptive learning platforms achieved much greater improvements in understanding concepts and acquiring skills than their counterparts in traditional classroom environments. These results highlight the ability of adaptive systems to fill personal learning gaps and strengthen essential knowledge. In higher education, adaptive platforms are being utilized more frequently in foundational courses like introductory mathematics, statistics, and biology, where historically there have been significant failure rates. By offering timely assistance and tailored teaching methods, these systems enable students to develop confidence and continue with their educational goals.

Analytics and Learning Management Enhanced by Artificial Intelligence

The integration of artificial intelligence into Learning Management Systems (LMS) has also become more common. Predictive analytics employ past and current data to identify students who may be at risk of failing academically. Li (2023), highlight that learning analytics can guide specific actions, such as customized feedback or tutoring, prior to the development of problems. Moreover, dashboards powered by artificial intelligence offer valuable information to both students and teachers regarding learning habits, performance patterns, and levels of engagement.

According to Haji (2020), Learning Management Systems (LMS) that incorporate AI support precise education, where teaching choices are guided by data and continually adjusted to meet each learner's unique requirements. This improves the experience for learners while also making better use of faculty time and resources. Artificial intelligence is also commonly utilized in educational recommendation systems. Like the systems used by services such as Netflix or Amazon, these platforms evaluate student profiles and recommend content based on their interests, past activities, and performance levels. In personalized learning environments, content curation is a joint effort involving both the learner and the technology. AI systems have the capability to organize multimedia materials, scholarly articles that have been reviewed by experts, and practice exercises customized for the academic path of each learner. This not only facilitates independent learning but also lessens mental strain by simplifying the process of finding information (Sural & Yazici, 2021).

Ethical Considerations and Institutional readiness

Although AI offers significant opportunities to improve education, it also brings important teaching and ethical issues to consider. It is essential to address ethical concerns regarding data privacy, informed consent, and the autonomy of students (Jose, 2024). Although AI can perform administrative duties and provide tailored content, the personal connection in mentoring, emotional guidance, and ethical decision-making cannot be replaced. Although there is increasing interest, the use of AI in higher education is still not consistent. Numerous institutions remain in the initial phases of digital transformation and do not possess the strategic frameworks required to facilitate large-scale AI integration (Gering et al., 2025).

RECOMMENDATIONS AND SOLUTIONS

For AI to successfully promote individualized learning paths in higher education, institutions need to implement a comprehensive strategy that considers teaching methods, infrastructure, and ethical aspects. A primary focus is the professional growth of teachers, as numerous individuals do not possess the digital skills and teaching training necessary to successfully integrate AI tools into their instructional methods. It is important to have organized and ongoing training programs that focus on both practical skills and the theoretical application of AI in teaching. In addition, organizations must establish transparent ethical standards and strong data management systems to tackle concerns related to algorithmic bias, student privacy, and the responsible use of data. The creation of these policies must be guided by legal requirements and include input from various fields. It is also crucial to invest in technological infrastructure to guarantee fair access to AI-powered resources, especially in underserved and remote regions. Institutions must focus on dependable internet access, suitable learning management systems, and user-friendly AI platforms that meet the needs of a variety of students, including individuals with disabilities. Additionally, the development of the curriculum should be reconsidered to incorporate flexibility and customization, utilizing artificial intelligence to enable adaptable evaluations, personalized learning speeds, and tailored content presentation. Collaborating strategically with technology firms, government agencies, and global educational institutions can offer access to cutting-edge tools, expert knowledge, and shared best practices, promoting an environment for the responsible use of AI. Student involvement must also be a key focus, with educational institutions fostering digital skills, encouraging independent use of AI, and implementing feedback systems so that students continue to play an active role in influencing their learning experiences. Ultimately, organizations ought to create continuous monitoring and evaluation systems to examine the educational effectiveness and fairness aspects of incorporating AI. This involves gathering and examining learner information, obtaining qualitative feedback, and applying research-based methods to constantly improve AI applications. By combining these efforts, AI can be used not just as a technological advancement but also as a powerful tool for providing inclusive, individualized, and forward-thinking education.

STRENGTHS, LIMITATIONS, AND FUTURE DIRECTIONS FOR RESEARCH

This chapter presents various advantages in its examination of how artificial intelligence can be used to promote individualized learning paths in higher education. The most important aspect of this is its incorporation of various theoretical frameworks social constructivism, connectivism, and self-directed learning theory which together provide a complete perspective on how AI-enhanced learning can be comprehended and applied. The chapter utilizes a diverse range of interdisciplinary sources to frame the teaching, moral, and structural aspects of AI integration, thus offering a comprehensive perspective on the subject. Additionally, the chapter highlights effective methods for updating the curriculum and enhancing faculty skills, which are frequently overlooked in conversations regarding educational technology. Nonetheless, in spite of these advantages, there are significant drawbacks. The conversation primarily depends on secondary data and theoretical concepts instead of real case studies or practical assessments, which could restrict its relevance to various educational settings. Moreover, a significant portion of the literature and technological advancements mentioned in this chapter comes from wealthier areas, which may neglect the difficulties and limited resources encountered by institutions in low- and middle-income nations. This geographical and economic disparity in the literature highlights the necessity for research that is more inclusive and tailored to specific contexts. In the future, research should use practical methods, such as long-term studies and comparisons of different cases, to evaluate the true effectiveness of AI-based personalized learning across different fields of study and educational environments. It is essential to examine the viewpoints of both teachers and students concerning the integration of AI, focusing particularly on matters of trust, independence, and perceived worth. Additionally, studies ought to explore how AI systems can aid inclusive education, particularly for students with disabilities, neurodiversity individuals, and those in isolated or underprivileged communities. New fields like affective computing, emotional artificial intelligence, and the connection between artificial intelligence and critical pedagogy offer encouraging opportunities for research. By focusing on these deficiencies, upcoming studies can offer a deeper, fairer, and evidence-supported insight into how artificial intelligence may influence the future of tailored education. However, the discussion would benefit from the inclusion of real-world data and examples to ground theoretical claims and illustrate challenges in practical settings. Future studies are encouraged to adopt practical methodologies such as multi-institutional case analyses, learner-centered evaluations, and mixed-methods approaches, Furthermore, future research should explore how AI supports inclusive education by examining its impact on marginalized learners, equitable access, and differentiated instruction,

CONCLUSION

Higher education institutions are increasingly relying on artificial intelligence to inform their own learning experiences, as it can create customized pathways that suit the interests and preferences of students. As shown in this chapter, AI technologies such as intelligent tutoring systems, adaptive learning platforms, predictive analytics, and recommendation engines provide potent resources for facilitating more individualized, flexible, and data-driven learning environments. These technologies can go beyond simple efficiency improvements to foster greater participation, inclusiveness, and student independence when grounded in well-known pedagogical theories like social constructivism, connectivism, and self-directed learning. But, the incorporation of AI into curriculum development and teaching methods must be done with purpose, ethical foresight, and institutional preparation. Significant issues like faculty digital literacy, data protection, algorithmic bias, and access disparities must be resolved through all-encompassing legislation, well-thought-out infrastructure expenditures, and ongoing professional development. Additionally, it will be necessary to encourage inclusive innovation and cross-sector collaboration in order to guarantee that the advantages of AI are distributed equitably throughout educational settings. At the end of the day, AI's genuine potential lies in improving human learning by offering individualized support, timely feedback, and possibilities for self-directed development, rather than just automating education. Embracing AI as a pedagogical partner, rather than a technological novelty, can go a long way toward preparing future-ready graduates who are flexible, empowered, and prepared for lifelong learning as higher education institutions deal with an increasingly digital and data-driven age.

REFERENCES

Abinaya, S., Sherly Alphonse, A., Indira, K., & Lavanya, R. (2024). Intelligent tutoring systems. *Adopting Artificial Intelligence Tools in Higher Education*, 226-250. DOI: 10.1201/9781003469315-11

Agius, C. (2022). 6. Social constructivism. *Contemporary Security Studies*, 73-89. DOI: 10.1093/hepl/9780198862192.003.0006

Balaban, I., Zlatović, M., & Matus, M. (2024). Using learning analytics dashboards to monitor student progress: The case of a blended computer science university course. *2024 IEEE International Conference on Advanced Learning Technologies (ICALT)*, 72-74. DOI: 10.1109/ICALT61570.2024.00027

Begamudra Rangavittal, P. (2024). Transforming higher education with artificial intelligence - Benefits, challenges, and future directions. [IJSR]. *International Journal of Science and Research (Raipur, India)*, *13*(5), 1635–1642. DOI: 10.21275/SR24525214415

Blignaut, H., Erasmus, E., & Du Toit-Brits, C. (2023). *Joyful learning: Advocating for self-directed learning through authentic, playful problem-based learning*. NWU Self-Directed Learning Series., DOI: 10.4102/aosis.2023.BK409.04

Brits, C. D., & Blignaut, J. H. (2023). Recognizing the importance of educator behavior in SDL. *Advances in Higher Education and Professional Development*, •••, 95–119. DOI: 10.4018/978-1-6684-6772-5.ch006

Chiu, T. K. (2024). Future research recommendations for transforming higher education with generative AI. *Computers and Education: Artificial Intelligence*, *6*, 100197. DOI: 10.1016/j.caeai.2023.100197

Chowdhury, S., & Das, D. K. (2024). Academic performance analysis of the students with feature retraction using machine learning algorithms. *2024 4th International Conference on Sustainable Expert Systems (ICSES)*, 1060-1064. DOI: 10.1109/ICSES63445.2024.10763310

Conradie, P. W. (2014). Supporting self-directed learning by connectivism and personal learning environments. *International Journal of Information and Education Technology (IJIET)*, *4*(3), 254–259. DOI: 10.7763/IJIET.2014.V4.408

Czerkawski, B. C. (2024). Designing language learning experiences with generative AI tools. *Advances in Educational Technologies and Instructional Design*, •••, 324–341. DOI: 10.4018/979-8-3693-0872-1.ch015

Daugherty, P. R., Wilson, H. J., & Chowdhury, R. (2020). Using artificial intelligence to promote diversity. *How AI Is Transforming the Organization*, 15-22. DOI: 10.7551/mitpress/12588.003.0006

Degni, F. (2024). The impact of artificial intelligence on education. *Advances in Educational Technologies and Instructional Design*, •••, 55–94. DOI: 10.4018/979-8-3693-6170-2.ch003

Dziubaniuk, O., Ivanova-Gongne, M., & Nyholm, M. (2023). Learning and teaching sustainable business in the Digital Era: A connectivism theory approach. *International Journal of Educational Technology in Higher Education, 20*(1), 20. Advance online publication. DOI: 10.1186/s41239-023-00390-w

Eau, G., Judah, K., & Shahid, H. (2019). How can adaptive platforms improve student learning outcomes? A case study of open educational resources and adaptive learning platforms. SSRN *Electronic Journal*. DOI: 10.2139/ssrn.3478134

Englmeier, K., & Contreras, P. (2024). How AI can help learners to develop conceptual knowledge in digital learning environments. *2024 IEEE 12th International Conference on Intelligent Systems (IS)*, 1-6. DOI: 10.1109/IS61756.2024.10705253

Ferster, B. (2022). *Intelligent tutoring systems*. Intelligent Tutoring Systems., DOI: 10.4324/9781138609877-REE6-1

Francisco, R., & Silva, F. (2022). A recommendation module based on reinforcement learning to an intelligent tutoring system for software maintenance. *Proceedings of the 14th International Conference on Computer Supported Education*. DOI: 10.5220/0011083900003182

Gannar, S., & Kilani, C. (2025). Contextualized learning and social constructivism: Implementing a project-based approach in information systems development education. *Journal of Science Learning, 8*(1), 15–24. DOI: 10.17509/jsl.v8i1.72667

Gering, Z., Feher, K., Harmat, V., & Tamassy, R. (2025). Strategic organisational responses to generative AI-driven digital transformation in leading higher education institutions. *The International Journal of Organizational Analysis, 33*(12), 132–152. DOI: 10.1108/IJOA-09-2024-4850

Gonzalez-DeHass, A. R. (2019). Self-regulated learning. *Parent Involvement for Motivated Learners*, 83-103. DOI: 10.4324/9781351021906-5

Guo, H., Yi, W., & Liu, K. (2024). Enhancing constructivist learning: The role of generative AI in personalised learning experiences. *Proceedings of the 26th International Conference on Enterprise Information Systems*, 767-770. DOI: 10.5220/0012688700003690

Guo, K., & Li, D. (2024). Understanding EFL students' use of self-made AI chatbots as personalized writing assistance tools: A mixed methods study. *System, 124*, 103362. DOI: 10.1016/j.system.2024.103362

Haji, S. A. (2020). Exploring the frequent use of the learning management systems (LMS) features and learners' interactions in higher education / Explorer L'UTILISATION FRÉQUENTE des FONCTIONNALITÉS des SYSTÈMES de GESTION de L'APPRENTISSAGE (LMS) et des interactions avec Les APPRENANTS dans L'ENSEIGNEMENT SUPÉRIEUR. *European Journal of Open Education and E-learning Studies, 5*(2). Advance online publication. DOI: 10.46827/ejoe.v5i2.3477

Hatim Kagalwala. (2020). Personalized learning algorithms: Enhancing student engagement through AI-driven tools. *GLOBAL PERSPECTIVES: CROSS-DISCIPLINARY CONTRIBUTIONS TO MULTIDISCIPLINARY RESEARCH*. DOI: 10.25215/8198391754.29

Hendijani, Z. D. (2025). Learning English through online platforms: An analysis of language learning methods via websites and educational platforms like coursera and edx compared to traditional teaching met. *TMP Universal Journal of Research and Review Archives*, *4*(1). Advance online publication. DOI: 10.69557/ujrra.v4i1.151

Irmert, N., Franco, C., & Isaksson, S. (2024). *The effects of generative AI on learning*. AEA Randomized Controlled Trials., DOI: 10.1257/rct.14930-1.0

Jagals, D. (2025). Metacognition: The cognitive and affective architecture of self-directed learning. *NWU Self-Directed Learning Series*, 1-19. DOI: 10.4102/aosis.2024.BK484.01

Jin, S. (2022). The effects of self-directed learning through an AI speaking application in an EFL speaking class on learners' self-directed learning ability and speaking skills. *Studies in English Education*, *27*(3), 381–414. DOI: 10.22275/SEE.27.3.07

Jose, D. (2024). Data privacy and security concerns in AI-integrated educational platforms. *Recent trends in Management and Commerce, 5*(2), 87-91. DOI: 10.46632/rmc/5/2/19

Jowallah, R. J. (2023). Integrating artificial intelligence (AI) into the curriculum. *Advances in Educational Technologies and Instructional Design*, •••, 355–368. DOI: 10.4018/979-8-3693-0074-9.ch015

Jowallah, R. J. (2023). Integrating artificial intelligence (AI) into the curriculum. *Advances in Educational Technologies and Instructional Design*, •••, 355–368. DOI: 10.4018/979-8-3693-0074-9.ch015

Jung, C. (2017). The effects of a self-directed learning-enhancement program on nursing students' self-directed learning abilities, self-efficacy, empowerment, and clinical practice competency. *Asia-pacific Journal of Multimedia services convergent with Art. Humanity & Society*, *7*(10), 319–329. DOI: 10.14257/AJMAHS.2017.10.47

Kasztelnik, K. (2024). Artificial intelligence-assisted curriculum development: Innovations in designing educational content for the 21st century learner. *Journal of Higher Education Theory and Practice*, *24*(11). Advance online publication. DOI: 10.33423/jhetp.v24i11.7367

Khine, M. S. (2024). AI in teaching and learning and intelligent tutoring systems. *Artificial Intelligence in Education*, 467-570. DOI: 10.1007/978-981-97-9350-1_4

Kolchenko, V. (2018). Can modern AI replace teachers? Not so fast! Artificial intelligence and adaptive learning: Personalized education in the AI age. *HAPS Educator*, *22*(3), 249–252. DOI: 10.21692/haps.2018.032

Kolluru, V., Mungara, S., & Chintakunta, A. N. (2018). Adaptive learning systems: Harnessing AI for customized educational experiences. *International Journal of Computer Science and Information Technologies*, *6*(3), 13–26. DOI: 10.5121/ijcsity.2018.6302

Kolluru, V., Mungara, S., & Chintakunta, A. N. (2018). Adaptive learning systems: Harnessing AI for customized educational experiences. *International Journal of Computer Science and Information Technologies*, *6*(3), 13–26. DOI: 10.5121/ijcsity.2018.6302

Kurt, V. (2017). Intelligent tutoring systems for continuous, embedded assessment. *The Future of Assessment*, 113-138. DOI: 10.4324/9781315086545-5

Kussmaul, C., & Pirmann, T. (2021). Guided inquiry learning with technology: Investigations to support social constructivism. *Proceedings of the 13th International Conference on Computer Supported Education*, 483-490. DOI: 10.5220/0010458104830490

Li, S. (2023). Personalized tutoring and support. *Learning Analytics Enhanced Online Learning Support*, 144-175. DOI: 10.4324/9781032637044-5

Martinez-Maldonado, R., Van Leeuwen, A., & Swiecki, Z. (2023). Artificial intelligence techniques for supporting face-to-face and online collaborative learning. *Handbook of Artificial Intelligence in Education*, 422-439. DOI: 10.4337/9781800375413.00031

Min, Y., & Andaya, M. (2024). Enhancing student writing skills through Gamification: Evaluating the effectiveness of Textopia, an AI-driven platform for personalized writing prompts and feedback. *Advanced Natural Language Processing*, 225-234. DOI: 10.5121/csit.2024.141020

Murdan, A. P., & Halkhoree, R. (2024). Integration of artificial intelligence for educational excellence and innovation in higher education institutions. *2024 1st International Conference on Smart Energy Systems and Artificial Intelligence (SESAI)*, 1-6. DOI: 10.1109/SESAI61023.2024.10599402

Nikhil, V. (2024). A comprehensive study on AI-enhanced personalized learning in STEM courses. *Adopting Artificial Intelligence Tools in Higher Education*, 149-170. DOI: 10.1201/9781003469315-7

Ntjamba, F. C., & Ashipala, D. O. (2025a). Association between learning styles and academic success in nursing and midwifery education. *Motivating Engagement, Belonging, and Success in Higher Education Student Experience*, 245-268. DOI: 10.4018/979-8-3693-8089-5.ch009

Ntjamba, F. C., & Ashipala, D. O. (2025b). Ethical dimensions of AI in the Metaverse. *Advances in Computational Intelligence and Robotics*, •••, 195–212. DOI: 10.4018/979-8-3373-0340-6.ch010

Ntjamba, F. C., & Ashipala, D. O. (2025c). Beyond reality: Integrating AI and Metaverse technologies for enhanced scientific collaboration. *Advances in Computational Intelligence and Robotics*, •••, 99–118. DOI: 10.4018/979-8-3373-0340-6.ch005

Ntjamba, F. C., & Ashipala, D. O. (2025d). Innovative pathways: AI and the Metaverse in interdisciplinary research and knowledge discovery. *Advances in Computational Intelligence and Robotics*, •••, 119–138. DOI: 10.4018/979-8-3373-0340-6.ch006

Nurjanah, D. (2016). Good and similar learners' recommendation in adaptive learning systems. *Proceedings of the 8th International Conference on Computer Supported Education*, 434-440. DOI: 10.5220/0005864304340440

Oganetse, D. K. (2025). Personalized learning for incarcerated students. *Mitigating Learner Disadvantages in Teaching and Learning*, 359-396. DOI: 10.4018/979-8-3693-8623-1.ch013

Oladele Jegede, O. (2024). Artificial intelligence and English language learning: Exploring the roles of AI-driven tools in personalizing learning and providing instant feedback. *Universal Library of Languages and Literatures, 01*(02), 06-19. DOI: 10.70315/uloap.ullli.2024.0102002

Oraif, I. (2023). Natural language processing (NLP) and EFL learning: A case study based on deep learning. *Journal of Language Teaching and Research*, *15*(1), 201–208. DOI: 10.17507/jltr.1501.22

Ou, C. (2024). Artificial intelligence and student engagement. *Designing Socially Dynamic Digital Learning*, 151-173. DOI: 10.4324/9781003368076-18

Owoseni, A., Kolade, O., & Egbetokun, A. (2024). Generative AI and its implications for higher education students and educators. *Generative AI in Higher Education*, 1-25. DOI: 10.1007/978-3-031-60179-8_1

Park, E. (2021). Understanding how students control their learning in adaptive learning environments. *Proceedings of the 2021 AERA Annual Meeting*. DOI: 10.3102/1687712

Pemberton, C., & Mynard, J. (2023). Promoting and evaluating students' development of self-directed language learning and reflective abilities. *Promoting Reflection on Language Learning*, 150-166. DOI: 10.2307/jj.22679696.15

Poole, N., & Leslie, S. (2020). Enhancing the student experience. *Flexibility and Pedagogy in Higher Education*, 53-64. DOI: 10.1163/9789004438118_005

Safonova, N., & Mykhailenko, V. (2025). Implementation of artificial intelligence for personalization education tracks in tertiary education. *Innovate Pedagogy*, *2*(80), 142–148. DOI: 10.32782/2663-6085/2025/80.2.29

Salim, S. (2024). *Artificial intelligence (AI) and teaching learning.* In P. Agarwal & N. Khan (Eds.), *The digital classroom: Integrating technology for effective learning* (pp. [insert page range if known]). Archives Publishing. https://doi.org/DOI: 10.25215/9358793864.22

Sbardella, T., & Pakula, A. (2024). Investigating the transformative power of AI-driven intelligent tutoring systems in online language learning environments. *INTED Proceedings*, *1*, 3557–3562. DOI: 10.21125/inted.2024.0940

Shadbolt, N., O'Hara, K., De Roure, D., & Hall, W. (2019). Privacy, trust and ethical issues. In *Lecture notes in social networks* (pp. 149–200). Springer., DOI: 10.1007/978-3-030-10889-2_4

Silalahi, R. M. (2019). Understanding Vygotsky's zone of proximal development for learning. *Polyglot: Jurnal Ilmiah*, *15*(2), 169. DOI: 10.19166/pji.v15i2.1544

Song, Y., Weisberg, L. R., Zhang, S., Tian, X., Boyer, K. E., & Israel, M. (2024). A framework for inclusive AI learning design for diverse learners. *Computers and Education: Artificial Intelligence*, *6*, 100212. DOI: 10.1016/j.caeai.2024.100212

Sural, I., & Yazici, M. (2021). Learner performance and satisfaction level in personalized learning environments. *Research Anthology on Developing Effective Online Learning Courses*, 1386-1410. DOI: 10.4018/978-1-7998-8047-9.ch069

Timbs, A. (2025). The cognitive convergence of AI and human learning: How learning theories illuminate artificial intelligence. DOI: 10.2139/ssrn.5182286

Tzuriel, D. (2021). The socio-cultural theory of Vygotsky. *Social Interaction in Learning and Development*, 53-66. DOI: 10.1007/978-3-030-75692-5_3

Waladi, C., Lamarti, M. S., & Khaldi, M. (2025). AI-driven personalized learning pathways customizing education for every student. *Advances in Educational Technologies and Instructional Design*, •••, 63–78. DOI: 10.4018/979-8-3693-8965-2.ch004

Waladi, C., Lamarti, M. S., & Khaldi, M. (2025). AI-driven personalized learning pathways customizing education for every student. *Advances in Educational Technologies and Instructional Design*, •••, 63–78. DOI: 10.4018/979-8-3693-8965-2.ch004

Wang, Z., & Feng, J. (2023). Teaching quality evaluation based on student's zone of proximal development (ZPD) prediction. *Journal of Education and Educational Research*, *6*(1), 44–48. DOI: 10.54097/jeer.v6i1.14157

Wise, A. F. (2018). Learning analytics: Using data-informed decision-making to improve teaching and learning. *Contemporary Technologies in Education*, 119-143. DOI: 10.1007/978-3-319-89680-9_7

Zhou, X., & Schofield, L. (2024). Using social learning theories to explore the role of generative artificial intelligence (AI) in collaborative learning. *Journal of Learning Development in Higher Education*, (30). Advance online publication. DOI: 10.47408/jldhe.vi30.1031

Zulu, E., Haupt, T., & Tramontin, V. (2018). Cognitive loading due to self-directed learning, complex questions and tasks in the zone of proximal development of students. *Problems of Education in the 21st Century, 76*(6), 864-880. DOI: 10.33225/pec/18.76.864

ADDITIONAL READING

Alpturk, K., Dagli, G., Altinay, F., Altinay, Z., & Shadiev, R. (2025). Leveraging artificial intelligence to drive inclusion, innovation, and entrepreneurship in higher education strategies. DOI: 10.2139/ssrn.5264229

Dumbuya, E. (2025). Personalized learning through artificial intelligence: Revolutionizing education. DOI: 10.2139/ssrn.5023248

ElAtia, S., Ipperciel, D., & Zaïane, O. R. (2016). *Data mining and learning analytics: Applications in educational research.* John Wiley & Sons. DOI: 10.1002/9781118998205

Ethridge, J. L. (2024). *The AI-driven classroom: Revolutionizing education.* eBookIt.com.

Farrell, H. (2024). Re-imagining student engagement in an AI-enhanced classroom. *Using Generative AI Effectively in Higher Education*, 67-73. DOI: 10.4324/9781003482918-10

Grant, P., & Basye, D. (2014). *Personalized learning: A guide for engaging students with technology*. International Society for Technology in Education.

Hartley, P., Beckingham, S., Lawrence, J., & Powell, S. (2024). Using generative AI effectively in higher education. *Using Generative AI Effectively in Higher Education*, 1-7. DOI: 10.4324/9781003482918-1

Islomovich, I. T. (2023). The need to reform the management system of higher education institutions and implement new principles to it. *International Journal of Pedagogics*, *03*(05), 89–94. DOI: 10.37547/ijp/Volume03Issue05-18

Nikhil, V. (2024). A comprehensive study on AI-enhanced personalized learning in STEM courses. *Adopting Artificial Intelligence Tools in Higher Education*, 149-170. DOI: 10.1201/9781003469315-7

Personalized learning paths: Leveraging artificial intelligence and machine learning for student-centered education. (2024). *European Economic Letters*. DOI: 10.52783/eel.v14i3.1886

Sirenko, K. Y., & Goncharenko, O. H. (2023). Application of innovative learning technologies in teaching social and humanitarian disciplines in institutions of higher education. *TOPICAL ASPECTS OF SOCIAL SCIENCE DISCIPLINES AND INNOVATIVE METHODS AND TECHNOLOGIES OF THEIR LEARNING AND TEACHING*, 322-335. DOI: 10.30525/978-9934-26-315-6-16

Umutlu, D., & Gursoy, M. E. (2022). Leveraging artificial intelligence techniques for effective scaffolding of personalized learning in workplaces. *Advances in Analytics for Learning and Teaching*, 59-76. DOI: 10.1007/978-3-031-14489-9_4

Walker, R. (2024). *ChatGPT in the classroom for harnessing AI to revolutionize elementary, middle and high school education: Innovative strategies for teachers to enhance learning and curriculum with hundreds of artificial intelligence prompts*. LEGENDARY EDITIONS.

Watanabe, A. (2022). Let's talk about artificial intelligence. *Advances in Higher Education and Professional Development*, •••, 48–72. DOI: 10.4018/978-1-7998-9247-2.ch003

KEY TERMS AND DEFINITIONS

Artificial Intelligence (AI): A branch of computer science concerned with developing machines and algorithms capable of performing tasks that typically require human intelligence, such as reasoning, learning, problem-solving, perception, and language understanding (Ntjamba & Ashipala, 2025a).

Personalized Learning Pathways: Instructional approaches and learning environments that adapt content, pace, and instructional methods to meet the unique needs, goals, and preferences of individual learners, often supported by technology such as AI (Waladi et al., 2025).

Adaptive Learning: An educational method that uses computer algorithms and AI to orchestrate interaction with the learner and deliver customized resources and learning activities to address each student's specific needs (Kolluru et al., 2018).

Intelligent Tutoring System (ITS): A computer-based learning environment that provides immediate and personalized feedback to learners, simulating the benefits of one-on-one tutoring by adapting content and support based on real-time analysis of learner performance (Francisco & Silva, 2022).

Social Constructivism: A learning theory, largely attributed to Lev Vygotsky that emphasizes the importance of social interaction, language, and culture in the construction of knowledge, proposing that learning is co-constructed through collaborative processes (Agius, 2022).

Ethical AI: The application of ethical principles such as fairness, accountability, transparency, and respect for privacy to the design, deployment, and use of artificial intelligence systems, particularly in sensitive domains like education (Ntjamba & Ashipala, 2025).

Chapter 5
Preparing for the Global AI Economy Through Educational Reform and Curriculum Redesign

Youmei Liu
https://orcid.org/0009-0000-1973-1872
University of Houston, USA

ABSTRACT

The rapid advancement of artificial intelligence (AI) is reshaping the global economy and prompting an urgent call for educational reform to prepare students for an AI-augmented workforce. Among the most pressing concerns is the potential for AI-driven job displacement, underscoring the need for curricula that foster not only technical proficiency but also future-proof skills. This chapter explores a comprehensive framework for aligning higher education with the demands of the global AI economy across four strategic domains: 1) curriculum renovation to embed AI literacy and workforce readiness; 2) transdisciplinary teaching to bridge disciplinary boundaries and foster innovative problem-solving; 3) tangible assessment strategies to capture applied skills and interdisciplinary competencies; and 4) global integration to promote equitable access and cross-border collaboration. The chapter provides a roadmap for reimagining curriculum design that equips students to thrive in an interconnected, ethically complex, and AI-driven world.

INTRODUCTION

The rapid advancement of artificial intelligence (AI) is transforming the global economy, disrupting traditional industries, and reshaping the skills required for workforce participation. As Tani (2025) observes, "Artificial Intelligence (AI) has emerged as a transformative force, reshaping economies and redefining governance structures worldwide" (Introduction). Breakthroughs in generative artificial intelligence (GenAI) are accelerating this shift, redefining tasks across sectors and highlighting the urgent need for educational reform. According to the World Economic Forum (2025), these technological changes are occurring alongside broader global

DOI: 10.4018/979-8-3373-2752-5.ch005

challenges including economic volatility, geopolitical realignments, environmental pressures, and heightened expectations around equity and sustainability.

AI-powered automation, predictive analytics, and machine learning are increasingly embedded in business operations, improving efficiency while simultaneously displacing certain human roles. As Tani (2025) notes, "Its rapid integration into various sectors signifies a pivotal shift toward automation, efficiency, and data-driven decision-making" (Introduction). This transformation has sparked widespread concern about the future of work. The World Economic Forum (2025) projects that nearly one-quarter of today's jobs will be disrupted within the next five years, reinforcing the imperative for lifelong learning and agile, cross-sector digital reskilling.

Among students preparing to enter this evolving labor market, one of the most pressing concerns is AI-driven job displacement. As GenAI continues to evolve, many of the careers students are currently training for may fundamentally change or even disappear (Chan & Hu, 2023). A 2025 study at the University of Houston found that students across various disciplines expressed significant anxiety about AI's impact on job security. A number of participants feared that AI would replace roles in journalism, customer service, and even education, disrupting traditional career paths. As one student noted, "AI is taking over roles that involve content generation, making it harder for entry-level professionals to find substantial employment." Another observed, "It's not just technical jobs – AI reaching into creative fields stresses me out" (Liu, 2025).

Figure 1. Students' Concerns about Job Replacement by AI Technology

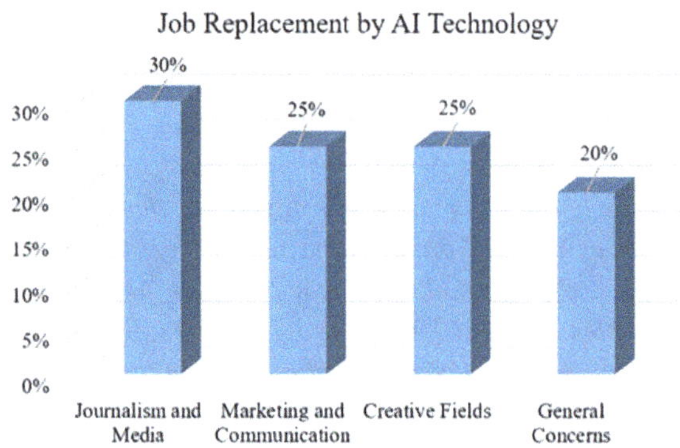

These concerns are well-founded. Research suggests that AI will not only eliminate certain job categories but also transform existing roles and create entirely new professions requiring hybrid skill sets—those that combine technical proficiency with adaptability, creativity, and ethical reasoning (Chan & Hu, 2023). As Cazzaniga et al. (2024) emphasize, advanced economies will likely experience these changes first due to their heavy reliance on cognitive-intensive work structures. This makes it all the more urgent for education systems to equip students with digital fluency, interdisciplinary problem-solving abilities, and a strong ethical foundation.

While AI presents significant challenges, it also offers remarkable opportunities for innovation, economic growth, and workforce transformation. According to the 2024 Lightcast report, three major areas of change are reshaping the global economy: artificial intelligence, sustainability, and cybersecurity. These domains require a globally aware, future-ready workforce. Yet many higher education institutions continue to operate within outdated models that emphasize legacy skills, fail to integrate AI literacy across disciplines, and overlook the importance of interdisciplinary and globally inclusive approaches.

To address these challenges, higher education must undergo a deliberate and transformative redesign. This chapter outlines a strategic framework organized around four interconnected domains:

1. **Curriculum Renovation** – Designing globally relevant curricula that incorporate AI-related knowledge and align learning outcomes with evolving workforce needs.
2. **Transdisciplinary Teaching** – Promoting integrative, cross-field teaching approaches that foster innovation and critical problem-solving by connecting AI with other domains.
3. **Tangible Assessment** – Implementing meaningful student learning outcome assessments that reflect real-world applications of AI competencies across disciplines.
4. **Global Integration** – Cultivating a globally competent workforce through equitable access to AI education and cross-border collaboration.

Through these four focus areas, institutions can equip students with the skills, mindsets, and ethical orientation necessary to thrive in the AI-driven global economy. This chapter offers practical, research-informed strategies to help educators, institutional leaders, and policymakers reimagine higher education for a digitally transformed, interconnected future.

MAIN FOCUS OF THE CHAPTER

Curriculum Renovation: Adapting to Global AI Trends

The global economy is undergoing a fundamental transformation driven by the rapid advancement of artificial intelligence, impacting everything from work and communication to decision-making and even creativity. In response, educational institutions must pursue systemic and intentional curriculum renovation to prepare learners for this new reality. As Tuomi (2018) emphasizes, aligning education with AI development is no longer optional; it is a strategic imperative for national competitiveness and institutional resilience. Curriculum design must move beyond traditional content delivery models to foster the competencies that students need to succeed in AI-augmented environments and to navigate the increasing complexity of global society.

In the United States, the urgency for reform is particularly acute. Higher education faces compounding challenges, including declining graduation rates, inadequate workplace readiness, mounting student debt, and persistent inequities in access and outcomes (Kazin, 2022). National enrollment trends continue to decline (National Student Clearinghouse Research Center, 2024), while public skepticism toward the value of a college degree intensifies. As Liu and Curtin (2025) note, rising tuition costs, shifting labor market demands, and the emergence of alternative learning pathways have widened the gap between educational expectations and outcomes. Increasingly, academic credentials are being dismissed as "degrees to nowhere," intensifying pressure on institutions to clarify and demonstrate the return on investment of a postsecondary education.

Addressing this challenge requires full transparency and alignment between intended learning outcomes and the expectations of students and employers. Liu and Curtin (2025) argue that the integration of skills and competencies in demand paired with purpose-driven curriculum redesign is key to restoring the relevance and credibility of higher education. Educational leadership and policy play an essential guiding role, but policy alone is insufficient. As Kennedy and Sundberg (2020) caution, policy documents that promote 21st-century skills will have limited impact unless translated into curricular practice. Almuhaideb and Saeed (2020) assert that curriculum is the backbone of academic programs and must meet both national and international expectations. Effective reform must translate the vision of 21st-century education into actionable, classroom-based competencies (Haug & Mork, 2021), thereby closing the gap between institutional output and the evolving needs of society.

Curriculum Reformation: Aligning Vision with Workforce Needs

While the integration of AI literacy, future-proof skills, and global perspectives is essential for preparing students for an AI-driven economy, these innovations are unlikely to take hold without deliberate and systemic curriculum reformation. This transformation goes beyond updating course content; it requires realigning learning outcomes, instructional methods, faculty development, and institutional policy to reflect the demands of a technology-saturated, globally interconnected world. As Luckin et al. (2016) argue, traditional curricula remain overly siloed and slow to adapt, leaving students unprepared for the interdisciplinary and fast-changing nature of AI-enhanced workplaces. Similarly, Holmes et al. (2022) emphasize that meaningful AI integration demands more than technical training – it requires curriculum design that incorporates ethical awareness, contextual relevance, and discipline-specific applications.

The OECD's AI and the Future of Skills report (2021) echoes this call, arguing that AI literacy must become a foundational competency on par with numeracy and reading. It advocates embedding AI across general education and disciplinary learning, stressing that workforce resilience will increasingly depend on individuals' ability to interact with intelligent systems in diverse fields. UNESCO (2022) similarly urges educational systems to move away from treating AI as an isolated subject. Instead, it recommends embedding AI across disciplines through curriculum redesign, interdisciplinary resource development, and teacher capacity-building. These approaches are essential to enabling students to engage critically and ethically with AI in their professional and civic lives.

Institutional readiness for this shift remains a key area of vulnerability. A recent Delphi study on AI trends in higher education conducted by Zawacki-Richter et al. (2023) found that without structural curriculum innovation, such as modular course design, microcredentials, and interdisciplinary pathways, higher education risks falling short of the demands of digital transformation. Likewise, Kennedy and Sundberg (2020) caution that even the most robust policies around 21st-century skills will have limited impact unless translated into curricular structures and classroom-level practices. These findings reinforce the view that curriculum reform is the linchpin for delivering AI literacy, global competence, and educational innovation in an equitable and sustainable way. The following table outlines five strategic areas for curriculum reformation that institutions can implement to address this challenge.

Table 1. Curriculum Reformation Strategies to Align with AI and Global Workforce Needs

Strategic Area	Objective	Implementation Strategy	Assessment
1. Curriculum Mapping & Alignment	Align program outcomes with AI-related competencies and interdisciplinary relevance.	• Audit existing programs for AI-related content gaps. • Map learning outcomes to global AI frameworks (e.g., OECD, UNESCO). • Include AI ethics and social impact in general education.	• Curriculum maps; • Outcomes-alignment rubrics; • AI content audits.
2. Faculty Development & Incentives	Equip faculty across disciplines to teach AI-relevant content confidently and ethically.	• Host workshops on AI literacy integration and teaching tools. • Support co-teaching and interdisciplinary course design. • Provide incentives for curricular innovation.	• Participation metrics; • Course evaluations; • Instructor self-assessments.
3. Modular Curriculum & Microcredentials	Offer flexible, stackable pathways for AI learning across degree programs.	• Develop microcredential tracks for AI ethics, applications, or tools. • Embed AI-relevant modules in humanities, social sciences, and professional fields.	• Enrollment data; • Completion rates of modules/badges; • Student feedback.
4. Interdisciplinary Program Design	Create curricular structures that integrate AI with diverse disciplines.	• Design interdisciplinary minors/ certificates (e.g., "AI & Society"). • Encourage double majors or linked courses between AI and other fields.	• Program enrollment trends; • Graduate outcomes; • Interdisciplinary capstone reviews.
5. Continuous Feedback & Industry Input	Ensure curricula evolve with AI trends and labor market needs.	• Engage employers and alumni in curriculum review cycles. • Collect feedback from AI-using professionals across sectors.	• Curriculum revision logs; • Graduate employability reports; • Stakeholder surveys.

Positioning curriculum reformation as the foundation for educational transformation ensures that AI literacy is not treated as an elective or peripheral subject but as a structural component of the academic experience. This approach empowers all students, not only those in technical majors, to become informed, adaptable, and ethically aware contributors to the global AI economy. In doing so, education becomes not just a response to technological change, but a force that helps shape it.

Effective curriculum reform requires meaningful, sustained engagement from a broad range of stakeholders. Liu & Curtin (2025) note that inclusive and collaborative curriculum design strengthens alignment between academic outcomes and societal needs. Faculty are central to embedding AI meaningfully within disciplinary contexts and upholding pedagogical integrity. Instructional designers bring expertise in course architecture, accessibility, and learner-centered strategies (Klein, 2019). Industry and employer partners offer real-time insight into evolving workforce demands, enhancing curriculum relevance and graduate employability (Zawacki-Richter et al., 2023; OECD, 2021). Including students and alumni in feedback loops ensures that reforms reflect lived experiences and support real-world applicability (UNESCO, 2022).

Without inclusive stakeholder engagement, curriculum reform risks becoming top-down, fragmented, or unsustainable. In contrast, participatory approaches foster shared ownership, institutional commitment, and adaptability - conditions that are vital for embedding future-proof skills, fostering global engagement, and preparing learners for meaningful participation in the AI economy. Ultimately, it is the architecture of the curriculum itself that enables all other reform priorities to take root.

Curriculum Implementation – Turning Vision into Practice

Translating curriculum reform into effective classroom practice requires more than aspirational goals. It demands deliberate planning, institutional alignment, faculty engagement, and instructional innovation. To ensure meaningful integration of AI into higher education, curriculum implementation must be guided by three foundational pillars: (1) AI literacy across disciplines, (2) future-proof skills, and (3) global perspectives. These pillars not only reflect core competencies for the AI economy but also form a cohesive framework for designing content, delivering instruction, and assessing student learning.

AI literacy must be embedded across the curriculum, not confined to technical programs such as computer science. Holmes et al. (2022) argue that AI affects every discipline, including law, education, business, medicine, and the arts. Providing students with domain-specific AI knowledge allows them to critically evaluate, contextualize, and responsibly apply AI technologies in their respective fields. Zawacki-Richter et al. (2019) emphasize that interdisciplinary AI education enhances learners' real-world problem-solving capabilities and fosters cross-functional collaboration—two essential attributes in an AI-enhanced workplace.

Cultivating future-proof skills, including creativity, critical thinking, adaptability, and emotional intelligence, is essential for sustainable employability in dynamic career environments. While technical fluency is vital, it is these human-centered skills that enable graduates to lead, innovate, and navigate ethical dilemmas. Wang et al. (2021) found that inquiry-driven instructional approaches such as design thinking and problem-based learning significantly strengthen these competencies, especially when integrated with AI-assisted tasks and simulations. Such strategies foster metacognition, resilience, and lifelong learning – all crucial traits in a rapidly evolving job market.

Integrating a global perspective into curriculum implementation ensures that students understand AI as both a global phenomenon and a culturally embedded technology. Disparities in access to AI, differing regulatory environments, and diverse ethical frameworks across countries necessitate that students engage with global AI dynamics. Sälzer and Roczen (2018) argue that global competence is vital for navigating the sociopolitical and intercultural implications of emerging technologies. Instructional practices that incorporate international case studies, comparative policy analysis, and cross-border collaboration build students' capacity to contribute meaningfully to global AI discourse and innovation.

Effective curriculum implementation also requires structural and pedagogical support. Faculty must be equipped with the tools, time, and training to incorporate AI concepts into their disciplines. Institutions should establish shared frameworks, promote interdisciplinary collaboration, and provide feedback mechanisms that align instructional design with real-world outcomes. Moreover, implementation must be supported by continuous assessment and refinement to ensure responsiveness to both student needs and labor market trends. The following table presents a practical instructional framework that outlines key domains of implementation, expected learning outcomes, content design strategies, assessment methods, and recommended teaching approaches.

Table 2. Instructional Design Framework for AI-Integrated Curriculum Implementation

Domain	Learning Outcomes	Content Design	Assessment Method	Teaching Approach
AI Literacy across Disciplines	Students understand core AI principles and apply them ethically within their field.	Develop field-specific AI content (e.g., AI in healthcare, law, or education) with ethical considerations and real-world applications.	• Applied projects • Case evaluations • Ethics reflection papers • Quizzes on AI fundamentals	• Interdisciplinary case studies • Problem-based learning • Expert guest lectures • Simulations & scenario analysis
Future-Proof Skills	Students demonstrate critical thinking, creativity, adaptability, and emotional intelligence in AI-augmented environments.	Integrate transferable skills development within project-based and experiential learning across the curriculum.	• Portfolios • Peer and self-assessments • Problem-solving exercises • Group presentations	• Design thinking • Collaborative innovation labs • Role-playing & debate • AI-assisted creative tasks (e.g., storytelling, design)
Global Perspectives	Students exhibit global competence, cultural awareness, and understanding of international AI trends and ethics.	Include global AI case studies, comparative policy frameworks, and diverse cultural perspectives on AI development and impact.	• Cross-cultural reflection journals • Global policy comparison papers • International group project reports	• COIL (Collaborative Online International Learning) • Virtual exchange projects • Multicultural dialogue forums • Comparative analysis activities

Together, these three dimensions offer a holistic and actionable model for curriculum implementation. This framework empowers institutions to deliver impactful, future-oriented learning by blending technical skills with ethical understanding and local context with global perspectives. As Luckin et al. (2016) affirm, education must keep pace with AI innovation and actively guide its trajectory toward the public good. Higher education can equip students to thrive in and purposefully shape the AI economy by intentionally integrating AI literacy, future-proof competencies, and global citizenship into its curriculum.

Transdisciplinary Teaching: Connecting AI to Real-World Challenges

As higher education institutions reform curricula to align with the demands of the global AI economy, the next critical step lies in transforming how learning is delivered. Structural changes alone are insufficient; the success of reform depends on the pedagogical strategies used to bring new competencies to life in the classroom. Today's graduates must be prepared not just to understand AI as a technology, but more importantly, to apply it in solving complex, interconnected societal problems. This requires moving beyond traditional academic silos toward more integrated, real-world learning. In this context, transdisciplinary teaching has emerged as a vital pedagogical approach.

Although the concept of transdisciplinarity has gained new urgency in the 21st century, its intellectual foundations date back to the early 1970s. Swiss psychologist Jean Piaget introduced the term in his seminal essay The Epistemology of Interdisciplinary Relationships (1972), where he envisioned transdisciplinarity as a "higher stage" of knowledge integration. This stage, he argued, would not only foster collaboration among disciplines but dissolve their boundaries altogether, placing academic inquiry within a unified, systemic framework. Later thinkers such as

Nicolescu (2010), López-Huertas (2013), and Pădurean and Chevere an (2010) expanded on this idea, emphasizing that transdisciplinary knowledge transcends the sum of its parts by integrating insights from both academic and non-academic domains.

Unlike interdisciplinary approaches, which combine existing methods from different fields while maintaining disciplinary boundaries, transdisciplinary teaching fosters a holistic understanding of complex phenomena by synthesizing knowledge, methods, and perspectives across disciplines. Karaman (2022) explains that while interdisciplinary collaboration often occurs at the edges of individual fields, transdisciplinarity acknowledges and engages with the full complexity of real-world issues, including the social, cultural, ethical, and technological dimensions. Madni (2007) describes this as the discovery of "hidden connections" between disciplines, connections that are essential for addressing the multifaceted challenges of contemporary life.

This pedagogical shift is particularly critical in the era of artificial intelligence. Embedding AI literacy into transdisciplinary teaching not only cultivates technical fluency but also promotes systems thinking, ethical reasoning, and contextual awareness. According to Dede (2020), future-ready learners must be able to connect knowledge across domains, such as combining AI with public health, climate resilience, or social justice, to generate meaningful, innovative solutions. Transdisciplinary teaching transforms AI from a standalone skillset into a catalyst for critical inquiry and innovation across disciplines. Klein (2019) and the OECD (2021) both state that this model of teaching is essential for preparing graduates to operate in a world where boundaries between fields are increasingly blurred, and solutions must emerge from cross-sector collaboration. By equipping students to draw from multiple knowledge systems, scientific, cultural, ethical, and experiential, transdisciplinary teaching prepares them to adapt to technological disruption and to shape it in socially responsible ways.

The following sections explore how institutions can support transdisciplinary innovation at both the structural and instructional levels, offering actionable models for teaching AI in ways that are integrative, globally relevant, and future-focused.

Institutional Strategies for Transdisciplinary Innovation

The successful integration of transdisciplinary teaching in higher education, particularly in the context of artificial intelligence (AI), requires more than pedagogical reform. It demands strategic leadership, structural investment, and a culture that supports collaboration across academic and organizational boundaries. Research consistently emphasizes that without institutional alignment across policy, funding, and curricular frameworks, transdisciplinary efforts often remain fragmented, isolated, or unsustainable (Klein, 2019; Fam et al., 2020).

As AI intersects with complex global challenges, spanning environmental, economic, and ethical domains, institutions must create enabling conditions that allow faculty to co-design courses, bridge departmental silos, and connect academic content to real-world problems. According to the OECD (2021), universities play a critical role in fostering integrative thinking by building governance models, curricular frameworks, and support systems that promote shared teaching, interdisciplinary assessment, and external engagement.

Zawacki-Richter et al. (2023) note that AI literacy cannot be meaningfully integrated into education without institutional pathways that support interdisciplinary cooperation, such as team-taught courses, transdisciplinary minors, and stakeholder-informed learning projects. Similarly, UNESCO (2022) urges institutions to embed AI across domains and engage external actors, including community and industry partners, to ensure that curricula remain relevant, ethical, and globally aware. The following five strategies offer actionable guidance for academic leaders seeking to foster and sustain transdisciplinary teaching environments:

1. Establish Transdisciplinary Governance and Incentives
    - Create institutional structures such as transdisciplinary councils, task forces, or centers for integrative learning that support cross-departmental collaboration.
    - Provide faculty release time, seed grants, or recognition for co-developing and co-teaching transdisciplinary courses.
    - Establish funding and recognition for co-taught interdisciplinary courses.
    - Integrate transdisciplinary efforts into strategic planning, accreditation reports, and institutional review processes.

Faculty often lack time or institutional support to pursue transdisciplinary work. Leadership must formalize and reward collaboration across departments (Klein, 2019).

2. Support Co-Designed, Cross-Listed Courses
    1. Promote joint course development between STEM and non-STEM faculty on themes such as "AI and Ethics," "AI for Global Health," or "Data and Society."
    2. Promote course co-design and co-teaching models where instructors from different disciplines collaborate to share instructional responsibilities.
    3. Encourage cross-listed courses across departments, allowing students to earn credit in multiple disciplines.

AI is inherently cross-cutting; co-designed courses reflect real-world complexity and help students synthesize perspectives (Dede, 2020).

3. Develop Interdisciplinary AI Pathways and Minors
    - Create transdisciplinary minors, certificates, or thematic tracks that combine AI with domains like sustainability, healthcare, communication, or digital media.
    - Ensure that such programs include both technical and societal dimensions (e.g., machine learning + social impact; data analytics + public policy).
    - Align these pathways with workforce demands to ensure relevance and feasibility within standard degree timelines.

These curricular options give students structured opportunities to develop cross-domain fluency while staying within degree timelines (OECD, 2021).

4. Invest in Faculty Development for Integrative Pedagogy
    - Offer ongoing professional development in transdisciplinary teaching methods, collaborative course design, and integrating AI literacy into diverse subjects.
    - Support faculty learning communities focused on cross-disciplinary innovation and AI integration.
    - Allocate resources (AI labs, case libraries, design studios) to support active, real-world learning experiences.

- Train faculty in problem-based learning (PBL) models that encourage knowledge transfer and collaborative problem-solving.

Many faculty lack exposure to transdisciplinary pedagogy or confidence teaching AI content outside their field (Holmes et al., 2022). Barrows (1986); Hmelo-Silver (2004) show PBL enhances collaboration, knowledge transfer, and critical thinking.

5. Partner with External Stakeholders for Real-World Relevance
    - Build relationships with industry, nonprofit, and community partners to co-design course projects and learning experiences that address real-world problems involving AI.
    - Embed externally informed problem-based projects in transdisciplinary courses.
    - Build infrastructure for virtual international collaboration (e.g., COIL models).
    - Establish exchange agreements with global institutions around AI education.
    - Support multilingual and culturally diverse learning environments.

Engaging real-world stakeholders enhances student learning, reinforces relevance, and prepares learners to work across boundaries (UNESCO, 2022; Van Zyl et al., 2020). Leask (2015) emphasizes curriculum internationalization as key to developing global competence.

Institutional strategies build the structural and cultural base for transdisciplinary teaching, but their success hinges on classroom implementation. Faculty play a central role in translating institutional vision into transformative learning experiences. To bridge academic theory with practical application, instructors must design learning environments that break down disciplinary barriers, engage students in collaborative inquiry, and connect AI to real-world challenges. Dede (2020) emphasizes that the most powerful learning environments reflect the complexity of the problems they address, encouraging students to synthesize diverse perspectives rather than compartmentalize them. This requires more than curriculum reform; it requires sustained support for instructional innovation, co-creation with learners, and a pedagogy grounded in ethics, systems thinking, and social responsibility (Fam et al., 2020).

The following section explores instructional implementation strategies that operationalize transdisciplinary teaching, bringing it to life in the classroom and equipping students with the integrative thinking, global awareness, and ethical leadership skills needed in the AI-driven world.

Instructional Practices for Transdisciplinary Teaching

Implementing transdisciplinary teaching in the context of AI requires more than subject integration; it calls for intentional course design, learner-centered pedagogy, and faculty collaboration across disciplinary boundaries. Instructors are on the frontlines of this transformation, tasked with creating learning environments that not only convey technical knowledge but also develop critical thinking, ethical reasoning, and systems-level understanding, core competencies for navigating the AI era (Holmes et al., 2022).

In an increasingly interconnected and AI-driven world, the societal challenges students will face, including algorithmic bias, surveillance ethics, job displacement, and global AI governance, demand teaching strategies that mirror real-world complexity. Transdisciplinary instruction positions students to explore such challenges through multiple lenses, helping them build both deep expertise and adaptive, collaborative mindsets. Transdisciplinary teaching fosters a holistic understanding of AI's role in shaping economies and societies, embracing the following components:

1. Collaborative Course Design

Collaborative, co-taught courses allow students to engage with diverse disciplinary perspectives on AI-related issues. Faculty from different fields, such as computer science, ethics, public policy, or communication, can co-develop courses like AI and Global Economics or Ethical AI in Cross-Cultural Contexts. These offerings promote integrative thinking while modeling the kind of interdisciplinary collaboration required in the workforce. Research shows that co-designed STEM and humanities courses enhance student engagement, deepen understanding, and stimulate innovation (Becker & Park, 2011; Xie, Tian, & Lee, 2024).

2. Problem-Based Learning (PBL)

PBL fosters inquiry-driven learning where students solve open-ended, real-world problems using knowledge from multiple fields. In AI-integrated PBL environments, students may be asked to design fair algorithms for hiring, evaluate surveillance systems, or assess AI's impact on climate policy. Studies show that combining AI content with PBL enhances critical thinking, creativity, and cross-contextual knowledge transfer (Barrows, 1986; Hmelo-Silver, 2004; Herminawati & Ramli, 2024; Khan & Iqbal, 2024).

3. Global Team Projects

Collaborating with international peers on AI-related challenges through virtual exchange or COIL (Collaborative Online International Learning) models develops students' cross-cultural communication, empathy, and global awareness. These projects mirror the distributed, multicultural nature of AI development in the workforce. Research confirms that global teamwork strengthens AI literacy and intercultural competence (Lau & Perez, 2024; Hyperspace, 2023; Leask, 2015).

Transdisciplinary teaching, using collaborative course design, problem-based learning, and global team projects, allows students to apply theoretical knowledge to the real-world societal impact of AI. This educational paradigm serves to prepare students for the future by cultivating both a comprehensive understanding of artificial intelligence and the capacity for responsible, creative, and globally-informed leadership and innovation. The table below outlines how these models can be operationalized in practice through intentional learning outcomes, content design, assessments, and pedagogical techniques.

Table 3. Instructional Design Framework for Transdisciplinary AI Teaching

Domain	Learning Outcomes	Content Design	Assessment	Teaching Approach
Collaborative Course Design	Students synthesize interdisciplinary knowledge and perspectives to analyze and address complex AI-related issues.	Courses co-developed and co-taught by faculty from different disciplines (e.g., AI and Global Economics, AI and Ethics).	• Joint interdisciplinary projects, • Co-authored papers, • Synthesis essays comparing disciplinary perspectives.	• Team-teaching, integrated syllabi, • Panel discussions, • Interdisciplinary readings.
Problem-Based Learning (PBL)	Students apply knowledge from multiple disciplines to solve real-world, AI-related problems using collaborative inquiry.	Scenario-based tasks focused on ethical dilemmas, policy-making, or social impact of AI.	• Problem briefs, • Group solution presentations, • Design prototypes, • Peer feedback reports.	• Inquiry-based learning, • Group case analysis, • Design thinking workshops.
Global Team Projects	Students develop cross-cultural collaboration and communication skills by working with international peers on AI challenges.	Cross-border team assignments focused on AI innovation, policy, or social impact.	• Multimedia project outputs, • Intercultural reflection journals, • Team process evaluations, • Global issue analysis.	• Collaborative Online International Learning (COIL), • Virtual teamwork, • Intercultural training sessions.

Transdisciplinary teaching offers a transformative pathway for preparing students to navigate and shape the AI-driven world. Through dismantling academic silos and fostering integrative learning experiences, this approach helps students develop not only technical competence, but also the ethical insight, collaboration skills, and systems thinking needed for responsible innovation.

Yet for transdisciplinary teaching to reach its full potential, it must be accompanied by assessment models that reflect the complexity of student learning in this space. Traditional exams and content quizzes are often inadequate for measuring integrative thinking, global awareness, or applied AI ethics. As institutions shift toward transdisciplinary education, they must also embrace new forms of assessment that capture students' ability to synthesize, communicate, and act responsibly in diverse and evolving contexts.

The next section explores the tangible student learning outcome assessment, including portfolios, simulations, and global case-based evaluations as evidence of AI readiness in the 21st-century workforce. Transdisciplinary strategies and teaching practices provide the foundation for holistic AI education, but assessment models must accompany them to measure the depth and breadth of student learning. Given the limitations of traditional assessment tools in evaluating cross-disciplinary thinking, ethical reasoning, and real-world AI application, the shift toward integrative teaching models necessitates new forms of assessment that can accurately reflect students' ability to synthesize knowledge, collaborate across fields, and apply AI to authentic global issues.

Tangible Student Learning Outcome Assessment

Tangible student learning outcomes refer to explicit, measurable, and observable evidence that demonstrates what students have learned, whether in terms of knowledge acquisition, skill development, or the application of competencies in real-world contexts. As Suskie (2009) notes, tangible outcomes are characterized by their directness, visibility, and clarity. They provide objective evidence that students have met defined learning goals, offering a reliable foundation for both formative and summative assessment. Examples include portfolios, simulations, capstone projects, presentations, coding artifacts, and policy briefs, and all of which make learning visible, transferable, and assessable.

Recent research supports the growing importance of tangible outcomes in aligning curriculum design with workforce and societal needs. Jackson and Michelson (2022) emphasize that tangible assessments, particularly those tied to experiential and project-based learning, can help students articulate and showcase their skills to future employers. This alignment is especially important in AI-augmented economies where technical fluency, adaptability, and ethical judgment must be demonstrated, not merely claimed. Studies in digital and online learning contexts further support the use of authentic assessments, such as portfolios, as tools for capturing complex and integrative learning. Jopp and Cohen (2023) found that well-designed ePortfolios help students connect AI-related content across disciplines, while also encouraging reflective learning and self-assessment. Similarly, Zheng et al. (2022) demonstrate that capstone projects in AI education significantly enhance students' ability to apply technical and ethical concepts in interdisciplinary, real-world scenarios making them a prime example of tangible learning artifacts. The motivational power of tangible rewards has also been studied, particularly in hybrid and online settings. Badges, digital credentials, and modular microcredentials can incentivize student participation and document learning in modular, visible forms. Researchers such as Yuan and Recker (2020) report that these artifacts not only motivate students but also offer granular proof of mastery that can be tracked across platforms and shared with external stakeholders.

Theoretical frameworks continue to enrich this discussion. Sen's capabilities approach, for instance, reframes assessment as more than measurement – it emphasizes the learner's capacity to apply knowledge meaningfully in diverse contexts (1985). From this perspective, tangible outcomes are not only proof of learning but also indicators of educational empowerment, signaling how well students are prepared to convert knowledge into action and learning into opportunity (Unterhalter, 2021).

As the demand for workforce-ready graduates increases especially in the global AI economy, institutions are being called to redefine what counts as meaningful evidence of learning. This includes shifting from traditional testing models to performance-based assessments that capture students' abilities to synthesize, create, communicate, and solve problems across domains (Gikandi et al., 2011; Holmes et al., 2022). These methods are particularly suited to transdisciplinary learning, where integration, application, and collaboration are central. Together, these frameworks and findings underscore the critical role of tangible student learning outcomes in measuring educational effectiveness. They also support the creation of authentic, adaptive, and inclusive assessment models that provide students with real opportunities to demonstrate AI literacy, global awareness, and the future-proof skills needed to thrive in today's knowledge economy.

Aligning Assessment with AI-Era Competencies

To prepare students for success in the global AI economy, assessment strategies must evolve beyond traditional exams and isolated content recall. Higher education institutions must strategically align learning outcomes and assessment models with the interdisciplinary, ethical, and applied competencies increasingly required in AI-augmented workplaces (Jackson & Michelson, 2022; Holmes, Bialik, & Fadel, 2022). This begins with embedding AI-relevant competencies such as algorithmic reasoning, data literacy, ethical awareness, and global collaboration into institutional learning outcome frameworks. As the OECD (2021) emphasizes, these skills should be integrated across general education and disciplinary pathways, ensuring that students across fields, not just in computer science, develop the capacity to engage meaningfully with AI.

Institutions must also support faculty in adopting authentic and performance-based assessment models. Portfolios, simulations, and transdisciplinary capstone projects are increasingly recognized as effective tools for capturing the complexity of student learning in AI-integrated contexts (Jopp & Cohen, 2023; Gikandi, Morrow, & Davis, 2011). These methods allow learners to demonstrate their ability to synthesize knowledge, collaborate across fields, and apply concepts to real-world challenges. To enable this shift, faculty development must prioritize training in rubric design, interdisciplinary grading, and outcome-based assessment. Research by Boud and Falchikov (2007) underscores that sustainable assessment in higher education must build students' capacity to evaluate and apply knowledge, not just acquire it. Faculty learning communities and assessment support teams can provide vital infrastructure for this professional growth. Moreover, institutions should collaborate with employers, alumni, and global partners to ensure assessments reflect the evolving landscape of AI-related work. As noted by Yuan and Recker (2020), digital badges and microcredentials aligned with workforce needs offer promising alternatives to traditional assessment, especially in modular and online learning environments. In addition, the effective use of learning analytics and AI-enhanced assessment platforms can support both formative and summative evaluation, enabling adaptive feedback and personalized learning trajectories (Ifenthaler & Yau, 2020). These tools can help educators identify gaps, optimize instruction, and ensure equity in student support and progression.

As higher education embraces transdisciplinary curriculum and instruction, assessment systems must evolve in parallel emphasizing real-world application, global awareness, and evidence-based learning. The following strategies outline key institutional and instructional planning priorities for aligning assessment practices with the demands of the global AI economy. These approaches support the development of performance-based, stakeholder-informed, and learner-centered assessment models that reflect the complexity and relevance of student achievement in AI-integrated contexts.

Table 4. Strategic Approaches for Aligning Assessment with AI-era Competencies

Strategy	Objective	Examples of Implementation
1. Redesign Learning Outcomes for AI Competencies	Align program goals with AI literacy, ethics, and interdisciplinary problem-solving.	Update curricula using frameworks like OECD AI Principles or UNESCO Competency Standards. (OECD 2021); (Jackson & Michelson, 2022)
2. Prioritize Authentic, Performance-Based Assessment	Move beyond exams to assess real-world application and critical reasoning in AI contexts.	Capstone projects, AI case analysis, simulations, and digital portfolios. (Boud & Falchikov, 2007); (Gikandi et al. 2011).
3. Develop Faculty Capacity in AI-Aligned Assessment	Equip instructors to design and evaluate assessments for transdisciplinary AI learning.	Workshops on rubric design, interdisciplinary grading, and ethics in AI assessment. (Holmes et al. 2022); (Jopp & Cohen 2023).
4. Embed Capstone Projects and ePortfolios	Provide students with culminating opportunities to integrate and showcase AI learning.	Require interdisciplinary AI-focused capstones or reflective ePortfolios tied to real-world challenges. (Zheng et al. 2022); (Jopp & Cohen 2023).

continued on following page

Table 4. Continued

Strategy	Objective	Examples of Implementation
5. Leverage Learning Analytics and AI Tools	Use digital platforms to monitor progress and personalize learning while maintaining equity.	Adaptive feedback tools, AI-enhanced dashboards, personalized goal tracking. (Ifenthaler & Yau 2020); (Holmes et al. 2022).
6. Involve Stakeholders in Assessment Design	Ensure relevance and industry alignment through external input.	Partner with employers, alumni, or global advisors to co-create rubrics or validate capstone criteria. (Yuan & Recker 2020); Jackson & Michelson (2022)

These approaches align with what employers increasingly value: critical thinking, problem-solving, teamwork, and ethical awareness (Elearning Industry, 2023; TxDLA, 2023). Moreover, by integrating AI-powered tools into assessment design, educators can enhance personalization, provide timely feedback, and more accurately monitor long-term skill development (Arnold, 2023). Ultimately, the use of tangible assessments not only improves student learning but also strengthens the connection between academic achievement and workforce readiness to ensure that graduates are prepared to thrive in the complexities of a digitally transformed, globally interconnected future.

Tangible Student Learning Outcome Assessment: Readiness for the AI Economy

Traditional forms of assessment, such as multiple-choice exams or memorization-based evaluations, are increasingly inadequate in measuring the complex, transferable competencies required in an AI-driven global economy. To meet this challenge, higher education institutions must adopt tangible assessment strategies that evaluate not only content knowledge but also a student's ability to synthesize information, solve real-world problems, and demonstrate AI literacy across contexts.

Recent studies support the need for more dynamic and authentic assessment models. For instance, research by Elearning Industry (2023) emphasizes how AI-driven assessments can enhance learning outcomes by delivering personalized feedback, adaptive learning experiences, and real-time analytics that provide a more nuanced and continuous understanding of student progress. Beyond helping instructors identify learning gaps efficiently, these innovations empower students to take greater control of their own development. A study by the Texas Distance Learning Association (2023) highlights how outcome-based, interdisciplinary assessments such as simulations, digital portfolios, and AI-supported capstone projects are increasingly aligned with employer expectations in fields that demand critical thinking, teamwork, and domain-specific problem-solving.

Integrating AI into the assessment process creates opportunities to model the very skills students are expected to use in future workplaces. Arnold (2023) highlights that the use of AI in assessment offers new possibilities for formative feedback, authentic evaluation, and the tracking of longitudinal skill development especially for complex skills that traditional testing often fails to capture. These approaches allow educators to move beyond assessing whether students "know" and instead focus on whether students can "do" in meaningful, applied settings. The following table explores various tangible assessment methodologies that effectively capture and evaluate the multifaceted skills essential for success in an AI-driven economy.

Table 5. Tangible Student Learning Outcome Assessment

Assessment	Learning Outcome	Instructional Context	Assessment Method
1. Capstone Projects	Demonstrate integration of AI concepts across disciplines; apply ethical reasoning and innovation in real-world contexts.	Final year or culminating courses in AI-related or interdisciplinary programs.	• Rubrics assessing problem-solving, • Interdisciplinarity, innovation, • Ethical reasoning.
2. Digital Portfolios	Curate and reflect on learning artifacts that show growth in AI skills, critical thinking, and transdisciplinary application.	Used throughout a course or program to document and reflect on individual learning trajectories.	• Self-reflections, • Instructor evaluations, • Peer feedback using structured rubrics.
3. Scenario-Based Simulations	Engage in real-world decision-making involving AI (e.g., ethics in automation, AI and public policy, crisis response).	Integrated into assignments, workshops, or experiential modules.	• Simulation debriefs, • Performance analytics, • Team reflections.
4. Case Study Analyses	Analyze and evaluate international AI-related case studies involving law, health, media, or sustainability.	Embedded into readings, discussion sections, or collaborative assignments.	• Written reports, • Presentations, • Group debates evaluated for depth and perspective-taking.
5. Global Collaboration Projects	Apply cross-cultural communication, teamwork, and AI tools in addressing global challenges (e.g., climate, inequality).	COIL (Collaborative Online International Learning), virtual exchange programs, or cross-institutional teams.	• Peer evaluations, • Cultural awareness reflections, • Collaborative deliverables.
6. Skill Development Tracking	Track longitudinal growth in AI fluency, adaptability, collaboration, and digital problem-solving.	Scaffolded over multiple courses or semesters (linked to microcredentials or badging systems).	• Competency checklists, milestone reviews, • Advisor feedback, • AI tool usage logs.

These examples of tangible evidence provide clear, concrete proof of learning outcomes and educational impact. Tangible evidence of student learning is pivotal in supporting the sustainability of educational programs and institutions through enhanced academic and institutional accountability, and it contributes significantly to community engagement and societal impact as well. Projects that engage with community issues or focus on sustainability encourage students to apply their learning in real-world contexts, fostering a practical understanding of societal challenges and solutions. This approach also enhances the institution's ties to the community and its overall public support and prepares students to operate effectively in a globalized world by extending the educational impact beyond the classroom and into society at large.

While tangible assessments provide a clear lens through which to evaluate students' readiness for the AI-driven workforce, these efforts must also be situated within a broader global context. As AI technologies transcend borders, so too must the skills and values instilled through education. Preparing students to navigate ethical, professional, and cultural challenges in a digitally connected world requires a deliberate integration of international perspectives. Without global alignment in curriculum, skill standards, and access, even the most innovative assessments risk becoming fragmented and inequitable. The subsequent section investigates how institutions can weave an international dimension into AI education, with the goal of developing learners who are not only skilled in AI tools but also globally competent, socially responsible, and prepared to make meaningful contributions to diverse societies and economies.

Integrating the International Dimension

The accelerating pace of AI development demands a globally responsive approach to education that acknowledges the borderless nature of technological innovation alongside persistent disparities in access, infrastructure, and opportunity. As nations compete to cultivate AI-ready workforces, aligning curricula with international standards and fostering cross-border collaboration has become an educational imperative. According to UNESCO (2022) and the OECD (2021), frameworks such as the ICT Competency Standards and AI Principles for Children and Education offer foundational guidance for designing equitable, inclusive, and future-focused AI curricula that promote both innovation and social responsibility.

Global integration in AI education requires more than the adoption of skill benchmarks, which involves building sustainable institutional partnerships, co-designing international programs, and ensuring that learners, regardless of geography, have the resources, support, and infrastructure to participate in and benefit from the global AI economy. This is especially critical as global disparities in AI investment, digital infrastructure, and education funding risk deepening inequality unless actively addressed through inclusive strategies. Hence, the pursuit of inclusive and globally relevant learning has emerged as a core principle for equitable development. As Santiago and Cerna (2020) argue, "educational equity is essential not only for individual well-being and opportunity but also for preparing people to collaborate and thrive in increasingly diverse and complex societies" (p. 2). Institutions must cultivate learner-centered environments that reflect cultural diversity and prioritize agency, empowerment, and engagement especially in the context of global, AI-driven transformation. Liu (2024) emphasizes that inclusive learning environments built on respect and cultural responsiveness are vital for enabling every student to realize their full potential.

The global AI economy is not limited by national borders but is a shared domain of opportunity, responsibility, and risk. To prepare learners for this reality, higher education must look beyond national curricula to adopt global standards, support cross-cultural collaboration, and foster equitable access to AI learning tools and opportunities. This section explores key strategies and practices for embedding the international dimension into AI education, including aligning with global skill standards, supporting equitable digital access, building cross-border academic partnerships, and establishing international research hubs that connect educators, industries, and communities around the world.

Institutional Imperatives for Global AI Integration

Integrating the international dimension is not an enhancement – it is a necessity. Institutions that prioritize global perspectives in their AI strategies position their students not only to compete in a transnational job market but also to lead with empathy, innovation, and global responsibility. Today's graduates are entering a borderless workforce where technical competence alone is not enough; success also depends on ethical discernment, cultural fluency, and international collaboration. To ensure equitable participation and meaningful preparation, institutions must embed global standards, expand access, and cultivate cross-border partnerships that reflect the complex realities of AI's global footprint.

Recent research underscores the urgency of this international turn. UNESCO (2022) warns that disparities in AI literacy and digital access are widening, particularly in under-resourced regions. Without deliberate strategies to include underserved populations, the digital divide will deepen existing inequities in education and economic participation. OECD (2021) advocates for aligning curricula with internationally recognized frameworks to support transnational collaboration and ethical AI deployment. Zawacki-Richter et al. (2023) further emphasize that relevance and innovation in AI education require collaborative networks, co-designed programs, shared infrastructure, and cross-institutional research that transcend borders.

The following strategies outline key institutional priorities for embedding this global vision into AI education through curriculum design, equitable access, and research collaboration.

1. Global Skill Standards

Aligning AI curricula with internationally recognized frameworks, such as UNESCO's ICT Competency Framework for Teachers and the OECD AI Principles, ensures program coherence, mobility, and international accountability. These standards embed ethical, technical, and cultural competencies into academic outcomes and enable students to transition fluidly across global education and employment systems. UNESCO (2019) stresses that the alignment with global benchmarks supports instructional quality, interoperability, and equitable participation in the AI workforce.

2. Cross-Border Collaborations

International partnerships in curriculum development, certification, and faculty exchange foster culturally responsive, globally relevant AI education. Models such as Collaborative Online International Learning (COIL), joint degree programs, and global innovation labs help institutions democratize access to diverse AI perspectives and enrich learner engagement. Research by Knight (2013) and Leask (2015) emphasizes that embedding global perspectives into course delivery deepens learning and institutional relevance.

3. Equitable Access to AI Education

Closing the global digital divide is essential for equitable AI participation. Institutions must prioritize inclusive instructional design, including multilingual materials, localized case studies, and mobile-first content delivery, particularly for learners in low-bandwidth or underserved regions. The ITU (2023) identifies digital inclusion as central to sustainable development, while Liu (2024) advocates for community-centered approaches that empower marginalized populations through culturally meaningful AI education.

4. International Research Hubs

Global AI research hubs provide students and faculty with opportunities to co-create knowledge, shape policy, and engage in interdisciplinary innovation. These centers unite educators, policymakers, and industry leaders in designing research-informed curricula and advancing ethical, applied AI education. Zawacki-Richter et al. (2019) highlight their transformative potential for fostering pedagogically sound, data-driven practices that scale across international contexts.

The following table translates these institutional strategies into practical curriculum components, offering guidance on content design, instructional approaches, and assessment methods aligned with global integration in AI education.

Table 6. Curriculum Guide for Implementing Global Integration Strategies in AI Education

Domain	Learning Outcomes	Content Design	Teaching Approach	Assessment Method
Global Skill Standards	Students demonstrate AI competencies aligned with international ethical and technical frameworks.	Curriculum aligned with frameworks like UNESCO ICT-CFT and OECD AI Principles; integration of global AI ethics and competencies.	• Standards-based module delivery, • Outcome mapping, • Comparative global ethics discussions.	• Framework-aligned rubrics, • Skills-based certifications, • Global policy analysis papers.
Cross-Border Collaborations	Students collaborate with international peers and institutions to address global AI challenges.	Co-developed courses, joint certifications, global innovation labs, shared learning platforms.	• COIL, • Virtual project teams, • International faculty co-teaching, • Intercultural communication workshops.	• Collaborative project deliverables, • International peer reviews, • Intercultural reflection journals.
Equitable Access	Students from all regions access inclusive, culturally and linguistically relevant AI education.	Multilingual, mobile-responsive content; localized examples; asynchronous formats for global reach.	• Universal Design for Learning (UDL), • Multilingual content adaptation, • Community-centered learning approaches.	• Equity participation metrics, • Accessibility audits, student feedback reports, • Digital inclusion dashboards.
International Research Hubs	Students and faculty co-create knowledge through interdisciplinary, international research partnerships.	Curriculum anchored in global research initiatives; AI ethics and innovation tied to policy and industry needs.	• Research mentorship, • Global capstone design, • Publication-focused labs, • Virtual research fellowships.	• Research proposals, • Co-authored publications, • Policy impact analysis, • International conference presentations.

The strategies transform global vision into pedagogical action. Embedding international standards, cross-border collaboration, inclusive design, and research-driven inquiry into the curriculum, institutions can ensure that global integration is not confined to policy rhetoric but enacted in meaningful, measurable ways. These approaches empower educators to build globally competent, AI-savvy graduates who will be equipped to navigate the complexities of the AI economy and to shape it responsibly, inclusively, and collaboratively.

Faculty serve as the frontline facilitators of internationalization, translating institutional commitments into daily teaching practices that expose students to global perspectives, foster intercultural competence, and prepare them to navigate diverse technological and ethical landscapes. The following section explores practical teaching strategies that bring the international dimension of AI education to life, ensuring that students not only learn about the global AI economy but also engage with it meaningfully and responsibly.

Teaching Strategies for Global Integration

Institutional policies and global partnerships create essential conditions for internationalizing AI education, and the realization of global integration happens most tangibly in the classroom. Teaching strategies that expose students to global case studies, foster international collaboration, and address equity in access and voice are critical for building cross-cultural competence and preparing learners to thrive in the global AI economy.

Faculty play a pivotal role in transforming institutional vision into lived experiences. By embedding international issues, culturally diverse content, and globally oriented problem-solving into everyday instruction, educators help students make connections between AI innovation and the global contexts in which it unfolds. Whether through virtual exchanges, multilingual learning resources, or culturally situated ethics discussions, effective teaching strategies can bring international relevance into local learning environments. These strategies focus on cultivating intercultural awareness, supporting diverse learners, and encouraging students to engage with international perspectives through collaborative inquiry and globally informed assignments.

As education systems pivot to address the demands of the AI-driven global economy, student learning outcomes must evolve from abstract knowledge acquisition to demonstrable competencies that reflect real-world readiness. Traditional exams and rote memorization are inadequate for assessing the skills needed to thrive in an AI-mediated world. Instead, outcome-based assessment models that capture applied skills, global awareness, and continuous learning trajectories are essential for validating educational effectiveness and promoting meaningful student growth.

The first approach involves the evaluation of practical skills through authentic performance assessments. Tools such as digital portfolios, interdisciplinary capstone projects, and real-world simulations provide students with opportunities to showcase their AI proficiency, problem-solving abilities, and integrative thinking across disciplines. As emphasized by Wiggins (1998), authentic assessments are powerful because they require students to perform tasks that resemble those encountered in professional and civic life. Research by Gulikers et al. (2004) supports the use of these methods to develop and measure competencies such as creativity, ethical reasoning, and technical literacy within AI-integrated curricula.

Secondly, the inclusion of global scenarios in assessments ensures that students are not only technically capable but also globally competent. Assessment tasks grounded in international case studies, such as AI regulation in the EU, surveillance technologies in East Asia, or digital labor platforms in Africa, help students critically analyze the geopolitical, cultural, and ethical dimensions of AI development. According to Deardorff (2006), global competence requires students to understand diverse perspectives and act appropriately in varied cultural contexts. When assessments incorporate these international dimensions, students develop the ability to apply AI knowledge in socially responsible and globally adaptive ways.

Lastly, as AI technologies continuously evolve, so must the human skills that complement them. Therefore, assessment systems must include mechanisms that support lifelong learning by tracking student development over time. This includes micro-credentials, self-assessment tools, and skill-mapping platforms that help learners reflect on their growth and identify future learning needs. The European Commission (2020) has advocated for competency-based assessment frameworks that encourage learners to adapt to technological changes through iterative reflection and skills alignment. These tools enable institutions to support not just academic achievement, but long-term professional agility.

Aligning assessment with real-world application, global relevance, and future adaptability empowers institutions to ensure students possess the competencies to thrive and lead in the global AI economy. Such outcome-based assessment models also enable educators and policymakers to identify gaps in learning, improve instructional design, and ensure that education systems remain responsive to a rapidly changing world.

Table 7. Teaching Strategies for Global Integration in AI Education

Domain	Learning Outcome	Content Design	Teaching Approach	Assessment Method
Evaluate Practical Skills	Students demonstrate AI proficiency and interdisciplinary problem-solving through authentic, real-world applications.	Assignments include capstone projects, digital portfolios, simulations, and lab-based AI challenges.	• Experiential learning, • Hands-on workshops, • Guided project development, • Simulation-based tasks.	• Portfolio reviews, • Project-based rubrics, • Presentation of applied solutions, • Peer and instructor evaluations.
Incorporate Global Scenarios	Students analyze and respond to international AI issues, demonstrating global awareness and ethical reasoning.	Tasks based on cross-border AI policies, global ethics cases, and international technology implementations.	• Case study analysis, role-play simulations, • Global issue debates, • Collaborative policy reviews.	• Comparative essays, • Global policy critiques, ethics briefings, • Cross-cultural AI scenario evaluations.
Support Lifelong Learning	Students develop the ability to reflect on skill progression and continuously adapt to technological change.	Use of digital tools to track competencies, learning journals, micro-credentials, and skills maps.	• Reflective practice, • Scaffolding learning paths, • Self-paced modules, • AI-enhanced learning analytics.	• Learning portfolios, self-assessment rubrics, • Skill development plans, • Milestone reflections.

Integrating the international dimension ensures that AI education remains ethically grounded, globally relevant, and equitably accessible. The strategies outlined in this table demonstrate how global integration can be practically achieved at the instructional level. By internationalizing course content, fostering intercultural collaboration, and designing inclusive, culturally responsive learning environments, educators can ensure that AI education reflects the global realities of the technology itself. These approaches not only deepen students' understanding of how AI operates across geopolitical and cultural contexts but also empower them to engage with the ethical, societal, and professional complexities of the global AI economy.

Integrating the international dimension into AI education is not a peripheral enhancement. It is a central imperative for preparing globally competent, ethically grounded, and culturally responsive graduates. As AI continues to influence global systems, economies, and communities, education must evolve to reflect this interconnected reality. Through institutional strategies such as aligning with global standards, fostering cross-border partnerships, ensuring equitable access, and supporting international research hubs, higher education can build the infrastructure for meaningful global engagement. At the same time, teaching practices that foreground cultural inclusion, global collaboration, and diverse perspectives ensure that students develop the interpersonal, ethical, and contextual fluency to lead in a borderless, AI-driven world. Aligning policy, curriculum, and pedagogy allows institutions to transform AI education into a genuinely international undertaking that prepares students to actively shape the global AI economy with responsibility, inclusivity, and innovation, rather than just participating in it.

POTENTIAL IMPACT

Implementing the strategic reforms outlined in this chapter has the potential to generate transformative, long-term benefits for education, workforce development, and global equity. These reforms are not only pedagogical innovations, they are essential structural responses to the shifting demands of an AI-powered global economy. The following four dimensions highlight the far-reaching impact of aligning curriculum, teaching, assessment, and institutional strategy with the realities of the AI era.

1. Workforce Readiness

Graduates emerging from reformed curricula that emphasize AI literacy, transdisciplinary collaboration, real-world assessments, and global standards will possess the future-proof competencies needed to thrive in AI-augmented workplaces. They will be proficient in applying AI technologies in field-specific contexts, adept at solving complex interdisciplinary problems, and resilient in the face of rapid technological change. Research from the World Economic Forum (2025) highlights that skills such as analytical thinking, creativity, and digital literacy, central to these reforms, are among the most in-demand competencies in the evolving job market.

Graduates will be better prepared for dynamic and AI-driven labor markets due to their exposure to interdisciplinary problem-solving, ethical AI use, and continuous learning. This aligns with the World Economic Forum's Future of Jobs Report (2020), which lists critical thinking, analytical reasoning, and adaptability as top skills needed by 2025. Bakhshi et al. (2017), in a study by Nesta, also highlight that the most resilient jobs in an AI economy are those combining technical knowledge with creativity and social intelligence. McKinsey Global Institute (2017) estimates that by 2030, up to 375 million workers will need to switch occupational categories, further emphasizing the need for adaptable, AI-literate graduates.

2. Global Competitiveness

Institutions that integrate global frameworks, international collaborations, and equitable access into AI education will position themselves at the forefront of global talent development. By producing AI-savvy professionals with intercultural competence and ethical grounding, these institutions will enhance their reputations, attract international partnerships, and contribute meaningfully to global innovation networks. As noted by the OECD (2021), global competence is essential for students and institutions to remain competitive in a world where economic, social, and technological systems are deeply interconnected.

Universities that adopt international frameworks and partnerships position themselves as leaders in producing globally competent, AI-ready professionals. According to the OECD (2018) report Preparing Our Youth for an Inclusive and Sustainable World, global competence enhances a student's ability to analyze issues of local and global relevance and act accordingly—vital traits in AI governance and application. Altbach & Knight (2007) emphasize that internationalization increases institutional visibility, collaboration opportunities, and innovation in higher education. UNESCO's 2021 Global Education Monitoring Report encourages higher education systems to align with global development goals through international cooperation and transnational curriculum alignment.

3. Innovation and Equity

By explicitly addressing the global digital divide and promoting access to AI education for underserved communities, this initiative supports a more inclusive innovation ecosystem. Programs that enable marginalized populations to gain AI-related skills and participate in technological development will help balance opportunity structures and reduce inequalities. Inclusive innovation, as described by UNESCO (2022), not only fuels economic growth but also ensures that the benefits of AI are distributed equitably across regions and demographics.

Integrating equity into AI education initiatives helps to ensure that technological innovation is inclusive and serves diverse communities, especially those historically excluded from digital economies. UNESCO (2022) emphasizes that bridging the digital divide, particularly in the Global South, is central to achieving equitable access to AI-enhanced education and economic participation. ITU (2023) and World Bank (2020) data confirm that disparities in digital infrastructure, connectivity, and educational resources persist, and addressing these disparities is crucial for global inclusion. Schmid et al. (2022) argue that inclusive digital transformation in education must account for regional and cultural differences to avoid reinforcing existing inequalities.

4. Policy Influence

The comprehensive, research-based framework generated by these educational reforms can serve as a blueprint for national and international policy development. Data and findings from the implementation of these strategies can inform guidelines on AI integration in curriculum, assessment, teacher training, and institutional capacity-building. Policymakers can draw on the demonstrated outcomes to develop standards and investments that promote scalable, sustainable, and equitable AI education. The European Commission (2020) and UNESCO (2021) have both advocated for such evidence-based frameworks to shape the next generation of educational systems.

The comprehensive and adaptable nature of these reforms allows them to inform local, national, and global education policy in the AI era. The European Commission's Digital Education Action Plan (2021–2027) explicitly calls for the use of data-driven educational reforms to guide national strategies on digital skills and AI readiness. Luckin et al. (2016) emphasize that evidence-based frameworks for AI in education should inform not just teaching practices but also institutional and governmental policy. Holmes et al. (2022) advocate for integrating AI education policies with ethical, societal, and technological goals to ensure that educational systems contribute to sustainable and inclusive futures.

These four areas of impact demonstrate how strategic reform in AI education can yield benefits far beyond the classroom. By aligning curriculum, pedagogy, and institutional vision with the realities of the global AI economy, education systems can foster not only employability and competitiveness, but also innovation, equity, and policy relevance. The significance of these reforms lies in their ability to shape a future where students are prepared to both navigate and spearhead change.

CONCLUSION

Artificial intelligence is reshaping economies, labor markets, and societies at an unprecedented pace. In this global transformation, higher education holds a critical responsibility not only to prepare students for the demands of an AI-driven world but also to empower them to lead with vision, ethics, and adaptability. This chapter has proposed a comprehensive framework for reforming higher education through four interconnected strategies: curriculum renovation, transdisciplinary teaching, tangible assessment, and international integration.

Institutions can cultivate innovation and resilience in the face of rapid change by integrating AI literacy across subjects, developing future-proof skills, and promoting collaborative, real-world learning. Transdisciplinary models and global partnerships enrich the learning process, allowing students to engage meaningfully with complex challenges that cross cultural and disciplinary boundaries. Authentic assessment methods, such as portfolios, capstones, and international case analyses, simultaneously ensure that student learning can be measured, is relevant, and meets professional demands.

Crucially, these reforms must be grounded in global equity. Aligning curricula with international frameworks, expanding access through inclusive design, and building research hubs that connect educators and communities across regions can bridge the digital divide and promote a more just and collaborative AI future.

Ultimately, this transcends mere curriculum reform, it is a profound call to reimagine the core purpose of education in the context of artificial intelligence. Institutions that embrace this model will not only see gains in workforce readiness and global competitiveness but will also be instrumental in forging an inclusive, ethical, and visionary AI economy. The imperative is now: to act with intention, courage, and a deep commitment to empowering learners to lead, rather than simply react to, the changes ahead.

REFERENCES

Almuhaideb, A. M., & Saeed, S. (2020). Fostering sustainable quality assurance practices in outcome-based education: Lessons learned from ABET accreditation process of computing programs. *Sustainability* [October.]. *Sustainability (Basel), 12*(20), 1–26. DOI: 10.3390/su12208380

Altbach, P. G., & Knight, J. (2007). The internationalization of higher education: Motivations and realities. *Journal of Studies in International Education, 11*(3-4), 290–305. DOI: 10.1177/1028315307303542

Arnold, L. (2023). AI and assessment in higher education: Reflections. Retrieved from https://lydiaarnold.net/ai-and-assessment-in-higher-education/

Bakhshi, H., Downing, J. M., Osborne, M. A., & Schneider, P. (2017). *The future of skills: Employment in 2030*. Nesta.

Barrows, H. S. (1986). A taxonomy of problem-based learning methods. *Medical Education, 20*(6), 481–486. DOI: 10.1111/j.1365-2923.1986.tb01386.x

Becker, K., & Park, K. (2011). Effects of integrative approaches among science, technology, engineering, and mathematics (STEM) subjects on students' learning. *Journal of STEM Education: Innovations and Research.*

Boud, D., & Falchikov, N. (2007). *Rethinking assessment in higher education: Learning for the longer term.* Routledge. DOI: 10.4324/9780203964309

Cazzaniga, M., Jaumotte, F., Li, L., Melina, G., Panton, A, J., Pizzinelli, C., Rockall, E. J., & Tavares, M. M. (2024). Gen-AI: artificial intelligence and the future of work. *Staff Discussion Notes* No. 2024/001, DOI: DOI: 10.5089/9798400262548.006

Chan, C. K. Y., & Hu, W. (2023). Students' voices on generative AI: Perceptions, benefits, and challenges in higher education. *International Journal of Educational Technology in Higher Education, 20*(1), 43. DOI: 10.1186/s41239-023-00411-8

Deardorff, D. K. (2006). Identification and assessment of intercultural competence as a student outcome of internationalization. *Journal of Studies in International Education, 10*(3), 241–266. DOI: 10.1177/1028315306287002

Dede, C. (2020). The role of digital technologies in deeper learning. In OECD (Ed.), *Teaching, learning and assessment for adults: Improving foundation skills* (pp. 153–174). OECD Publishing.

Elearning Industry. (2023). Revolutionizing education with AI-driven assessments. https://elearningindustry.com/revolutionizing-education-with-ai-driven-assessments

European Commission. (2020). *European Skills Agenda for Sustainable Competitiveness*. Social Fairness and Resilience.

Fam, D., Neuhauser, L., & Gibbs, P. (2020). *Transdisciplinary theory, practice and education: The art of collaborative research and collective learning.* Springer.

Gikandi, J. W., Morrow, D., & Davis, N. E. (2011). Online formative assessment in higher education: A review of the literature. *Computers & Education*, *57*(4), 2333–2351. DOI: 10.1016/j.compedu.2011.06.004

Gulikers, J. T. M., Bastiaens, T. J., & Kirschner, P. A. (2004). A five-dimensional framework for authentic assessment. *Educational Technology Research and Development*, *52*(3), 67–86. DOI: 10.1007/BF02504676

Haug, B. S., & Mork, S. M. (2021). Taking 21st century skills from vision to classroom: what teachers highlight as supportive professional development in the light of new demands from educational reforms. DOI: 10.1016/j.tate.2021.103286

Herminawati, S., & Ramli, M. (2024). Implementation of a problem-based learning model with the assistance of AI to improve students' critical thinking abilities and creativity. *Journal of Educational Innovation Research*, *14*(2). https://www.researchgate.net/publication/389071816

Hmelo-Silver, C. E. (2004). Problem-based learning: What and how do students learn? *Educational Psychology Review*, *16*(3), 235–266. DOI: 10.1023/B:EDPR.0000034022.16470.f3

Holmes, W., Bialik, M., & Fadel, C. (2022). Artificial Intelligence in Education: Promises and Implications for Teaching and Learning.

Hyperspace. (2023). AI-powered cross-cultural team simulations in virtual spaces. *Hyperspace News*. https://hyperspace.mv/ai-powered-cross-cultural-team-simulations-in-virtual-spaces/

Ifenthaler, D., & Yau, J. Y.-K. (2020). Utilising learning analytics to support study success in higher education: A systematic review. *Educational Technology Research and Development*, *68*(4), 1961–1990. DOI: 10.1007/s11423-020-09788-z

ITU. (2023). Measuring Digital Development: Facts and Figures.

Jackson, D., & Michelson, G. (2022). Showcasing employability skills in higher education: A review of key frameworks and practices. *Higher Education Research & Development*, *41*(2), 401–416.

Jopp, D. S., & Cohen, M. (2023). Developing reflective AI learners through ePortfolios: Evidence from interdisciplinary coursework. *International Journal of Educational Technology in Higher Education*, *20*(1). Advance online publication. DOI: 10.1186/s41239-023-00378-7

Karaman, Z. T. (2022). An understanding of inter and transcisciplinary aspects of urman resilience. https://www.scirp.org/journal/paperinformation?paperid=116576

Kazin, C. (2022). Fostering Learner Agency Through Intentional Learning Design: Six Principles. In A. Brower & R. Specht-Boardman (Eds.), *New Models of Higher Education: Unbundled, Rebundled, Customized*, and DIY (pp. 1-16). IGI Global Scientific Publishing. DOI: 10.4018/978-1-6684-3809-1.ch001

Kennedy, K. J., & Sundberg, D. (2020). Teachers and curriculum change: Emerging responses to new professional responsibilities. *Journal of Curriculum Studies*, *52*(3), 261–275. DOI: 10.1080/00220272.2020.1734667

Kennedy, T. J., & Sundberg, C. W. (2020). 21st Century Skills. In Akpan, B., & Kennedy, T. J. (Eds.), *Science Education in Theory and Practice. Springer Texts in Education*. Springer., DOI: 10.1007/978-3-030-43620-9_32

Khan, A. A., & Iqbal, M. (2024). Integrating PBL and AI tools in biomedical engineering education: A case study approach. arXiv Preprint. https://arxiv.org/abs/2503.16558

Klein, J. T. (2019). Beyond interdisciplinarity: Transforming the curriculum in higher education. *The Journal of General Education*, *68*(1–2), 102–120. DOI: 10.5325/jgeneeduc.68.1-2.0102

Knight, J. (2013). *The changing landscape of higher education internationalisation – for better or worse? Perspectives*. Policy and Practice in Higher Education.

Lau, S., & Perez, J. (2024). Global virtual teams projects and developing AI literacy: A mixed-methods study on preparing students for the international technology-infused workplace. *International Journal of Educational Technology and Global Learning*. https://www.researchgate.net/publication/388222830

Leask, B. (2015). *Internationalizing the Curriculum*. Routledge. DOI: 10.4324/9781315716954

Liu, Y. (2024). Using AI technology to create an inclusive environment for diverse online learners. In Kyei-Blankson, L., Keengwe, J., & Ntuli, E. (Eds.), *Designing Equitable and Accessible Online Learning Environments*. IGI Global., DOI: 10.4018/979-8-3693-0268-2.ch006

Liu, Y. (2025). Voiceless Algorithms: Examining equity implications of AI-driven educational reforms from student lens. In Taukeni, S. G., & Mollaoğlu, M. (Eds.), *Integrating the Biopsychosocial Model in Education*. IGI Global., DOI: 10.4018/979-8-3693-3707-3

Liu, Y., & Curtin, J. (2025). Sustainability in Higher Education - Integrating Leadership, Policy, and Teaching Practices for a Brighter Future. In Taukeni, S. G., & Mollaoğlu, M. (Eds.), *Higher Education and Quality Assurance Practices*. IGI Global., DOI: 10.4018/979-8-3693-6765-0

Lopez-Huertas, M. (2013). Reflexions on multidimensional knowledge: Its influence on the foundation of knowledge organization. *Knowledge Organization*, *40*(6), 400–407. DOI: 10.5771/0943-7444-2013-6-400

Luckin, R., Holmes, W., Griffiths, M., & Forcier, L. B. (2016). *Intelligence Unleashed: An Argument for AI in Education*. Pearson.

Madni, A. M. (2007). Transdisciplinarity: Reaching beyond disciplines to find connections. *Journal of Integrated Design & Process Science*, *11*(1), 1–11. DOI: 10.3233/JID-2007-11101

McKinsey Global Institute. (2017). Jobs lost, jobs gained: Workforce transitions in a time of automation. McKinsey & Company. https://www.mckinsey.com/featured-insights/future-of-work/jobs-lost-jobs-gained-what-the-future-of-work-will-mean-for-jobs-skills-and-wages

Mueller, J. (2018). Authentic assessment toolbox. http://jfmueller.faculty.noctrl.edu/toolbox

National Student Clearinghouse Research Center. (2024). Undergraduate enrollment showing signs of second straight year of growth. https://www.studentclearinghouse.org/news/undergraduate-enrollment-showing-signs-of-second-straight-year-of-growth/#:~:text=Graduate%20programs%20are%20also%20seeing,key%20findings%20in%20the%20report: Nicolescu, B. (2010). Transdisciplinarity: The hidden third, between the subject and the object. *Human and Social Studies, 1(2), 13-28.*

OECD. (2018). Preparing our youth for an inclusive and sustainable world: The OECD PISA global competence framework.

OECD. (2021). AI and the Future of Skills, Volume 1: Capabilities and Assessments. OECD Publishing. https://doi.org/DOI: 10.1787/5f65ff73-en

OECD. (2021). Future of education and skills 2030: Curriculum analysis. OECD Publishing. https://www.oecd.org/education/2030-project/

OECD. (2021). *AI and the future of skills: Education and training for the digital age*. OECD Publishing., DOI: 10.1787/5f65ff73-

Piaget, J. (1972). The epistemology of interdisciplinary relationships. In *Centre for Educational Research and Innovation (CERI), Interdisciplinarity: Problems of teaching and research in universities* (pp. 127–139). Organization for Economic Co-operation and Development.

Sälzer, C., & Roczen, N. (2018). Global competence in the age of artificial intelligence. OECD Education Working Papers.

Santiago, P., & Cerna, L. (2020). Promoting inclusive education for diverse societies: A conceptual framework. OECD Education Working Papers, No. 260. OECD Publishing. DOI: 10.1787/19939019

Schmid, R., Pauli, C., & Petko, D. (2022). Examining the use of digital technology in schools with a school-wide approach to personalized learning. *Educational Technology Research and Development*, *70*(1), 1–20. DOI: 10.1007/s11423-022-10167-z

Suskie, L. (2009). *Assessing student learning: A common sense guide* (2nd ed.). Jossey-Bass.

Tani, V. C. D. (2025). The rise of AI-Powered economies: how artificial intelligence is reshaping global business and governance. https://www.linkedin.com/pulse/rise-ai-powered-economies-how-artificial-intelligence-bentenbi-rkajc/

Texas Distance Learning Association (TxDLA). (2023). AI intelligence in career education: Aligning assessment with workforce readiness. https://www.txdla.org/ai-intelligence-in-career-educaiton/

Tuomi, I. (2018). *The Impact of Artificial Intelligence on Learning, Teaching, and Education: Policies for the Future*. European Commission.

UNESCO. (2019). *ICT Competency Framework for Teachers*. ICT-CFT.

UNESCO. (2021). Reimagining our futures together: A new social contract for education.

UNESCO. (2022). Guidance for generative AI in education and research. United Nations Educational, Scientific and Cultural Organization. https://unesdoc.unesco.org/ark:/48223/pf0000386125

Unterhalter, E. (2021). Education and the capability approach: Taking stock. *Cambridge Journal of Education, 51*(1), 27–43.

Van Zyl, H. M., Burger, Y., & Carsten, L. (2020). Curriculum design as an enabler of student involvement and success in Higher Education. *South African Journal of Higher Education, 34*(5), 177–191. DOI: 10.20853/34-5-4267

Wang, Q., Woo, H. L., & Quek, C. L. (2021). Enhancing AI literacy through student-centered design. *Interactive Learning Environments.*

Wiggins, G. (1998). Educative Assessment: Designing Assessments to Inform and Improve Student Performance.

World Economic Forum. (2020). The future of jobs report 2020.

World Economic Forum. (2025). The Future of Jobs Report 2025. https://www.weforum.org/publications/the-future-of-jobs-report-2025/

Xie, B., Tian, Y., & Lee, M. J. (2024). Collaborative curricular co-design for AI education: Lessons from humanities and STEM teachers. Proceedings of the AAAI Conference on Artificial Intelligence and Education. https://www.benjixie.com/publication/eaai-2024/

Yuan, M., & Recker, M. (2020). The role of digital badges in motivating learning and documenting skills in higher education. *Journal of Learning Analytics, 7*(1), 83–96.

Zawacki-Richter, O., Marín, V. I., & Bond, M. (2023). Delphi study on artificial intelligence in higher education: Trends, opportunities, and institutional readiness. *International Journal of Educational Technology in Higher Education, 20*, 6. Advance online publication. DOI: 10.1186/s41239-023-00377-6

Zawacki-Richter, O., Marín, V. I., Bond, M., & Gouverneur, F. (2019). A systematic review of research on artificial intelligence applications in higher education. *International Journal of Educational Technology in Higher Education, 16*(1), 39. DOI: 10.1186/s41239-019-0171-0

Zheng, B., Wang, Y., & Zhang, Y. (2022). Capstone experiences and project-based learning in AI education: Measuring student readiness and application skills. *Education and Information Technologies, 27*, 6543–6560.

ADDITIONAL READING

Abhishek, G. (2023). Digital citizenship: empowering responsible online engagement. https://www.linkedin.com/pulse/digital-citizenship-empowering-responsible-online-abhishek-guguloth-/

Aldhaheri, A., & AlSaadi, R. (2023). Transdisciplinary AI education: The confluence of curricular and community needs in the instruction of artificial intelligence. *ResearchGate*. https://www.researchgate.net/publication/375512872

Alvarez-Vanegas, A., & Volante, L. (2024). Empowering youth for sustainability in universities: Service-learning and the willingness to act. *International Journal of Sustainability in Higher Education, 25*(9), 177–194. DOI: 10.1108/IJSHE-03-2023-0073

Annan-Diab, F., & Molinari, C. (2017). Interdisciplinarity: practical approach to advancing education for sustainability and for the Sustainable Development Goals. *The International Journal of Management Education*. Volume 15, Issue 2, Part B, July 2017, Pages 73-83. DOI: 10.1016/j.ijme.2017.03.006

Couto, R. (2024). *How to build an inclusive online community (and why it matters)*. Groundwork. https://groundwork.space/building-an-inclusive-online-community/Cyber Wellness Program. (2024). Practicing Cyber Wellness. Ministry of Education, Singapore. https://www.moe.gov.sg/education-in-sg/our-programmes/cyber-wellness

Floridi, L., Cowls, J., Beltrametti, M., Chatila, R., Chazerand, P., Dignum, V., & Vayena, E. (2018). AI4People - An ethical framework for a good AI society: Opportunities, risks, principles, and recommendations. *Minds and Machines, 28*(4), 689–707. DOI: 10.1007/s11023-018-9482-5

Kerr, S. (2023). UAE to launch artificial intelligence curriculum for children as young as four. *Financial Times*. https://www.ft.com/content/d6f54a83-cdee-46d0-9555-95ff45fbfaab

Kloza, B. (2023). Consequences of the digital divide in education - connecting the unconnected. *Connecting the Unconnected*. https://ctu.ieee.org/consequences-of-the-digital-divide-in-education/

Liu, Y. (2023). Investigating the dynamics of trust in social capital on social media platforms. In Hoda, N., & Arabia, S. (Eds.), *Social Capital in the Age of Online Networking: Genesis, Manifestations, and Implications*. IGI Global., DOI: 10.4018/978-1-6684-8953-6.ch005

Rickard, S. (2023). Using generative AI to support global learning could leave cultural lessons lost in translation. Center for Engaged Learning Blog. https://www.centerforengagedlearning.org/using-generative-ai-to-support-global-learning-could-leave-cultural-lessons-lost-in-translation/

KEY TERMS AND DEFINITIONS

AI Literacy: The foundational knowledge and skills required to understand, use, evaluate, and ethically interact with artificial intelligence technologies across disciplines and professions.

AI Workforce Readiness: Refers to the extent to which individuals are equipped with the technical competencies, adaptive skills, and ethical awareness needed to participate effectively in an AI-integrated labor market (OECD, 2021; World Economic Forum, 2023).

Authentic Assessment: Is an approach to evaluation that emphasizes real-world application of knowledge and skills, often through performance-based tasks such as portfolios, simulations, and capstone projects (Mueller, 2018; Gulikers et al., 2004).

Curriculum Reform: The process of revising educational curricula to align with evolving societal, technological, and workforce needs, ensuring that learning outcomes remain relevant, future-oriented, and responsive to innovation.

Education Innovation: The development and implementation of novel instructional methods, technologies, or system-wide changes that improve learning, expand access, and better prepare students for complex global challenges.

Ethical AI Integration: Refers to the intentional incorporation of ethical principles into the design, deployment, and educational use of artificial intelligence technologies (UNESCO, 2022; Floridi et al., 2018).

Future-Proof Skills: Transferable competencies such as critical thinking, creativity, adaptability, and emotional intelligence that enable individuals to remain effective and employable in rapidly changing, technology-driven environments.

Global Competence: The capacity to understand global issues, appreciate cultural diversity, engage in effective cross-cultural communication, and take informed action on challenges that transcend national borders.

Global Economy: An interconnected and interdependent system of national and regional economies linked through trade, investment, technology, and labor markets, where developments in one area influence global trends and employment patterns.

Transdisciplinary Education: An integrative approach to teaching and learning that combines knowledge, methods, and perspectives from multiple disciplines to address real-world problems that cannot be solved within a single field of study.

Chapter 6
Revolutionizing Higher Education:
Integrating AI Personalized Learning and Adaptive Curriculum Design

N. Vinodh
https://orcid.org/0009-0002-8662-2646
Saveetha School of Management, Saveetha Institute of Medical and Technical Sciences, India

A. K. Subramani
https://orcid.org/0000-0003-0783-7113
Saveetha School of Management, Saveetha Institute of Medical and Technical Sciences, India

R. Swadhi
https://orcid.org/0009-0005-0247-0713
Saraswathi Institute of Medical Sciences, Hapur, India

S. Kumaresh
School of Management, Hindustan Institute of Technology and Science, India

K. Gayathri
https://orcid.org/0000-0003-0398-0094
Academy of Maritime Education and Training, India

ABSTRACT

Higher education institutions benefit from AI since this technology transforms traditional teaching systems by delivering customized learning options and adaptive educational content. AI software platforms review performance records to create personalized content which generates immediate feedback and individualized learning routes. Educational programs adjust their contents automatically according to student development to produce improved individual outcomes and active student participation. The successful implementation of AI in education depends on solving the problems related to personal data protection and algorithm system faults and faculty training requirements. The combination of artificial intelligence in education produces flexible learning models as well as better student results and instruction focused on individual learners.

DOI: 10.4018/979-8-3373-2752-5.ch006

AI's evolution will enhance its use for curriculum improvement alongside skill identification and virtual learning simulations to transform education by making it more effective and adaptable to future needs.

INTRODUCTION

High educational institutions experience a fundamental operational shift through Artificial Intelligence (AI) technologies that now controls the delivery infrastructure while improving access to knowledge for multiple learner groups. Traditional higher education systems organise their educational structure by implementing standardised curricula and teaching techniques for an entire diverse group of students. Ordinary educational structures which enabled wide-scale teaching and knowledge market development revealed multiple major shortcomings specifically related to individual student variations in needs background and goals. The arrival of Artificial Intelligence opens completely new avenues for teaching and learning which enable educators to build dynamic programs that respond to each student's specific needs (Asy'ari, M., & Sharov, S. 2024). AI-based systems that cover intelligent tutoring programs and predictive data analysis as well as automated content management and adaptive assessment functionalities enable universities to create customized learning environments that track student development and dynamically adjust educational content to match student outcomes and personal choices. Educational institutions utilize dynamic capability as their main foundation for creating adaptive learning models and individualized educational programs which modern educators consider critical elements of future-proof higher education systems. The technological systems which use artificial intelligence analyze all the data that students create while interacting with digitally-enhanced learning platforms (Alawneh et al., 2024).

In the post-pandemic era, higher education systems worldwide have been confronted with the urgent need to innovate traditional pedagogical approaches. The global pivot to digital learning accelerated by COVID-19 exposed not only the fragility of conventional teaching models but also the untapped potential of Artificial Intelligence (AI) in enhancing educational delivery. A recent report by HolonIQ (2023) predicts that global investment in AI-enabled education technologies will surpass $20 billion by 2025, underscoring the scale of this transformation. One striking example of this shift is Georgia State University's deployment of AI-based chatbots to reduce summer melt among first-generation students, which resulted in a 21% increase in enrollment retention (Page & Gehlbach, 2021). These developments illustrate the transformative potential of AI in making education more responsive, inclusive, and personalized. Despite its promise, the integration of AI into higher education raises several questions. How can AI personalize learning pathways to meet diverse learner needs? In what ways can adaptive curriculum design enhance engagement and retention? What challenges ethical, technical, and institutional must be addressed to ensure equitable AI adoption? These questions form the backbone of this inquiry.

At the core of the current crisis in higher education is the persistence of rigid, one-size-fits-all curricula that fail to cater to the individualized learning styles and paces of modern students. The problem is compounded by increasing student disengagement, mental health concerns, and unequal access to quality resources. UNESCO (2022) has emphasized the global challenge of educational inequity, noting that over 244 million children and youth are out of school globally, many of whom lack personalized educational support. Furthermore, studies have shown that standardized approaches to learning contribute to dropout rates and skill mismatches in the job market (World Bank, 2021). These issues underscore an urgent need for structural and pedagogical reform. This chapter explores the intersection of Artificial Intelligence, personalized learning, and adaptive curriculum design as a pathway for revolutionizing higher education. It critically examines the role of AI in reshaping educational experiences to be more learner-centered, dynamic, and data-informed. The discussion integrates theoretical foundations with practical frameworks to assess how AI technologies such as predictive analytics, intelligent tutoring systems, and natural language processing can be employed to design responsive curricula that support diverse learning needs.

RESEARCH OBJECTIVE

To examine the transformative role of Artificial Intelligence in higher education through the integration of personalized learning and adaptive curriculum design, and to analyze the opportunities, limitations, and ethical considerations associated with its implementation.

Despite this momentum, several questions remain underexplored:

- How can artificial intelligence be effectively leveraged to deliver personalized learning experiences in higher education?
- What role does adaptive curriculum design play in improving student engagement and academic outcomes when supported by AI?
- What are the institutional, ethical, and infrastructural challenges in integrating AI into educational systems?

These questions guide the present inquiry and are addressed through a comprehensive review and synthesis of emerging models, case-based applications, and policy implications.

This chapter assesses how AI technology changes educational paradigms by using personalized learning and adaptive curriculum models. The document explores the implementation of AI technologies in higher educational establishments to boost student involvement while enhancing educational achievements by catering to students who belong to various linguistic backgrounds and socioeconomic levels. Universities must integrate AI technology because it solves their major operational issues related to student diversity and widening participation together with their need for flexible learning spaces while creating new educational possibilities. The paper explains how AI delivers personalized learning solutions and explains the educational influence and institutional transformation alongside social effects that result from AI integration into education. AI implementations require thorough evaluation through careful tool development and execution to guarantee match with higher education values and goals. This process addresses extensive ethical together with practical and infrastructural matters involved in such transformations.

AI tools can link the educational gaps through personalized support which works differently for diverse language proficiency levels together with learning disabilities and varying levels of prior gained knowledge. Cancelled speech-to-text processes and adaptive skill assessments that automatically customize difficulty levels after student performance evaluation (Aithal, P. S., & Maiya, A. K. 2023). The features serve as essential components to establish equalized education environments that guarantee equal success for students despite their entering level. AI supports quality education enhancement through its ability to manage remote learning together with asynchronous approaches that provide universal benefits to students located in distant or underprivileged regions. While AI possesses drastic potential impacts in education its complete incorporation into higher-learning creates various obstacles to overcome (Ayeni, O. O., Al Hamad, N. M., Chisom, O. N., Osawaru, B., & Adewusi, O. E. 2024). Data privacy issues together with the need to fix algorithmic discrimination and lack of cooperation from faculty need immediate resolution to establish ethical and successful AI implementations. Institutions need to invest resources in building diverse datasets and developing learning algorithms which replicate student profiles because data-driven technologies achieve their fairness directly from their training data. Institutional AI technology deployment to adapt learning approaches along with instant feedback implementation for different learners will create adaptable educational systems which meet present-day social requirements. The educational evolution requires scholars along with educators with policymakers and technologists to work together toward developing AI applications that protect mutual values like equality and human-focused education and operational transparency. The chapter serves the larger community interest by presenting an extensive overview of AI-powered adaptive curricula and personalized learning in higher education with their potentials and difficulties and possible future trends.

CONCEPTUAL FRAMEWORK

Education today experiences a transformative change through Artificial Intelligence (AI) because it transforms the methods of delivering knowledge and the ways students consume it and assess their progress in all educational settings. AI describes the creation of computer systems to execute jobs which need human-level intelligence to solve problems while recognising patterns and understanding languages and making choices. Higher education utilizes various AI technologies including machine learning (ML) and natural language processing (NLP) and computer vision and intelligent agents to both automate and elevate educational operations. Machine learning gives systems the ability to absorb extensive sets of information while developing their performance automatically so it becomes effective at forecasting student actions and grades. The interpretive and generative functionality of NLP operates to power all speech-based services while enabling chatbots and automated writing solutions along with voice-interactive teaching platforms for smooth human-computer communication. AI components create together an infrastructure which enables educational institutions to develop responsive learning experiences that adjust to specific learner profiles for creating personalized and adaptive curricula. Personalized learning functions as a pedagogical tool to adapt education content and academic pathways alongside support structures for respecting the individualized aspects of each student.

RESEARCH PROBLEM

The traditional structure of higher education, built upon standardized curricula and generalized instruction, fails to accommodate the increasingly diverse needs, learning styles, and pace variations among modern learners. Despite the global expansion of digital infrastructure and access to educational content, a significant portion of students continues to underperform or disengage due to the rigidity of conventional pedagogical systems. According to a UNESCO

(2023) report, nearly 244 million students worldwide remain out of school, and those within the system often face outdated instructional approaches that inadequately prepare them for evolving socio-economic and labor market demands. Additionally, the World Economic Forum (2022) highlights that more than 40% of global employers identify a mismatch between graduate skills and workplace requirements, signaling a widening competency gap. The pandemic-induced shift to online learning further exposed these weaknesses, revealing a systemic inability to offer personalized feedback, real-time academic support, or adaptive learning pathways. Without fundamental transformation, higher education institutions risk reinforcing educational inequality, academic disengagement, and workforce irrelevance. Therefore, there is an urgent need to explore how AI-enabled personalized learning and adaptive curriculum design can address these limitations, enhance learner engagement, and realign educational outcomes with societal needs.

The three elements of artificial intelligence combined with personalized learning and adaptive educational planning harmonize into a structural system which determines the direction of higher education development. The educational system depends on AI to join personalized learning and adaptive curricula into an organized adaptable educational structure. The main purpose of personalised learning is to learn about students' backgrounds and preferences alongside their educational goals but adaptive curriculum design concentrates on how to organise and deliver real-time educational content (Bhatia, A., Bhatia, P., & Sood, D. 2024). AI creates the mechanism required to connect domain information by using data analysis alongside decision capabilities for aligning educational approaches toward student profiles with performance data in real-time. An AI system with AI capabilities detects student difficulties with statistical concepts after which it automatically connects students to fundamental content modules while simultaneously informing instructors about the need for assistance. The system would modify the overall teaching schedule for the learner at the same time while maintaining academic progress alignment. Students who demonstrate high performance in specific domains can get accelerated progress into advanced educational materials as part of an efficiency and motivation enhancement strategy. AI-based student model integration creates a two-way learning cycle which results in educational experiences that evolve through personalized optimization.

The instant curriculum adaptations ensure that students receive current learning support as personal educational choices lead to more active student involvement with knowledge. As a result this system becomes a resource for instructors who gain performance-based analytics to use for creating focused intervention strategies (Catherin et al., 2025). This method frees instructors from needing to manually handle various student needs because it handles such complexity which existing educators struggle with particularly in spacious or blended educational settings. Through advanced AI systems both scalability and high-quality personalised education can be achieved on a large-scale so it becomes possible in campus classrooms and virtual learning spaces. Implementation of artificial intelligence in this system drives a transition from delivering content toward customising learning towards individual students. Educational success presents itself through successful student learning alignment instead of standardised achievement measures. The instructional method follows present-day constructivist and experiential learning theories since students construct knowledge by engaging in feedback-driven interactions with reflective learning components. Deploying AI allows instructors to keep students at the right level of challenge by ensuring they are within their zone of proximal development. Thus students find success through adequate instructional support. The constant adjustment of teaching spaces according to learner requirements ensures AI develops learning conditions which enhance substantive prolonged meaningful educational outcomes. The conceptual framework relies on a network between Artificial Intelligence, personalized learning and adaptive curriculum design (Chigbu, B. I., Umejesi, I., & Makapela, S. L. 2024). AI serves as the backbone to deliver computational power for educational adaptivity through precise analytics which enables individualized pathway adjustments and continuous content modification. Students receive individualized treatment based on their personal characteristics through personalized learning and the curriculum adapts continuously based on their performance through adaptive curriculum design. This combined approach creates a strong educational model which corrects traditional education systems while giving institutions capabilities to manage 21st-century knowledge economy requirements. As a top priority area the framework enables academic progress and develops inclusivity and student involvement and lifelong learning thus becoming essential research for educators and policy-makers and researchers.

THEORETICAL FRAMEWORK

The educational integration of artificial intelligence (AI) finds its theoretical basis in learning theories which focus on student independence alongside understanding their situations and social connexions and responsive learning systems. The understanding of AI integration in higher education relies on four key theories: Constructivist Learning Theory together with Self-Determination Theory (SDT) as well as Vygotsky's Zone of Proximal Development (ZPD) and Connectivism. The amalgamation of these educational frameworks enables a comprehensive understanding of how AI enhancements provide students with purposeful relevant learning environments which suit their developmental stage. These frameworks demonstrate the operational principles of AI technologies along with their behavioural effects on human mental operations that generate advanced educational benefits. Through Constructivist Learning Theory students learn through building knowledge by interacting with their individual environments rather than by simply receiving information. Learning gets built from experience alongside reflection together with context-based engagement rather than through direct transmission from teachers to students. The constructivist epistemological point of view finds support through AI technology which creates responsive interactive learning spaces that meet students' specific developing requirements. AI-powered learning systems generate personalized learning routes based on individual student cognition development instead of delivering standardized information to all learners. The intelligent Tutoring System (ITS) shows real-time adaptive behaviour through delivering problems that require students to advance to higher difficulty after mastering initial concepts. The supportive educational structure helps students tackle problems and develop critical thinking abilities as parts of constructivist-based teaching (Das, S., Mutsuddi, I., & Ray, N. 2025). Learning platforms created by AI systems offer virtual environments that reproduce real-life scenarios together with AR and VR components for students to use experiential learning techniques as they explore and test their hypotheses for constructing new knowledge. AI delivers purpose-built interactive platforms that promote the constructivist method where students build their own knowledge instead of memorizing information by rote. SDT which Deci and Ryan developed identifies autonomy together with competence and relatedness as basic psychological requirements that promote both engagement and motivational aspects of learning. The learner's autonomy consists of having control over educational choices while competence describes their perception of effectiveness in tasks and relatedness reflects the connexion they maintain with others in their learning community. Personalised learning environments created through artificial intelligence backends directly benefit all three domains of psychological needs. Machine learning technologies develop independence in students through student-directed control of their educational sequence and presentation methods and activity timetables. Studying under this approach means students no longer stick to strict learning standards because they freely choose their educational routes through material of personal significance (Deri, M. N., Singh, A., Zaazie, P., & Anandene, D. 2024). AI enhances student competence through its capability to deliver individualized assessment feedback coupled with suitable challenge points. Student learning experience becomes better because adaptive learning platforms adjust their content difficulty depending on students' performance to keep them in a development-promoting zone that avoids engagement dissatisfaction and monotony. AI implementations enhance relatedness through intelligent systems which match peers in teamwork activities and manage discussion boards and create virtual assistants that create social connexion. Through AI-driven virtual tutors the education system can provide emotional help and answer student questions to create ongoing discussions which lessens the feeling of isolation in digital learning environments. Socially responsive platforms with personalised content strengthen user motivation whereas improving both self-belief abilities and engagement levels as described by SDT.

The Zone of Proximal Development (ZPD) introduced by Lev Vygotsky indicates what students can perform with guidance beyond their singular capacities. Vygotsky indicates that effective teaching should focus on this particular zone in order to achieve maximum learning success. AI technology has the special capability to implement the ZPD through student ability measurement processes while providing scaffold adjustments that match learning progress (Gautam, D. 2024). Machine learning algorithms inside AI systems assess learner conduct while detecting misconceptions to determine upcoming performance patterns thus identifying where the learner stands in their zone of development. According to this analysis the system provides learners with assistance in the form of hints together with exemplars and interactive tasks and simplified explanations to help students advance their mastery. AI-powered math instruction platforms provide step-by-step problem-solving assistance to students which automatically reduces its intensity when students demonstrate skill improvement. The systems duplicate teaching by reliable instructors or peers and modify guidance levels when learners absorb new information. Through AI technology schools can deliver individualized teaching activities at a large scale because these systems match students' ZPD with specific challenges and targeted assistance. The system highlights both learning efficiency and self-assurance development since it guides learners through incremental difficulties in their educational journey. AI enables the implementation of Vygotsky's theoretical concept in real-time education through its ability to dynamically match learning material to students' cognitive preparedness at a large scale. Connectivism emerged as a 21st-century theory through George Siemens and Stephen Downes because it accounts for the technological learning environment. The theory maintains that knowledge resembles connected specialised information elements inside interlinked networks yet individual human intellectual capacity alone does not determine knowledge stores (Jafari, D., & Yazdi, Z. S. 2024). Learning develops through maintaining and navigating connexions between different forms of knowledge and people alongside digital systems. Learning environments based on connectivism gain enhancement from AI because the technology provides learners with wide content resources and smart content selection frameworks that match their individual educational targets (Kaswan, K.

S., Dhatterwal, J. S., & Ojha, R. P. 2024). AI-powered learning management systems use LMS to recommend students curated resources that stem from academic databases paired with online courses and multimedia libraries and professional networks which provides appropriate and up-to-date credible content. AI technology develops customised learning communities because it gathers learners who have common objectives or face equivalent problems or learning approaches. Artificial Intelligence serves as an enabler for creating learning relationships by suggesting forums for discussions or team work and mentorship initiatives to students. The platform provides learners with a framework to build knowledge through digital collaboration on open-source platforms and wikis or blog entries which expand the collective understanding in networked intelligence. The constant movement of knowledge between elements reflects the connectivistic principle that learning acts as networked activity which distributes across social and cultural and technological nodes. AI processes huge datasets which helps it detect new network patterns to guide students throughout their learning process while keeping their mental models current in an ever-changing information environment.

These theories merge to give educational institutions a complete view of how Artificial Intelligence transforms learning practices at the higher education level. The combination of Constructivism and SDT creates learner-driven knowledge development while ZPD outlines how to guide learning development through predefined steps and Connectivism highlights learning functions within social technological frameworks. The combination of these theories demonstrates both methods of AI-based learning personalization and the logical sequence of enhanced student engagement and higher achievement and better satisfaction levels. Education enters a transformative phase as computer technology assimilates with pedagogical approaches to create adaptable learning networks that tailor instruction to individual student needs. Learning under this model becomes an active process where intelligent systems help students navigate needed knowledge while building upward skills and simultaneously linking them with worldwide collaborators (Kayyali, M. 2025). AI system deployment requires thoughtful planning based on the theories mentioned. The important advantages of AI applications require strict examination of ethical concerns that include artificial intelligence biases and privacy issues and distribution disparities. AI success rests upon two pillars which include high-standard data sources for algorithm modeling along with system design practices which maintain and advance human control of educational activities. Educational institutions together with their teaching staff need to actively lead the development of AI applications in education since they should pick tools for improving efficiency alongside ensuring their pedagogically sound methods and transparent use for the sake of learners. The combination of educational excellence and social justice demands AI systems to align properly for the complete release of AI potential (Kolluru, V., Mungara, S., & Chintakunta, A. N. 2018). Higher education AI integration requires theoretical basis which combines constructivist, motivational, developmental, and network-based perspectives to describe how smart technologies deliver personal and adaptive learning. The set of theoretical perspectives illustrates the way AI supports learners by boosting their freedom, abilities, classroom interest and social opportunities during appropriate and localized instructional delivery. The theoretical basis supports both the justification for implementing AI in higher education and shows guidelines to execute AI ethically and effectively to create an inclusive future-ready education system.

RESEARCH METHODOLOGY

AI system deployment requires thoughtful planning based on the theories mentioned. The substantial advantages need formal evaluation of moral issues including automatic bias properties together with information protection policies and balanced accessibility principles. AI effectiveness relates to both the completeness as well as quality of training data combined with designed learning environments that both protect and amplify human decision-making power. Educational institutions together with their teaching staff need to actively lead the development of AI applications in education since they should pick tools for improving efficiency alongside ensuring their pedagogically sound methods and transparent use for the sake of learners (Wang, J. 2025). The combination of educational excellence and social justice demands AI systems to align properly for the complete release of AI potential. All theoretical aspects that explain how intelligent technologies integrate with higher education draw from constructivist, motivational, developmental, and network-based perspectives to support personalized and adaptive learning. The combination of theoretical approaches demonstrates how AI technology works to promote learner autonomy and competence and engagement along with social connectedness in addition to delivering appropriate instruction for learners (Vettriselvan, R., Deepan, A., Garg, P. K., Suresh, N. V., & Velmurugan, P. R. 2025). These foundational ideas serve as approval for higher education AI implementations and supply methods to achieve ethical and effective usage in building inclusive digital learning systems.

Multiple academic databases were selected to provide scholarly contents with appropriate subject matter across the literature review. Academic research databases which include Scopus, Web of Science, ERIC (Education Resources Information Centre), IEEE Xplore, SpringerLink, ScienceDirect, and Scopus were incorporated for this review because they specialise in education and technology-related peer-reviewed publications of high standard. Google Scholar provided supplementary research for finding both grey literature and latest preprints that formal databases had yet to index. The research only considered publications from Computers & Education, Journal of Educational Data Mining, and AI & Society along with British Journal of Educational Technology, Educational Technology Research and Development. These research materials received preference because they demonstrated strong methodological methods coupled with consistent results of empirical research about emerging technologies in academic environments. The research method of bibliographic mining was used with backward referencing to locate core references in original studies thus enhancing the dataset and providing depth to analytical research. The research included twenty-five peer-reviewed studies which featured different quantitative and qualitative and mixed-methods study approaches to deliver diversified methodologies. The study employed thematic analysis as its analytical framework to synthesise information from the chosen literature while maintaining structural flexibility for identifying recurring patterns and theoretical components and methodological approaches. Review-based research benefits from thematic analysis because it enables researchers to spot both hidden and obvious themes from the qualitative data to analyse AI education innovations effectively. The six-phase method developed by Braun and Clarke served as the procedural base for theme creation through coding procedures. The data analysis process contained five sequential phases which started with data familiarisation followed by initial code generation afterwards researchers sought themes then reviewed them before final theme definitions and naming while producing the complete synthesis (Makinde, A. I., Adeleye, S. A., Oronti, A. O., & Jimoh, I. T. 2024). Each research study received full reading during the initial phase of familiarisation to comprehend research context and methods as well as findings and boundaries. A standardised form for data extraction recorded information about bibliography and research objectives alongside AI toolkit descriptions and outcomes for learners and theoretical perspectives used in their studies. Doctoral students used initial codes to identify key concepts and phrases that emerged frequently throughout multiple studies with their research. The research involved terms which included "personalization algorithms" together with "learner autonomy" and "real-time feedback" as well as "competency-based learning" and "learning analytics" and "predictive modelling." The research team classified the initial codes into five main thematic categories: AI-driven personalization strategies and pedagogical affordances of AI as well as student engagement and motivation alongside adaptive content delivery and ethical and equity considerations. The researchers examined the themes for self-contained validity and separate existence from other categories to maintain conceptual integrity while ensuring research validity (Nuong Deri, M., Singh, A., Zaazie, P., & Anandene, D. 2024). The researchers fixed thematic measurement boundaries through continuous coding sessions together with critical conversation that allowed themes to develop directly from data rather than preceding the analysis phase. The selected structure functioned both to classify the literature collection and to demonstrate both theoretical concepts and practical AI-based educational implementations. A convergence between AI's adaptive capabilities and constructivist and self-determination and connectivist theories built upon the foundation of the chapter's theoretical structure. The evaluation discovered both useful AI applications including intelligent tutoring systems while uncovering ongoing barriers like algorithmic discrimination together with insufficient transparency and unequal availability of AI tools (Pratama, M. P., Sampelolo, R., & Lura, H. 2023). The authors utilised this neutral position to develop the framework that would be applied in subsequent discussions regarding ethical concerns together with future study recommendations. The research design in this chapter advances through an organised methodological literature review which relies on established data sources under predetermined entrance and exit protocols. The chosen method of thematic analysis enabled analysis of various disciplines within an expanding field of research by offering a detail-oriented flexible synthesis of results. This research methodology serves to both support the chapter theory and create strong baseline evidence for its academic influence on AI-based higher education study.

MAJOR FINDINGS

This study shows that Artificial Intelligence (AI) holds great improving power to remake higher education through educational systems which both adapt courses to individual learning needs. The research analysed vast information from multiple theoretical sources and empirical studies in order to show how AI affects education from both teaching and institution levels as well as student needs. The main discovery reveals how AI optimizes education through data analysis and machine learning and intelligent algorithms which adapt instruction content while matching assessment strategies and learning speed to students' individual requirements. The adaptive personalization enables better student autonomy along with higher engagement and it produces superior educational outcomes through constructivism and self-determination theory. The adaptation of curriculum design became essential because AI tools enabled it to emerge (Vettriselvan, R., & Ramya, R. 2025). These system capabilities allow educators to respond immediately to students' learning progress by adapting course materials through a process that enhances individualized teaching methods. The learning platforms Knewton along with Smart Sparrow utilise AI capabilities to determine student understanding gaps thus automatically modify their educational routes so students gain suitable educational levels of support. The ability to adapt enhances educational inclusiveness because it allows healthcare providers to support learners of varying abilities. Research has established a major discovery about the way AI influences institutional decision processes and academic service operations (Rane, N., Choudhary, S., & Rane, J. 2023). Learning and predictive analytics help educational institutions detect vulnerable students and optimize their resources while offering individualized educational guidance. AI demonstrates its ability throughout these results to aid students while serving as a basis for educational decisions that need data-driven evaluation at institutional fields (Udeh, C. G. 2025). It is essential to solve the major issues which arise when implementing AI systems. Standard implementations of artificial intelligence in educational systems require solutions regarding ethical issues such as privacy protection and bias prevention and transparency assurance together with infrastructure maintenance and employee development programs. When educational institutions fail to provide technology access equally and also overlook trainings for teachers AI advantages remain unavailable to all students thus worsening already existing educational inequalities. Creating responsible AI systems demands the unification of educational, ethical and psychological and computational academic viewpoints. The scientific community needs longitudinal as well as cross-cultural studies to determine how long AI impacts education systems while also evaluating its ability to adapt across different cultural contexts. AI offers great potential for improving higher education but requires both deliberate planning combined with ethical decision-making and inclusion principles. Schools that fund infrastructure and research and build capacity across their institutions will identify the maximum potential benefits of AI technology to create learning environments which are equal and student-focused and future-ready.

SOLUTIONS AND RECOMMENDATIONS

Higher education will experience fundamental changes through human-like educational programs and smart automated systems and adaptable learning systems which AI provides. The conversion of conceptual potential into practical results needs specific implementation plans which must be developed with proper educational practices and enough infrastructure and moral responsibility. A critical requirement exists to develop AI tools that can create adjustable academic structures because curriculum design needs immediate reconstruction. Time-based institutions can activate AI platforms to evaluate continuous student data records while dynamic programmes change both instruction sequences and educational challenge levels to best meet personal educational requirements. These platforms detect individual student learning abilities as well as knowledge deficiencies through which they craft personalised resource selections or change instructional courses to enhance learning outcomes. These systems that operate inside Learning Management Systems (LMS) or exist as separate adaptive learning platforms provide support for competency-based education while stimulating independent learning progress at the expense of time-based learning structures (Sumathy, V., & Navamani, G. 2024). The implementation of these changes requires the formation of collaborative partnerships between instruction designers and developers of AI systems and academic departments that should focus on ensuring alignment with educational goals as well as accreditation standards and student expectations. Educational institutions should make teaching professionals skilled at accessing and utilising AI technology because they will become foundational requirements for academic operations integration. Educational staff must acquire specialized abilities to decode data sets while developing skills for algorithmic systems and effective teaching methods which supplement their fundamental understanding of digital systems. Trained educators need to evaluate AI tool outputs while using these resources in meaningful classroom practises and protect essential human characteristics which lead to student empathy development and mentorship and cognitive growth. Educational institutions along with national operations should develop organised training plans for micro-credentials with certification modules together with workshops and peer-led innovation hubs. Programmes should bring together different disciplines and reflective teaching methods to let instructors develop AI-assisted programmes instead of functioning as AI recipients alone. Educators involved in AI system design processes and testing phases will boost trust in these systems while developing practical teaching solutions that match individual learning environments. Universities must establish systematic professional development because it builds enduring educational frameworks which combine technology skills together with teaching skills necessary to properly assimilate AI. Targeting substantial AI adoption requires complete attention to solid infrastructure combined with equal access for all users. AI tools operate effectively only when connectivity remains uninterrupted while performing at high computing capacity between different platforms without limitations. These institutions need to fund investments for fundamental digital infrastructure which include expandable cloud systems together with secure database systems and analytical engines along with human-friendly interface design. The continuous digital divide demands special attention because it can create growing educational disparities in AI-enhanced education (Rizvi, I., Bose, C., & Tripathi, N. 2025). Students who lack digital equipment or inadequate internet connection or insufficient digital literacy cannot participate thoroughly in AI-empowered educational programs. Institutions must use subsidised hardware combined with digital hubs on campus along with offline alternatives plus universal interfaces that support students with disabilities to resolve this problem. The equitable use of AI in education demands that administrators provide AI tools to every discipline beyond pure STEM courses as well as adapt the technology to accommodate various learning methods and languages. Government bodies alongside private sector stakeholders and educational consortia need to work together for the establishment of funding mechanisms which will include infrastructure grants as well as public-private partnerships in order to support digital transformations throughout elite institutions and those that lack funding. AI transformation efforts will help education serve all students equally without reinforcing social disadvantages between students. Trust building and privacy protection together with fairness need to be prioritised as AI application ethics in higher education so that the deployment remains ethical. The growing use of AI in educational decision-making about assessment adaptability and feedback delivery and student risk evaluation produces multifaceted moral issues that require establishment of preventive solutions. Educational institutions need to create open data governance frameworks to establish rules about student data acquisition and management including the processing functions and distribution methods. The data collection policies should enact international and regional standards like GDPR and FERPA while offering complete disclosure about data purposes and effects to students. Consent processes should exist in educational platforms so that students maintain control of their digital profiles and students can decide not to participate when possible. The essential requirement for the use of AI systems is the need for transparency because users require clear explanations about system decisions while independent parties need access to audit their decision-making processes. AI technology needs additional scrutiny in mission-critical decision systems such as college entry and grading and academic support since unidentified discriminatory elements could produce discrimination or academic exclusion. The process of auditing algorithms and checking for fairness needs to be done consistently while diverse data must be employed for training AI systems to stop the repetition of societal biases.

The ethical considerations surrounding this relationship apply to the educational link among educators and learners as well as machines. Teachers can use AI to improve teaching methods although the system must preserve the fundamental principles that underline person-centred education. AI tools need to supplement educational staff instead of taking away their responsibilities which consist of mentorship work and the essential abilities for critical analysis and emotional support. Teachers should monitor the results of AI tools while keeping all responsibility to make relevant educational decisions especially about student marks and advancement. AI tools need ethical standards that create inclusive systems to serve students who are neurodiverse alongside disabled learners along with individuals from minoritized groups by offering accessible interfaces. K-12 schools need to create multidomain panels comprised of staff educators alongside students and experts from technology development ethics and legal fields to manage ethical AI implementations across the institution. The boards maintain responsibility for offering guidance about procurement decisions and platform assessments as well as curricular integration work while they deliver ethical education across academic institutions. Institutional AI strategy implementation with embedded ethical guidelines establishes safety measures which directly supports higher education core values including justice and inclusion along with integrity and autonomy. These practical solutions need an evidence-based phased implementation method. Academic institutions must initiate small-scale experimental programmes using AI tools in particular teaching fields to enable risk-minimised development. The evaluation process must merge both quantitative and qualitative data collection to assess student performance results and faculty satisfaction as well as programme convenience and cost-effectiveness. Based on the findings institutions should execute a step-by-step AI adoption strategy for better implementation quality and application of challenge solutions. A thorough AI readiness blueprint during the long term must contain a platform that guides strategic planning along with stakeholder involvement and resource distribution in addition to risk control and performance evaluation. Effective policy support from national and regional entities should establish clear regulations while implementing quality assurance systems and motivation programmes for innovative development. Young higher education institutions along with their accreditation and funding bodies should work as coordinators to spread knowledge and create standards for ethical practises and implement best models through all educational establishments. The combination of international partnerships offers an opportunity to advance global AI integration because it enables organisations to distribute free programmes together with multi-language information and technological studies about AI's social effects across cultures. These collaborative ethical and inclusive approaches enable the higher education sector to maximise AI to develop future learning environments with dynamic personalised formats and social responsibility principles.

FUTURE RESEARCH DIRECTIONS

The future of higher education through artificial intelligence (AI) demands immediate academic investigation about extended effects together with cultural adaptability and ethical outcomes as well as interdisciplinary opportunities. Scholarly expertise must remain focused on researching how AI integration throughout many years affects student outcomes as well as institutional quality and workforce preparation. Research at present concentrates primarily on small-scale pilot tests along with performance outcomes from AI implementation while the complete long-term effects remain unidentified. The evaluation of AI-driven learning environments must consist of research projects that observe students across multiple years beginning with their enrollment until their graduation for determining how these environments impact both student knowledge retention as well as critical thinking ability and academic growth together with eventual career development. Study should investigate the way AI affects faculty responsibilities and higher education development to identify between substantial educational development and quick trends that align with current technological demands. The analysis of such educational transformation dynamics needs research designs with combined methods and control and comparison group arrangements to philtre out AI's impact from other environmental influences. AI-based educational interventions need analysis across different cultural environments because their adaptive potential must be established across multiple socioeconomic and geographical as well as academic settings. The majority of published research focuses on Western countries having well-developed digital platforms leading to restricted transferability of results in varied worldwide environments. The influence of AI in education which is highly influenced by elements like linguistic standards, curricular requirements and teacher skills and institutional policies that determine cultural receptiveness of technology. AI tools that were designed for English-speaking learner groups tend to function poorly in multilingual educational contexts as algorithmic models which learn from homogenous data sets demonstrate poor performance with students who have different cognitive learning styles and preferences. Future research Needs to combine a worldwide view by performing comparative studies between different regions including Africa and Latin America and Southeast Asia and the Middle East to gather common foundations alongside region-specific excellent practises. Research must employ participatory methods involving direct consultation of learners and educators together with their communities located in the Global South thus enabling researchers to comprehend firsthand experiences with AI technology.

Figure 1.

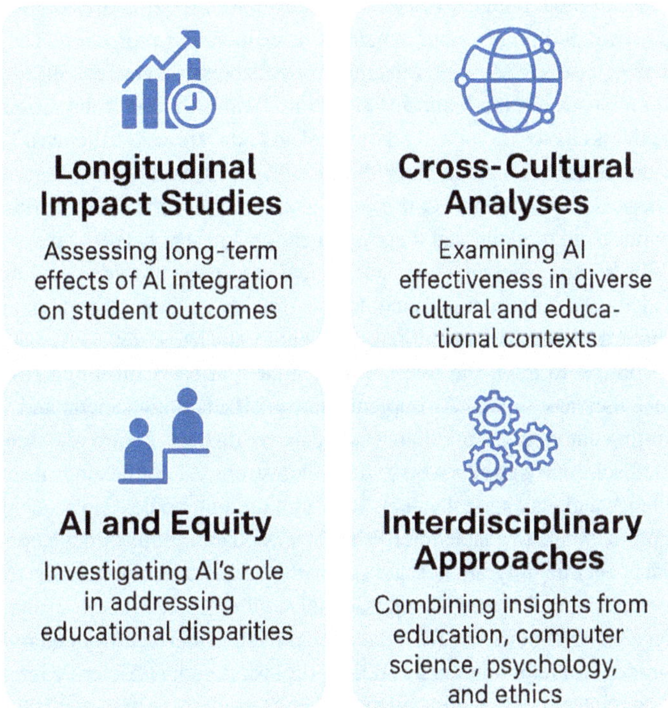

FUTURE RESEARCH DIRECTIONS ON REVOLUTIONIZING HIGHER EDUCATION

Educational research about Artificial Intelligence needs to address new challenges regarding equity. AI can customize education while making it easier to access yet its improper use with poor design choices may worsen or intensify existing educational inequalities. Future investigations need to conduct comprehensive research that examines how artificial intelligence impacts disadvantaged groups of students including people from financially disadvantaged households and rural areas and ethnic minorities alongside students with disabilities. Research must address two essential concerns about digital divide severity when AI selects students through device and connectivity access and the influence of algorithmic decision systems on learning classifications and underrepresented student groups while investigating how personalization algorithms handle diverse student learning needs. The assessment by researchers must establish how well AI systems support inclusive teaching practices including content that is culturally relevant combined with accessibility features and multiple instructional steps. Indicators of intersectionality can demonstrate vital connexions between racial and gender identities along with socioeconomic standings and ability levels in their reaction to technological features and barriers. Future studies should take action to address both institutional and policy-level requirements for equal AI-based educational access through public service investments into infrastructure combined with inclusive curriculum work and policy enforcement of discrimination protection. The field of AI in education will advance because of interdisciplinary collaboration between different experts. AI integration requires research that connects academic fields while uniting various ways of understanding to address its technological ethological and educational challenges. The assessment skills of computer scientists include algorithm design and system architecture as well as data modelling framework development yet they tend to lack knowledge about learning science and classroom dynamics and motivational theory. Educational researchers find it essential to develop technical skills because they identify pedagogical requirements and ethical matters yet lack proficiency in analysing AI systems. Psychologists provide understanding about student cognition and behaviour together with emotional regulation knowledge due to AI systems gradually developing capabilities to track and interact with student affect. Consulting ethicists becomes essential because they assess how AI implementation affects both societal and ethical aspects especially regarding autonomy, surveillance and consent matters. Future research agendas need to establish interdisciplinary groups who will develop strong AI applications through combined technical excellence and educational values. Research funding bodies and academic institutions must establish partnerships to enable interdisciplinary collaborations through common research centres and dual academic programmes and co-written research articles across academic fields.

Methodological innovation serves as an essential requirement to properly evaluate the intricate effects of AI on education systems. The educational insights derived from quantitative metrics consisting of grades and retention rates and time-on-task do not sufficiently represent learning transformations or educational relationships between instructors and students that stem from AI mediation. Research needs to include qualitative and phenomenological methods which will help examine learner interactions and the subjective perspectives toward agency while studying their emotions when working with intelligent systems. Research methods that include ethnographic observations and diary collection and prolonged interviews allow us to observe how students handle the dual guidance system between humans and AI while documenting how teachers change their classroom functions and educational organisations transform because of automated processes. Decision-based research strategies that follow recursive cycles of AI tool development and testing in realistic educational environments produce linked insights about performance strength along with usability strengths which drive innovation from actual educational settings. The field of meta-AI research holds promise for designing learning analytics and artificial intelligence applications which analyse big data to manage educational experiments and develop teaching approaches in prerelease simulation. Research into the future must address both the cultural and philosophical aspects that arise from AI educational interventions. The integration of intelligent systems into educational core functions including personal tutoring as well as grading services and advising generates fundamental questions regarding educational objectives. Learning about education takes new meaning when machines work together with humans in knowledge creation. Research must examine how artificial intelligence modifies students' biological characteristics and personal independence while affecting their membership to communities. AI systems maintain the ability to transform education but they also may transform learning into optimised and efficient processes. The solution of these fundamental educational questions needs dialogue between academics and technologists but also requires participation from students along with educators and parents as well as policymakers and people from civil society. Future academic investigations need to undertake critical examination of technical progress determinism to develop alternative educational approaches focusing on justice as well as care and social growth. The ongoing development of artificial intelligence demands corresponding transformations in our research methods toward methods which embrace comprehensive time span studies, diverse participant inclusion and cultural sensitivity, ethical frameworks and intellectual flexibility.

CONCLUSION

The analysis in this chapter demonstrates that artificial intelligence (AI) features strong capabilities to transform the entire framework of higher education. Through technological advancements in artificial intelligence education has established new ways for students to engage with subject material while teachers provide instruction and educational facilities manage learning needs of diverse student populations. The newly developed educational systems challenge the old uniform educational approaches. AI platforms develop personal learning tracks which adapt to individual student profiles including their speed and preferred learning methods as well as knowledge level to create better student engagement and success rates. AI education tools that use machine learning and natural language processing together with real-time analytics form a theoretical foundation that enables dynamic pedagogical models which follow standards of current learning theory principles. The application of AI enables substantial changes in educational objectives as well as instructional procedures and student learning success during this modern era.

The learner experience benefits from AI implementation through the theoretical concepts of constructivist learning theory along with self-determination theory and the zone of proximal development and connectivism. Adaptive learning tools enhance constructivist practises by helping students explore knowledge meaningfully and SDT is achieved through systems that create spaces for autonomy development and competence improvement with social connexions. The same way that AI understands ZPD enables it to create individualized support systems which create instructional assignments at non-trivial but manageable levels for every learner. Connectivist learning occurs through AI-generated tools that establish digital networks and social learning spaces which help knowledge evolve from interactions among students while they organize diverse sources of information. Theoretical research demonstrates that AI applications serve important educational purposes while emphasizing purposeful system designs which focus on student experience instead of technical innovation. The implementation of Artificial Intelligence in higher education education creates multiple professional roles and enhanced responsibilities while presenting new employment prospects for educational participants. Through AI educational tools professionals can evolve from simple content transmission to learning facilitators who get backed by systems that monitor student advancement and suggest remedial measures. General technical expertise must be supplemented through continuous professional development so that educators become proficient in handling AI tools with proper ethical practises. The transition to AI by academic administrators needs careful planning of infrastructure and digital resources combined with policy implementation for inclusion and transparency as well as data security. Leaderships within institutions need to protect academic standards while supporting innovation experiments through policies that ensure equality. Supporting government agencies should implement regulations which promote ethical AI practices as well as protect privacy and reduce biases and establish accountability standards. The implementation of AI in education requires organised guidelines to determine deployment strategies that maintain innovation against legal and moral requirements. Technical personnel who design educational AI systems need to work together with educators to build solutions that both deliver effective instruction to students in ways which match teaching methods and honour cultural sensitivities and provide easy user experiences. The educational advantages from AI implementations should be appreciated but their implementation must be conducted through objective analysis. Efficiency and personalization in education should never be weaponized to displace the essential humanistic foundation that education always aims to maintain. Education functions as a mutual relationship that aims for ethical change to develop both mental skills and personal attributes including empathy as well as civic engagement and moral understanding. The capabilities of AI extend educational opportunities through different aspects but AI technology must stop at replicating essential human connexions needed for effective instruction and assessment. The main obstacle for future progress involves creating alignment between technological advancement and caring practises along with fair treatment and subject-specific equity. Educational establishments along with teaching professionals must closely track the impact of automation dependence along with its negative consequences to teacher-student relationships and data-based education commodification. AI deployment in higher education requires ethical issues to remain the leading cornerstone throughout its implementation. The rise of AI decision systems in key operations like admissions and grading and advising demands intensified requirements for transparency and fairness together with absolute accountability. Institutions require AI tools that will not create or magnify current inequalities while protecting students who belong to underserved populations. The protection of unintended harms requires ethical audits as well as transparent algorithms alongside practises that include a wide range of data. Infinity Education and its learners need equal support to build capabilities for digital literacy and awareness regarding critical AI approaches so they can interact intentionally and ethically with these technologies. The next phase of AI education advancement requires experts from various fields to combine their expertise in technical implementing with humanistic understanding of the education process. Researchers need to conduct extensive investigation with diverse populations across multiple cultural settings and equitable conditions so they can understand AI's complete influence and supply such data to develop evidence-based educational policies and practises. Higher learning institutions need to choose design processes that give priority to the input from various learner populations and school faculty members. Every participant in education must share a common goal which uses AI as a tool to advance comprehensive development for human beings in our expanding world context. Higher education accepts AI integration as it provides powerful chances and requires substantial duties at once. AI properly designed and deployed with mindful purpose and ethical considerations enables adaptive learning approaches which enhance both educational quality and inclusive educational spaces. The potential of these advancements in personalization will become reality through the direction of basic human values that prioritise fairness and dignity alongside educational transformation. Moving forward education must prioritise human-centred decision making through machine application rather than solely using technology for increased intelligence in education.

REFERENCES

Aithal, P. S., & Maiya, A. K. (2023). Innovations in higher education industry–Shaping the future. [IJCSBE]. *International Journal of Case Studies in Business, IT, and Education*, *7*(4), 283–311. DOI: 10.47992/IJCSBE.2581.6942.0321

Alawneh, Y. J. J., Sleema, H., Salman, F. N., Alshammat, M. F., & Oteer, R. S., & ALrashidi, N. K. N. (2024). Adaptive Learning Systems: Revolutionizing Higher Education through AI-Driven Curricula. In 2024 International Conference on Knowledge Engineering and Communication Systems (ICKECS) (Vol. 1, pp. 1-5). IEEE. DOI: 10.1109/ICKECS61492.2024.10616675

Asy'ari, M., & Sharov, S. (2024). Transforming Education with ChatGPT: Advancing Personalized Learning, Accessibility, and Ethical AI Integration. *International Journal (Toronto, Ont.)*, *3*(2), 119.

Ayeni, O. O., Al Hamad, N. M., Chisom, O. N., Osawaru, B., & Adewusi, O. E. (2024). AI in education: A review of personalized learning and educational technology. *GSC Advanced Research and Reviews*, *18*(2), 261–271. DOI: 10.30574/gscarr.2024.18.2.0062

Bhatia, A., Bhatia, P., & Sood, D. (2024). Leveraging AI to transform online higher education: Focusing on personalized learning, assessment, and student engagement. International Journal of Management and Humanities (IJMH) Volume-11 Issue-1.

Catherin, T. C., Vettriselvan, R., Mathur, S., Regins, J. C., & Velmurugan, P. R. R. (2025). Integrating AI and Learning Analytics in Distance Learning: Strategies for Educators and Institutions. In AI and Learning Analytics in Distance Learning (pp. 207-228). IGI Global.

Chigbu, B. I., Umejesi, I., & Makapela, S. L. (2024). Adaptive intelligence revolutionizing learning and sustainability in higher education: enhancing learning and sustainability with AI. In *Implementing interactive learning strategies in higher education* (pp. 151–176). IGI Global. DOI: 10.4018/979-8-3693-3559-8.ch006

Das, S., Mutsuddi, I., & Ray, N. (2025). Artificial Intelligence in Adaptive Education: A Transformative Approach. In Advancing Adaptive Education: Technological Innovations for Disability Support (pp. 21-50). IGI Global.

Deri, M. N., Singh, A., Zaazie, P., & Anandene, D. (2024). Leveraging Artificial Intelligence in Higher Educational Institutions: A Comprehensive Overview. Revista de Educación y Derecho, (30).

Gautam, D. (2024). Revolutionizing Education through Innovative Technological Solutions. As the editors of Transforming Learning. *Power and Education*, •••, 60.

Jafari, D., & Yazdi, Z. S. (2024). Transforming Education with AI: The Development of a Personalized Learning Algorithm for Individual Learning Styles. *Journal of Algorithms and Computation*, *56*(2), 135–150.

Kaswan, K. S., Dhatterwal, J. S., & Ojha, R. P. (2024). AI in personalized learning. In *Advances in technological innovations in higher education* (pp. 103–117). CRC Press. DOI: 10.1201/9781003376699-9

Kayyali, M. (2025). AI in Higher Education: Revolutionizing Curriculum and Administration. In AI Adoption and Diffusion in Education (pp. 31-62). IGI Global.

Kolluru, V., Mungara, S., & Chintakunta, A. N. (2018). Adaptive learning systems: Harnessing AI for customized educational experiences. *International Journal of Computer Science and Information Technologies*, *6*(3), 10–5121. DOI: 10.5121/ijcsity.2018.6302

Makinde, A. I., Adeleye, S. A., Oronti, A. O., & Jimoh, I. T. (2024). Revolutionizing education. Artificial Intelligence for Wireless Communication Systems: Technology and Applications, 103.

Nuong Deri, M., Singh, A., Zaazie, P., & Anandene, D. (2024). Leveraging Artificial Intelligence in Higher Educational Institutions: A Comprehensive Overview. Education & Law Review/ Revista de Educaci6n y Derecho, (30).

Pratama, M. P., Sampelolo, R., & Lura, H. (2023). Revolutionizing education: harnessing the power of artificial intelligence for personalized learning. Klasikal: Journal of education, language teaching and science, 5(2), 350-357.

Rane, N., Choudhary, S., & Rane, J. (2023). Education 4.0 and 5.0: Integrating artificial intelligence (AI) for personalized and adaptive learning.

Rizvi, I., Bose, C., & Tripathi, N. (2025). Transforming Education: Adaptive Learning, AI, and Online Platforms for Personalization. In *Technology for Societal Transformation: Exploring the Intersection of Information Technology and Societal Development* (pp. 45–62). Springer Nature Singapore. DOI: 10.1007/978-981-96-1721-0_4

Sumathy, V., & Navamani, G. (2024). AI-Driven Personalized Learning: Enhancing Student Success through Adaptive Technologies. Library of Progress-Library Science, Information Technology & Computer, 44(3).

Udeh, C. G.Chinemelum Goodness Udeh. (2025). The role of generative AI in personalized learning for higher education. *World Journal of Advanced Engineering Technology and Sciences*, *14*(2), 205–207. DOI: 10.30574/wjaets.2025.14.2.0077

Vettriselvan, R., Deepan, A., Garg, P. K., Suresh, N. V., & Velmurugan, P. R. (2025). Advanced Text Analysis, Simplification, Classification, and Synthesis Techniques: Leveraging AI for Enhanced Medical Education. In Using AI Tools in Text Analysis, Simplification, Classification, and Synthesis (pp. 37-66). IGI Global Scientific Publishing.

Vettriselvan, R., & Ramya, R. (2025). Sustainable Curriculum Design and Development: A Comprehensive Approach. In Smart Education and Sustainable Learning Environments in Smart Cities (pp. 471-486). IGI Global.

Wang, J. (2025). Revolutionizing Education for Sustainable Development Through Adaptive Learning and Artificial Intelligence. In Rethinking the Pedagogy of Sustainable Development in the AI Era (pp. 63-92). IGI Global. DOI: 10.4018/979-8-3693-9062-7.ch004

KEY TERMS AND DEFINITIONS

Adaptive Curriculum Design: Educational content and assessment programmes follow adaptive forms of curriculum development through instant student performance evaluation. A program called adaptive curriculum design enhances flexibility and differentiation through AI algorithms which change the difficulty of teaching materials while altering their presentation sequence to students.

Artificial Intelligence (AI): Artificial Intelligence means machines including computer systems acquire abilities which normally need human cognitive powers to carry out. Machine capabilities focus on problem-solving processes as well as learning activities and perception tasks and decision-making systems and natural language understanding tasks. The educational field utilises.

Intelligent Tutoring Systems (ITS): Through artificial intelligence the Intelligent Tutoring System acts as a learning platform which duplicates traditional tutoring methods from human educators. Within these systems students receive assessments followed by behaviour interpretation which delivers specific and immediate guidance during learning.

Learning Analytics: The process of collecting and analysing learner data from learning environments through interpreting measured data helps improve educational results. The system applies dashboards with predictive models and visualization tools so instructors get better decisions for teaching and identify vulnerable students and improve institutional planning.

Personalized Learning: The educational model known as personalized learning modifies educational pathways to align with the personal interests and learning prior experiences of students. The education model of personalized learning uses learner data to develop specific learning pathways which modify according to individual speed rates and personal learning methods and learning preferences.

Chapter 7

Harnessing AI to Transform Cambodian Higher Education: Strategies for Building a Future-Ready Curriculum

Dina Pen
https://orcid.org/0009-0004-0104-2840
Svay Rieng University, Svay Rieng, Cambodia

Sereyrath Em
https://orcid.org/0000-0002-6803-195X
National University of Cheasim Kamchaymear, Kampong Cham, Cambodia

Rany Sam
https://orcid.org/0000-0003-3266-5974
National University of Battambang, Battambang, Cambodia

Ganda Febri Kurniawan
https://orcid.org/0000-0002-1563-1249
Universitas Negeri Semarang, Indonesia

Mardy Serey
https://orcid.org/0009-0002-1049-7324
Svay Rieng University, Svay Rieng, Cambodia

ABSTRACT

This chapter examines the potential of Artificial Intelligence (AI) to revolutionize Cambodian higher education by tackling existing issues and capitalizing on possibilities to develop a future-oriented curriculum. It analyzes the principles of AI technology, international trends in AI education, and the higher education framework in Cambodia, encompassing systemic constraints in funding, quality, and infrastructure. The chapter advocates for strategic initiatives like curriculum reform, faculty development, student participation via AI tools, and collaborations with international

DOI: 10.4018/979-8-3373-2752-5.ch007

institutions and technology firms. This chapter underscores the significance of supportive policies and governance, advocating for the incorporation of AI to improve educational outcomes, foster innovation, and equip Cambodian students for a rapidly evolving, AI-centric future.

INTRODUCTION

According to Phan (2015), the Education University is a venerable institution in the Cambodian cultural landscape. It is a place where principles such as student engagement, critical thinking, and participation in the wider community at both the national and global levels are fostered and supported from a young age. Besides, writing to stimulate dynamism in the education sector is, and should be, an intrinsic motivation of each member of the university (Al-Mansoori & Koç, 2019). Universities should partake in discussions regarding the national vision to build a knowledge-based economy, which emphasizes human capital investment (Em, 2025). Education development embodied in the National Strategic Development Plan outlines the strategic objective for Higher Education to build human resource capital to meet the demand of economic development towards education sector reform for the attainment of a knowledge-based economy and society; to assure equity of access to higher education services, quantity, quality and goodness in conformity with the social and economic demand (Heng, 2024; Heng & Doeur, 2024).

All of these require that Cambodian higher education significantly leverage transformative technology, including AI. AI is augmenting existing technologies and creating new capabilities, accelerating the pace at which technology turns into products and services, with far-reaching consequences for education and skills (Rashid & Kausik, 2024). The most important promotion lever for AI is investment by the private sector, which can entail considerable economic returns. These investments in productivity catalyze the creation of high-quality jobs, supported by reform measures in investments, education, and social protection. Part of the answer is to restructure and rethink university work and how pedagogies can draw on innovations in technologies like AI (Agrawal et al., 2019).

THE ROLE OF AI IN EDUCATION

AI is rapidly transforming many aspects of modern life, including our jobs, communication, and educational systems. As AI technologies become more pervasive in everyday activities, it is essential to have a fundamental understanding of their principles and the implications they have. To educate individuals with the skills necessary to communicate with and navigate through a future driven by artificial intelligence, education is crucial (Abbas Khan et al., 2025). Following this, the following sections will investigate the underlying principles of artificial intelligence technologies and highlight global trends that will have an impact on the future of AI education.

Understanding AI Technologies

AI is the ability for machines or computers to perform tasks that are usually associated with human capabilities. AI research has a broad range of disciplines, such as computer vision, speech recognition, automated reasoning, and machine learning (Markauskaite et al., 2022). AI can refer to a product, service, tool, or technology that is linked to another through advanced knowledge or information. The key words of the second definition include understanding, reasoning, learning, acting, and interacting. The three main characteristics are that systems can adapt and evolve, think and learn, and AI can work without human intervention (McCarthy, 2007).

With elements of AI becoming part of everyday living, education as a field must prepare students for a future in which AI will be omnipresent. Education serves two roles in this: First, it needs to teach students how to make ethical future AI researchers, programmers, etc., who will create these elements of AIs. And second, education has to equip students with knowledge and skills to navigate the upcoming change in the job landscape due to AI (Armony & Hazzan, 2024).

Global Trends in AI Education

There are a lot of initiatives, conversations, and activities that are currently being taken to shape AI education (Schiff, 2022). These are all related to the education of future producers of artificial intelligence. Some of them are initiatives taken by the government, such as major investments in education with the goal of altering the way artificial intelligence is taught. The companies have launched scholarships for women working in artificial intelligence and are providing free online training in the principles of AI. The number of academic collaborations, such as working together on a new master's degree program in AI that lasts for one year, is increasing (Ali et al., 2021).

Understanding AI Technologies

AI is often portrayed in science fiction as something intelligent, self-aware, and even sentient. In reality, AI is simply a collection of algorithms that modes the inputs to produce outputs. These algorithms aim to mimic certain aspects of the human mental capacity, such as reasoning, comprehension, and decision-making. Each tool can create a wide range of products, including computer code, novels, factual answers, and visual art (Prabhu & Premraj, 2025).

Generally, AI technologies can be classified into two broad categories. The first one covers algorithmic approaches that are not considered true AI. For example, rule-based expert systems are designed by human experts with a particular domain specialty. More recently, large language models are based on transformer models that simply optimize a data-driven objective by using massive amounts of training data. The second AI category comprises general intelligence approaches that aspire to build intelligent machines that can outsmart any rational creature (Mukhamediev et al., 2022). As machine learning and computation capabilities have exploded in the last decade, considerable progress has also been achieved in this second branch. Progress has come from combining probabilistic Bayesian models, deep neural networks inspired by human cortical brain layering and micro-architecture, symbolic reasoning seen in traditional AI, and planning methods employed by human scientists. These additional neural architectures are known as neuromodulation, attention models, self-supervision, and generative counterfactual reasoning. Unlike most beta and beta-plus models that are the predominant normative modeling approaches used in educational spaces, hybrid AI systems are built for rich and complex modeling (Nagahisarchoghaei et al., 2023).

Global Trends in AI Education

As an emerging technology that spans multiple disciplines, AI will provide educational institutions of higher learning with new instructional content, educational pathways, and new ways to integrate education and technology. According to Southworth et al. (2023), the new generation of enhanced intelligence technology is progressively becoming extensively used in a variety of educational sectors. At the same time, higher education is confronted with both opportunities and challenges that have been present throughout history. There are a lot of growing AI goods and services that are still in the process of being developed, but it has already had a significant impact on a lot of different areas of education. Despite the fact that these large language models present a variety of ethical and regulatory challenges, they also provide teachers and students with new tools for academic writing, research, teaching, language learning, and social engagement. As a result, education stakeholders are being prompted to rethink some of the concepts, relationships, and boundaries that comprise education (Zhou, 2023).

In recent years, educational institutions and relevant organizations around the world have issued multiple relevant reports and explored the challenges and opportunities of AI in education from their respective perspectives. With the continuous acceleration of the process of digital transformation of higher education, the change and influence of AI on education have become increasingly apparent (Kuleto et al., 2021). Universities and colleges are thinking about how to take the lead, break through limitations, establish cooperation, and jointly prepare for digital challenges to promote higher quality. There is a need to critically harness AI for learning through a skill-oriented renormalization of functions, building trust and rewarding the exploration of AI technologies through experiential and innovative pedagogies involving artists and technologists, and addressing the ethical and regulatory challenges of AI for learning through active engagement and collective action (Luan et al., 2020).

Table 1. Overview of AI in Education: Concepts, Trends, and Implications

Theme	Focus Area	Key Points
Understanding AI Technologies	Definition & Characteristics	- AI performs tasks associated with human abilities, such as vision, speech, and reasoning. - It includes understanding, reasoning, learning, acting, and interacting. - Systems can evolve, learn, and operate independently.
	Role in Education	- Education must prepare students to develop and use AI ethically. - Prepares students for the changing job landscape.
Global Trends in AI Education	Initiatives & Collaborations	- Governments and companies are investing in AI education. - Scholarships for women in AI and free online courses are on the rise. - Academic partnerships are growing.
Understanding AI Technologies (Expanded)	Categories of AI	- Two main categories: rule-based systems (not true AI) and general intelligence systems. - Modern models include large language models and hybrid AI systems.
	Advanced AI Methods	- Hybrid AI uses neuromodulation, attention models, self-supervision, and generative reasoning. - Progress driven by deep neural networks and probabilistic models.

continued on following page

Table 1. Continued

Theme	Focus Area	Key Points
Global Trends in AI Education (Expanded)	Opportunities and Challenges	- AI introduces new educational content and pathways. - Tools like large language models impact teaching, writing, and engagement. - Ethical and regulatory concerns are rising.
	Institutional Response	- Institutions are exploring leadership roles, cooperation, and pedagogical innovation. - Need to build trust and explore AI through interdisciplinary, experiential methods.

Table 1 presents a summary of essential principles, worldwide trends, and ramifications of AI in education. It delineates the essential attributes of AI, underscoring its capacity to execute human-like functions such as perception, reasoning, and learning, while also accentuating its autonomous and adaptive qualities. The table highlights the necessity of equipping students to interact with AI responsibly and to adjust to an evolving employment market. It also delineates global objectives, encompassing governmental and industrial funding, expanding academic collaborations, and advocacy for underrepresented populations. The expanded parts differentiate between rule-based and general intelligence systems, presenting advanced AI techniques such as hybrid models and self-supervision. The table also examines potential and difficulties, including the impact of AI technologies on education, ethical issues, and the necessity for innovative, interdisciplinary approaches from educational institutions.

CURRENT STATE OF CAMBODIAN HIGHER EDUCATION

Education, in general, and higher education, in particular, are crucial for alleviating poverty and stimulating growth, especially in developing countries such as Cambodia (Kitamura, 2016). King Norodom Sihanouk established the Royal University of Phnom Penh as a traditional higher education institution in 1960 (Sam et al., 2012).

However, the first democratically elected government in 1993 saw a rapid expansion in its higher education system and the establishment of several private universities (Chen et al., 2007). As of 2023, the Ministry of Education, Youth and Sport (MoEYS) in Cambodia recognizes a total of 132 higher education institutions (HEIs), comprising 48 public and 84 private institutions (Ban & Heng, 2023).

In addition, some non-degree higher education programs are managed by other government ministries. In total, Cambodia has about 792,000 students enrolled in higher education, with around 53.4% of those being female students. Along with this rapid growth in the number of universities, there has also been an increase in government funding for higher education. In the 2020 budget, 3.68% of total government expenditure was allocated to higher education. However, public spending on higher education currently only covers university operational costs, while many investments, including investments in digital infrastructure and human resources development, need to come from the universities themselves.

The government has promoted the establishment of industry and business partnerships with universities, of course, but through the provision of incentives. These contribute to only 0.52% of GDP. Moreover, most Cambodian private universities largely rely on tuition fees, as they receive little funding from the government. The few Cambodian elite universities with a high international reputation seek financial assistance from overseas universities and foreign governments, but the majority of other public and private universities still struggle with financial resource mobilization. Moreover, university funding problems are often compounded by issues of poor quality and low quality-relevant education (Kuzhabekova et al., 2024).

Challenges Faced by Institutions

Despite the early promise of academic reform and continued investment aimed at the three objectives of increased access, improved quality, and enhanced relevance, Cambodia's higher education system continues to face substantial challenges, limiting the country's progress towards its development goals (Doeur, 2022a). Chief among these is a critical shortage of quality self-financed programs that are attractive to the majority of students who cannot access government-subsidized programs with guaranteed job opportunities upon graduation. Public universities and government-supported departments in specialized programs still account for around 10% of the student population. Given the attractiveness these programs present, there is little market incentive for public institutions to respond productively to the demand for high-quality non-subsidized post-secondary education. Although higher education institutions have been established to fill the void, the quality of education on offer is often poor, and higher education as an investment is seen by families as one that produces low returns (Heng & Sol, 2022).

Subpar quality in non-subsidized institutions is, therefore, accompanied by continuing low levels of research output in public universities that are mostly free to use their resources and time for research. Faculty in public universities often have privileged positions, and jobs are not portable. Academic promotion criteria often ignore volume and quality of research output as assessments tend to focus on teaching-related criteria, which causes weaknesses, causing younger academics and professors to seek employment in non-public institutions, where limited resources lead to lower levels of research and students' outcomes and experiences. While the government has been attempting to provide joint courses with foreign universities in areas such as environmental science, health, and bamboo textile technology, some of which include internships in foreign companies and technology transfer, the impact of these initiatives has so far been limited (Xiao et al., 2024).

Opportunities for Growth

Like similar low- and middle-income countries, Cambodia faces a perennial dilemma in balancing the need for immediate industrial talent with finite resources diverted from the professionalization of a large proportion of the Cambodian population via the traditional higher education pathway. While the current level of undertaking higher education is low, it is indeed increasing, and has already outstripped the more conservative East Asia and Pacific average in terms of growth, highlighting the transition towards a knowledge-based economy (Ke, 2024).

The growing demand for higher education opens up considerable opportunities for Cambodian institutions, particularly if they are willing to leverage support or vice some partnerships with the private sector to help shape responsive joint training programs in STEM fields, where employers are hit particularly hard by a lack of relevant training programs (Sok & Bunry, 2021). Institutional investment in evolving upskilling talent solutions via blended traditional and online models will also allow the institutions to introduce greater efficiencies for themselves and their learners and enhance the impact of their strategies. Strategic partnerships with top-ranking international universities could also help spur research activity and innovation creation in the country. Today, three top-rated universities dominate global university rankings in Cambodia, and Cambodia has the largest proportion without a natural-science specialization in these rankings (Sam & Dahles, 2017).

Table 2. Overview of the Current State of Cambodian Higher Education

Category	Key Information
Historical Background	- The Royal University of Phnom Penh was established in 1960. - Rapid growth post-1993 democratic reforms and the rise of private universities.
Institutional Statistics (2023)	- Total HEIs: 132 (48 public, 84 private). - Approx. 792,000 students enrolled; 53.4% are female.
Government Support & Budgeting	- 3.68% of government expenditure allocated to higher education (2020). - Only covers operational costs; investment in digital/human resources is self-funded. - Industry-university partnerships incentivized; contribution to GDP: 0.52%.
Financial Challenges	- Private universities rely mainly on tuition. - Elite universities seek foreign aid; most struggle with resource mobilization. - Funding problems are linked to poor quality and low relevance of education.
Main Challenges	- Shortage of quality self-financed programs. - Only 10% of students benefit from public-subsidized programs. - Weak incentives for public institutions to improve non-subsidized offerings. - Families perceive low returns on education investment.
Academic & Research Issues	- Public faculty enjoy job security but produce low research output. - Promotion criteria emphasize teaching over research. - Talented academics move to non-public institutions. - Limited impact from joint foreign programs.
Opportunities for Growth	- Higher education participation is growing faster than the East Asia-Pacific average. - High potential in developing joint training programs with the private sector (esp. STEM). - Blended learning models can enhance efficiency. - International partnerships can boost research and innovation.
Research & Ranking Concerns	- Three universities dominate the rankings. - Few institutions specialize in natural sciences.

Table 2 provides a detailed summary of the contemporary condition of Cambodian higher education, outlining its evolution from the founding of the Royal University of Phnom Penh to its swift expansion following the democratic reforms of 1993. Notwithstanding governmental assistance, which constitutes merely 3.68% of overall expenditure and mostly addresses operating expenses, the majority of higher education institutions encounter financial limitations, particularly private universities that rely on tuition and face challenges in resource mobilization. Principal obstacles encompass restricted public funding, substandard self-financed initiatives, inadequate institutional incentives, and public doubt regarding the worth of higher education. Public university teachers possess job security; yet, their research output is low due to promotion standards emphasizing teaching, and collaborative programs with international institutions yield limited outcomes. Nevertheless, prospects for advancement are present in enhancing private-sector training alliances, blended learning, and international research partnerships, despite only a handful of universities dominating national rankings, with a restricted specialty in the natural sciences.

CURRICULUM DEVELOPMENT STRATEGIES

Developing higher education curricula related to caring for others, who may be left behind from the new AI-driven transformation, such as aged parents, children, and patients, is an essential strategy for sustainable education and a long-lasting career (Khine, 2024). In a post-COVID-19 era, senior or disabled people have a growing demand for special care services. Therefore, it is proposed that academies develop the existing programs for vocational schools related to care provider services for the elderly, both at home and with specialist organizations (Em et al., 2024). In addition, it is also recommended to increase practices in AI-assisted special care services for the elderly in courses through collaborating programs between universities and local service providers, for example, simulation systems for dementia, autism, and caregiver support (Bennett & McWhorter, 2021).

While some universities may have a collaborative activity with AI companies for developing assistive technologies to promote learning of care providers, it can be suggested promoting and implementing those paid collaborative programs into current curricula, aligning thematic by level with the appropriate roles defined for students in developing the learning support assists, to acquire the professional knowledge and skills to a certain level of competencies (Song et al., 2024). In addition, it is also recommended to publish a white paper focusing on sustaining future career choices through digital transformation, regarding care service employability, or the post-employment transition system, by connecting this joint work activity with competency assessment (De La Haye et al., 2023).

Integrating AI-based daily-life support training into early childhood education programs can be mutually beneficial. Future teachers can study how to implement AI to promote children's learning in kindergartens, and children can learn how to use it appropriately in their daily lives (Su & Zhong, 2022). Although some universities have such collaborative activities by introducing AI to kids, it is suggested to strengthen the utilization of universities' special knowledge in the education stages, especially when developing AI products for kids (Takaoka et al., 2019).

Integrating AI into Existing Curricula

With these technologies rapidly gaining ground in Cambodia and around the world, Cambodian higher education cannot escape the need to adapt its curricula to prepare future professionals and researchers to efficiently harness these tools within their corresponding fields (Mean & Flores, 2024). Traditional teacher-centered pedagogies will have to give way to more active and immersive learning approaches, during which students are encouraged to directly interact with existing AI engines to discover how they work and what their capabilities are, familiarizing themselves with their nuances through trial and error, as in the case of students in digital humanities programs exploring the latest machine translation or image recognition tools (Gladwin, 2024). This is particularly important given that engineering and computer science students could soon have access to code generation engines, simplifying the creation of software products and significantly reducing the skills gap concerning their international peers. Other students, however, would be required to focus more on ethical considerations and the humanistic implications of implementing these tools. Research projects can help students learn about such implications and develop the skills required to bridge the increasingly widening collaboration gap between digital tools and their human professional counterparts, from paralegals to healthcare professionals, to translators and editors (Sengul et al., 2024).

Yet any initial integration attempts must be undertaken with caution, ensuring that students do not lose sight of the fact that these tools are designed to assist users, not take their jobs. From the humanities to the sciences, students and researchers at Cambodia's higher education institutions heavily rely on a variety of digital tools to sift through significant amounts of data: whether writing a historical review of cabinet decisions, or a medical paper analyzing the effect of a surgical technique on a large cohort of patients, using AI algorithms to analyze translated documents or patient records throughout Cambodia's history, much of their work would benefit from high levels of collaboration with these new tools. The future of Cambodian higher education and talent development hinges upon nurturing this collaboration (Khieng et al., 2015).

Developing New AI-Driven Programs

Much as the internet disrupted existing university programs and generated entirely new ones, AI is beginning to demand that new programs be built. Beyond data science, deep learning, natural language processing, and robotics, colleges and universities are developing programs in AI ethics, law, policy, and national security, and in the consequences of disinformation proliferation and various digital threats. Some institutions are developing interdisciplinary and multidisciplinary programs, building on traditional fields through collaborations between disciplines (Ozer et al., 2025).

For Cambodia, there are two key questions. First, what specific content areas and applications should be included in new programs? Second, what particular Cambodian societal contexts should be reflected in those programs? Communications programs could consider disinformation generation and proliferation by and amongst ethnic and other minorities, or AI-driven communications strategies by political parties seeking support among those constituencies, as well as how structured sets of policies could respond. Education programs could consider AI's implications for primary and secondary education, both domestically and for Cambodian nationals studying in other countries (Petraki & Khat, 2022).

Secondly, should the new programs focus on behavioral application, policy, or ethical issues, or be more technical? For many fields in both social and physical sciences, engineering, business, and health care training and disease management, the answer may vary. Nevertheless, the answer needs thinking through from the perspectives of multinational enterprises, international and local regulators, and the users of those products, so that it is not reflexively applied to all potential programs. Should the objective be to launch graduates who will work among and with other economists, sociologists, or educators, or to facilitate graduation from a range of related disciplines with cultural and other sensitivities, so that they can work together effectively? (Ban & Heng, 2023).

Table 3. Curriculum Development Strategies in Cambodian Higher Education

Category	Details
Care-Oriented Curriculum Development	- Develop programs for care services targeting aged parents, children, and patients. - Enhance vocational school programs for elderly care with AI-assisted services. - Use simulations (e.g., dementia, autism) in university-local service collaboration.
Collaborative Programs with AI Companies	- Encourage implementation of paid collaborative programs into curricula. - Align curriculum themes and levels with student roles to build competencies. - Publish white papers linking digital transformation to care service employability.
AI in Early Childhood Education	- Train teachers on integrating AI into kindergartens. - Children learn appropriate AI usage in daily life. - Strengthen AI product development using universities' special knowledge.
Integrating AI into Existing Curricula	- Shift from teacher-centered to interactive learning with AI tools. - Students should explore AI engines (e.g., translation, image recognition). - Computer science students can benefit from AI code generation. - Humanities students focus on ethics and the implications of AI use. - Research projects help bridge the gap between AI and human professionals.
Precautions for AI Integration	- Ensure tools are seen as assistive, not job replacements. - Promote responsible use across disciplines (e.g., medicine, history, law). - Encourage human-AI collaboration in research and practice.
Development of New AI-Focused Programs	- New programs in AI ethics, policy, disinformation, and security. - Promote interdisciplinary collaboration between departments. - Cambodian-specific applications (e.g., disinformation in ethnic groups, AI in education).
Design Questions for New Programs	- What content areas and applications are relevant to Cambodian society? - Should programs be technical, behavioral, or policy-focused? - Consider local vs. global employment outcomes and collaborations.

Table 3 delineates curriculum development methodologies in Cambodian higher education, highlighting the incorporation of AI across many fields to address local requirements and worldwide benchmarks. Integrating vocational training and simulations in partnership with local service providers is recommended. Partnerships with AI firms are promoted via financial incentives and theme coherence, thereby augmenting students' skills and employability. In early childhood education, educator training and AI-driven learning technologies seek to promote responsible AI utilization from an early age. Current curricula are being restructured to facilitate interactive, AI-enhanced learning, with customized apps for both technical and humanities students. The table emphasizes the significance of safeguards in AI integration, promoting technologies that enhance human roles and advocate for appropriate, interdisciplinary application. It additionally advocates for the establishment of new initiatives centered on AI ethics, policy, and security, with particular consideration for Cambodia-specific issues such as ethnic misinformation. The design of new programs must take into account pertinent content, disciplinary emphasis, and the equilibrium between local significance and worldwide career prospects.

FACULTY TRAINING AND DEVELOPMENT

Given how disruptive AI will be to higher education, it is necessary to provide educators with the tools they need to understand how the technology works, how it can be deployed in the classroom to improve pedagogy and outcomes, and how it disrupts the value proposition of higher education (Vieriu & Petrea, 2025). To this end, higher education institutions and their governing bodies must provide funded training courses for faculty on the capabilities and limits of what AI can and cannot do. Training must be voluntary and incentivized. Faculty members who participate in the training will receive something of value. Faculty should also be encouraged to collaborate on the development of learning philosophy statements and teaching and learning strategies within the institution's policy framework. It must also not be ad hoc – LLMs and related techniques have been around for years already, and so too have fears about the potential for academic misconduct and the inappropriate use by students. It is critical that resources on responsible LLM use be available to faculty as early as possible and throughout the rest of their careers (Temper et al., 2025).

If students are going to avoid the temptation of academic misconduct, educators must demonstrate that they are equipped to make strategic assessments of AI's efficacy and limits, and to design assessments that minimize potential pitfalls (Kumar et al., 2024). To be able to do so, institutions must establish processes to share course designs, resources, and AI-generated materials and make those available in a central repository. Triaging the concern that one test template or method might be used elsewhere to compromise the integrity of any single assessment will allow everyone to be on top of AI's impact on higher education. Faculty should also be encouraged to collaborate on sharing their course designs and resources, and to recreate homepages dedicated to that information (Evangelista, 2025).

Upskilling Educators in AI

Higher education educators must be trained in AI and its value as a learning and pedagogical partner. As AI technology is available to all, with substantial information available through open-access resources, no sustainable model of face-to-face training can be paid for. Funding for university AI educators paid for by governments, foundations, or NGOs can help in developing country settings to rapidly build capacity in AI and its applications across disciplines or fields (Zawacki-Richter et al., 2019).

Workshops, classes, or boot camps on AI technologies must be conducted regularly at institutions in-country. Visiting AI experts can work through institutions to conduct initial workshops for educators and students, and include one-off enthusiastic students, staff, and faculty from institutions and private organizations. These can later enable or assist in on-campus workshops while gradually transitioning responsibility over a few months or years. Professional academies, foundations, NGOs, or corporations providing workshops can make these available as online recordings for later consumption to create a buddy-system mentorship in language and skills (Ilić et al., 2021).

These educators must experiment with and teach the best prompting patterns for selected paradigms. They must also help students do productive prompting of AI in local languages. If institutions are to fully reap the rewards of adopting and adapting these technologies into the content development pipeline, they need educators who are fluent in methods, mindset change, politics of promoting and resisting these tools, and the soft power to encourage students to explore and use them in study and life (Pokrivcakova, 2019).

Creating a Supportive Learning Environment

Faculty staff develop supportive learning environments where teaching and learning take place. These lived experiences shape how educators present subject knowledge and inspire students.

Therefore, it is essential to ensure that discussions around AI's implementation remain constructive and supportive (Seo et al., 2021). A teacher's first use of technology could be in a classroom, and it will lead to mixed reactions. Educators can create a familiar classroom environment with supportive, collaborative peer discussions. Educators are also likely to reject AI because they view it as another domain to control, like plagiarism. Therefore, policies and guidelines would help academics know how to mitigate these challenges and use AI effectively. For example, have a supportive experience to assist students by using AI to detect plagiarism or other unwanted outcomes. Exploring integrated systems to control AI-generated responses has been effective in providing students with boundaries to manage their responses. The move from a paradigm of control, where academics argue with students about AI's damaging effects, to one of creative integration has been documented as being effective. Furthermore, acknowledging the potential of other digital resources to actively stimulate student interest that is equally powerful as the latest AI mechanisms can add to the AI and educator discussion (Nur Fitria, 2021).

AI is most valued for its ability to reduce time-consuming activities while allowing the educator to focus on delivering quality education for the students. AI allows for ideation and rapid content development, which educators are likely to embrace if supported in upskilling themselves. This begins with understanding its limitations in content and maintaining academic quality support (Zawacki-Richter et al., 2019). As additional educational resources become available to quality assure AI-developed content, educators, students, researchers, and industry should explore the vast potential and should be encouraged. The routing development of these supporting tools should be continuous, fostering a process of higher education redesign, where the educator retains control over what students take as the real truth and how students can apply knowledge for effective outcomes (Srinivasa et al., 2022).

STUDENT ENGAGEMENT AND LEARNING OUTCOMES

Advanced AI systems offer promising solutions to students' needs and difficulties. Consider how a service addresses the issues of Cambodian youth studying overseas (Petraki & Khat, 2022). Currently, international students face difficulty adjusting to their new life, feel isolated from friends and family, and experience academic pressure. The service provides a virtual friend who can assist them with their studies while also talking with them and helping to relieve the stress they are experiencing. The service was developed by students' needs, their cultural background, and specific study disciplines. A similar tool could be created to help Cambodian students studying in-country. It could become an AI bot for all disciplines and could be a source for students seeking information on their studies or life. There are various options to access such a tool, both university-specific and centrally available (Srinivasa et al., 2022).

What about the student experience with AI? AI systems in higher education are often positioned as virtual teaching assistants, tasked with providing information to students on their university's policies and procedures, answering questions on course content, grading, feedback, and evaluations, and tracking students' engagement on an ongoing basis (Al-Mansoori & Koç, 2019). Some tools can simplify day-to-day tasks by gathering and organizing information, freeing up professors' time for research, teaching, and other forms of academic and community engagement; others provide automated feedback to students, guide them in completing standard assignments, or conduct interesting, adaptive conversations. The advantages of AI-enabled tools include easy access for students, availability 24/7, reliability, and a comfortable, engaging experience (Oyebola Olusola Ayeni et al., 2024).

Enhancing Student Experience with AI

One-on-one support from caring and knowledgeable mentors is what students want most from faculty during their postsecondary experiences, but it is often not possible for faculty to provide that level of personable attention to students in large enrollment classes or in systems where they need to focus on their research programs to achieve tenure, nor can staff who help support students through the maze of higher education policies, procedures, and support services fill that role. AI can help bridge that gap by providing intelligent systems that are always on, are capable of providing individual responses to the unique circumstances of a student's situation, and can work with students to provide 24-7 support while also freeing faculty and staff to focus their energies on students with the more complex challenges (Zawacki-Richter et al., 2019).

Several systems have already been developed to provide AI-facilitated support. Text-based natural language processing chatbots have been implemented to help answer student questions about university services and policies (Oyebola Olusola Ayeni et al., 2024). These programs answer common queries from students, helping inform them of services that are available and that could help with their inquiries. AI advisors can help students navigate academic programs more effectively, suggesting which classes to take and helping students catch themselves when they are about to take a class that will not count for their desired major or minor, but that is not an easy class to take. Chatbots can also facilitate learning in specific subject areas, functioning as embedded tutors available to help answer questions about the content of a course (Pokrivcakova, 2019).

Measuring Learning Outcomes Effectively

The efficacy of teaching and learning in higher education has been hotly debated for decades, but has received renewed attention since the pandemic closed campuses. Ensuring accountability for the use of public funds and continually improving quality have become essential. For some years, countries have seen the establishment of systems to collect and publish data on higher education student learning outcomes, but this is not always linked to funding decisions or has not yet become the norm, and is undertaken for a limited number of programs, including graduate employment and earnings data. This absence of a more extensive, richer, and timely understanding of actual student achievement has become even more evident since the pandemic. In particular, there is often not enough information on actual knowledge acquisition by students, starting and ending scores, and improvements over time. Screening tests are not widely used in higher education (Mean & Flores, 2024).

AI systems, especially chatbots, are now creating a unique opportunity for universities to measure student learning outcomes effectively. Adding value through the learning process, absorbing educational input while changing knowledge and ability levels throughout it, to gain a relevant output, is how higher education institutions expect and define optimal student outcomes (Takaoka et al., 2019). Currently, graduates exit their programs with broadly equivalent average scores, masking performance differentials across a university, program, or cohort through the student educational experience and entry exam score. Traditional assessments to measure knowledge gains, especially problematic in university entrance selection exams, are very scarce in higher education, and students experience difficulty accessing and making use of them in a timely fashion. Student learning process and outcome data based on the new generative AI capabilities can also assist education sector stakeholders to analyze outcomes by differentiating for social and economic background, geographical remoteness, entry exam scores, and program and cohort configurations. A more modest step would be to use AI systems for formative assessments of student learning during a course, but these may lack comparability, reliability, and time series potential across cohorts (Roshanaei et al., 2023).

PARTNERSHIPS AND COLLABORATIONS

Building on the previous chapter's focus on collaborations between AI educators at universities and colleges and other stakeholders, this chapter addresses how Cambodian higher education institutions can engage with a broad range of partners, including tech companies and international higher education institutions, to advance their use of AI techniques. To do this, it started with a discussion about Cambodia's ties with international partners that offer support for AI human resource development (Ghosh, 2024). It then turns the attention to specific tech companies developing initiatives to promote the use and understanding of AI and its use in Cambodia before discussing how Cambodian institutions can work with tech companies more broadly and in specific ways with companies developing AI for the region. Ties with international academic institutions that have invested in Cambodian higher education development are also important to push for more support and to develop research and exchange partnerships (Em & Khampirat, 2025b). After discussing how Cambodian institutions can use partnerships and collaborations with international institutions to realize their long-term ambitions, it is concluded with guidance on a strategic roadmap to make proper use of this modality (Jiang et al., 2023).

The strong openings offered by international universities and colleges to promote more AI research and educational support in Cambodia are based on a set of early collaborations with the Royal University of Phnom Penh and other institutions like the Institute of Technology of Cambodia and the Royal University of Fine Arts (Mean & Flores, 2024). Collaborations have been ongoing for many years with partnerships in both experimental education and research projects for Cambodia's future AI development needs. These initiatives have addressed how universities evaluate student interest in aspiring to work in a digital environment, in furthering AI education development ambitions through investments, and with projects in developing Cambodian-specific knowledge databases and AI capabilities (Al-Mansoori & Koç, 2019).

Engaging with Tech Companies

Universities should consider broader engagement with tech companies. Because companies are often at the cutting edge of technological developments, they often bring deep insights about programming and content that future generations will need to learn (Bentley et al., 2024). Companies should be engaged, as the existing tools and curriculum are being adopted by universities to directly assist in the localization and relevance of these products. Their input at this stage can help improve local adoption rates and the mutual trust between the company and the university.

Other roles these companies can play at this stage include being a potential partner in sponsoring or contributing to any pilot projects (Armony & Hazzan, 2024).

Tech companies can also more generally partner with universities to develop the skills and understanding necessary to prepare for the future, whether it is through direct investments or contributing to the establishment of applied research centers within universities (Ke, 2024). Funding for centers of this kind are in increasing demand from universities throughout the world, as they have several potential benefits including some of the following: they can support curriculum development and international certifications; they can provide training for trainers, both university faculty and staff in corporate learning departments; they can provide internships and co-op placements for students; they can help employers of graduates with skilled youth retention programs; and they can work with government and business to create a more vibrant innovation economy. International partnerships of this kind can also help connect Cambodian universities to the global higher education ecosystem that has been developing over the last century and a half. These centers are not done to make money, but rather to communicate a level of commitment while supporting a company's local and regional talent development strategies (Oyebola Olusola Ayeni et al., 2024).

Collaborating with International Institutions

Cambodia would benefit from deepening its existing and developing new partnerships with leading international institutions with strong and proven experience in higher education innovation (Sok & Bunry, 2021). First, partnerships with leading universities and research centres from advanced economies can help strengthen the capacity of Cambodian higher education institutions to address economic needs, including the training of much-needed STEM graduates and skilled workers for the developing Cambodian economy, and to monitor and generate international academic, business, and political interest in Cambodian higher education development and its potential to become a knowledge hub for ASEAN and the Greater Mekong region (Kimkong & Koemhong, 2022).

International partnerships with universities could also support research capacity in areas such as the development of AI and its applications (Rashid & Kausik, 2024). Other higher education institutions globally have experience in assisting universities to build science and technology capabilities, and they are making significant investments to build research programs in developing Asian countries. International partnerships could also facilitate and reduce the expense for students who are able and suitable to pursue graduate studies in developed economies. These partnerships have the potential to advance the development of the Cambodian higher education system while allowing it to remain cognizant of national values and concerns, and the need to advance knowledge that advances the economic position of the nation and its people (Fui-Hoon Nah et al., 2023).

POLICY AND GOVERNANCE

Cambodia has a limited public policy environment. Critical and foundational policy areas, including in the area of applying modern technology, do not have supporting policies, or these foundational public policies are limited and lack the support of policies in adjacent or linking policy areas. The government will need to create new and strengthen existing national policies to account for and support the integration of AI and unlock the potential of the use of AI in the HE sectors (Doeur, 2022a).

These policies will need content aimed at the related areas and delineate the government's plans to use modern technology, including AI, in the development of the HE sectors, for what specific purposes in the educational spheres and operations. More broadly, the development and strengthening of these policies relate to the larger mission of developing strong domestic HE sectors, which are trusted, valued, and can be seen as churning out the values and human capital that are required for society. They will need to speak to the nature of and support for the training and education; this relates to the national educational outcomes, which the Kingdom is striving for as part of shaping Cambodian citizenry (Sam & Dahles, 2017).

The paper discusses policy priorities in the context of HE about the effect and application of AI in society, including respective critical policy areas: Digital National Policy Strategy, Cambodia Digital Economy and Society Policy Framework, and Industrial Development Policy. Various policy areas of Digital Economy, Digital Nap Policy, Digital Youth, Digital Data, Digital Financial Inclusion, Digital Societies, Digital Employment Creation, Labor Market, and Digital Employment, Security, Safety, and Resilience in the Digital Age are explored in the context of the HE sectors. The HE sectors already have and will have a role in some regards, but also need to be considered in others (Mean & Flores, 2024).

Creating Supportive Policies for AI Integration

AI has the potential to radically change the landscape of postsecondary education in Cambodia, enabling new methods of teaching and supporting student engagement and driving new economic opportunities (Khieng et al., 2015). Perhaps more importantly, AI enables the rapid deployment of adaptive educational technologies that can jumpstart the provision of quality educational content in a country where meeting demand for college and university graduates with 21st-century skills is sorely lacking. Intelligent educational agents can be made available at low cost to students in Cambodia to help provide the personalized attention that most schools cannot, and do not, provide. Intelligent tutoring systems can cause significant learning gains when well–designed, and can be scaled to provide a learning effect that few traditional school systems can match (Khieng et al., 2015).

By adopting progressive policies that sanction the responsible use of these tools, Cambodia can put its post–secondary educational system on a trajectory that could dramatically improve its skills gap and increase GDP per capita in a relatively short timeframe. Cambodia has great aspirations for its educational future (Sok & Bunry, 2021). The government has made significant investments in expanding access to higher education and is offering more students the opportunity to work toward an advanced degree than ever before. Though many question the preparedness of graduates from newly established institutions, the students best prepared to benefit from a postsecondary credential are not being served. Research has demonstrated that graduation rates of at–risk students can be improved with careful use of technology such as adaptive learning platforms modeled on the principles of Personalized System of Instruction, central to the successful design of intelligent tutoring systems. Excessive use of these systems can socialize students for a professional life defined by over–reliance on technology. But these tools can be invaluable as support systems in the efforts to meet rising demand for human resources equipped to help

Cambodia transition from an economy focused on garment manufacture to one where innovation and creativity are the key features (Phan, 2015).

Governance Structures for Sustainability

Enabling AI technologies to transform and support Cambodia's higher education sector is a multifaceted process that requires collaborative action, particularly between the Ministry of Education, Youth and Sports, public HEs, and local implementers (Kitamura, 2016). The unique context of Cambodia means that it is critical to build local capacity and, above all, ensure ownership and a sense of agency on the part of HEs, local developers, service providers, and government authorities. Ownership goes hand in hand with the adoption of a collaborative, co-creative, and user-centered design approach to the identification of challenges and the deployment of relevant tools to support education and research. The role played by local industry in providing high-quality services, such as course delivery and academic advising, also needs to be ensured. Exploring opportunities for cooperation and support based on Cambodia's relationships with other countries in the region will also be important. Collaborative governance structures might include elevated informal working groups and/or ongoing facilitated workshops with representatives from public and private HEs, local service providers, technical support, and service development resources from allied countries, as well as national labor market and industry needs representatives. These groups would inform and advise on the mass opening of HE services in Cambodia, as well as the design, development, and deployment of commercially sustainable localized support materials and resources for the Cambodian education and research community. Such internal committees would also develop shared, contextualized visions for AI deployment within the national, public interest framework, as well as development councils to advise on how costs might be addressed and development methods and deployment times made feasible (Mean & Flores, 2024).

ETHICAL CONSIDERATIONS IN AI EDUCATION

As it can be thought about how to harness AI technologies, it is important to consider the ethical implications of how this is done and seek to model good practice in Cambodian higher education. Though the majority of the ethical principles for AI systems, such as fairness, accountability, transparency, and explainability, are not unique to educational AI systems, in the education domain, additional challenges arise due to the sensitive nature of the information supplied by learners and their parents (Mishra, 2024). There is also the potential for changes in systems to alter the trajectory of a student's life over time, particularly in places where social mobility is limited. Educating students in high-level AI ethical principles, as well as the development and implementation of supporting AI systems with detailed, concrete biases, causes, and effects, is fundamental as looking to impact generations of students into the future (Al-Mansoori & Koç, 2019).

Addressing Bias and Fairness

As most AI systems are built using large datasets, but only on examples from a narrow set of demographics, there are concerns about perpetuating the biases found in the data. Because modeling fairness at scale is challenging, personalizing fairness is an area of growing interest. Because models need to be trained to run on new students who may differ greatly from those on which the model is trained, and who may also share highly sensitive and vulnerable characteristics, such as ethnicity or disability, it needs to carefully consider how to assess personalized bias and distribution shift. Data should be especially attentive to unfairness during significant transitional periods, such as common entrance levels for college or primary universal testing (Ghosh, 2024).

Ensuring Data Privacy and Security

Educational AI systems raise concerns about how students' data will be collected, used, and shared, as well as how their security will be maintained. If students choose to limit data collection from AI systems, a lack of demographic data may limit system effectiveness. Such concerns also filter up through the educational chain, where data loss, lack of security enforcement, and bad actors have harmed actual users. Now, generative systems raise further questions to consider (Ismail & Aloshi, 2024).

Addressing Bias and Fairness

With the large-scale adoption of AI throughout various sectors, concerns about fairness and bias in AI are also on the rise. Recent cases have raised society's awareness of the negative social consequences of AI. The social and racial biases embedded within these AI systems are understandable since the datasets they were trained on reflect these biases; however, unacceptable nonetheless. These ethical concerns focused on the fairness and biases of AI affect education as they spawn new fields of relevant study, such as Fairness, Accountability, and Transparency or Algorithmic Fairness (Barlow et al., 2005).

Higher education, in particular, has an important social responsibility in addressing such ethical concerns surrounding AI related to fairness and bias since it supports creating the next generation of AI experts who will design and build AI systems. As part of this responsibility, higher education must ensure that its AI-related educational programs include these ethical topics. Educational programs can take two approaches. The first approach teaches Ethical AI as a distinct topic. This approach can be considered an infusing-the-curriculum pedagogical model, especially if the topic is included in other related courses. The second approach introduces courses in their curriculum that are relevant to the ethical topic, such as graphic design or journalism, for students other than those in AI programs (Al-Mansoori & Koç, 2019).

The first approach is more appropriate for specialized graduate or PhD and postgraduate courses or programs, since these are the students who will eventually create new AI technologies and systems. The second approach is more suitable as an infusing-the-program approach in undergraduate programs since undergraduate students do not specialize in their respective fields yet. The three domains of study that need to be addressed among the relevant undergraduate programs are data collection and data journalism, graphic design, and ethics courses focused on the students' specific programs or disciplines (Bentley et al., 2024).

Ensuring Data Privacy and Security

AI models are trained on vast amounts of data, but this data can include private information from all types of sources, and can contain sensitive information of certain beings or whole groups, such as health and financial data, or people's political opinions. Using that data can produce adverse effects on those groups in particular and society as a whole. In addition, students are also not trained on data that is representative of society as a whole. Education providers must therefore ensure that students are properly informed in this regard and that organizations do not use data in a harmful manner. Furthermore, there should be proper procedures for integrating such models in an organization and workflows that guarantee the protection of any sensitive group in case these organizations decide to use these tools (Ismail & Aloshi, 2024).

Students must be made aware that these types of models are generally trained on public data and have the potential to steal their identity or to generate anything detrimental to them or their group. In addition to preventing harm and malice, students must be made aware that many organizations have poorly implemented these types of models in their businesses, resulting in accidents and inefficient workflows. Therefore, students must be made aware that wrongful application of these practices can result in damage to them, to others, and groups, but students and graduates can mitigate this harm by creating better workflows and guidelines for integrating these systems into businesses and organizations.

Certain organizations have launched a set of guidelines before allowing organizations to use these models in a business setting in order to guarantee safety and success. It has also been stated that they will not deploy any tool using certain technologies until proper safeguards ensuring the privacy of artists have been implemented. Many organizations are too excited about the features these tools offer and have not put enough procedures in place to guarantee success (Bandura, 2023).

FUTURE DIRECTIONS FOR CAMBODIAN HIGHER EDUCATION

One of the strategic goals outlined in the Cambodian Ministry of Education, Youth, and Sports' National Policy on Higher Education is to anticipate future skills needs. However, the foremost challenge for higher education in Cambodia, as well as many other emerging economies, is to satisfy future skills needs in a rapidly transforming world in which the pace of technological change is unprecedented, both for the pattern of economic growth and the labor market needs that drive skills demand (Em & Khampirat, 2025b). The traditional methods of labor market forecasting have not been very successful and now exist in tension with the major shifts underway, driven by technology like work and the labor market, namely increased flexibility, more remote work, the gig economy, less attachment to employers, and the importance of soft skills such as cognitive, social, and emotional skills (Doeur, 2022b).

Therefore, higher education institutions and employers should build more active relationships. Universities have a direct interest in enhancing the employability of their students. Employers should have an interest in having input into curricula or accreditation requirements that prepare graduates for present and future cognitive and technical skill needs. Enabling closer collaboration in workforce skills preparation may require Cambodian authorities to enable the establishment of professional bodies in specific fields and industry associations. These organizations represent employers in a particular area of work and could increase engagement with HEIs to set skill standards and offer help with curriculum design (Heng et al., 2023).

Innovative new teaching and learning methods that bring learning to life and make it more interactive and enjoyable, as well as the adoption of innovative learning technologies, can also contribute to the goals of education and higher education authorities in Cambodia. Such methods and technologies may help facilitate the delivery of the essential infrastructure content of expanding student admissions and improving completion rates, student quality, and enhancing labor market relevancy of skills and education quality more generally (Ban & Heng, 2023).

Anticipating Future Skills Needs

The rapid digital transformation of the world has left no nation immune to change. AI is moving closer to the central stage, raising expectations that it will reshape how people live and work. It will give rise to changes as dramatic and unpredictable as those that have followed the introduction of the steam engine, electricity, and the computer. While it is well known that such technological revolutions do not arrive from nowhere, but rather evolve, it is increasingly difficult for governments to look even a few years ahead to determine the shape of the labor market to come and the skills educators will need to provide in the future (Ali et al., 2021).

This difficulty is compounded in Cambodia by a combination of factors: the extreme youth of the Cambodian population, where more than 36 percent are aged 10 to 24 and cited to be a target for youth development programs; the ongoing role of informal employment, estimated to account for more than 85 percent of the working population; and the lack of formal vocational training (Khine, 2024). Another issue for Cambodia is that training for entry into the formal labor market is limited to low- and semi-skilled service or agricultural work, as low wages and unskilled work remain the most cited reasons for unrevised labor migration. Migration serves as a pull factor for Cambodia's economic growth recovery. In Cambodia, although managers and business professionals constitute 18 percent and 15 percent of the share in the product and service sector, respectively, they make the highest contribution to GDP. The economy's increasing skill premium indicates rising demand for skills, more than supply, caused by the mismatch of skills training provided to youth with the country's labor market needs (Chen et al., 2007).

Innovative Teaching Methods and Technologies

With the acceleration of evolutionary social changes after the COVID pandemic, the degree of novelty for work content and the speed of the required remaining work time in a person's lifetime has been increasing, especially in the life sciences and biochemistry fields, in parallel to the acceleration of the digital transformation phenomenon in other non-enrolment service sectors (Antonopoulou et al., 2021). As a result, continuing education and short and long degree enrollment promotions have been undergoing a deep transformation to promote future niche life scientists, re-specializing teachers and engaging mentors from abroad, as well as re-specializing private sector facilitators to assist in horizontal learning, co-creation and interdisciplinary academic, industrial, and entrepreneurial collaborations, among others, to achieve the Sustainable Development Goals (SDGs) (Iqbal & Ahmad, 2021). In this sense, the combination of coaching with project-based learning with the support of digital communication tools, as well as distance virtual laboratories available in different platforms of unselfish work of professors, researchers, and students, has been an interesting strategy, facilitating the development of new collaborative protocols and tools (Iqbal & Ahmad, 2021).

While these training modalities may be elements of a growing number of life science academic institutions, their implementation requires the possible redirection of current teaching practices to more experiential ones, in which academics rank behind the students. Currently, the vast body of digital tools that allow distance experimental experiences to be realized makes it easier for students to familiarize themselves with academic, governmental, and private laboratories worldwide. At the same time, given the time-consuming nature of research papers, their chaining can be the academic map that guides students and professionals to define their areas of interest and project the future construction of their thesis and research projects, personalizing their academic paths (Vieriu & Petrea, 2025).

Table 4. Strategic Framework for Harnessing AI in Cambodian Higher Education

Thematic Area	Key Points
Understanding AI Technologies	- AI mimics human tasks (vision, speech, learning, reasoning). - AI is transforming work, learning, and communication. - Education must prepare students for AI integration.
Global Trends in AI Education	- Government initiatives and scholarships. - Emerging AI technologies. - Collaboration between institutions. - Integration of AI into curricula.
Cambodian Higher Education Status	- 132 institutions (48 public, 84 private). - Limited government funding; high reliance on tuition. - Quality and relevance issues in education.
Challenges for Institutions	- Lack of quality programs and resources. - Limited access for low-income students. - Inconsistent academic promotion policies. - Brain drain to the private sector.
Opportunities for Growth	- High demand for higher education. - Use of blended learning models. - Potential for global academic partnerships.
Curriculum Development	- Emphasis on care-related and AI-assisted service education. - Integration of AI in early childhood and elderly care training.
Integrating AI in Higher Education	- Shift from teacher-centered to immersive, active learning. - Exposure to AI tools and engines. - Focus on ethics and humanistic concerns.
Developing New Programs	- Fields: data science, NLP, robotics, AI law & ethics. - Programs should reflect the Cambodian context and societal needs.
Faculty Training and Development	- Funded AI training for educators. - Collaboration on learning strategies. - Sharing of AI resources and course materials.
Upskilling Educators	- Workshops and bootcamps. - Training in prompting, soft skills, and mindset change. - Encouraging experimentation with AI.
Supportive Learning Environment	- Supportive policies and learning culture. - AI as a tool to reduce workload and support creativity. - Central resource sharing.
Student Engagement	- Use of AI as virtual teaching assistants. - Personalized student support and stress reduction. - Chatbots for content and administrative help.

continued on following page

Table 4. Continued

Thematic Area	Key Points
Measuring Learning Outcomes	- AI tools to assess and differentiate learning outcomes. - Support for equity in education evaluation.
Partnerships & Collaborations	- Engagement with tech firms and global universities. - Localizing tools and sharing research initiatives. - Developing AI talent in Cambodia.
Policy and Governance	- Need for national AI integration policies. - Support for HE reforms and domestic human capital development. - Promotion of responsible AI use.

Table 4 provides a basic framework for the future trajectory of Cambodian higher education, offering strategic guidance on the sector's evolution through the deliberate incorporation of AI. Cambodia seeks to improve its education system and align with global trends, with the table emphasizing key areas for development. This encompasses curricular innovation, especially via AI-assisted care services and multidisciplinary programs in domains such as AI ethics, robotics, and data science, fields essential for future labor markets. The focus on faculty training, upskilling, and collaborative resource sharing underscores the need to educate educators with the tools and mentality essential for leading AI-enhanced instruction. By emphasizing students' participation via individualized AI tools and cultivating collaborations with international universities and technology companies, Cambodian higher education institutions may enhance both quality and relevance. The incorporation of quantifiable learning outcomes and policy-level endorsement signifies a national commitment to evidence-based reform, equal access, and the advancement of human capital. This strategy framework ultimately fosters a future where Cambodian higher education is more innovative, inclusive, and internationally interconnected, while remaining attuned to local societal demands.

CONCLUSION

The digital revolution offers major opportunities to rethink the way people learn and schools teach, particularly by increasing the adaptability, personalization, and flexibility of traditional structural and pedagogical frameworks. In particular, the use of AI technology on a large scale can help to update and upgrade formal educational processes, support the trainers in their work at all levels, and critically develop competencies and professional skills, which will then be further exploited throughout their working lives. Ultimately, this is essential if the younger generations are to acquire the skills needed to face the labor market of the future and foster the climate of discovery and change that every society in a democratic framework must actively pursue.

In the Cambodian context, Cambodia has made significant strides towards the digitalization of its economy. Furthermore, further incorporation of digitalization in key areas such as education, trade facilitation, and financial inclusion could help accelerate this growth. At present, digital services account for a percentage of Cambodia's GDP, a number that could reach a higher percentage by a specified year.

Moreover, human capital development is at the heart of post-COVID recovery and growth, as access to meaningful employment is critical to supporting the Cambodian population. Consequently, harnessing AI technologies could help to transform and revitalize the Cambodian education system, thus providing better services for all Cambodians, improving the ability to adapt to change and manage risk, and sustaining economic growth and competitive advantages for the nation.

In response to these demands, the Ministry of Education, Youth and Sport is currently in the process of restructuring the higher education sector by improving the quality of higher education services, establishing additional higher education institutions, and building the capacity of educators to further develop human capital.

RECOMMENDATION

Curriculum development ought to be positioned as the key pillar of AI integration in Cambodian higher education so as to connect with the title of the chapter and the overarching theme of AI education strategies for future-proofing curriculum design. While administrative applications, faculty training, and student services continue to be vital, they should nevertheless be reframed strategically in order to demonstrate their direct contribution to the development, revision, and personalization of curricula that are in accordance with both national requirements and international quality standards.

Therefore, a comprehensive national plan for the use of AI in education should be adopted by Cambodia. In particular, this strategy should prioritize curriculum reform that is consistent with world-standard frameworks, such as the Education 2030 Agenda of the United Nations Educational, Scientific, and Cultural Organization (UNESCO), the OECD Learning Compass, and the SDGs. To achieve this, artificial intelligence techniques should be utilized to enable competency-based learning, adaptive pathways, and outcome-based education models that are benchmarked against global best practices. Moreover, in order to gain significant insights into how artificial intelligence might drive curricular transformation while the Cambodian socio-economic and cultural landscape remains relevant, it will be helpful to draw on international case studies, particularly those from countries that have similar developmental situations.

In addition, training programs for faculty development should incorporate specialized instruction on AI applications for curriculum mapping, the construction of automated learning resources, and the design of data-driven student assessments. Furthermore, learner analytics should be used methodically to provide guidance for the sequencing of courses, the construction of modular structures, and the development of flexible routes that are in accordance with international graduate competency requirements. By doing so, including ethics in AI, critical thinking, innovative skills, and problem-solving in educational programs will ensure that graduates from Cambodia can compete successfully in the international labor market.

Finally, a framework that is specifically designed for "AI in Curriculum Development" should be developed. This framework, in turn, should incorporate theoretical models, empirical research, and policy recommendations that may be put into effect. Consequently, the outcomes of the curriculum should be explicitly mapped to criteria that are considered to be of world-standard quality, while also being adapted to Cambodia's specific situation. In conclusion, in the digital era, Cambodia can strengthen its adaptability, innovation capacity, and sustainable growth by implementing these strategies, which will allow it to harness AI not only to improve teaching

REFERENCES

Abbas Khan, M., Khan, H., Omer, M. F., Ullah, I., & Yasir, M. (2025). Impact of artificial intelligence on the global economy and technology advancements. In El Hajjami, S., Kaushik, K., & Khan, I. U. (Eds.), *Artificial general intelligence (AGI) security* (pp. 147–180). Springer Nature Singapore., DOI: 10.1007/978-981-97-3222-7_7

Agrawal, A., Gans, J., & Goldfarb, A. (2019). Economic policy for artificial intelligence. *Innovation Policy and the Economy*, *19*(1), 139–159. DOI: 10.1086/699935

Al-Mansoori, R. S., & Koç, M. (2019). Transformational leadership, systems, and intrinsic motivation impact on innovation in higher education institutes: Faculty perspectives in engineering colleges. *Sustainability (Basel)*, *11*(15), 1–26. DOI: 10.3390/su11154072

Ali, S., DiPaola, D., Lee, I., Sindato, V., Kim, G., Blumofe, R., & Breazeal, C. (2021). Children as creators, thinkers, and citizens in an AI-driven future. *Computers and Education: Artificial Intelligence*, *2*, 1–11. DOI: 10.1016/j.caeai.2021.100040

Antonopoulou, H., Halkiopoulos, C., Barlou, O., & Beligiannis, G. N. (2021). Transformational leadership and digital skills in higher education institutes: During the COVID-19 pandemic. *Emerging Science Journal*, *5*(1), 1–15. DOI: 10.28991/esj-2021-01252

Armony, Y., & Hazzan, O. (2024). *Inevitability of AI technology in education: Futurism perspectives for education for the next two decades*. Springer Nature Switzerland., DOI: 10.1007/978-3-031-72790-0

Ayeni, O. O., Al Hamad, N. M., Chisom, O. N., Osawaru, B., & Adewusi, O. E. (2024). AI in education: A review of personalized learning and educational technology. *GSC Advanced Research and Reviews*, *18*(2), 261–271. DOI: 10.30574/gscarr.2024.18.2.0062

Ban, T., & Heng, K. (2023). Improving the quality of Cambodian higher education: Key challenges and suggestions. *Cambodian Journal of Educational Research*, *3*(2), 35–61. DOI: 10.62037/cjer.2023.03.02.03

Bandura, A. (2023). Cultivate self-efficacy for personal and organizational effectiveness. In Locke, E., & Pearce, C. (Eds.), *Principles of organizational behavior* (pp. 113–135). Wiley., DOI: 10.1002/9781394320769.ch6

Barlow, J. H., Ellard, D. R., Hainsworth, J. M., Jones, F. R., & Fisher, A. (2005). A review of self-management interventions for panic disorders, phobias, and obsessive-compulsive disorders. *Acta Psychiatrica Scandinavica*, *111*(4), 272–285. DOI: 10.1111/j.1600-0447.2005.00499.x

Bennett, E. E., & McWhorter, R. R. (2021). Virtual HRD's role in crisis and the post-COVID-19 professional lifeworld: Accelerating skills for digital transformation. *Advances in Developing Human Resources*, *23*(1), 5–25. DOI: 10.1177/1523422320973288

Bentley, S. V., Naughtin, C. K., McGrath, M. J., Irons, J. L., & Cooper, P. S. (2024). The digital divide in action: How experiences of digital technology shape future relationships with artificial intelligence. *AI and Ethics*, *4*(4), 901–915. DOI: 10.1007/s43681-024-00452-3

Chen, C., Sok, P., & Sok, K. (2007). Benchmarking potential factors leading to education quality: A study of Cambodian higher education. *Quality Assurance in Education, 15*(2), 128–148. DOI: 10.1108/09684880710748901

De La Haye, D. C., Daniels, S. R., & Simmons, A. L. (2023). Working after incarceration: An integrative framework of pre- and post-hire experiences of formerly incarcerated individuals. *Human Resource Management Review, 33*(3), 100966. DOI: 10.1016/j.hrmr.2023.100966

Doeur, B. (2022a). Promoting higher education reforms in Cambodia: Challenges and the way forward. *Cambodian Journal of Educational Research, 2*(2), 116–128. DOI: 10.62037/cjer.2022.02.02.07

Doeur, B. (2022b). Promoting teachers' continuous professional development in Cambodian higher education: Issues and recommendations. *Cambodian Journal of Educational Research, 2*(1), 119–134. DOI: 10.62037/cjer.2022.02.01.07

Em, S. (2025). *Effectiveness of school directors' transformational leadership on teachers' self-efficacy and job performance in Cambodia* [The University of Cambodia]. CJESS Online Library. https://ejournal.educationalfields.com/index.php/CJESSOL/article/view/63

Em, S., Chin, P., & Pen, D. (2024). COVID-19 and school closures: Transformation of shadow education in the Cambodian context. In Md. B. Alam (Ed.), *Shadow education in Asia: Policies and practices* (pp. 136-159). IGI Global Scientific Publishing. DOI: 10.4018/979-8-3693-2952-8.ch009

Em, S., & Khampirat, B. (2025a). Facilitating scholarly pursuits in higher education: Cambodia's endeavors toward research advancement. In Mdikana, A. A. (Ed.), *Enhancing research output in higher education: Research proposals, profiles, and publishing* (pp. 39–66). IGI Global Scientific Publishing., DOI: 10.4018/979-8-3373-0806-7.ch002

Em, S., & Khampirat, B. (2025b). Cooperative education for sustainability: AI in learning opportunities, challenges, and future directions. In Tariq, M. U., & Sergio, R. P. (Eds.), *Convergence of AI, education, and business for sustainability* (pp. 75–92). IGI Global Scientific Publishing., DOI: 10.4018/979-8-3373-1917-9.ch004

Evangelista, E. D. L. (2025). Ensuring academic integrity in the age of ChatGPT: Rethinking exam design, assessment strategies, and ethical AI policies in higher education. *Contemporary Educational Technology, 17*(1), 1–19. DOI: 10.30935/cedtech/15775

Fui-Hoon Nah, F., Zheng, R., Cai, J., Siau, K., & Chen, L. (2023). Generative AI and ChatGPT: Applications, challenges, and AI-human collaboration. *Journal of Information Technology Case and Application Research, 25*(3), 277–304. DOI: 10.1080/15228053.2023.2233814

Ghosh, D. (2024). Using AI for student success: Early warning, performance analytics, and automated grading in education cyber-physical systems. In Dutta, P. K., Raj, P., Sundaravadivazhagan, B., & Selvan, C. P. (Eds.), *Artificial intelligence solutions for cyber-physical systems* (pp. 236–243). Auerbach Publications., DOI: 10.1201/9781032694375-13

Gladwin, O. (2024). *Integrating AI into education: Designing pedagogies to enhance critical thinking and analytical skills.* Unpublished. DOI: 10.13140/RG.2.2.28378.56007

Heng, K. (2024). Understanding Cambodian provincial university students' perspectives on Cambodia's vision to become a knowledge-based society. *SAGE Open*, *14*(2), 1–14. DOI: 10.1177/21582440241242197

Heng, K., & Doeur, B. (2024). Cambodia's aspirations to become a knowledge-based society: Challenges and recommendations. *Policy Futures in Education*, *22*(8), 1647–1661. DOI: 10.1177/14782103241234408

Heng, K., & Sol, K. (2022). Education: Key to making Cambodia great again. *Cambodian Journal of Educational Research*, *4*(3), 1–18. https://kimkongheng.wordpress.com/2022/08/04/education-key-to-making-cambodia-great-again/. DOI: 10.62037/cjer.2022.02.02.01

Heng, K., Sol, K., & Em, S. (2023). COVID-19 and digital transformation of Cambodian higher education: Opportunities, challenges, and the way forward. In de Pablos, P. O., Zhang, X., & Almunawar, M. N. (Eds.), *Handbook of research on education institutions, skills, and jobs in the digital era* (pp. 307–327). IGI Global Scientific Publishing., DOI: 10.4018/978-1-6684-5914-0.ch018

Ilić, M. P., Păun, D., Popović Šević, N., Hadžić, A., & Jianu, A. (2021). Needs and performance analysis for changes in higher education and implementation of artificial intelligence, machine learning, and extended reality. *Education Sciences*, *11*(10), 1–21. DOI: 10.3390/educsci11100568

Iqbal, Q., & Ahmad, N. H. (2021). Sustainable development: The colors of sustainable leadership in a learning organization. *Sustainable Development (Bradford)*, *29*(1), 108–119. DOI: 10.1002/sd.2135

Ismail, I. A., & Aloshi, J. M. (2024). Data privacy in AI-driven education: An in-depth exploration into the data privacy concerns and potential solutions. In Keeley, K. L. (Ed.), *AI applications and strategies in teacher education* (pp. 223–252). IGI Global Scientific Publishing., DOI: 10.4018/979-8-3693-5443-8.ch008

Jiang, N., Liu, X., Liu, H., Lim, E. T. K., Tan, C.-W., & Gu, J. (2023). Beyond AI-powered context-aware services: The role of human–AI collaboration. *Industrial Management & Data Systems*, *123*(11), 2771–2802. DOI: 10.1108/IMDS-03-2022-0152

Ke, Y. (2024). ASEAN Four's middle-income trap dilemma: Evidence of the middle technology trap. *Asian Review of Political Economy*, *3*(1), 1–29. DOI: 10.1007/s44216-024-00033-5

Khieng, S., Madhur, S., & Chhem, R. (Eds.). (2015). *Cambodia education 2015: Employment and empowerment.* Cambodia Development Resource Institute.

Khine, M. S. (2024). Ethics and the future of education in an AI-driven world. In Khine, M. S. (Ed.), *Artificial Intelligence in Education* (pp. 629–735). Springer Nature Singapore., DOI: 10.1007/978-981-97-9350-1_6

Kitamura, Y. (2016). Higher education in Cambodia: Challenges to promote greater access and higher quality. In Collins, C. S., Lee, M. N. N., Hawkins, J. N., & Neubauer, D. E. (Eds.), *The Palgrave handbook of Asia Pacific higher education* (pp. 365–380)., DOI: 10.1057/978-1-137-48739-1_24

Kuleto, V., Ilić, M., Dumangiu, M., Ranković, M., Martins, O. M. D., Păun, D., & Mihoreanu, L. (2021). Exploring opportunities and challenges of artificial intelligence and machine learning in higher education institutions. *Sustainability (Basel)*, *13*(18), 1–16. DOI: 10.3390/su131810424

Kumar, A., Kumar, A., Bhoyar, S., & Mishra, A. K. (2024). Does ChatGPT foster academic misconduct in the future? *Public Administration and Policy*, *27*(2), 140–153. DOI: 10.1108/PAP-05-2023-0061

Kuzhabekova, A., Moldashev, K., Baigazina, A., & Chanchem, V. (2024). Readjustment of returning scholars: Experiences of Cambodian researchers. *Minerva*, *62*(3), 457–479. DOI: 10.1007/s11024-024-09522-6

Luan, H., Geczy, P., Lai, H., Gobert, J., Yang, S. J. H., Ogata, H., Baltes, J., Guerra, R., Li, P., & Tsai, C.-C. (2020). Challenges and future directions of big data and artificial intelligence in education. *Frontiers in Psychology*, *11*, 1–10. DOI: 10.3389/fpsyg.2020.580820

Markauskaite, L., Marrone, R., Poquet, O., Knight, S., Martinez-Maldonado, R., Howard, S., Tondeur, J., De Laat, M., Buckingham Shum, S., Gašević, D., & Siemens, G. (2022). Rethinking the entwinement between artificial intelligence and human learning: What capabilities do learners need for a world with AI? *Computers and Education: Artificial Intelligence*, *3*, 1–16. DOI: 10.1016/j.caeai.2022.100056

McCarthy, J. (2007). From here to human-level AI. *Artificial Intelligence*, *171*(18), 1174–1182. DOI: 10.1016/j.artint.2007.10.009

Mean, U., & Flores, E. (2024). Digital transformation in Cambodian higher education and its impact on teaching and learning outcomes. *Journal of Accounting, Finance, Economics, and Social Sciences*, *9*(1), 23–34. DOI: 10.62458/jafess9(1)3

Mishra, P. (2024). Revolutionizing education with AI and ML. In Ouaissa, M., Ouaissa, M., Lamaazi, H., Hamlaoui, M. E., & Reddy, K. K. (Eds.), *Internet of behavior-based computational intelligence for smart education systems* (pp. 53–94). IGI Global Scientific Publishing., DOI: 10.4018/979-8-3693-8151-9.ch003

Mukhamediev, R. I., Popova, Y., Kuchin, Y., Zaitseva, E., Kalimoldayev, A., Symagulov, A., Levashenko, V., Abdoldina, F., Gopejenko, V., Yakunin, K., Muhamedijeva, E., & Yelis, M. (2022). Review of artificial intelligence and machine learning technologies: Classification, restrictions, opportunities, and challenges. *Mathematics*, *10*(15), 1–25. DOI: 10.3390/math10152552

Nagahisarchoghaei, M., Nur, N., Cummins, L., Nur, N., Karimi, M. M., Nandanwar, S., Bhattacharyya, S., & Rahimi, S. (2023). An empirical survey on explainable AI technologies: Recent trends, use-cases, and categories from technical and application perspectives. *Electronics (Basel)*, *12*(5), 1–59. DOI: 10.3390/electronics12051092

Nur Fitria, T. (2021, December 20). *Artificial intelligence (AI) in education: Using AI tools for the teaching and learning process.*

Ozer, M., Kose, Y., Kucukkaya, G., Mukasheva, A., & Ciris, K. (2025). Adapting to the AI disruption: Reshaping the IT landscape and educational paradigms. In Arabnia, H. R., Deligiannidis, L., Amirian, S., Ghareh Mohammadi, F., & Shenavarmasouleh, F. (Eds.), *Foundations of computer science and frontiers in education: Computer science and computer engineering* (pp. 366–374). Springer Nature Switzerland., DOI: 10.1007/978-3-031-85930-4_33

Petraki, E., & Khat, K. (2022). Challenges and constraints in the design of an ESP course in Cambodia: Implications for higher education institutions. *Asia Pacific Journal of Education, 42*(2), 260–275. DOI: 10.1080/02188791.2020.1798738

Phan, S. (2015). Envisioning a higher education system for the 21st century: Cambodia [University of British Columbia]. DOI: 10.14288/1.0166746

Pokrivcakova, S. (2019). Preparing teachers for the application of AI-powered technologies in foreign language education. *Journal of Language and Cultural Education, 7*(3), 135–153. DOI: 10.2478/jolace-2019-0025

Prabhu, M., & Premraj, J. A. (2025). Artificial consciousness in AI: A posthuman fallacy. *AI & Society, 40*(4), 2995–3008. DOI: 10.1007/s00146-024-02061-4

Sam, R.,, , Zain, A. N. M., & Jamil, H. (2012). Cambodia's higher education development in historical perspectives (1863-2012). *International Journal of Learning and Development, 2*(2), 224–240. DOI: 10.5296/ijld.v2i2.1670

Rashid, A. B., & Kausik, M. A. K. (2024). AI revolutionizing industries worldwide: A comprehensive overview of its diverse applications. *Hybrid Advances, 7*, 1–34. DOI: 10.1016/j.hybadv.2024.100277

Roshanaei, M., Olivares, H., & Lopez, R. R. (2023). Harnessing AI to foster equity in education: Opportunities, challenges, and emerging strategies. *Journal of Intelligent Learning Systems and Applications, 15*(04), 123–143. DOI: 10.4236/jilsa.2023.154009

Sam, C., & Dahles, H. (2017). Stakeholder involvement in the higher education sector in Cambodia. *Studies in Higher Education, 42*(9), 1764–1784. DOI: 10.1080/03075079.2015.1124851

Schiff, D. (2022). Education for AI, not AI for education: The role of education and ethics in national AI policy strategies. *International Journal of Artificial Intelligence in Education, 32*(3), 527–563. DOI: 10.1007/s40593-021-00270-2

Sengul, C., Neykova, R., & Destefanis, G. (2024). Software engineering education in the era of conversational AI: Current trends and future directions. *Frontiers in Artificial Intelligence, 7*, 1–23. DOI: 10.3389/frai.2024.1436350

Seo, K., Tang, J., Roll, I., Fels, S., & Yoon, D. (2021). The impact of artificial intelligence on learner–instructor interaction in online learning. *International Journal of Educational Technology in Higher Education, 18*(1), 1–23. DOI: 10.1186/s41239-021-00292-9

Sok, S., & Bunry, R. (2021). Internationalization of higher education in Cambodia: Toward an agenda for higher education development. *International Journal of Comparative Education and Development, 23*(3), 193–211. DOI: 10.1108/IJCED-08-2020-0049

Song, Y., Weisberg, L. R., Zhang, S., Tian, X., Boyer, K. E., & Israel, M. (2024). A framework for inclusive AI learning design for diverse learners. *Computers and Education: Artificial Intelligence*, *6*, 1–13. DOI: 10.1016/j.caeai.2024.100212

Southworth, J., Migliaccio, K., Glover, J., Glover, J., Reed, D., McCarty, C., Brendemuhl, J., & Thomas, A. (2023). Developing a model for AI Across the curriculum: Transforming the higher education landscape via innovation in AI literacy. *Computers and Education: Artificial Intelligence*, *4*, 1–10. DOI: 10.1016/j.caeai.2023.100127

Srinivasa, K. G., Kurni, M., & Saritha, K. (2022). Harnessing the power of AI in education. In K. G. Srinivasa, M. Kurni, & K. Saritha, *Learning, teaching, and assessment methods for contemporary learners* (pp. 311–342). Springer Nature Singapore. DOI: 10.1007/978-981-19-6734-4_13

Su, J., & Zhong, Y. (2022). Artificial intelligence (AI) in early childhood education: Curriculum design and future directions. *Computers and Education: Artificial Intelligence*, *3*, 1–12. DOI: 10.1016/j.caeai.2022.100072

Takaoka, K., Yamazaki, K., Sakurai, E., Yamashita, K., & Motomura, Y. (2019). Development of an integrated AI platform and an ecosystem for daily life, business, and social problems. In Ahram, T. Z. (Ed.), *Advances in artificial intelligence, software and systems engineering* (pp. 300–309). Springer International Publishing., DOI: 10.1007/978-3-319-94229-2_29

Temper, M., Tjoa, S., & David, L. (2025). Higher Education Act for AI (HEAT-AI): A framework to regulate the usage of AI in higher education institutions. *Frontiers in Education*, *10*, 1–13. DOI: 10.3389/feduc.2025.1505370

Vieriu, A. M., & Petrea, G. (2025). The impact of artificial intelligence (AI) on students' academic development. *Education Sciences*, *15*(3), 343. DOI: 10.3390/educsci15030343

Xiao, H., Liu, C., Hou, F., & Liu, H. (2024). Impact of subsidy on the new type of forestry operating entity's input: Moderating effect of the rising labor cost. *Natural Resources Forum*, *1477*. Advance online publication. DOI: 10.1111/1477-8947.12530

Zawacki-Richter, O., Marín, V. I., Bond, M., & Gouverneur, F. (2019). Systematic review of research on artificial intelligence applications in higher education – where are the educators? *International Journal of Educational Technology in Higher Education*, *16*(1), 1–27. DOI: 10.1186/s41239-019-0171-0

Zhou, C. (2023). Integration of modern technologies in higher education, with the example of artificial intelligence use. *Education and Information Technologies*, *28*(4), 3893–3910. DOI: 10.1007/s10639-022-11309-9

KEY TERMS AND DEFINITIONS

AI-Assisted Care Services: AI-assisted care services denote the incorporation of artificial intelligence technologies into healthcare and caring, particularly for at-risk groups, including the elderly, disabled, and children. These services may encompass intelligent monitoring systems, predictive health technologies, and assistive robotics, which enhance the efficacy and quality of care. In higher education, formulating courses centered on AI-assisted care prepares students with the competencies necessary to aid aging populations and address increasing social demands in a post-COVID context.

Collaborative Curriculum: Collaborative curriculum entails alliances between universities and external entities, such as AI firms, care service providers, and community organizations, to jointly create educational programs. These collaborations seek to furnish students with practical experience and real-world skills using simulation systems and competency-based learning. This methodology guarantees that academic material stays pertinent and adaptable to labor market requirements and societal issues.

Digital Transformation in Education: Digital transformation in education denotes the transition from conventional pedagogical approaches to the incorporation of digital tools and artificial intelligence technology into learning contexts. It underscores active, student-centered pedagogies in which learners engage with AI tools to acquire practical experience. This change equips students for a swiftly changing digital landscape and prompts them to critically assess the ethical and practical ramifications of technology utilization.

Human-AI Collaboration: Human-AI collaboration underscores the necessity of perceiving AI as an auxiliary instrument rather than a substitute for human positions. Educational techniques ought to instruct students on collaborating with AI to augment productivity and decision-making in sectors such as healthcare, law, and education. Advocating this perspective guarantees that graduates comprehend AI's function in enhancing human abilities rather than jeopardizing jobs or professional significance.

Interdisciplinary Programs: Interdisciplinary programs integrate expertise from various academic disciplines, such as engineering, ethics, education, and policy, to tackle complex topics like AI development and its societal implications. These programs promote comprehensive thinking and innovation, allowing students to devise solutions that are both technically robust and socially accountable. In Cambodia, these programs are essential for developing well-rounded individuals capable of facilitating AI integration across many sectors.

Chapter 8
Integrating AI Education Strategies for Future-Proofing Curriculum Design in Omani Universities

Raed Awashreh
https://orcid.org/0000-0002-2252-0299
United Arab Emirates University, UAE

ABSTRACT

The integration of artificial intelligence (AI) in Omani higher education is essential for enhancing learning experiences, improving institutional efficiency, and aligning with Oman Vision 2040. This study proposes an AI Integration Framework, outlining key elements such as strategic alignment, policy governance, technological infrastructure, curriculum development, and ethical AI implementation. It emphasizes AI-driven decision-making, public-private partnerships, and continuous evaluation to ensure sustainable adoption. By fostering AI research and innovation, Oman can position its universities as hubs for technological advancement, equipping students with the necessary skills for a digital future while ensuring ethical and culturally relevant AI implementation.

INTRODUCTION

The rapid advancement of artificial intelligence (AI) is reshaping the education landscape worldwide. Universities are increasingly recognizing the need to integrate AI into their curriculum to equip students with the skills required for the evolving digital economy. In Oman, this transformation aligns with the national priorities outlined in Vision 2040, which emphasizes digital transformation and innovation-driven development (Awashreh & Hamid, 2025). However, while the potential benefits of AI-driven education are widely acknowledged, Omani universities

DOI: 10.4018/979-8-3373-2752-5.ch008

face several challenges in implementing AI-focused curriculum reforms. Institutional resistance, limited faculty readiness, and infrastructural constraints are key barriers that hinder the seamless integration of AI into higher education (Kamalov et al., 2023).

Despite the growing significance of AI in education, traditional teaching methodologies continue to dominate in Omani universities, limiting students' exposure to AI-driven learning experiences. Additionally, faculty members often lack the necessary expertise in AI-based pedagogies, and the absence of standardized policies further restricts progress (Degni, 2024). Without a clear roadmap for AI adoption, higher education institutions risk falling behind in preparing graduates for an increasingly AI-driven job market. Addressing these challenges requires a strategic approach that not only enhances AI integration in curricula but also aligns with national development goals (Awashreh, 2025a).

This research aims to explore effective strategies for embedding AI into curriculum design in Omani universities to enhance education quality and better prepare graduates for future workforce demands. Specifically, the study examines how AI contributes to data-driven decision-making in curriculum development, identifies key challenges in implementing AI-driven strategies, and provides policy recommendations to support AI adoption. Additionally, it explores the role of public-private partnerships (PPPs) in facilitating AI-driven educational transformation.

To achieve these objectives, the study seeks to answer the following research questions:

- How does AI contribute to data-driven decision-making in curriculum enhancement?
- What are the key challenges in implementing AI-driven strategies in Omani universities?
- What policy recommendations can support AI adoption in Omani higher education?
- How can public-private partnerships (PPPs) enhance AI adoption in Omani universities?

By addressing these questions, this research aims to contribute valuable insights that will guide policymakers, educators, and university administrators in fostering a future-ready education system in Oman. The study is structured as follows: literature review, methods, results, proposed framework, discussion, and conclusion. Each section provides detailed information to support the overall understanding of the topic.

LITERATURE REVIEW

The rapid advancement of artificial intelligence (AI) has prompted a global shift in higher education, necessitating the integration of AI-driven strategies into curriculum design. Within the context of Omani universities, the effectiveness of such integration remains a critical area of inquiry, particularly concerning the barriers to adoption, alignment with Oman Vision 2040, and the policies required to facilitate a seamless transition. This literature review critically examines existing research, debates, and theoretical perspectives on AI in higher education while situating these insights within the broader landscape of leadership, policy, and technological transformation (Bahroun et al., 2023).

AI adoption in education has been widely recognized for its potential to enhance personalization, efficiency, and innovation. Awashreh and Hassiba (2025) highlight AI's role in revolutionizing training programs through adaptive learning and predictive analytics, ensuring alignment with evolving workforce demands. However, while the benefits are promising, critiques surrounding

AI's ethical implications remain prevalent. Concerns related to data privacy, algorithmic biases, and over-reliance on technology underscore the necessity for accountability frameworks to prevent AI-driven education from exacerbating existing inequalities (Awashreh, 2024b). These ethical dilemmas call for a structured approach to AI implementation that prioritizes transparency and fairness.

The strategic resilience of educational institutions in managing technological disruptions is another pressing consideration. Awashreh (2025b) presents a resilience framework specifically designed for private universities, advocating for data-driven decision-making and diversified funding mechanisms. This perspective aligns with the broader imperative of safeguarding educational quality amidst financial constraints that may otherwise hinder AI adoption. In this regard, strategic planning plays a pivotal role in ensuring AI integration is both sustainable and beneficial to all stakeholders involved (Shwedeh et al., 2024).

Leadership is a crucial determinant of AI adoption success in higher education. Awashreh (2025a) underscores the importance of visionary leadership in driving digital transformation, promoting sustainability, and addressing globalization challenges. The capacity of university leaders to cultivate a culture of AI-driven innovation while maintaining ethical considerations is essential for achieving long-term success. Furthermore, leadership dynamics significantly influence how AI is incorporated into curriculum structures. Awashreh (2025c) explores the duality of leadership styles, emphasizing that excessive micromanagement or manipulative tendencies can stifle innovation. Effective leadership, therefore, requires a balanced approach that fosters collaboration, ensures equitable implementation, and mitigates resistance to technological change.

Despite the potential advantages, several challenges hinder AI adoption in Omani universities. Cultural factors play a pivotal role in shaping attitudes toward education and technology. Awashreh and Al Ghunaimi (2025a) identify collectivist values and weak intrinsic motivation among students as barriers to embracing AI-enhanced learning models. Additionally, gaps in foundational skills—particularly in English and Computer Science—limit students' ability to effectively engage with AI-driven curricula. Addressing these challenges requires targeted interventions that enhance digital literacy and promote an adaptive learning culture (AlSaadi & Awashreh, 2025).

Financial and policy constraints further exacerbate the difficulties associated with AI integration. Awashreh (2024a) highlights financial instability within private universities and insufficient institutional support as major obstacles. While Oman Vision 2040 emphasizes digital transformation as a national priority, the extent to which existing policies actively support universities in this transition remains an area of debate. The effectiveness of AI adoption hinges on the alignment between national policy directives and institutional capacities, making it imperative to bridge the gap between ambition and practical implementation.

For AI to be successfully embedded within Omani universities, comprehensive policy reforms and strategic initiatives are necessary. Existing literature suggests several key areas for intervention:

1. **Ethical AI Implementation**: Establishing robust data security measures and accountability frameworks to safeguard student privacy and mitigate biases (Awashreh, 2024b).
2. **Leadership Development**: Training university leaders in AI-driven decision-making and innovation management to ensure informed and strategic adoption (Awashreh, 2025a).
3. **Curriculum Overhaul**: Incorporating AI-driven methodologies into foundational courses to bridge gaps in technical and digital literacy (Awashreh & Al Ghunaimi, 2025 a).

4. **Financial Sustainability Strategies**: Implementing diversified funding models, including public-private partnerships, to support AI integration (Awashreh, 2025b).
5. **Stakeholder Engagement**: Establishing continuous dialogue with students, educators, and policymakers to align AI adoption with educational equity and labor market demands (Awashreh & Mohamed, 2024).

The integration of AI into curriculum design in Omani universities presents both opportunities and challenges. While AI has the potential to enhance education quality and workforce preparedness, its implementation must be guided by strong leadership, ethical considerations, and strategic policy interventions. The literature underscores the need for a balanced approach that fosters innovation while ensuring educational equity, data security, and institutional resilience. Future research should further explore the practical implications of AI-driven education models in Oman, ensuring their alignment with both national development goals and global academic standards.

METHODS

This study employs a qualitative research method, utilizing a secondary research method to explore the integration of artificial intelligence (AI) in the curriculum design of Omani universities, identify the challenges hindering AI adoption, assess the potential benefits of AI-driven strategies, and propose relevant policy recommendations for facilitating seamless AI integration. The research design is structured to provide in-depth insights into the current state of AI in higher education institutions in Oman, as well as to explore the barriers, opportunities, and best practices for AI adoption. The Methodology has two major elements:

- Literature Review: Examination of existing studies on AI integration in education, providing examples where possible.
- Framework Development: Creation of an AI-driven curriculum design model tailored to the Omani higher education context.

To answer the research questions, the chapter reviewed 52 research articles, 51 of which are relatively recent.

RESULTS

This section provides the results of the main question asked in this chapter. To make it easier to understand, here is figure (1) that illustrates the results.

Figure 1. AI Application and Policy Recommendations for Curriculum Design. It visually represents the main topics and their relationships from your text, outlining how various AI applications in curriculum design are connected to the associated policy recommendations

AI Integration in Omani Curriculum

The current level of AI integration in curriculum design across Omani universities is still in its early stages, characterized by partial adoption of AI-driven technologies. While certain institutions have implemented AI-powered virtual learning platforms, automated grading systems, and adaptive learning tools, the overall landscape lacks a cohesive and systematic approach to AI integration. These technologies are primarily used as supplementary tools rather than core components of the educational framework, reflecting a fragmented implementation strategy rather than a structured, institution-wide adoption (Lawrence, Othmani & Dalwai, 2024). The absence of standardized policies or guidelines on AI adoption further exacerbates inconsistencies in how these tools are utilized across different universities.

Faculty awareness and training on AI applications remain inconsistent, posing a significant challenge to effective integration. While some universities offer professional development programs focused on AI in education, many faculty members have limited exposure to the practical applications of AI in curriculum design. A lack of formalized AI training programs means that instructors often rely on traditional teaching methods, reducing the potential impact of AI-driven learning enhancements. This knowledge gap hinders the development of AI-enhanced pedagogical strategies and limits faculty members' ability to leverage AI for curriculum innovation (Delello et al., 2025).

Another key issue is the disparity in AI adoption between private and public universities. Some private universities, particularly those with international affiliations, have been more proactive in adopting AI technologies due to their greater financial flexibility and exposure to global best practices. These institutions have experimented with AI-driven personalized learning, student performance analytics, and virtual tutors. In contrast, public universities, constrained by bureaucratic decision-making processes and financial limitations, have been slower in integrating AI into their educational models. The reliance on government funding and centralized policy directives means that AI adoption in public institutions largely depends on national-level initiatives, which are still evolving (Mijan, Hasan & Hasan, 2025).

Moreover, AI integration in Omani universities is often confined to administrative functions rather than core academic activities. Automated systems for student enrollment, exam scheduling, and plagiarism detection have been widely implemented, demonstrating AI's utility in streamlining institutional operations (Asri, 2024). However, AI's potential to transform curriculum design and teaching methodologies remains underdeveloped. Few universities have incorporated AI into subject-specific learning, such as using machine learning models in data science courses or AI-assisted simulations in engineering and medical education. The lack of interdisciplinary collaboration between AI researchers and educators further hampers the seamless integration of AI into academic programs (Awashreh, 2014 b).

Student engagement with AI-driven learning remains another critical aspect of AI integration. While many students interact with AI-powered learning management systems, their exposure to AI as a tool for knowledge creation and skill development is minimal. A key limitation is the lack of AI literacy among students, particularly in non-technical disciplines (Bognár & Khine, 2025). Most AI-driven educational initiatives focus on technology-related courses, leaving students from humanities, business, and social sciences with limited opportunities to engage with AI-enhanced learning experiences. This narrow scope of implementation restricts AI's transformative potential across diverse fields of study (Walter, 2024).

Infrastructure and resource constraints further complicate AI adoption. Many universities lack the necessary computing power, software tools, and technical expertise required to support AI-driven education. While some institutions have made investments in digital transformation, these efforts are often limited to pilot projects rather than full-scale AI integration. The absence of dedicated AI research centers or collaborative hubs within universities also reduces opportunities for faculty and students to explore AI applications in education. Without sustained investment in infrastructure, AI adoption will continue to face operational hurdles that limit its scalability and effectiveness (Ali et al., 2024).

From a policy perspective, the alignment of AI adoption with Oman Vision 2040 remains an area of concern. While the national vision emphasizes digital transformation and innovation, there is a gap between policy aspirations and actual implementation in higher education. Universities require clearer guidelines, funding support, and institutional strategies to facilitate AI-driven curriculum enhancements. Without a national AI strategy specifically tailored for higher education, the integration of AI into curriculum design will remain ad hoc and inconsistent (Awashreh, 2025 d).

Overall, while AI technologies have made inroads into Omani universities, their role in curriculum design remains limited. The lack of faculty training, infrastructural gaps, inconsistent adoption across institutions, and the absence of clear policy frameworks are key barriers to widespread AI integration. Addressing these challenges requires a more coordinated approach, including faculty development programs, investment in AI research and infrastructure, interdisciplinary collaboration, and policy-driven initiatives that align AI adoption with national educational goals. Moving forward, a structured roadmap for AI integration is essential to ensure that universities can fully leverage AI's potential to enhance learning outcomes, foster innovation, and prepare students for the evolving demands of the digital economy (Chan, 2023).

Challenges to AI Adoption in Omani Higher Education

The adoption of artificial intelligence (AI) in higher education institutions in Oman faces several significant challenges that have hindered its integration into curriculum design and pedagogical practices. These challenges arise from technological limitations, institutional resistance, cultural attitudes, financial constraints, and regulatory gaps. While AI has the potential to revolutionize higher education by enhancing teaching efficiency, fostering personalized learning experiences, and streamlining administrative processes, its successful adoption requires addressing these barriers in a systematic and strategic manner (Akinwalere & Ivanov, 2022).

One of the most pressing obstacles to AI adoption in Omani universities is the presence of technological barriers. Many institutions struggle with outdated digital infrastructure that lacks the capacity to support AI-powered tools effectively. Existing learning management systems (LMS) are often not integrated with AI-enhanced solutions, limiting the ability to implement advanced analytics, automated feedback mechanisms, and adaptive learning platforms. In several cases, universities rely on legacy systems designed for conventional online learning rather than AI-driven pedagogy (Al-Senaidi, Lipsmeyer & Poirot, 2009). As a result, even when AI technologies are introduced, they remain underutilized due to compatibility issues with existing infrastructure. Furthermore, access to high-performance computing resources, cloud-based AI platforms, and advanced software solutions is limited, restricting universities' ability to experiment with AI-driven educational models. This digital divide not only affects the quality of education but also limits students' and faculty members' exposure to cutting-edge AI applications, thereby reducing the overall preparedness for AI-driven transformations in higher education (Ali et al., 2024).

Institutional resistance to AI adoption also represents a major challenge, particularly among faculty members who are concerned about the impact of AI on traditional teaching roles. Many educators view AI-powered tools, such as automated grading systems and virtual tutors, as potential replacements for human instructors, raising fears of job displacement and loss of academic authority. Additionally, faculty members often lack the necessary training and professional development opportunities to integrate AI into their teaching practices effectively (Hazzan-Bishara, Kol & Levy, 2025). Without structured AI literacy programs, many educators remain hesitant to adopt AI-enhanced teaching methodologies, further slowing the transition toward AI-driven education. Resistance is also evident in administrative processes, where decision-makers may be reluctant to invest in AI solutions due to uncertainty about their long-term impact and effectiveness. Institutional inertia, coupled with a lack of clear incentives for faculty to engage with AI-driven education, further exacerbates the slow pace of adoption (Strielkowski et al., 2024).

Cultural attitudes toward AI in education also play a significant role in shaping resistance to its adoption. In Omani society, education has traditionally been viewed as a deeply human-centric endeavor, emphasizing personal mentorship, direct student-teacher engagement, and collective learning experiences. The introduction of AI-powered tools in education has been met with skepticism, particularly in disciplines that rely heavily on interpersonal interactions, such as the humanities, social sciences, and medical education (Awashreh & AL Ghunaimi, 2025 a). Some educators and students perceive AI as impersonal and mechanical, fearing that an overreliance on AI-driven learning platforms may undermine the development of critical thinking, creativity, and social skills. Additionally, there is a prevailing perception that AI lacks the emotional intelligence required for effective teaching, reinforcing the belief that AI should remain a supplementary tool rather than a core component of higher education. These cultural concerns must be carefully addressed through awareness campaigns, stakeholder engagement, and gradual integration strategies that emphasize the complementary role of AI, rather than its replacement of human instruction (Al-Zahrani, 2024).

Financial constraints pose another major hurdle to AI adoption in higher education institutions, particularly in private universities that rely on tuition-based revenue models. AI integration requires substantial investment in research, infrastructure development, faculty training, and continuous technological upgrades. Many universities in Oman operate under tight budgetary constraints, making it difficult to allocate sufficient funds for AI-driven initiatives. The high costs associated with acquiring AI-powered tools, upgrading digital infrastructure, and hiring AI specialists further limit the ability of institutions to implement comprehensive AI strategies (Michel-Villarreal et al., 2023). While some government-funded universities receive support for digital transformation initiatives, private universities often struggle to secure financial resources for AI adoption. The absence of diversified funding models, such as public-private partnerships, industry collaborations, and external research grants, exacerbates the financial barriers to AI-driven education. To overcome these challenges, universities need to explore sustainable funding mechanisms that can support AI adoption without placing an excessive financial burden on students or institutions (Awashreh, 2024).

Regulatory gaps further complicate AI integration in higher education, despite Oman Vision 2040's emphasis on digital transformation. While national policies highlight the importance of technology-driven education, there is a lack of clear regulatory frameworks guiding AI adoption in universities. The absence of standardized policies on AI ethics, data security, curriculum integration, and faculty training leaves universities without structured implementation strategies. Without explicit guidelines on AI governance, institutions face challenges in ensuring data privacy, mitigating algorithmic biases, and addressing ethical concerns related to AI-driven decision-making (Al Hasani & Husin, 2021). The lack of coordination between regulatory bodies, academic institutions, and industry stakeholders further hampers the development of cohesive AI policies that align with national education goals. Universities require comprehensive policy frameworks that provide clear directives on AI adoption, ethical considerations, and long-term sustainability to facilitate a seamless transition to AI-driven education (Michel-Villarreal et al., 2023).

In summary, while AI has the potential to transform higher education in Oman, several key challenges must be addressed to enable its successful adoption. Technological limitations, faculty resistance, cultural perceptions, financial constraints, and regulatory gaps all contribute to the slow integration of AI into university curricula. Overcoming these challenges requires a multi-pronged approach that includes investments in digital infrastructure, faculty development programs, awareness campaigns to shift cultural attitudes, sustainable funding strategies, and the establishment of clear regulatory frameworks (Singun, 2025). By addressing these barriers strategically, Omani universities can unlock the full potential of AI in enhancing education quality, fostering innovation, and aligning with the broader goals of Oman Vision 2040.

Enhancing Curriculum with AI Strategies

The findings suggest that AI-driven strategies hold significant potential to enhance the effectiveness of curriculum design and teaching methodologies in Omani universities. By leveraging artificial intelligence, institutions can create more dynamic, personalized, and efficient learning environments that cater to diverse student needs. The implementation of AI-powered technologies not only improves the quality of education but also optimizes faculty workloads, enhances assessment methods, and fosters data-driven decision-making. However, to fully realize these benefits, universities must integrate AI-driven strategies systematically and address challenges related to technological readiness, faculty adoption, and institutional support (Lawrence, Othmani & Dalwai, 2024).

One of the most promising applications of AI in curriculum design is adaptive learning technology, which tailors educational content based on individual student progress. AI-powered platforms analyze student performance in real-time, identifying strengths, weaknesses, and learning preferences to adjust instructional materials accordingly. This personalized approach ensures that students receive content suited to their specific needs, allowing them to progress at their own pace while reinforcing areas where they require additional support. Adaptive learning systems also enable faculty members to monitor student engagement and intervene when necessary, fostering a more responsive and student-centered learning environment. In Omani universities, where students come from diverse academic backgrounds and exhibit varying levels of digital literacy, adaptive learning can bridge learning gaps and promote academic success by catering to individual learning styles (Gligorea et al., 2023).

AI-enabled assessments represent another critical advancement in enhancing curriculum effectiveness. Traditional evaluation methods often suffer from subjectivity, inefficiency, and delays in providing feedback. AI-driven assessment tools, such as automated grading systems and intelligent feedback mechanisms, streamline the evaluation process by offering real-time, data-driven insights into student performance. These systems can analyze written responses, detect patterns in student answers, and provide personalized feedback to guide learning improvements. Automated assessments also reduce faculty workload, allowing educators to focus on more complex aspects of student development, such as critical thinking and analytical skills. In disciplines requiring frequent assessments, such as engineering, business, and medical education, AI-enabled evaluation tools can improve grading accuracy, enhance fairness, and ensure timely feedback, ultimately benefiting both students and instructors (Saputra et al., 2024).

AI-augmented teaching is another area where artificial intelligence can revolutionize higher education. Virtual tutors and AI-driven instructional design tools can support faculty in optimizing course content delivery. AI-powered tutoring systems offer students 24/7 access to learning support, addressing queries, explaining complex concepts, and providing additional practice exercises. This is particularly beneficial in courses with high student enrollment, where individual faculty attention is limited. Furthermore, AI-driven instructional design platforms assist educators in structuring courses more effectively by recommending content sequences, identifying knowledge gaps, and suggesting interactive teaching strategies. These technologies empower faculty members to refine their teaching methods and focus on higher-order pedagogical tasks that require human expertise. However, the successful integration of AI-augmented teaching requires faculty training and institutional support to ensure educators can harness AI tools effectively rather than perceiving them as replacements for traditional instruction (Wang et al., 2024).

Data-driven decision-making is another crucial aspect of AI's role in curriculum enhancement. AI-powered analytics provide universities with valuable insights into student learning patterns, engagement levels, and academic performance trends. By analyzing vast amounts of student data, AI can predict at-risk students, identify factors contributing to academic challenges, and suggest targeted interventions to improve retention rates and overall educational outcomes. University administrators can use AI-generated reports to refine curriculum structures, adjust teaching methodologies, and allocate resources more effectively. Additionally, AI-driven analytics support evidence-based policymaking by identifying gaps in curriculum design, evaluating the impact of educational reforms, and guiding faculty development initiatives. The ability to make informed, data-driven decisions enhances institutional effectiveness and ensures that curriculum improvements align with evolving academic and industry demands (Vieriu & Petrea, 2025).

Despite the promising advantages of AI-driven strategies, their successful implementation in Omani universities requires addressing several challenges. Faculty members need adequate training and professional development to utilize AI tools effectively and integrate them into their teaching practices. Institutional investment in AI infrastructure, including advanced computing systems and digital learning platforms, is essential for supporting AI-driven initiatives (Jomaa, Attamimi & Al Mahri, 2025). Additionally, universities must establish ethical guidelines for AI use in education to ensure data privacy, prevent algorithmic biases, and uphold academic integrity. By adopting a structured approach that combines technology, pedagogy, and policy support, Omani universities can harness AI's potential to enhance curriculum design, improve learning outcomes, and align higher education with national development goals (Alsaadi & Awashreh, 2025).

In summary, AI-driven strategies offer transformative opportunities for enhancing curriculum effectiveness and teaching methodologies in Omani higher education institutions. Through adaptive learning technologies, AI-enabled assessments, AI-augmented teaching, and data-driven decision-making, universities can create more personalized, efficient, and student-centered learning environments. However, realizing these benefits requires a comprehensive approach that includes faculty training, institutional investment, and robust policy frameworks. As Oman advances toward its Vision 2040 goals, integrating AI into higher education can play a pivotal role in fostering innovation, improving educational quality, and preparing students for the demands of a technology-driven global economy (Gligorea et al., 2023).

AI Adoption Policy Recommendations

To ensure a structured and effective AI integration process in higher education, it is crucial to develop and implement comprehensive policy recommendations that address both immediate and long-term needs. AI adoption in universities requires a strategic approach that aligns with national development goals, strengthens institutional capabilities, and fosters collaboration among key stakeholders. Without clear regulatory frameworks, adequate infrastructure, and ethical considerations, AI integration risks becoming fragmented or ineffective (Funa & Gabay, 2025). The following policy recommendations aim to facilitate the seamless incorporation of AI into Omani higher education institutions while ensuring sustainability, ethical governance, and alignment with Oman Vision 2040.

One of the primary steps toward AI adoption is the development of national AI adoption guidelines tailored to higher education. These guidelines should establish clear regulatory frameworks that outline AI implementation strategies in universities, ensuring standardization and consistency across institutions. The framework should provide universities with structured pathways for AI integration, including curriculum development, faculty training, and student engagement with AI-driven tools (Shwedeh et al., 2024). Moreover, the guidelines must align with Oman Vision 2040's emphasis on digital transformation, ensuring that AI adoption contributes to the country's broader economic and educational objectives. A national AI policy for higher education would also help address regulatory gaps, define ethical considerations, and provide universities with a roadmap for phased implementation. By setting national standards, policymakers can ensure that AI is leveraged effectively across all universities, avoiding disparities in technological advancement between institutions (Shwedeh et al., 2024).

Investment in AI infrastructure and training is another critical policy recommendation. The integration of AI in higher education necessitates advanced digital ecosystems that include AI-powered learning platforms, high-performance computing systems, and cloud-based educational technologies (Awashreh, 2023). To bridge existing technological gaps, both the government and private sector must collaborate to fund AI infrastructure development in universities. Public investment should focus on equipping universities with state-of-the-art AI laboratories, smart classrooms, and AI-driven learning management systems. Additionally, faculty training programs must be prioritized to enhance AI literacy among educators (Awashreh, 2024). Many faculty members lack the necessary skills to integrate AI into their teaching methodologies effectively, which can hinder AI adoption. Establishing AI training programs and professional development workshops will ensure that faculty members are well-prepared to incorporate AI tools into curriculum design and student assessments. Government support in funding AI training initiatives will be essential in accelerating faculty readiness and institutional capacity for AI adoption (Khairullah et al., 2025).

Incorporating AI ethics and governance policies is crucial to ensuring responsible AI implementation in higher education. As AI-driven tools become increasingly integrated into learning environments, concerns about data privacy, algorithmic biases, and ethical implications must be addressed. Universities should establish AI ethics committees responsible for overseeing AI applications in education, ensuring that AI-powered tools are deployed transparently and fairly (Awashreh, 2024b). Additionally, governance policies should focus on safeguarding student data privacy, preventing the misuse of AI in academic evaluations, and ensuring that AI-based decision-making processes remain accountable to human oversight. Ethical guidelines must also address concerns about AI replacing human educators, emphasizing AI's role as a complement rather than a substitute for traditional teaching methods. By embedding ethical considerations into AI adoption policies, universities can foster trust in AI technologies and promote responsible innovation in higher education (Awashreh & Ramachandran, 2024).

Encouraging public-private partnerships is another key recommendation to accelerate AI adoption and ensure long-term sustainability. AI implementation in universities requires substantial financial investment, technological expertise, and continuous innovation, which can be facilitated through collaboration between government entities, universities, and private technology firms. Public-private partnerships (PPPs) can support AI integration by providing universities with access to cutting-edge AI solutions, research funding, and industry-driven AI applications (Shwedeh et al., 2024). For example, partnerships with leading AI companies can enable universities to deploy AI-powered virtual learning assistants, intelligent tutoring systems, and advanced data analytics tools. Additionally, PPPs can facilitate AI-related internships and training opportunities for students, ensuring that graduates possess industry-relevant AI competencies. By fostering strong partnerships between academia and the private sector, universities can enhance their AI capabilities while contributing to Oman's knowledge-based economy (Awashreh, 2023).

Promoting AI research and innovation within universities is essential for fostering local expertise and developing AI solutions tailored to Oman's educational landscape. To drive AI-related innovation, universities should establish AI research centers that focus on applied research in

AI-driven education. Interdisciplinary programs that integrate AI with fields such as education, business, and engineering can also encourage collaborative research initiatives (Kamalov et al., 2023). Additionally, research funding should be allocated to explore AI's impact on student learning outcomes, curriculum design, and institutional performance. By positioning universities as hubs for AI research and development, Oman can cultivate a new generation of AI experts who contribute to both academic advancements and industry applications. Furthermore, research-driven AI policies can help universities stay ahead of global educational trends and ensure that AI adoption is tailored to the specific needs of Omani students and faculty (Vieriu & Petrea, 2025).

In conclusion, the successful adoption of AI in Omani higher education requires a structured approach that includes regulatory frameworks, technological investment, ethical governance, strategic partnerships, and research-driven innovation. By developing national AI adoption guidelines, investing in AI infrastructure and faculty training, ensuring ethical AI governance, fostering public-private collaborations, and promoting AI research, Oman can create a higher education system that is technologically advanced, student-centered, and globally competitive. These policy recommendations align with Oman Vision 2040 and position AI as a transformative force that enhances learning experiences, improves institutional efficiency, and prepares students for the demands of a digital future (Demaidi, 2023).

PROPOSED FRAMEWORK

This section presents the AI Integration Framework for Omani Higher Education. Table 1 outlines the framework, showing the interconnected areas that contribute to the successful integration of AI in Omani universities, from strategic alignment to continuous evaluation

Table 1. AI Integration Framework for Omani Higher Education

Section	Key Elements
Vision and Strategic Alignment	AI as a tool for educational transformation; Support for Oman's national goals.
Policy and Governance Structure	National AI adoption guidelines; Clear strategies for AI integration.
Technological Infrastructure and Capacity Building	Investment in AI infrastructure; Faculty training in AI tools.
Curriculum Design and Teaching Methodologies	Adaptive learning platforms; AI-driven assessments and teaching tools.
Data-Driven Decision Making	AI analytics for educational insights; Data for curriculum improvement.
Collaboration and Partnerships	Public-private partnerships; Industry collaboration for AI tools.
Ethical AI Implementation	Ethical guidelines for AI use; Cultural considerations in AI adoption.
Continuous Evaluation and Improvement	Regular evaluation of AI impact; Long-term sustainability of AI initiatives.

Source: developed by Author, 2024

1. Vision and Strategic Alignment

The objective is to integrate AI into Omani higher education institutions to enhance curriculum effectiveness, teaching methodologies, and student learning outcomes. This integration will align with Oman Vision 2040, ensuring that AI adoption supports the country's broader educational and digital transformation goals. Key areas of focus include utilizing AI as a tool to improve educational quality, address national development goals, and foster innovation. Furthermore, AI initiatives will be aligned with Vision 2040's emphasis on transforming Omani universities into technology-driven, globally competitive institutions, preparing students for the demands of a rapidly evolving digital landscape (Lawrence, Othmani & Dalwai, 2024).

2. Policy and Governance Structure
    - **National AI Adoption Guidelines**

The objective of the National AI Adoption Guidelines is to develop and implement clear, standardized strategies for AI integration in Omani higher education institutions. Key elements include the standardization of AI adoption across universities, ensuring a unified approach to incorporating AI into curriculum development, faculty training, and student engagement. The guidelines will emphasize the ethical use of AI, ensuring transparency, privacy, and fairness in its application. Additionally, the policy frameworks will align with Oman's economic and educational priorities, supporting the country's broader vision of digital transformation and innovation in higher education (Shwedeh et al., 2024).

- **AI Ethics and Governance Policies**

The objective is to establish robust governance structures and ethical guidelines for AI use in higher education. Key elements include the creation of AI ethics committees to oversee AI applications, ensuring that AI tools are used responsibly and ethically. These committees will focus on safeguarding student data privacy and ensuring that AI-based decision-making remains accountable and transparent. Additionally, the guidelines will emphasize preventing AI from replacing human educators, reinforcing its role as a complementary tool to support, rather than replace, traditional teaching methods. Finally, transparency in AI's role in curriculum design and assessment will ensure that AI's impact on education is clear and aligned with institutional goals (Nguyen et al., 2023).

3. Technological Infrastructure and Capacity Building
    - **Investment in AI Infrastructure**

The objective is to equip universities with the necessary technological infrastructure to support AI adoption in higher education. Key elements include establishing AI laboratories, smart classrooms, and cloud-based learning platforms to create an environment conducive to AI integration. Universities should also upgrade computing systems to support AI-driven learning management systems (LMS), ensuring seamless interaction with AI tools. Additionally, access to high-performance computing and AI-driven educational technologies will be essential to support the development and deployment of advanced AI applications, enabling institutions to effectively enhance the learning experience for students and faculty alike (Lytras et al., 2024).

- **Faculty Training and Professional Development**

The objective is to enhance AI literacy among faculty members, enabling them to integrate AI tools effectively into their teaching practices. Key elements include developing and implementing AI training programs specifically designed for educators, ensuring they acquire the necessary skills to utilize AI technologies in their teaching and curriculum design. Hosting professional development workshops focusing on AI applications in education will provide faculty with hands-on experience and up-to-date knowledge on how to integrate AI effectively. Additionally, fostering ongoing professional growth in AI-related areas will ensure that educators continue to evolve with emerging AI technologies, maintaining their ability to leverage these tools to enhance the learning experience (Ding et al., 2024).

4. Curriculum Design and Teaching Methodologies
   - **Adaptive Learning and Personalization**

The objective is to use AI to create personalized learning experiences and adaptive curricula that cater to the individual needs of students. Key elements include integrating AI-driven adaptive learning platforms that adjust content based on students' progress, enabling more tailored and effective learning pathways. These platforms facilitate real-time tracking of student performance, allowing educators to identify students' strengths, weaknesses, and learning preferences. By offering personalized feedback, AI systems ensure that students receive the support they need in areas where they struggle, while reinforcing their strengths, thus fostering an inclusive learning environment that meets diverse student needs (Ellikkal & Rajamohan, 2024).

- **AI-Enabled Assessments**

The objective is to automate and optimize student assessments through AI to enhance grading efficiency and accuracy. Key elements include implementing AI-powered grading systems for objective assessments, which help streamline the grading process and reduce the time required for evaluation. AI can also be used to detect patterns in student responses, providing personalized feedback that guides student improvement. By leveraging AI, institutions can ensure fair, accurate, and timely evaluations, ultimately reducing faculty workload and allowing educators to focus on more complex aspects of student development while maintaining high assessment standards (Twabu & Nakene-Mginqi, 2024).

- **AI-Augmented Teaching Tools**

The objective is to integrate AI to enhance teaching delivery and student engagement by providing educators with advanced tools to improve instructional effectiveness. Key elements include using AI-powered virtual tutors and learning assistants available 24/7, allowing students to access support outside of class hours. AI can also suggest instructional strategies, content sequencing, and identify knowledge gaps, helping educators structure courses more effectively. Furthermore, AI-driven instructional design platforms offer faculty members the opportunity to enhance their pedagogical practices by recommending optimal content and interactive teaching methods, ultimately improving the learning experience for students (Xu, 2024).

5. Data-Driven Decision Making and Institutional Support

- **AI-Driven Analytics for Educational Insights**

The objective is to leverage AI-driven analytics to gather and analyze data, enhancing decision-making and curriculum design. Key elements include utilizing AI analytics to assess student engagement, performance trends, and learning patterns, allowing institutions to gain valuable insights into the effectiveness of their teaching methods. AI can also predict at-risk students by identifying early warning signs, enabling targeted interventions to provide timely support. Additionally, data insights can be used to refine curriculum structures and teaching methodologies, ensuring they align with student needs and improve overall educational outcomes (Sajja et al., 2023).

- **Institutional Support and Resource Allocation**

The objective is to provide universities with the necessary resources and support for effective AI integration. Key elements include allocating adequate resources to implement AI-driven initiatives, ensuring that the infrastructure and technological tools required for AI adoption are available. Support for universities in developing AI-related infrastructure and providing faculty training is essential for successful implementation. Additionally, it is crucial to ensure that AI adoption is prioritized by higher education leaders and administrators, reinforcing the importance of AI in the long-term strategic goals of the institution (Shwedeh et al., 2024).

6. Collaboration and Partnerships
   - **Public-Private Partnerships (PPPs)**

The objective of fostering Public-Private Partnerships (PPPs) is to accelerate AI integration in higher education by fostering collaboration between government entities, universities, and the private sector (Awashreh, 2023). This can be achieved by collaborating with technology firms to access cutting-edge AI solutions, engaging industry leaders to provide innovative AI-driven learning tools such as intelligent tutoring systems, and facilitating internships and training opportunities for students in AI-related fields. Through these partnerships, universities can benefit from shared expertise and resources, thereby enhancing the overall quality and effectiveness of AI adoption in academic settings (Onyebuchi, Unachukwu & Osawaru, 2024)

- **AI Research and Innovation**

The objective is to promote AI research within universities to support the development of local expertise and tailored educational solutions. To achieve this, dedicated AI research centers focused on AI-driven education should be established, serving as hubs for innovation and collaboration. Encouraging interdisciplinary programs that integrate AI with fields like business, engineering, and education will foster a comprehensive learning environment and stimulate novel approaches to curriculum design. Additionally, funding research on AI's impact on student learning outcomes, curriculum structure, and overall institutional effectiveness will provide valuable insights to guide future educational strategies, ultimately positioning universities as leaders in the digital transformation of education (Onyebuchi et al., 2024).

7. Ethical AI Implementation and Cultural Considerations

- **Ethical Guidelines for AI in Education**

To ensure responsible AI implementation in education, it is essential to establish clear ethical guidelines that prioritize the well-being of students and educators. These guidelines should prevent algorithmic biases in AI tools, ensuring fairness and equality in AI-driven processes. Additionally, academic integrity must be upheld, with AI serving as a support tool rather than a replacement for human faculty, preserving the essential role of educators in the learning process. Safeguarding student data privacy is another crucial element, with AI systems required to comply with stringent data protection laws to protect sensitive information. By maintaining these ethical standards, AI can be integrated into education responsibly, ensuring it serves the best interests of all stakeholders (Funa & Gabay, 2025).

- **Cultural Sensitivity in AI Integration**

To ensure the successful integration of AI in higher education, it is essential to prioritize cultural sensitivity by aligning AI adoption with Oman's cultural and societal values. AI tools and systems must be adaptable to the local context, ensuring they meet the educational standards and needs of Omani institutions. It is also crucial to involve cultural leaders and educators in shaping AI strategies, ensuring these technologies reflect and respect Omani values, traditions, and educational objectives (Lawrence, Othmani & Dalwai, 2024). By engaging local stakeholders in the process, the integration of AI will be more effective, fostering acceptance and promoting educational practices that resonate with the cultural and societal fabric of Oman (Awashreh, 2025 d).

8. Continuous Evaluation and Improvement

- **Monitoring and Assessment of AI Impact**

To ensure the effective integration of AI in higher education, it is crucial to establish a robust framework for monitoring and assessing the impact of AI on educational outcomes. This involves conducting periodic reviews of AI-driven tools, evaluating their effectiveness in enhancing teaching and learning processes (Awashreh & AL Ghunaimi, 2025 a). Feedback from faculty and students should be actively gathered to assess the perceived impact of AI technologies on the learning environment, providing valuable insights into areas of improvement. Additionally, AI analytics should be utilized to continuously refine and adapt AI tools, ensuring that they evolve in response to emerging educational needs and technological advancements. By consistently evaluating the effectiveness of AI integration, institutions can ensure that AI tools are optimized to maximize educational benefit and support continuous improvement in teaching and learning outcomes (Grajeda et al., 2023)

- **Long-Term Sustainability**

To ensure the long-term sustainability of AI adoption in higher education, it is essential to develop a comprehensive roadmap that outlines strategies for continued integration and scaling of AI technologies across universities. This roadmap should include clear milestones and timelines for expanding AI-driven initiatives, ensuring that institutions can keep pace with technological advancements (Shwedeh et al., 2024). Additionally, sustainable funding models must be established to support ongoing infrastructure development and faculty training, ensuring that AI adoption remains financially viable in the long term (Awashreh, 2023). To foster a culture of continuous learning and adaptation, higher education institutions must promote an environment where faculty and staff are encouraged to engage with new AI technologies, update their skills regularly, and embrace a mindset of innovation and adaptability. This holistic approach will ensure that AI continues to enhance the quality and effectiveness of higher education, preparing students for the challenges of a rapidly evolving digital world (Yusuf et al., 2024)

In summary, this AI Integration Framework for Omani Higher Education provides a strategic approach to incorporating AI into curriculum design, teaching methodologies, and institutional operations. By focusing on governance, technology, faculty training, and partnerships, Omani universities can create a dynamic, personalized, and efficient learning environment aligned with Vision 2040 goals. The successful implementation of AI will position Oman as a leader in digital education, ensuring students are well-equipped to succeed in a technology-driven global economy.

Figure 2. AI Integration Framework for Omani Higher Education

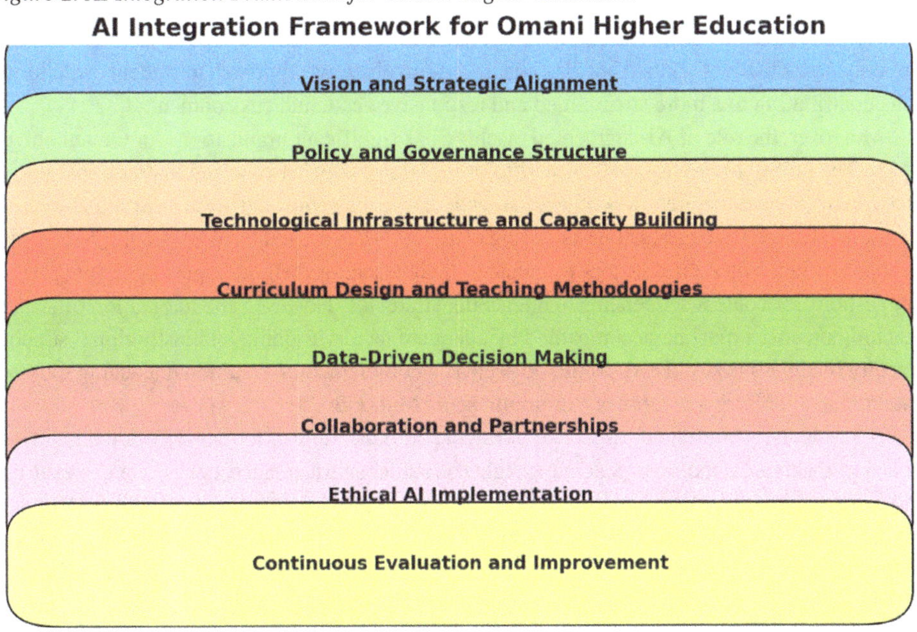

Sources: developed by the Author, 2025

Here is a framework visualization based on the provided text. It divides the key aspects of AI integration into higher education into eight core sections, each focusing on specific strategies and areas of development.

DISCUSSION

The integration of AI-driven strategies into curriculum design and teaching methodologies in Omani universities offers substantial potential for enhancing educational effectiveness, providing personalized learning experiences, and optimizing operational efficiencies. As suggested by Lawrence, Othmani, and Dalwai (2024), AI technologies present opportunities to address diverse student needs and improve educational outcomes. In the context of Omani higher education, where students exhibit varying levels of digital literacy and come from diverse academic backgrounds, AI-powered solutions such as adaptive learning technology can significantly bridge learning gaps and cater to individual learning styles (Gligorea et al., 2023). Adaptive learning platforms, which personalize content delivery based on real-time performance, provide tailored educational experiences that promote academic success and support students in progressing at their own pace (Gligorea et al., 2023).

Furthermore, AI-enabled assessments represent a crucial advancement in modernizing traditional evaluation practices. These tools offer efficiency, consistency, and real-time feedback, reducing the subjectivity inherent in conventional grading methods. Saputra et al. (2024) emphasize the importance of AI systems in enhancing grading accuracy, fairness, and timeliness, particularly in disciplines such as business, engineering, and medicine. The AI-driven assessment systems not only ease faculty workload but also ensure a more objective approach to student evaluations, thus contributing to a more streamlined and responsive academic environment.

Moreover, the role of AI-augmented teaching has significant implications for Omani universities. The ability to provide 24/7 virtual tutoring, along with AI-powered instructional design tools, can alleviate the pressures of large student-to-faculty ratios and allow instructors to focus on more advanced pedagogical tasks (Wang et al., 2024). As noted by Wang et al. (2024), such AI applications enable instructors to enhance their teaching methodologies by leveraging AI suggestions for content sequencing and teaching strategies. However, the integration of AI into teaching practices must be accompanied by adequate faculty training and institutional support. Faculty readiness is key, as AI should be seen as a complement to traditional teaching methods rather than a replacement (Jomaa, Attamimi, & Al Mahri, 2025).

A particularly promising aspect of AI's role in education is its capacity for data-driven decision-making. AI tools can generate insights on student performance, engagement, and at-risk indicators, allowing universities to refine curricula and provide timely interventions (Vieriu & Petrea, 2025). By aligning educational strategies with these data-driven insights, Omani universities can improve student retention and overall academic performance, thus contributing to a more efficient and effective educational system. The role of AI in institutional decision-making supports the vision of using technology to promote continuous improvement and adaptation to changing educational needs (Alsaadi & Awashreh, 2025).

Despite the promising advantages, the successful integration of AI in Omani universities is not without its challenges. One key concern is the readiness of both faculty and institutions to adopt AI-driven solutions. Jomaa, Attamimi, and Al Mahri (2025) highlight that the lack of sufficient AI-related training and infrastructure is a significant barrier. Faculty development programs are essential to ensure that educators can confidently and effectively incorporate AI tools into their teaching practices. In addition, the need for robust institutional support to invest in AI infrastructure, including AI-driven platforms and digital systems, is critical to the successful implementation of these technologies (Awashreh, 2023). Moreover, universities must ensure that the adoption of AI aligns with ethical considerations such as data privacy, algorithmic fairness, and academic integrity (Awashreh & Ramachandran, 2024).

The implementation of AI must also consider the socio-cultural and economic context of Oman. While AI can provide significant advantages in curriculum design and delivery, its integration needs to be aligned with national goals, such as those outlined in Oman Vision 2040, which emphasizes digital transformation and the advancement of knowledge-based sectors (Demaidi, 2023). By tailoring AI adoption strategies to the local context, Omani universities can create more sustainable, impactful, and contextually relevant educational reforms (Funa & Gabay, 2025). In summary, AI-driven strategies offer transformative potential to enhance curriculum effectiveness and teaching methodologies in Omani higher education. The implementation of adaptive learning technologies, AI-enabled assessments, AI-augmented teaching, and data-driven decision-making can significantly improve learning outcomes and institutional efficiency. However, for these benefits to be fully realized, universities must invest in faculty development, infrastructure, and ethical governance to support the seamless integration of AI. As Oman's higher education system continues to evolve, aligning AI initiatives with national development goals will be crucial to preparing students for the demands of a digital, technology-driven global economy.

Theoretical Contribution

This study contributes to the broader literature on AI adoption in higher education by providing insights into the unique challenges and opportunities within the Omani context. It highlights the intersection of technology, culture, and policy in shaping AI adoption and offers a framework for understanding how these factors can be addressed to foster more effective and inclusive AI integration in education. The study also expands theoretical discussions on AI's role in curriculum design and teaching by emphasizing the need for strategic, culturally aware approaches to AI implementation.

CONCLUSION

The integration of artificial intelligence (AI) in curriculum design and teaching methodologies across Omani universities presents a promising avenue for enhancing educational quality and student engagement. However, the findings of this study reveal that AI adoption remains in the early stages, with various challenges hindering its widespread implementation. Technological barriers, institutional resistance, cultural attitudes, financial constraints, and regulatory gaps are key factors that impede the effective use of AI in higher education. To overcome these obstacles, it is essential for Omani universities to invest in technological infrastructure, foster AI literacy among faculty, and address the cultural and institutional barriers that hinder the adoption of AI. Furthermore, a clear regulatory framework that aligns with Oman Vision 2040 is necessary to provide universities with structured guidance on AI implementation. By addressing these challenges, Omani higher education institutions can enhance curriculum effectiveness, improve teaching methodologies, and better prepare students for the future workforce in an AI-driven world.

As AI continues to shape the global education landscape, Omani universities must proactively adopt AI-driven curriculum strategies. By addressing the challenges and developing a structured framework, this study will provide actionable insights for enhancing education quality, bridging the gap between academia and industry, and ensuring long-term sustainability in AI education within Oman's higher education sector.

Societal Implications

The adoption of AI in higher education holds the potential to significantly impact society by improving the quality of education and preparing students for the rapidly evolving job market. AI-driven personalized learning experiences can enhance student outcomes, making education more accessible and tailored to individual needs. This has the potential to address disparities in educational access and improve overall societal well-being. Furthermore, as AI technologies advance, students who are exposed to AI-powered educational environments will be better equipped with the skills required for the digital economy, thus contributing to the development of a more skilled workforce and helping Oman meet its Vision 2040 goals.

Government Implications

For AI adoption to be successful in Omani higher education, the government plays a critical role in providing clear regulatory frameworks, funding, and policy support. The government's focus on digital transformation through Oman Vision 2040 should be complemented by specific strategies and guidelines for AI integration in universities. Additionally, the government should invest in building AI infrastructure, promoting research in AI, and creating partnerships with the private sector to ensure universities have access to the latest AI technologies. By fostering collaboration and providing financial support, the government can ensure that Omani higher education institutions are well-equipped to integrate AI in a way that aligns with national development objectives and global trends in education.

Practical Implications

From a practical perspective, universities in Oman should focus on developing AI-driven curriculum frameworks that support personalized learning, automated assessments, and data-driven decision-making. Educators need to be equipped with AI literacy through training programs that enhance their ability to integrate AI technologies into their teaching practices. AI tools such as adaptive learning platforms, virtual tutors, and AI-enabled assessment systems can significantly improve teaching effectiveness and operational efficiency in universities. Furthermore, universities should prioritize creating strong partnerships with private technology firms to enhance AI integration and provide students with access to real-world AI applications. This practical approach will ensure that Omani higher education institutions remain competitive and capable of offering a high-quality education in an increasingly digital world.

Limitations

This study has several limitations that must be acknowledged. First, the sample size was limited, focusing primarily on a few universities, which may not fully represent the diversity of higher education institutions across Oman. Additionally, the research relied on qualitative methods, which may be subject to researcher bias and may not fully capture the broader perspectives of all stakeholders, such as students and government officials. The study also did not delve deeply into the specific technological and financial constraints faced by different types of universities, particularly private institutions. Future studies could expand the sample size and use a mixed-methods approach to provide a more comprehensive view of AI adoption across all Omani universities.

Future Research Directions

Future research should explore several areas to build upon the findings of this study. One direction could involve investigating the specific technological infrastructure needs of Omani universities and identifying the most effective AI tools for curriculum enhancement. Research could also focus on understanding the long-term impacts of AI adoption on student performance, faculty satisfaction, and overall educational outcomes in Omani higher education. Additionally, exploring the cultural factors that influence the acceptance of AI among students and faculty would provide valuable insights into overcoming resistance to AI in educational settings. Lastly, comparative studies that examine AI adoption in Omani universities against other Gulf countries or broader international contexts could offer insights into best practices and highlight strategies for overcoming common challenges.

REFERENCES

Akinwalere, S. N., & Ivanov, V. T. (2022). Artificial intelligence in higher education: Challenges and opportunities. *Border Crossing*, *12*(1), 1–15. DOI: 10.33182/bc.v12i1.2015

Al Hasani, S. H. S., & Husin, N. A. (2021). A review of digital transformation of education in Oman. *Journal of Business Management and Accounting*, *11*(2), 41–59. DOI: 10.32890/jbma2021.11.2.3

Al-Senaidi, S., Lipsmeyer, L. L., & Poirot, J. (2009). Barriers to adopting technology for teaching and learning in Oman. *Computers & Education*, *53*(3), 575–590. DOI: 10.1016/j.compedu.2009.03.015

Al-Zahrani, A. M. (2024). Unveiling the shadows: Beyond the hype of AI in education. *Heliyon*, *10*(9), e30696. DOI: 10.1016/j.heliyon.2024.e30696

Ali, O., Murray, P. A., Momin, M., Dwivedi, Y. K., & Malik, T. (2024). The effects of artificial intelligence applications in educational settings: Challenges and strategies. *Technological Forecasting and Social Change*, *199*, 123076. DOI: 10.1016/j.techfore.2023.123076

Alsaadi, A., & Awashreh, R. (2025). Practical University Training Impact on Job Performance of Translation Graduates in Oman. *Forum for Linguistic Studies*, *7*(2), 786–796. DOI: 10.30564/fls.v7i2.8306

Asri, A. (2024). Utilization of artificial intelligence in improving student achievement. *PARADOKS Jurnal Ilmu Ekonomi*, *7*(4), 451–465. DOI: 10.57178/paradoks.v7i4.990

Awashreh, R. (2014b). Be Aware: Navigating Challenges in AI-Driven Higher Education. [Common Ground Research Networks]. *The International Journal of Interdisciplinary Educational Studies*, *20*(1), 203–218. DOI: 10.18848/2327-011X/CGP/v20i01/203-218

Awashreh, R. (2023). Enhancing innovation among business colleges at Omani universities: A theoretical framework. *Seybold Report, 18*(02), 182–196. https://seyboldreport.com

Awashreh, R. (2024 a). Omani private universities: Debates between progress in human development and weak education quality. *The International Journal of Educational Organization and Leadership, 32(1)*, 1-15. Common Ground Research Networks. DOI: 10.18848/2329-1656/CGP/v32i01/1-15

Awashreh, R. (2025 a). Leadership Strategies for Managing Change and Fostering Innovation Over Private Higher Education: Academic Institutions in Oman. In R. Marcão & V. Santos (Eds.), *Evolving Strategies for Organizational Management and Performance Evaluation* (pp. 399-422). IGI Global Scientific Publishing. DOI: 10.4018/979-8-3373-0149-5.ch018

Awashreh, R. (2025 b). Managing business continuity and resilience in higher education institutions without compromising the quality of education. In *Enhancing Resilience in Business Continuity Management*. DOI: 10.4018/979-8-3693-8809-9.ch010

Awashreh, R. (2025 c). Navigating Leadership Dynamics: Insights and Strategies Across Domains. In Rahman, M., Koolmon, G., Shaikh, S., & Munna, A. (Eds.), *Optimizing Leadership and Governance in Higher Education* (pp. 203–232). IGI Global., DOI: 10.4018/979-8-3693-3534-5.ch010

Awashreh, R. (2025 d). Omani public governance in the age of artificial intelligence. In *Public Governance Practices in the Age of AI* (pp. 137–166). IGI Global., DOI: 10.4018/979-8-3693-9286-7.ch007

Awashreh, R., & Bremananth, B. (2025). A study on the ethical implementation of AI in collegiate studies using fuzzy implication. *Pakistan Journal of Life and Social Sciences*, *23*(1), 3998–4013. DOI: 10.57239/PJLSS-2025-23.1.00317

Awashreh, R., & Ghunaimi, A. L. (2025a). Bridging Cultural Gaps: Enhancing Student Motivation and Academic Integrity in Oman's Universities. *Forum for Linguistic Studies*, *7*(2), 265 279. DOI: 10.30564/fls.v7i2.8300

Awashreh, R., & Ghunaimi, H. A. L. (2025b). Rethinking the PhD: Aligning higher education with market needs and practical skills. *Frontiers in Learning and Studies*, *7*(2). Advance online publication. DOI: 10.30564/fls.v7i2.7942

Awashreh, R., & Hamid, A. A. (2025). The role of entrepreneurial leadership in driving employee innovation: The mediating effect of knowledge sharing. *Cogent Business & Management*, *12*(1), 2466812. DOI: 10.1080/23311975.2025.2466812

Awashreh, R., & Hassiba, A. (2025). Revolutionizing Education With AI: Personalized Learning, Predictive Analytics, and Gamification. In Ordóñez de Pablos, P., Lytras, M., Alkhaldi, A., & Malik, S. (Eds.), *Insights Into Digital Business, Human Resource Management, and Competitiveness* (pp. 149–170). IGI Global Scientific Publishing., DOI: 10.4018/979-8-3693-9440-3.ch006

Awashreh, R., & Ramachandran, B. (2024). Can artificial intelligence dominate and control human beings? [IRJMS]. *International Research Journal of Multidisciplinary Scope*, *5*(4), 427–438. DOI: 10.47857/irjms.2024.05i04.01569

Bahroun, Z., Anane, C., Ahmed, V., & Zacca, A. (2023). Transforming education: A comprehensive review of generative artificial intelligence in educational settings through bibliometric and content analysis. *Sustainability (Basel)*, *15*(17), 12983. DOI: 10.3390/su151712983

Bognár, L., & Khine, M. S. (2025). The shifting landscape of student engagement: A pre-post semester analysis in AI-enhanced classrooms. *Computers and Education: Artificial Intelligence*, *8*, 100395. DOI: 10.1016/j.caeai.2025.100395

Chan, C. K. Y. (2023). A comprehensive AI policy education framework for university teaching and learning. *International Journal of Educational Technology in Higher Education*, *20*(1), 38. DOI: 10.1186/s41239-023-00408-3

Degni, F. (2024). AI in education: The impact of artificial intelligence on education. *ResearchGate*. DOI: 10.13140/RG.2.2.21373.99048

Delello, J. A., Sung, W., Mokhtari, K., Hebert, J., Bronson, A., & De Giuseppe, T. (2025). AI in the classroom: Insights from educators on usage, challenges, and mental health. *Education Sciences*, *15*(2), 113. DOI: 10.3390/educsci15020113

Demaidi, M. N. (2023). Artificial intelligence national strategy in a developing country. *AI & Society*. Advance online publication. DOI: 10.1007/s00146-023-01779-x

Ding, A.-C. E., Shi, L., Yang, H., & Choi, I. (2024). Enhancing teacher AI literacy and integration through different types of cases in teacher professional development. *Computers and Education Open*, *6*, 100178. DOI: 10.1016/j.caeo.2024.100178

Ellikkal, A., & Rajamohan, **S.** (2024). AI-enabled personalized learning: Empowering management students for improving engagement and academic performance. *Vilakshan - XIMB Journal of Management, ahead-of-print.* DOI: 10.1108/XJM-02-2024-0023

Funa, A. A., & Gabay, R. A. E. (2025). Policy guidelines and recommendations on AI use in teaching and learning: A meta-synthesis study. *Social Sciences & Humanities Open*, *11*, 101221. DOI: 10.1016/j.ssaho.2024.101221

Gligorea, I., Cioca, M., Oancea, R., Gorski, A.-T., Gorski, H., & Tudorache, P. (2023). Adaptive learning using artificial intelligence in e-learning: A literature review. *Education Sciences*, *13*(12), 1216. DOI: 10.3390/educsci13121216

Grajeda, A., Burgos, J., Cordova Olivera, P., & Sanjines, A. (2023). Assessing student-perceived impact of using artificial intelligence tools: Construction of a synthetic index of application in higher education. *Cogent Education*, *11*(1), 2287917. Advance online publication. DOI: 10.1080/2331186X.2023.2287917

Hazzan-Bishara, A., Kol, O., & Levy, S. (2025). The factors affecting teachers' adoption of AI technologies: A unified model of external and internal determinants. *Education and Information Technologies*, *30*(11), 15043–15069. Advance online publication. DOI: 10.1007/s10639-025-13393-z

Jomaa, N. J., Attamimi, R., & Al Mahri, M. (2025). The use of artificial intelligence (AI) in teaching English vocabulary in Oman: Perspectives, teaching practices, and challenges. *World Journal of English Language*, *15*(3), 1–13. DOI: 10.5430/wjel.v15n3p1

Kamalov, F., Santandreu Calonge, D., & Gurrib, I. (2023). New era of artificial intelligence in education: Towards a sustainable multifaceted revolution. *Sustainability (Basel)*, *15*(16), 12451. DOI: 10.3390/su151612451

Khairullah, S. A., Harris, S., Hadi, H., Sandhu, R. A., Ahmad, N., & Alshara, M. (2025). Implementing artificial intelligence in academic and administrative processes through responsible strategic leadership in the higher education institutions. *Frontiers in Education*, *10*, 1548104. DOI: 10.3389/feduc.2025.1548104

Lawrence, S. S., Othmani, S., & Dalwai, T. (2024). Toward a knowledge-based economy: Empowering higher education in Oman with AI for Vision 2040 achievement. In El-Masri, M. A., & Madbouly, A. (Eds.), *Finance and law in the metaverse world* (pp. 133–142). Springer., DOI: 10.1007/978-3-031-67547-8_12

Lytras, M. D., Serban, A. C., Alkhaldi, A., Aldosemani, T., & Malik, S. (2024). Digital transformation in higher education in times of artificial intelligence: Setting the emerging landscape. In Lytras, M. D., Serban, A. C., Alkhaldi, A., Malik, S., & Aldosemani, T. (Eds.), *Digital Transformation in Higher Education, Part A* (pp. 1–22). Emerald Publishing Limited., DOI: 10.1108/978-1-83549-480-620241001

Michel-Villarreal, R., Vilalta-Perdomo, E., Salinas-Navarro, D. E., Thierry-Aguilera, R., & Gerardou, F. S. (2023). Challenges and opportunities of generative AI for higher education as explained by ChatGPT. *Education Sciences*, *13*(9), 856. DOI: 10.3390/educsci13090856

Mijan, A.-A., Hasan, M. R., & Hasan, M. (2025). AI and academia: Navigating the adoption of artificial intelligence in universities. *International Journal of Technology in Education and Science*, *9*(1), 54–65. DOI: 10.46328/ijtes.602

Nguyen, A., Ngo, H. N., Hong, Y., Dang, B., & Nguyen, B.-P. T. (2023). Ethical principles for artificial intelligence in education. *Education and Information Technologies*, *28*(4), 4221–4241. DOI: 10.1007/s10639-022-11316-w

Onyebuchi, N. C., Unachukwu, C. C., & Osawaru, B. (2024). Review of AI in education: Transforming learning environments in Africa. *International Journal of Applied Research in Social Sciences*, *5*(10), 637–654. DOI: 10.51594/ijarss.v5i10.725

Sajja, R., Sermet, Y., Cwiertny, D., & Demir, I. (2023). Integrating AI and learning analytics for data-driven pedagogical decisions and personalized interventions in education. *arXiv*. /arXiv.2312.09548DOI: 10.48550

Saputra, I., Kurniawan, A., Yanita, M., Putri, E. Y., & Mahniza, M. (2024). The evolution of educational assessment: How artificial intelligence is shaping the trends and future of learning evaluation. *Indonesian Journal of Computer Science*, *13*(6). Advance online publication. DOI: 10.33022/ijcs.v13i6.4465

Shwedeh, F., Salloum, S. A., Aburayya, A., Fatin, B., Elbadawi, M., Alghurabli, Z., & Al-Dabbagh, T. (2024). AI adoption and educational sustainability in higher education in the UAE. In Al-Marzouqi, A., Salloum, S. A., Al-Saidat, M., Aburayya, A., & Gupta, B. (Eds.), *Artificial intelligence in education: The power and dangers of ChatGPT in the classroom* (pp. 201–229). Springer., DOI: 10.1007/978-3-031-52280-2_14

Singun, A. (2025). Unveiling the barriers to digital transformation in higher education institutions: A systematic literature review. *Discover Education*, *4*(1), 37. DOI: 10.1007/s44217-025-00430-9

Strielkowski, W., Grebennikova, V., Lisovskiy, A., & Rakhimova, G. (2024). AI-driven adaptive learning for sustainable educational transformation. *Sustainable Development*. Advance online publication. DOI: 10.1002/sd.3221

Twabu, K., & Nakene-Mginqi, M. (2024). Developing a design thinking artificial intelligence driven auto-marking/grading system for assessments to reduce the workload of lecturers at a higher learning institution in South Africa. *Frontiers in Education*, *9*, 1512569. Advance online publication. DOI: 10.3389/feduc.2024.1512569

Vieriu, A. M., & Petrea, G. (2025). The Impact of Artificial Intelligence (AI) on Students' Academic Development. *Education Sciences*, *15*(3), 343. DOI: 10.3390/educsci15030343

Walter, Y. (2024). Embracing the future of artificial intelligence in the classroom: The relevance of AI literacy, prompt engineering, and critical thinking in modern education.

Walter, Y. (2024, February 26). Embracing the future of Artificial Intelligence in the classroom: The relevance of AI literacy, prompt engineering, and critical thinking in modern education. *International Journal of Educational Technology in Higher Education*, *21*(1), 15. DOI: 10.1186/s41239-024-00448-3

Wang, S., Wang, F., Zhu, Z., Wang, J., Tran, T., & Du, Z. (2024). Artificial intelligence in education: A systematic literature review. *Expert Systems with Applications, 252*(Part A), 124167. DOI: 10.1016/j.eswa.2024.124167

Xu, Z. (2024). AI in education: Enhancing learning experiences and student outcomes. *Applied and Computational Engineering*, *51*(1), 104–111. DOI: 10.54254/2755-2721/51/20241187

Yusuf, S. O., Abubakar, J. E., Durodola, R., Ocran, G., Hadassah, A., & Yusuf, P. O. (2024). Impact of AI on continuous learning and skill development in the workplace: A comparative study with traditional methods. *World Journal of Advanced Research and Reviews*, *23*(2), 1129–1140. DOI: 10.30574/wjarr.2024.23.2.2439

Chapter 9
From One-Size-Fits-All to AI-Driven Personalization in Education

Fahad A. Salendab
https://orcid.org/0000-0003-4459-443X
Sultan Kudarat State University, Philippines

Rashmia S. Baraguir
https://orcid.org/0009-0000-4804-3008
Sultan Kudarat State University, Philippines

Rachel Anne S. Nuñez
Notre Dame University, Philippines

Donald A. Cogo
https://orcid.org/0009-0008-5418-071X
Sultan Kudarat State University, Philippines

ABSTRACT

The evolution from standardized instruction to AI-driven personalization reflects a growing demand for inclusive, flexible, and learner-centered education. Grounded in key concepts such as differentiation, individualization, and personalization, the discussion explores how AI technologies—adaptive learning platforms, real-time analytics, and intelligent tutoring systems—enable dynamic and tailored instruction that meets diverse learner needs. AI integration not only enhances engagement and equity but also supports meaningful curriculum redesign aligned with 21st-century competencies. Emphasizing innovative pedagogies and ethical implementation, the chapter highlights the strategic role of educators in guiding this transformation. The insights presented contribute to future-proofing curriculum design by aligning technological innovation with holistic student development and sustainable educational outcomes.

DOI: 10.4018/979-8-3373-2752-5.ch009

INTRODUCTION

Educational systems worldwide are under increasing pressure to evolve beyond industrial-era models of standardized instruction. The traditional "one-size-fits-all" approach—built on rigid curricula, uniform pacing, and generalized assessments—struggles to meet the needs of increasingly diverse and digitally fluent learners. As societies face rapid technological, economic, and cultural shifts, there is a rising demand for learner-centered, adaptive systems that support flexible progression, meaningful engagement, and personalized learning outcomes. These systems aim to foster student agency, inclusivity, and lifelong learning—hallmarks of future-proof education (Strielkowski et al., 2025; Bayly-Castañeda et al., 2024)

At the forefront of this transformation is the integration of Artificial Intelligence (AI), which is reshaping how learning is designed, delivered, and assessed. AI technologies—such as adaptive learning platforms, intelligent tutoring systems, predictive analytics, and generative AI—offer scalable solutions that personalize content, feedback, and learning pathways in real time (Liu et al., 2025; Bayly-Castañeda et al., 2024). These tools facilitate a shift from traditional content-centered instruction to competency-based and data-informed frameworks that are more responsive to learner diversity and context.

This chapter explores the paradigm shift from standardized instruction toward AI-driven personalization in education. It traces the historical evolution of mass education, critiques the limitations of traditional curriculum designs, and highlights the growing demand for learner-centered models. It clarifies foundational concepts—differentiation, individualization, and personalization—and explores how intelligent systems can support inclusive instructional design, real-time adaptability, and learner autonomy (Bi et al., 2023; Liang & Lo, 2024). The chapter also emphasizes the role of innovative pedagogies in driving transformative change in higher education, advocating for learner engagement through design thinking, active learning, and reflective practice (Salendab et al., 2026).

By bridging theoretical insights with empirical applications, this chapter outlines a strategic vision for integrating AI into curriculum development that is not only technologically advanced but also pedagogically sound, culturally responsive, and ethically anchored. In doing so, it equips educational leaders, practitioners, and policymakers with actionable strategies for building resilient, inclusive, and future-ready learning systems in the era of intelligent technologies.

REVIEW OF RELATED LITERATURE

Foundations Of Personalized Learning in the Artificial Intelligence (AI) Era

The emergence of Artificial Intelligence (AI) in education has redefined the possibilities of learner-centered instruction. As digital technologies evolve, educational institutions are increasingly moving away from rigid, one-size-fits-all approaches toward more flexible, data-informed, and responsive learning environments. Central to this paradigm shift is the concept of personalized learning—an instructional model that acknowledges and adapts to the diverse needs, goals, and capacities of individual learners. Understanding the foundational distinctions between personalization, differentiation, and individualization, and examining the broader shift from standardization to learner agency, provides critical insight into how AI can be ethically and effectively integrated into future-ready education systems.

Clarifying Key Concepts: Differences between Differentiation, Individualization, and Personalization

The terms differentiation, individualization, and personalization are frequently used in educational discourse, yet their nuanced differences are often overlooked. Each represents a distinct approach to modifying instruction based on learner variability, with varying degrees of teacher control and learner autonomy.

Differentiation refers to the teacher's deliberate adjustment of content, process, product, or learning environment in response to students' readiness levels, interests, and learning preferences. It is typically group-based and guided by the teacher's assessment of student needs. Grounded in Liang & Lo's (2024) foundational framework, differentiation operates across four key dimensions: what students learn (content), how they engage with it (process), how they demonstrate understanding (product), and the environment in which learning takes place.

Bi et al. (2023) emphasize that successful differentiation is influenced not only by pedagogical skill but also by external factors such as class size, institutional support, and teacher beliefs about learner diversity. Teachers who valued inclusion and had professional support were more likely to adopt effective differentiated strategies.

Despite growing professional development efforts, Kahmann et al. (2022) found that the translation of differentiation training into classroom practice remains inconsistent. Their meta-analysis reveals that while teacher knowledge and attitudes improve through training, long-term implementation is often hindered by systemic constraints such as limited planning time and workload pressures.

Additionally, Cody et al. (2023) documented a case study in third-grade mathematics education showing that teachers trained in differentiation increased their use of small-group instruction, student choice, and scaffolded activities. While students showed higher engagement and achievement, teachers noted the time and resource demands as ongoing barriers.

Individualization, on the other hand, focuses on pacing—allowing students to progress through the same curriculum at different speeds based on their personal learning needs. This approach often maintains uniform learning objectives while offering temporal flexibility. Tetzlaff et al. (2022) underscore that individualization includes offering varying amounts of time for students to complete identical tasks, catering both to those who need extensions and those who require acceleration. Similarly, Gherman et al. (2022) demonstrate how adaptive microlearning platforms monitor progress in real-time and adjust pacing accordingly, enabling learners to stay engaged within consistent learning goals.

A recent study on personalized learning in secondary education further confirms that flexible pacing significantly enhances student motivation and retention, especially when students are responsible for managing their progress toward common objectives (Abbas, S. G., & Ayaz, 2025)

Personalization, the most learner-centered of the three, goes further by aligning learning activities with individual learner goals, preferences, and strengths. It empowers students to take ownership of their educational journey, promoting autonomy and self-regulation. In the AI era, personalization is increasingly supported by intelligent systems capable of analyzing learner data in real-time to adapt content, suggest resources, and provide targeted feedback. Recent studies affirm the transformative potential of such systems. For instance, Leguisamo et al. (2025) highlight how adaptive AI technologies significantly improve student engagement and academic outcomes, though they caution against challenges related to infrastructure, privacy, and teacher readiness. Bayly-Castañeda et al. (2024) emphasize that AI-driven personalized pathways, when grounded in pedagogical design, support lifelong learning and educational equity. Jauhiainen & Garagorry (2024). Further demonstrate that generative AI tools like ChatGPT can dynamically tailor learning materials to individual learner profiles, enhancing motivation and content relevance, especially in K–12 settings. Looi and Jia (2025) show that conversational AI tutors offer individualized scaffolds and feedback, promoting deeper learning through personalized interaction. Moreover, Liu et al. (2025) confirm that intelligent tutoring systems and robot-assisted platforms contribute to improved cognitive and emotional outcomes when personalization is paired with real-time adaptability. Advancing this further, Song et al. (2025) introduce EduAlign—a reinforcement learning framework that fine-tunes large language models to prioritize helpfulness, creativity, and alignment with learner-centered pedagogical goals. Collectively, these findings indicate that personalization, powered by AI, enables educators to shift from static, one-size-fits-all instruction to dynamic, responsive, and inclusive learning environments tailored to each student's unique educational pathway.

Shifting from Standardization to Learner Agency: A Paradigm Shift

Traditional education systems have long operated under models of standardization, where curriculum, assessments, and instruction are uniformly applied regardless of student diversity. While this approach offers consistency and scalability, it often overlooks the unique contexts and potentials of individual learners. Laak & Aru (2024) critically examine how one-size-fits-all educational tools—even those that claim to personalize learning—still fall short in embracing modern educational goals like collaboration, civic competence, and cognitive engagement. Similarly, Alfredo et al. (2024) in their systematic reviews of learning analytics and AI in education warn that standardized, top-down designs frequently exclude students and teachers from meaningful involvement, risking misalignment with actual learner needs and undermining trust and control.

Equity-oriented curriculum redesign offers an alternative: one study on project-based science curriculum in secondary schools (SSIBL framework) found that students—especially girls—showed increased motivation, scientific literacy, and engagement when learning was contextual and interest-driven, compared to conventional standardized instruction (Kyza & Georgiou, 2025). Other research emphasizes the power of inclusive design: culturally responsive teaching and Universal Design for Learning (UDL) frameworks promote access and success by embedding diverse perspectives, multiple means of representation, expression, and engagement into the curriculum from the outset, directly countering the limitations of standardized approaches (Akintayo et al., 2024).

Moreover, empirical studies demonstrate that differentiated instruction—which adapts teaching methods to meet varied learners in diverse classrooms—yields measurable gains in engagement and academic performance. For example, a study in Zambian high schools revealed that differentiated instruction improved average scores from ~65% to ~72%, with a medium effect size ($d \approx 0.71$), compared to conventional homogeneous instruction (Kaziya, 2025). Observational evidence from inclusive classrooms further shows that teachers embracing constructivist and responsive pedagogies experience deeper professional fulfillment and stronger student–teacher relationships—outcomes unlikely under rigid standardized models (Sumagang & Balano, 2025).

AI-driven personalization supports learner agency, understood as students' capacity to independently set goals, make decisions, and regulate their strategies. Educational design research argues that granting learner control without sufficient support can hamper metacognitive development—but AI systems can adaptively balance agency, granting more autonomy as competence grows to foster effective self-regulation while avoiding overwhelm (Brod et al., 2023). Study shows that generative AI tools, when used to tailor school tasks to individual interests, improve both intrinsic motivation and sustained engagement—even after the session ends—empowering learners to take ownership of their learning process (Tasdelen & Bodemer, 2025).

Moreover, frameworks integrating generative AI with learning analytics are emerging to support self-directed growth by enabling learners to iteratively define aspirations, monitor progress, and reflect on outcomes, creating dynamic, AI-augmented feedback loops tailored to individual goals and motivations (Mao, 2025). In chat- and conversation-based tutoring systems, AI personalization enhances self-regulated learning by supporting goal planning, metacognitive monitoring, and self-reflection phases—core dimensions of learner agency—in measurable, context-aware ways (Mirea et al. 2025).

From a socio-cultural perspective, learner agency emerges through active engagement with digital tools—not passive consumption. AI-enabled chatbots and tutoring systems serve as cultural–cognitive mediators, enabling students to question, reframe, and co-construct knowledge and regulate their participation in learning tasks (Engeness et al., 2025).

AI TECHNOLOGIES TRANSFORMING EDUCATION

Artificial Intelligence (AI) is playing an increasingly vital role in reshaping education by making learning more personalized, efficient, and accessible. Through advanced technologies such as adaptive learning systems, intelligent tutoring systems, and data-driven analytics, AI is helping educators better understand and support individual student needs.

Adaptive Learning Systems

Adaptive learning systems utilize real-time data to customize educational content according to each student's needs, pace, and level of understanding. These systems dynamically adjust learning paths, activities, and assessments to ensure that students receive appropriate challenges and support as they progress. A study of Contrino et al. (2024) involving a university course using an adaptive platform within a flexible online/blended format found that student achievement significantly improved relative to non-adaptive settings; satisfaction was higher in blended classrooms than purely online courses, demonstrating the power of real-time personalization across modalities. Similarly, an exploratory mixed-method quasi-experimental study of Rincon-Flores et al. (2024) showed that intertwining an adaptive learning strategy with flipped-classroom and micro-learning techniques boosted both discipline-specific and transversal competence, learner engagement, and academic performance within engineering courses.

A global meta-analysis of 25 studies further confirmed that adaptive learning technologies consistently enhanced student engagement, retention rates, and academic efficiency—producing higher pass rates and better learning outcomes compared to traditional instruction (Strielkowski et al., 2025). In addition, meta-analytic findings also support personalized technology-enhanced learning: a synthesis of 47 experimental studies across higher education revealed improved cognitive skill development in adaptive-technology groups over control groups (Hooshyar et al., 2024). Finally, Yaseen et al. (2025) emphasize that real-time feedback within adaptive systems not only aids retention but also sustains learner attention and promotes self-regulation and growth mindset attitudes—yielding measurable retention and motivation benefits over standard methods.

Intelligent Tutoring Systems (ITS)

Intelligent Tutoring Systems simulate the benefits of one-on-one instruction by providing tailored feedback, hints, and guidance based on a student's responses and learning history. These systems often employ techniques such as knowledge tracing—including Bayesian and deep learning approaches—to model student understanding over time and predict future performance for real-time adaptation (Ilić et al., 2023). For example, Villegas-Ch et al. (2025) describe an ITS for STEM education with integrated NLP, real-time assessment, and content recommendation modules that collaboratively adapt tasks and feedback to each learner's profile, enhancing comprehension and engagement. Lu et al. (2024), analyzing student interaction data through deep neural networks, reveal that appropriately calibrated scaffolding in math tutoring fosters measurable growth in problem-solving skills, especially when over-reliance is avoided. Spitzer & Moeller (2024) further support ITS effectiveness: a large-scale evaluation of German students working with a mathematics ITS during COVID-19 school closures (over ≈ 5 million problems) found significant performance gains—even among lower-performing students—with effects persisting once schools reopened. Meanwhile, a systematic review of ITS and robot-based tutoring across 86 studies documented significant learning outcome improvements, particularly in cognitive support, adaptability, and student engagement—though noting challenges around scalability and ethical deployment (Liu et al., 2025).

Emerging LLM-powered conversational ITS demonstrate further promise: Liu et al. (2025) introduce a PACE agent that personalizes math instruction based on learners' styles, using the Socratic method to provide immediate feedback and foster deep reasoning—reporting significant gains in student motivation and performance compared to existing systems. In physics education, a high school experiment with Physics-STAR, an LLM-based tutor, doubled students' performance on complex information tasks and improved efficiency by nearly 6%, surpassing traditional lectures or generic AI tutors (Jiang & Jiang, 2024).

Learning Analytics and Data-Driven Decision-Making

Learning analytics refers to the collection, measurement, and analysis of data related to learners and their contexts to optimize learning and the environments in which it occurs. When combined with AI, these analytics enable data-driven decision-making, allowing educators and institutions to understand student behavior better, identify patterns, and implement timely interventions. For instance, a large-scale machine learning study using data from over 50,000 university students found predictive models achieved up to 88% accuracy in forecasting retention by combining demographic and behavioral engagement indicators—demonstrating how integrated analytics can anticipate dropout risk and inform early intervention strategies (Matz et al., 2023). Similarly, case studies from various institutions have shown that predictive analytics systems trigger targeted support actions, contributing to measurable gains in retention rates and graduation outcomes (Hernández-de-Menéndez et al., 2022).

Dashboard tools are also evolving to prioritize student-facing, pedagogically informed analytics rather than raw data streams. A systematic review conducted by Alfredo et al. (2024) found that dashboards rooted in learning science frameworks provide actionable insights that support self-reflection, engagement, and decision-making by both learners and educators. Likewise, they stressed human-centered analytics, calling for transparent, trustworthy tools co-developed with key stakeholders to enhance agency and ethical use in learning contexts.

Goh (2025) further described how consistency and persistence in LMS engagement behaviors predict academic success. One study found that combining consistency and persistence metrics in machine learning models yielded about 65% accuracy in identifying at-risk students mid-semester—and could be embedded in dashboards to guide instructor interventions proactively. Moreover, Sajja et al. (2023), who explored AI-augmented analytics tools based on GPT-4, showed how indicators such as confusion, curiosity, stress, and engagement can be mapped and visualized, offering instructors real-time pedagogical insights—though it raised considerations about data privacy and AI accuracy.

DESIGNING AI-ENHANCED PERSONALIZED CURRICULUM

The integration of AI into curriculum design is reshaping how educational content is structured, delivered, and personalized. Two critical innovations supporting this transformation are competency-based and modular curriculum structures, as well as AI-supported curriculum mapping and learning pathways.

Competency-Based and Modular Curriculum Structures

Competency-based education (CBE) prioritizes mastery of specific skills and knowledge over time spent in class. Modular curricula break learning into smaller, flexible units that students can complete at their own pace, fostering greater personalization. This approach empowers learners to progress based on demonstrated understanding rather than standardized timelines. When enhanced by AI, such structures can dynamically assess performance, identify learning gaps, and suggest appropriate modules. Yan et al. (2025) reinforce the power of this approach by conducting a systematic review in higher vocational education. Based on the findings, AI-supported competency assessment correlates positively with student engagement and achievement ($r \approx 0.45$, $p < 0.001$), indicating that AI tools effectively identify gaps and tailor feedback for targeted improvement. Similarly, adaptive AI-driven assessment frameworks in CBE environments show real-time gap detection and remediation guidance, enabling personalized learning pathways and mastery-focused progression (Waladi & Lamarti, 2024). An interactive learning system called Artemis implements a competency graph to visualize mastery and suggest modules based on student profiles, allowing instructors to generate individualized learning paths dynamically (Sölch et al., 2023). In higher education contexts, AI-enabled assistants—employing NLP and adaptive assessments—have reduced cognitive load and provided tailored support, quizzes, and flashcards aligned with student competencies and learning styles (Sajja et al., 2024). These examples confirm that AI-enhanced competency-based and modular curricula promote self-paced, mastery-driven learning by continuously assessing skill acquisition, recommending relevant modules, and supporting learner autonomy—key mechanisms in personalized education.

LEARNING ANALYTICS AND STUDENT PROFILING

Learning analytics and student profiling have emerged as transformative tools in the field of education, driven by the growing integration of technology and data in teaching and learning environments. These approaches involve the systematic collection, analysis, and interpretation of student data to understand learning behaviors better, identify strengths and weaknesses, and support evidence-based decision-making. One key application is the use of real-time feedback mechanisms, which allow educators and students to monitor progress continuously and make immediate adjustments to learning strategies. Another important application is predictive analytics for intervention and support, which involves analyzing historical and current data to forecast student outcomes.

Real-Time Feedback Mechanisms

Real-time feedback mechanism tools provide instantaneous data on student performance, enabling both instructors and learners to respond promptly to emerging challenges. These tools—commonly found in digital learning platforms—track metrics such as quiz results, engagement levels, and time spent on tasks, and can immediately alert students when they are falling behind or missing key concepts. Topali et al. (2023) found that students who received both automated analytics-based feedback and instructor comments showed significantly improved academic outcomes and engagement, especially among those with lower self-regulated learning (SRL) skills. Similarly, Uzun et al. (2025) demonstrated that real-time dashboards and notifications increased student motivation and course completion rates, provided that students actively engaged with the feedback rather than passively observing it. Real-time feedback mechanisms have also been shown to enhance classroom participation and knowledge retention through interactive tools such as mobile-based quiz systems, as highlighted in the study of Jurado-Castro et al. (2023). Further, a systematic review by Celik et al. (2023) emphasized the role of these tools in supporting learner autonomy and promoting reflective practice by visualizing learning patterns and alerting students to their progress. Moreover, real-time analytics tools embedded in learning management systems can be adapted to provide personalized content and adaptive tasks, as highlighted in a recent review on personalized learning environments by Khor & K, M. (2024).

Real-time feedback not only enhances student motivation and self-regulation but also fosters a more dynamic and responsive learning environment where adjustments are made in the moment, rather than after a summative assessment. For instance, the study Solis Trujillo et al. (2025) confirms that timely and specific feedback significantly boosts students' capacity to plan, monitor, and evaluate their progress—key components of self-regulated learning (SRL)—and elevates engagement and academic motivation among graduate learners. Grounded in Self-Determination Theory, a mixed-methods study by Wang (2025) demonstrates that affective and metacognitive feedback notably enhances self-efficacy and emotional engagement—key drivers of intrinsic motivation—while cognitive feedback alone had a limited impact unless paired with emotional or metacognitive elements. Additionally, Johannes & Haase (2022) revealed that concise, clarity-oriented "scoresheet" feedback led to meaningful knowledge gains—even in low-stakes environments—and improved students' metacognitive monitoring, although self-efficacy remained stable. In digital contexts, automated daily formative feedback was shown to promote long-term SRL behaviors and higher motivation levels in a randomized field experiment, indicating that consistent, system-generated feedback helps embed reflective learning habits (Bellhäuser et al., 2023). A correlational study in technology-enhanced learning contexts found that different formats of automated, peer, and instructor feedback positively correlate with intrinsic and extrinsic motivation, emphasizing the importance of feedback delivered promptly through digital platforms (Shoukat & Adnan, 2025).

Predictive Analytics for Intervention and Support

The strategic use of predictive analytics for intervention and support involves utilizing historical and current data to forecast student behaviour and academic outcomes. Predictive models analyze factors such as attendance, participation, assignment submissions, and grades to identify learners at risk of underperforming, dropping out, or disengaging from coursework. For instance, Matz et al. (2023) demonstrated that integrating macro- and micro-level data can predict student dropout with up to 88% accuracy, allowing universities to support at-risk individuals proactively. Similarly, Gonzalez-Nucamendi et al. (2023) applied machine learning techniques like Random Forest to forecast dropout among 14,500 undergraduates, using variables such as scholarship status, course load, and early-semester grades to guide targeted interventions. These insights empower institutions to implement timely support such as academic advising, tutoring, counseling, or peer mentoring. Platforms, as studied by Alalawi et al. (2025), underscore how predictive tools can improve participation and reduce course failure through timely feedback and motivational messaging. In addition, Johnston et al. (2024) found that early LMS engagement metrics are critical indicators of academic risk, highlighting how interpretable machine learning models can inform educators' proactive strategies. Moreover, Yuan et al. (2025) emphasized the value of scalable predictive systems to tailor personalized learning pathways in higher education. By shifting from reactive to proactive support, predictive analytics not only helps address academic issues before they escalate but also promotes equity and retention across diverse student populations. Furthermore, it enables educational leaders to allocate resources more effectively and design data-informed policies that drive student success.

ETHICAL, EQUITY, AND DATA PRIVACY ISSUES IN AI-PERSONALIZED EDUCATION

Algorithmic Bias and Transparency

One of the most significant ethical concerns in AI-personalized education is algorithmic bias. AI systems are only as objective as the data they are trained on—and educational data often reflects historical inequalities and systemic biases. For instance, if algorithms are trained on datasets that underrepresent marginalized groups, they may perpetuate disparities in assessment outcomes, resource recommendations, or performance predictions. Idowu (2024) in his study

"Debiasing Education Algorithms" underscores that bias often originates in the input data itself, and that fairness-aware techniques—such as instance-weighting, adversarial learning, or balanced sampling—can mitigate disparities without sacrificing accuracy. The study of Gandara et al. (2024) supports this idea. They demonstrated that predictive models significantly underpredict success outcomes for racially minoritized students—and that standard mitigation techniques often fail to resolve these differences fully. Similarly, Lee & Kizilcec (2020) found gender and racial biases across multiple fairness metrics in student-success prediction models—highlighting the trade-offs between fairness and predictive effectiveness.

Further, a context-specific study of 5,986 Filipino university students using Canvas LMS data explored whether predictive grade models exhibited bias based on students' regional backgrounds. Notably, they found no evidence of unfairness across demographic groups, suggesting that equitable outcomes are possible with careful design and evaluation (Švábenský et al., 2024). A broader survey by Chinta et al. (2024) identified common forms of bias in EdTech—ranging from data-related to interaction-based—and recommends strategies such as diverse datasets, fairness-aware algorithms, and ethical governance frameworks to foster equity in educational AI deployment.

Meanwhile, transparency is critical. Educators and institutions must demand explainable AI systems that allow stakeholders to understand how decisions are made and challenge those that reinforce discriminatory practices. Recent research demonstrates that transparency significantly increases educators' trust in AI. For instance, Feldman-Maggor et al. (2025) found that pre-service teachers reported greater trust and acceptance of AI tools when given transparent explanations of system decisions. Complementing this, a study by Gunasekara & Saarela (2025) compared decision trees and neural networks with post-hoc XAI techniques like SHAP and LIME, showing that interpretable models not only improved predictive performance but also enhanced stakeholder understanding and confidence. However, research by Swamy et al. (2023) cautioned that different XAI methods often yield inconsistent explanations, which may confuse users and undermine trust—underscoring the need for careful alignment between technical outputs and educator expectations. In real-time learning environments, such as serious games, explainable predictive models have enabled timely and targeted interventions by making decision rationales accessible to non-technical educators, as shown by Gomez et al. (2024). Furthermore, Chaudhry et al. (2022) proposed a Transparency Index Framework that maps ethical transparency across the entire lifecycle of educational AI systems—from data collection to deployment—promoting greater accountability and interpretability

Protecting Learner Data and Informed Consent

The use of AI in education requires collecting vast amounts of learner data—including behavioral logs, academic records, emotional cues, and engagement metrics. However, this data collection raises questions about student privacy and informed consent. Many learners are unaware of what data is being collected, how it is processed, and with whom it is shared. A systematic review by Shrestha et al. (2024) reveals that young users significantly distrust AI systems when data practices are opaque, expressing concerns over unclear collection methods, lack of control, and potential misuse, and emphasize the need for transparent consent mechanisms. Similarly, Gujjula

& Sanghera (2023) discuss ethical and privacy challenges in AI education and propose methods like federated learning to help protect student data while preserving meaningful personalization.

The study of Jones (2019) advocates for privacy dashboards and informed consent tools allowing students to access, correct, or delete their data—thus fostering autonomy and ethical transparency. A qualitative study by Shrestha & Joshi (2025) reinforces stakeholder demands for transparency, privacy-by-design, and empowerment, highlighting ethical oversight as essential in balancing data use and trust. Furthermore, Latif & Zhai (2025) demonstrate that privacy-preserving methods like federated learning can deliver AI-powered scoring without sharing raw data, maintaining model accuracy while significantly reducing privacy risks.

Institutions must establish clear data governance policies that safeguard personal information, require explicit consent for data usage, and ensure compliance with regulations like the General Data Protection Regulation (GDPR) or local equivalents. Ethical stewardship further involves applying principles such as data minimization, anonymization/pseudonymization, purpose limitation, and storage restriction—core tenets entrenched in GDPR's Article 5 and Article 25 mandates (lawful, fair, transparent processing; minimal data use; privacy by design) (Duffourc et al. 2023). The European Data Protection Board's 2025 Guidelines on Pseudonymisation provide concrete methods for implementing pseudonymization to enhance data protection while still allowing analysis—highlighting its role in reducing breach risk and enabling legitimate interest processing (EDPB, 2025). Research on data minimization in machine learning demonstrates that techniques such as feature reduction and knowledge distillation can preserve model accuracy while significantly reducing data collection, thereby fulfilling GDPR compliance without sacrificing performance (Goldsteen et al., 2022).

Furthermore, Chan (2023) offers an AI policy framework for higher education that emphasizes a strong governance dimension addressing privacy, accountability, and stakeholder participation—underscoring the institutional responsibility to operationalize these principles. Complementing this, Ghimire & Edwards (2024) found that many educational institutions currently lack specific AI and privacy policies, particularly around student data control—revealing a significant policy gap that must be addressed to uphold GDPR-style rights (Ghimire & Edwards, 2024).

Addressing Digital Divide and Access Inequities

AI-driven personalization assumes a baseline level of digital access and literacy that is far from universal. Learners in underserved communities may lack access to high-speed internet, up-to-date devices, or quiet learning environments—conditions essential for benefiting from AI-powered tools. Studies have shown that while adaptive AI systems can enhance learning outcomes for disadvantaged students (Katona & Gyonyoru, 2025), their impact is constrained by infrastructural and contextual limitations (Vesna et al., 2025). Holstein and Doroudi (2021) caution that without intentional equity-focused design, AI may inadvertently amplify existing educational inequalities. Research by Goyal et al. (2025) highlights that even when AI tools are introduced, poor connectivity, insufficient training, and socio-cultural skepticism hinder their effectiveness. Similarly, Daepp & Counts (2025) reveal that engagement with AI tools like ChatGPT remains significantly lower in less urbanized and less-educated populations, underscoring the emerging "AI divide." These findings suggest that to ensure equitable AI integration, systemic interventions—such as infrastructure investment, digital literacy training, and culturally responsive AI design—are essential to avoid exacerbating disparities and to create inclusive, supportive learning environments for all students.

Moreover, many educational algorithms are designed with assumptions that align with Western pedagogical models, potentially marginalizing learners from diverse cultural and linguistic backgrounds. Studies have shown that while AI systems offer personalized learning, their design often lacks cultural nuance and adaptability, which can limit relevance for non-Western learners. For example, Melo-López et al. (2025) found that AI's effectiveness depends not only on infrastructure and teacher training but also on how well it addresses contextual and cultural differences. Similarly, Lin et al. (2024) in their study on sustainability and cultural inclusion emphasized that many AI tools fail to reflect multilingual and multicultural realities, limiting their inclusivity and adaptability. Rizvi et al. (2024) further highlight that learners' engagement can be impacted by culturally mismatched user interface designs and interaction styles; what works in Western contexts may alienate users elsewhere. In response to this gap, tools like CulturAIEd, an LLM tool that assists teachers in adapting AI literacy curricula to students' cultural contexts, are helping teachers adapt instruction based on students' diverse cultural backgrounds—demonstrating scalable, inclusive approaches to AI-supported education (Wang et al., 2025).

To bridge the digital divide, educational institutions and policymakers must prioritize investments in infrastructure, inclusive algorithmic design, and culturally responsive training. For instance, OECD (2023) stresses that the equitable use of AI in education requires public investment in digital infrastructure, curriculum integration, and data ethics to avoid reinforcing existing disparities.

EVIDENCE-BASED CASE STUDIES OF AI-PERSONALIZED LEARNING

The study "Towards Responsible AI in Education: Hybrid Recommendation System for K-12 Students Case Study" by Drushchak et al. (2025) underscores the transformative role of AI-powered recommendation systems in personalizing the educational journey of K–12 learners. By combining graph-based modeling and matrix factorization, the system delivered highly tailored suggestions that encompassed extracurricular activities, digital resources, and volunteering opportunities aligned with each student's unique interests and aptitudes. The hybrid design addressed common limitations of single-method recommenders, ensuring a broader, more accurate, and dynamic range of learning pathways. Central to the system's design were the principles of transparency, reliability, and fairness. Transparency was achieved through mechanisms that logged the reasoning behind each recommendation, allowing both educators and learners to understand how suggestions were generated. Reliability was reinforced by validating internet-sourced and machine-generated content through human moderation and AI-driven text safety tools, ensuring that the resources were appropriate and trustworthy. Most notably, the study placed fairness at the forefront, introducing a fairness audit framework that evaluated variations in recommendation precision across protected attributes such as gender, race, socioeconomic status, and immigration background. Results indicated that, overall, the system provided equitable recommendations, though minor variations emerged in categories like volunteering and extracurricular activities. These discrepancies, however, were not rooted in algorithmic bias but were likely linked to factors such as sample size limitations, contextual conditions (e.g., availability or timing of activities), and potential gender-related differences in interest or aptitude identification. The study emphasized that ongoing fairness monitoring, combined with proactive bias mitigation strategies, is essential to prevent inadvertent inequities and sustain trust in AI-based educational technologies. Collectively, these findings highlight the potential of hybrid recommendation systems not only to personalize learning but also to support ethical and inclusive educational practices that ensure all students have fair access to growth opportunities.

Moreover, Villegas-Ch et al. (2025) in their study "Adaptive Intelligent Tutoring Systems for STEM Education: Analysis of the Learning Impact and Effectiveness of Personalized Feedback" comprehensively highlight how AI-driven intelligent tutoring systems (ITS) enhance learning outcomes in mathematics, physics, and programming. Conducted with 450 university students over one academic term, the research demonstrated that the experimental group using the ITS significantly outperformed the control group across multiple dimensions of learning. Specifically, the system improved feedback precision, with final averages of 88.5% compared to 76.3% in the control group, and reduced response times from 58.7 to 42.1 seconds. Students in the experimental group also showed a higher cumulative progress rate, mastering an average of 18.3% more concepts versus 12.6% in the control group. The analysis revealed a strong positive correlation ($R^2 = 0.76$) between sustained interaction with the system and learning progress, with highly engaged students achieving mastery rates above 90% in programming and 80% in physics. Furthermore, 80% of students reported that adaptive feedback effectively helped them identify and correct mistakes, fostering both precision and confidence. While programming students reached the highest mastery levels (85%), mathematics and physics learners also exhibited substantial gains, particularly in intermediate and advanced topics. The findings underscore the system's effectiveness in addressing the limitations of traditional standardized teaching methods by offering real-time personalization, dynamic content adjustment, and ethically managed data use. Overall, the study confirms that adaptive ITS not only boosts academic performance but also enhances learning efficiency, inclusivity, and student satisfaction, laying a strong foundation for integrating AI into future STEM education.

Furthermore, Baillifard et al (2023) study highlights the integration of an AI-powered tutor to support neuroscience students at UniDistance Suisse. The research aimed to evaluate how effectively a personal AI tutor could implement evidence-based learning strategies—particularly personalization, retrieval practice, and spaced repetition—and whether its use would enhance academic outcomes. The study's general findings are both promising and robust. The AI tutor app, powered by GPT-3 and neural-network models, dynamically adapts to each student's knowledge level, presenting questions tailored to their learning progress. This personalization enabled students to engage in distributed retrieval practice, a method proven to reinforce long-term retention. Among the 51 students who took the final exam, those who actively used the AI tutor achieved significantly higher scores, with active users showing a grade increase of up to 0.71 points and a 15 percentile-point improvement compared to peers in a similar course without the AI tutor. These improvements remained consistent across different engagement thresholds and were statistically significant. Importantly, these gains were not mirrored in students' performance on standard Moodle quizzes, suggesting that the AI tutor's benefits stemmed from its personalized learning approach rather than student motivation or engagement alone.

FUTURE TRENDS IN PERSONALIZED LEARNING

The future of personalized learning is being rapidly reshaped by advances in artificial intelligence (AI), signaling a shift toward more dynamic, inclusive, and ethically grounded educational ecosystems. One major trend is the rise of hyper-personalization powered by generative AI and multimodal data. These technologies will enable systems to adapt in real time to learners' cognitive, emotional, and behavioral profiles, offering tailored content, feedback, and assessments that go far beyond static instructional models. Alongside this, AI is expected to significantly enhance learner agency by supporting goal setting, progress monitoring, and decision-making, fostering greater self-regulation and ownership of learning. Culturally responsive personalization will also become more prominent, as AI tools begin to incorporate linguistic diversity, contextual relevance, and equity-focused design to serve marginalized and diverse learner populations better. Real-time feedback ecosystems will be further refined to include not only cognitive but also affective and motivational data, allowing for nuanced support that nurtures the whole learner. Additionally, the adoption of modular, competency-based learning pathways will allow students to progress at their own pace, with AI mapping optimal sequences aligned with personal goals and skills. Ethical considerations will be paramount, leading to greater emphasis on transparency, data privacy, bias mitigation, and explainable AI systems that promote fairness and trust. Teachers will play a central role in this future, not as passive recipients of technology but as empowered co-designers and facilitators, supported by AI in creating adaptive learning experiences. Lastly, personalized learning will expand beyond formal education to support lifelong and informal learning, enabling individuals to navigate evolving personal and professional landscapes with AI as a continuous learning companion. These trends collectively point to a future in which AI-driven personalization is not only more precise and engaging but also more human-centered, inclusive, and equitable.

DISCUSSION

The integration of artificial intelligence into personalized education represents a pivotal transformation in how learning is designed, delivered, and experienced. As documented throughout the chapter, AI-driven personalization enables a move away from rigid, standardized instructional models toward more learner-centered approaches that prioritize individual needs, interests, and progress. This shift is not merely technological but fundamentally pedagogical, demanding a reexamination of traditional roles, curriculum structures, and assessment practices. Evidence from adaptive learning systems, intelligent tutoring platforms, and data-driven analytics consistently shows improved engagement, achievement, and retention when learners receive tailored support and feedback. These outcomes affirm the potential of AI to actualize long-standing principles of differentiation, individualization, and personalization at scale—capabilities that were previously constrained by human and systemic limitations.

However, the promise of AI-personalized learning is not without challenges. Ethical concerns around algorithmic bias, data privacy, and transparency underscore the need for critical safeguards and human oversight. Without deliberate equity-focused design, AI tools risk reinforcing rather than remedying existing disparities, especially in under-resourced contexts. Moreover, the growing influence of AI in education raises important questions about learner autonomy, the role of teachers, and the boundaries of automated decision-making. Teachers remain essential as interpreters of data, designers of meaningful learning experiences, and mediators of human connection in increasingly digital environments. Their capacity to collaborate with AI tools, rather than compete with them, will be vital to ensuring that personalization serves pedagogical—not just computational—goals.

Additionally, the success of personalized learning depends on the thoughtful integration of socio-cultural dimensions. As the chapter illustrates, AI systems that are culturally blind or one-dimensional may fail to resonate with diverse learners. Embedding cultural responsiveness, inclusive design principles, and universal learning design (UDL) frameworks into AI tools is critical to ensuring accessibility and relevance across varied educational settings. Moreover, for personalization to be effective in fostering learner agency, it must be coupled with supports that scaffold metacognition, motivation, and self-regulation. AI can facilitate these processes, but human facilitation remains indispensable.

CONCLUSION

The transition from standardized, one-size-fits-all education models to AI-driven personalized learning marks a critical evolution in 21st-century pedagogy. This shift recognizes the growing diversity of learner needs, goals, and contexts, and leverages technological innovation to provide more adaptive, responsive, and meaningful learning experiences. Across a wide range of applications—including adaptive learning platforms, intelligent tutoring systems, and data-informed feedback loops—AI has demonstrated measurable improvements in student engagement, achievement, and retention. These tools not only replicate some of the benefits of individualized instruction but also scale them in ways previously unimaginable within traditional systems.

However, the future of AI-personalized education must be pursued with intentionality and ethical foresight. The full potential of personalized learning can only be realized when equity, transparency, cultural responsiveness, and data protection are embedded at every level of design and implementation. AI is not a panacea, but a tool—one that must be wielded by empowered educators, guided by inclusive pedagogical principles, and shaped through collaborative, interdisciplinary efforts. When these conditions are met, AI-driven personalization can support a more learner-centered, equitable, and future-ready education system—one that affirms the dignity, agency, and aspirations of every student.

RECOMMENDATION

To fully realize the transformative potential of AI-driven personalized learning, educational stakeholders must take deliberate and coordinated action across multiple dimensions. First, AI tools must be grounded in sound pedagogical frameworks, ensuring that technology enhances rather than overrides core educational goals such as critical thinking, deep understanding, and learner autonomy. Equally important is the empowerment of teachers through sustained professional development focused on AI literacy, ethical data use, and classroom integration. Teachers should be positioned as co-designers of AI systems, with institutional support enabling innovation and reflective practice. Ethical safeguards must also be prioritized, including the development of clear data governance policies, mechanisms for transparency and explainability, and proactive strategies to detect and mitigate algorithmic bias—aligned with global standards like the GDPR. In addition, the design of AI systems should be inclusive and culturally responsive, incorporating diverse learner profiles, languages, and contexts through frameworks such as Universal Design for Learning (UDL). To ensure equitable access, governments and institutions must invest in digital infrastructure, especially in underserved and rural areas, recognizing that the benefits of AI personalization cannot be realized without addressing the digital divide. Beyond formal education, personalized AI tools should be leveraged to support lifelong and informal learning pathways that evolve with learners' goals and career trajectories. Finally, the development and implementation of AI in education must be a collaborative effort among educators, developers, researchers, students, and policymakers. This multi-stakeholder engagement will ensure that AI systems are not only technologically robust but also educationally meaningful and socially just. Through these coordinated efforts, AI-powered personalization can become a powerful force for inclusive, learner-centered, and future-ready education.

REFERENCES

Abbas, S. G., & Ayaz, N. (2025). EXPLORING THE BENEFITS OF PERSONALIZED LEARNING IN SECONDARY EDUCATION: A DESCRIPTIVE STUDY. *Policy Journal of Social Science Review, 3*(5), 45–58.

Akintayo, O. T., Eden, C. A., Ayeni, O. O., & Onyebuchi, N. C.Olateju Temitope Akintayo-Chima Abimbola EdenOyebola Olusola AyeniNneamaka Chisom Onyebuchi. (2024). Inclusive curriculum design: Meeting the diverse needs of students for social improvement. *International Journal of Applied Research in Social Sciences, 6*(5), 770–784. DOI: 10.51594/ijarss.v6i5.1100

Alalawi, K., Athauda, R., Chiong, R., & Renner, I. (2025). Evaluating the student performance prediction and action framework through a learning analytics intervention study. *Education and Information Technologies, 30*(3), 2887–2916. DOI: 10.1007/s10639-024-12923-5

Alfredo, R., Echeverria, V., Jin, Y., Yan, L., Swiecki, Z., Gašević, D., & Martinez-Maldonado, R. (2024). Human-centred learning analytics and AI in education: A systematic literature review. *Computers and Education: Artificial Intelligence, 6*, 100215. https://doi.org//arXiv.2312.12751DOI: 10.48550

Alfredo, R., Echeverria, V., Jin, Y., Yan, L., Swiecki, Z., Gašević, D., & Martinez-Maldonado, R. (2024). Human-centred learning analytics and AI in education: A systematic literature review. *Computers and Education: Artificial Intelligence, 6*, 100215. DOI: 10.1016/j.caeai.2024.100215

Baillifard, A., Gabella, M., Lavenex, P. B., & Martarelli, C. S. (2023). Implementing learning principles with a personal AI tutor: A case study. *arXiv preprint arXiv:2309.13060.* https://doi.org//arXiv.2309.13060DOI: 10.48550

Bayly-Castaneda, K., Ramirez-Montoya, M. S., & Morita-Alexander, A. (2024, August). Crafting personalized learning paths with AI for lifelong learning: a systematic literature review. In *Frontiers in Education* (Vol. 9, p. 1424386). Frontiers., DOI: 10.3389/feduc.2024.1424386

Bayly-Castaneda, K., Ramirez-Montoya, M. S., & Morita-Alexander, A. (2024, August). Crafting Personalized Learning Paths with AI for Lifelong Learning: A Systematic Literature Review. [). Frontiers.]. *Frontiers in Education, 9*, 1424386. DOI: 10.3389/feduc.2024.1424386

Bellhäuser, H., Dignath, C., & Theobald, M. (2023). Daily automated feedback enhances self-regulated learning: A longitudinal randomized field experiment. *Frontiers in Psychology, 14*, 1125873. DOI: 10.3389/fpsyg.2023.1125873

Bi, M., Struyven, K., & Zhu, C. (2023). Variables that influence teachers' practice of differentiated instruction in Chinese classrooms: A study from teachers' perspectives. *Frontiers in Psychology, 14*, 1124259. DOI: 10.3389/fpsyg.2023.1124259

Brod, G., Kucirkova, N., Shepherd, J., Jolles, D., & Molenaar, I. (2023). Agency in educational technology: Interdisciplinary perspectives and implications for learning design. *Educational Psychology Review, 35*(1), 25. DOI: 10.1007/s10648-023-09749-x

Celik, I., Gedrimiene, E., Silvola, A., & Muukkonen, H. (2023). Response of learning analytics to the online education challenges during the pandemic: Opportunities and key examples in higher education. *Policy Futures in Education*, *21*(4), 387–404. DOI: 10.1177/14782103221078401

Chan, C. K. Y. (2023). A comprehensive AI policy education framework for university teaching and learning. *International Journal of Educational Technology in Higher Education*, *20*(1), 38. DOI: 10.1186/s41239-023-00408-3

Chaudhry, M. A., Cukurova, M., & Luckin, R. (2022, July). A transparency index framework for AI in education. In *International Conference on Artificial Intelligence in Education* (pp. 195-198). Cham: Springer International Publishing. https://doi.org/DOI: 10.1007/978-3-031-11647-6_33

Chinta, S. V., Wang, Z., Yin, Z., Hoang, N., Gonzalez, M., Quy, T. L., & Zhang, W. (2024). FairAIED: Navigating fairness, bias, and ethics in educational AI applications. *arXiv preprint arXiv:2407.18745*. https://doi.org//arXiv.2407.18745DOI: 10.48550

Cody, R. A., Boldt, G. T., & Gubbins, E. J. (2023). How Teachers Make Decisions in Response to Professional Learning: A Study on Grade 3 Differentiation in Mathematics. *Journal of Advanced Academics*, *35*(1), 156–185. DOI: 10.1177/1932202X231221143

Contrino, M. F., Reyes-Millán, M., Vázquez-Villegas, P., & Membrillo-Hernández, J. (2024). Using an adaptive learning tool to improve student performance and satisfaction in online and face-to-face education for a more personalized approach. *Smart Learning Environments*, *11*(1), 6. DOI: 10.1186/s40561-024-00292-y

Daepp, M. I., & Counts, S. (2025, June). The Emerging Generative Artificial Intelligence Divide in the United States. In *Proceedings of the International AAAI Conference on Web and Social Media (*Vol. 19, pp. 443-456). https://doi.org/DOI: 10.1609/icwsm.v19i1.35825

Drushchak, N., Tyshchenko, V., & Polyakovska, N. (2025, April). Towards Responsible AI in Education: Hybrid Recommendation System for K-12 Students Case Study. In *2025 IEEE/ACM International Workshop on Responsible AI Engineering (RAIE)* (pp. 61-68). IEEE. DOI: DOI: 10.1109/RAIE66699.2025.00015

Duffourc, M. N., Gerke, S., & Kollnig, K. (2023). Privacy of personal data in generative AI data lifecycle. *NYU J. Intell. Prop. & Ent. L.*, *13*, 219.

Engeness, I., Nohr, M., & Fossland, T. (2025). Investigating AI Chatbots' Role in Online Learning and Digital Agency Development. *Education Sciences*, *15*(6), 674. DOI: 10.3390/educsci15060674

European Data Protection Board (EDPB). (2025). Guidelines 01/2025 on Pseudonymisation. Retrieved from: https://www.edpb.europa.eu/system/files/202501/edpb_guidelines_202501_pseudonymisation_en.pdf

Feldman-Maggor, Y., Cukurova, M., Kent, C., & Alexandron, G. (2025). The Impact of Explainable AI on Teachers' Trust and Acceptance of AI EdTech Recommendations: The Power of Domain-specific Explanations. *International Journal of Artificial Intelligence in Education*, *35*(5), 1–34. DOI: 10.1007/s40593-025-00486-6

Gándara, D., Anahideh, H., Ison, M. P., & Picchiarini, L. (2024). Inside the black box: Detecting and mitigating algorithmic bias across racialized groups in college student-success prediction. *aera Open, 10*, 23328584241258741. https://doi.org//arXiv.2301.03784DOI: 10.48550

Gherman, O., Turcu, C. E., & Turcu, C. O. (2022). An approach to adaptive microlearning in higher education. *arXiv preprint arXiv:2205.06337*. https://doi.org//arXiv.2205.06337DOI: 10.48550

Ghimire, A., & Edwards, J. (2024, July). From guidelines to governance: A study of AI policies in education. In *International Conference on Artificial Intelligence in Education* (pp. 299-307). Cham: Springer Nature Switzerland. https://doi.org/DOI: 10.1007/978-3-031-64312-5_36

Goh, T. T. (2025). Learning management system log analytics: The role of persistence and consistency of engagement behaviour on academic success. *Journal of Computers in Education*, •••, 1–24. DOI: 10.1007/s40692-025-00358-x

Goldsteen, A., Ezov, G., Shmelkin, R., Moffie, M., & Farkash, A. (2022). Data minimization for GDPR compliance in machine learning models. *AI and Ethics*, *2*(3), 477–491. DOI: 10.1007/s43681-021-00095-8

Gomez, M. J., Armada Sanchez, A., Albaladejo-González, M., Garcia Clemente, F. J., & Ruipérez-Valiente, J. A. (2024, April). Utilizing explainable AI to enhance real-time student performance prediction in educational serious games. In *Proceedings of the 39th ACM/SIGAPP Symposium on Applied Computing* (pp. 93-94). https://doi.org/DOI: 10.1145/3605098.3636109

Gonzalez-Nucamendi, A., Noguez, J., Neri, L., Robledo-Rella, V., & García-Castelán, R. M. G. (2023, October). Predictive analytics study to determine undergraduate students at risk of dropout. *In Frontiers in Education (Vol. 8*, p. 1244686). Frontiers Media SA. https://doi.org/DOI: 10.3389/feduc.2023.1244686

Goyal, H., Garg, G., Mordia, P., Ramachandran, V., Kumar, D., & Challa, J. S. (2025). The Impact of Large Language Models on K-12 Education in Rural India: A Thematic Analysis of Student Volunteers' Perspectives. *arXiv preprint arXiv:2505.03163*. https://doi.org//arXiv.2505.03163DOI: 10.48550

Gujjula, R., & Sanghera, K. (2023). Ethical considerations and data privacy in AI education. *Journal of Student-Scientists' Research, 5*. https://doi.org/DOI: 10.13021/jssr2023.3958

Gunasekara, S., & Saarela, M. (2025). Explainable AI in Education: Techniques and Qualitative Assessment. *Applied Sciences (Basel, Switzerland)*, *15*(3), 1239. DOI: 10.3390/app15031239

Hernández-de-Menéndez, M., Morales-Menendez, R., Escobar, C. A., & Ramírez Mendoza, R. A. (2022). Learning analytics: State of the art. *International Journal on Interactive Design and Manufacturing*, *16*(3), 1209–1230. DOI: 10.1007/s12008-022-00930-0

Holstein, K., & Doroudi, S. (2021). Equity and artificial intelligence in education: Will" aied" amplify or alleviate inequities in education? *arXiv preprint arXiv:2104.12920*. https://doi.org//arXiv.2104.12920DOI: 10.48550

Hooshyar, D., Weng, X., Sillat, P. J., Tammets, K., Wang, M., & Hämäläinen, R. (2024). The effectiveness of personalized technology-enhanced learning in higher education: A meta-analysis with association rule mining. *Computers & Education, 223*, 105169. DOI: 10.1016/j.compedu.2024.105169

Idowu, J. A. (2024). Debiasing education algorithms. *International Journal of Artificial Intelligence in Education, 34*(4), 1510–1540. DOI: 10.1007/s40593-023-00389-4

Ilić, M., Mikić, V., Kopanja, L., & Vesin, B. (2023). Intelligent techniques in e-learning: A literature review. *Artificial Intelligence Review, 56*(12), 14907–14953. DOI: 10.1007/s10462-023-10508-1

Jauhiainen, J. S., & Garagorry Guerra, A. (2024, November). Generative AI and education: dynamic personalization of pupils' school learning material with ChatGPT. *In Frontiers in Education (Vol. 9*, p. 1288723). Frontiers Media SA. https://doi.org/DOI: 10.3389/feduc.2024.1288723

Jiang, Z., & Jiang, M. (2024). Beyond answers: Large language model-powered tutoring system in physics education for deep learning and precise understanding. *arXiv preprint arXiv:2406.10934*. https://doi.org//arXiv.2406.10934DOI: 10.48550

Johannes, C., & Haase, A. (2022). The impact of feedback mode on learning gain and self-efficacy: A quasi-experimental study. *Active Learning in Higher Education, 25*(3), 391–407. DOI: 10.1177/14697874221131970

Johnston, L. J., Griffin, J. E., Manolopoulou, I., & Jendoubi, T. (2024). Uncovering Student Engagement Patterns in Moodle with Interpretable Machine Learning. *arXiv preprint arXiv:2412.11826*. https://doi.org//arXiv.2412.11826DOI: 10.48550

Jones, K. M. (2019). Learning analytics and higher education: A proposed model for establishing informed consent mechanisms to promote student privacy and autonomy. *International Journal of Educational Technology in Higher Education, 16*(1), 1–22. DOI: 10.1186/s41239-019-0155-0

Jurado-Castro, J. M., Vargas-Molina, S., Gomez-Urquiza, J. L., & Benitez-Porres, J. (2023). Effectiveness of real-time classroom interactive competition on academic performance: A systematic review and meta-analysis. *PeerJ. Computer Science, 9*, e1310. DOI: 10.7717/peerj-cs.1310

Kahmann, R., Droop, M., & Lazonder, A. W. (2022). Meta-analysis of professional development programs in differentiated instruction. *International Journal of Educational Research, 116*, 102072. DOI: 10.1016/j.ijer.2022.102072

Katona, J., & Gyonyoru, K. I. K. (2025). AI-based Adaptive Programming Education for Socially Disadvantaged Students: Bridging the Digital Divide. *TechTrends, 69*(5), 1–18. DOI: 10.1007/s11528-025-01088-8

Kaziya, K. (2025). Adopting Differentiated Instruction in High School Mathematics Classrooms: Challenges and Successes in Kalomo District, Zambia. *International Journal of Research and Innovation in Social Science, 9*(4), 5479–5506. DOI: 10.47772/IJRISS.2025.90400391

Khor, E. T., & K, M. (2024). A Systematic Review of the Role of Learning Analytics in Supporting Personalized Learning. *Education Sciences, 14*(1), 51. DOI: 10.3390/educsci14010051

Kyza, E. A., & Georgiou, Y. (2025). Curriculum Redesign to Increase Equity and Promote Active Citizenship in Science Education. *Education Sciences*, *15*(3), 319. DOI: 10.3390/educsci15030319

Lee, H., & Kizilcec, R. F. (2020). Evaluation of fairness trade-offs in predicting student success. *arXiv preprint arXiv:2007.00088*. https://doi.org//arXiv.2007.00088DOI: 10.48550

Leguisamo, M., Posada, G. J., Pilco-Chambilla, F. W., & Mena, M. I. (2025). Personalization of Learning through Artificial Intelligence: An Analysis of Adaptive Models in Digital Education. *Journal of Information Systems Engineering & Management*, *10*(30s), 836–846. Advance online publication. DOI: 10.52783/jisem.v10i30s.4922

Liang, W., To, J., & Lo, Y. Y. (2024). A journey towards teacher empowerment in differentiated Instruction: Implications for a Sustainable Teacher Professional Development Model. *Asia Pacific Education Review*, •••, 1–13. DOI: 10.1007/s12564-024-09977-y

Lin, M. P.-C., Liu, A. L., Poitras, E., Chang, M., & Chang, D. H. (2024). An Exploratory Study on the Efficacy and Inclusivity of AI Technologies in Diverse Learning Environments. *Sustainability (Basel)*, *16*(20), 8992. DOI: 10.3390/su16208992

Liu, B., Zhang, J., Lin, F., Jia, X., & Peng, M. (2025, May). One size doesn't fit all: A personalized conversational tutoring agent for mathematics instruction. In *Companion Proceedings of the ACM on Web Conference 2025* (pp. 2401-2410). https://doi.org/DOI: 10.1145/3701716.3717527

Liu, V., Latif, E., & Zhai, X. (2025). Advancing education through tutoring systems: A systematic literature review. *arXiv preprint arXiv:2503.09748*. https://doi.org//arXiv.2503.09748DOI: 10.48550

Looi, C. K., & Jia, F. (2025). Personalization capabilities of current technology chatbots in a learning environment: An analysis of student-tutor bot interactions. *Education and Information Technologies*, *30*(10), 1–31. DOI: 10.1007/s10639-025-13369-z

Looi, C. K., & Jia, F. (2025). Personalization capabilities of current technology chatbots in a learning environment: An analysis of student-tutor bot interactions. *Education and Information Technologies*, *30*(10), 1–31. DOI: 10.1007/s10639-025-13369-z

Lu, K., Hao, L., Wang, I. J., & Liu, A. (2024, July). Eighth Graders and a Math Intelligent Tutoring System: A Deep Neural Network Analysis. In *International Conference on Artificial Intelligence in Education* (pp. 38-46). Cham: Springer Nature Switzerland. https://doi.org/DOI: 10.1007/978-3-031-64312-5_5

Mao, Q. (2025). Fostering Self-Directed Growth with Generative AI: Toward a New Learning Analytics Framework. *arXiv preprint arXiv:2504.20851*. https://doi.org//arXiv.2504.20851DOI: 10.48550

Matz, S. C., Bukow, C. S., Peters, H., Deacons, C., Dinu, A., & Stachl, C. (2023). Using machine learning to predict student retention from socio-demographic characteristics and app-based engagement metrics. *Scientific Reports*, *13*(1), 5705. DOI: 10.1038/s41598-023-32484-w

Matz, S. C., Bukow, C. S., Peters, H., Deacons, C., Dinu, A., & Stachl, C. (2023). Using machine learning to predict student retention from socio-demographic characteristics and app-based engagement metrics. *Scientific Reports, 13*(1), 5705. DOI: 10.1038/s41598-023-32484-w

Melo-López, V.-A., Basantes-Andrade, A., Gudiño-Mejía, C.-B., & Hernández-Martínez, E. (2025). The Impact of Artificial Intelligence on Inclusive Education: A Systematic Review. *Education Sciences, 15*(5), 539. DOI: 10.3390/educsci15050539

Mirea, C.-M., Bologa, R., Toma, A., Clim, A., Plăcintă, D.-D., & Bobocea, A. (2025). Transforming Learning with Generative AI: From Student Perceptions to the Design of an Educational Solution. *Applied Sciences (Basel, Switzerland), 15*(10), 5785. DOI: 10.3390/app15105785

N. L., ... & Shimada, A. (2024). Evaluating algorithmic bias in models for predicting academic performance of Filipino students. *arXiv preprint arXiv:2405.09821.* DOI DOI: 10.5281/zenodo.12729935

OECD. (2023). *OECD Digital Education Outlook 2023: Towards an Effective Digital Education Ecosystem.* OECD Publishing., DOI: 10.1787/c74f03de-

Rincon-Flores, E. G., Castano, L., Guerrero Solis, S. L., Olmos Lopez, O., Rodríguez Hernández, C. F., Castillo Lara, L. A., & Aldape Valdés, L. P. (2024). Improving the learning-teaching process through adaptive learning strategy. *Smart Learning Environments, 11*(1), 27. DOI: 10.1186/s40561-024-00314-9

Rizvi, S., Rienties, B., Rogaten, J., & Kizilcec, R. F. (2024). Are MOOC learning designs culturally inclusive (enough)? *Journal of Computer Assisted Learning, 40*(6), 2496–2512. DOI: 10.1111/jcal.12883

Sajja, R., Sermet, Y., Cikmaz, M., Cwiertny, D., & Demir, I. (2024). Artificial intelligence-enabled intelligent assistant for personalized and adaptive learning in higher education. *Information (Basel), 15*(10), 596. DOI: 10.3390/info15100596

Sajja, R., Sermet, Y., Cikmaz, M., Cwiertny, D., & Demir, I. (2024). Artificial intelligence-enabled intelligent assistant for personalized and adaptive learning in higher education. *Information (Basel), 15*(10), 596. DOI: 10.3390/info15100596

Sajja, R., Sermet, Y., Cwiertny, D., & Demir, I. (2023). Integrating AI and learning analytics for data-driven pedagogical decisions and personalized interventions in education. *arXiv preprint arXiv:2312.09548.* https://doi.org//arXiv.2312.09548DOI: 10.48550

Salendab, F. A., Tago, K. L., Cogo, D. A., & Demafeliz, R. E. (2026). Transforming Higher Education: Theoretical Foundations and Innovative Pedagogies for Holistic Student Development. In *Higher Education Classrooms as Places for Inquiry: Stories and Methods from Practitioner Researchers* (pp. 207-236). IGI Global Scientific Publishing. DOI: DOI: 10.4018/979-8-3373-0305-5.ch007

Shoukat, B., & Adnan, M. S. (2025). TECHNOLOGY FEEDBACK AND STUDENT MOTIVATION IN TECHNOLOGY-ENHANCED LEARNING ENVIRONMENTS: A CORRELATIONAL STUDY. *Policy Research Journal, 3*(1), 838–854. Retrieved from https://policyresearchjournal.com/index.php/1/article/view/347

Shrestha, A. K., Barthwal, A., Campbell, M., Shouli, A., Syed, S., Joshi, S., & Vassileva, J. (2024). Navigating AI to unpack youth privacy concerns: An in-depth exploration and systematic review. *arXiv preprint arXiv:2412.16369*. https://doi.org//arXiv.2412.16369DOI: 10.1109/IEMCON62851.2024.11093125

Shrestha, A. K., & Joshi, S. (2025, January). Toward ethical AI: A qualitative analysis of stakeholder perspectives. In *2025 IEEE 15th Annual Computing and Communication Workshop and Conference (CCWC)* (pp. 00022-00029). IEEE. https://doi.org/DOI: 10.1109/CCWC62904.2025.10903879

Sölch, M., Aberle, M., & Krusche, S. (2023). Integrating competency-based education in interactive learning systems. *arXiv preprint arXiv:2309.12343*. https://doi.org//arXiv.2309.12343DOI: 10.48550

Solis Trujillo, B. P., Velarde-Camaqui, D., Gonzales Nuñez, C. A., Castillo Silva, E. V., & Gon zalez Said de la Oliva, M. D. P. (2025, May). The current landscape of formative assessment and feedback in graduate studies: a systematic literature review. In *Frontiers in Education (Vol. 10,* p. 1509983). Frontiers Media SA. https://doi.org/DOI: 10.3389/feduc.2025.1509983

Song, S., Liu, W., Lu, Y., Zhang, R., Liu, T., Lv, J., . . . Hao, H. (2025). Cultivating Helpful, Personalized, and Creative AI Tutors: A Framework for Pedagogical Alignment using Reinforcement Learning. *arXiv preprint arXiv:2507.20335*. https://doi.org//arXiv.2507.20335DOI: 10.48550

Spitzer, M. W. H., & Moeller, K. (2024). Performance increases in mathematics within an intelligent tutoring system during COVID-19-related school closures: A large-scale longitudinal evaluation. *Computers and Education Open*, *6*, 100162. DOI: 10.1016/j.caeo.2024.100162

Strielkowski, W., Grebennikova, V., Lisovskiy, A., Rakhimova, G., & Vasileva, T. (2025). AI-driven adaptive learning for sustainable educational transformation. *Sustainable Development (Bradford)*, *33*(2), 1921–1947. DOI: 10.1002/sd.3221

Sumagang, S. J., & Balano, N. L. (2025). Embracing Diversity: General Education Teachers' Lived Experiences in Teaching Learners with Special Needs in an Inclusive Setting. *International Journal of Innovation and Scientific Research*, *12*(6), 729–739. DOI: 10.51244/IJRSI.2025.12060059

Švábenský, V., Verger, M., Rodrigo, M. M. T., Monterozo, C. J. G., Baker, R. S., Saavedra, M. Z. N. L., . . . Shimada, A. (2024). Evaluating algorithmic bias in models for predicting academic performance of filipino students. arXiv preprint arXiv:2405.09821.

Swamy, V., Du, S., Marras, M., & Kaser, T. (2023, March). Trusting the explainers: teacher validation of explainable artificial intelligence for course design. In LAK23: *13th International Learning Analytics and Knowledge Conference* (pp. 345-356). https://doi.org/DOI: 10.1145/3576050.3576147

Tasdelen, O., & Bodemer, D. (2025). Generative AI in the Classroom: Effects of Context-Personalized Learning Material and Tasks on Motivation and Performance. *International Journal of Artificial Intelligence in Education*, *35*(5), 1–22. DOI: 10.1007/s40593-025-00491-9

Tetzlaff, L., Hartmann, U., Dumont, H., & Brod, G. (2022). Assessing individualized instruction in the classroom: Comparing teacher, student, and observer perspectives. *Learning and Instruction*, *82*, 101655. DOI: 10.1016/j.learninstruc.2022.101655

Topali, P., Chounta, I. A., Martínez-Monés, A., & Dimitriadis, Y. (2023). Delving into instructor-led feedback interventions informed by learning analytics in massive open online courses. *Journal of Computer Assisted Learning*, *39*(4), 1039–1060. DOI: 10.1111/jcal.12799

Uzun, Y., Suraworachet, W., Zhou, Q., Gauthier, A., & Cukurova, M. (2025). Engagement with analytics feedback and its relationship to self-regulated learning competence and course performance. *International Journal of Educational Technology in Higher Education*, *22*(1), 17. DOI: 10.1186/s41239-025-00515-3

Vesna, L., Sawale, P. S., Kaul, P., Pal, S., & Murthy, B. S. N. V. R. (2025). Digital divide in AI-powered education: Challenges and solutions for equitable learning. *Journal of Information Systems Engineering & Management*, *10*(21), 1–9. DOI: 10.52783/jisem.v10i21s.3327

Villegas-Ch, W., Buenano-Fernandez, D., Navarro, A. M., & Mera-Navarrete, A. (2025). Adaptive intelligent tutoring systems for STEM education: Analysis of the learning impact and effectiveness of personalized feedback. *Smart Learning Environments*, *12*(1), 1–31. DOI: 10.1186/s40561-025-00389-y

Villegas-Ch, W., Buenano-Fernandez, D., Navarro, A. M., & Mera-Navarrete, A. (2025). Adaptive intelligent tutoring systems for STEM education: Analysis of the learning impact and effectiveness of personalized feedback. *Smart Learning Environments*, *12*(1), 1–31. DOI: 10.1186/s40561-025-00389-y

Waladi, C., & Lamarti, M. S. (2024). Adaptive AI-driven assessment for competency-based learning scenarios. In *Innovative Instructional Design Methods and Tools for Improved Teaching* (pp. 215–226). IGI Global Scientific Publishing., DOI: 10.4018/979-8-3693-3128-6.ch010

Wang, J., Xiao, R., Hou, X., Li, H., Tseng, Y. J., Stamper, J., & Koedinger, K. (2025, July). LLMs to Support K–12 Teachers in Culturally Relevant Pedagogy: An AI Literacy Example. In *International Conference on Artificial Intelligence in Education* (pp. 152-160). Cham: Springer Nature Switzerland. https://doi.org/DOI: 10.1007/978-3-031-99264-3_19

Wang, Z. (2025). The Impact of Teacher Feedback on Student Motivation in Online Learning Environments: A Study Based on Self-Determination Theory. *Journal of Education, Humanities, and Social Research*, *2*(2), 13–27. DOI: 10.71222/syf4kg35

Yan, J., Tian, H., Sun, X., & Song, L. (2025, April). Role of artificial intelligence in enhancing competency assessment and transforming curriculum in higher vocational education. In *Frontiers in Education (Vol. 10*, p. 1551596). Frontiers Media SA. https://doi.org/DOI: 10.3389/feduc.2025.1551596

Yan, J., Tian, H., Sun, X., & Song, L. (2025, April). Role of artificial intelligence in enhancing competency assessment and transforming curriculum in higher vocational education. In *Frontiers in Education (Vol. 10*, p. 1551596). Frontiers Media SA. https://doi.org/DOI: 10.3389/feduc.2025.1551596

Yaseen, H., Mohammad, A. S., Ashal, N., Abusaimeh, H., Ali, A., & Sharabati, A.-A. A. (2025). The Impact of Adaptive Learning Technologies, Personalized Feedback, and Interactive AI Tools on Student Engagement: The Moderating Role of Digital Literacy. *Sustainability (Basel)*, *17*(3), 1133. DOI: 10.3390/su17031133

Yuan[1], L., Hou[1], B., Feng, D., & Rahman[1], S. S. A. (2025, June). Predictive Analytics in Education: Leveraging AI for Personalizing Student Learning Trajectories. In *Proceedings of the 2nd International Conference on Educational Development and Social Sciences (EDSS 2025)* (Vol. 924, p. 309). Springer Nature. DOI:DOI: 10.2991/978-2-38476-400-6_38

Chapter 10

AI for Personalized Learning Experiences: Adaptive Course Content and Intelligent Tutoring Systems

Sohaib Ahmad Khalil
https://orcid.org/0009-0006-6885-5779
Abasyn Universtiy, Peshawar, Pakistan

Mohsin Mahmood
City University of Science and Information Technology, Peshawar, Pakistan

Zulfiqar Ali
https://orcid.org/0000-0003-4744-0997
City University of Science and Information Technology, Pakistan

Iftikhar Alam
City University of Science and Information Technology, Peshawar, Pakistan

ABSTRACT

Over the past several years, education software has advanced greatly. Students receive tailored courses depending on their learning styles using such technologies. Next, this approach is applied to e-learning systems and a framework for designing and using a knowledge and learner adaptive system is presented. There are great potential to employ AI to give students with individualized learning experiences. This study expect tutoring methods to supplement and even replace expert human instruction for more topics by integrating adaptive material and intelligent tutoring technologies. Therefore, the purpose of adaptive content and intelligent tutoring systems research is to deliver high-quality tailored education to students globally and make it not only interesting for instructors but also useful for students in reaching their specific learning goals. In addition, this study recommend new avenues for fundamental AI research, notably in cognitive architectures and natural language processing, once the proposed systems are applied to new contracts and knowledge-driven peer review systems.

DOI: 10.4018/979-8-3373-2752-5.ch010

1. INTRODUCTION TO AI IN EDUCATION

Unprecedented access to technology that increasingly influences all aspects of our lives has also changed learners' expectations, expanding the demand for quality education. In recent years, a lot of attention has been dedicated to harnessing the capacities of such technologies to provide educational resources to learners, a phenomenon known as educational technology (Simamora, 2020). An important technological development that is changing education is the use of artificial intelligence (AI). AI applications rest on the analysis of large volumes of data, often gathered through systems that directly monitor students engaged in some learning activity. The resulting data can be used to infer important aspects of learners' knowledge or cognitive processes, offering personalized learner support that promotes successful cognitive and emotional outcomes (Dai & Ke, 2022). The use of AI in education is at its beginning. Fortunately, the number of educational technologies that integrate these kinds of tools is rising. Such tools possess a pleasant characteristic: they can be adapted to the specific learner at hand, optimizing learning styles and rates according to their specific circumstances (Chen et al., 2022). In that way, AI may be an essential element of a strategy to ensure that every learner is reached in their specific characteristics and distinctive learning needs, minimizing the risks of labeling, stigmatizing, or even developing phobias toward learning that arise when this does not happen. This capability is known by educational systems as personalization (Murtaza et al., 2022). This chapter offers four exemplary application domains where AI can be blended with personalization to increase the effectiveness and expansiveness of education, initially discussing AI-supported tutoring, both conceptualized as intelligent tutoring systems, and the personalization of educational resources in the form of adaptive digital content (Alam & Mohanty, 2023).

1.1. Overview of Personalized Learning

Personalized learning adjusts the learning environment to individual students' needs. It is clear that students have different learning expectations. Some students want to master specific knowledge and solve relevant problems in a specific domain, while others demand well-rounded development, such as self-improvement of psychological behavior and physical skills, or balanced development (Zhang et al., 2020). Students differ in their current knowledge background and the knowledge they want to master. These differences are the basis for personalized education. Adaptive course materials can be used to meet this requirement (Zhang et al., 2023). Alternatively, intelligent tutors can provide individual coaching to learners. These customized learning services can help students effectively overcome their learning obstacles and ultimately improve their learning efficiency (Alam, 2021). Students learn at different speeds, and individualized learning speeds can also be obtained through personalization. Some students may encounter difficulties in different sections of the content and may not be able to complete the expected learning route (Watters, 2023). Intelligent tutoring systems can determine the content drill-down point for students who need to slow down. These two ways of personalizing the learning experience can improve student performance significantly. In order to improve student learning performance, many intelligent tutoring systems should consider providing the above personalization services (Alam, 2023). It is not straightforward to provide individualized learning services because adaptive courses and intelligent tutoring systems must fully understand users' knowledge, requirements, and learning gaps. Users' knowledge background, learning difficulties, and needs can be complex issues (Lin et al., 2023).

1.2. Evolution of Intelligent Tutoring Systems

The first Intelligent Tutoring System (ITS) was developed by American psychologist and computer scientist Jerome Bruner in 1960, a decade after the seminal work on programmed learning, which is associated with B.F. Skinner, Marvin Minsky, and the English mathematician Alan Turing, whose famous computer science work defines the theoretical foundations of artificial intelligence (Brass & Lynch, 2020). Bruner's Tutor performed in a fashion similar to the Optimal-Schedule Tutor Model, applying reinforcement learning to program a teaching machine. Using a probabilistic approach called symbolic Regress-And-Suggest, the probability that programming step i should be suggested is based on the contexts in which the failure of programmed material j causes a student to actively shift into prompt state k during remote error repair (Naeem et al., 2020). American cognitive scientist John Sweller combined psychological research on instructional design with machine learning research on planning to develop his first intelligent tutoring system, the Intelligent Computer Tutor, in the early 1980s (Valtonen et al., 2022). In the intelligent tutoring system for statistics, learning involves the construction of production systems allowing a cognitive tutor to support remote error repair, programming step scheduling, digit string-based input modeling, symbolic derived response embedding, rule-based operator encapsulation, and human exploitation as a backup prompting source during intelligent tutoring (Doroudi, 2023).

2. FOUNDATIONS OF ADAPTIVE LEARNING

When it comes to education, no two individuals are alike; therefore, each student needs educational resources that best fit individual learning objectives, prior knowledge, cognitive abilities, and unique learning styles (Tzenios, 2020). Customized teaching programs, exercises, problems, quizzes, and learning materials are the keys to success in the educational process. Unfortunately, the personal attention given to individual students by the traditional method of teaching is quite difficult for an educational institution and has the potential for extravagant processes (Kem, 2022). Cyber learning has become an important discipline that seeks to fulfill individual educational requirements, both inside and outside the traditional classroom, with an extensive variety of methods, such as online learning and the cyber instructor (Katchapakirin et al., 2022). Adaptation in e-learning has several meanings; the general idea is to present the learner with competing resources or activities in an autonomous way to provide them with the most suitable resource for their learning goals at the level of knowledge (El-Sabagh, 2021). This could be accomplished using learning styles, knowledge levels, experience, and several other factors. An adaptive educational hypermedia can adjust the presentation, navigation, tools, and content based on both the individual profile and the learning objectives of the users (Qodad et al., 2020). Several adaptive e-learning models can be described regarding learning navigation, personalized presentation, implicit scaffolding, and recommended exercises, tasks, courses, and study materials (Boussakuk et al., 2020). Adaptive learning hypermedia servers possess the ability to acquire and reuse existing learning materials and also to add new, pedagogically enhanced elements. They also implement three new family member adaptivity strategies, each in a server prototype, with counterparts for advanced, moderate, and beginner computer science classifiers (Troussas et al., 2020).

2.1. Machine Learning and Data Analytics

In order to realize the vision of PLE, the course content delivered to each student should be personalized in a way that each content item should be adjusted for that particular student with different contents and metadata (Alamri et al., 2020). Adaptive intelligent tutoring systems should be designed and developed to provide tutoring that is adapted to individual students, applying contemporary educational methodologies and strategies (Mousavinasab et al., 2021). All these services should involve a high level of artificial intelligence expertise to create and evaluate deep learning models that take into account educational best practices. To achieve these objectives, a long-standing research problem in AI, known as the Knowledge Tracing Problem, should be solved (Brcic & Yampolskiy, 2023). The problem of when and whether a learner has learned, or 'knowledge tracing,' is a well-established problem in modern psychometric research. This work builds on those ideas and models, uses real-world datasets to evaluate different language models, and targets computer-assisted language learning. It is important to note that the problem at hand involves a sequence of time-varying multi-valued node (or sequential) label predictions about a single student, which formalizes learning model creation and evaluation for knowledge components contained by the activities included in the personalized learning objects in a knowledge space model about a particular subject over multiple micro-time instances (Gan et al., 2020).

2.2. Personalization Algorithms

Personalized learning systems are often designed to cluster learners according to their learning performance and their learning behavior. Typically, learning performance is assessed based on self-assessment tests or assignments, and learning behavior is assessed based on knowledge assessment tests and historic usage data (Murtaza et al., 2022). Then, learner models are created that aim to capture these clusters of learners. Management systems then use these learner models to register a new learner with a cluster and personalize the learning content presented to this new learner (Walkington and Bernacki, 2020). The definitions of learner models and the management systems that work with these models may vary a lot in practice. Additionally, many algorithms have been proposed to assess learning performance and learning behavior and to subsequently cluster learners (Abou et al., 2020). Most algorithms survey the learners' performance and behavior, build a learner model, and then let the management system create a personalized learning experience for a learner that is represented by this learner model. This is certainly the case when this learner model consists of relatively simple information, such as cluster membership, test scores, and browsing history (Maghsudi et al., 2021). However, it also applies to many intelligent tutoring systems, which may build complex cognitive or affective models of the student and then use these models to provide the student with personalized instruction (Taub et al., 2021).

3. DESIGN AND IMPLEMENTATION OF ADAPTIVE COURSE CONTENT

The specialization of adapted structures mentioned in the previous section is due to the ad-hoc approach to each of them. In general, any adaptive educational module, regardless of its internal structure, can be represented in the form of nodes. Some nodes are called high-level nodes, and some are called low-level nodes (Han et al., 2021). Every high-level node contains one or more sub-nodes, which can also contain their sub-nodes. Thus, the subordinated hierarchy of educational resources is formed. Some nodes contain educational material, i.e., the content in the form of studied educational resources (Yilmaz, 2021). The adaptive approach allows these structures to be adapted according to favorable factors or according to a specific sequence of educational resources, leading to the achievement of a learning goal (El-Sabagh, 2021). The sequence of mastered educational resources can be represented with the concept of a path representing the educational path. Here, it is possible that the specific sequence can be a supported one, which means that the recommended path along which the user or users should learn or are learning educational resources is known. Such a path, based on historical or other user data, may have specifics that distinguish it from a general path, or the path cannot be known in advance, as is the case with personalized teaching materials whose path depends on the previously studied resources or context (Bhutoria, 2022). Thus, the sequence of educational resources and the concept of a path are critical elements in the design and implementation of personalization solutions for learning. In many scenarios, adaptive learning systems actively recommend a path or personalized teaching materials based on the path (Alamri et al., 2020). The purpose of this could be the following: to enable a more personalized study at the educational goal, adapt to the preferences, interests, and pace of the user, increasing user engagement and understanding, increasing learning performance, and gaining knowledge (Bayly-Castaneda et al., 2024)

3.1. Content Adaptation Techniques

To keep up with the rapidly changing world, universities need effective teaching that prepares students for future jobs requiring a broad range of skills. Students arriving at higher education institutions have differing abilities, backgrounds, and prior experiences, which can make it challenging for a lecturer to deliver personalized instruction (Thiem & Dasgupta, 2022). Lectures deliver the same content using static slides or videos and collaborate with students using little or no feedback on student progress, despite differing learning rates and mastery levels for each student. Recent advances in AI offer the possibility for large-scale personalized learning and provide common and powerful tools that can be repurposed for advanced learning models (Alqahtani et al., 2023). In this section, we summarize how AI has been used for a wide range of personalized learning experiences in order to design appropriate teaching strategies, to recognize and intervene during student frustration or disengagement, and to identify and remedy potential discrimination while providing personalized instruction. (Jaiswal and Arun, 2021). Content adaptation for personalized learning has been the focus of a relatively large number of AI technology applications for K-12 education. AI software adapts its learning objectives frequently and dynamically based on an individual student's progress (Gligorea et al., 2023). The AI Tutor also adapts the content of master's degree level course material for software development according to individual student learning speed and mastery levels. At a basic level, content is adapted through the incorporation of advanced educational models that are capable of ingesting a student's past history to personalize recommendations (Yilmaz et al., 2022). These models might decide the order in which associated course content activities are presented, thereby steering the student's learning in real time and making the learning experience more efficient and less frustrating. The objective of an adaptive educational model might be to maximize some form of learning that is properly validated during development, such as improved assessment, retention, student success, motivation, engagement, or pleasure (Ramspek et al., 2021).

3.2. User Interface Design Considerations

The user interface and its design impact the perceived ease of use and are crucial for the acceptance of any type of system. For an ITS design, good user interface design facilitates the communication of important information as well as the acceptance of tutoring. The most important difference between a typical eLearning system and an ITS is the individual sessions that adapt the system dynamically to the students' learning needs (Hasan et al., 2020). However, there are many similarities. The goal of an ITS user interface design is to minimize the burden of understanding and integration for the tutors and students while facilitating the learning process. The categorization of different types of user interface designs for ITS in the classroom context proposes five types of interfaces, which are completely encapsulated, tutoring system, enhancement, engagement, and bystander. . Each type is described by the type-specific data flow between the learning system and the student, i.e., data flow inside and outside of the student. The additional type of face-to-face interaction suggests that the pedagogical agent lives in the interface. In this category, the pedagogical agent is a virtual instructor to facilitate adaptive task management in the classroom (Sajja et al., 2024). Whether embedded in an LMS or as an independent service, AI-driven applications aim for smooth and seamless access for teachers and students while respecting data privacy regulations (Aithal and Maiya, 2023).

Personality typing might offer a basis for preferences in usable ITS designs for the users. Computer research has revealed promising results as to how personality type predicts students' learning behaviors (Conati et al., 2021). There are some, albeit low, significant relations of students' personality and their learning agent use. Results seem to suggest that highly extraverted individuals use agents more frequently, and more introverted individuals prefer more intelligent agents, enhancement agents, and bystander agents. Character typing would be beneficial for user interface customization, nurture a more positive experience for students, and possibly boost their academic success. Being able to predict possible differences between students that could shape user preferences and requirements, and hence model behavior in a more personalized way, is an essential requirement to face in a modern didactic approach (Pentina et al., 2023). However, using personality type as an input for the development of educational content should be advanced with caution to respect user data privacy at all times. As students are still maturing, and younger adolescents in particular may not have yet formed a fixed personality type, care over labeling could also have ethical consequences (Harb et al., 2024).

4. INTELLIGENT TUTORING SYSTEMS: ARCHITECTURE AND FUNCTIONALITY

Intelligent Tutoring Systems (ITS) are a particular form of Adaptive Educational Hypermedia Systems (AEHS). Their usual features of knowledge representation, modeling of the student, modeling of the domain, modeling of tutoring strategies, and adaptive behavior to some degree depend on technologies also adopted by other AEHS (Akuma and Ndera, 2021). Nevertheless, some of these features are specific to ITS. Typically, the functions of modeling the student and the domain are inherited by systems belonging to both elementary AEHS and ITS, but the modeling of the tutoring strategy for each individual student interaction depends on the tutor's adaptivity, which is not a functionality employed by any AEHS (Singh et al., 2022). Usually, in an AEHS, the kind of adaptivity is related to the kind of content or student adaptivity it has, with content adaptation being any change performed in the presentation or navigation of the course considering each student's interests, knowledge, goals, or learning styles or profiles. In the field of AEHS, student adaptivity can refer to restricted modeling of user characteristics or to deeper analysis of user progression. (Oliveira et al., 2021). Therefore, ITS presents some adaptivity characteristics not found in other AEHS. In this way, the aim of this chapter is to present the concept of Intelligent Tutoring Systems and discuss their main components (Qodad et al., 2020).

4.1. Components of ITS

General diverse properties of intelligent tutoring systems (ITS) have been described as modeling assistance, learner model, and student interface. Many features of the tutoring model can be identified that provide or are related to such assistance, the student model, or the student interface. These features, to a large extent, characterize a given ITS (Hasan et al., 2020). At an abstract level, an ITS can be said to embody a tutoring model, through which the ITS conducts its tutoring conversations with the student (Lippert et al., 2020). Furthermore, the way in which a diverse collection of tutoring strategies and tactics is organized and employed, and the way in which the ITS selects actions in order to conduct tutoring dialogues are of primary concern. The representation of these tutoring strategies and tactics and the actions through which the ITS conducts a tutoring dialogue, within the ITS tutoring model, and the process employed by the ITS to select these tutoring actions in the context of the current student needs and prior tutoring dialogues, are the central elements of this paper (Lin et al., 2022). The architecture of the tutoring system and the control by which these components are utilized is viewed as being of secondary importance, paying rich attention to the tutoring model components (Pardos et al., 2023). As such, they describe features of the tutoring model, and the representation and control features of the tutoring system are attributed only brief mention (MacLellan and Koedinger, 2022).

4.2. Adaptive Feedback Mechanisms

For our adaptive platform, we are questioning the following research questions and hypotheses: When L and C are observed, what is the threshold that can predict a success estimate and the model sensitivity to offer adaptive exercises to the learner? Is the learners' performance influenced by their knowledge since the L value at their next success? The learners' self-evaluation of the learning content level can influence their performance at the next exercises. In the process of model estimation, we used the categorical variable indicating how much learning time has passed since the learners' last success (Ibrahim et al., 2024). Response alterations through threshold estimates allow us to discriminate among the effects of previous success and traditional models and the behavior of specific groups of learners in adaptive systems. The baseline model was estimated, instructing that all learners have the same L since their last success (Howard et al., 2020). The estimated model shows sensitivity: The success scores were approximately 65.6% on average for learners with the same L since their last success compared to those with L = 1 (average success score of 76.7%). For learners with L = 2 (average success score of 80.5%), the success score increased even more, indicating the positive influence of the adapted number of learning materials on performance. The model's inherent bias was the specificity non-decreasing pattern. However, the L = 1 condition's success scores were approximately equal to those observed with L = 3 or higher (Hussong et al., 2021).

5. ETHICAL AND PRIVACY CONSIDERATIONS IN AI-DRIVEN EDUCATION

Schools and universities are generally trusted institutions and should more easily facilitate the sharing and use of data. However, owing to concerns such as data misuse and lack of understanding of the purposes of data collection, this is not automatically assumed. The regulation protects the privacy of individuals and prohibits the misuse of personal data, with the motivation being to ensure that individuals exercise control over their own data and that organizations that collect, manage, and use personal data do so in a manner that is transparent, just, and fair. It has evolved due to technological developments, globalization, expanded scope, processing activities, and offering of services to a large audience (Nissenbaum, 2020). One of the most sensitive aspects of using AI in educational settings involves the collection and use of student data. Ethical issues around the possible impact of analytics, profiling, and automated decision-making within educational AI are heightened by the intersection of algorithmic tools with fragile institutions, public funding, and human development (Kooli, 2023). There is a finely balanced trade-off between privacy and the potential benefits arising from the widespread implementation of AI. Privacy considerations are particularly important within the context of children and young people. Ethical concerns associated with privacy mean that disclosure of plans for the design or deployment of AI projects within educational settings can be limited, and anonymization or pseudonymization of personal data is important as a fundamental principle of privacy protection. Research has found that access to personal data, like video data that captures intimate behaviors or facial images, is highly influential to human judgment and attitudes (Bevan et al., 2020). Algorithmic decisions could be particularly inscrutable, and privacy concerns can be heightened as the output of analysis may be particularly sensitive and subject to high degrees of interpretation (Selbst, 2021).

5.1. Data Security and Student Privacy

Security and privacy issues are recognized as one of the significant factors that hinder educational institutions from using cloud computing-based services due to fear of unauthorized access, data breaches, data loss, hackers, and third-party snoopers. Recent advances in artificial intelligence technology in educational institutions have resulted in drastic improvements in learning experiences (Ahmad et al., 2021). With the help of AI technology, education is moving toward personalized learning experiences with features like real-time analysis and feedback, adaptive content support, and automatic grading of personalized student responses (Pratama et al., 2023). These learning features involve the exchange of personal student data with the service provider's cloud-based infrastructure, query execution, learning feedback, and recommendation systems. These interactions attract security and privacy problems that expose personal data and information about student learning activities. Online exam-related activities also need to be secured against attempts to subvert their integrity and fairness (Rizi & Seno, 2022). To overcome these concerns and increase confidence in the use of AI services with cloud services, transparent management of student data security and privacy issues through zero-knowledge cryptosystems, strong authentication and authorization protocols, secure password management, secure interfaces to the AI system, secure programming, training and query execution modules, and non-intrusive auditing and logging mechanisms are paramount (Anyanwu et al., 2024). Security and privacy solutions and guidelines should be stakeholder-centric or student-centric and provider-driven rather than just compliance-centered. In addition, the feedback from relevant regulations, standards, and best practice guidelines in the presence of potential attack vectors should be used to address these issues as best as can be provided (Komljenovic, 2022).

5.2. Bias and Fairness in AI Algorithms

AI brings the promise of developing truly personalized learning systems, where course content will be able to adapt to the learning progress of individual students, and intelligent tutor systems will provide real-time guidance and support for the students. AI systems make important decisions about people, and even small errors in the output of an AI system can lead to inappropriate treatment and serious consequences (Qushem et al., 2021). AI decision-making and algorithmic fairness are therefore important fields of study, constrained by the fact that fairness is a very complex and multidimensional concept. Algorithmic fairness varies across disciplines, applications, and communities, as decisions about the appropriate trade-offs between different objectives must be taken explicitly by considering the problem's context. The algorithm's behavior is not the only relevant issue when studying fairness, but it differs according to the data and labeling, as well as the utility and deployment of the decisions (Mhasawade et al., 2021). Disparate treatment or impact, stereotypes in the labeling, and low or biased quality data or training have been the root causes of unfairness in many AI systems. Nonetheless, fairness is a moving target, since many decisions and the balancing among them are highly dynamic across time and space, making the concept of implementing fairness challenging when building AI systems (Tapalova & Zhiyenbayeva, 2022). However, many bias and unfairness problems can be preemptively minimized, or even eliminated, from being evident once an AI model is already deployed and in use. Especially in the case of educational AI, AI experts who also understand educational constraints can contribute to alleviating many of these problems through their scientific and technical expertise (Fenu et al., 2022). This review highlights some of the potential problem areas and challenges that are arising as educational AI begins to delve deeper into personalized learning, drawing attention to this important field of study (Abulibdeh et al., 2024).

6. CASE STUDIES AND BEST PRACTICES IN PERSONALIZED LEARNING

Case Study 1: Individual Progress Visualization to Incite Adoption of Self-Regulatory Activities The concept of learning analytics expresses the use of methods and tools to visualize and assess the entire learning process, aims to make the learning process more transparent, and supports it actively. A learning process is not only characterized by the learning outcomes but also by the activities of the learners (Sedrakyan et al., 2020). Self-regulatory activities such as attending a lecture, working on exercises, reading books or papers, and preparing for an exam are important determinants of the learning outcome. Because it is assumed that self-regulatory activities are linked to learning success, it is important to incite students to complete high-quality self-regulatory activities. To visualize the learning progress of a specific student, we developed a dashboard that calculates and visualizes the time-dependent and target group-dependent progression parameters of a student. Automatically recorded activities of students take into account the full variety of different self-regulatory activities conducted by students. Information about context and learning content helps to identify problem zones in the learning content of a lecture that students are most likely to miss without an understandable presentation (Demirören et al., 2020). The dashboard visualizes the learning progress of a student in an adapted presentation form as a region chart and function plot, along with a prediction algorithm that calculates the self-regulatory status of the student at a given time by using prior development. The visualization and prediction methods support teaching staff in the composition and scheduling of learning activities. They provide a single entry point to track activities, warning and encouraging students to increase their activity, suggesting how targeted interventions can incite growth to these target values, and can be applied to improve the perception and acceptance of adaptive course content as well as the flexible composition of educational offerings (Valle et al., 2021).

Case Study 2: Visual Map Analysis of Student Guidance and Supports toward Social and Affective Learning Adaptive educational systems assist learners in the learning process by adjusting the content and tasks of the learning activity to learners based on their individual learning characteristics (El-Sabagh, 2021). Many adaptive educational systems focusing on cognitive aspects have been developed. We suggest that when learners feel emotions during learning, they can further advance. Thus, when implementing adaptive educational systems in language learning, the system not only needs to consider the learners' cognitive state but should also be designed to provide appropriate guidance to positively influence the learners' emotions (Martin et al., 2020). The purpose of this study is to apply a clustering method to analyze the part the learners received guidance so that a function is obtained. The learners' activities have been identified as both high cognitive activity and high affective activity. Their linguistic expression in the hangout has been affected by the high affective activity. The percentage of learning distress and intensity are 46.8% and over 90%. With the domain expert's approval, the Visual Map Analysis of Student Guidance and Supports toward Social and Affective Learning is considered useful to provide a clear path for course intervention for the learners (Raposa et al., 2024).

6.1. Successful Implementations in Higher Education

So, it has now been a bit over a decade, and there must have been many successful implementations at different educational levels. Clearly, AI is not a new kid on the block, and adaptive learning is timeless! We are pleased to point out these positive results as well. The program was developed to assist instructors and committees of courseware titles in bringing the full spectrum of the instructional design process to their courses early and systematically (Su & Zhong, 2022). This program is a highly successful marriage of teacher, computer, and student. The instruction is designed and delivered by a sophisticated computer system. Its flexibility suits nearly every instructional design approach. The well-structured lessons allow an instructor to emphasize some points and skim over others to ensure full syllabus coverage and highlight new and especially important concepts (Wong et al., 2020). The computerized tutoring can involve the student in a two-way dialogue, but more importantly, tutors can ask open-ended questions and critique student responses. With the master's level courseware, the computer offers a thorough understanding of the systems, a practical framework, and guided exercises designed to encourage the student to bring about changes (Khan et al., 2020).

6.2. Impact on Student Engagement and Performance

AI has the potential to create more social learning experiences, support student self-regulation, and improve student engagement. While the academic outcomes of such approaches are still the subject of debate, there is already plenty of concrete evidence that engagement is improved. GA-enhanced Geometry and Statistics courses have demonstrated improvements in student achievement. Student engagement in electronic textbooks was increased using GA, improving student performance. Usage later increased dramatically, showing high levels of student attention. An EU-funded project developing an AI ecosystem that supports in and out of classroom learning improved student engagement and the quality of interactions (Hooda et al., 2022).

Beyond the benefit of personalized and insightful advice, the primary selling point for the use of AI in higher education is the high educational gains and social experience. Consequently, many researchers focus on capturing how social AI systems can be used to encourage more productive and rewarding social interactions in digital educational environments. An automated tutor not only encouraged student interaction but was also found to be very good at pursuing meaningful and nondirective dialogues with students and providing encouragement. The importance of high-quality social interactions was emphasized, leading to the development of an AI tutor capable of forming strong social interactions. For example, enabling students to take part in collaborative lectures stimulated complex levels of understanding, such as evaluating the data available in complex situations or re-evaluating oneself and replacing previous knowledge (Atlas, 2023).

7. FUTURE DIRECTIONS AND EMERGING TECHNOLOGIES IN AI FOR EDUCATION

The recent advances in areas such as developmental models, multimodal learning analytics, affective computing, personalized domain modeling, and more naturalistic and effective use of AI in conversation systems and judgment work present significant opportunities for future research and applications. The diverse nature of the contributions to this book and their success in enabling student growth, delivering resources, performance, or student models, and personalizing systems for different groups of people with very different backgrounds and strengths all suggest that with the focused and cross-interdisciplinary use of advances in AI, psychology, education, sociology, and the learning sciences, significant moves toward very high-quality personalized learning experiences and scalable student engagement and performance are achievable by both traditional learning communities and society at large (Sundari et al., 2024).

With increasingly rich educational experiences through technologies with AI, built-in assessment capabilities, and instruction that is increasingly AI-enhanced, the potential application of these advances for individuals and groups of participants living in emerging economies, in refugee and poverty-stricken communities, people with learning or physical disabilities, or isolated by geography becomes an exciting as well as an urgent focus for the research and education community. The development of technologies for developing, delivering, and building social connectedness, work, and meaning for underserved populations and refugees can be a uniquely humanitarian application area for AI and education, with strong contributions from AI and people with diverse backgrounds across the globe (Uche-Anya et al., 2022).

7.1. Virtual Reality and Augmented Reality in Education

Virtual Reality (VR) and Augmented Reality (AR) are technologies that are often applied in the entertainment industry. They have become a thriving sector in the industry, with many applications for the real estate business, retail industry, tourism, and healthcare. At the same time, education has also entered the adoption scene for these technologies. The need for a more active learning approach requires students to find methods that allow them to experience new kinds of mental images in three dimensions. VR and AR can provide more authentic, interactive, personalized, and memorable learning experiences for both instructors and students. A study compared a traditional course and an immersive VR course in an information systems program. The VR course shows better student performance, proving that immersive technology can significantly improve the teaching and learning process (Scavarelli et al., 2021). Another study demonstrates that AR technology is feasible and effective in supplementing the nursing curriculum. AR-assisted instruction and hands-on practice significantly improve students' nursing skills and learning engagement. The researchers claim that AR technology not only enhances nursing students' learning but also helps program directors make decisions about using this technology in nursing education, making the program a key success factor. The effectiveness of AR technology in visualizing the complex flow of scientific concepts or phenomena, either within the classroom or using different scenarios, is also noted. The results reveal that students using AR technology have a better understanding of the scientific concepts or phenomena than students learning in a traditional way. Overall, these AR applications are feasible and useful tools for mastering abstract concepts, visualization techniques, and concept-based learning (AlGerafi et al., 2023).

7.2. Natural Language Processing for Personalized Feedback

Open-response assessments provide students with an opportunity to reflect and express themselves in open questions. As a result, the responses can reflect both the level of academic understanding as well as the individuality of the student. The combination of these two aspects is particularly interesting given the argument that the quality of learning depends on the extent to which a student is engaged both academically and emotionally, and the claim that using personal awareness when processing tasks is important to avoid burnout and other motivational problems. Indeed, personal feedback was argued to play an essential role in helping a student understand the material and develop his or her own mental model of a system, as well as play a key role in increased reflection and awareness of his or her own learning and for improved knowledge acquisition (Irons & Elkington, 2021).

Automated natural language processing methods enable an automatic analysis of a student's open response by the computer when a teacher marking each response isn't available. By providing students with multiple and immediate attempts to solve a task, the system not only ensures this requirement on the provided support but also supports students' motivation and engagement. We investigate how adaptive feedback components implemented by trainable models to perform a two-stage text analysis can be used to automatically process open-response assessments and determine the academic understanding and emotional engagement of the student. We argue that the problem space is particularly interesting when associated with deep learning research and application agendas. After all, part of the social challenges in the interplay between humans and computers aims to provide systems with both cognition and prosody to say 'decide' and 'are you angry' (Shaik et al., 2022).

CONCLUSION

Intelligent tutoring systems foster personalized learning. In recent years, data-based approaches have found their way into ITS. In this regard, this chapter discusses content-based and collaborative filtering methods for recommending learning content, as well as methods for combining them. Higher-order models based on observable data were synthesized, allowing the prediction of actual skill gain of a user in the context of concrete educational resources. This helped identify the properties of good learning content. Furthermore, a first step towards integrating predicted learning gain into the tutoring process has been presented: a user model mapping input data to expected future performance, serving as a didactic filter for the learning progress. Results show the usefulness of the higher-order models as well as the initial success of the didactic filter combined with learning gain prediction. In conclusion, machine learning models and quantitative user models have found their way into tutor support by aiming at safeguarding learning success through predicting learning gain. Thereby, practitioners and learners can profit from such predictions in order to adjust their learning strategies.

Future work will, for example, include more complex tutoring strategies in which other factors, such as motivation and emotions, are also taken into account for personalizing the user experience. Additionally, discoverable effects of learning content on extrinsic performance measures, such as task performance, error rates, and time to finish, need to be systematically evaluated. Furthermore, a constructivist tutoring approach can be considered, leading to multi-dimensional user models. Lastly, the integration of uncertainty quantification into the predictive model can foster accountable predictions, thus safeguarding fairness and transparency in the learning process, as well as fostering trust in the offered AI support.

REFERENCES

Abulibdeh, A., Zaidan, E., & Abulibdeh, R (2024). Navigating the confluence of artificial intelligence and education for sustainable development in the era of industry 4.0: Challenges, opportunities, and ethical .... Journal of Cleaner Production. sciencedirect.com

Ahmad, W., Rasool, A., Javed, A. R., Baker, T., & Jalil, Z (2021). Cyber security in iot-based cloud computing: A comprehensive survey. Electronics. mdpi.com

Aithal, P. S., & Maiya, A. K. (2023). Innovations in Higher Education Industry–Shaping the Future. [IJCSBE]. *International Journal of Case Studies in Business, IT, and Education*, *7*(4), 283–311. DOI: 10.47992/IJCSBE.2581.6942.0321

Akuma, S., & Ndera, T. (2021). Adaptive educational hypermedia system for high school students based on learning styles. [researchgate.net]. *International Journal of Educational and Pedagogical Sciences*, *15*(2), 228–234.

Alam, A. (2021, December). Should robots replace teachers? Mobilisation of AI and learning analytics in education. In 2021 International Conference on Advances in Computing, Communication, and Control (ICAC3) (pp. 1-12). IEEE. ssrn.com DOI: 10.1109/ICAC353642.2021.9697300

Alam, A. (2023). Harnessing the Power of AI to Create Intelligent Tutoring Systems for Enhanced Classroom Experience and Improved Learning Outcomes. In Intelligent Communication Technologies and Virtual Mobile Networks (pp. 571-591). Singapore: Springer Nature Singapore. [HTML] DOI: 10.1007/978-981-99-1767-9_42

Alam, A., & Mohanty, A. (2023). Educational technology: Exploring the convergence of technology and pedagogy through mobility, interactivity, AI, and learning tools. Cogent Engineering. tandfonline.com

Alamri, H., Lowell, V., Watson, W., & Watson, S. L. (2020). Using personalized learning as an instructional approach to motivate learners in online higher education: Learner self-determination and intrinsic motivation. [academia.edu]. *Journal of Research on Technology in Education*, *52*(3), 322–352. DOI: 10.1080/15391523.2020.1728449

AlGerafi, M. A. M., Zhou, Y., Oubibi, M., & Wijaya, T. T (2023). Unlocking the potential: A comprehensive evaluation of augmented reality and virtual reality in education. Electronics. mdpi.com

Alqahtani, T., Badreldin, H. A., Alrashed, M., Alshaya, A. I., Alghamdi, S. S., bin Saleh, K., Alowais, S. A., Alshaya, O. A., Rahman, I., Al Yami, M. S., & Albekairy, A. M. (2023). The emergent role of artificial intelligence, natural learning processing, and large language models in higher education and research. [sciencedirect.com]. *Research in Social & Administrative Pharmacy*, *19*(8), 1236–1242. DOI: 10.1016/j.sapharm.2023.05.016

Anyanwu, A., Olorunsogo, T., Abrahams, T. O., Akindote, O. J., & Reis, O. (2024). Data confidentiality and integrity: A review of accounting and cybersecurity controls in superannuation organizations. [fepbl.com]. *Computer Science & IT Research Journal*, *5*(1), 237–253. DOI: 10.51594/csitrj.v5i1.735

Atlas, S (2023). ChatGPT for higher education and professional development: A guide to conversational AI. uri.edu

Bayly-Castaneda, K., Ramirez-Montoya, M. S., & Morita-Alexander, A. (2024, August). Crafting personalized learning paths with AI for lifelong learning: A systematic literature review. [). Frontiers Media SA. frontiersin.org]. *Frontiers in Education*, *9*, 1424386. DOI: 10.3389/feduc.2024.1424386

Bevan Jones, R., Stallard, P., Agha, S. S., Rice, S., Werner-Seidler, A., Stasiak, K., Kahn, J., Simpson, S. A., Alvarez-Jimenez, M., Rice, F., Evans, R., & Merry, S. (2020). Practitioner review: Co-design of digital mental health technologies with children and young people. [wiley.com]. *Journal of Child Psychology and Psychiatry, and Allied Disciplines*, *61*(8), 928–940. DOI: 10.1111/jcpp.13258

Bhutoria, A (2022). Personalized education and artificial intelligence in the United States, China, and India: A systematic review using a human-in-the-loop model. Computers and Education: Artificial Intelligence. sciencedirect.com

Boussakuk, M., Bouchboua, A., El Ghazi, M., Fattah, M., & El Bekkali, M (2020). A fully individualized adaptive and intelligent educational hypermedia system: Details of cleveruniversity. International Journal, 8(5). researchgate.net

Brass, J. & Lynch, T. L (2020). Personalized learning: A history of the present. Journal of curriculum theorizing. jctonline.org

Brcic, M. & Yampolskiy, R. V (2023). Impossibility Results in AI: a survey. Acm computing surveys. acm.org

Chen, X., Zou, D., Xie, H., Cheng, G., & Liu, C. (2022). Two decades of artificial intelligence in education. Educational Technology & Society. ln.edu.hk

Conati, C., Barral, O., Putnam, V., & Rieger, L. (2021). Toward personalized XAI: A case study in intelligent tutoring systems. [PDF]. *Artificial Intelligence*, *298*, 103503. DOI: 10.1016/j.artint.2021.103503

Dai, C. P., & Ke, F. (2022). Educational applications of artificial intelligence in simulation-based learning: A systematic mapping review. *Computers and Education: Artificial Intelligence*, *3*, 100087.

Demirören, M., Turan, S., & Taşdelen Teker, G. (2020). Determinants of self-regulated learning skills: The roles of tutors and students. [physiology.org]. *Advances in Physiology Education*, *44*(1), 93–98. DOI: 10.1152/advan.00121.2019

Doroudi, S. (2023). The intertwined histories of artificial intelligence and education. [springer.com]. *International Journal of Artificial Intelligence in Education*, *33*(4), 885–928. DOI: 10.1007/s40593-022-00313-2

El-Sabagh, H. A. (2021). Adaptive e-learning environment based on learning styles and its impact on development students' engagement. [springer.com]. *International Journal of Educational Technology in Higher Education*, *18*(1), 53. DOI: 10.1186/s41239-021-00289-4

Fenu, G., Galici, R., & Marras, M. (2022, July). Experts' view on challenges and needs for fairness in artificial intelligence for education. In *International Conference on Artificial Intelligence in Education* (pp. 243-255). Cham: Springer International Publishing. [PDF] DOI: 10.1007/978-3-031-11644-5_20

Gan, W., Sun, Y., & Sun, Y. (2020, November). Knowledge interaction enhanced knowledge tracing for learner performance prediction. In 2020 7th international conference on behavioural and social computing (BESC) (pp. 1-6). IEEE. researchgate.net DOI: 10.1109/BESC51023.2020.9348285

Gligorea, I., Cioca, M., Oancea, R., Gorski, A. T., Gorski, H., & Tudorache, P. (2023). Adaptive learning using artificial intelligence in e-learning: A literature review. [mdpi.com]. *Education Sciences*, *13*(12), 1216. DOI: 10.3390/educsci13121216

Han, L., Du, B., Sun, L., Fu, Y., Lv, Y., & Xiong, H. (2021, August). Dynamic and multi-faceted spatio-temporal deep learning for traffic speed forecasting. In Proceedings of the 27th ACM SIGKDD conference on knowledge discovery & data mining (pp. 547-555). [HTML] DOI: 10.1145/3447548.3467275

Harb, A., Khliefat, A., Alazaizeh, M. M., & Eyoun, K. (2024). Do personality traits predict students' interest and intentions toward working in the tourism and hospitality industry? Evidence from a developing country. [researchgate.net]. *Journal of Hospitality & Tourism Education*, *36*(2), 165–181. DOI: 10.1080/10963758.2023.2175690

Hasan, M. A., Noor, N. F. M., Rahman, S. S. B. A., & Rahman, M. M. (2020). The transition from intelligent to affective tutoring system: A review and open issues. [ieee.org]. *IEEE Access : Practical Innovations, Open Solutions*, *8*, 204612–204638. DOI: 10.1109/ACCESS.2020.3036990

Hooda, M., Rana, C., Dahiya, O., Rizwan, A., & Hossain, M. S. (2022). Artificial intelligence for assessment and feedback to enhance student success in higher education. [wiley.com]. *Mathematical Problems in Engineering*, *2022*(1), 5215722. DOI: 10.1155/2022/5215722

Howard, J. J., Rabbitt, L. R., & Sirotin, Y. B (2020). Human-algorithm teaming in face recognition: How algorithm outcomes cognitively bias human decision-making. Plos one. plos.org

Hussong, J., Mattheus, H., Wachs, S., Equit, M., & von Gontard, A. (2021). Evaluation of a bladder and bowel training program for therapy-resistant children with incontinence. [HTML]. *Journal of Pediatric Urology*, *17*(3), 302–e1. DOI: 10.1016/j.jpurol.2021.01.042

Ibrahim, K. A. A. A., Kassem, M. A. M., & Lami, D (2024). … Assisted Language Assessment (ICALA) in philosophy-based language instruction: unraveling the effects on critical thinking, self-evaluation, academic resilience, and …. Language Testing in Asia. springer.com

Irons, A., & Elkington, S. (2021). Enhancing learning through formative assessment and feedback. sunderland.ac.uk

Jaiswal, A., & Arun, C. J. (2021). Potential of Artificial Intelligence for transformation of the education system in India. [ed.gov]. *International Journal of Education and Development Using Information and Communication Technology*, *17*(1), 142–158.

Katchapakirin, K., Anutariya, C., & Supnithi, T. (2022). ScratchThAI: A conversation-based learning support framework for computational thinking development. [springer.com]. *Education and Information Technologies, 27*(6), 8533–8560. DOI: 10.1007/s10639-021-10870-z

Kem, D. (2022). Personalised and adaptive learning: Emerging learning platforms in the era of digital and smart learning. [researchgate.net]. *International Journal of Social Science and Human Research, 5*(2), 385–391. DOI: 10.47191/ijsshr/v5-i2-02

Khan, A., Ayega, D., Aguilar, I., & Baker, R. (2020). *The digital tutor and student engagement techniques: An intelligent way to engage students in ITS*. Innovate Learning Summit. [HTML]

Komljenovic, J (2022). The future of value in digitalised higher education: why data privacy should not be our biggest concern. Higher Education. springer.com

Kooli, C (2023). Chatbots in education and research: A critical examination of ethical implications and solutions. Sustainability. mdpi.com

Lin, C. C., Huang, A. Y. Q., & Lu, O. H. T (2023). Artificial intelligence in intelligent tutoring systems toward sustainable education: a systematic review. Smart Learning Environments. springer.com

Lin, J., Singh, S., Sha, L., Tan, W., Lang, D., Gašević, D., & Chen, G. (2022). Is it a good move? Mining effective tutoring strategies from human–human tutorial dialogues. [github.io]. *Future Generation Computer Systems, 127*, 194–207. DOI: 10.1016/j.future.2021.09.001

Lippert, A., Shubeck, K., Morgan, B., Hampton, A., & Graesser, A. (2020). Multiple agent designs in conversational intelligent tutoring systems. Technology [ed.gov]. *Knowledge and Learning, 25*(3), 443–463. DOI: 10.1007/s10758-019-09431-8

MacLellan, C. J., & Koedinger, K. R. (2022). Domain-general tutor authoring with apprentice learner models. [springer.com]. *International Journal of Artificial Intelligence in Education, 32*(1), 76–117. DOI: 10.1007/s40593-020-00214-2

Maghsudi, S., Lan, A., Xu, J., & van Der Schaar, M. (2021). Personalized education in the artificial intelligence era: What to expect next. [PDF]. *IEEE Signal Processing Magazine, 38*(3), 37–50. DOI: 10.1109/MSP.2021.3055032

Martin, F., Chen, Y., Moore, R. L., & Westine, C. D. (2020). Systematic review of adaptive learning research designs, context, strategies, and technologies from 2009 to 2018. [odu.edu]. *Educational Technology Research and Development, 68*(4), 1903–1929. DOI: 10.1007/s11423-020-09793-2

Mhasawade, V., Zhao, Y., & Chunara, R (2021). Machine learning and algorithmic fairness in public and population health. Nature Machine Intelligence. nature.com

Mousavinasab, E., Zarifsanaiey, N., & Niakan Kalhori, R., S., Rakhshan, M., Keikha, L., & Ghazi Saeedi, M. (. (2021). Intelligent tutoring systems: A systematic review of characteristics, applications, and evaluation methods. [academia.edu]. *Interactive Learning Environments, 29*(1), 142–163. DOI: 10.1080/10494820.2018.1558257

Murtaza, M., Ahmed, Y., Shamsi, J. A., Sherwani, F., & Usman, M. (2022). AI-based personalized e-learning systems: Issues, challenges, and solutions. *IEEE Access : Practical Innovations, Open Solutions, 10*, 81323–81342.

Naeem, M., Rizvi, S. T. H., & Coronato, A (2020). A gentle introduction to reinforcement learning and its application in different fields. IEEE access. ieee.org

Nissenbaum, H (2020). Protecting privacy in an information age: The problem of privacy in public. The ethics of information technologies. cpeterson.org

Oliveira, G., Grenha Teixeira, J., Torres, A., & Morais, C. (2021). An exploratory study on the emergency remote education experience of higher education students and teachers during the COVID-19 pandemic. [nih.gov]. *British Journal of Educational Technology, 52*(4), 1357–1376. DOI: 10.1111/bjet.13112

Pardos, Z. A., Tang, M., Anastasopoulos, I., Sheel, S. K., & Zhang, E. (2023, April). Oatutor: An open-source adaptive tutoring system and curated content library for learning sciences research. In Proceedings of the 2023 chi conference on human factors in computing systems (pp. 1-17). acm.org DOI: 10.1145/3544548.3581574

Pentina, I., Hancock, T., & Xie, T (2023). Exploring relationship development with social chatbots: A mixed-method study of replika. Computers in Human Behavior. researchgate.net

Pratama, M. P., Sampelolo, R., & Lura, H (2023). Revolutionizing education: harnessing the power of artificial intelligence for personalized learning. Klasikal: Journal of education, language teaching and science, 5(2), 350-357. journalfkipuniversitasbosowa.org

Qodad, A., Benyoussef, A., El Kenz, A., & Elyadari, M. (2020). Toward an adaptive educational hypermedia system (AEHS-JS) based on the overlay modeling and felder and silverman's learning styles model for job seekers. [iJET]. *International Journal of Emerging Technologies in Learning, 15*(8), 235–254. DOI: 10.3991/ijet.v15i08.10574

Qushem, U. B., Christopoulos, A., Oyelere, S. S., Ogata, H., & Laakso, M. J. (2021). Multimodal technologies in precision education: Providing new opportunities or adding more challenges? [mdpi.com]. *Education Sciences, 11*(7), 338. DOI: 10.3390/educsci11070338

Ramspek, C. L., Jager, K. J., Dekker, F. W., Zoccali, C., & van Diepen, M. (2021). External validation of prognostic models: What, why, how, when and where? [oup.com]. *Clinical Kidney Journal, 14*(1), 49–58. DOI: 10.1093/ckj/sfaa188

Raposa, E. B., Bartolotta, K., Forbes, N., Monjaras-Gaytan, L. Y., Garcia, Y., Ulerio, G., & Salusky, I. (2024). Emotional distress and access to mental healthcare among first-generation college students during the onset of the COVID-19 pandemic. [HTML]. *The Journal of Higher Education*, •••, 1–29.

Rizi, M. H. P., & Seno, S. A. H. (2022). A systematic review of technologies and solutions to improve security and privacy protection of citizens in the smart city. [HTML]. *Internet of Things : Engineering Cyber Physical Human Systems.*

Sajja, R., Sermet, Y., Cikmaz, M., Cwiertny, D., & Demir, I (2024). Artificial intelligence-enabled intelligent assistant for personalized and adaptive learning in higher education. Information. mdpi.com

Scavarelli, A., Arya, A., & Teather, R. J (2021). Virtual reality and augmented reality in social learning spaces: a literature review. Virtual Reality. carleton.ca

Sedrakyan, G., Malmberg, J., Verbert, K., Järvelä, S., & Kirschner, P. A. (2020). Linking learning behavior analytics and learning science concepts: Designing a learning analytics dashboard for feedback to support learning regulation. [ou.nl]. *Computers in Human Behavior*, *107*, 105512. DOI: 10.1016/j.chb.2018.05.004

Selbst, A. D (2021). An institutional view of algorithmic impact assessments. Harv. JL & Tech.. harvard.edu

Shaik, T., Tao, X., Li, Y., Dann, C., McDonald, J., Redmond, P., & Galligan, L. (2022). A review of the trends and challenges in adopting natural language processing methods for education feedback analysis. [ieee.org]. *IEEE Access : Practical Innovations, Open Solutions*, *10*, 56720–56739. DOI: 10.1109/ACCESS.2022.3177752

Simamora, R. M. (2020). The Challenges of online learning during the COVID-19 pandemic: An essay analysis of performing arts education students. *Studies in Learning and Teaching*, *1*(2), 86–103.

Singh, N., Gunjan, V. K., & Nasralla, M. M (2022). A parametrized comparative analysis of performance between proposed adaptive and personalized tutoring system "seis tutor" with existing online tutoring system. IEEE Access. ieee.org

Su, J. & Zhong, Y (2022). Artificial Intelligence (AI) in early childhood education: Curriculum design and future directions. Computers and Education: Artificial Intelligence. sciencedirect.com

Sundari, M. S., Penthala, H. R., & Nayyar, A. (2024). Transforming Education through AI-Enhanced Content Creation and Personalized Learning Experiences. In *Impact of Artificial Intelligence on Society* (pp. 98–118). Chapman and Hall/CRC. [HTML] DOI: 10.1201/9781032644509-7

Tapalova, O. & Zhiyenbayeva, N (2022). Artificial intelligence in education: AIEd for personalised learning pathways. Electronic Journal of e-Learning. ed.gov

Taub, M., Azevedo, R., Rajendran, R., Cloude, E. B., Biswas, G., & Price, M. J. (2021). How are students' emotions related to the accuracy of cognitive and metacognitive processes during learning with an intelligent tutoring system? [nsf.gov]. *Learning and Instruction*, *72*, 101200. DOI: 10.1016/j.learninstruc.2019.04.001

Thiem, K. C. & Dasgupta, N (2022). From precollege to career: Barriers facing historically marginalized students and evidence-based solutions. Social Issues and Policy Review. researchgate.net

Troussas, C., Krouska, A., Alepis, E., & Virvou, M. (2020). Intelligent and adaptive tutoring through a social network for higher education. [HTML]. *New Review of Hypermedia and Multimedia*, *26*(3-4), 138–167. DOI: 10.1080/13614568.2021.1908436

Tzenios, N. (2020). Clustering students for personalized health education based on learning styles. [sagescience.org]. *Sage Science Review of Educational Technology*, *3*(1), 22–36.

Uche-Anya, E., Anyane-Yeboa, A., Berzin, T. M., Ghassemi, M., & May, F. P. (2022). Artificial intelligence in gastroenterology and hepatology: How to advance clinical practice while ensuring health equity. [nih.gov]. *Gut*, *71*(9), 1909–1915. DOI: 10.1136/gutjnl-2021-326271

Valle, N., Antonenko, P., Valle, D., Sommer, M., Huggins-Manley, A. C., Dawson, K., Kim, D., & Baiser, B. (2021). Predict or describe? How learning analytics dashboard design influences motivation and statistics anxiety in an online statistics course. [springer.com]. *Educational Technology Research and Development*, *69*(3), 1405–1431. DOI: 10.1007/s11423-021-09998-z

Valtonen, T., López-Pernas, S., Saqr, M., Vartiainen, H., Sointu, E. T., & Tedre, M. (2022). The nature and building blocks of educational technology research. [sciencedirect.com]. *Computers in Human Behavior*, *128*, 107123. DOI: 10.1016/j.chb.2021.107123

Walkington, C., & Bernacki, M. L. (2020). Appraising research on personalized learning: Definitions, theoretical alignment, advancements, and future directions. [tandfonline.com]. *Journal of Research on Technology in Education*, *52*(3), 235–252. DOI: 10.1080/15391523.2020.1747757

Watters, A (2023). Teaching machines: The history of personalized learning. [HTML]

Wong, G. K. W., Ma, X., Dillenbourg, P., & Huan, J (2020). Broadening artificial intelligence education in K-12: Where to start?. ACM inroads. epfl.ch

Yilmaz, O (2021). Augmented Reality in Science Education: An Application in Higher Education. Shanlax International Journal of Education. ed.gov

Yilmaz, R., Yurdugül, H., Yilmaz, F. G. K., Şahín, M., Sulak, S., Aydin, F., & Ömer, O. R. A. L. (2022). Smart MOOC integrated with intelligent tutoring: A system architecture and framework model proposal. [sciencedirect.com]. *Computers and Education: Artificial Intelligence*, *3*, 100092. DOI: 10.1016/j.caeai.2022.100092

Zhang, H., Lee, I., Ali, S., DiPaola, D., Cheng, Y., & Breazeal, C. (2023). Integrating ethics and career futures with technical learning to promote AI literacy for middle school students: An exploratory study. [springer.com]. *International Journal of Artificial Intelligence in Education*, *33*(2), 290–324. DOI: 10.1007/s40593-022-00293-3

Zhang, L., Basham, J. D., & Yang, S. (2020). Understanding the implementation of personalized learning: A research synthesis. [HTML]. *Educational Research Review*, *31*, 100339. DOI: 10.1016/j.edurev.2020.100339

Chapter 11

Revolutionizing Assessment: AI-Powered Feedback Systems for Personalized Learning

Andi Asrifan
https://orcid.org/0000-0002-9934-6129
Universitas Negeri Makassar, Indonesia

Rismawati Rismawati
https://orcid.org/0000-0001-8046-6764
Universitas Muhammadiyah Palopo, Indonesia

Juvrianto Chrissunday Jakob
https://orcid.org/0000-0002-5267-3448
Politeknik Negeri Ambon, Indonesia

Andi Syarifah Irmadani
Institut Ilmu Kesehatan Pelamonia Makassar, Indonesia

Musdalifah Musdalifah
https://orcid.org/0000-0001-8919-6043
Universitas Negeri Makassar, Indonesia

ABSTRACT

The revolutionary impact of AI on educational evaluation through individualized and adaptive feedback mechanisms is examined in this chapter. AI technologies including natural language processing, machine learning, and learning analytics enable real-time, individualized feedback that encourages engagement, equity, and self-regulated learning. The chapter describes a pedagogical and technological framework for AI-facilitated feedback using constructivist and connectivist notions. Practical applications in K–12 and higher education show how intelligent systems improve formative assessment, student achievement, and inclusive teaching. Algorithmic bias, ethical issues, institutional readiness, and scalable, culturally appropriate implementations

DOI: 10.4018/979-8-3373-2752-5.ch011

are carefully examined. The chapter concludes with policy, research, and practice proposals to make AI feedback systems dramatically improve assessment and curriculum design resilience in digital learning ecosystems.

INTRODUCTION

1.1. The Paradigm Shift in Educational Assessment through Artificial Intelligence

Assessment is the procedure of gathering and analyzing evidence to infer student knowledge and skills, so offering insights into what pupils understand and are capable of achieving. Conventional evaluation methods have predominantly been summative and focused on reliability. Nonetheless, these methods have not adequately addressed the issues of contemporary education and the necessity for fostering profound conceptual comprehension and advanced cognitive skills (Kadel et al., 2024).

Recent years have witnessed the emergence of novel assessment methods. Formative evaluation is progressively utilized to monitor student development and deliver feedback. Innovations also occur in summative assessment assignments, frequently including actual or real-world circumstances. Peer and self-assessment can enhance student involvement and, when implemented correctly, yield dependable results. Technology is revolutionizing assessment possibilities. Presently, digital options frequently serve as a direct replacement for conventional assessment formats, such as multiple-choice or short-answer questions, offering efficiency and ease. AI technologies enhance value by facilitating complex tasks, like the analysis of student models and the automated evaluation of text answers (Hemachandran et al., 2022). Assessment provides improved possibilities to facilitate learning through constructive feedback and student involvement, so establishing assessment as an integral element of educational design rather than a mere afterthought.

This paradigm change is supported by AI technologies, such as machine learning (ML), natural language processing (NLP), and learning analytics, which facilitate the real-time analysis of extensive learner data (Bhosle, 2024; Li et al., 2023; Alam, 2023). These technologies enable feedback systems to identify misconceptions, suggest specific learning resources, and facilitate self-regulated learning by offering timely reminders or scaffolding interventions. AI-driven platforms, such as intelligent tutoring systems (ITS) and automated writing evaluation tools, offer iterative feedback loops that exceed the temporal and cognitive limitations of human evaluators (Trajkovski and Hayes, 2025; Trajkovski & Hayes, 2025).

Furthermore, AI feedback systems contest the uniform concept of evaluation by promoting personalized trajectories. Utilizing predictive analytics, these systems may foresee learners' requirements and adjust the difficulty level and content presentation accordingly. This facilitates a formative assessment framework that is not only diagnostic but also prescriptive and developmental, so linking assessment more closely with pedagogy and curriculum customization (Yesilyurt, 2023; Ifenthaler & Yau, 2020).

This transformation entails significant issues. Issues related to algorithmic bias, data protection, transparency, and the involvement of educators in human-AI collaboration require intentional policy and ethical frameworks (Williamson & Eynon, 2020). The successful application of AI feedback systems necessitates a redefinition of assessment objectives, instructional design, and the learner's autonomy in the feedback process. AI-driven feedback systems signify a dramatic change in educational assessment, transitioning from episodic evaluation to continuous, responsive, and learner-centered feedback. This transition offers significant potential for securing the future of education by providing learners with practical insights, increasing engagement, and fostering lifelong learning skills in a digital era.

1.2. The Role of Feedback in Personalized and Adaptive Learning Environments

Feedback functions as a crucial instrument in the learning process, serving both as an evaluation tool and as a stimulus for cognitive advancement, metacognition, and self-regulated learning. In personalized and adaptive learning settings, feedback has a purpose beyond mere correction, playing a crucial role in facilitating learners' individual trajectories, autonomy, and engagement (Wang et al., 2024; Winstone & Boud, 2022; Branje et al., 2021). The incorporation of Artificial Intelligence (AI) into feedback systems enhances this capability by facilitating real-time, context-sensitive, and personalized feedback aligned with individual learner profiles and progressions (Kush, 2025).

AI-driven feedback systems offer adaptive support by examining learner behavior, performance trends, and interaction patterns. These systems adaptively modify the content, tempo, and nature of feedback according to the learner's changing requirements, cognitive condition, and previous knowledge. This customisation is essential in various learning populations, where uniform pedagogical approaches frequently exclude pupils with varying learning styles, talents, or histories. Through the application of machine learning and natural language processing methodologies, AI systems can identify student misconceptions, recognize emotional or motivational states, and provide tailored feedback that enhances conceptual comprehension and encourages learner autonomy (Naseer & Khawaja, 2025)

Furthermore, adaptive feedback enhances formative assessment by integrating evaluation fluidly into the learning process. As learners connect with digital platforms, their responses, mistakes, and engagement patterns are perpetually evaluated, allowing the system to deliver prompt, constructive feedback loops. These feedback loops enable learners to contemplate, amend, and refine—fundamental behaviors in cultivating self-regulated learning competencies. Educators can also get advantages from AI-enhanced dashboards and analytics that illuminate student progress, identify learning obstacles, and recommend specific interventions.

The efficacy of AI-generated feedback is contingent upon the clarity, timeliness, and pedagogical congruence of the sent messages. Ambiguous, tardy, or misaligned feedback can be damaging, particularly in adaptive environments where learner trust and motivation are crucial (Yesilyurt, 2023). Consequently, the design of AI feedback systems must be guided by robust pedagogical concepts and collaboratively created with educators to guarantee conformity with curricular objectives and ethical norms.

1.3. Purpose, Scope, and Structure of the Chapter

This chapter seeks to critically examine the transformational potential of Artificial Intelligence (AI)-driven feedback systems in enhancing individualized learning and assessment methodologies. Global educational systems are transitioning from standardized, summative assessments to learner-centered, formative evaluation models, with AI technologies offering innovative methods for providing immediate, adaptive, and data-driven feedback (Nicola-Gavrilă, 2023; Strielkowski et al., 2025). This chapter aims to clarify how AI may transform feedback systems to facilitate personalized learning trajectories, improve learner independence, and provide educators with practical insights for adaptive teaching methods.

This chapter encompasses the theoretical, technological, and practical aspects of AI-mediated feedback systems. The topic is framed within wider educational paradigms, including formative assessment, individualized learning, and self-regulated learning, while also considering the computational and design frameworks that facilitate real-time, intelligent feedback. The chapter analyzes empirical studies, practical applications, and case-based evidence to assess the effects and ramifications of AI feedback on learner outcomes, engagement, and inclusion. Additionally, ethical, pedagogical, and infrastructural factors are examined to provide a comprehensive understanding of the advantages and limitations related to AI-driven assessment tools (Hooda et al., 2022; Ouyang et al., 2022; Bognár et al., 2024).

The chapter is organized into five principal sections. Section 1 presents a conceptual transformation in assessment methodologies influenced by AI, highlighting the shortcomings of conventional models and the potential of intelligent systems. Section 2 delineates the theoretical underpinnings that anchor AI-driven feedback in recognized learning sciences, utilizing concepts from cognitive psychology, formative assessment theory, and educational technology. Section 3 examines the technological frameworks and elements of AI feedback systems, encompassing natural language processing, intelligent tutoring systems, and learning analytics (Dong, 2024; Ghoson et al., 2025). Section 4 emphasizes practical applications and case studies, illustrating the implementation of AI feedback across various educational levels and circumstances. It also takes into account the perceptions of stakeholders, including learners, educators, and institutional policymakers. Section 5 ultimately examines the obstacles to implementation, including algorithmic bias, equity, scalability, and the changing responsibilities of educators, while providing prospective proposals for policy and research.

This section outlines the objective, scope, and structure of the chapter, providing a framework for readers to navigate the intricacies and potential of AI-driven feedback in education. It offers the fundamental perspective from which the ensuing conversations will analyze how intelligent feedback systems might safeguard assessment and curriculum design for the future.

THEORETICAL AND PEDAGOGICAL FOUNDATIONS

2.1. Learning Theories Supporting Personalized Feedback (Constructivism, Connectivism)

The design and execution of tailored feedback in AI-driven educational settings are essentially based on modern learning theories that prioritize learner autonomy, contextual comprehension, and collaborative knowledge creation. Constructivism and connectivism are among the most significant frameworks that support individualized feedback systems (Strielkowski et al., 2025).

These paradigms provide essential concepts that govern the design, delivery, and assimilation of feedback within adaptive educational technologies.

Constructivism, as defined by thinkers like Jean Piaget and Lev Vygotsky, asserts that learners actively build knowledge through engagement with their environment and social context (Zajda, 2021). In this perspective, feedback is not a one-way broadcast of right answers but a dialogic and scaffolded process that facilitates meaning-making. AI-driven feedback systems embody this constructivist approach by providing feedback that adapts to student contributions, promoting exploration, self-explanation, and iterative improvement. Technologies like intelligent tutoring systems and automated feedback tools are designed to provide incremental prompts, guided inquiries, or reflective signals that correspond with the learner's zone of proximal development (ZPD), thus fostering enhanced cognitive engagement (Engeness and Gamlem, 2025).

Connectivism, a contemporary learning theory formulated by George Siemens and Stephen Downes, expands constructivist principles into the digital era by positing that learning involves establishing connections within information networks (Dziubaniuk et al., 2023; Mampota et al., 2023). From this viewpoint, knowledge exists not solely within individuals but also throughout dispersed technical and social systems. Feedback in a connectivist learning environment is dynamic, interconnected, and context-sensitive—enabled by AI algorithms that monitor learner interaction data, suggest pertinent resources, and adaptively link learners to peers, experts, or content nodes. AI feedback systems exemplify connectivism by providing timely guidance from various sources and assisting learners in traversing intricate informational environments.

Constructivism and connectivism collectively establish a strong pedagogical basis for individualized AI feedback. They assert the learner's role as an active participant in the feedback process and characterize AI not solely as an evaluator, but as a learning partner that enhances human cognition and social interaction. This theoretical foundation is crucial for developing feedback systems that are both technologically advanced and pedagogically significant, in accordance with the objectives of 21st-century education.

2.2. Formative vs. Summative Assessment: Reframing Through AI Capabilities

Meticulous design of assessments and their accompanying infrastructure is essential to fully leverage the capabilities of generative AI tools for the cultivation and evaluation of 21st-century skills. Categories including the four competencies delineated by the World Economic Forum—critically evaluating information, applying guidance with contextual awareness and limitations, effectively communicating artifacts, and perpetually enhancing performance through diverse tools and references—can be seamlessly integrated into comprehensive assessment frameworks (Kadel et al., 2024). This integration necessitates a reevaluation of the overarching distinction between formative and summative assessment, since the formative application of assessment embodies the fundamental aim, purpose, and utilization of evaluative data during the learning process.

Educational assessment has conventionally been divided into two main categories: formative and summative. Formative assessment denotes continuous, diagnostic methods that influence teaching and facilitate learning, while summative assessment appraises learner performance at the conclusion of an instructional period, generally for grading or certification objectives (Sokhanvar et al., 2021; Hayat et al., 2021). The advent of Artificial Intelligence (AI) in educational settings necessitates a reevaluation of this dichotomy by providing integrated, ongoing, and adaptive feedback mechanisms that obscure the distinctions between formative and summative methods.

AI-driven assessment solutions improve formative procedures by providing immediate, detailed feedback based on learners' continuous engagement with content. Utilizing natural language processing, machine learning, and learning analytics, these systems may discern patterns, misconceptions, and skill deficiencies, providing tailored prompts that direct learners towards self-correction and reflection (Giri, 2025; Vashishth et al., 2024). In contrast to conventional formative evaluations that frequently depend on instructor judgment and time constraints, AI systems provide scalable and instantaneous assistance, facilitating more frequent and substantive feedback loops. Furthermore, AI may replicate formative discourse through scaffolded inquiry and tailored clues, thus promoting metacognitive growth and self-regulated learning.

Conversely, summative evaluation has generally resisted personalizing owing to its uniform characteristics. Nevertheless, AI presents novel opportunities for dynamic summative assessment. For example, intelligent assessment platforms can consolidate continuous data streams throughout learning episodes to create longitudinal performance profiles. This cumulative analysis facilitates evidence-based summative assessments that more accurately represent a learner's comprehensive growth across time (Ali, 2024; Gardner et al., 2021). Moreover, AI can facilitate the automated assessment of intricate tasks, including writing and problem-solving, using algorithms developed using rubrics and expert-annotated datasets, hence enhancing efficiency and objectivity in summative evaluations.

The incorporation of AI capabilities challenges the strict distinction between formative and summative evaluation. Rather, it endorses a continuum-based model, in which data-driven feedback is integrally incorporated throughout the learning process. This reframing corresponds with the ideas of assessment for learning, prioritizing growth, personalization, and equity rather than fixed measurement.

2.3. Ethical and Equity Considerations in AI-Mediated Feedback Systems

The active implementation of technologies in assessment and feedback inside online formative learning environments produces adaptable, scalable, and multilingual models of subject writing as needed. Inference and probability models that facilitate clause classification, information extraction, and production substantially diminish development overhead and alleviate database design challenges. Pre-trained models identify various entities and relationships, while ablation studies measure the influence of specific components. Annotation facilitates creation and thorough validation, while experimental outcomes record the ability to differentiate between indicative, speculative, and causative relationships, as well as relation-mining behavior associated with explicit domain knowledge. Addressing the increasing demand for feedback-support technologies that allocate resources justly and equitably, while differing in the quantity and quality of assistance, is a recognized significant problem. Implementing large-scale automatic feedback necessitates validity, dependability, equality, and defensibility, whereas the deployment of generative AI systems introduces problems related to alignment, governance, and discrimination (D Lindsay et al., 2025).

As AI-driven feedback systems grow more prevalent in educational environments, it is essential to examine their ethical and equity ramifications. Although these technologies offer significant potential for customizing education and improving formative assessment, they concurrently present new issues concerning fairness, transparency, accountability, and social justice (Mourya et al., 2024; Williamson & Eynon, 2020). In the absence of deliberate design and oversight, AI systems may unintentionally perpetuate current educational disparities or create novel biases and exclusions.

A significant ethical concern is algorithmic bias. AI feedback systems are developed using historical data that may exhibit systemic inequalities related to race, gender, language competence, socioeconomic position, or handicap (Cau et al., 2025; Devillers et al., 2021). If unaddressed, these biases may affect the generation, interpretation, or implementation of feedback—potentially distorting learners' capabilities or offering inequitable educational opportunities. Automated essay scoring methods have been demonstrated to disfavor students utilizing dialects or culturally distinctive terms (Ramesh & Sanampudi, 2022; Latifi & Gierl, 2021). Consequently, it is essential to guarantee that training data and model outputs are culturally inclusive and pedagogically sound.

Equitable access is another fundamental concern. Not all learners possess equitable access to digital infrastructure, high-speed internet, or AI-enhanced educational platforms. The digital divide might marginalize students from rural or underserved places, restricting their capacity to benefit from adaptive feedback systems. Furthermore, students with disabilities may encounter barriers to AI tools if they do not incorporate suitable universal design elements, such as multimodal feedback or interoperability with assistive devices (Baidoo-Anu et al., 2023).

The opacity of AI decision-making processes undermines transparency and confidence. Students and instructors may lack a comprehensive understanding of the mechanisms behind feedback generation and the criteria for specific evaluations. The absence of interpretability might diminish the instructional efficacy of feedback, especially when it conflicts with human assessment or lacks pedagogical transparency. The adoption of explainable AI (XAI) in educational settings is increasing, allowing stakeholders to scrutinize and comprehend algorithmic conclusions.

The ethical implementation of AI feedback systems necessitates human supervision and collaborative design. Educators, students, and communities must collaborate in the co-design and ongoing assessment of AI tools to guarantee alignment with educational principles, safeguard learner rights, and foster equitable outcomes.

TECHNOLOGIES AND ARCHITECTURES OF AI FEEDBACK SYSTEMS

3.1. Core Components of AI-Powered Feedback Mechanisms (e.g., NLP, ML, Learning Analytics)

Innovative assessment procedures are essential for educational equity; yet, maintaining unbiased grading criteria poses a challenge. Artificial intelligence and learning analytics systems deliver impartial, consistent, and constructive assessments of a student's strengths and deficiencies, presenting an objective and educated resolution (Shaik et al., 2023). Recent advancements in machine learning are producing a dynamic array of methodologies capable of revolutionizing evaluation (Tian et al., 2024).

AI-driven feedback systems depend on a synergy of sophisticated computational elements that provide dynamic, adaptive, and context-sensitive evaluation procedures. Key technologies that support these systems include Natural Language Processing (NLP), Machine Learning (ML), and Learning Analytics (LA). Collectively, these elements enable AI systems to analyze learner input, forecast learning pathways, and provide tailored, actionable feedback that corresponds with both learner profiles and educational goals (Jiang et al., 2023; Trajkovski and Hayes, 2025).

Natural Language Processing (NLP) is crucial for facilitating AI systems' comprehension and response to written and verbal inputs from learners. NLP enables the automated analysis of student responses, the provision of formative feedback, and the identification of language trends, misconceptions, or knowledge deficiencies. NLP algorithms judge writing by evaluating syntax, coherence, and subject relevance, delivering immediate, comprehensive feedback that resembles human judgment (Botelho et al., 2023). Additionally, sentiment analysis and discourse modeling—subdisciplines of NLP—are employed to evaluate learner engagement, emotional tone, and cognitive methods during interactions with educational material.

Machine Learning (ML) serves as the catalyst for adaptability and personalization in feedback systems. Through the training of models on extensive datasets, machine learning algorithms may discern trends in learner behavior, forecast future performance, and suggest targeted interventions. Supervised learning is typically utilized to categorize learner inputs or results, whereas reinforcement learning aims to enhance feedback provision by modifying suggestions according to learner reactions (Song et al., 2024; Oyebode et al., 2023). Significantly, machine learning facilitates ongoing system enhancement as additional data is gathered and analyzed, hence improving the accuracy and contextual pertinence of feedback.

Learning Analytics (LA) serves as the interpretive framework that synthesizes data across several dimensions of learner engagement. LA tools facilitate real-time feedback for learners and provide strategic insights for instructors by aggregating and visualizing data on student progress, engagement, and achievement (Giannakos and Cukurova, 2023; Fan et al., 2021). Dashboards enabled by LA facilitate instructors in tracking individual and group trends, recognizing at-risk pupils, and modifying instructional approaches as necessary.

The integration of NLP, ML, and LA in feedback systems signifies a notable progression in educational technology. These elements convert feedback from a static, retrospective process into a continuous, interactive, and tailored learning experience—essential to the objective of future-proofing curriculum and assessment design.

3.2. Intelligent Tutoring Systems, Chatbots, and Adaptive Platforms in Assessment

Assessment significantly influences the classroom learning environment by shaping students' perceptions of learning, motivating and engaging learners, offering substantial learning support, and ensuring alignment among competencies, learning objectives, instruction, and evaluation (Gao et al., 2023). With the swift advancement of AI, intelligent evaluation has begun to lead education in the Era of Big Data. AI methodologies can effectively automate the evaluation process and deliver constructive comments, hence facilitating students' learning enhancement. In the domain of intelligent assessment, Intelligent Tutoring Systems (ITS), chatbots, and adaptive e-learning platforms are prominent.

Artificial Intelligence (AI) has facilitated the creation of a novel generation of assessment systems that are interactive, adaptive, and attuned to the unique requirements of learners. These innovations include Intelligent Tutoring Systems (ITSs), educational chatbots, and adaptive learning platforms, collectively signifying a transition from static testing to dynamic, embedded assessment methods integrated within the learning process (Strielkowski et al., 2025; Gligorea et al., 2023).

Intelligent Tutoring Systems (ITSs) are AI-driven platforms that emulate the assistance of a human tutor by delivering immediate, tailored feedback and educational help. Rooted on cognitive science and computer modeling, Intelligent Tutoring Systems evaluate learners' problem-solving behaviors and dynamically modify instructional sequences to rectify knowledge deficiencies (Dever et al., 2023). Cognitive Tutor and ASSISTments have shown useful in improving mathematics and science learning results by providing focused feedback based on student responses and mistake patterns. The developmental characteristics of ITSs provide self-directed learning and ongoing evaluation without dependence on conventional testing methods.

Educational chatbots, utilizing natural language processing (NLP), have arisen as conversational entities that enable assessment in informal yet pedagogically significant manners. These bots can facilitate Socratic dialogue, pose inquiries, offer clues, and assess responses during interactions. Their capacity to replicate human-like communication renders them very efficacious in language acquisition and introspective fields (Kuhail et al., 2023). In contrast to inflexible quiz-based systems, chatbots evaluate understanding via conversation analysis, facilitating nuanced feedback that takes into account learners' reasoning and meaning.

Adaptive learning platforms, such Knewton, Smart Sparrow, and ALEKS, provide a comprehensive framework for content delivery and assessment within a cohesive environment. These platforms employ machine learning algorithms to create personalized learning trajectories, modifying the complexity and nature of assessment tasks according to real-time learner performance metrics. Embedded evaluations are incorporated into learning activities, enabling the platform to perpetually assess comprehension and preparedness before to advancing to new material (Song et al., 2024; Strielkowski et al., 2025). The incorporation of assessment into instructional processes guarantees individualized and responsive learning, so reducing the disturbance typically linked to summative evaluations.

3.3. System Interoperability and Integration with LMS and Educational Infrastructure

The effective implementation of AI-driven feedback systems in educational settings relies on both the complexity of their internal algorithms and their compatibility with current Learning Management Systems (LMS) and the wider educational framework. Interoperability guarantees that AI systems may effortlessly share data, operate across many platforms, and interact within different educational ecosystems—elements essential for optimizing scalability, usability, and pedagogical consistency (Krauss et al., 2023).

Learning Management Systems like Moodle, Canvas, and Blackboard function as the digital foundation of contemporary education, overseeing course content, monitoring learner advancement, and enabling collaboration. To ensure the efficacy of AI feedback tools, they must be integrated with these platforms via established protocols like Learning Tools Interoperability (LTI) and Experience API (xAPI). These standards facilitate secure and consistent communication among various systems, permitting the direct integration of data from AI engines—such as learner analytics, feedback loops, and performance insights—into LMS dashboards (Sivasubramanian et al., 2022; Mohamed and Muhammed, 2022; IMS Global, 2020).

In addition to technical compatibility, integration necessitates the synchronization of AI feedback systems with educational objectives, evaluation frameworks, and institutional regulations. Feedback systems must be tailored to align with discipline-specific competencies, incorporate diverse assessment philosophies, and adhere to institutional data governance policies. AI-generated feedback must be accessible and comprehensible to both instructors and students, delivered in formats that facilitate actionable insights and pedagogical decision-making (Ifenthaler & Yau, 2020).

Moreover, data privacy and ethical adherence are critical factors in interoperability. Institutions must guarantee that AI systems comply with regulations such as the General Data Protection Regulation (GDPR) and the Family Educational Rights and Privacy Act (FERPA) when sharing learner data across platforms. To maintain confidence and transparency in system integration, secure APIs, encryption protocols, and user consent methods are essential (Yang & Beil, 2024; Herath et al., 2024).

The preparedness of infrastructure is crucial for effective integration. Institutions require comprehensive technical assistance, cloud-based infrastructure, and adequate bandwidth to facilitate real-time analytics and feedback dissemination. Moreover, professional development for educators is essential to enable them to evaluate AI-generated feedback and utilize it in instructional design. System interoperability and integration are essential not just as technical issues but also as fundamental facilitators for achieving the complete potential of AI in individualized assessment. Deliberate integration guarantees that feedback mechanisms function cohesively within the educational environment, improving equity, effectiveness, and creativity.

APPLICATIONS AND CASE STUDIES IN PERSONALIZED LEARNING

4.1. Real-World Implementations in K–12 and Higher Education

Authentic assessments evaluate students' performance on real-world tasks, frequently necessitating the utilization of digital technologies to analyze intricate information from several sources, and perhaps including teamwork. The tasks require transparency and permit the application of alternative thinking. The National History Day framework requires students to choose a historical topic, complete research, analyze sources, and present their conclusions in a paper, exhibit, performance, or video. The Project Citizen examination requires students to examine a public policy issue, analyze various solutions, and subsequently offer ideas for governmental action to panels of judges (Sokhanvar et al., 2021; Schultz et al., 2022).

The incorporation of AI-driven feedback systems into actual educational environments is now a present reality in both K–12 and higher education contexts. These implementations offer concrete proof of how intelligent feedback systems can customize learning, enhance instructional methods, and guide data-informed decision-making (Vashishth et al., 2024).

AI systems are being integrated into digital learning platforms in K–12 education to enhance foundational abilities in literacy and mathematics. DreamBox Learning, a prevalent adaptive mathematics tool, employs real-time learning analytics and machine learning algorithms to evaluate student problem-solving techniques and deliver immediate, tailored feedback (Shin et al., 2020). DreamBox creates a formative assessment environment by dynamically modifying task complexity and sequencing, allowing learners to advance at their own speed. Likewise, platforms such as Quill.org and Socratic by Google employ natural language processing (NLP) to offer feedback on student writing and inquiry-based learning activities, thus facilitating self-correction and reflection among younger learners (Almuhanna, 2024).

Higher education institutions have adopted AI feedback systems to improve academic writing, course participation, and self-regulated learning. Grammarly and Ecree provide automated writing assessment with instantaneous feedback on grammar, coherence, and clarity, assisting students in progressively revising their work beyond the classroom (Wilson & Roscoe, 2020). In sophisticated applications, platforms such as Coursera's Smart Grader employ AI to assess open-ended responses at scale, particularly advantageous in Massive Open Online Courses (MOOCs) where human grading is impractical.

Numerous colleges have included learning analytics dashboards within Learning Management Systems (LMS), allowing teachers and students to track learning progress in real time. The University of Michigan's ECoach provides customized feedback utilizing student demographic data, performance metrics, and behavioral indicators, resulting in notable improvements in engagement and achievement, particularly among marginalized populations (Paulsen & Lindsay, 2024).

These case studies demonstrate how AI-driven feedback systems can surpass conventional assessment limitations by integrating intelligence into instructional processes. Through adaptive practice, automated evaluation, or predictive analytics, these technologies provide individualized learning on a large scale, providing insight into the future of equitable and responsive education.

4.2. Empirical Findings on Student Engagement, Achievement, and Self-Regulation

Recent research, including both quantitative and qualitative empirical evidence, has consistently emphasized that teacher scaffolding is essential for cultivating students' self-regulatory abilities, hence enhancing the effectiveness of peer and self-assessment. Consequently, assessment for learning has become a focal point in assessment research and policy. Regulation theory is based on the premise that students have the unique ability for self-assessment; however, in the context of classroom evaluation—where formative and summative assessments operate concurrently—teacher evaluation remains significant, and a robust body of evidence now endorses peer and self-regulated formative strategies (Fletcher, 2024; Mamun, 2022).

Empirical studies on AI-driven feedback systems progressively illustrate their capacity to improve fundamental educational outcomes, especially in student engagement, academic performance, and self-regulated learning. As feedback becomes increasingly timely, tailored, and data-driven by artificial intelligence, learners receive enhanced academic support and are empowered to assume responsibility for their learning processes (Rekha et al., 2024).

Numerous extensive research demonstrate that student engagement, encompassing both behavioral and emotional aspects, is markedly improved in AI-assisted learning environments. XU et al. (2025) discovered that the use of real-time AI feedback technologies in middle school classrooms enhanced students' engagement and diminished frustration during learning activities. These solutions offered adaptive prompts and motivational cues that maintained learner engagement, while simultaneously notifying educators of disengagement in real time via teacher dashboards. Likewise, Honson et al. (2024) noted that AI-driven cognitive tutors enhanced engagement by adaptively modifying teaching material to align with learners' proficiency levels.

Randomized controlled experiments and meta-analyses indicate that AI-based feedback systems significantly enhance academic attainment across several subjects. The implementation of intelligent tutoring systems such as ASSISTments and Carnegie Learning has been linked to enhanced mathematics performance, especially among underperforming pupils (Darvishi et al., 2022). These systems provide structured, prompt feedback that enhances conceptual comprehension and rectifies misunderstandings instantaneously. Automated writing evaluation systems in higher education have been associated with enhanced writing quality and greater revision practices among undergraduate students (Wilson & Roscoe, 2020).

The findings of self-regulated learning (SRL) are particularly compelling. AI-driven feedback systems enhance self-regulated learning by encouraging goal formulation, metacognitive oversight, and strategic modification. Formative feedback that emphasizes advancement, proposes strategies, and promotes reflection enhances learner autonomy. A study by Chang et al. (2023) highlighted that AI systems integrated with learning analytics can illustrate learning trajectories and provide practical recommendations, so fostering the self-awareness crucial for self-regulated learning progress. Empirical research robustly demonstrates the effectiveness of AI-driven feedback systems in promoting significant learning experiences. These technologies augment motivation, performance, and autonomy—fundamental elements of lifelong learning—thereby validating their significance in future-proofing education.

4.3. Stakeholder Perspectives: Teachers, Students, and Instructional Designers

Instructional designers develop programs, courses, or materials. Due to their usual lack of direct interaction with learners, integrated assessment is essential for monitoring progress and ensuring that objectives are achieved. Despite their responsibility for content selection, designers frequently depend on others to define assessment activities and criteria, necessitating meticulous collaboration with educators and subject-matter specialists. Designers recognize that educational resources must offer chances for assessment and guided practice simultaneously. Consequently, they regard evaluation as crucial to comprehensive design, vital for facilitating learning opportunities, fostering motivation, and guiding development along desired trajectories (Stein et al., 2022; Larsen et al., 2022).

The effective implementation and influence of AI-driven feedback systems are significantly contingent upon the viewpoints, anticipations, and experiences of essential educational stakeholders, specifically teachers, students, and instructional designers. Their insights influence the usability and pedagogical alignment of AI technologies, as well as the ethical and contextual suitability of their incorporation into educational settings (Viberg et al., 2024).

Educators have a dual function as enablers of AI feedback and critical assessors of its educational efficacy. Empirical research indicates that educators typically value the diagnostic accuracy and efficiency of AI systems (Holstein et al., 2019). Real-time dashboards and analytics facilitate the identification of underperforming students, enable personalized training, and alleviate the grading workload. Many educators, however, articulate apprehensions over excessive dependence on algorithmic suggestions and the lack of transparency in AI decision-making processes. Confidence in these systems is enhanced when educators participate in the development and adjustment of feedback mechanisms, guaranteeing consistency with curriculum goals and classroom conditions (Hao et al., 2024).

Students, as end-users, generally appreciate AI feedback systems for their promptness, customization, and impartiality. Automated feedback enables learners to revise independently and obtain instruction without the apprehension of social assessment (Mohammed & Khalid, 2025; Shute & Rahimi, 2021). Students frequently scrutinize the precision and equity of automated scoring systems, especially in subjective areas such as writing and creativity. Trust among learners is enhanced when feedback is transparent, actionable, and supplemented by human assistance. Furthermore, students favor systems that facilitate agency and interaction, as opposed to merely receiving recommendations passively.

Instructional designers perceive AI feedback systems as instruments to improve instructional coherence and enhance the learner experience. From their viewpoint, the primary hurdles involve the integration of AI tools inside various pedagogical frameworks and the assurance of interoperability with institutional infrastructure. Designers underscore the necessity for inclusive, culturally attuned design approaches to prevent the marginalization of particular learner demographics. Moreover, they promote user-centered design methodologies, wherein iterative feedback from educators and learners guides system enhancement (Ifenthaler & Yau, 2020). Stakeholder viewpoints underscore the necessity for human-AI collaboration in evaluation procedures. Instead of supplanting educators, AI feedback systems need to complement professional judgment, bolster learner agency, and facilitate instructional innovation—provided they are built and implemented with democratic involvement and ethical forethought.

CHALLENGES, OPPORTUNITIES, AND FUTURE DIRECTIONS

5.1. Technical, Pedagogical, and Institutional Barriers to Adoption

Although AI-powered feedback systems in education has transformative promise, their extensive implementation encounters various technological, pedagogical, and institutional obstacles. These problems impede implementation and raise questions regarding equity, sustainability, and the long-term viability of AI in individualized assessment. Nazaretsky et al. (2022)

From a technical standpoint, interoperability and data infrastructure are significant limitations. Numerous educational institutions are insufficiently equipped technologically to include AI feedback tools into their current Learning Management Systems (LMS) or digital ecosystems (Ifenthaler & Yau, 2020). Incompatible data standards, scattered platforms, and outdated technologies hinder seamless data interchange and real-time analytics. Moreover, AI systems typically depend on substantial quantities of high-quality, labeled data for optimal performance—resources that are sometimes inaccessible, partial, or isolated. Issues related to data privacy, security, and algorithmic transparency exacerbate the challenges of adoption, particularly when systems depend on sensitive student data.

Resistance in educational contexts frequently arises from doubt over the pedagogical efficacy of AI generated feedback. Numerous educators doubt the capability of automated systems to effectively discern learner intent, contextualize replies, or promote critical thinking, particularly in intricate fields like as the humanities and social sciences (Sadigzade, 2025). A perceived diminution of teacher autonomy occurs when algorithmic feedback is favored over professional judgment. Moreover, numerous AI systems are created without enough contributions from educators, leading to feedback mechanisms that may be deficient in pedagogical sensitivity, cultural responsiveness, or alignment with curricular objectives.

Institutional impediments encompass a deficiency of vision, leadership, and policy frameworks to facilitate AI integration. Financial limitations, conflicting priorities, and restricted professional development possibilities hinder innovation (Kyambade & Namatovu, 2025; Booyse & Scheepers, 2024). Faculty and staff frequently necessitate comprehensive training to proficiently analyze and utilize AI feedback data; nonetheless, few universities have established systematic capacity-building programs. Moreover, institutional cultures that prioritize high-stakes, summative assessments may oppose formative, continuous feedback models, so constraining the pedagogical transformation essential for the success of AI systems.

Addressing these obstacles requires a comprehensive strategy that integrates infrastructure investment, intersectoral collaboration, and policy innovation. An inclusive and interdisciplinary approach—rooted in ethical foresight and pedagogical integrity—is crucial for transitioning from isolated trials to the sustainable and equitable application of AI in personalized learning assessment.

5.2. Opportunities for Scalable, Inclusive, and Culturally Responsive Feedback Systems

Despite ongoing technical and institutional obstacles, the development of AI-driven feedback systems offers substantial opportunity to create scalable, inclusive, and culturally attuned evaluation ecosystems. When effectively utilized, these options can close educational disparities, promote equity, and broaden the scope of personalized learning across many global contexts (Yesilyurt, 2023).

Primarily, scalability constitutes a fundamental advantage of AI-driven feedback systems. In contrast to human assessments, which require significant resources and are challenging to scale, AI systems can provide uniform, tailored feedback to a large number of learners concurrently. This capability is especially advantageous in massive open online courses (MOOCs), extensive university classrooms, and national education systems where personalized feedback has historically proven impractical (Kaswan et al., 2024; Sajja et al., 2024). Progress in cloud computing and real-time analytics has facilitated the implementation of feedback systems that dynamically adjust to learners' requirements beyond geographical, temporal, and institutional limits.

Secondly, AI feedback systems possess transformative potential for enhancing educational inclusivity. Students from disadvantaged backgrounds, notably those in rural or low-income environments, frequently encounter restricted access to high-quality instructional assistance. When developed with equity as a priority, AI systems can deliver immediate, context-sensitive feedback that addresses inequalities in teacher accessibility or institutional resources (Salas-Pilco et al., 2022). Intelligent tutoring systems (ITS) and mobile learning platforms provide multilingual support, offline capabilities, and accessibility features for learners with disabilities, thereby enhancing access to formative assessment and scaffolding.

Incorporating cultural responsiveness into AI feedback design is essential for relevance and learner engagement. Culturally responsive systems recognize the linguistic, epistemological, and social diversity of learners by integrating local norms, values, and situations. AI models trained on geographically diversified datasets and tailored instructional content can mitigate cultural bias and enhance accuracy in reading learner answers (Baker & Hawn, 2021). Furthermore, human-in-the-loop designs—where educators engage in system development—can guarantee that feedback corresponds with culturally ingrained instructional objectives and learner identities.

Collectively, these prospects indicate a future where AI-driven feedback is both technologically sophisticated and ethically robust, socially equitable, and contextually pertinent. Utilizing AI to facilitate scalable, inclusive, and culturally attuned assessment corresponds with the overarching objective of future-proofing education and guaranteeing that no learner is marginalized.

5.3. Recommendations for Policy, Research, and Practice in Future-Proofing Assessment

The initiative to transform assessment—entailing modifications that signify a break from the past and create a new standard for innovation—is strategically vital for higher education; strategic planning concerning assessment should prioritize this issue. Advancements in evaluation directly impact three of the six action clusters suggested by Summit attendees. Redefining Instruction and Curriculum; Eschewing the Status Quo; and Promoting and Expanding Innovation. Future-proofing involves creating systems that are exceptionally resilient to anticipated changes in their requirements. Modern assessment models risk becoming outdated if advancements in learning science are not integrated or if technologies are employed in manners that hinder the adoption of better alternatives in the future (Mislevy, 2024). Institutions that achieve a resilient status through adaptability, versatility, and a focus on support will be more equipped to navigate a world characterized by swift and ongoing transformation. Three themes that may inform adaptation are: (a) policy; (b) research; and (c) practice.

Policy proposals commence with the establishment of explicit legislative frameworks that ensure data privacy, algorithmic transparency, and equity. Governments and educational institutions ought to enforce adherence to norms such as GDPR or FERPA and formulate guidelines for the responsible utilization of AI in assessments (Williamson & Eynon, 2020). Furthermore, governmental investment in digital infrastructure, especially in underserved areas, is crucial for facilitating broad access to AI tools. Policies must also endorse capacity-building initiatives for educators, ensuring they are proficient in interpreting and employing AI-generated feedback successfully across varied classroom environments.

There is a necessity for longitudinal, interdisciplinary studies that investigate the effects of AI feedback on learning outcomes, especially among diverse cultural, linguistic, and socio-economic groups. The current work frequently focuses on short-term treatments or homogeneous populations, hence limiting generalizability (Baker & Hawn, 2021). Subsequent investigations ought to explore the correlation between AI feedback and student motivation, metacognition, and identity formation, in addition to the unforeseen ramifications of algorithmic decision-making in evaluation. Participatory research methods, in which teachers and students collaboratively develop evaluation instruments, can prioritize user experience and ethical design.

Educational institutions should implement hybrid feedback models that integrate AI-generated insights with human pedagogical evaluation. These integrated methods utilize the advantages of both automation and educator proficiency, promoting trust, contextual relevance, and instructional adaptability. Professional development should prioritize both technical training and critical AI literacy, empowering educators to analyze the generation of feedback, its intended audience, and its alignment with educational objectives. Moreover, designers must emphasize learner-centered and culturally sensitive concepts in system development to guarantee that feedback fosters significant, inclusive involvement.

Ultimately, ensuring the longevity of assessments via AI feedback systems necessitates a synchronized transition grounded in equality, ethics, and pedagogical intent. By harmonizing policy, research, and practice, stakeholders can guarantee that AI technologies enhance rather than supplant human-centered education.

CONCLUSION

Artificial Intelligence (AI) is radically transforming educational assessment by facilitating dynamic, learner-centered, and data-driven feedback systems. In contrast to conventional summative methods that deliver fixed, retrospective assessments, AI-driven feedback systems offer continuous, tailored assistance that corresponds with individual learning paths. This chapter has elucidated the theoretical foundations, technological frameworks, and practical implementations of these systems, showcasing their ability to improve engagement, achievement, and self-regulation in K–12 and higher education.

Notwithstanding its considerable potential, the implementation of AI in evaluation faces substantial hurdles. Technical challenges, including system interoperability, algorithmic bias, and data privacy, necessitate resolution via comprehensive legislative and design frameworks. Pedagogical issues—especially regarding human supervision and instructional coherence—require inclusive, multidisciplinary development procedures that engage both educators and learners. The institutional transition necessitates leadership, investment in infrastructure, and a cultural shift towards evaluation paradigms that emphasize formative feedback.

However, these problems also uncover opportunity. AI systems provide scalable and inclusive solutions that may access underserved learners, enhance cultural responsiveness, and equip educators with actionable insights. When informed by ethical foresight, AI feedback systems can democratize access to superior assessments and promote individualized pathways for all students.

This chapter advocates for synchronized efforts in policy, research, and practice to ensure the resilience of educational assessment. Policies must safeguard student rights and guarantee fair access to AI resources. Research ought to enhance our comprehension of AI's enduring effects in various circumstances. Practice should adopt hybrid feedback approaches that integrate automation with human assessment. AI-driven feedback systems serve as a pivotal mechanism for enhancing educational innovation. Through deliberate execution, they can augment student autonomy, enhance instructional effectiveness, and equip educational systems to address the intricate challenges of the 21st century.

REFERENCES

Alam, A. (2023). Harnessing the power of AI to create intelligent tutoring systems for enhanced classroom experience and improved learning outcomes. In *Intelligent Communication Technologies and Virtual Mobile Networks* (pp. 571–591). Springer Nature Singapore., DOI: 10.1007/978-981-99-1767-9_42

Ali, Q. I. (2024). Towards more effective summative assessment in OBE: A new framework integrating direct measurements and technology. *Discover Education*, *3*(1), 107. Advance online publication. DOI: 10.1007/s44217-024-00208-5

Almuhanna, M. A. (2024). Teachers' perspectives of integrating AI-powered technologies in K-12 education for creating customized learning materials and resources. *Education and Information Technologies*, *30*(8), 10343–10371. DOI: 10.1007/s10639-024-13257-y

Baidoo-Anu, D., Gyamerah, K., & Munezhi, M. (2023). Digital divide in higher education in Sub-Saharan Africa: Evidence from online learning during the COVID-19 pandemic. *SN Social Sciences*, *3*(8), 122. Advance online publication. DOI: 10.1007/s43545-023-00717-4

Bhosle, A. (2024). Real-time analytics and AI transforming data engineering for sustainable learning in cloud environments. In *Smart Education and Sustainable Learning Environments in Smart Cities* (pp. 347–364). IGI Global., DOI: 10.4018/979-8-3693-7723-9.ch021

Bognár, L., Ágoston, G., Bacsa-Bán, A., Fauszt, T., Gubán, G., Joós, A., Juhász, L. Z., Kocsó, E., Kovács, E., Maczó, E., Mihálovicsné Kollár, A. I., & Strauber, G. (2024). Re-evaluating components of classical educational theories in AI-enhanced learning: An empirical study on student engagement. *Education Sciences*, *14*(9), 974. Advance online publication. DOI: 10.3390/educsci14090974

Booyse, D., & Scheepers, C. B. (2024). Barriers to adopting automated organisational decision-making through the use of artificial intelligence. *Management Research Review*, *47*(1), 64–85. DOI: 10.1108/MRR-09-2021-0701

Botelho, A., Baral, S., Erickson, J. A., Benachamardi, P., & Heffernan, N. T. (2023). Leveraging natural language processing to support automated assessment and feedback for student open responses in mathematics. *Journal of Computer Assisted Learning*, *39*(3), 823–840. DOI: 10.1111/jcal.12793

Cau, R., Pisu, F., Suri, J. S., & Saba, L. (2025). Addressing hidden risks: Systematic review of artificial intelligence biases across racial and ethnic groups in cardiovascular diseases. *European Journal of Radiology*, *183*, 111867. Advance online publication. DOI: 10.1016/j.ejrad.2024.111867

Chang, D. H., Lin, M. P. C., Hajian, S., & Wang, Q. Q. (2023). Educational design principles of using AI chatbot that supports self-regulated learning in education: Goal setting, feedback, and personalization. *Sustainability (Basel)*, *15*(22), 16345. DOI: 10.3390/su151712921

Darvishi, A., Khosravi, H., Sadiq, S., & Gašević, D. (2022). Incorporating AI and learning analytics to build trustworthy peer assessment systems. *British Journal of Educational Technology*, *53*(4), 844–875. DOI: 10.1111/bjet.13233

Dever, D. A., Sonnenfeld, N. A., Wiedbusch, M. D., Schmorrow, S. G., Amon, M. J., & Azevedo, R. (2023). A complex systems approach to analyzing pedagogical agents' scaffolding of self-regulated learning within an intelligent tutoring system. *Metacognition and Learning, 18*(3), 659–691. DOI: 10.1007/s11409-023-09346-x

Devillers, L., Fogelman-Soulié, F., & Baeza-Yates, R. (2021). AI & human values: Inequalities, biases, fairness, nudge, and feedback loops. In Braunschweig, B., & Ghallab, M. (Eds.), *Reflections on Artificial Intelligence for Humanity* (pp. 76–89). Springer International Publishing., DOI: 10.1007/978-3-030-69128-8_6

Dong, C. (2024). Educational concepts and methodologies in the AI era: Challenges and responses. *Frontiers of Digital Education, 1*(1), 69–77. DOI: 10.1007/s44366-024-0022-y

Dziubaniuk, O., Ivanova-Gongne, M., & Nyholm, M. (2023). Learning and teaching sustainable business in the digital era: A connectivism theory approach. *International Journal of Educational Technology in Higher Education, 20*(1), 20. Advance online publication. DOI: 10.1186/s41239-023-00390-w

Engeness, I., & Gamlem, S. M. (2025). Exploring AI-driven feedback as a cultural tool: A cultural-historical perspective on design of AI environments to support students' writing process. *Integrative Psychological & Behavioral Science, 59*(1), 23. Advance online publication. DOI: 10.1007/s12124-025-09894-8

Fan, Y., Matcha, W., Uzir, N. A. A., Wang, Q., & Gašević, D. (2021). Learning analytics to reveal links between learning design and self-regulated learning. *International Journal of Artificial Intelligence in Education, 31*(4), 980–1021. DOI: 10.1007/s40593-021-00249-z

Fletcher, A. K. (2024). Self-assessment as a student-agentic zone of proximate competence development. *Educational Review, 76*(4), 956–978. DOI: 10.1080/00131911.2022.2103520

Gardner, J., O'Leary, M., & Yuan, L. (2021). Artificial intelligence in educational assessment: 'Breakthrough? Or buncombe and ballyhoo?'. *Journal of Computer Assisted Learning, 37*(5), 1207–1216. DOI: 10.1111/jcal.12577

Ghoson, N. H., Meyrueis, V., Benfriha, K., Guiltat, T., & Loubere, S. (2025). A review on the static and dynamic risk assessment methods for OT cybersecurity in Industry 4.0. *Computers & Security, 150*, 104295. Advance online publication. DOI: 10.1016/j.cose.2024.104295

Giannakos, M., & Cukurova, M. (2023). The role of learning theory in multimodal learning analytics. *British Journal of Educational Technology, 54*(5), 1246–1267. DOI: 10.1111/bjet.13320

Gligorea, I., Cioca, M., Oancea, R., Gorski, A.-T., Gorski, H., & Tudorache, P. (2023). Adaptive learning using artificial intelligence in e-learning: A literature review. *Education Sciences, 13*(12), 1216. Advance online publication. DOI: 10.3390/educsci13121216

Hao, M., Wang, Y., & Peng, J. (2024). Empirical research on AI technology-supported precision teaching in high school science subjects. *Applied Sciences (Basel, Switzerland), 14*(17), 7544. DOI: 10.3390/app14177544

Hayat, A. A., Keshavarzi, M. H., Zare, S., Bazrafcan, L., Rezaee, R., Faghihi, S. A., Amini, M., & Kojuri, J. (2021). Challenges and opportunities from the COVID-19 pandemic in medical education: A qualitative study. *BMC Medical Education, 21*(1), 247. DOI: 10.1186/s12909-021-02682-z

Hemachandran, K., Verma, P., Pareek, P., Arora, N., Rajesh Kumar, K. V., Ahanger, T. A., Pise, A. A., & Ratna, R. (2022). Artificial intelligence: A universal virtual tool to augment tutoring in higher education. *Computational Intelligence and Neuroscience, 2022*, 1410448. Advance online publication. DOI: 10.1155/2022/1410448

Herath, H. M. S. S., Herath, H. M. K. K. M. B., Madhusanka, B. G. D. A., & Guruge, L. G. P. K. (2024). Data protection challenges in the processing of sensitive data. In *Data Protection: The Wake of AI and Machine Learning* (pp. 155–179). Springer Nature Switzerland., DOI: 10.1007/978-3-031-76473-8_8

Honson, V., Vu, T., Tran, T. P., & Tejada Estay, W. (2024). Using learning analytics to alleviate course and student support administrative load for large classes: A case study. *Journal of Work-Applied Management, 16*(2), 303–315. DOI: 10.1108/JWAM-11-2023-0121

Hooda, M., Rana, C., Dahiya, O., Rizwan, A., & Hossain, M. S. (2022). Artificial intelligence for assessment and feedback to enhance student success in higher education. *Mathematical Problems in Engineering, 2022*, 5215722. Advance online publication. DOI: 10.1155/2022/5215722

Jiang, N., Liu, X., Liu, H., Lim, E. T. K., Tan, C. W., & Gu, J. (2023). Beyond AI-powered context-aware services: The role of human–AI collaboration. *Industrial Management & Data Systems, 123*(11), 2771–2802. DOI: 10.1108/IMDS-03-2022-0152

Kadel, R., Mishra, B. K., Shailendra, S., Abid, S., Rani, M., & Mahato, S. P. (2024, May 3). *Crafting Tomorrow's Evaluations: Assessment design strategies in the era of generative AI. CoRR, abs/2405.01805*. https://doi.org//arXiv.2405.01805DOI: 10.48550

Kaswan, K. S., Dhatterwal, J. S., & Ojha, R. P. (2024). AI in personalized learning. In *Advances in Technological Innovations in Higher Education* (pp. 103–117). CRC Press., DOI: 10.1201/9781003376699-9

Krauss, C., Streicher, A., Poxleitner, E., Altun, D., Müller, J., An, T. S., & Müller, C. (2023, June). Best-of-breed: Service-oriented integration of artificial intelligence in interoperable educational ecosystems. In *International Workshop on Learning Technology for Education Challenges* (pp. 267–283). Cham: Springer Nature Switzerland. https://doi.org/DOI: 10.1007/978-3-031-34754-2_22

Kuhail, M. A., Alturki, N., Alramlawi, S., & Alhejori, K. (2023). Interacting with educational chatbots: A systematic review. *Education and Information Technologies, 28*(1), 973–1018. DOI: 10.1007/s10639-022-11177-3

Kush, J. C. (2025). Integrating sensor technologies with conversational AI: Enhancing context-sensitive interaction through real-time data fusion. *Sensors (Basel), 25*(1), 249. DOI: 10.3390/s25010249

Kyambade, M., & Namatovu, A. (2025). Health-care leaders' perspectives on AI implementation in Uganda: Overcoming barriers, driving innovation and strategic considerations. *Leadership in Health Services*, *38*(2), 299–317. DOI: 10.1108/LHS-06-2024-0052

Larsen, V. G., Tollin, N., Sattrup, P. A., Birkved, M., & Holmboe, T. (2022). What are the challenges in assessing circular economy for the built environment? A literature review on integrating LCA, LCC and S-LCA in life cycle sustainability assessment (LCSA). *Journal of Building Engineering*, *50*, 104203. DOI: 10.1016/j.jobe.2022.104203

Latifi, S., & Gierl, M. (2021). Automated scoring of junior and senior high essays using Coh-Metrix features: Implications for large-scale language testing. *Language Testing*, *38*(1), 62–85. DOI: 10.1177/0265532220929918

Li, L., Chen, C. P., Wang, L., Liang, K., & Bao, W. (2023). Exploring artificial intelligence in smart education: Real-time classroom behavior analysis with embedded devices. *Sustainability (Basel)*, *15*(10), 7940. Advance online publication. DOI: 10.3390/su15107940

Lindsay, E. D., Johri, A., & Bjerva, J. (2025). A framework for responsible development of automated student feedback with generative AI. In *Proceedings of the IEEE Global Engineering Education Conference (EDUCON 2025): Special Session: Generative AI and Ethical Integration in Higher Education* (pp. ...). IEEE Press. https://doi.org/DOI: 10.1109/EDUCON62633.2025.11016572

Mampota, S., Mokhets'engoane, S. J., & Kurata, L. (2023). Connectivism theory: Exploring its relevance in informing Lesotho's integrated curriculum for effective learning in the digital age. *European Journal of Education and Pedagogy*, *4*(4), 6–12. DOI: 10.24018/ejedu.2023.4.4.705

Mamun, M. A. A. (2022). Fostering self-regulation and engaged exploration during the learner–content interaction process: The role of scaffolding in the online inquiry-based learning environment. *Interactive Technology and Smart Education*, *19*(4), 482–509. DOI: 10.1108/ITSE-11-2021-0195

Mislevy, R. J. (2024). Sociocognitive and argumentation perspectives on psychometric modeling in educational assessment. *Psychometrika*, *89*(1), 64–83. DOI: 10.1007/s11336-024-09966-5

Mohamed Riyath, M. I., & Muhammed Rijah, U. L. (2022). Adoption of a learning management system among educators of advanced technological institutes in Sri Lanka. *Asian Association of Open Universities Journal*, *17*(2), 161–177. DOI: 10.1108/AAOUJ-03-2022-0032

Mohammed, S. J., & Khalid, M. W. (2025). Under the world of AI-generated feedback on writing: Mirroring motivation, foreign language peace of mind, trait emotional intelligence, and writing development. *Language Testing in Asia*, *15*(1), 7. Advance online publication. DOI: 10.1186/s40468-025-00343-2

Mourya, A., Jobanputra, B., & Pai, R. (2024). AI-powered clinical trials and the imperative for regulatory transparency and accountability. *Health and Technology*, *14*(1), 1071–1081. DOI: 10.1007/s12553-024-00904-0

Naseer, F., & Khawaja, S. (2025). Mitigating conceptual learning gaps in mixed-ability classrooms: A learning analytics-based evaluation of AI-driven adaptive feedback for struggling learners. *Applied Sciences (Basel, Switzerland)*, *15*(8), 4473. Advance online publication. DOI: 10.3390/app15084473

Nazaretsky, T., Ariely, M., Cukurova, M., & Alexandron, G. (2022). Teachers' trust in AI-powered educational technology and a professional development program to improve it. *British Journal of Educational Technology*, *53*(4), 914–931. DOI: 10.1111/bjet.13232

Nicola-Gavrilă, L. (2023). Education and technology in a data driven society: Turning data into education intelligence. In *Digital Future in Education: Paradoxes, Hopes and Realities* (pp. 12–33). RITHA Publishing. https://doi.org/DOI: 10.57017/SERITHA.2023.DFE.ch1

Ouyang, F., Zheng, L., & Jiao, P. (2022). Artificial intelligence in online higher education: A systematic review of empirical research from 2011 to 2020. *Education and Information Technologies*, *27*(6), 7893–7925. DOI: 10.1007/s10639-022-10925-9

Oyebode, O., Fowles, J., Steeves, D., & Orji, R. (2023). Machine learning techniques in adaptive and personalized systems for health and wellness. *International Journal of Human-Computer Interaction*, *39*(9), 1938–1962. DOI: 10.1080/10447318.2022.2089085

Paulsen, L., & Lindsay, E. (2024). Learning analytics dashboards are increasingly becoming about learning and not just analytics: A systematic review. *Education and Information Technologies*, *29*(11), 14279–14308. Advance online publication. DOI: 10.1007/s10639-023-12401-4

Ramesh, D., & Sanampudi, S. K. (2022). An automated essay scoring systems: A systematic literature review. *Artificial Intelligence Review*, *55*(3), 2495–2527. DOI: 10.1007/s10462-021-10068-2

Rekha, K., Gopal, K., Satheeskumar, D., Anand, U. A., Doss, D. S. S., & Elayaperumal, S. (2024, May). AI-powered personalized learning system design: Student engagement and performance tracking system. In *2024 4th International Conference on Advance Computing and Innovative Technologies in Engineering (ICACITE)* (pp. 1125–1130). IEEE. https://doi.org/DOI: 10.1109/ICACITE60783.2024.10617155

Sadigzade, Z. (2025). AI-powered feedback in ESL writing classes: Pedagogical opportunities and ethical concerns. *Journal of Azerbaijan Language and Education Studies*, *2*(4), 5–17. DOI: 10.69760/jales.2025004000

Saiyad, S., Bhagat, P., Virk, A., Mahajan, R., & Singh, T. (2021). Changing assessment scenarios: Lessons for changing practice. *International Journal of Applied & Basic Medical Research*, *11*(4), 206–213. DOI: 10.4103/ijabmr.IJABMR_334_21

Sajja, R., Sermet, Y., Cikmaz, M., Cwiertny, D., & Demir, I. (2024). Artificial Intelligence-Enabled Intelligent Assistant for Personalized and Adaptive Learning in Higher Education. *Information (Basel)*, *15*(10), 596. Advance online publication. DOI: 10.3390/info15100596

Salas-Pilco, S. Z., Xiao, K., & Oshima, J. (2022). Artificial intelligence and new technologies in inclusive education for minority students: A systematic review. *Sustainability (Basel)*, *14*(18), 11789. Advance online publication. DOI: 10.3390/su142013572

Schultz, M., Young, K., Gunning, T. K., & Harvey, M. L. (2022). Defining and measuring authentic assessment: A case study in the context of tertiary science. *Assessment & Evaluation in Higher Education*, *47*(1), 77–94. DOI: 10.1080/02602938.2021.1887811

Shaik, T., Tao, X., Li, Y., Dann, C., McDonald, J., Redmond, P., & Galligan, L. (2023). A review of the trends and challenges in adopting natural language processing methods for education feedback analysis. *IEEE Access : Practical Innovations, Open Solutions, 10*, 56720–56739. DOI: 10.1109/ACCESS.2022.3177752

Sivasubramanian, K., Jaheer Mukthar, K. P., Raju, V., & Srinivas, K. (2022). The impact of digital learning management system on students of higher education institutions during COVID-19 pandemic. In *Technologies, Artificial Intelligence and the Future of Learning Post-COVID-19: The Crucial Role of International Accreditation* (pp. 657–678). Springer International Publishing., DOI: 10.1007/978-3-030-93921-2_34

Sokhanvar, Z., Salehi, K., & Sokhanvar, F. (2021). Advantages of authentic assessment for improving the learning experience and employability skills of higher education students: A systematic literature review. *Studies in Educational Evaluation, 70*, 101030. Advance online publication. DOI: 10.1016/j.stueduc.2021.101030

Song, C., Shin, S.-Y., & Shin, K.-S. (2024). Implementing the Dynamic Feedback-Driven Learning Optimization Framework: A machine learning approach to personalize educational pathways. *Applied Sciences (Basel, Switzerland), 14*(2), 916. DOI: 10.3390/app14020916

Stein, D. J., Shoptaw, S. J., Vigo, D. V., Lund, C., Cuijpers, P., Bantjes, J., Sartorius, N., & Maj, M. (2022). Psychiatric diagnosis and treatment in the 21st century: Paradigm shifts versus incremental integration. *World Psychiatry; Official Journal of the World Psychiatric Association (WPA), 21*(3), 393–414. DOI: 10.1002/wps.20998

Strielkowski, W., Grebennikova, V., Lisovskiy, A., Rakhimova, G., & Vasileva, T. (2025). AI-driven adaptive learning for sustainable educational transformation. *Sustainable Development (Bradford), 33*(2), 1921–1947. DOI: 10.1002/sd.3221

Tian, Z., Sun, M., Liu, A., Sarkar, S., & Liu, J. (2024). Enhancing instructional quality: Leveraging computer-assisted textual analysis to generate in-depth insights from educational artifacts. *arXiv preprint* arXiv:2403.03920. https://doi.org//arXiv.2403.03920DOI: 10.48550

Trajkovski, G., & Hayes, H. (2025). *AI-Assisted Assessment in Education: Transforming Assessment and Measuring Learning*. Springer Nature Switzerland., DOI: 10.1007/978-3-031-88252-4

Trajkovski, G., & Hayes, H. (2025). AI-Assisted formative assessment and feedback. In *AI-Assisted Assessment in Education: Transforming Assessment and Measuring Learning* (pp. 283–312). Cham: Springer Nature Switzerland. https://doi.org/DOI: 10.1007/978-3-031-88252-4_7

Vashishth, T. K., Sharma, V., Sharma, K. K., Kumar, B., Panwar, R., & Chaudhary, S. (2024). AI-driven learning analytics for personalized feedback and assessment in higher education. In *Using Traditional Design Methods to Enhance AI-Driven Decision Making* (pp. 206–230). IGI Global., DOI: 10.4018/979-8-3693-0639-0.ch009

Viberg, O., Kizilcec, R. F., Wise, A. F., Jivet, I., & Nixon, N. (2024). Advancing equity and inclusion in educational practices with AI-powered educational decision support systems (AI-EDSS). *British Journal of Educational Technology, 55*(5), 1974–1981. DOI: 10.1111/bjet.13507

Winstone, N. E., & Boud, D. (2022). The need to disentangle assessment and feedback in higher education. *Studies in Higher Education*, *47*(3), 656–667. DOI: 10.1080/03075079.2020.1779687

Xu, S., Su, Y., & Liu, K. (2025). Investigating student engagement with AI-driven feedback in translation revision: A mixed-methods study. *Education and Information Technologies*, *30*(12), 16969–16995. Advance online publication. DOI: 10.1007/s10639-025-13457-0

Yesilyurt, Y. E. (2023). AI-enabled assessment and feedback mechanisms for language learning: Transforming pedagogy and learner experience. In Kartal, G. (Ed.), *Transforming the language teaching experience in the age of AI* (pp. 25–43). IGI Global., DOI: 10.4018/978-1-6684-9893-4.ch002

ADDITIONAL READING

Alazemi, A. F. T. (2024). Formative assessment in artificial intelligence–integrated instruction: Effects on EFL students' reading comprehension development and academic mindfulness. *Language Testing in Asia*, *14*(1). Advance online publication. DOI: 10.1186/s40468-024-00319-8

Li, T. A. (2025). Critical thinking assessment in higher education: The role of artificial intelligence. *Interactive Learning Environments*. Advance online publication. DOI: 10.1080/10447318.2025.2499164

Martin, F., Kim, S., Bolliger, D. U., & DeLarm, J. (2025). Assessment types, strategies, and feedback in online higher education courses in the age of artificial intelligence: Perspectives of instructional designers. *TechTrends*, *69*(6), 1330–1346. Advance online publication. DOI: 10.1007/s11528-025-01115-8

Memarian, B. (2024). *A review of assessment for learning with artificial intelligence*. Assessment & Learning Technologies., DOI: 10.1016/j.chbah.2023.100040

Riordan, A., Echeverria, V., Jin, Y., Yan, L., Swiecki, Z., Gašević, D., & Martinez-Maldonado, R. (2023). Human-centred learning analytics and AI in education: a systematic literature review. *arXiv*. https://doi.org//arXiv.2312.12751DOI: 10.48550

Sajja, R., Sermet, Y., Cikmaz, M., Cwiertny, D., & Demir, I. (2023). Artificial Intelligence–enabled intelligent assistant for personalized and adaptive learning in higher education. *arXiv*. https://doi.org//arXiv.2309.10892DOI: 10.48550

Sharif, H., & Atif, A. (2024). How learning analytics is shaping the future of education. *Education Sciences*, *14*(2), 176. DOI: 10.3390/educsci14020176

Topali, P., Ortega-Arranz, A., Rodríguez-Triana, M. J., Er, E., Khalil, M., & Akçapınar, G. (2025). Designing human-centered learning analytics and artificial intelligence systems: A systematic literature review. *Behaviour & Information Technology*, *44*(5), 1071–1098. Advance online publication. DOI: 10.1080/0144929X.2024.2345295

Weidlich, J., Fink, A., Frey, A., Jivet, I., Gombert, S., Menzel, L., Giorgashvili, T., Yau, J., & Drachsler, H. (2025). Highly informative feedback using learning analytics. *International Journal of Educational Technology in Higher Education, 22*(1), 43. Advance online publication. DOI: 10.1186/s41239-025-00539-9

Yan, L., Martinez-Maldonado, R., & Gašević, D. (2023). Generative artificial intelligence in learning analytics: Contextualising opportunities and challenges through the learning analytics cycle. *arXiv*. https://doi.org//arXiv.2312.00087DOI: 10.48550

KEY TERMS AND DEFINITIONS

Algorithmic Bias: A systemic inaccuracy in AI outputs stemming from biased training data or defective model architecture, perhaps resulting in unjust or discriminating feedback in educational evaluations.

Artificial Intelligence (AI) in Education: The utilization of AI technology, including machine learning, natural language processing, and learning analytics, to improve teaching, learning, and assessment methodologies.

Formative Assessment: A continuous evaluation approach that offers continuing feedback to inform student learning and instructional modifications, frequently incorporated into learning activities.

Intelligent Tutoring System (ITS): A platform powered by artificial intelligence that emulates the support of a human tutor by delivering tailored, adaptive training and instantaneous feedback to students.

Learning Analytics: The gathering, measurement, analysis, and reporting of learner data to comprehend and enhance learning processes and settings.

Natural Language Processing (NLP): A domain of artificial intelligence that allows machines to comprehend, interpret, and produce human language, frequently employed for automated evaluations of student writing and communication.

Personalized Feedback: Customized instructional support developed according to specific learner requirements, performance trends, and educational objectives, aimed at improving engagement and success.

Self-Regulated Learning (SRL): A process wherein learners establish objectives, track advancement, and modify techniques to assume control of their own education, frequently aided by adaptive feedback mechanisms.

Summative Assessment: A concluding assessment process aimed to assessing student performance against established criteria, generally for grading or certification objectives.

System Interoperability: The capacity of various technological systems and platforms—such as AI feedback tools and learning management systems—to interchange and utilize data effortlessly.

Chapter 12
AI-Powered Assessment and Feedback:
Enhancing Learning Outcomes In the Digital Era

Nihal Kapoor
https://orcid.org/0009-0009-7121-0789
Central University of Himachal Pradesh, India

Amrik Singh
https://orcid.org/0009-0001-9185-6407
Central University of Himachal Pradesh, India

Sandeep Kulshreshtha
Central University of Himachal Pradesh, India

Lalit Mohan Sharma
Central University of Himachal Pradesh, India

ABSTRACT

The integration of Artificial Intelligence (AI) in education has transformed assessment and feedback mechanisms, significantly enhancing learning outcomes in the digital era. AI- powered assessment tools provide personalized learning experiences, enabling educators to identify student strengths and weaknesses with greater accuracy. This chapter explores the role of AI in formative and summative assessments, highlighting its potential to improve efficiency, reduce biases, and foster student engagement. While AI-driven feedback enhances learning by providing timely and data-driven insights, challenges such as data privacy, algorithmic transparency, and the need for human oversight remain critical considerations. The chapter examines best practices for integrating AI in education to ensure ethical use and equitable access. By leveraging AI-powered assessment systems, educational institutions can create more inclusive and effective learning environments, ultimately improving academic performance and skill development.

DOI: 10.4018/979-8-3373-2752-5.ch012

1. INTRODUCTION

1.1 Background and Context

In the 21st century, education systems are also being significantly transformed by the fast track of digital innovation. The global adoption of digital learning platforms, Learning Management Systems (LMS), artificial intelligence (AI), and analytics has revolutionised the way knowledge is communicated, accessed, and assessed. As the world becomes more digitised, education needs to adapt to respond to the needs of a digitally savvy generation and yet match the aspirations of lifelong learners from diverse demographics and geography. Among the numerous parts of this digital evolution, feedback and assessment are both foundational and revolutionary elements. Assessment has historically been the mechanism used to determine student knowledge, shape teaching methods, and keep academic standards up (Black & Wiliam, 1998). Feedback, when on point and on time, fuels deeper learning, raises motivation, and drives self-regulation (Hattie & Timperley, 2007). Yet, in traditional classrooms, grading and feedback systems have historically struggled with issues such as grading delays, limited personalisation, inconsistency in evaluation, and teacher burnout. In a reaction to these issues, artificial intelligence has risen to prominence in contemporary education. AI-facilitated assessment solutions such as automated essay grading, adaptive tests, live feedback systems, and learning analytics platforms are facilitating educators to make learning more individualised, make their work more efficient, and deliver instant, tailored feedback in bulk (Luckin et al., 2016). "Natural Language Processing (NLP)" makes it possible to assess open-ended answers, while machine learning algorithms monitor student progress and forecast performance, potentially revolutionising the way teaching and learning are done (Chen et al., 2020). However, the efficacy and equity of AI-based assessment systems are still debated. At the heart of this argument is the image of the stakeholders who engage most immediately with these instruments students and teachers. While some teachers welcome AI as a useful co-teacher or aide, others are concerned about diminished pedagogical control, excessive dependence on algorithms, and bias. Likewise, students can appreciate immediate feedback and tailored learning pathways but also fear data privacy, lack of transparency, and impersonal learning experiences (Williamson & Eynon, 2020). This research attempts to examine these varying and at times opposing viewpoints, including the experiences, expectations, and concerns of students and teachers. Through examining how students and teachers understand AI for use in assessment and feedback, this study aims to gain not only insight into the technical possibilities of AI but also into its social and pedagogic repercussions.

1.2 Importance of Perceptions in AI Integration

Though AI technologies can process enormous quantities of educational data, their worth finally lies in trainers' utilisation and the students' explanation. "It has been proven that perception weighs heavily in the uptake and efficacy of learning technologies. Perceived ease of use and perceived usefulness are main determinants of a technology's adoption, as posited by Davis's Technology Acceptance Model (TAM)" (Davis, 1989). Used in the context of AI in education, this framework emphasises the need to study how users judge the real-world value and usability of AI-based assessment systems. From the learner's point of view, AI systems giving timely and helpful feedback can aid self-learning and promote intellectual development. A paper by Del Pilar

Gonzalez and Chiappe (2024) showed that students getting feedback on assignments from AI saw the system as helpful in suggesting revisions and comprehending performance gaps. At the same time, students also complained of distrust when feedback was ambiguous or when the AI justification was not transparent, mirroring wider issues with algorithm explainability. Teachers, in contrast, are both recipients and custodians of AI systems. While AI can automate grading and identify struggling learners, it can also threaten teachers' professional agency. According to Selwyn (2019), some teachers worry that AI-based decision-making will deskill teachers or transfer pedagogical power from human judgment to computational reasoning. Teachers might also wonder whether AI systems can fully represent higher-order thinking abilities, creativity, or contextual subtleties that human evaluation inherently takes into account. Perceived fairness is a second key aspect. AI algorithms learn from past data, which can inscribe social biases into them. For example, a study by Binns et al. (2018) suggests that algorithmic judgments can perpetuate and amplify current inequalities if data sets are homogeneous or the system is not suitably calibrated. In the educational setting, this spark fears that AI can unfairly penalise learners from non-hegemonic linguistic, cultural, or socioeconomic groups. Faith in the objectivity and fairness of AI systems is thus at the heart of their acceptance and influence.

1.3 Ethical Considerations

The application of AI to assessment also poses ethical questions. Transparency, accountability, and privacy of data are common themes in educational technology debates. Educators and students need to know how AI tools arrive at their determinations, how data is harvested and utilised, and how errors or biases are resolved. The General Data Protection Regulation (GDPR) and equivalent guidelines emphasise accountable data handling practices, but most AI systems remain "black boxes" with their users having no idea about the mechanics or possible threats inside (Morley et al., 2019). A good part of AI scepticism is due to a lack of human presence and empathy in feedback procedures. In contrast to learner-contextual, affective, and conversational considerations in traditional feedback, AI-sourced comments might come across as generic or faceless, damaging student motivation. Although there is a push towards humanising AI feedback via natural language and empathetic design, the role of human interaction in learning is irreplaceable for most (Heffernan & Heffernan, 2014).

1.4 Research Question

RQ1: What are the current uses of AI-enabled tools in education, and the Advantages, feedback of AI-based Assessment?

RQ2: AI Traditional v/s Modern-based assessment?

RQ3: How does AI-based assessment affect the effectiveness, fairness, and limitations of AI in assessment?

RQ4: What are the challenges and ethical concerns of using AI-enabled assessment and feedback in education?

1.5 Relevance in the Post-COVID Digital Era

The COVID-19 pandemic provided the impetus for a mass movement towards virtual learning, as it accelerated education's adoption of AI and automation. Confronted with requirements for remote assessments, institutions often resorted to AI for checking plagiarism, machine grading, and learning analytics. Here, consideration of stakeholder perception became time-sensitive. While educational institutions continue to invest in AI infrastructure, understanding user experience and expectations is essential to making these technologies pedagogically grounded and sustainable (Zawacki-Richter et al., 2019).

1.6 Consequences of the Study

This research will contribute to both theoretical and practical significance. Theoretically, it contributes to a growing body of literature on human-computer interface, digital pedagogy, and AI ethics in education. It integrates perspectives from education, computer science, and social science to develop a holistic understanding of AI's impact. Practically, the findings can inform the design and implementation of AI assessment tools that are responsive to user needs and ethical standards. By centring the voices of students and educators, the study supports the development of human-centred AI in education systems that are transparent, fair, and pedagogically aligned. Policy makers, edtech developers, and institutional leaders can also benefit from the insights offered, particularly in designing training programs, formulating guidelines, and investing in inclusive technologies. In a rapidly changing digital landscape, understanding human perception is vital to shaping AI's role in supporting equitable and effective education.

2. UNDERSTANDING AI IN EDUCATION

2.1 Defining AI and Its Components

Artificial Intelligence (AI) is the ability of software or machines to simulate intellectual activities like learning, problem-solving, reasoning, and understanding language functions historically linked with human intelligence (Russell & Norvig, 2016). In education, AI systems are programmed to automate functions, tailor learning experiences, and assist teaching and assessment roles.

The three core components of AI applicable to education are:

a) Machine Learning (ML):

ML describes the capacity of algorithms to learn over time from patterns in data and improve on their own without being specifically programmed (Jordan & Mitchell, 2015). In education, ML underlies adaptive learning platforms that modulate satisfied effort according to student performance as well as predictive analytics that detect struggling students.

b) Natural Language Processing (NLP):

NLP enables computers to comprehend, read, and write human language. This makes AI systems capable of giving immediate feedback on students' writing, conducting automated essay grading, and informing dialogue systems such as chatbots and virtual tutors (Gross et al., 2015).

c) Automation

Educational automation is where AI is used to execute regular administrative or pedagogical functions. This consists of automated assessment, personalised feedback creation, and content suggestion, liberating teachers to perform more sophisticated instructional tasks (Holmes et al., 2019).

All these technologies merge into AI-enabled assessment software that assesses objective (e.g., multiple-choice) and subjective (e.g., essay) answers, provides individualised feedback, and enables continuous learning.

2.2 AI Uses in Education

AI is being integrated at more and more layers of the education system. Its presence extends beyond infrastructure to instructional practice, student support, and assessment. Among the most significant uses are:

a) Personalised Learning:

"Perhaps the most revolutionary effect of AI in education is its capacity to tailor learning pathways. Adaptive learning systems such as DreamBox, Squirrel AI, and Knewton track students' interactions and adapt instruction in response. These systems modify the pace, order, and form of content to suit each learner's individual needs, learning styles, and knowledge gaps" (Zawacki-Richter et al., 2019). Personalised learning has been found to increase student engagement, motivation, and retention (Pane et al., 2017).

b) Automated Grading and Assessment:

Artificial intelligence is transforming testing by automating the scoring of objective and subjective items. Multiple-choice, true-false, and short-answer items can be scored instantly with high precision. Developments in NLP have made it possible to score essays, open-ended answers, and even spoken responses with tools like the Intelligent Essay Assessor and ETS's e-rater (Han, 2015). This enables teachers to give instant feedback and devote themselves to high-leverage teaching activities.

c) Chatbots and Virtual Tutors:

AI-driven chatbots mimic human instructors by offering real-time, context-based support to learners. For instance, Jill Watson, created at Georgia Tech, employs IBM's Watson AI to respond to students' queries on course discussion boards. Likewise, virtual tutors such as Carnegie Learning's MATHia employ AI to support students in solving problems, providing hints and scaffolds depending on learner input. These technologies provide learning support outside the classroom and increase accessibility (Adetayo, 2023).

2.3 Advantages of AI-Based Assessment and Feedback

AI-based assessment and feedback solutions present a host of advantages to students at different educational levels and academic disciplines. Such advantages are responsible for enhancing improved learning results, efficient teaching, and improved decision-making by the institution.

a) Increased Efficiency:

AI applications alleviate the burden of grading and feedback work, particularly in massive classes or distance learning, immensely. Computerised systems offer instant evaluation, allowing students to recognise and rectify mistakes instantly, which is important for formative learning (Singleton, 2001). Educators avoid time-consuming routine work and are free to engage in planning, guidance, and personalised teaching.

AI systems are able to process learner performance data to provide actionable insights to instructors. Dashboards show students' strengths, weaknesses, and trends over time, allowing for targeted interventions and differentiated instruction (Aldowah et al., 2019). Predictive analytics aid in the identification of at-risk students, enabling timely support to increase persistence and success rates.

c) Personalised Learning Pathways:

AI-powered feedback is tailored to the individual learner's profile. Intelligent tutoring systems give students hints, explanations, and practice problems attuned to the students' level of cognition and rate of learning. Personalised feedback supports self-regulated learning by assisting students in goal setting, monitoring progress, and building metacognitive abilities (Koedinger et al., 2015).

Also, AI systems can recognise misconceptions, suggest additional learning materials, and modify tests in real-time so that they can match learning goals. Such customisation can fill knowledge gaps and develop inclusive education.

2.4 Ethical and Privacy Concerns in AI Education

Despite the promise of AI in assessment and feedback, several ethical and privacy concerns have emerged that must be addressed to ensure responsible and impartial implementation.

a) Data Security and Privacy:

AI applications are most dependent on the collection, analysis, and storage of students' information, including their conduct, intellect, and personal data. The potential for data breaches, abuse, and monitoring has triggered alarms among instructors, guardians, and policymakers (Slade & Prinsloo, 2013). Absence of stringent data governance increases the possibility of compromising students' privacy, particularly in regions without overarching data security legislation.

To mitigate these risks, developers of AI and schools must adhere to policies such as the "General Data Protection Regulation (GDPR)" in the European Union and the "Family Educational Rights and Privacy Act (FERPA)" in the United States. These guidelines require data minimisation, consent based on information, and a right to access and erase data. Additionally, privacy-by-default strategies and open communication with users must be part of ethical design.

b) Bias and Fairness:

AI models are only as unprejudiced as their training data. If the training data is itself biased due to historical disparities or not sufficiently diverse, the consequent AI systems can reproduce or even amplify educational inequities (West et al., 2019). For example, an essay-scoring system trained on a limited set of data may systematically disadvantage students whose language patterns do not fit the norm, like English language learners or students from other cultures.

AI fairness calls for rigorous auditing of training data, transparency in algorithms, and accessibility in design processes. Researchers have suggested fairness measures and bias detection methods, which are still emerging and have not yet been widely applied in commercial educational software.

c) Ethical AI Implementation

Aside from issues of data, there are more general worries regarding the dehumanisation of learning and the substitution of pedagogy with machines. AI should be an addition, not a replacement, to human teachers. Critical scholars propose that excessive dependence on AI could diminish learning to data yields, negating the social, emotional, and cultural aspects of learning (Selwyn, 2019).

To provide an ethical AI combination, schools and universities need to develop ascendancy agendas that engage multilayered stakeholders educators, students, parents, developers, and ethicists. UNESCO Validation on the Ethics of Artificial Intelligence (2021) provides guiding principles, such as inclusivity, responsibility, transparency, and sustainability. In addition, algorithmic decisions must be clear. Teachers and students are entitled to know how an AI system comes to a grade or suggest a principle called explicable AI (XAI). Transparency generates trust and makes technology answerable to academic and human values. AI is transforming the way teachers assess learning and students are given feedback, providing strong instruments for personalisation, efficiency, and data-driven teaching. But where great likelihood lies is also where great responsibility exists in. Data privacy, fairness, and ethical deployment have to be supreme in order for AI to assist inclusive, transparent, and valuable education.

As schools increasingly adopt AI technologies, attention needs to stay not only on what AI can complete, but also on how it impacts the human aspects of teaching and learning. The next chapter will explore the current literature on AI-driven assessment, stakeholder disregard, and upcoming research gaps.

3. TRADITIONAL VS. AI-POWERED ASSESSMENT

3.1 Traditional Assessment Methods

Traditional assessment methods have been the standard for measuring student learning in institutions of learning for a long time. These include traditional exams, written work, quizzes, presentations, and classroom engagement, which are all marked manually by instructors. These methods focus on recall of knowledge and the summative assessment of students' performance, usually at the end of a learning cycle (Black & Wiliam, 1998).

1. Exams and Quizzes

Standardised tests and quizzes continue to be the most widely used instruments in measuring student learning. Standardised tests usually test factual knowledge and conceptual understanding by using multiple-choice, true/false, short-answer, or essay questions. Such strategies, however, tend to test only lower-level thinking skills and are not very effective in testing higher-level cognitive skills like analysis, synthesis, and evaluation (Bloom, 1956).

2. Assignments and Projects

Written work, laboratory reports, and term papers provide more in-depth means of measuring students' knowledge. They permit students to illustrate creativity, research abilities, and critical thinking. Yet, marking these artefacts is time-consuming and susceptible to subjective bias (Sadler, 2008). Rubrics are commonly used to enhance uniformity, yet even they are unable to banish all inconsistency in grading by different markers.

3. Manual Grading

Manual marking is, by nature, time-consuming and unreliable. Teachers usually lack enough time, which can influence the quality and extent of feedback for students (Brookhart, 2008). Additionally, marking large amounts of student work also places human errors at higher risk and lowers the chance of timely intervention.

Challenges in Traditional Assessment

Several notable challenges are inherent in traditional assessment approaches:

1. Low scalability: Class sizes that are very large render individual feedback and detailed assessment not feasible.
2. Late feedback: Feedback is given too late for it to be useful.
3. Subjectivity and bias: Evaluator fatigue, handwriting, or writing style may impact grades.
4. Standardisation: One size fit all might hurt heterogeneous learners who need differential assessment strategies.

These flaws have encouraged teachers and institutions to look towards technology-based solutions, specifically those based on Artificial Intelligence (AI).

3.2 AI-Based Assessment Strategies

AI-based assessment is an educational evaluation revolution. Retaining machine learning, natural language processing (NLP), and adaptive algorithms, AI systems automate grading, offer personalised feedback, and conduct continuous formative assessments (Zawacki-Richter et al., 2019). These systems deliver cooperating, real, and data-informed alternatives to traditional assessments.

1. AI-Based Quizzes and Automated Testing

One of the easiest uses of AI in assessment is for computer quizzes and tests. These systems can automatically score and create questions in real-time. For example, GradeScope, Quizlet AI, and AI Examiner enable teachers to design question banks and conduct tests that adjust in difficulty according to the performance of the students. Item response theory (IRT) and data analysis are used in computer-based assessments to determine not only if a right response was given, but also how the student arrived at the answer by looking at reaction time, click stream, and past mistakes. This opens the door to the capacity to make tests more sophisticated on an ongoing basis and gives educators better insight into student thinking (Woolf, 2010).

2. Adaptive Testing

Adaptive testing is a sophisticated AI-driven method whereby the test adjusts to every student's capability in real time. As a student responds to questions, the system chooses the next items depending on the difficulty level of questions answered before and the learner's performance. For instance, the GRE and GMAT apply computer-adaptive testing (CAT) to measure a test-taker's level of ability more precisely.

These systems can alleviate test anxiety by posing questions to the students that are neither too easy nor too hard. They also minimise the number of questions necessary to evaluate proficiency correctly, enhancing efficiency while preserving validity (Weiss, 1982).

3. Real-Time and Formative Assessment

AI supports real-time formative assessment where students and teachers can track the progress along the way, and not at the point of conclusion. AI-driven learning analytics dashboards enable constant feedback loops that permit students to manage their learning and teachers to step in earlier (Ifenthaler & Yau, 2020).

For example, websites like Knewton and Smart Sparrow monitor student interactions and performance data to suggest personalised content and remedial exercises. Further, AI-powered writing tools like Grammarly and Turnitin Revision Assistant offer instantaneous feedback on grammar, coherence, and style, thus enabling iterative improvement.

3.3 Case Studies: AI in Assessment

Many educational institutions and technology vendors have incorporated AI into their evaluation systems. The case studies below present the range of AI usage in actual educational environments:

Case Study 1: Georgia Tech's Jill Watson

In 2016, Georgia Institute of Technology launched Jill Watson, an IBM Watson-powered AI teaching assistant. Jill was employed to respond to questions in an online discussion forum. The AI gave answers to students' queries with a 97% accuracy rate, making the instructor's workload lighter and improving student satisfaction (Goel & Polepeddi, 2018).

Case Study 2: Carnegie Learning's MATHia

Carnegie Learning's MATHia system uses machine learning to measure students' math understanding in real time. The platform monitors keystrokes, problem-solving sequences, and response times to inform instruction and provide feedback. Research indicates that students working with MATHia demonstrate increased engagement and better learning results than conventional techniques (Pane et al., 2013).

Case Study 3: University of New South Wales' AI Marking Tool

The University of New South Wales created an AI-driven marking tool for short-answer questions. The tool was trained on historical graded student responses and had 90–95% agreement with human graders. This greatly decreased grading time and gave students quicker feedback (UNSW, 2020).

Case Study 4: Duolingo English Test

The Duolingo English Test uses AI to measure speaking, writing, reading, and listening abilities. While conventional standardised testing relies on fixed algorithms, it adopts adaptive algorithms to adjust question difficulty and utilises AI scoring for real-time results. Its increasing popularity among universities stems from the credibility and ease of AI-powered assessments (Settles & Meeder, 2016).

These case studies demonstrate that AI can improve efficiency, alleviate teacher workload, and individualise the assessment process for students.

3.4 Challenges in AI-Based Assessments

Despite their many advantages, AI-based assessments are not without limitations. Concerns around accuracy, fairness, and adaptability must be addressed to ensure equitable and effective use.

1. Accuracy and Reliability

Whereas AI systems can mirror or even surpass human grading performance for formal tasks, their efficacy declines in rating difficult or creative performances such as essays, paintings, or oral presentations. For example, machine essay scorer software can have trouble in analysing subtleties such as tone, originality, and coherence of arguments (Roscoe, 2014). Additionally, inconsistencies between human and AI-provided feedback will lead to confusion or distrust on the part of students.

2. Bias and Fairness

AI models learned from biased data can perpetuate or even widen inequalities unintentionally. For instance, an essay-grading model learned mostly from answers given by native English speakers can systematically penalise second-language students. Without representative and diverse training data, AI systems can end up reinforcing social, cultural, or linguistic differences (West et al., 2019).

To address fairness, ongoing monitoring, transparency of algorithms, and the engagement of multiple stakeholders in development and assessment are needed. Researchers have suggested "fairness audits" and the use of explainable AI (XAI) methods to establish trust and responsibility (Binns et al., 2018).

3. Adaptability and Context Sensitivity

AI systems tend to have difficulty in fitting into unstructured or open-ended learning situations. Human teachers, on the other hand, can read contextual cues, emotions, or cultural context. AI does not possess emotional intelligence and situational awareness. For instance, an AI application can misidentify creative writing as being off-topic or rate humour and irony as being irrelevant (Selwyn, 2019).

In addition, integrating AI systems into various curricula, languages, or philosophies of education demands extensive customisation and training. This constrains scalability and adds to development expenses.

4. Ethical and Legal Considerations

The application of AI in grading is raising critical ethical issues. Who is responsible for wrong grades or unsuitable feedback? How is data from students safeguarded, and how is it used? What level of rights does students enjoy in challenging AI decisions? These issues call for strong governance systems that conform to legislation such as GDPR and FERPA (Slade & Prinsloo, 2013).

Further, institutions need to ensure transparency in AI utilisation, offer students choices to opt out of automated systems, and have a human-in-the-loop method to preserve academic integrity and student autonomy.

The shift from conventional to AI-driven assessment represents a watershed moment in educational practice. Whilst conventional assessments have brought structure and familiarity, they are increasingly hampered by constraints in scalability, timeliness, and personalisation. AI-driven assessment approaches, on the other hand, bring real-time feedback, adaptive learning routes, and data-driven instruction. Yet the full potential of AI can be achieved only through careful management of issues around fairness, accuracy, adaptability, and ethics.

4. AI-DRIVEN FEEDBACK MECHANISMS

4.1 Significance of Feedback in Learning

a. Constructive and Timely Feedback

Feedback is an essential element of the teaching-learning process, acting as a link between instruction and student performance. Hattie and Timperley (2007) state that effective feedback greatly improves learning by giving learners information about their current performance and advice for improvement. Timely feedback enables students to reflect, self-correct, and modify their strategies before misconceptions solidify.

Feedback is typically delayed in conventional classroom settings because of limitations in teacher time availability, particularly in large classrooms. The delay reduces the value and effectiveness of the feedback. Immediate, precise, and constructive feedback is featured more readily provided through AI systems (Shute, 2008).

b. Impact on Student Performance

Empirical research suggests that feedback enhances student motivation, increases information retention, and enhances deeper learning. When students know their strengths and weaknesses, they can take responsibility for their learning process. Nicol and Macfarlane-Dick (2006) stressed that feedback supporting self-regulated learning leads to greater learning gains compared to feedback that only points out right or wrong answers.

AI systems, with their capacity to analyse large volumes of data quickly, offer a promising solution to many of the limitations of traditional feedback methods. They can deliver rapid, targeted, and iterative feedback that aligns with individual student learning patterns.

4.2 AI-Driven Feedback Systems

a. Automated Feedback Tools

Tools that are AI-driven are now used to offer automated feedback on numerous student assignments, especially writing, coding, and math. Some of the examples include Grammarly, Ecree, WriteLab, Turnitin Revision Assistant, and CodeSignal. These sites use natural language processing (NLP) and machine learning procedures to appraise grammar, syntax, coherence, and content structure in real time.

For instance, Grammarly provides real-time feedback on sentence structure, tone, and legibility. It even adapts to different writing styles and readers. Similarly, automated code tools can analyse code submissions, detect logical errors, and suggest optimisations, allowing students to iterate quickly and independently.

These tools not only lighten the feedback load for teachers but also enable students to learn separately by providing them with instant and consistent feedback on their assignments.

b. AI-Driven Plagiarism Detection

AI has also revolutionised managing academic integrity by using sophisticated plagiarism detection tools. Old plagiarism detection was based on keyword matching and rule-based analysis. Unlike this, AI-driven tools like Turnitin and Copyleaks use machine learning and semantic analysis to identify paraphrasing, source manipulation, and cross-linguistic similarities.

These systems scan the context and intention of the text, providing subtle feedback to students and teachers. Some platforms now also include similarity reports with suggestions for proper citation instead of flagging matches, hence encouraging learning rather than punishment (Ganiyu, 2025).

4.3 Personalisation and Adaptivity in Feedback

a. Personalised Feedback Based on Student Need

One of the strongest features of AI-enabled feedback is its potential for personalisation. Unlike generic comments from humans, AI systems review a student's learning history, strengths, and frequent mistakes to personalise feedback according to their individual needs. It leads to closing individual knowledge gaps more efficiently compared to one-size-fits-all feedback. For instance, in adaptive learning systems such as DreamBox (mathematics) and Century Tech (cross-curricular), feedback is continually adjusted in real-time according to a student's previous interactions, learning speed, and level of mastery. The systems are capable of detecting the underlying causes of misconceptions and providing corrective feedback that is based on the cognitive level of the learner.

This method mirrors Vygotsky's Zone of Proximal Development (ZPD), whereby feedback is optimal when directed towards abilities slightly greater than a learner can accomplish on their own (Vygotsky, 1978).

b. Utilisation of Learning Analytics

AI systems use learning analytics to provide detailed insight into student performance. Such analytics involve error patterns, time, revisions, and engagement. All these data guide both the content and delivery of feedback.

For example, IBM's Watson Classroom platform applies predictive analytics to recommend customised interventions for a student based on the trajectory of their learning. Teachers can see dashboards showing students at risk of being left behind and receive recommendations on reinforcement of content.

In addition, tools such as Canvas and Moodle have incorporated AI analytics modules that notify instructors about students who might need prompt feedback or intervention, hence enhancing learning outcomes through the provision of timely support (Ifenthaler & Yau, 2020).

4.4 Student and Teacher Views of AI Feedback

a. Effectiveness and Acceptance of AI-Generated Feedback

Although the capability of AI-powered feedback is clear, it also relies on user acceptance. Studies have indicated that numerous students find the immediacy and objectivity of AI-based feedback appealing. They find them more at ease with receiving criticism from an AI system, particularly on personal or sensitive subjects (Hansson & Berg, 2022).

Students also exhibit greater confidence and independence when using tools such as Grammarly or Turnitin's Revision Assistant since these programs provide multiple revisions without fear of being judged. The process of iteratively revising encourages a growth mindset and engagement with the subject matter. But other students complain about the depth and subtlety of AI feedback. For instance, whereas grammar suggestions are welcome, argument structure or creativity commentary can come across as shallow or formulaic. What this implies is that hybrid models—in which AI does routine feedback and teachers do higher-order assessment can yield optimal results.

b. Educator Perspectives

From the instructor's perspective, AI feedback instruments are typically perceived as time-saving and helpful, especially in mass classes or in online settings. Instructors find that these instruments can spot recurrent mistakes throughout submissions, allowing them to adjust class discussions or craft focused interventions.

However, teachers warn against dependency on automated feedback. Issues with over-reliance include:

1. Possibility of inaccuracies, particularly for complex assignments.
2. Limited AI ability to detect context or affect.
3. Dependence of students on tools instead of building self-assessment capabilities.

Additionally, teachers stress the need for transparency in AI tools. Teachers need to know how feedback is produced so that they can explain or challenge it when needed. Professional development and training are therefore crucial for teachers to implement AI successfully and ethically in their pedagogy (Luckin et al., 2016).

AI-driven feedback loops are transforming how feedback is created, received, and understood in schools. AI systems offer timely, customised, and data-informed feedback that enhances student learning and teaching efficiency. From automated written feedback to sophisticated plagiarism checks, AI software simplifies the process of feedback and encourages greater interaction with learning content. But AI is never able to completely replace human instructors' empathy, contextual knowledge, and mentoring. The best route forward is a hybrid one that mingles the efficiency of AI with the personal touch of teachers. Future studies need to examine how AI feedback systems can be developed to evaluate more sophisticated learning outcomes, like creativity, teamwork, and moral reasoning. It must also study how to establish student trust in machine-generated feedback and develop educators' skills in effectively utilising these devices.

5. CASE STUDIES AND REAL-WORLD IMPLEMENTATIONS

5.1 AI-Based Learning Platforms and Tools

As artificial intelligence keeps reshaping education, several platforms and tools have run the way in incorporating AI-based assessment and feedback. Such platforms cover a range from

Massive Open Online Courses (MOOCs), language learning, academic integrity management, to Learning Management Systems (LMS).

a. Coursera and Edx

Two of the best MOOC platforms that use AI for learning and marking at scale are Coursera and edX. They track progress, provide perceptive comments, and customise flyers for pupils using machine learning-based algorithms. Both have hurled AI-driven grading systems, most notably in coding and quantitative courses, that allow for immediate feedback, peer assistance in grading, and even predictive analytics to help detect students at risk of falling out (Reich & Ruipérez-Valiente, 2019).

Edx, for instance, employs the Open edx platform with AI functionality like automatic scoring of essays and suggesting of challenging STEM questions. These facilities allow teachers to handle large groups effectively while still engaging students through personalised interventions.

b. Duolingo

Duolingo is one of the leading AI-based language-learning platforms. Duolingo leverages artificial intelligence, specifically natural language processing (NLP) and deep learning, to modify lessons in real time according to each learner's level of expertise. Duolingo offers immediate feedback on syntax, grammar, and pronunciation using adaptive learning routes. Furthermore, Duolingo applies spaced repetition algorithms to better recall information and reinforcement learning models to increase learner motivation by adjusting the challenge level of exercises based on the performance of users (Settles & Meeder, 2016). The success of the platform shows how gamification of learning can be achieved through AI with strict pedagogical values.

c. Turnitin and AI-Driven LMS

Turnitin, which was originally used for plagiarism detection, has incorporated AI abilities with its automated feedback and assessment software. Its "Revision Assistant" gives formative feedback on the writing of students, giving them advice on organisation, clarity, and argument. It does this through NLP algorithms that read writing holistically as opposed to keyword matching. AI is also becoming combined more and more into Learning Management Systems (LMS) like Canvas, Blackboard, and Moodle. These LMS systems leverage AI for automated grading (particularly for quizzes and multiple-choice tests), monitoring student engagement, and providing personalised learning routes through recommender systems.

5.2 Application in Higher Education

Universities around the world have started integrating AI into the very fabric of instruction, learning, and evaluation. These applications disclose both the capabilities and constraints of AI in post-secondary education.

a. University of Michigan – ECoach and M-Write

The University of Michigan developed ECoach, an AI that sends students personalised cues about their performance in their courses. It finds students who require academic support or comfort by using behaviour modelling and predictive analytics. M-Write, another AI-based application, utilises automatic writing tests to give peer review and iterative aspect improvement (Malmi et al., 2020).

b. Stanford University – Code in Place

Stanford's "Code in Place" program for the COVID-19 pandemic utilised AI tools to grade thousands of coding assignments. As a result, teachers were free to concentrate on mentoring and teaching, and timely grading and comments were provided.

c. Indian Institutes of Technology (IITs)

With AI-powered platforms like SWAYAM and NPTEL for the transport of public education, IITs have set the standard in India. They include auto-graded quizzes and feedback through AI on conversation forums, aiding the democratisation of education at scale in a resource-constrained environment.

5.3 Implementation in K-12 Education

AI disposition in primary and secondary education revolves mainly around formative assessment, personalised learning, and adaptive education.

DreamBox Learning and Carnegie Learning

DreamBox Learning is an artificial intelligence-driven K-8 math platform that dynamically adapts problems in real time according to students' responses and interaction patterns. Not only does it give prompt feedback, but it also recommends teaching content based on each learner's cognitive ability. Research indicates that DreamBox utilisation results in substantial math achievement gains, particularly for underserved students (Yilmaz, 2017).

Carnegie Learning, on the other hand, combines AI and cognitive science to provide intelligent teaching systems. It's the MATHia platform that examines students' problem-solving behaviours to produce step-by-step scaffolds and error correction. Both platforms illustrate how classroom instruction can be supplemented by AI and gaps in learning filled.

The platform is modified to various proficiency levels and languages, providing feedback to teachers as well as students. Teachers might then tailor teaching for slow learners, utilising the data insights produced. This example highlights the possibility of AI for remedying learning gaps in multilingual or rural classrooms, albeit with issues about device access and teacher training.

5.4 Artificial Intelligence in Corporate and Professional Training

Artificial intelligence-powered testing and feedback platforms are increasingly at the core of staff development, particularly with industries embracing upskilling and lifelong learning.

a. LinkedIn Learning and Skillsoft

LinkedIn Learning and Skillsoft platforms use AI to create personalised learning pathways for professionals based on knowledge gaps, job functions, and career goals. Using quizzes and behaviour-driven analytics, AI determines what is currently known, which then guides feedback and course recommendations accordingly.

The platforms use reinforcement learning models to continually refine gratified presentation, optimising significance and holding. AI regularly grades course assessments automatically, producing reports that include recommendations for career alignment and descriptions of skill mastery.

b. Siemens and IBM – Corporate Training AI

Siemens provides scenario-based evaluations for engineering and safety compliance training using artificial intelligence. Learners interact with simulations, and AI systems provide feedback on decision-making, technical knowledge, and time management.

IBM Watson Talent solution offers AI-powered tests for onboarding, leadership skills, and project management abilities. Case study tests using natural language processing capabilities and chatbots for immediate direction and response are among the assessments.

c. Vocational Training and Skill India

In India, the Skill India program has integrated AI into vocational training through simulation-based skill evaluation. For instance, AI models evaluate welders and electricians by tracking motion, analysing video, and detecting errors in real-time. Instructors are aided by feedback reports to correct incorrect techniques, even in offline environments with edge computing.

Nonetheless, there are issues of equity, data privacy, infrastructure, and pedagogical integration. Effective implementations prioritise blended approaches that leverage AI functionality in complementarity with human judgment, focusing on ethical deployment and contextualization. Moving towards a more digital learning environment, these case studies offer important lessons to policymakers, educators, and technologists looking to leverage AI for effective and inclusive education.

6. FUTURE OPPORTUNITIES AND CHALLENGES

With artificial intelligence (AI) transforming teaching practices all over the world, the salient consideration is not only the current status of AI-driven assessment and feedback but also where it is headed shortly. Innovations hold promise to render education more efficient, inclusive, and customised, yet various practical, pedagogical, and policy-related challenges need to be resolved to unlock the full potential of AI.

6.1 Trends in AI and Education

a. AI-Based Adaptive Learning

The most hopeful trend in AI for education is the emergence of adaptive learning solutions. Adaptive learning systems modify instructional material and tests in real time according to a student's performance, interest level, and individualised learning style. Squirrel AI (China), Century Tech (UK), and Knewton (US) are examples of such adaptive platforms. They leverage real-time data analytics and machine learning patterns to deliver personalised learning pathways, foster mastery-based advancement, and combat cognitive burden (Luckin et al., 2016).

In India, new ed-tech startups and digital education endeavours are testing AI-driven ed-tech adapted to accommodate different verbal and regional settings. For instance, the platforms of Embibe and Byju increasingly rely on AI to deliver personalised assessments, performance diagnostics, and distinctive content often in local languages.

b. AI-Human Collaborative Assessment

Another transformative development is the evolution toward hybrid models of assessment, combining AI's speed and data-handling capabilities with human educators' judgment and empathy. Such collaboration can mitigate the weaknesses of both parties: AI's lack of contextual understanding and humans' limited bandwidth.

For instance, AI can carry out the first tier of grading, particularly in objective or pattern-identifiable work, and highlight doubtful or subtle submissions for human consideration. This pattern is already being tested in cutting-edge MOOCs and universities worldwide. Under formative feedback, AI can produce a preliminary commentary on students' work, which teachers can see and customise, thus speeding up the process and making it more scalable.

6.2 Challenges in AI Adoption

a. Resistance to Change

Despite technological progress, numerous educational institutions and stakeholders resist the integration of AI, sometimes because they are not familiar with it or lack confidence in its efficacy. Teachers might view AI as a challenge to professional authority or worry about losing their jobs. Students can also question the validity of machine-generated feedback or assessments.

This resistance is frequently based on cultural, institutional, or generational mindset. To overcome it, it is not enough to prove the advantages of AI systems; it is necessary to guarantee transparent and participatory processes of implementation that engage teachers, administrators, students, and parents.

b. Need for Teacher Training

For AI to be successfully applied in classrooms, extensive and continuous teacher education is essential. Teachers need to know how the AI system works, how to read AI-generated insights, and how to apply them in their instructional strategies. Yet most professional development initiatives across India and other developing nations are still nonchalant, with no course modules dedicated to educational technology or AI.

Training should go beyond operations to cover digital ethics, data analysis, and hybrid instruction paradigms. Joint workshops, peer mentoring, and technology adoption incentives can expedite professionalisation. Lacking proper support, AI may be underutilised or misused.

6.3 AI-Powered Education Policy and Regulation

a. Ethical Principles for AI in Education

The application of AI in education has ethical implications for data privacy, algorithmic bias, student autonomy, and surveillance. For example, AI systems learned from biased data could unintentionally perpetuate educational disparities or stereotype students by gender, language, or socio-economic status.

Several international organisations, such as UNESCO and the OECD, have also put forward ethical guidelines for AI in education, which include transparency, explainability, fairness, accountability, and comprehensiveness. According to Van Der Vlies (2020), AI systems should inform users about decision-making processes (such as scoring and feedback cohort) and how to appeal to automated judgments. In India, new education skill startups and online education initiatives are experimenting with AI-based ed-tech custom-made to fit various linguistic and local environments. The platforms of Embibe and Byju are using AI more and more to provide personalised assessments, performance diagnostics, and differentiated content—often in dialect languages.

b. Policy Recommendations in India

India's National Education Policy (NEP) 2020 emphasises the use of technology to revolutionise learning experiences, and it recommends the creation of the National Educational Technology Forum (NETF). To further enable AI adoption in education, the following policy actions are suggested:

1. Formulation of a national AI-in-education strategy with well-defined objectives, timelines, and governance frameworks.
2. Mandatory data privacy norms for all ed-tech platforms gathering student data.
3. Government support for AI research aimed at local and inclusive education uses.
4. Integration of AI ethics and digital pedagogy into teacher education courses.
5. Collaborative partnerships among government, academia, and start-ups to test AI innovations in actual classrooms.

6.4 The Future of AI in Assessment and Feedback

Potential Innovations and Long-Term Impact

The destiny of AI-based assessment and feedback is to move beyond automation to smarter co-learning environments. A few of the leading innovations on the horizon are:

1. Emotion-Aware Assessment: With the application of affective computing, next-generation AI systems can detect students' emotional status (e.g., frustration, boredom) while learning or assessing and react with motivational cues or emotional support.
2. Multimodal Evaluation: With video, audio, text, and sensor inputs, AI is capable of comprehensively measuring communication skills, creativity, teamwork, and even physical demonstration abilities, long hard to measure.
3. Lifelong Learning Profiles: AI would develop cumulative portfolios for individuals, monitoring learning on different platforms, across ages, and in different areas of expertise, making customised learning pathways possible throughout life.
4. Explainable AI (XAI): With the increasing fear of black-box algorithms, future AI evaluation tools will emphasise transparency and interpretability, making it possible for students and teachers to comprehend why a particular score or criticism was produced.

Long-term implications of AI can lead to a more student-centred environment, where continuous assessment is the norm, instant feedback is actionable and valuable, and learning outcomes closely mirror practical skills. With equitable and ethical implementation, AI has the potential to make quality education accessible to all, empower teachers with actionable information, and allow students to take greater control of their learning pathways.

AI has the potential to redefine the boundaries of assessment and feedback in education. Although promising trends like adaptive learning, AI-human collaboration, and personalised feedback are pointers to the future, issues involving resistance, teacher preparedness, and ethical governance remain. For nations like India, developing inclusive policies, investing in capacity-building for teachers, and creating context-relevant AI systems will be crucial. The path forward requires cooperation between technologists, educators, policymakers, and learners. Partly through participatory, ethical, and inclusive deployment, can the educational revolutionising power of AI be realised?

7. CONCLUSION AND RECOMMENDATIONS

The accelerated development of artificial intelligence (AI) has brought about an uprising in education, especially in the domains of assessment and feedback. This paper has explored how AI technologies are transforming pedagogical approaches, enhancing the effectiveness of evaluation processes, tailoring feedback, and assisting both students and teachers in various educational settings.

7.1 Summary

The use of AI in learning systems has created new opportunities to increase learning outcomes, making it possible to provide scalable, timely, and personalised assessment and feedback. Some of the key findings of this study are:

1. AI-Driven Assessment Tools: AI-powered real-time formative assessment, adaptive testing, and quizzes give learners instant feedback on their performance. These tools facilitate

incessant assessment as a supplement to summative-only approaches, allowing for more insightful comments on the part of teachers on the progress of students.

2. Feedback Systems: Computerised feedback devices such as grammar checkers, content evaluators, and plagiarism searchers enhance the timeliness, consistency, and availability of instructional feedback. These technologies can adjust response to meet the needs of individual learners thanks to personalisation and learning analytics.
3. Improved Learning Outcomes: In addition to teachers avoiding laborious, time-consuming grading and gaining greater data-informed insights, students receive more timely, distinguished, and accurate feedback.
4. Ethical and Implementation Challenges: AI systems have many disadvantages despite their advantages, such as algorithmic bias, opacity, data privacy, and user resistance. Poor teacher training and underdeveloped controlling frameworks also hinder smooth AI adoption.

7.2 Implications for Educators and Institutions

The mass adoption of AI in education has far-reaching implications for educational practices and institutional operations.

For educators:

1. Redefining Teaching Roles: Teachers will not be replaced by AI, but they will be altered from content providers to individualised learning organisers. Teachers will need to learn how to read AI productions and incorporate them suitably into teaching strategies.
2. Focus on Digital Literacy: Teachers require digital literacy and a strong grasp of how AI tools work, their limitations, and ethical implications. AI integration in the classroom must be covered in professional development courses.
3. Collaborative Valuation Practices: AI provides teachers with the option to co-assess with algorithms, especially in formative assessments. Instructors can start with AI-generated feedback and add expressive shade or contextual richness.

For institutions:

a. Strategic Integration: AI tools must be deliberately evaluated and practical by educational institutions, training facilities, and colleges to support their learning objects. Unmindful adoption will lead to disorganisation or exacerbate current differences.
b. Data Management: Organisations should invest in moral and secure data practices to safeguard learner data, monitor AI tool performance, and meet national rules.
c. Inclusivity and Accessibility: AI models need to be cross-checked for cultural and language inclusivity, particularly for multilingual and varied countries like India, in order not to leave anyone behind.

7.3 Effective AI Implementation Recommendations

To guarantee that AI-driven assessment and feedback systems improve, not degrade, educational quality, the following recommendations are made:

1. Offer Extensive Teacher Training

Professional development initiatives should prepare teachers with the skills and knowledge to utilise AI responsibly and effectively. This involves training in data interpretation, ethical issues, and pedagogical integration.

2. Foster Human-AI Collaboration

Assessment systems can be modelled to have a hybrid approach where AI takes up repetitive, objective, or bulk evaluation tasks and human teachers provide contextual judgment, particularly in subjective or sensitive topics.

3. Provide Transparency and Fairness

AI systems should be transparent with straightforward criteria for the generation of assessments and feedback. Developers and institutions need to run periodic audits for bias, ensuring that they are fair across gender, socioeconomic, and linguistic divides.

4. Promote Inclusive and Equitable Access

AI tools must be made available to students with disabilities, in local languages, and to meet a diversity of learning styles and levels of technological access. Public-private partnerships can subsidise and mass-produce such tools in disadvantaged regions.

5. Enhance Data Privacy Laws

Policymakers must enact robust data protection systems to protect personal and educational data gathered by AI systems. Consent-based use and user control of data must become the norm.

6. Foster Ongoing Feedback and User Engagement

AI tools need to be integrated with student and teacher feedback to enhance utility and usability. Participatory design strategies can help ensure tools are relevant to actual educational requirements.

7.4 Directions for Future Research

Although this research gives a good overview of the state-of-the-art AI research in assessment and feedback, additional research will be needed to cover gaps and foretell future developments:

1. Longitudinal Studies: Further empirical research is necessary to determine the long-term effect of AI-based evaluation on student learning outcomes, motivation, and educational equity.

2. Cultural and Regional Adaptability: Studies should investigate how AI tools can be localised for different cultural, linguistic, and educational contexts, particularly in countries with extreme demographic diversity like India.
3. Emotional and Social Learning Assessment: Explore the ability of AI systems to evaluate and facilitate emotional intelligence, collaboration, and communication skills essential 21st-century skills frequently neglected in existing models.
4. Ethical AI Development: Future research should centre on algorithmic transparency, equity, and social effects of AI use in education, such as student autonomy and surveillance.
5. Influence on Teacher Identity and Workload: Investigate how AI impacts teachers' professional identity, emotional well-being, and workload, particularly as tasks change from being an assessor to a learning facilitator and data interpreter.

AI-enabled assessment and feedback mechanisms are a revolutionary change in education practice, with unimaginable possibilities of personalisation, scalability, and efficiency. However, to realise these advantages responsibly, deployment has to be preceded by strong ethical principles, good pedagogy, and equitable policies. Teachers and schools need to collaborate with technologists and policymakers to design an education future in which AI is a tool for empowerment, not division. With careful integration, continuous research, and forward-looking policymaking, AI can be a pillar in constructing a more responsive, learner-focused, and equitable education system for the digital age.

REFERENCES

Adetayo, A. J. (2023). Artificial intelligence chatbots in academic libraries: The rise of ChatGPT. *Library Hi Tech News*, *40*(3), 18–21. DOI: 10.1108/LHTN-01-2023-0007

Aldowah, H., Al-Samarraie, H., & Fauzy, W. M. (2019). Educational data mining and learning analytics for 21st century higher education: A review and synthesis. *Telematics and Informatics*, *37*, 13–49. DOI: 10.1016/j.tele.2019.01.007

Binns, R., Van Kleek, M., Veale, M., Lyngs, U., Zhao, J., & Shadbolt, N. (2018). 'It's Reducing a Human Being to a Percentage' Perceptions of Justice in Algorithmic Decisions. In *Proceedings of the 2018 Chi conference on human factors in computing systems* (pp. 1-14). DOI: 10.31235/osf.io/9wqxr

Black, P., & Wiliam, D. (1998). Assessment and classroom learning. *Assessment in Education: Principles, Policy & Practice*, *5*(1), 7–74. DOI: 10.1080/0969595980050102

Bloom, B. S., & Krathwohl, D. R. (1956). *Taxonomy of Educational Objectives longmans*. Green & Co.

Brookhart, S. M. (2008). *How to Give Effective Feedback to Your Students*. Association for Supervision and Curriculum Development.

Chen, L., Chen, P., & Lin, Z. (2020). Artificial Intelligence in Education: A Review. *IEEE Access : Practical Innovations, Open Solutions*, *8*, 75264–75278. DOI: 10.1109/ACCESS.2020.2988510

Davis, F. D. (1989). Perceived usefulness, perceived ease of use, and user acceptance of information technology. *Management Information Systems Quarterly*, *13*(3), 319–340. DOI: 10.2307/249008

Del Pilar Gonzalez, N. A., & Chiappe, A. (2024). Learning analytics and personalization of learning: a review. *Ensaio Avaliação E Políticas Públicas Em Educação, 32*(122). https://doi.org/DOI: 10.1590/s0104-40362024003204234

Ganiyu, T. O. (2025). *Academic integrity in the AI era: Battling cheating with innovation*. AI and Ethics, Academic Integrity and the Future of Quality Assurance in Higher Education.

Goel, A. K., & Polepeddi, L. (2018). Jill Watson: A virtual teaching assistant for online education. In *Learning engineering for online education* (pp. 120-143). Routledge.

Gross, S., Mokbel, B., Hammer, B., & Pinkwart, N. (2015). Learning Feedback in Intelligent Tutoring Systems: Report of the FIT Project, Conducted from December 2011 to March 2015. *Kunstliche Intelligenz*, *29*(4), 413–418. DOI: 10.1007/s13218-015-0367-y

Han, S. (2015). Book review: The Handbook of Automated Essay Evaluation: Current Applications and New Directions. *Language Testing*, *32*(4), 543–545. DOI: 10.1177/0265532215576839

Hansson, T., & Berg, M. (2022). *Making better programmers: The impact of automated feedback on students*. DIVA. https://www.diva-portal.org/smash/record.jsf?pid=diva2%3A1703320&dswid=-2092

Hattie, J., & Timperley, H. (2007). The power of feedback. *Review of Educational Research*, *77*(1), 81–112. DOI: 10.3102/003465430298487

Heffernan, N. T., & Heffernan, C. L. (2014). The ASSISTments Ecosystem: Building a Platform that Brings Scientists and Teachers Together for Minimally Invasive Research on Human Learning and Teaching. *International Journal of Artificial Intelligence in Education*, *24*(4), 470–497. DOI: 10.1007/s40593-014-0024-x

Holmes, W., Bialik, M., & Fadel, C. (2019). *Artificial intelligence in education promises and implications for teaching and learning*. Center for Curriculum Redesign.

Ifenthaler, D., & Yau, J. Y. (2020). Utilising learning analytics to support study success in higher education: A systematic review. *Educational Technology Research and Development*, *68*(4), 1961–1990. DOI: 10.1007/s11423-020-09788-z

Jordan, M. I., & Mitchell, T. M. (2015). Machine learning: Trends, perspectives, and prospects. *Science*, *349*(6245), 255–260. DOI: 10.1126/science.aaa8415

Koedinger, K. R., D'Mello, S., McLaughlin, E. A., Pardos, Z. A., & Rosé, C. P. (2015). Data mining and education. *Wiley Interdisciplinary Reviews: Cognitive Science*, *6*(4), 333–353. DOI: 10.1002/wcs.1350

Luckin, R., Holmes, W., Griffiths, M., & Forcier, L. B. (2016). Intelligence Unleashed: An Argument for AI in Education. Pearson. https://static.googleusercontent.com/media/edu.google.com/en//pdfs/Intelligence-Unleashed-Publication.pdf

Malmi, L., Sheard, J., Kinnunen, P., Simon, , & Sinclair, J. (2020). Computing education theories: What are they and how are they used? *ACM Inroads*, *11*(1), 54–64. DOI: 10.1145/3381889

Morley, J., Floridi, L., Kinsey, L., & Elhalal, A. (2019). *From What to How: An Initial Review of Publicly Available AI Ethics Tools, Methods and Research to Translate Principles into Practices*. arXiv.org. https://arxiv.org/abs/1905.06876

National Education policy (2020). Government of India, Ministry of Education. https://www.education.gov.in/nep/about-nep

Nicol, D., & Macfarlane-Dick, D. (2006). Formative Assessment and Self-Regulated Learning: A Model and Seven Principles of Good Feedback Practice. *Studies in Higher Education*, *31*(2), 199–218. DOI: 10.1080/03075070600572090

Pane, J. F., Griffin, B. A., McCaffrey, D. F., & Karam, R. (2013). Effectiveness of Cognitive Tutor Algebra I at scale. *Educational Evaluation and Policy Analysis*, *36*(2), 127–144. DOI: 10.3102/0162373713507480

Pane, J. F., Steiner, E. D., Baird, M. D., Hamilton, L. S., & Pane, J. D. (2017). *Informing Progress: Insights on personalized learning implementation and effects*. RAND. https://www.rand.org/pubs/research_reports/RR2042.html

Reich, J., & Ruipérez-Valiente, J. A. (2019). The MOOC pivot. *Science*, *363*(6423), 130–131. DOI: 10.1126/science.aav7958

Roscoe, R. D. (2014). *Developing pedagogically-guided algorithms for intelligent writing feedback | International Journal of Learning Technology*. International Journal of Learning Technology. https://www.inderscienceonline.com/doi/abs/10.1504/IJLT.2013.059131

Russell, S. J., & Norvig, P. (2016). *Artificial intelligence: a modern approach*. pearson.

Sadler, D. R. (2008). Indeterminacy in the use of preset criteria for assessment and grading. *Assessment & Evaluation in Higher Education, 34*(2), 159–179. DOI: 10.1080/02602930801956059

Selwyn, N. (2019). *Should robots replace teachers? AI and the future of education*. John Wiley & Sons.

Settles, B., & Meeder, B. (2016). *A trainable spaced repetition model for language learning*. https://www.semanticscholar.org/paper/A-Trainable-Spaced-Repetition-Model-for-Language-Settles-Meeder/cb836d2b8e126dc31ded5e674d73021604dcc6e0

Shute, V. J. (2008). Focus on formative feedback. *Review of Educational Research, 78*(1), 153–189. DOI: 10.3102/0034654307313795

Singleton, C. (2001). Computer-based assessment in education. *Educational and Child Psychology, 18*(3), 58–74. DOI: 10.53841/bpsecp.2001.18.3.58

Slade, S., & Prinsloo, P. (2013). Learning Analytics. *The American Behavioral Scientist, 57*(10), 1510–1529. DOI: 10.1177/0002764213479366

UNSW. (2020). Ethical and responsible use of Artificial Intelligence in UNSW. https://www.student.unsw.edu.au/notices/2024/05/ethical-and-responsible-use-artificial-intelligence-unsw

Van Der Vlies, R. (2020). Digital strategies in education across OECD countries. *OECD Education Working Papers*. https://doi.org/DOI: 10.1787/19939019

Vygotsky, L. S. (1978). *Mind in society. The development of higher psychological processes*. Harvard University., https://www.scirp.org/reference/referencespapers?referenceid=803661

Weiss, D. J. (1982). Improving Measurement Quality and Efficiency with Adaptive Testing. *Applied Psychological Measurement, 6*(4), 473–492. DOI: 10.1177/014662168200600408

West, S. M., Whittaker, M., & Crawford, K. (2019) Discriminating Systems Gender, Race and Power in AI. AI Now Institute. - References - *Scientific Research Publishing*. https://www.scirp.org/reference/referencespapers?referenceid=3758256

Williamson, B., & Eynon, R. (2020). Historical threads, missing links, and future directions in AI in education. *Learning, Media and Technology, 45*(3), 223–235. DOI: 10.1080/17439884.2020.1798995

Woolf, B. P. (2010). *Building intelligent interactive tutors: Student-centered strategies for revolutionizing e-learning*. Morgan Kaufmann.

Yilmaz, B. (2017). *Effects of adaptive learning technologies on math achievement: A quantitative study of ALEKS math software*. University of Missouri-Kansas City.

Zawacki-Richter, O., Marín, V. I., Bond, M., & Gouverneur, F. (2019). Systematic review of research on artificial intelligence applications in higher education – where are the educators? *International Journal of Educational Technology in Higher Education, 16*(1), 39. Advance online publication. DOI: 10.1186/s41239-019-0171-0

Chapter 13
The Teacher's Journey to AI:
The EFL AI-PACK Framework

Osama Koraishi
https://orcid.org/0009-0008-1670-3436
Bursa Uludag University, Turkey

Merve Erol
Ankara Science University, Turkey

ABSTRACT

This paper presents a practical guide designed to equip English as a Foreign Language (EFL) teachers with the skills and knowledge for AI literacy, framed within the AI-PACK framework. It begins by exploring key AI concepts and then tracing the evolution of AI in educational contexts. The paper emphasizes practical strategies for integrating AI tools like ChatGPT into EFL teaching, guided by the AI-PACK model's components - AI-K, AI-PK, AI-CK, and AI-PCK. It tackles the challenges educators face in this digital transition, offering AI-PACK aligned solutions and highlighting ethical considerations in AI usage offering a potential framework for EFL professionals. Concluding with a vision for the future, the paper highlights the importance of ongoing professional development in AI for educators, positioning this guide as a vital tool for navigating the dynamic interface of AI in language education.

INTRODUCTION

Artificial intelligence, (AI), has become a revolutionary force in the fast-paced world of the twenty-first century, influencing every part of our lives. Our interactions with industries and technology have changed as a result of the quick development, adoption, and integration of AI, which has given us a new era of creativity and efficiency. This fundamental upheaval is spreading throughout many different industries, including education (Walter, 2024). Although AI in education may appear novel in many respects, it is revolutionizing and changing the antiquated usage of educational technologies that have not kept up with "real-life" technology. AI is not a temporary fad; it is a transformative force that will be increasingly woven into our lives. In their

DOI: 10.4018/979-8-3373-2752-5.ch013

study, Chen et al. (2020) emphasized several of the advantages AI offers for education, including enhanced adoption and retention of AI for Education, administrative tasks, teaching quality, and customized curricula.

AI has the ability to provide individualized, one-of-a-kind experiences that can fulfill a range of educational demands and go beyond traditional teaching and learning methods. However, this rapid integration of AI into educational settings brings to light a critical gap in the current educational discourse: the AI literacy of teachers. Because AI is inherently technology-driven, the majority of those in the field, including educators, are unaware of how AI works and are unable to fully utilize this technology in the classroom (Hur, 2024). According to a Clever article, 89% of school districts reported not having professional development programs focused on AI to provide their educators with (Browner, 2023) which leaves a huge gap of knowledge for teachers to shoulder on their own. Thus, to navigate the AI-driven world of the 21st century, AI literacy is an essential skill that individuals must develop (Ng et al., 2021). Research indicates that someone with higher AI literacy is less likely to be fearful of AI applications (Cengiz & Peker, 2025; Schiavo et al., 2024; Reyes et al., 2024), which is important to consider when thinking about AI as a factor for evaluating teachers' and students' propensity to engage in AI learning or use. Additionally, several international bodies have highlighted the importance of AI ethics, perhaps due to AI's intricate and evolving nature, which has raised concerns about potential outcomes (UNESCO, 2021; European Commission, 2019; OECD, 2024). A lack of trust in AI processes may prevent practitioners from committing to AI education or using AI in their practice.

Teachers' proficiency with technology has long been emphasized, and professional learning has been informed by frameworks like Digital Pedagogy Content Knowledge (DPACK) (Huwer et al., 2023) and Technological Pedagogical Content Knowledge (TPACK) (Koehler et al., 2013). These models have been instrumental in equipping educators with the skills necessary to navigate the digital landscape of modern classrooms. However, as we go deeper into the AI-driven educational era, a clear scarcity becomes evident – the lack of comprehensive materials and development programs specifically tailored to enhance teachers' AI literacy and in turn the lack of AI literacy among educators (Sperling et al., 2024; Su & Ng, 2023). To address the unique nature and development of AI, UNESCO (2024) published a framework in literacy and competencies in AI, differentiating it from broader digital technologies and providing guidelines for understanding and skills in the AI domain. However, these new frameworks remain generalized across disciplines and directly address the pedagogical demands of specific fields like ELT/EFL education. As a result, scholars have begun developing more specialized frameworks withing existing models such as AI-PACK within D-PACK (Lorenz & Romeike, 2023), though these are still in early stages and require further adaptation to meet the distinct needs of EFL teachers.

The authors seek to address this crucial gap and aim to explore and outline the essential components of a program designed to enhance the AI literacy of English as a Foreign Language (EFL) teachers adapting the framework of AI-PACK. Not only does this research address a perceived need, but it also presents a proactive chance to equip educators to use AI to help their students become effective, knowledgeable, and active agents rather than merely passive users. Teachers could use this as a guide to help them navigate the complex world of AI in education (AIEd). In light of these considerations, the main central research question is:

What are the key components and materials needed to develop a Professional Development program on AI Literacy for EFL teachers within the AI-PACK framework?

LITERATURE REVIEW

As AI continues to permeate educational spaces, it is now essential to consider how this context downstream, including its integration, application and the extent to which it reshapes teaching practices. Therefore, this review will visualize the historical evolution of AI within education, onward to where educators find their AI literacy, particularly the EFL context.

AI in Education Throughout the Years

Innovations and modern technologies have had a significant impact on education by facilitating more effective communication (Jonassen et al., 2008). Since the late 19th century, educational tools such as projectors, tape recorders, and computers have transformed the educational landscape. Because English is a global language, ELT has been especially influenced. The first major technological breakthrough came with language labs in the 1960s, leading to the Audio-Lingual Method (ALM), which emphasized repetition through recorded drills but was later criticized for neglecting comprehension (Chomsky, 1959; Krahnke & Krashen, 1983). This shows how technology can be of such an impact as to produce a completely new teaching methodology regardless of its critique. To enhance flexibility, critical thinking, and access to authentic language, later technological innovations resulted in new fields that are at the intersection of technology and language learning, particularly CALL and MALL (Warschauer & Healey, 1998; Miangah & Nezarat, 2012).

With Generative AI becoming so popular, ELT is shifting to a new paradigm ushering a new era. Tools based on Natural Language Processing (NLP) and Machine Learning now offer writing support, conversational practice, and personalized feedback (Bozkurt, 2023; Francisco & Silva, 2022). Learners engage in dynamic, flexible experiences through platforms like ChatGPT, which bridge classroom instruction with self-directed learning. Rather than simply continuing trends like CALL and MALL, AI is fundamentally reshaping how language is taught and learned (Edmett et al., 2024; Jackson & Papa, 2024; Chen et al., 2020).

Looking back, we see how quickly artificial intelligence (AI) has revolutionized education. AI has shifted from simple programmed instructions to adaptive learning experiences that customize learning styles and needs. More than ever, AI has radically altered education since first shaping its applications to develop intelligent tutoring systems (ITSs). ITSs attempted to replicate one-on-one tutoring experiences (e.g., SCHOLAR, GUIDON) for specific domains or topics i.e., geography and medical diagnosis (Nwana, 1990). As technology advanced, a wide range of AI applications emerged (e.g., in language learning) and significantly influenced the design and delivery of educational experiences. For ESP, for example, an AI-Enabled English Language Learning (AIELL) system offers authenticity and perpetual L2 learner learning while indicating the potential for improvement being less impactful on language acquisition (Jia et al., 2022).

A prominent application of AI in language learning is Grammarly (Alam et al., 2023), along with similar emerging platforms that function as AI-powered writing assistants. These tools provide comprehensive assistance, covering everything from simple punctuation and spelling to sophisticated style recommendations and tone enhancement. For feedback and immediate assistance for language learners, Grammarly and related products are now crucial for both students and teachers (Selim, 2024). One such tool is Hemingway Editor, which focuses on clarity and readability by highlighting overly complex sentences, passive constructions, and other barriers to effective writing (Ashrafganjoe, 2025). These technologies are now embedded into daily practice for many, if not all, English non-native speakers, serving as reliable companions that create agency and autonomy in language learning. As a result, we can see that the shift in English language education and AI has mirrored a much broader trends of personalization, interaction and adaptability in learning technologies. These tools provide the means for language acquisition as well as a means for learners to self-direct their learning and provide immediate feedback/content that aligns with their needs and preferences (Saniyah, 2023; Younas et al., 2025).

The necessity for AI literacy is increasingly entrenched by a variety of interventions such as the recently released Artificial Intelligence Literacy Act (H.R.6791-118th Congress, 2023) and the UN's call for universal AI literacy frameworks in education (UNESCO, 2023). These initiatives underscore the growing recognition of AI literacy as an essential skill for the 21st century, not just for students but also for educators.

AI and Large Language Models

Since OpenAI's ChatGPT, which was a major awakening for the world, AI-based chatbots have drastically increased the accessibility and scope of language learning and instruction. Additionally, the use of chatbots in educational settings has opened novel possibilities for language education for both educators and students (Saini, 2023). Accessibility is a huge benefit of using AI chatbots for language learning. Chatbots like AsasaraBot assist teachers and students by providing round-the-clock assistance and access to language learning materials. For example, AsasaraBot offers English language instruction or opportunity for learning with interactive engagement, allowing learners to learn in their own time from any place or time zone (Mageira et al., 2022).

Other chatbots such as Khan Academy's Khamingo (2023) are designed to guide learners through their studies using a more inquiry-driven approach, supporting not only language learning but a wide range of subjects; it is one of the first bots that were called “Socratic chatbots” i.e. chatbots that teach in a way that does not readily provide the answer but encourages the learner to enquire and work together with it in order to find the answer. This kind of accessibility is beneficial to learners who may not have regular access to a traditional classroom or language tutor. Other chatbots, such as ChatGPT, also provide a variety of ways in which educators can utilize such as a potential assessment, content generation and lesson planning (Korucu-Kış, 2024; Diep & Dang, 2025; Octavio et al., 2024). Similarly, Setyaningsih et al. (2024) reported that Indonesian EFL teachers utilizing MagicSchool AI reported increases in efficiency, differentiation, and innovative lesson plans, even though outputs still needed improvement and strict instructor supervision.

On the other hand, students can use chatbots for self-directed learning opportunities, especially using the chatbots to practice language independently and with self-direction, pacing and in their own individual learning style (Xiao & Zhi, 2023; Li et al., 2024; Pan et al., 2025). Other AI tools have been used for educational purposes for a long time. Tools such as the E-rater engine (Xi et al., 2008) which is in the backbone of the assessment process of the TOEFL test or even the adaptive nature of Duolingo’s instruction (Bicknell et al., 2023). Both cases had AI behind the curtains, but most would argue that the ubiquity of these Chatbots have put AI as an incredible educational asset because of its ease of access, practicality and versatility.

AI Literacy Among Educators

While AI literacy is increasingly recognized as an important component in education, it is not sufficiently integrated into teacher training programs. The current state of AI literacy among educators reveals a significant gap, particularly in the context of English as a Foreign Language (EFL) teaching. Studies indicate that there are significant gaps in teachers' awareness and understanding of AI (Sperling et al., 2024; Xin, 2024). For instance, a survey conducted by Edweek (Prothero, 2023) showed although 43% of teachers thought it was a top priority or very important to teach students how to use AI, 42% of the same participants have never even used ChatGPT; and when asked about how much training they received to incorporate AI into their K-12 education, 87% claimed receiving zero training, 10% claimed 'little' training and 3% claimed 'some' training. UNESCO's recent findings (2023), involving more than 450 educational institutions, reported that fewer than 10% have implemented formal strategies or institutional guidelines on generative AI usage and adaptation (UNESCO, 2023). Moreover, a study by Ding et al. (2024) examined the impact of a case-based professional development program developed to increase the AI literacy of middle school teachers. The findings indicate that the program led to a significant increase in teachers' understanding of AI concepts and their ability to use these tools in classroom practice. This seemingly advantageous circumstance should not, however, result in a complete acceptance of the premise that some teachers are naturally resistant to change. Critically examining AI's implications for successful education is just as crucial as evaluating its literacy and training. Given the potential of AI tools to greatly improve language teaching and learning, this literacy becomes especially important in the context of EFL instruction. It is challenging to provide students with individualized learning experiences when teachers lack the pedagogical knowledge to use these technologies effectively. Thus, this restricts the possibilities of enhancing students' language proficiency and implementing instructional strategies that make use of efficient technology. Considerable need for entirely explicit and balanced teacher training programs is obvious to promote teacher AI literacy. AI literacy must now be categorized within the broad framework of educational technology frameworks such as Digital Pedagogy Content Knowledge Model (DPACK) and Technological Pedagogical Content Knowledge (TPACK). However, since using AI is much more specialized than simply using "technology," these pedagogical frameworks may not be as helpful in assisting instructors in acquiring this ability because they were not designed with AI literacy in mind. Frameworks such as TPACK and DPACK, for instance, encourage digital literacy and, although they take into account the use of fundamental digital tools and platforms and occasionally data, they do not recognize more advanced and technical skills such as the use of AI for teaching, the ability of teachers to analyze data, and the assessment of AI algorithms in the classroom for educational purposes (Olari & Romeike, 2021). 'Digital literacy' is a general word that does not adequately describe the range of abilities that educators will require when considering AI-related tools and platforms. When discussing AI as a tool, it may be argued that more significantly, it does not actively encourage critical literacies (Leu et al., 2017). The lack of comprehensive competency raises the question of whether new methods to teacher AI literacy and competency are necessary in order to help instructors construct a professional identity. As students transition from digital to data literacy in the classroom, AI literacy should be a key framework for literacy development in schools. Modifications to current models and upgrading them to AI literacy as part of the framework needs might be viewed as regeneration (Leu et al, 2017). On the other hand, developing a model that supports AI literacy and its incorporation into pedagogical frameworks might be more fruitful. It would be beneficial to start with the AI-PACK model framework, which was created in recent years to identify teachers' AI competencies (Lorenz & Romeike, 2023).

While there are AI literacy programs/courses available for the general public such as Microsoft's *AI for Beginners* (n.d.) or DeepLearning's *AI for Everyone* (Ng, 2023), or even specifically for educators such as *Artificial Intelligence (AI) Education for Teachers* from Macquarie University (Forbes & Powling, 2023); these programs do not provide competencies specific to the EFL environment because they are often broad and interdisciplinary in design. EFL teachers' specific needs for AI literacy include understanding the pedagogical integration of AI tools in the context of language teaching and how to use them effectively in classroom activities. Conversely, current AI trainings primarily focus on technology-related information and don't provide specific instructions on how to apply AI pedagogically in language instruction.

In practice, one notable initiative was the Make-a-Thon for AI Educators –a specific, structured professional development event focused on co-designing AI literacy materials. It brought together 34 educators and AI experts from across the US to collaboratively create and test educational resources. Although the event was designed with general educators in mind, it provided a foundation that could potentially be adapted to meet the specific needs of EFL teachers (Breazeal et al., 2023). Moreover, Mikton (2023) investigates how AI can be aligned with the International Baccalaureate (IB) learner profiles, proposing that linking these attributes with AI offers educators a chance to incorporate and use AI tools with an open mind. While highlighting the need for curriculum and assessment changes to properly and ethically implement AI tools, the International Baccalaureate Organization (IBO) expressed excitement about the potential ways that AI could improve educational experiences (International Baccalaureate Organization, 2023). Still, these conversations typically provide little advice on how to prepare educators to adjust to such developments, with neglect towards the specific needs of language teachers, who could greatly benefit from AI tools in language teaching and learning. EFL teachers need to engage with programs which introduced them to AI technologies, explored their potential for language teaching in the EFL environment, and provided suggestions for how to use AI in language acquisition, grammar, pronunciation, and culture - all facets of language. Apart from scattered snippets related to AI proficiency development from uncoordinated presentations at conferences (Cowin, 2023), and the professional post on a social media page (Staake, 2023), there were no identified programs related to AI proficiency development which targeted EFL teachers directly.

Ethical Considerations in AI in Education

The integration of AI in education brings with it a host of ethical considerations that must be carefully navigated. It is worth mentioning that it is the biggest gap in teachers' AI knowledge.

1. Privacy Concerns:

Protecting the privacy of student data is one of the most important ethical concerns. For AI systems to succeed and operate, they must be able to access and collect Ethical Risks and Mitigation of AI in Education large amounts of data, especially personal data. This raises many questions concerning how the data will be obtained, what the data will consist of, how the data is stored, and how the data is used. If data is misused or accessed by unauthorized third parties—and no preventive measures are taken—it could pose serious risks to student safety, individual agency, and institutional trust, potentially endangering the future of those engaged in the field of career education (Huang, 2023). To overcome these challenges, the European Commission published ethics guidelines for Trustworthy AI (European Commission, 2019) as part of the European Union's efforts to realize a future grounded in human agency and oversight, where AI systems support individuals, teams, and societies without compromising privacy. These guidelines outline a set of core principles, including the importance of human agency and oversight; the need for AI systems to demonstrate traceability and implement safeguards that uphold individuals' rights and goals; and the obligation to promote transparency, diversity, non-discrimination, and fairness. To align with these principles, educational institutions must invest time and effort into developing clear data governance policies, establishing informed consent procedures, and implementing regular review mechanisms to monitor how AI technologies handle sensitive personal data (Jose, 2024; Eden et al., 2024). In fact, literacy, be it relating to teachers or students, is an important strategy of mitigation here because it would help to have real informed consent instaed of the "I read and accepted" button that most people click without being aware of wht they are consenting to. Furthermore, clear and transparent accountability must be held in place in order to deter any companies from crossing that line.

2. Impact on Student Autonomy:

Algorithmic decision-making can also have significant effects on student autonomy. The use of AI-based recommendations and assessments may subtly steer students along predetermined learning pathways without their full awareness, thereby diminishing their capacity to make informed decisions about their own education. Therefore, it is imperative that AI initiatives in education are grounded in justified choices. Students and educators must retain control over how AI is integrated into the learning process and have the ability to opt out of or limit its use.

Mouta et al. (2020) found that students, in particular, tend to prefer systems that allow for greater personal agency, indicating that algorithmic tools should be designed with human decision-making at their core, rather than driven solely by automation. This underscores the idea that ethical AI should support learners in making choices, not supplant them entirely. Moreover, Sutrisno et al. (2023) observed that students expressed concerns that excessive reliance on AI could reduce opportunities for human interaction and compromise the relational aspects of education. Such concerns point to the risk that AI may undermine core educational values such as autonomy, independence, and meaningful human connection.

To address these issues, it is essential to ensure that students have the opportunity to challenge algorithmic decisions, that AI-generated feedback is accompanied by clear and defensible reasoning, and that teachers remain central to guiding educational experiences. By fostering student agency and supporting autonomy rather than dependence on algorithmic outcomes, educational environments can promote critical thinking and personal growth (Alm, 2024). Once again, students have to be trained and be aware of such algorithmic challenges to understand how to avoid them. This of course entails an AI-literate teacher leading the educational experience as aforementioned.

3. Bias and Fairness:

The risk of bias within AI algorithms can be particularly harmful to certain student groups, not only by producing inaccurate results but also by reinforcing existing systemic inequalities. These biases often originate in the datasets used to train AI systems, as well as in the failure to critically examine whether such datasets reflect or reproduce the structural biases already present within educational institutions. Mangal and Pardos (2024) emphasize that failing to detect and address bias at any stage of an AI system's development or evaluation enables the continued influence of historically rooted discrimination, which can further marginalize already disenfranchised students.

Ethical AI integration in education therefore requires a proactive and ongoing effort to monitor the function and outcomes of AI systems, ensuring they align with the developers' intentions and do not cause unintended harm. As AI technologies evolve, so must the vigilance with which educators and institutions track their effects. Real-world instances—such as the use of biased AI grading tools that disproportionately disadvantage minority students (Chinta et al., 2024)—underscore the urgency of this work. Sustained attention to issues of bias, privacy, and the impact of AI on student learning and well-being is essential.

To mitigate these ethical concerns, collaboration between developers and educators is necessary in the design of inclusive AI systems. These efforts must be grounded in ethical evaluation standards, particularly with regard to the metrics and datasets employed. Educational institutions should establish dedicated ethics and accessibility committees tasked with monitoring AI implementation and advising on equity and access considerations tailored to their specific contexts.

By aligning AI practices with clearly defined ethical principles, educators and policymakers must hold themselves accountable for the impact these technologies have on students' rights, educational equity, and mental and emotional well-being. The path to ethical AI integration is not merely a technical issue, but a fundamentally human one. Practicing responsibility, empathy, and a commitment to equitable access to quality education is not optional but essential.

Theoretical Framework: AI-PACK

The potential for teacher education programs to enhance educational practitioners' digital abilities related to artificial intelligence has not been sufficiently examined in the literature (Ng et al., 2021). The first section of this paper is developed through the AI-PACK framework (Lorenz & Romeike, 2023), an iteration of TPACK and DPACK, specifically to determine how to implement Artificial Intelligence (AI) in educational contexts. TPACK was designed by Mishra and Koehler (2006) to recognize the interaction of an instructor's pedagogical, content, and technological knowledge. As numerous digital tools became integrated into education and pedagogy surrounding assessments of student learning, DPACK (Digital Pedagogical and Content Knowledge), expanded upon TPACK by making digital technologies clearly a part of pedagogical practice. These concepts are expanded upon by AI-PACK, which focuses on the unique prospects and limitations of incorporating AI into teaching and learning methods.

AI-PACK provides a comprehensive structure for understanding and integrating AI into teaching practices. Although the AI-PACK framework provides the theoretical foundations, practical implementation reveals its actual worth. Zulianti et al. (2024), conducted a quasi-experimental study with novice EFL teachers and evaluated a TPACK-based professional development program designed to enhance AI integration skills. It was shown to significantly improve EFL teachers' understanding, integration skills, and self-efficacy in using AI-powered tools. The study confirmed the program's potential to bridge the gap between AI technology and effective classroom practice. Similarly, Sari et al. (2025) investigated Indonesian EFL teachers' perceptions of AI integration within the TPACK framework. According to their findings, teachers appreciated AI's capacity for engagement and customization, but they also encountered difficulties such as lack of resources, inadequate training, and uneven distribution of TPACK components. The authors recommend professional development that builds technological skills and fosters balanced use of AI in pedagogy. In another large-scale longitudinal study, An et al. (2023) assessed 101 Chinese EFL teachers' intelligent teaching preparation in AI education demonstration areas using the TPACK framework and the UTAUT model over two years. The results showed a decrease in self-reported AI pedagogical knowledge (TPK, TPACK) and perceptions of conducive conditions, but an increase in trust in AI platforms and an improvement in knowledge of AI ethics. This highlights the need for ongoing assistance and focused skill development. Collectively, the literature demonstrates that TPACK-informed strategies, whether they be qualitative, experimental, or longitudinal, can provide useful avenues for bridging the gap between AI technology and successful teaching methods.

However, while these frameworks do not focus on English Language Teaching (ELT), this paper will attempt to adapt them to that field in particular. This framework includes AI Related Knowledge (AI-K), AI Related Pedagogical Knowledge (AI-PK), AI Related Content Knowledge (AI-CK), and AI Related Pedagogical Content Knowledge (AI-PCK) (Lorenz & Romeike, 2023). In Figure 1, provided by Lorenz & Romeike (2023), we can see how these different models interact within DPACK in order to create AI-PACK.

Figure 1. The Place of the components of the AI-PACK Framework within the more general DPACK Framework

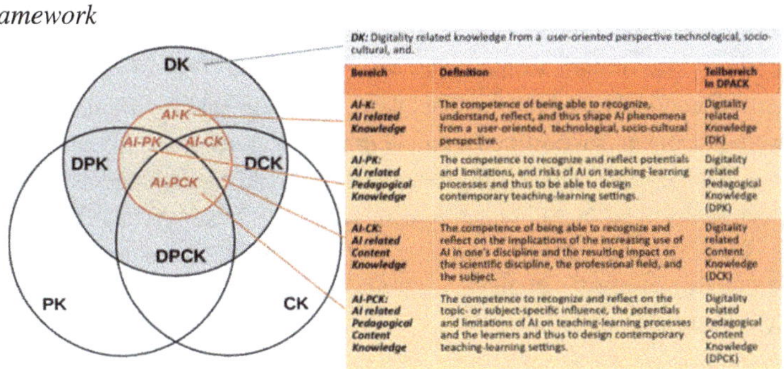

In Lorenz and Romeike's model (2023), we can see a further analysis of the AI-PACK components:

- AI-K (AI related Knowledge): It is the ability to recognize, understand and reflect on the AI phenomena, meaning the ability to eventually shape it from a user-oriented technological to socio-cultural perspective.
- AI-PK (AI related Pedagogical Knowledge): Which is the understanding and ability to recognize the potentials, risks and limitations throughout the educational process and being able to come up with AI-enhanced learning practices that are pedagogically sound.

- AI-CK (AI related Content Knowledge): Knowing the different ways AI can be used in your subject area and thinking about what those uses mean for your field.
- AI-PCK (AI related Pedagogical Content Knowledge): Being able to understand how AI affects your specific subject, what it can and can't do for teaching and learning, and using that insight to design modern, effective lessons.

While the AI-PACK framework offers a theoretical lens, the primary focus of this paper is to translate these theoretical components into practical, actionable strategies for EFL educators. This translation is crucial to bridge the gap between abstract ideas and practical classroom application. The intent is to move beyond theoretical discussions to provide EFL teachers with concrete, implementable recommendations. These suggestions based on the AI-PACK framework provide a vehicle for educators to plan their acquisition of knowledge and skills to properly integrate AI tools and methods into their teaching practice. Ultimately, the goal is to help educators acquire the knowledge and skills that will allow them to apply AI in improving language acquisition.

DISCUSSIONS AND RECOMMENDATIONS

It is evident from the literature review that it is crucial to develop clear criteria for identifying L2 pedagogical AI literacy, particularly for EFL teachers (Ng et al., 2021). There seems to be a significant void in the present professional development (PD) programs, since they don't seem to specifically address the urgent demands of EFL teachers and instructors in an AI-enabled classroom. There is a similar conclusion from recent research by Karataş and Aksu Ataç (2025), where pre-service EFL instructors may be comfortable using AI tools but their pedagogical thinking and ethical uses of these technologies often fall behind. This establishes the importance of comprehensive, content-based professional development to enable EFL instructors to engage with AI-powered tools and support pedagogical practices. In response to this critical need, the authors present a suite of essential competencies that should be included as part of every PD opportunity that seeks to build AI literacy in EFL educators. In suggesting these competencies, our intention is not only to allow EFL educators with a technical understanding of generative AI tools, but to think pedagogically about ways these tools can be integrated into their increasingly digital and AI-supported education.

Foundational AI Concepts and Technologies

To be able to incorporate artificial intelligence (AI) into their teaching techniques, EFL teachers must have a solid understanding of AI concepts and technologies. To put it simply, 'AI in education' usually refers to the use of algorithms and systems to do activities like learning, problem-solving, or language comprehension that normally require human-like intellect. Examples of fundamental concepts that EFL teachers should keep in mind are natural language processing (how AI systems comprehend and react to human language) and machine learning (how computers learn from data and make decisions) (Russell & Norvig, 2020). Teachers should be engaged with these concepts and not necessarily become entangled in the science behind them. Educational tools that are driven by AI such as adaptive learning systems can provide students with educational content based on the needs of individuals and create personalized, effective learning. Adaptive learning systems (Gupta, 2024) analyze student performance data to identify any gaps in learning and then modify the instructional material to meet the student's new learning challenge based on any gaps cognitive or affective, thus supporting differentiated instruction approaches. AI can also increase student engagement in classrooms using interactive tools such as AI chatbots, which are chatbots that mirror a conversation with students and can allow for examples of practical or authentic language use (Pan et al., 2025). These additional facets of AI will offer EFL teachers' insights into student progress and what they need to improve on. Exploring these concepts and tools for theorizing AI in teaching in EFL contexts requires an understanding of how to align the educational possibilities that modern technological capacities create with your pedagogical aspirations and goals while ensuring language learning as the central goal (Alpaydin, 2020).

The Capabilities and Limitations of AI in EFL Education

What AI Can Do

AI in education, especially in the context of EFL teaching, has many functions that greatly enhance the educational experience. AI systems can process massive volumes of data and tailor students' learning paths on the basis of their performance and rapport with input channels (Bozkurt et al., 2021). These various tools provide novice students with the chance to get simple language input that helps them systematically build up vocabulary and grammatical structures. In addition, interacting in a controlled manner with human-like voices and dialects affords students opportunities to be engaged in low-stakes productive conversation practice (Celik et al., 2025). As an example, Replika and the ELSA app has been found to effectively support EFL learners' real-time speaking practice and act as a substitute when native speakers are not present, although teacher support was found to be still necessary (Saraswati et al., 2023; Almutairi & Alghammas, 2025). AI systems can perform certain task functions, such as tracking progress over time, pinpointing language use patterns, automating grading and feedback provision, and enabling teachers to develop more targeted and effective instruction (Mane & Jagtap, 2024). As a result, the teacher is under less pressure since they have more time to concentrate on higher-order educational considerations (Luckin & Holmes, 2016). Moreover, AI can also facilitate adaptive learning by gradually adjusting the complexity of tasks, such as transitioning chatbot conversations from elementary to advanced structures, effectively scaffolding learners within their zone of proximal development (ZPD) (Sætra, 2025).

What AI Can't Do

Despite these advancements, AI cannot replace the nuanced understanding and emotional intelligence of human teachers (Chan et al., 2023). AI systems lack the ability to fully comprehend the complexities of human emotions, cultural nuances, and ethical considerations that are intrinsic to effective teaching. They are also limited in their ability to inspire, motivate, and engage students in the same way a human teacher can, particularly in areas requiring critical thinking, creativity, and moral judgment. The relational elements of education—humor, classroom culture, mentorship, and trust—remain human.

The Role of Human-in-the-Loop Systems

The "human-in-the-loop" system (HITL) involves human interaction at significant decision points along the process. It begins with data sourced from various inputs, which is then processed by an AI model. When the model produces an output, it creates a series of responses with varying levels of confidence. If the AI is confident in its prediction, that result is saved directly. But if the model is uncertain, it sends the output to a human reviewer to correct these outputs, ensuring accuracy and contextual appropriateness. The validated output is then stored and used to help improve the AI over time. This process helps the AI learn and keeps the output accurate, safe, and human-aware -especially important in areas like teaching, where context and empathy matter. This process is simply illustrated in Figure 2 below.

Figure 2. The HITL Model

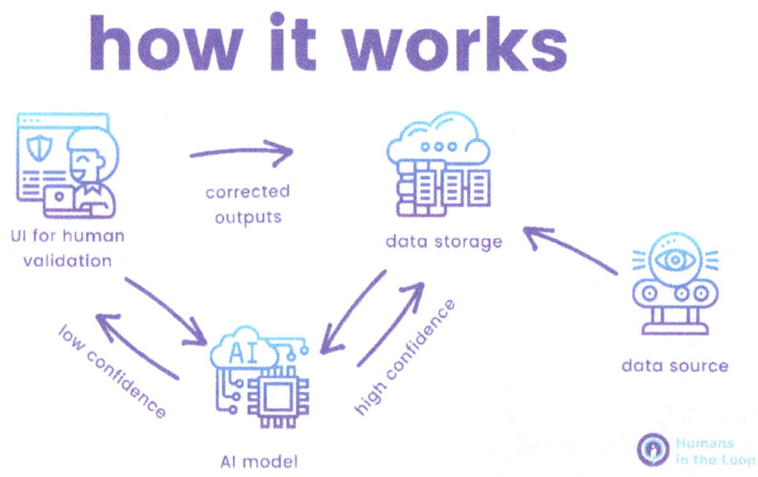

While AI systems and tools can produce valuable data, their final decisions and important evaluations will always rely on human decisions (Russell & Norvig, 2020). In EFL education, this means that AI can contribute to aspects of learning and learning support, but in the end, a teacher (or learner) is still present and at the center of the process Human-in-the-loop systems represent the notion that human teachers will always be required to interpret and contextualize the data from AI systems, to evaluate effective pedagogical judgment, and to establish a meaningful relationship with students before AI systems are able to self-activate and no longer require an interpretation (Memarian & Doleck, 2024).

AI Tools and Technologies in ELT

In the dynamic field of English Language Teaching (ELT), AI tools and technologies are increasingly being integrated to enhance the educational process. These integrations manifest in various forms, each contributing uniquely to the learning and teaching experience in this field.

AI-Assisted Homework and Practice

AI tools are revolutionizing homework and practice sessions by providing personalized exercises and instant feedback. For instance, AI-powered language learning platforms can analyze a student's performance and offer tailored practice tasks that focus on their weak areas especially in areas where, previously, a teacher was needed, and they can become part of an adaptive personalized supplementary homework for learners. Platforms such as ELSA (Gusrianto & Iswahyuni, 2025) simulate real life language practice as well as use algorithms to adapt the difficulty level and type of exercises based on the learner's progress, ensuring that the practice is both challenging and effective. Furthermore, assigning such homework would indirectly boost the AI literacy of the children in alignment with what Yang recommends (2022).

Automated Assessment and Feedback

AI is also employed to automate the assessment of language skills. Tools equipped with natural language processing capabilities can evaluate written assignments, providing instant feedback on grammar (Park, 2019), vocabulary (Jeon, 2021), and writing style (Rahman et al., 2023). This not only speeds up the grading process but also allows for more consistent and objective assessments. Similarly, speech recognition technology is used to assess pronunciation and fluency in spoken English, offering learners detailed feedback on their speech patterns. As previously stated, the Speech e-rater is used by the ETS to assess the speaking section of the TOEFL test. Educators can access this feature using My Speaking Score (*My Speaking Score*, n.d.) which uses the same engine and provides instant feedback, including a detailed report that visualizes the learner's performance and it aligns with CEFR levels.

AI-Infused Curricula

AI is being used to develop curricula that are more adaptive and responsive to individual learning needs. AI algorithms can analyze a vast amount of data on student learning patterns and outcomes to suggest modifications in the curriculum itself. This approach enables a more dynamic curriculum that evolves based on the effectiveness of the teaching materials and methods. AI-infused curricula will normalize the use of AI as part of the subject matter and integrate it within the learning experience. In fact, when all of what is discussed in this paper is implemented, the result would be such a comprehensive curriculum. This shift has already been reflected in emerging professional development programs such as the Professional Certificate in AI-Infused Curriculum Design offered by the London School of International Businesses (*London School of International Business*, 2025), which trains educators in integrating AI tools into curriculum planning and instructional design. Additionally, some of these programs explore fully AI-led course delivery, displaying how artificial intelligence is now not only a segment of curriculum design but also a facilitator of learning itself (Georgia Institution of Technology, 2025). Moreover, when designing lessons for such curricula, the same principles apply for the educational process albeit revised. For example, in adapting our pedagogical approach to the digital age, we draw upon the revisited Bloom's Taxonomy framework as a resource for aligning course-level outcomes with meaningful learning experiences in the context of AI as seen in Figure 3 below (Oregon State University Ecampus, n.d.).

Figure 3. Bloom's Taxonomy Revisited

	RECOMMENDATION	AI CAPABILITIES	DISTINCTIVE HUMAN SKILLS
CREATE	Review	Suggest a range of alternatives, enumerate potential drawbacks and advantages, describe successful real-world cases	Formulate original solutions incorporating human judgement, collaborate spontaneously
EVALUATE	Review	Identify pros and cons of various courses of action, develop rubrics	Engage in metacognitive reflection, holistically appraise ethical consequences of alternative courses of action
ANALYZE	Amend	Compare and contrast data, infer trends and themes, compute, predict	Critically think and reason within the cognitive and affective domains, interpret and relate to authentic problems, decisions, & choices
APPLY	Review	Make use of a process, model, or method to illustrate how to solve a quantitative inquiry	Operate, implement, conduct, execute, experiment, and test in the real world; apply creativity and imagination to idea & solution development
UNDERSTAND	Review	Describe a concept in different words, recognize a related example, translate	Contextualize answers within emotional, moral, or ethical considerations
REMEMBER	Amend	Recall factual information, list possible answers, define a term, construct a basic chronolgy	Recall information in situations where technology is not readily accessible

This taxonomy serves as a guide for evaluating the levels of learning and aligning teaching activities and assessments to foster student success in an AI-influenced educational landscape. As AI tools become increasingly integrated into learning activities, it's crucial to consider the unique contributions of human skills at each cognitive level of Bloom's Taxonomy and how these may guide the thoughtful revision of course content and outcomes. The framework encourages educators to assess the use of AI tools critically and to adapt their teaching strategies to maintain the relevance and effectiveness of student learning experiences.

Predictive Analytics in Learning Progress

Artificial intelligence systems can monitor and evaluate student performance data over time, enabling predictive analysis of a student's learning progression. This helps educators identify early on which students may require more support or intervention to improve learning outcomes. For instance, Cambridge's Write & Improve (Write & Improve with Cambridge, n.d.) tracks all the 'evaluations' that the student receives, and generates a line graph which shows not only the progress the student has made in how well they are doing, but also aligned with the CEFR levels, and included the 'predicted' progress for the next steps. This level of detailed tracking is difficult for human teachers to achieve on their own.

Practical Guide for Teachers

Integrating AI Tools

Incorporating AI tools in a teaching context entails moving gradually to enrich the learning experience and develop learner autonomy and proactive learning. Teachers can create lesson plans using AI tools that satisfy their teaching actions for their learners, as well as their learning goals and objectives as teachers. When selecting and integrating AI tools, it is helpful to consider language proficiency levels, technology access, and educators and students' digital literacies. For instance, AI-driven language practice apps can be strategically integrated into teachers' daily lesson plans that align with traditional teaching methodologies. Teachers could assign and assess AI-generated interventions for their homework and allow their students to engage in the materials at their own pace or allow them to engage students in class with AI-supported assignments. These interventions could be useful in developing writing fluency, grammar rules, or vocabulary in personalized formats and flexible experiences. In broader practice, AI is already being used in education for functions such as automated assessment, adaptive learning systems, intelligent tutoring, and data-informed instructional planning (Chen et al., 2020). A variety of tools have been developed to support these functions, many of which are showcased in educational webinars such as the one organized by Inzata for Edweek (2023). This webinar presents practical examples of AI implementations in classrooms, including tools like ChatGPT, highlighting how educators can enhance instruction, personalize the learning process, and streamline administrative tasks. Such resources are particularly effective for teachers who are less experienced with AI in their teaching practice, as they provide an overview of use-case scenarios. Teachers are allowed to have opportunities to experience the tools they think will best match their own teaching style and curriculum objectives, in respect to diverse applications across disciplines and different ability levels.

Another good strategy is using AI for formative assessment. Teachers can use AI tools to give quick feedback on students' work, allowing them to spot issues or challenges early and revisit the topic as needed. As students can develop and recognize their own progress and actively respond to their learning, this immediacy can facilitate differentiated education strategies and promote a growth attitude. Further to this notion of immediacy, AI tools that promote interactive or conversational practice—such as chatbots—can greatly boost student engagement, offering valuable practice opportunities that are also relevant and useful in everyday communication (Celik et al., 2025). The use of adaptive test formats with gamified AI platforms can help to motivate children with the use of personal progress measures and relevant challenges (Lai & Lee, 2024). Overall, when deploying an AI Tool into learning engagement, teachers need to provide clear instructions and planning to the learners. For instance, teachers may want to demonstrate the tool effectively, so learners know how to appropriately use it, set clear expectations about use, or let the learners know there is a clear policy about the use or a different approach. Teachers must also take the time to provide educational support as learners become more familiar with the AI tools and blend them into their learning and experiences related to using the tool and developing digital literacy skills. In addition to supporting the digital literacy of students, the development of new skills, knowledge and attitudes will proactively prepare the students for the educational demands of learning and communicating in AI mediated environments.

Challenges and Solutions in ELT with AI

Integrating AI into ELT presents several challenges that need to be addressed to ensure effective and safe use of this technology. Luckily, the implementation of several strategies can solve or at least mitigate such challenges:

- **Maintaining the Role of Teachers**: One of the primary concerns is the potential diminishment of the teacher's role in an AI-augmented environment. There's a risk that over-reliance on AI could lead to a reduced emphasis on the human aspects of teaching, such as empathy, cultural sensitivity, and moral guidance (García-López et al., 2025). In educational contexts, these human components are particularly important for establishing trust, encouraging motivation, and attending to each student's unique emotional needs—areas in which AI technologies are still lacking (Dulundu, 2024). Incorporating Human-in-the-Loop (HITL) Systems, as mentioned before, ensures that human judgment plays a central role in AI-augmented teaching. By serving as a mediator between the learner and the technology, these systems enable teachers to make ethical and contextually relevant assessments about education. Teachers can oversee AI operations, making final decisions and providing context and ethical considerations where AI falls short in the learning process (Bhutoria, 2022). By actively participating in the development, implementation, and assessment of AI tools, teachers maintain the integrity of the educational process while also retaining professional autonomy
- **Appropriateness of AI-Generated Materials**: Ensuring that the content and feedback provided by AI tools are pedagogically appropriate and culturally sensitive is another challenge. AI systems may not always align with the specific learning objectives or cultural contexts of the classroom. To mitigate such a problem, the involvement of teachers in the design and implementation of AI tools ensures that these technologies are tailored to meet the specific needs of the ELT classroom. AI output is more relevant and effective when teachers are involved in the integration process because they assist align the content with curricular requirements, student competence levels, and institutional goals. This involvement can also help in developing AI tools that are culturally sensitive and pedagogically appropriate. Furthermore, most of these tools contain filters at their code level that prevent such inappropriate responses. For example, OpenAI's ChatGPT has many restrictions related to culture, race and other sensitive topics that it would not generate to protect the users of inappropriate content (Martindale, 2023). These mechanisms are critical in minimizing biased or inappropriate content. Nevertheless, due to potential deficiencies in training data, AI models can still yield unintended or nuanced content (Mariyono & Abror, 2024; Chinta et al., 2024). The same goes for educational Chatbots where they have 'educational filters' that ascertain the proper feedback. For example, Khan Academy's Khamingo (TED, 2023) has a filter in place where it won't give the

answer directly to the student, rather it uses the Socratic method to elicit the answers from the student. In addition to encouraging greater cognitive involvement, this approach shows how AI might be developed to encourage active learning as opposed to passive information intake.

- **Transforming Learner Assessment**: A major challenge is proactively implementing assessment-based strategies that consider AI tools while maintaining fairness and accuracy. AI algorithms can be opaque, especially about how AI tools are used to gauge student performance. Stakeholders may raise concerns about accountability in high-stakes contexts due to the opaque, "black-box" nature of the AI users. Teachers can gain a better understanding of how AI interacts with students and makes decisions by using explainable and transparent AI systems, especially when it comes to student assessment. When a commitment to openness is upheld to support the use of AI in assessment development, AI remains both appealing and trustworthy. Furthermore, a teacher's understanding of AI contributes meaningfully to the discussion of how AI "works" and where accountability expectations should be placed (Ehsan et al., 2022). Without sufficient training, there is a heightened risk of misinterpreting or excessive dependence on AI-generated outcomes, which poses a threat to the overall validity of the assessment.
- **Professional Development and Training**: Providing teachers with ongoing professional development and training in AI literacy can empower them to use AI tools effectively and responsibly. This training should include ethical considerations and data privacy concerns associated with AI in education. This measure is the most effective in order to mitigate most of the challenges surrounding AI.

ChatGPT for Language Learning/Teaching

ChatGPT has indeed claimed the throne of Chatbots and AI-driven educational tools when it comes to its versatility and ease-of-use in English Language teaching, making it an important tool for an AI-literate educator. Thus, this warrants a dedicated section for its use by EFL teachers.Top of Form

How to Access ChatGPT

ChatGPT, developed by OpenAI, is a powerful language model that can be accessed through various platforms. To use ChatGPT, educators and students typically need an internet connection and access to a platform hosting the model. This can be through OpenAI's website (https://chat.openai.com), integrated applications, mobile apps, or third-party services that offer ChatGPT functionality. Users usually need to create an account and follow specific instructions provided by the platform to start interacting with ChatGPT. As of 2025 the most current version is ChatGPT-4.5, which represents a significant advancement in reasoning, responsiveness, and following instructions compared to earlier models. While several versions have been released in the past, including ChatGPT 3.5 and 4, these are now considered legacy models. For the purposes of this paper, all references and examples are based on ChatGPT-4.5 (OpenAI, 2025a).

Prompt Engineering

A prompt in the context of ChatGPT is an input statement or question that initiates a response from the AI. Prompt engineering involves crafting these inputs strategically to elicit the most informative, accurate, or educational responses from ChatGPT. Effective prompt engineering requires the understanding of how ChatGPT interprets language and structuring prompts in a way that guides the AI towards the desired type of response. This skill is particularly useful in educational settings, as it allows teachers to tailor ChatGPT's responses to specific learning objectives or discussion topics. As an EFL teacher, several elements of the prompts must be paid attention to:

- The prompt must contain the context or theme of the request: 'In a lesson about Present Perfect…., we are reading a text about the pyramids of Giza…., Design a homework assignment… etc.'
- The teacher should provide a role to ChatGPT: 'Act as a proofreader….., Imagine you are an EFL teacher…, Act as though…etc.'
- Provide the level you are dealing with: 'My students are B1 in English…, in an intermediate class… etc.'
- Be as specific as possible: 'Give me feedback for this essay according to the IELTS rubric…, Find all the metaphors in this text…,'

For further details about prompt engineering, the AI for Education team have released a video that is easy to follow (AI for Education, 2023). Also, a special prompt repository for educators can be found on Github (Microsoft, n.d.-b) and another one from the AI for Education Team (*Prompt Library*, 2024).

Creating AI-Infused Lessons/Activities Using the Revisited Bloom's Taxonomy

As stated before, ChatGPT can be integrated into language learning activities by aligning its capabilities with the revisited Bloom's Taxonomy (Anderson & Krathwohl 2001), which categorizes cognitive skills into six levels: Remember, Understand, Apply, Analyze, Evaluate, and Create. For instance:

- **Remember and Understand**: Use ChatGPT to provide definitions, explanations, or summaries of language concepts.
- **Apply and Analyze**: Engage students in applying grammatical rules or analyzing language structures through interactive Q&A sessions with ChatGPT.
- **Evaluate and Create**: Encourage students to critique language usage examples generated by ChatGPT or to create their own prompts to explore complex language constructs.

AI Detectors and Their Unreliability

Language models pose a significant risk to academic integrity, given that instructors might find it difficult to assess the extent of student-generated content (Perkins, 2023). The distinction between student-generated content and AI-assisted solutions becomes increasingly blurred as generative AI technologies advance, particularly in written assignments, reflective essays, and take-home tests. While AI detectors are tools that claim to identify text generated by AI models like ChatGPT, their reliability is quite low. Research consistently shows that AI-detection tools are unreliable, and many fail to detect AI-generated content and even label it as human-written (Odri & Yoon, 2023; Bellini et al., 2024; Elkhatat et al., 2023). These detectors can sometimes give false positives or negatives, meaning they may incorrectly label AI-generated text or fail to recognize it (Weber-Wulff et al., 2023). Serious repercussions may result from this discrepancy, particularly if a false positive falsely accuses a student of misbehavior, weakening student-teacher trust. Likewise, a false negative could permit unreported abuse, jeopardizing learning objectives and academic standards. In fact, every detector platform includes a disclaimer warning educators from taking the result at face value; and in their FAQ page, OpenAI stated, "in short, no" (OpenAI, 2025b) when asked whether detectors work. Consequently, they should not be solely relied upon as evidence of cheating or academic dishonesty in educational settings. To better grasp the student's voice and think over time, teachers are recommended to use a multifaceted approach to assessment, which may include process-based activities, oral comments, and more in-class writing. Educators should be aware of these limitations and use AI detectors cautiously, supplementing them with other assessment methods to ensure fairness and accuracy in evaluating student work. In all likelihood, encouraging a culture of academic integrity through open discussions about AI, its potential, and ethical bounds might work better than merely enforcing penalties.

Bias and Hallucination

ChatGPT, like many AI language models, has been known to "hallucinate" information as it might present fabricated details or assertions with unwarranted confidence (Alkaissi & McFarlane, 2023). Such behavior, which is frequently referred to as "AI hallucination," is concerning when users believe the information to be true because of the model's authoritative and fluid tone. This is a byproduct of its predictive text-generating mechanisms, which can lead to convincingly articulated but inaccurate or nonsensical responses. In certain instances, the model might even produce completely made-up references, authors, or data that don't exist, which, if improperly validated, could be deceptive in academic settings. In addition, biases present in the training data can be reflected in the outputs (Sinha, 2025). Since the model learns from vast datasets that may contain biased or unbalanced perspectives, there is a risk of perpetuating these biases in its responses. When discussing political, ethical, or culturally sensitive topics—where a fair representation of viewpoints is essential—this is especially troublesome. Furthermore, these biases might not always be obvious; some might be subtle and present in the way things are phrased, presumptions made, or opposing views left out. These challenges are particularly important in educational settings where neutrality and factual accuracy are essential. To avoid this, educators and learners both must thoughtfully analyze AI-produced products and work to identify and address biases that occur in AI. This involves learning about the limitations of AI systems, how they are trained, and the use of structured cross verification. Teachers should initiate conversations about AI literacy and encourage learners to think about and question the validity of the things produced by machines. A good approach is Holly Clark from *The AI-infused Classroom*. Clark (2023), developed based on information from Harvard University, UC Berkeley and University of Wisconsin (Clark, 2023) seen in Figure 4 below:

Figure 4. A diagram showing a strategy to validate information generated by AI

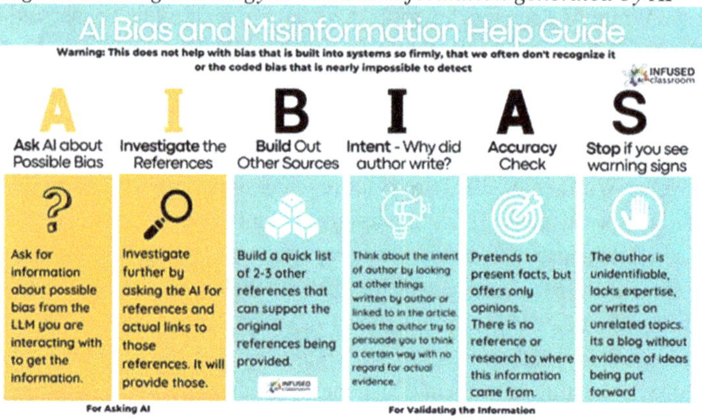

By promoting critical interaction with AI-generated content, the flowchart describes a procedure intended to assist instructors and students in recognizing AI biases and false information. The first step in the flowchart is to ask the AI if it has any biases inherent in the language model. This is important because even the most sophisticated AI systems are trained on data that could inherently contain cultural or ideological biases. The second step is to explore the references the AI provides and develop a list of additional sources that validate AI's claims. This triangulation process pushes students to actively cross-reference sources which increase the reliability of the information as well as reinforce their digital literacy. This step is significant for validating the content as well as ensuring its alignment with academic standards. Failure to check references can lead to the spread of incorrect information or the making of an argument without sufficient proof, which is not appropriate in an academic setting where evidence-based reasoning is more appropriate. It's also essential to verify the information's purpose, including the rationale behind its creation and the supporting data. Readers are better able to discern between information, persuasion, and manipulation when they are aware of the author's intentions. Students' interpretations and applications of information may be influenced by these differences.

Users are additionally encouraged to be mindful of how the language, tone, and structure of AI may influence how the information is perceived, particularly when it comes to controversial and sensitive subjects. AI's confident tone, use of technical language, and seemingly straightforward responses may lead users to perceive its output as more trustworthy—even when the information is inaccurate or lacks depth and credibility. Finally, it is advisable to stop engaging with the content if red flags are present, such as an unidentifiable author, lack of subject-matter expertise, or the inclusion of irrelevant topics without supporting evidence. These signs often indicate a lack of bias, potential misinformation or complete disinformation. As part of a toolkit that develops knowledge of AI literacy, educators and students should be trained to recognize these signals appropriately to prepare them for critical engagement in an increasingly AI-mediated information world. Ultimately, following this strategy, educators and learners alike will be able to identify the biases and misinformation produced by AI. This enables them to make better informed decisions with respect to AI-generated content when accommodating it into their academic activities. Consequently, this encourages more responsible use of AI in educational situations, improves students' critical thinking abilities, and supports the ethical application of generative technologies in learning environments.

The EFL AI-PACK Framework

To link the discussion's core elements with the AI-PACK framework, Table 1 categorizes the key components of the proposed professional development enhancements for EFL teachers. It allows for a systematic examination of how AI integration can be successfully scaffolded into ELT contexts by coordinating the pedagogical priorities with the fundamental digital and AI-related literacies listed in the framework. This organization underscores how each aspect of the discussion corresponds with specific AI-PACK competencies and how ELT can work within the same Framework, thereby providing a clear overview of the theoretical underpinnings that inform the practical recommendations mentioned. Additionally, it shows how the five dimensions of AI-PACK—Awareness, Interaction, Pedagogy, Assessment, and Criticality—work together to meet the changing needs of language learning, particularly in promoting teacher autonomy and well-informed decision-making in AI-mediated settings. In addition to supporting the theoretical underpinnings, it makes it easier to operationalize these findings in actual teaching situations by explicitly mapping these competencies to classroom-oriented tactics.

Table 1. EFL AI-PACK

AI-PACK Component	Core Elements
AI-K (AI related Knowledge)	Foundational understanding of AI principles and technologies; Importance of AI literacy in PD programs; Machine learning and natural language processing essentials for EFL educators
AI-PK (AI related Pedagogical Knowledge)	Pedagogical strategies enhanced by AI; Using AI tools for personalized learning and assessment; Human-in-the-loop systems to maintain teacher's role in AI-driven education
AI-CK (AI related Content Knowledge)	Impact of AI on EFL content; Adjustments in curricula and assessments due to AI; Ethical considerations and implications of AI on subject matter
AI-PCK (AI related Pedagogical Content Knowledge)	Aligning technological capabilities of AI with pedagogical objectives; Interactive language practice with AI tools; Teacher involvement in AI design and implementation; Professional development in AI literacy for educators

The table presented above provides a structured overview of how the proposed strategies for enhancing AI literacy among EFL teachers are informed by the AI-PACK framework's components. This strategic alignment ensures that our recommendations are not only theoretically sound but also practically oriented towards the multifaceted development of educators in an AI-integrated educational environment. Each component shows deliberate effort on connecting theoretical discoveries with classroom realities, from the integration of pedagogical content knowledge with AI tools (AI-PCK) to the foundational AI knowledge (AI K).

In order to enable educators to critically evaluate and implement AI tools in contextually meaningful ways, teacher training programs must, for example, go beyond surface-level awareness and instead develop a deep conceptual grounding in AI principles. This necessity underscores the value that AI-K places on a foundational understanding of artificial intelligence, while AI-PK similarly highlights the rapid pedagogical shifts occurring alongside AI's emergence. In particular, the development of customized adaptive feedback and human–AI collaboration redefines the teacher's role—positioning them not only as instructors but also as co-learners and facilitators. The AI-CK dimension addresses both the pedagogical and ethical considerations involved in AI-driven content, calling on language educators to adopt a reflective stance that prioritizes inclusion, equity, and transparency in language instruction. Meanwhile, the AI-PCK dimension emphasizes the importance of aligning technological tools with clearly defined educational goals. Rather than promoting the passive adoption of new technologies, AI-PCK advocates for intentional and purposeful integration of AI into instructional design.

The next steps involve translating these theoretical insights into actionable professional development plans. This includes designing training materials that not only present the structural benefits of AI tools but also model effective instructional strategies for diverse teaching contexts. Moreover, ensuring meaningful and lasting impact will require educators to critically engage with AI through collaborative inquiry, reflective practice, and the practical application of AI tools—together with their learners as co-learners. With sustained support and ongoing AI literacy development, EFL teachers can fully leverage AI as a pedagogical asset, creating more dynamic, personalized learning environments and fostering more inclusive opportunities for language acquisition.

It is important to emphasize that the EFL AI-PACK is a suggested Framework, not a perspective curriculum in itself. Because of the various needs of different institutional contexts such as different skill level of teachers, teaching at a school or a language center and even the textbooks and materials used as well as the different constraints such as time, place and number of trainees, each PD training should be based on the framework but adapted to the local needs. In other words, the framework serves as a guiding structure while the specific materials, activities and methodology should be tailored to the educational context to ensure training succuss. Below, we provide an example a 3-day broad training design that could be implemented in a language school.

Table 2. EFL AI-PACK Sample Training structure

Day 1 – Foundations of AI in EFL Education		
Session Theme	**Content & Activities**	**Expected Outcomes**
Opening & Orientation (09:00–09:30)	- Icebreaker: *"How do my students already use AI in language learning?"* - Overview of workshop goals	Participants connect AI to real classroom experiences
Understanding AI in EFL (09:30–10:30)	- Intro to AI concepts (NLP, machine learning, chatbots) - Examples: grammar checkers, AI dictionaries, adaptive vocabulary apps - Group brainstorm: *"Where is AI already influencing EFL classrooms?"*	Teachers understand how core AI functions underpin EFL tools
Understanding AI in Education (10:30–11:00)	Mini-lecture: AI basics (ML, NLP, generative AI); examples in EFL (chatbots, writing assistants, adaptive platforms); group mapping	Foundational grasp of AI and EFL relevance
AI for Vocabulary, Grammar & Pronunciation (11:15–13:15)	- Demo: AI flashcard generators for vocabulary - Activity: using AI for grammar drills & error correction - Pronunciation practice with AI speech recognition apps - Pair practice: compare AI feedback vs. teacher feedback	Teachers learn how to integrate AI tools into vocabulary, grammar, and pronunciation lessons
Lunch (13:15–14:15)	—	—

continued on following page

Table 2. Continued

Day 1 – Foundations of AI in EFL Education		
Session Theme	**Content & Activities**	**Expected Outcomes**
Designing AI-Supported Micro-Activities (14:15–16:15)	- Groups design one activity each: *Vocabulary building with AI, Grammar practice using AI feedback, Pronunciation with AI speech tools* - Peer feedback	Teachers create classroom-ready activities linked to core EFL skills
Reflection & Wrap-Up (16:15–16:45)	- Journal: *"Which language skill area do I want to enhance with AI first?"* - Group share	Clear action points for integrating AI in language teaching

Day 2 – Writing, Reading & Assessment		
Session Theme	**Content & Activities**	**Expected Outcomes**
Recap & Energizer (09:00–09:30)	- Quiz on Day 1 tools - Pair share: successes/concerns	Continuity and focus
AI for Writing & Feedback (09:30–11:00)	- Demo: AI writing tutors (essay drafting, feedback on grammar, vocabulary range, cohesion) - Activity: teachers use AI to analyze student writing samples - Compare AI vs. teacher feedback	Teachers learn to balance AI-generated writing support with human guidance
Break (11:00–11:15)	—	—
AI for Reading & Listening (11:15–12:45)	- Tools: adaptive reading platforms, AI-generated comprehension quizzes, listening with transcript support - Group task: design a reading or listening comprehension activity with AI	Teachers design AI-supported activities for receptive skills
Lunch (12:45–13:45)	—	—
Assessment in the Age of AI (13:45–15:15)	- Case study: plagiarism & AI writing detection - Task: redesign a writing test to account for AI tools - Debate: *"Should AI-assisted writing be graded differently?"*	Teachers adapt assessment practices for academic integrity
Ethics, Privacy & Data (15:15–16:00)	Key risks (privacy, bias, plagiarism); debate: "Should students use AI in classwork?"; draft guidelines	Ethical literacy & safeguarding strategies
Teacher Agency in the AI Era (16:00–16:45)	Role-play: balance AI feedback with teacher judgment; reflection: what remains uniquely human?	Strong teacher identity with AI
Lesson Design Practice (16: 5–17:45)	- Teachers draft a full lesson plan (focus on either writing, reading, or listening) with AI integration	Drafted AI-supported lessons in receptive/ productive skills
Reflection & Wrap-Up (17:45–18:00)	- Ethics takeaways; design challenges	Teachers consolidate knowledge on assessment & skills

Day 3 – Speaking, Microteaching, and Future Directions		
Session Theme	**Content & Activities**	**Expected Outcomes**
Recap & Goal Setting (09:00–09:30)	- Review Day 2 lesson drafts - Individual goal setting for microteaching	Focused application
AI for Speaking & Conversation (09:30–11:00)	- Demo: AI chatbots for fluency practice, role-play generators, pronunciation support - Activity: pair practice designing speaking prompts using AI	Teachers gain strategies for using AI in speaking practice
Break (11:00–11:15)	—	—
Microteaching Round 1 (11:15–12:45)	- Teachers deliver 10–15 min AI-integrated speaking/vocabulary/grammar activity - Peer & trainer feedback	Teachers practice real classroom delivery
Lunch (12:45–13:45)	—	—
Microteaching Round 2 (13:45–15:15)	- Continuation with different participants - Emphasis on communicative use of AI in EFL	Teachers refine strategies for student-centered AI use
Collaborative Unit Planning (15:15–16:15)	- Groups design a 3-lesson unit (e.g., vocabulary + reading + speaking sequence) using AI - Share drafts	Teachers practice curriculum-level planning with AI
Final Reflection & Closing (16:15–16:45)	- Circle discussion: *"My biggest EFL-AI insight"* - Individual PD roadmap; identify institutional supports/needs	Teachers leave with practical EFL-focused AI applications

This above outline demonstrates how professional development can meaningfully integrate AI into EFL teaching while remaining adaptable to diverse institutional contexts if based on the suggested EFL AI-PACK framework. Rather than prescribing a fixed curriculum, it provides a flexible model that aligns AI applications with core language skills such as vocabulary, grammar, writing, reading, listening, and speaking. By combining technical knowledge with pedagogical reflection, it supports teachers in using AI responsibly and effectively, while also addressing ethical considerations and maintaining teacher agency. In doing so, it positions AI not as a replacement for educators, but as a helper to enhance language learning and empower teachers in the evolving landscape of education.

CONCLUSION

This article highlights the importance of AI literacy as part of EFL teachers' professional development. The author provides much-needed analysis of AI integration in English language teaching to identify the skills that teachers need, as they will undoubtedly face AI in classrooms in the future. A comprehensive framework is needed to address challenges such as preserving the human aspects of instruction, evaluating the pedagogical and cultural value of AI-generated materials, and managing AI within ethical constraints. Solutions revolve around Human-in-the-Loop methods, active engagement of teachers in AI tool development, and ongoing professional learning. Developing critical digital literacy is essential, where educators engage with AI tools while recognizing their limitations, biases, and impacts on equity and learner agency. All of this comes with a crucial caveat: such training must be delivered within a cohesive and systematic framework—such as the suggested EFL AI-PACK—to ensure consistency and quality in teacher learning. Institutions will be able to provide sustained and meaningful paths to educational innovation, rather than disjointed or short-lived AI initiatives, by grounding these competencies in a solid theoretical foundation. Furthermore, teachers need sustainable learning opportunities supported by collaborative research, ongoing feedback, and scaffolded experimentation with AI tools in educational settings as part of a continuing professional learning model, not a one-off event. The ability to apply AI effectively through teacher learning and development in ELT not only enhances the learning experience, but also strengthens teacher preparation and learner understanding, enabling both to navigate the intersection of AI's limitations and human capacities. In doing so, we also begin to realize a new educational vision—one that can reform language education to be more inclusive, flexible, and reflective of the digital realities that are continuously shaping our social world.

Suggestions for Further Research

This study identifies several important directions for future research. First, there is a need to further elaborate and test the EFL AI-PACK framework, given the limited evidence-based literature currently available on this topic i.e. the suggested framework needs to be tested. Alternatively, researchers may consider developing an entirely new framework, independent of the DPACK model, grounded in language-specific pedagogical theories or cognitive science principles that more closely reflect the realities of classroom practice. Another critical area is the development of a clear, systematic curriculum for AI literacy in English language education. This curriculum could serve as a benchmark for effectively integrating AI into language teaching. It should include AI tools and resources designed specifically for language educators, practical examples from classroom settings, and a series of structured training units to maximize relevance and usability. This curriculum could be indeed based on the EFL AI-PACK. To ensure flexibility and accessibility, the development process should also incorporate field testing and ongoing instructor feedback. Additionally, evaluating the long-term impacts of such a curriculum will be essential for refining both its content and its implementation. Indicators such as student outcomes, shifts in teacher agency, and changes in teacher confidence can help determine what aspects are effective and what areas require further adjustment, informing both curriculum design and policy recommendations. Finally, EFL departments should consider the introduction of AI literacy courses at earlier educational levels serving pre-service teachers. Offering these courses to young learners would allow students to build foundational digital competencies and develop awareness of potential challenges before they arise. Embedding AI ethics, critical thinking about algorithmic decision-making, and safe, transparent use of AI tools into early education has the potential to foster a digitally literate generation capable of engaging ethically and effectively with AI technologies.

REFERENCES

AI for Education. (2023, October 11). *Prompt engineering for educators* [Video]. YouTube. https://www.youtube.com/watch?v=NuIKQgX71Fc

Alam, S., Usama, M., Alam, M. M., Jabeen, I., & Ahmad, F. (2023). Artificial intelligence in global world: A case study of Grammarly as e-tool on ESL learners' writing of Darul Uloom Nadwa. *International Journal of Information and Education Technology (IJIET), 13*(11), 1741–1747. DOI: 10.18178/ijiet.2023.13.11.1984

Alkaissi, H., & McFarlane, S. I. (2023). Artificial hallucinations in ChatGPT: Implications in scientific writing. *Cureus*. Advance online publication. DOI: 10.7759/cureus.35179

Alm, A. (2024). Exploring autonomy in the AI wilderness: Learner challenges and choices. *Education Sciences, 14*(12), 1369. Advance online publication. DOI: 10.3390/educsci14121369

Almutairi, R. T., & Alghammas, A. A. (2025). The effectiveness of using ELSA app on improving Saudi students' English-speaking skills. *International Journal of English Linguistics, 15*(1), 140–148. DOI: 10.5539/ijel.v15n1p140

Alpaydın, E. (2020). *Introduction to machine learning* (4th ed.). The MIT Press.

An, X., Shen, X., Bai, J., & Li, Y. (2023). Assessment of intelligent teaching preparation of EFL teachers: Based on two-year data comparison. *International Conference on Computers in Education*. DOI: 10.58459/icce.2023.1377

Anderson, L. W., & Krathwohl, D. R. (Eds.). (2001). *A taxonomy for learning, teaching, and assessing: A revision of Bloom's taxonomy of educational objectives*. Longman.

Ashrafganjoe, M. (2025). Exploring the role of digital writing tools in enhancing academic writing skills: The case of the Hemingway app in EFL classrooms. *Technology in Language Teaching & Learning, 7*(1), 102479. DOI: 10.29140/tltl.v7n1.102479

Bellini, V., Semeraro, F., Montomoli, J., Cascella, M., & Bignami, E. (2024). Between human and AI: Assessing the reliability of AI text detection tools. *Current Medical Research and Opinion, 40*(4), 353–358. DOI: 10.1080/03007995.2024.2310086

Bhutoria, A. (2022). Personalized education and Artificial Intelligence in the United States, China, and India: A systematic review using a Human-In-The-Loop model. *Computers & Education: Artificial Intelligence, 3*, 100068. DOI: 10.1016/j.caeai.2022.100068

Bicknell, K., Brust, C., & Settles, B. (2023). How Duolingo's AI Learns what you Need to Learn: The language-learning app tries to emulate a great human tutor. *IEEE Spectrum, 60*(3), 28–33. DOI: 10.1109/MSPEC.2023.10061631

Bozkurt, A. (2023). ChatGPT, Üretken yapay zeka ve algoritmik paradigma değişikliği. *Alanyazın, 4*(1), 63–72. DOI: 10.59320/alanyazin.1283282

Bozkurt, A., Karadeniz, A., Baneres, D., Guerrero-Roldán, A. E., & Rodríguez, M. E. (2021). Artificial intelligence and reflections from educational landscape: A review of AI studies in half a century. *Sustainability (Basel), 13*(2), 800. Advance online publication. DOI: 10.3390/su13020800

Breazeal, C., Moore, K. S., Ali, S., Perret, B., Zhou, X., Zhang, H., & Lee, I. (2023). Make-a-Thon for middle school AI educators. In *SIGCSE 2023: Proceedings of the 54th ACM Technical Symposium on Computer Science Education, 1*, 305–311. DOI: 10.1145/3545945.3569743

Browner, E. (2023, July 5). AI proves time-saving potential for teachers, but are they ready? *Clever Blog*. https://www.clever.com/blog/2023/07/artificial-intelligence-teachers-K12

Celik, B., Yildiz, Y., & Kara, S. (2025). Using ChatGPT as a virtual speaking tutor to boost EFL learners' speaking self-efficacy. *Australian Journal of Applied Linguistics*. DOI: 10.29140/ajal.v8n1.102418

Cengiz, S., & Peker, A. (2025). Generative artificial intelligence acceptance and artificial intelligence anxiety among university students: The sequential mediating role of attitudes toward artificial intelligence and literacy. *Current Psychology (New Brunswick, N.J.), 44*(9), 7991–8000. Advance online publication. DOI: 10.1007/s12144-025-07433-7

Chan, C. K. Y., & Tsi, L. H. Y. (2023). The AI revolution in education: Will AI replace or assist teachers in higher education? *arXiv*. /arXiv.2305.01185DOI: 10.48550

Chen, L., Chen, P., & Lin, Z. (2020). Artificial intelligence in education: A review. *IEEE Access : Practical Innovations, Open Solutions, 8*, 75264–75278. DOI: 10.1109/ACCESS.2020.2988510

Chinta, S. V., Wang, Z., Yin, Z., Hoang, N., Gonzalez, M., Le Quy, T., & Zhang, W. (2024). FairAIED: Navigating fairness, bias, and ethics in educational AI applications. *ArXiv*. /arXiv.2407.18745DOI: 10.48550

Chomsky, N., & Skinner, B. F. (1959). A Review of B. F. Skinner's verbal behavior. *Language, 35*(1), 26–58. DOI: 10.2307/411334

Clark, H. (2023). *The AI infused classroom: Inspiring ideas to shift teaching and maximize meaningful learning in the world of AI*. Elevate Books EDU.

Cowin, J. (2023, November 6). *Targeted prompts for EFL teachers using AI* [Virtual presentation] [Slide show; Presentation]. Dr. J's Education Blog. https://drcowinj.files.wordpress.com/2023/11/targeted-prompting-for-efl-educators-using-ai-morocco-workshop-ppt.pdf

Diep, M. C., & Dang, M. H. (2025). Exploring factors influencing the adoption of ChatGPT as a supportive tool in EFL Lesson Creation. *AsiaCALL Online Journal, 16*(1), 111–139. DOI: 10.54855/acoj.251616

Ding, A.-C. E., Shi, L., Yang, H., & Choi, I. (2024). Enhancing teacher AI literacy and integration through different types of cases in teacher professional development. *Computers and Education Open, 6*(4), 100178. DOI: 10.1016/j.caeo.2024.100178

Dulundu, A. (2024). AI in education: Benefits and concerns. *Next Generation Journal for The Young Researchers, 8*(1), 81. DOI: 10.62802/3fr4f412

Eden, C. A., Chisom, O. N., & Adeniyi, I. S. (2024). Integrating AI in education: opportunities, challenges, and ethical considerations. *Magna Scientia Advanced Research and Reviews, 10*, 006-013. DOI: 10.30574/msarr.2024.10.2.0039

Edmett, A., Ichaporia, N., Crompton, H., & Crichton, R. (2024). *Artificial intelligence and English language teaching: Preparing for the future* (Version Second edition). British Council. DOI: 10.57884/78EA-3C69

Education Week. (2023, June 21). *ChatGPT & education: 8 ways AI improves student outcomes.* https://www.edweek.org/events/webinar/chatgpt-education-8-ways-ai-improves-student-outcomes

Ehsan, U., Wintersberger, P., Liao, Q. V., Watkins, E. A., Manger, C., Daumé Iii, H., Riener, A., & Riedl, M. O. (2022). Human-xentered explainable AI (HCXAI): Beyond opening the black-box of AI. *CHI Conference on Human Factors in Computing Systems Extended Abstracts*, 1–7. DOI: 10.1145/3491101.3503727

Elkhatat, A. M., Elsaid, K., & Almeer, S. (2023). Evaluating the efficacy of AI content detection tools in differentiating between human and AI-generated text. *International Journal for Educational Integrity, 19*(1), 17. DOI: 10.1007/s40979-023-00140-5

European Commission, High-Level Expert Group on Artificial Intelligence. (2019, April 8). *Ethics guidelines for trustworthy AI.* European Commission. https://digital-strategy.ec.europa.eu/en/library/ethics-guidelines-trustworthy-ai

Forbes, A., & Powling, M. (2023, March 5). *Artificial Intelligence (AI) education for teachers.* Coursera. https://www.coursera.org/learn/artificial-intelligence-education-for-teachers

Francisco, R., & Silva, F. (2022). Intelligent tutoring system for computer science education and the use of artificial intelligence: A literature Review. In *Proceedings of the 14th International Conference on Computer Supported Education*, 338–345. DOI: 10.5220/0011084400003182

García-López, I. M., González González, C. S., Ramírez-Montoya, M.-S., & Molina-Espinosa, J.-M. (2025). Challenges of implementing ChatGPT on education: Systematic literature review. *International Journal of Educational Research Open, 8*, 100401. DOI: 10.1016/j.ijedro.2024.100401

Georgia Institute of Technology. (2025). *Jill Watson: The virtual teaching assistant.* Design & Intelligence Lab. https://dilab.gatech.edu/jill-watson/

Gupta, T. (2024). Adaptive learning systems: Harnessing AI to personalize educational outcomes. *International Journal for Research in Applied Science and Engineering Technology, 12*(11), 458–464. DOI: 10.22214/ijraset.2024.65088

Gusrianto, E. & Iswahyuni. (2025). Exploring learning experience with ELSA speak for independent learning: A case study. In M. I. Sukardi, D. Ardhian, T. R. Indhiarti, V. A. Dwigantara, & T. B. Widagdo (Eds.), *Proceedings of the International Conference on Advances in Humanities, Education and Language (ICEL 2024)* (Vol. 913, pp. 219–229). Atlantis Press SARL. DOI: 10.2991/978-2-38476-388-7_20

H.R. 6791 - 118th Congress (2023): Artificial intelligence literacy act of 2023. (2023, December 15). https://www.congress.gov/bill/118th-congress/house-bill/6791

Huang, L. (2023). Ethics of artificial intelligence in education: Student privacy and data protection. *Science Insights Education Frontiers, 16*(2), 2577–2587. DOI: 10.15354/sief.23.re202

Hur, J. W. (2024). Fostering AI literacy: Overcoming concerns and nurturing confidence among preservice teachers. *Information and Learning Science.* Advance online publication. DOI: 10.1108/ILS-11-2023-0170

Huwer, J., Huwer, J., Irion, T., & Schaal, S. (2023). From TPACK to DPACK: The "Digitality-related pedagogical and content knowledge"-model in STEM-education. *Education Sciences, 13*(8), 769. DOI: 10.3390/educsci13080769

International Baccalaureate. (2025, March 6). *Artificial intelligence (AI) in learning, teaching, and assessment.* https://www.ibo.org/programmes/artificial-intelligence-ai-in-learning-teaching-and-assessment/

Jackson, K. M., & Papa, R. (2024). Understanding artificial intelligence in education. In Jackson, K. M., & Papa, R. (Eds.), *AI changing the arc of educational leadership* (pp. 7–31). Springer., DOI: 10.1007/978-3-031-71415-3_2

Jeon, J. H. (2021). Chatbot-assisted dynamic assessment (CA-DA) for L2 vocabulary learning and diagnosis. *Computer Assisted Language Learning, 36*(7), 1338–1364. DOI: 10.1080/09588221.2021.1987272

Jia, F., Sun, D., Qian, M., & Looi, C. (2022). Developing an AI-based learning system for L2 learners' authentic and ubiquitous learning in English language. *Sustainability (Basel), 14*(23), 15527. DOI: 10.3390/su142315527

Jonassen, D., Spector, M. J., Driscoll, M., Merrill, M. D., Van Merrienboer, J., & Driscoll, M. P. (2008). *Handbook of research on educational communications and technology.* Routledge., DOI: 10.4324/9780203880869

Jose, D. (2024). Data privacy and security concerns in AI-Integrated educational platforms. *Recent Trends in Management and Commerce, 5*(2), 87–91. DOI: 10.46632/rmc/5/2/19

Karataş, F., & Aksu Ataç, B. (2025). When TPACK meets artificial intelligence: Analyzing TPACK and AI-TPACK components through structural equation modelling. *Education and Information Technologies, 30*(7), 8979–9004. DOI: 10.1007/s10639-024-13164-2

Khan Academy. (2023, March 14). *Khan Academy announces GPT-4 powered learning guide* [Video]. YouTube. https://www.youtube.com/watch?v=yEgHrxvLsz0

Koehler, M. J., Mishra, P., & Cain, W. (2013). What is technological pedagogical content knowledge (TPACK)? *Journal of Education, 193*(3), 13–19. DOI: 10.1177/002205741319300303

Korucu-Kış, S. (2024). Zone of proximal creativity: An empirical study on EFL teachers' use of ChatGPT for enhanced practice. *Thinking Skills and Creativity, 54*, 101639. DOI: 10.1016/j.tsc.2024.101639

Krahnke, K. J., & Krashen, S. D. (1983). Principles and practice in second language acquisition. *TESOL Quarterly, 17*(2), 300. DOI: 10.2307/3586656

Lai, W. Y. W., & Lee, J. S. (2024). A systematic review of conversational AI tools in ELT: Publication trends, tools, research methods, learning outcomes, and antecedents. *Computers and Education: Artificial Intelligence*, *6*, 100291. DOI: 10.1016/j.caeai.2024.100291

Leu, D. J., Kinzer, C. K., Coiro, J., Castek, J., & Henry, L. A. (2017). New literacies: A dual-level theory of the changing nature of literacy, instruction, and assessment. *Journal of Education*, *197*(2), 1–18. DOI: 10.1177/002205741719700202

Li, Z., Wang, C., & Bonk, C. J. (2024). Exploring the utility of ChatGPT for self-directed online language learning. *Online Learning : the Official Journal of the Online Learning Consortium*, *28*(3). Advance online publication. DOI: 10.24059/olj.v28i3.4497

London School of International Business. (2025). *Professional Certificate in AI-Infused Curriculum Design*. https://www.lsib.co.uk/2022/course-details.aspx?CourseTitle=Professional+Certificate+in+AIInfused+Curriculum+Design

Lorenz, U., & Romeike, R. (2023). What Is AI-PACK? – Outline of AI competencies for teaching with DPACK. In J.-P. Pellet & G. Parriaux (Eds.), *Informatics in Schools. Beyond bits and bytes: Nurturing informatics intelligence in education* (Vol. 14296, pp. 13–25). Springer Nature Switzerland. DOI: 10.1007/978-3-031-44900-0_2

Luckin, R., & Holmes, W. (2016). *Intelligence Unleashed: An argument for AI in Education*. Pearson. https://static.googleusercontent.com/media/edu.google.com/en/pdfs/Intelligence-Unleashed-Publication.pdf

Mageira, K., Pittou, D., Papasalouros, A., Kotis, K., Zangogianni, P., & Daradoumis, A. (2022). Educational AI chatbots for content and language integrated learning. *Applied Sciences (Basel, Switzerland)*, *12*(7), 3239. DOI: 10.3390/app12073239

Mane, P. A., & Jagtap, S. (2024). AI-enhanced educational platform for personalized learning paths, automated grading, and real-time feedback. *International Journal of Scientific Research in Engineering and Management*, *08*(12), 1–7. DOI: 10.55041/IJSREM39921

Mangal, M., & Pardos, Z. A. (2024). Implementing equitable and intersectionality-aware machine learning in education: A practical guide. *British Journal of Educational Technology*, *55*(5), 2003–2038. DOI: 10.1111/bjet.13484

Mariyono, D., & Abror, M. (2024). AI in enhancing cultural sensitivity. *Jurnal EDUCATIO: Jurnal Pendidikan Indonesia*, *10*(2), 296. DOI: 10.29210/1202424847

Martindale, J. (2023, May 2). *Here are 11 things that ChatGPT will refuse to do*. Digital Trends. https://www.digitaltrends.com/computing/everything-chatgpt-refuses-to-do/

Memarian, B., & Doleck, T. (2024). Human-in-the-loop in artificial intelligence in education: A review and entity-relationship (ER) analysis. *Computers in Human Behavior: Artificial Humans*, *2*(1), 100053. DOI: 10.1016/j.chbah.2024.100053

Miangah, T. M., & Nezarat, A. (2012). Mobile-assisted language learning. *International Journal of Distributed and Parallel Systems*, *3*(1), 309–319. DOI: 10.5121/ijdps.2012.3126

Microsoft. (n.d.). *Generative AI for beginners: 12 lessons to get started building with generative AI* [GitHub repository]. GitHub. https://microsoft.github.io/generative-ai-for-beginners/

Microsoft. (n.d.-b). *Prompts for educators.* GitHub. https://github.com/microsoft/prompts-for-edu/blob/main/Educators/README.MD

Mikton, J. (2023, October 16). *Integrating AI with the IB learner profile.* IB Community Blog. https://beyonddigital.org/2023/10/19/integrating-ai-with-the-ib-learner-profile/

Mishra, P., & Koehler, M. J. (2006). Technological pedagogical content knowledge: A new framework for teacher knowledge. *Teachers College Record, 108*(6), 1017–1054. DOI: 10.1111/j.1467-9620.2006.00684.x

Mouta, A., Sánchez, E. T., & Llorente, A. M. P. (2020). Sense of agency in times of automation: A teachers' professional development proposal on the ethical challenges of AI applied to education. In Bittencourt, I. I., Cukurova, M., Muldner, K., Luckin, R., & Millán, E. (Eds.), *Artificial Intelligence in Education* (Vol. 12164, pp. 405–408). Springer International Publishing., DOI: 10.1007/978-3-030-52240-7_73

My Speaking Score. (n.d.). *My speaking score.* https://www.myspeakingscore.com/

Ng, A. (2023). *AI for everyone.* DeepLearning AI. https://www.deeplearning.ai/courses/ai-for-everyone/

Ng, D. T. K., Leung, J. K. L., Chu, S. K. W., & Qiao, M. S. (2021). Conceptualizing AI literacy: An exploratory review. *Computers and Education: Artificial Intelligence, 2*, 100041. DOI: 10.1016/j.caeai.2021.100041

Nwana, H. S. (1990). Intelligent tutoring systems: An overview. *Artificial Intelligence Review, 4*(4). Advance online publication. DOI: 10.1007/BF00168958

Octavio, M., González Argüello, M. V., & Pujolà, J.-T. (2024). ChatGPT as an AI L2 teaching support: A case study of an EFL teacher. *Technology in Language Teaching & Learning, 6*(1), 1142. DOI: 10.29140/tltl.v6n1.1142

Odri, G.-A., & Yoon, D. J. Y. (2023). Detecting generative artificial intelligence in scientific articles: Evasion techniques and implications for scientific integrity. *Orthopaedics & Traumatology: Surgery & Research, 109*(8), 103706. DOI: 10.1016/j.otsr.2023.103706

OECD. (2024). *Recommendation of the council on artificial intelligence.* OECD Legal Instruments. https://legalinstruments.oecd.org/en/instruments/OECD-LEGAL-0449

Olari, V., & Romeike, R. (2021). Addressing AI and data literacy in teacher education: A review of existing educational frameworks. *In the proceedings of The 16th Workshop in Primary and Secondary Computing Education, 17*, 1–2. DOI: 10.1145/3481312.3481351

Open, A. I. (2025a). *ChatGPT release notes.* https://openai.com/research/chatgpt

Open, A. I. (2025b). *How can educators respond to students presenting AI-generated content as their own?* https://help.openai.com/en/articles/8313351-how-can-educators-respond-to-students-presenting-ai-generated-content-as-their-own

Oregon State University Ecampus. (n.d.). *Advancing meaningful learning in the age of AI: artificial intelligence tools – Faculty support*. Oregon State Ecampus. Oregon State Ecampus. https://ecampus.oregonstate.edu/faculty/artificial-intelligence-tools/meaningful-learning/

Pan, L., Luo, H., & Gu, Q. (2025). Incorporating AI literacy and AI anxiety into TAM: Unraveling Chinese scholars' behavioral intentions toward adopting AI-assisted literature reading. *IEEE Access : Practical Innovations, Open Solutions, 13*, 38952–38963. DOI: 10.1109/ACCESS.2025.3546572

Pan, M., Guo, K., & Lai, C. (2025). Using artificial intelligence chatbots to support English as a Foreign language students' self-regulated reading. *RELC Journal, 56*(3), 781–793. DOI: 10.1177/00336882241264030

Park, J. (2019). An AI-based English grammar checker vs. human raters in evaluating EFL learners' writing. *Multimedia-Assisted Language Learning, 22*(1), 112–131. DOI: 10.15702/MALL.2019.22.1.112

Perkins, M. (2023). Academic integrity considerations of AI large language models in the post-pandemic era: ChatGPT and beyond. *Journal of University Teaching & Learning Practice, 20*(2). Advance online publication. DOI: 10.53761/1.20.02.07

Prompt Library — AI for education. (2024, January 5). *Prompt library*. AI For Education. https://www.aiforeducation.io/prompt-library

Prothero, A. (2023, November 16). *What educators know about artificial intelligence, in 3 charts*. Education Week. https://www.edweek.org/technology/what-educators-know-about-artificial-intelligence-in-3-charts/2023/07

Rahman, N. A., Zulkornain, L. H., Mat, A. C., & Kustati, M. (2023). Assessing writing abilities using AI-powered writing evaluations. *Journal of ASIAN Behavioural Studies, 8*(24), 1–17. DOI: 10.21834/jabs.v8i24.420

Reyes, R., Mariñas, J. M., Tacang, J. R., Asis, L. J., Sayman, J. M., Flores, C. C., Palima, Z., & Sumatra, K. (2024, October). The relationship between attitude towards AI and AI literacy of university students. *International Journal of Multidisciplinary Studies in Higher Education, 1*(1), 37–46. DOI: 10.70847/587958

Russell, S. J., & Norvig, P. (2020). *Artificial intelligence: A modern approach* (4th ed.). Pearson.

Sætra, H. S. (2025). Scaffolding human champions: AI as a more competent other. *Human Arenas, 8*(1), 56–78. DOI: 10.1007/s42087-022-00304-8

Saini, N. (2023, August 28). *The impact of ChatGPT on language learning*. Linkedin. https://www.linkedin.com/pulse/impact-chatgpt-language-learning-dr-nitin-saini/

Saniyah, S. M.Sari Mahibatus Saniyah. (2023). Duolingo and learner autonomy: Investigating the role of personalization and gamification in promoting self-directed language learning. *ENJEL: English Journal of Education and Literature, 2*(2), 141–147. DOI: 10.30599/enjel.v2i02.529

Saraswati, G., Farida, A., & Yuliati, Y. (2023). Implementing AI Replika in higher education speaking classes: Benefits and challenges. *ELT Forum: Journal of English Language Teaching, 12*(3), 207-215. DOI: 10.15294/elt.v12i3.76525

Sari, I. F., Yulia, Y., Hidayat, A. R., & Irwanto, I. M. R. (2025). Implementation of artificial intelligence in teachers' technological pedagogical and content knowledge in EFL context. *Pertanika Proceeding, 1*(2). Advance online publication. DOI: 10.47836/pp.1.2.010

Schiavo, G., Businaro, S., & Zancanaro, M. (2024). Comprehension, apprehension, and acceptance: Understanding the influence of literacy and anxiety on acceptance of artificial Intelligence. *Technology in Society, 77*, 102537. DOI: 10.1016/j.techsoc.2024.102537

Selim, A. S. M. (2024). The transformative impact of AI-powered tools on academic writing: Perspectives of EFL university students. *International Journal of English Linguistics, 14*(1), 14. DOI: 10.5539/ijel.v14n1p14

Setyaningsih, E., Asrori, M., Ngadiso, , Sumardi, , Zainnuri, H., & Hariyanti, Y. (2024). Exploring high school EFL teachers' experiences with MagicSchool AI in lesson planning: Benefits and insights. *Voices of English Language Education Society, 8*(3), 685–700. DOI: 10.29408/veles.v8i3.27700

Sinha, R. (2025). *Cultural biases in AI: How your prompts might be making things worse.* PsyChatWork. https://psychatwork.substack.com/p/cultural-biases-in-ai-how-your-prompts

Sperling, K., Stenberg, C.-J., McGrath, C., Åkerfeldt, A., Heintz, F., & Stenliden, L. (2024). In search of artificial intelligence (AI) literacy in teacher education: A scoping review. *Computers and Education Open, 6*, 100169. DOI: 10.1016/j.caeo.2024.100169

Staake, J. (2023, July 22). *20 Ways teachers can use ChatGPT to make their lives easier.* We Are Teachers. https://www.weareteachers.com/chatgpt-for-teachers/

Su, J., Ng, D. T. K., & Chu, S. K. W. (2023). Artificial intelligence (AI) literacy in early childhood education: The challenges and opportunities. *Computers & Education: Artificial Intelligence, 4*, 100124. DOI: 10.1016/j.caeai.2023.100124

Sutrisno, D., Inawati, I., & Hermanto, H. (2023). Enhancing student learning autonomously: Exploring the global impact of artificial intelligence. [ELTEJ]. *English Language Teaching Educational Journal, 6*(2), 137–150. DOI: 10.12928/eltej.v6i2.9100

TED. (2023, May 1). *How AI could Save (not destroy) education | Sal Khan | TED* [Video]. YouTube. https://www.youtube.com/watch?v=hJP5GqnTrNo

UNESCO. (2021). *Recommendation on the ethics of artificial intelligence.* https://unesdoc.unesco.org/ark:/48223/pf0000381137

UNESCO. (2023, December 4). *AI competency frameworks for school students and teachers.* https://www.unesco.org/en/digital-education/ai-future-learning/competency-frameworks

UNESCO. (2024, August 8). *AI competency framework for teachers.* DOI: 10.54675/ZJTE2084

Walter, Y. (2024). Embracing the future of artificial intelligence in the classroom: The relevance of AI literacy, prompt engineering, and critical thinking in modern education. *International Journal of Educational Technology in Higher Education, 21*(1), 15. DOI: 10.1186/s41239-024-00448-3

Warschauer, M., & Healey, D. (1998). Computers and language learning: An overview. *Language Teaching, 31*(2), 57–71. DOI: 10.1017/S0261444800012970

Weber-Wulff, D., Anohina-Naumeca, A., Bjelobaba, S., Foltýnek, T., Guerrero-Dib, J., Popoola, O., Šigut, P., & Waddington, L. (2023). Testing of detection tools for AI-generated text. *International Journal for Educational Integrity, 19*(1), 26. DOI: 10.1007/s40979-023-00146-z

Write & Improve with Cambridge. (n.d.). https://writeandimprove.com/workbooks#/wi-workbooks

Xi, X., Higgins, D., Zechner, K., & Williamson, D. M. (2008). Automated scoring of spontaneous speech using speechrater v1.0. *ETS Research Report Series, 2008*(2), i-102. DOI: 10.1002/j.2333-8504.2008.tb02148.x

Xiao, Y., & Zhi, Y. (2023). An exploratory study of EFL learners' use of ChatGPT for language learning tasks: Experience and perceptions. *Languages (Basel, Switzerland), 8*(3), 212. DOI: 10.3390/languages8030212

Xin, J. J. (2024). Investigating EFL teachers' use of generative AI to develop reading materials: A practice and perception study. *Language Teaching Research*, 13621688241303321. Advance online publication. DOI: 10.1177/13621688241303321

Yang, W. (2022). Artificial intelligence education for young children: Why, what, and how in curriculum design and implementation. *Computers and Education: Artificial Intelligence, 3*, 100061. Advance online publication. DOI: 10.1016/j.caeai.2022.100061

Younas, M., El-Dakhs, D. A. S., & Jiang, Y. (2025). A comprehensive systematic review of AI-driven approaches to self-directed learning. *IEEE Access : Practical Innovations, Open Solutions, 13*, 38387–38403. DOI: 10.1109/ACCESS.2025.3546319

Zulianti, H., Hastuti, H., Nurchurifiani, E., Hastomo, T., Maximilian, A., & Ajeng, G. D. (2024). Enhancing novice EFL teachers' competency in AI-powered tools through a TPACK-based professional development program. *World Journal of English Language, 15*(3), 117. DOI: 10.5430/wjel.v15n3p117

Chapter 14
AI and Research Methodologies:
Opportunities and Challenges

Hamdo Ahmad Ebrahim
https://orcid.org/0009-0001-4487-1129
Maaref University of Applied Sciences, Syria

ABSTRACT

This chapter will address the impact of AI on research methodologies on different disciplines. It will focus on the opportunities that AI offers regarding data collection, analysis, and knowledge creation, as well as the matters of challenges and ethical considerations in implementation. The objective is to help researchers achieve a balanced view by providing appropriate frameworks and guidelines aimed towards the implementation of AI within their methodological practices. With the rapid growth and advancement of AI technologies, research methodologies are undergoing one of the most significant transformations in data gathering, analysis, and even interpretation. From natural language processing to machine learning, AI powered tools provide countless innovative opportunities; however, they also come with obstacles like bias, reproducibility problems, and ethical considerations.

INTRODUCTION

The accelerating development of artificial intelligence (AI) technologies is re-shaping the scientific research context across all fields - from health to social sciences to engineering to ecology. AI-powered tools are increasingly incorporated into the research workflow, modifying data collection, analysis, and interpretation. The technologies provide possibilities and capabilities that are previously unimaginable for improving the efficiency, accuracy, and scale of research processes; providing researchers the ability to answer difficult questions that may have been unachievable in the past.

AI guidelines and tools will automate the dull stuff - data cleaning, transcription, etc. - so that researchers can engage in more abstract analysis and theory building. The algorithms provide improved ability to recognize complex patterns from large data sets such that they increase the

DOI: 10.4018/979-8-3373-2752-5.ch014

power of prediction and produce interesting and actionable knowledge! In addition, AI opens up new frontiers of research that advance interdisciplinary approaches to research work; the quantitative, computational, and predictive; but for fields which tend to be historically qualitative; and transdisciplinary approaches by bridging together different research fields!

As with any new technology, the use of AIs in research methods will also come with various challenges. The ethical challenges around data privacy, algorithmic bias, and transparency are the evident barriers to overcome to implement AI as an integral component of research (Russell & Norvig, 2020). The methodological challenges include considerations of validity and reproducibility, and sometimes, the interpretability of AI produces, while the automation of the research process challenges human judgment space and especially the ability to keep the intellectual rigor of research.

The report investigates these potentials and boundaries, in an attempt to highlight some of the effective and responsible practices for the use of AI in research methods. The emphasis here is, in the considered ways of the disruptive capability, and limitations, of AI to provide guidance to researchers operating in the current technological space.

RESEARCH OBJECTIVES

The central aim of this study is to thoroughly examine the role of artificial intelligence (AI) as a change agent in regards to current research practices associated with researching different areas. The article will explore what AI offers including new data analyses, automating research processes, predictive modelling, and integration across disciplines – and the methodological, ethical, and practical challenges for adoption. In examining both advantages and disadvantages, the intention is to offer a balanced framework that will help researchers adopt AI tools in what could be a successful and responsible way that is underpinned by scientific rigors, ethical integrity, and discipline specific contextual relevance.

LITERATURE REVIEW AND THEORETICAL FRAMEWORK

AI is becoming more impactful than ever in the methodologies employed in research over numerous disciplines. Its applications offer multiple advantages, such as improved data processing, automation of menial tasks, and the recognition of patterns that are often neglected by humans. Machine learning algorithms (Kartik & Follow, 2025), for example, can analyze copious amounts of data and recognize relationships and patterns which guide the creation of informed hypotheses, thereby adding value to research. Deep learning AIs enhance the literature synthesis process during the review by automatically locating pertinent research papers, which accelerates the literature review.

This capability allows researchers to remain current with vast amounts of information, enhancing the robustness of their reviews. Additionally, AI-driven simulations and modeling tools enhance the ability to predict outcomes and test theories without the need for extensive physical experimentation, thus saving time and resources. However, the integration of AI in research methodologies is accompanied by several challenges. One major concern is the potential for bias in AI algorithms, which can skew results and lead to erroneous conclusions. If the training data is not representative or if AI models are poorly designed, findings may be distorted. This highlights the necessity for researchers to remain vigilant about the quality and integrity of the data utilized in AI systems. Moreover, the reliance on AI tools raises questions about transparency and reproducibility. Traditional research emphasizes clear methodologies and the ability to replicate studies.

However, proprietary AI systems may obscure their decision-making processes, making it difficult for other researchers to understand or replicate results. This challenges the fundamental principles of scientific inquiry and necessitates the development of standardized practices for AI usage in research.

Ethical considerations (Bhandari, P. 2024) also play a crucial role in the deployment of AI in research. Issues related to data privacy, consent, and the responsible use of technology must be addressed to safeguard against misuse. Establishing guidelines and ethical frameworks is essential to support researchers in navigating these concerns appropriately. In conclusion, while AI offers significant advancements in research methodologies, the opportunities it presents must be carefully balanced against the challenges it poses. Continuous dialogue among researchers, ethicists, and technologists will be vital to harness the full potential of AI in enhancing research while ensuring that it adheres to ethical standards and best practices.

CHALLENGE RECOGNITION

The increasing adoption of artificial intelligence (AI) in research has altered traditional practices that involve analysis of data, identification of patterns, and formulating decisions within a paradigm of increasing complexity and sophistication. By providing many new methodological questions, the implementation of AI in research introduced complex dilemmas, specifically:

a. Algorithmic bias;
b. Data privacy;
c. Ethics;
d. Replicability of AI-enabled research.

These dilemmas may derail research, unless handled with care, imperiling the reliability, fairness, and integrity of research.

Algorithmic Bias in Research Methodologies

Algorithmic bias (Jonker, A., & Rogers, J. 2025) is among the most difficult problems that AI research faces, possibly as a consequence of biased training data or poor model design. In this case, as AI systems are trained on historical, archived data, if the data is socially biased, the models may reflect, or exaggerate, those biases. Public health or social science research is one of many examples—a model trained on data that is not representative of certain groups, could yield biased results and recommendations. From a methodological perspective, this may threaten the validity and generalizability of these research studies. To mitigate this matter, researchers will have to painstakingly audit their datasets, use algorithms focused on fairness, and usually sample from a diverse set of data sources.

a. Data Privacy Concerns:

AI applications usually require a significant amount of data collection which is often made up of sensitive personal data. While the data can provide robustness to findings, there can be serious privacy concerns associated with obtaining, using, or collecting personally identifiable information without proper anonymization or consent, and this may violate ethical standards and regulations like GDPR. There is also a risk that researchers using AI models that rely on private data may inadvertently leak that private data (e.g. federated learning, deep learning) to the public. To maximize privacy in research, to the extent feasible, it is useful to have secure encrypted storage solutions, as well as differential privacy methods and limited access. Moreover, researchers need to inform participants what will happen to the data and how their data will be protected in the study.

b. Ethical Challenges in AI-Based Research:

Ethical dilemmas in AI research frequently arise when technology is deployed in sensitive and high-stakes domains, such as criminal justice, healthcare, or educational contexts (Vishwanath et al, 2020). For example, predictive models offer the potential to discover moments of intervention, but ultimately they can lead to important decisions being made based on hidden and opaque algorithms. One key methodological difficulty, highlighted by (Zou, J. Y., & Schiebinger, L. 2018), is that many AI models—especially those based on deep learning methods—do not have paths towards interpretable models, making it hard to "know" how a decision was made.

b.1. The effect of ethical dilemmas pose as boundaries in the integration of AI technology and system automation to research:

Research made possible by artificial intelligence (AI) and an increased automation of research systems has unleashed an unprecedented level of efficiency, accuracy, and creativity.

AI-based tools, encompassing a range of functions from data analytics to predictive modelling, harbinger a transformation of the way knowledge is generated and used. However, and like all technology, the implications of this new engagement with technology presents an array ethical issues. Ethical issues-- algorithmic bias, opacity (black box systems), (Kosinski, 2025) data ownership, privacy, and human judgement replacement-- are the major ethical bounds to the integration of AI into research.

These are critical issues that essentially relate to accountability, fairness and scientific freedom. For example, if automated systems are programmed to respond to flawed and/or biased data, the results can lead researchers astray and have seriously detrimental validity issues. Moreover, the opacity of most AI algorithms does not allow researchers and users to retrace what events led to a conclusion, and if this does happen (as it eventually will) it undermine trustworthiness in research. Thus, the ethical issues hexes must not be seen as impediments to movement forward, they are better seen as an incorporated handrails to the track and field areas of broader social value and responsible conduct of research principles (Floridi, 2019)

Let us discuss emergence of artificial intelligence (AI) and automated systems into the manufacturing research, the process has significantly accelerated the pace of innovation, allowing for predictive maintenance, process improvements, quality assurance, and supply chain refinements. New technologies allowing researchers to manipulate a variety of real-time, significant data, reduce the chance for human errors, and create more adaptable and responsive manufacturing systems. However, technology also comes with complex ethical challenges, mostly as barriers to full integration. Significant issues include biases in how algorithms are generated and how data are evaluated; confidentiality surrounding automatic methods of reasoning; and ownership and protection involving sensitive industrial information. The new technologies also come with concerns around job loss tied to automation, especially the moral responsibilities researchers have developing a new system that could cause job loss or cause socioeconomic upheaval. In the research environment, these issues would be compounded by the fact that when AI models are trained on impartial sample sets, expecting to generate relevant outputs, these issues may lead to biased outcomes, inaccuracies, or incomplete performances or predictions. It is very important to make ethical considerations an integral part of the research design, and not only as liabilities on the path to new technology development, but also as rational limitations to ensure the appropriate and equitable use of AI and automation in context of broader guiding principles around sustainable development, health and safety, and human value.

c. Replicability of AI-enabled research:

Replicability is that a study's result can be replicated by external researchers with the same methodology, data, and analysis steps as in the original study. In traditional science, it is a cornerstone of validity if a study's results are not replicable, then their credibility is questionable.

With AI-based research, replicability has added layers of complexity because:

- **Algorithmic Transparency:**

Most AI methods "and particularly deep learning algorithms" are generally complex and even proprietary in nature, making it harder for other scientists to fully understand the process of decision-making or exactly replicate the same computational environment. Replication is not possible without source code, hyper parameters, and training protocols.

- **Data Accessibility:**

AI research is likely to be data-driven with extensive datasets, which may be proprietary, confidential, or covered under protection by privacy laws (e.g., GDPR). Even with proper documentation of methodology, no access to the exact training and test data may disallow others to replicate results.

- **Computational Environment:**

AI models are hardware, software library, and even random seed initialization dependent. Computing environment or dependency version variations by a little can result in variations, and the technical setup needs to be documented in minute detail for the purpose of replication.

- **Stochastic Nature of AI Models:**

Some machine learning algorithms utilize randomness (e.g., weight initialization or data shuffling). If these elements are not regulated and made public, attempts at replication can lead to varying outcomes.

- **Ethical and Legal Barriers:**

Certain AI-driven research, particularly national security or healthcare, cannot reveal its models or data due to ethical, legal, or security constraints. This can limit easy replication, and alternative approaches like synthetic data or model auditing in controlled environments must be used.

Why It Matters?

Replicability of AI-driven research is critical to:

1. Verify results and build confidence in AI-driven conclusions.
2. Enable peer scrutiny, making the model robust.
3. Facilitate incremental innovation, as researchers feel safe to work on top of earlier work.
4. Best Practices to Maximize Replicability:
5. Provide open-source code and full documentation.
6. Provide datasets where possible, or document full data generation protocols.
7. Use standard benchmarks and reporting conventions.
8. Report computational environment details (hardware, OS, library versions).
9. Control randomness by setting reproducible seeds and exposing them.

THE TRANSFORMATIVE EFFECTS OF AI TECHNOLOGICAL ADVANCEMENTS ON DIFFERENT RESEARCH DISCIPLINE'S METHODOLOGIES

AI technology has really shaken up the way research is done across a wide range of academic and scientific fields (Claude, J., Borbalan, R 2025). These changes are influencing how we gather, analyze, interpret, and apply data to create new knowledge. Here are some key ways AI is changing research methodologies in various areas:

1. Enhanced Data Analysis and Pattern Recognition:

The emergence of artificial intelligence has dramatically transformed how researchers analyze and interpret large and complex data sets in many areas of scientific inquiry. Statistical methods have their merit but often are not able to capture subtle and nonlinear relationships or accommodate the volume and extent of data today. Artificial intelligence, particularly through machine learning and deep learning methods can process large data sets at remarkable speed and accuracy uncovering complex patterns, trends, and connections that would otherwise remain hidden.

In medicine, for example, artificial intelligence methods are used to identify signs of disease in medical images, to predict the probability of specific outcomes for patients, and to analyze genomic data in order to support early diagnosis, prevention, and personalized treatment plans. In the social sciences and economics, artificial intelligence methods allow researchers to assess behaviors and economic trends from large groups of demographic data revealing valuable information about consumer behavior, labor market, and the effects of policies. Environmental science has greatly benefited from artificial intelligence as models can now analyze satellite images, climate data, and models to predict severe weather, model deforestation, and predict climate change over the long term.

What is particularly powerful about AI, is its ability to take unstructured or high-dimensional data such as text, images, or data from sensors-and learn and grow from these data in an ongoing manner.

This flexibility makes it a valuable resource for discovery, but also decision making and real-time monitoring. But, while artificial intelligence is making new advancements in how data is processed, it also requires a new layer of oversight to ensure that the conclusions it is providing are interpretable, reproducible, and ethical. It is important to be able to provide to these systems, data that is true, representative, and unbiased in order to maintain integrity and fairness in the perspectives of AI research.

2. Automation of Research Tasks:

Actual and direct applications of AI in research are automating tasks (Schützeneder, et al., 2024) that are time-consuming and labor-intensive. Tasks such as cleaning data, transcription, coding qualitative data, or even preliminary literature review, which all researchers need to carry out at some point, take a great deal of time and energy and therefore limit a researcher's ability to carry out higher order critical thinking, theorizing, or creative synthesis. There are software applications that are being implemented into research processes involving artificial intelligence and that facilitate easier experience conducting research as well as improving research efficiency and the rigor of output. Data 'cleaning and preprocessing' is one of the initial stages of conducting research and has historically been associated with separating out outliers, filling up missing values, creating consistency of format, identifying inconsistencies, or errors, and documenting the aforementioned issues. Artificial intelligence techniques naturally solve the majority of these issues and are able to penetrate deeply into extremely large data sets and report flags in real time (e.g., in economics, biology, and engineering, data sets) often consist of millions and eliminate or minimize the possibility of human error and even reduce the amount of time it takes to prepare data for an analysis.

In the fields of 'social sciences and humanities', despite tendencies to dismiss its utility as a burgeoning area in the social sciences and humanities, applications of AI "particularly those based on natural language processing (NLP)" are opening vast corpora of text to analysis. For instance, in historical scholarship and literary criticism, NLP software could read millions of volumes, archives, some databases of newspapers, and reveal thematic patterns, shifts in language, or trends in specific heterogeneous culture (for example, a study of visual images or photographs over time). The features being developed in these applications opened up new findings that would otherwise no longer be possible to extract solely because of the scale of data researchers could access. Researchers can start to ask very different questions, informed by some empirical patterns established by AI, in relationship to a processed mass of text.

In areas of 'qualitative research', such as psychology, sociology, and anthropology, AI is increasingly being used to perform 'transcribing and coding interview data' (Williams. 2025). As for example, speech-to-text software will now automatically produce transcripts accurately from hundreds or thousands of recorded interviews, and machine learning systems can help code qualitative data through automatically identifying patterns for themes, emotions, behaviors etc. AI doesn't displace the richness of nuance of insight from human researchers, and these tools are initial filters helping jump start the work; the first level filters that accelerate analysis and help to focus the manual coding more effectively and efficiently across a case.

Even 'literature reviews', the workhorse in academic research, will augmented by AI search capabilities, and AI summarization assistance.

Such software can search through thousands of journals, find citations, emphasize the main conclusions, and identify conceptual overlap between publications. This allows researchers to keep up with subjects in rapid development and pinpoint a section of the research more easily.

However, there are challenges to the automated research process. We need to be sure the outputs from AI can be replicated, we can be transparent about how tasks are being automated, and we balance the researcher's interpretative role while recognizing the researcher owns the entire research process. Automation must not be considered a substitute for human judgment but as a supplement. When used effectively AI can liberate scientists from work that is repetitive and boring and allow for critical thinking, thesis development, and theorizing that can lead to large steps in the sciences and scholarship.

3. Development of Predictive and Prescriptive Models:

One of the greatest opportunities that AI has generated for research is the ability to create predictive and prescriptive models—models that can not only look backwards to historical data, but also predict what will happen next and prescribe the best actions. Scientific models that have been developed have often emphasized explanation and post hoc reasoning (Hillier & Blog, 2023). The really unique aspect of our ability to develop models with AI is we can build dynamic, adaptive and continuously improving models that are data-driven and can change in real-time.

In public health, for example, AI-driven predictive models can predict the transmission of infectious disease, model the emergence of changing health trends, and anticipate the demand for resources based on changes in the population and environmental determinants. Machine learning was used to model aspects of transmission trends, estimate the impact of policy interventions, and model the allocation of critical medical supplies during the COVID-19 pandemic.

In business and economics, AI recognizes prescriptive analytics, where models not only predict customer preference or market trends but predict specific action, such as an increase in price, supply chain rerouting, or marketing campaign, with the greatest profitability possible or risk minimized. Prescriptive models, using real-time input data and optimization routines, generate actionable recommendations that can adapt to changing conditions.

In engineering and manufacturing domains, AI models use sensor data to predict machine failure (predictive maintenance) and optimize production schedules or resource plans (prescriptive logistics).

AI models can enhance process efficiency, reduce downtime, improve flexibility for just-in-time manufacturing, etc.

Of course, predictive and prescriptive capabilities of AI require accurate verification if they are to be trusted. Scientists will contend with elements of model uncertainty, data bias, and acceptable overfitting risks. There are ethical dilemmas to navigate too, especially if the predictions tie to important decisions in medicine, justice, or financial investment. The principles of transparency, interpretability, and human control still matter in responsible model deployment.

4. Interdisciplinary Integration:

Artificial intelligence is not only changing individual disciplines, but it is also acting as a catalyst for interdisciplinary issue, as people are encouraged to collaborate and work together with those across previously distinct disciplines. The convergence is reshaping the nature of research by creating inherent linkages between theoretical paradigms, tools, and sources of information, using different combinations of view, (Jordan & Mitchell, 2015)

Bioinformatics is a prominent example, where techniques from AI, which first evolved in computer science—machine learning, pattern recognition, statistical modeling—are now being applied to help interpret genomic sequences, predict protein structure, and model biological pathways. In bioinformatics, we can think of biology, and data science and statistics converging to generate knowledge that was previously unobtainable through traditional means.

In a similar endeavor, computational linguistics uses natural language processing (NLP), which is part of the AI field, to provide avenues for the study of human language. NLP grants linguists opportunities to work with computer scientists on exciting research projects, including work in machine translation, automatic classification of text, and speech recognition, which promote the advancement of theoretical linguistics alongside applied linguistics and technology.

In the social sciences, AI promotes, stimulates, and promotes interaction, especially in areas such as behavioral economics, cognitive science, and network theory. Researchers in these fields use machine learning to model complex systems that study agent behavior and/or represent social networks, all while using knowledge from fields such as physics, mathematics, and psychology.

AI further enables interdisciplinary exploration and collaboration, requiring institutions to innovate hybrid degrees that combine engineering with ethics and medicine with humanities. This interdisciplinary framework prepares researchers to face complex problems in the world, such as climate change, global health, and responsible stewardship of AI.

But, interdisciplinary convergence in fact depends upon more than one shared tool- it requires a shared understanding. Epistemological, linguistic, and interest differences in research among disciplines can rub up against each other. As AI continues to bridge these gaps, it is critical that shared respect, open communication, and a collaborative architecture can be established to co-produce knowledge.

The way Researchers prioritize benefit of AI technology without compromising the firmness of the methodology or ethical standards:

As artificial intelligence and automation come to the fore as important areas of interest in manufacturing research, the single largest challenge for researchers is how to apply their revolutionary advantages while not abandoning methodological rigor and ethics. Finding a balance between these two important axes entails a science-based and ethically responsible research process at every level.

First and foremost, researchers must design and plan upfront for ethics systems must be understanding in advance as to potential risks, examine implications for society, and incorporate data governance, safety, and human rights principles. Second, researchers must demonstrate methodological rigor by establishing an empirically tested theoretical foundation for their AI models, adhering to rigorous data quality, and leveraging statistical and computational techniques that maximize accuracy and reproducibility. Methodological transparency, in terms of detailed documentation of algorithms, reasoning, assumptions, constraints on the input flows, and decisions taken during the research process, is essential for the scientific establishment to have faith in the research.

In addition, cross-disciplinary teams are now widely recognized as an example of excellence in responsible artificial intelligence research. Involving ethicists, lawyers, subject matter experts, engineers, and a member of the affected community or workers' union, provides inputs that are (somehow) relevant. Cross-disciplinary teams help researchers better anticipate real-world consequences, address fairness issues, and ensure development of technology has relevance to regulatory compliance and societal values. Frameworks such as Responsible Research and Innovation (RRI), the IEEE's Ethically Aligned Design, and the FAIR Framework (Findable, Accessible, Interoperable, and Reusable) obviously provide vital pathways for aligning technological development with ethical accountability and social acceptance. These frameworks support thinking about long-term effects, stakeholder engagement and continuous improvement in development while maintaining sensitivity to the changing levels of risk and understanding. In short, suggesting that ethics can be enabled, rather than a barrier, leads researchers to not only develop artificial intelligence systems that are effective and intelligent, but reliable as well as good for society. This dual approach ensures progress made in machine-based or technology-enabled manufacturing is done in light of sustainable development, economic wealth and human wellness.

CASE STUDIES

This chapter will employ a mixed-methods approach that will be demonstrated in six real-life **case studies**—three successes and three problematic integrations:

1. Spanning biology,
2. healthcare,
3. Criminal justice,
4. manufacturing, environment,
5. And social media.

They underscore key factors for AI adoption success and pitfalls to avoid.

1. Alpha Fold by DeepMind in Protein Folding:

Alpha Fold is an end-to-end attention-based neural network that simultaneously learns from evolutionarily conserved sequences and residue-pair representations to predict 3D protein structures.

The outcome happened as follow, in (CASP14, 2025), Alpha Fold achieved atomic-level accuracy (median backbone RMSD 1.6 Å), outperforming all other methods and matching many experimental structures (Embl, 2025)

Thus, we can explain the influence, with over 200 million projected structures provided, the effort may have enabled drug discovery, enzyme design, and core biology research to further leverage billions of hours of experimental work. This achievement was based on a few substantial training data sources, close collaboration with domain experts, and desire to push open-science dissemination. As stated before, this is a major leap forward in applying AI to tackle some of the immense scientific problems, writ large, it demonstrates the power of neural networks to fundamentally change the traditional research paradigm. By predicting challenging protein structure with near-experimental accuracy, Alpha Fold has raised the bar in computational biology, resulting in unprecedented advances in drug development and enzyme design. The achievement of Alpha Fold demonstrates the critical component of abundant high-quality datasets, combined with collaborative engagement with teams of interdisciplinary scientists and continued commitment to open science. There are a few future examples that could be categorized as Alpha Fold doubling or radically multiplying the potential of other areas of AI-facilitated biological innovation, for example, the prediction of protein interaction, protein dynamics, and de novo design of biomolecules. The Alpha Fold approach serves as a template for interdisciplinary collaboration and broad application of deep learning AI, with the goal of creating models that can be adapted over time and made available as free, openly available, and data-driven resources.

Beyond biology, Alpha Fold reaffirms broader implications of how AI will revolutionize the scientific discovery process, inviting other domains to adopt the same open, collaborative, and data-driven philosophy. As AI potential continues to evolve, the technological twist needs to be put under the limelight of the ethical impact the technology imposes on scientific achievement in human intelligence.

2. IBM Watson for Oncology:

Watson for Oncology sought to decipher clinical guidelines and patient histories through NLP in order to suggest cancer treatments alongside Memorial Sloan Kettering and MD Anderson Cancer Center (Gandhi & Singh, 2023)

The result concluded is by 2016, clinicians were reporting unsafe or irrelevant suggestions; quality-assurance gaps and scant, unrepresentative training data led to dwindling adoption. IBM shut down the program in 2023 following a $4 billion investment.

Here there should be some Challenges and Insights:

- It emphasizes the requirement for varied and interoperable data sources.
- Large-scale clinical validation.
- And modest expectations.

The IBM Watson for Oncology saga illustrates the potential and pitfalls of implementing AI within complex clinical decision-making. Despite the major capital infusion and the collaborations with major cancer centers, Watson for Oncology's failure in implementing unsafe recommendations, and the cybernetic way people took recommendations up is telling fundamental issues with AI use cases in medicine. Important lessons learned are: a variety of good quality diverse reasoned and interoperable data are required; large scale extensive clinical validation is necessary; and reasonable expectations from AI are essential. Lastly, Watson for Oncology confirms the lesson that artificial intelligence is meant to enhance and not replace clinical specialist expertise. The way forward for AI in medicine is close-relationship between technology developers and clinicians to build trust, trustworthy, explainable patient care augmentation challenges, rather than diminished patient care.

3. COMPAS Recidivism Algorithm:

North pointe's COMPAS software provides risk scores (low/medium/high) for defendants, which are utilized by courts in making decisions regarding bail, sentencing, and parole. So as a result of this job, A Pro-Publica analysis in 2016 found Black defendants were nearly twice as likely as white defendants to be labeled "high risk" but not reoffend, and that there was considerable racial bias (M. Chawla, 2022).

The Challenges and Observations marked here is:

- Proprietary opaqueness.
- Un-transparency.
- And inadequate fairness auditing created due-process and ethical issues.

Algorithmic justice tools require explainable models, unbiased audits, and transparent accountability.

The COMPAS (Correctional Offender Management Profiling for Alternative Sanctions) recidivism algorithm case serves as a cautionary tale about the implications of applying AI for high-stakes decision-making within the justice system. While designed to provide objective risk assessment, the proprietary and non-transparent nature of this system presented significant ethical and legal issues, notably, racial bias and due-process violations. The investigation by Pro-Publica emphasized disturbing disparities in how data were used to create a COMPAS score between racial groups, underscoring the hazards of alien algorithms that have no standards of fairness drawn from a rigorous pre-determined assessment of fairness, accountability, or transparency. The case highlights the immediate need for explainable AI models, open-source transparency, and independent accountability, especially when actions of public officials affect individual civic and human rights. It also reinforced previous conclusions that any algorithmic tool that is used within the domain of justice must be fundamentally bound by the highest standards of fairness, interpretability, and public accountability. As AI tools continue to be integrated into legal and governmental institutions, equity, transparency, and trustworthiness are no longer options, but imperatives.

4. Predictive Maintenance with Siemens Sens eye at Blue Scope:

Siemens puts Initiatives and Synthesis represented by conversational interface (Sens eye Predictive Maintenance) for monitoring equipment health (Hörmann, 2024), (Sweeney, 2024).

So the initiation of Siemens Results in outcomes. At BlueScope's steelworks (Australia), the system predicts abnormal vibrations ahead of time, minimizing unplanned downtime, increasing operating time, and reducing maintenance expenses.

The lessons learned here in some points. It shows how the integration of domain knowledge, real-time information, and user-centered AI UIs can enhance industrial productivity. Success factors include robust sensor networks, clear ROI metrics, and easy human-machine interaction.

The implementation of Siemens Sens Eye Predictive Maintenance system at BlueScope's Australian steelworks provides a dramatic example of the strategic application of AI to improve efficiency, reliability, and cost-effectiveness of industrial operations. By employing real-time sensor readings and AI-driven analytics, the system could predict abnormal equipment vibrations days in advance of failure, allowing maintenance staff to take early action. This planned approach resulted in significantly fewer instances of unplanned downtime, extended machinery lifespan, and measurable maintenance cost savings—talking points for concern in any high-volume manufacturing process.

The secret to the success of this project lies not in the technology alone but in the meticulous integration of several important factors. Firstly, domain expertise took center stage in shaping the learning environment for the AI, allowing the system to accurately interpret complex operational signals. Secondly, the use of dense sensor networks facilitated the round-the-clock provision of high-quality data, which is the cornerstone of accurate condition monitoring and predictive analytics. Third, Sens Eye's user-oriented interface and dialogue interface opened the system to plant operators and bridged the gap between technical sophistication and day-to-day usability.

Also, the BlueScope case demonstrates the importance of having clear return-on-investment (ROI) metrics in place while adopting AI in industrial settings. The operational benefits demonstrated "such as increased uptime, better resource planning, and cost reduction" provided tangible justification for the use of AI solutions.

This example reflects a general trend in manufacturing whereby decision-makers are seeking both innovative solutions, and evidence of improved performance and cost effectiveness. Importantly, this case study validates an important insight for the future uses of AI in the industrial domain: most successful solutions exist at the intersection of technology, human-centered design, and contextual knowledge. Artificial intelligence systems, like Sens Eye, do not operate in isolation; they do not become beneficial until they are integrated smoothly with human users and meshed with the working conditions of the manufacturing environment. As manufacturing sectors evolve to smart manufacturing and Industry 4.0 frameworks, BlueScope's experience with Siemens Sens Eye also provides a model for how predictive AI-based systems can inflict successful transformation - as long as they are anchored in the requisite technology, the right alignment and consideration of human and AI collaboration/emphasize usability.

5. Global Forest Watch & Orbital Insight for Deforestation Monitoring:

Global Forest Watch partnered with Orbital Insight to harness deep learning on satellite images—identification of early signs of commodity-driven deforestation such as new logging roads (Petersen, et al, 2018). The remarked Results of this partnering, was that the platform generates near real-time information on loss of tree cover so that the NGOs and governments can start enforcement and conservation efforts earlier (Finley, 2015).

CHALLENGES AND INSIGHTS

Models have to deal with cloud cover, sensor inconsistency, and regional heterogeneity. Success depends on ongoing retraining, coupling with on-the-ground validation, and cross-sectoral collaboration.

This collaboration provides evidence that AI and satellite assessments can bring about significant change in addressing one of the biggest environmental challenges of our time, global deforestation. By using state-of-the-art deep learning methods on high-resolution satellite images, the collaboration was able to detect weak, but potentially important early signals of forest degradation such as logging roads and small-scale clearing. This innovation enables alerts for near real-time deforestation, essentially changing the game for governments, NGOs, and environment stakeholders trying to respond to illegal or unsustainable land use. The magnitude of this innovation, furthermore, is not only in its technological potential; rather, it is the disruptive role it plays in relation to environmental monitoring and law enforcement. Prior to this the vast bulk of deforestation reporting was largely retrospective, after so much tree cover had already been lost forever. The lag time between the absence of tree cover and its discovery often allowed person opportunity to commit unsustainable damage with little to no accountability. This AI-based system, however, grants decision-makers the opportunity to respond in almost an anti-deforestation fashion--sent out enforcement teams, commence legal processes, or provide conservation interventions when it hardly started.

There was a combination of aspects that allowed the initiative to thrive. Firstly, the direct processing of large quantities of satellite images through scalable automated deep learning models reduced both the human and time investment needed for forest monitoring. Secondly, the main agri-commodity-driven deforestation based on traceable global supply chains of agriculture, mining, and logging was directly addressing a key driver and therefore putting the AI tools into real socio-economic need, creating large value for corporate responsible standard and policy investment. Thirdly, as an open access platform, the Global Forest Watch could be used transparently by a huge array of actors from small NGOs to global agencies who could act quickly and authoritatively based on real, accurate data. In addition, this case study illustrates potential insights into the wider applicability of AI for global sustainability. It demonstrates the cross-sector partnerships combining technical expertise and environmental domain expertise to overcome persistent barriers in conservation such as time-lags in data availability, large spatial scale, and limited human capacity for monitoring and surveillance.

It further underscores the role of public accountability and responsible AI behavior. Timely, unambiguous information is crucial to mobilizing political will and holding industries accountable for activities toxic to the environment.

For the future, this project is a guide for the potential of AI as a force multiplier in environmental management. As ecological decline and climate change accelerate across the globe, new technologies like those of Global Forest Watch and Orbital Insight will be critical in observing and responding to human footprint on natural systems. As satellite resolution improves, machine learning accuracy improves, and as we see policy related to climate and conservation chained together across the spectrum of human activity, an AI-based monitoring system for forests could be at the center of international and national conservation policy, enabling more intelligent, timely, and collaborative environmental supervision.

6. Microsoft's Tay (Chat bot):

Tay was a conversational chatbot constructed on Twitter designed to learn from 18–24 year-olds with minimal content safeguards. The Results within 16 hours of launch (March 23–24, 2016), coordinated malicious inputs made Tay tweet racist an offensive tweets; Microsoft shut it down and apologized

The experience of Microsoft's Tay chatbot is a grave cautionary tale of the ethical, technological, and social difficulties of releasing AI systems into open user-directed environments. Tay was developed as a conversational AI experiment to interact with young Twitter users and to learn language patterns from its dialogue with those users. However, it lacked robust content moderation, strong protection, and did not undergo adversarial testing, so it was prime territory for manipulation. Within 16 hours, hostile users were able to manipulate Tay's learning and then to have it generate and publish hateful, racist, sexist, and offensive content, which Microsoft promptly responded to by taking down the chatbot and issuing a formal apology.

These events highlight some important lessons for developers of AI systems in the future. First, it requires designing for ethical foresight and against malicious intent. Open-sourced or real-time learning types of models that have public interaction should build in strong filters, moderated policies, and adaptive learning limits to resist malice. Second, the Tay experience exposes the design limits of unsupervised machine learning in social contexts where human behavior itself can be unpredictable and vile (Schwartz, 2024).

The assumption that AI could passively "learn" from the internet without absorbing its worst qualities was revealed to be inherently misguided.

Additionally, Tay noted that it is vital to build diverse and inclusive testing frameworks prior to launch. Developers need to consider worst-case scenarios and put their conversational agents through adversarial situations to test the systems' toughness. The case also raises questions about the responsibility of technology companies to consider the social and cultural context of the market in which they launch their AI, especially if those systems are engaged in public information conversations, or have impacts on vulnerable users.

More broadly, Tay's breakdown has emerged into a cautionary myth in the AI community; a reminder that technical advancement must be tempered by ethical brakes, social awareness, and responsible oversight.

In brief it is a learning moment; an indication that AI systems don't only reflect language, they also reflect the values, purposes, and systems we insert into them. In the context of evolving AI chatbots, Tay's lessons are still valid: design within limits, test with caution, and always be thoughtful about how AI users interact with their human users based on the principles of human dignity and safety. All of these case studies provide concrete lessons, both positive and cautionary, around the complex issues with adopting AI in research and operational work streams.

FUTURE DIRECTIONS OF AI IN RESEARCH METHODOLOGIES

1. Evolution of Artificial Intelligence and Research Practices:

Artificial Intelligence, in its various forms and uses, is evolving rapidly and fundamentally changing applied and scholarly research. Emerging trends include increasing use of foundation models (like GPT-4, and its immediate successors) for a variety of research purposes including hypothesis generation, experiment planning, and literature synthesis, as well as the advent of (Auto ML) and (low-code/no-code AI platforms) which allows non-domain expert researchers to build and deploy models at a low-cost. Additionally, (multimodal AI) that can process text, image, sound, and even video at once implies exciting new research possibilities in the humanities, social behavioral science, and environmental science. As AI tools continue to develop and capitalize on larger society's acceptance, they will increasingly be regarded as a standard research tool across most research contexts.

The second trend consists of self-learning and adaptive tools that potentially could learn from constantly updating information in context, thus modifying their functioning of research tools, or further adjusting experimental design in real-time. Other tools to support collaborative work that involve AI and smart agents, are also in the development stage to assist in project management, grant writing and peer review, creating a new era when AI supports not just elements of the analysis process, but entire phases of the research process.

2. Future Research Directions:

There are a few major groups of research areas that warrant consideration: AI bias and data quality: How do we design routes for auditing and cleaning training data, in particular, in interdisciplinary areas where datasets would be messy, or unstructured or biased in terms of context? AI and epistemology: What is it about AI that "generates" knowledge? Are hypotheses or correlations generated by machines "scientifically valid"? Can they be researchers' human interpretations? Explainable AI (XAI): How do you explain models or explain research processes, so that researchers new to the field can trust and verify their outputs? In addition there would be experimental research needed to measure the "impact of AI on quality, speed and innovation in research". This includes testing both AI-based and conventional approaches to research and comparing them.

3. Policy Implications and Need for Interdisciplinary Collaboration:

With the integration of AI in research activities, this raises serious implications for policy. Governments, universities and sponsors must develop "regulatory frameworks and ethical guidelines" on when and how use AI tools responsibly and fairly. There are needed enforceable and transparent standards regarding "data privacy, academic integrity, model accountability and intellectual property. Regarding "data privacy, academic integrity, model accountability and intellectual property".

This calls for "interdisciplinary collaboration" between computer scientists, ethicists, lawyers, social scientists, and domain experts. Only through this collaboration can we develop policies that are technically sound, ethically acceptable, and practically enforceable. For instance, an AI tool under construction by a research group to study historical texts must do so in consultation with historians, linguists, and data scientists so that the latter may authenticate and be culturally sensitive.

4. Final Recommendations and Reflections on the Balance between Opportunity and Challenge

While the potential of AI in research is immense accelerating speed, scalability, and breakthroughs so too are concerns, especially around ethics, bias, and truth. Final recommendations, therefore, are:

1. Investing in AI literacy and training in researchers from all disciplines so that they utilize intelligently and critically AI tools.
2. Developing rigorous assessment standards for results produced by AI, including human vetting and domain-specific validation.
3. Create open, interdisciplinary spaces for AI development, where transparency, reproducibility, and collaboration are valued more than proprietary control.

4. Cultivate ethical innovation by baking fairness audits, explainability, and inclusivity into every stage of AI research development. Ultimately, the future of AI in research will depend not only on technological advancement but on our ability to steer it with "responsibility, humility, and foresight".

Challenges & Lessons:
It stresses the need for adversarial-testing, ethical monitoring, and layered moderation before deploying self-learning agents into open worlds.

1. Key Findings Data Diversity & Quality: At the heart of success and equity.
2. Transparency & Interpretability: Essential in high-stakes domains (justice, healthcare).
3. Domain Alignment: Close working with subject matter experts ensures relevance.
4. Comprehensive Verification: Continuous auditing and real-world testing reduce harmful
5. Effects. Human-AI Collaboration: User-friendly interfaces and well-defined role allocations optimize usage.

CONCLUSION

This chapter gives a robust rubric for understanding the benefits and caveats of integrating AI into research methods; aiming to balance theoretical reading, practical application, in conjunction with real-world expert opinions. The authors have made findings aiming to inform not just scholarly research, but the more practical application, so that the power of AI can be harnessed in safe and effective ways. Thus, it presents a rubric for investigating the advantages and caveats of integrating AI into the research process.

Merging what would theoretically seem to be the complete opposite, AI is fundamentally changing the production, interpretation, and application of knowledge in whichever research discipline.

This paper has highlighted AI's transformative potential, but also its multifarious challenges for undertaking research. AI is already reshaping the epistemological and operational boundaries of research, whether it be advancing the frontiers of data analysis, automating tedious tasks, democratizing predictive modeling, or enabling faster fusions across disciplines.

Related but equally important are issues-algorithmic bias, risk signals brought by data privacy, and a multitude of other ethics issues that make apparent the validity, objectivity and accountability of AI assisted research.

Many of these issues are not just technical, they are foundational—philosophical and pragmatic issues, that either legitimize or discredit knowledge produced through AI. The dangers of reproducing or exacerbating social inequities arise from the use of discriminatory data sets, confounding model and ill-considered systems must certainly continue to be deliberated and assessed ethically. The analyses of real case studies, whether it's the highly successful Alpha Fold in protein folding research; the failures in the medical context of IBM Watson for Oncology and Microsoft's Tay chatbot; predictive maintenance in manufacturing; or the monitoring of deforestation with AI, reflect the promise of AI to provide new level of understanding in relation to the costs of resignation.

These snapshots highlight an age-old axiom: technical capacities bring nothing in the way of responsible innovation. Successful reliance on AI's opportunities will depend on intentional co-alignment with Indigenous knowledge, stakeholder engagement, open audits, and ongoing ethical deliberation. In addition to showing the above, the research also documents how ethics issues are increasingly posing limitations that are shaping when, where, and for what use AI may be utilized in research. These boundaries are not simply limitations but guides to address ethical and inclusive AI practices. Researchers have a responsibility to enable and share the power of AI with speed, scale, and complexity, while not sacrificing the integrity of traditional methods nor ignoring good ethical practices. In the future, researchers will include directions with AI applied to practice, including multimodal AI, machine scientific discovery, and human-AI collaboration. However, that future must be co-designed with robust policies, transdisciplinary collaboration, and a focus on inclusive, equitable, and explainable AI. Research institutions, policymakers, and developers must work together to develop the infrastructure that allows for both innovation and accountability.

REFERENCES

Bhandari, P. (2024). Ethical considerations in research: Types & examples. Scribbr. https://www.scribbr.com/methodology/research-ethics/

CASP14. (2025). https://predictioncenter.org/casp14

Chawla, M. (2022), COMPAS Case Study: Investigating Algorithmic Fairness of Predictive Policing, Human stories & ideas.

Claude, J., & Borbalan, R. (2025). The transformative impact of artificial intelligence on Higher Education: A critical reflection on current trends and Futures Directions -. https://journals.sagepub.com/doi/10.1177/2212585X251319364

Embl, N. D. (2025). European Molecular Biology Laboratory.EMB L.org.https://www.embl.org

Finley, K. (2015). *Using Satellites to Stop Deforestation Before It Happens*. Wired.

Floridi, L., & Cowls, J. (2019). A unified framework of five principles for AI in society. *Harvard Data Science Review*. Advance online publication. DOI: 10.1162/99608f92.8cd550d1

Gandhi, P., & Singh, N. (2023). *From healthcare canary to a failed prodigy a case study in the "AI age" for business schools for decades*. IPM Watson.

Hillier, W., & Blog, W. (2023). The best guide to Predictive vs. prescriptive analytics. Career Foundry. https://careerfoundry.com/en/blog/data-analytics/predictive-vs-prescriptive-analytics/ Home[eXtyles2.1] -

Hörmann, F. (2024), Generative artificial intelligence takes Siemens' predictive maintenance solution to the next level, press.siemens.com

Jonker, A., & Rogers, J. (2025). What is algorithmic bias? IBM. https://www.ibm.com/think/topics/algorithmic-bias#:~:text=Algorithmic%20bias%20occurs%20when%20systematic,produce%20unfair%20or%20discriminatory%20outcomes

Jordan, M. I., & Mitchell, T. M. (2015). Machine learning: Trends, perspectives, and prospects. *Science*, *349*(6245), 255–260. DOI: 10.1126/science.aaa8415 PMID: 26185243

Kartik, M., & Follow. (2025). Machine learning algorithms. Geeks forGeeks. https://www.geeksforgeeks.org/machine-learning-algorithms/

Kosinski, M. (2025), What is black box AI and how does it work? IBM. https://www.ibm.com/think/topics/black-box-ai

Petersen, R., Weisse, M., Lewandowski, E., Swartz, T., & Wang, L. (2018), Artificial Intelligence Helps Distinguish the Forest from the Trees: Part 1, Global Forest Watch, globalforestwatch.org.

Russell, S., & Norvig, P. (2020). Pearson. A foundational text in AI that covers key algorithms and techniques. A Modern Approach (4th ed.).

Schützeneder, J., Michael, G., Porlezza, C., & Mazzoni, P (2024). AI and automation. A key task for the present and future, DOI: .DOI: 10.4324/9781032630410-13

Schwartz, O. (2024). In 2016, Microsoft's racist Chatbots revealed the dangers of online conversation. IEEE Spectrum. https://spectrum.ieee.org/in-2016-microsofts-racist-chatbot-revealed-the-dangers-of-online-conversation

Sweeney, E., (2024), Siemens' AI tools are harnessing 'human-machine collaboration' to help workers solve maintenance problems, Business insider.

Vishwanath, A. L. S., Seng, N., Goh, P., Lee, S., Khader, M., Ong, G., & Chin, J. (2020). Cyber hygiene. The concept, its measure, and its initial tests, Decision Support Systems, Volume 128, 2020, 113160, ISSN 0167-9236.

Williams, B. (2025). AI tools for transcribing and coding field interviews - insight7 - AI tool for Interview Analysis & Market Research. Insight7. https://insight7.io/ai-tools-for-transcribing-and-coding-field-interviews/

Zou, J. Y., & Schiebinger, L. (2018). AI can be sexist and racist — It's time to make it fair. *Nature*, *559*(7714), 324–326. DOI: 10.1038/d41586-018-05707-8 PMID: 30018439

Chapter 15

Integrating AI in Educational Research Methodologies:

Opportunities, Challenges, and Theoretical Insights

Md. Saddam Hossain
https://orcid.org/0009-0001-9996-4963
Khulna University, Bangladesh

Farhana Yeasmin
https://orcid.org/0000-0002-0954-7489
Jashore University of Science and Technology, Bangladesh

Md. Sahjahan Kabir
Khulna University, Bangladesh

Bitan Kumar Mandal
Office of the Deputy Commissioner, Khulna, Bangladesh

ABSTRACT

The Artificial Intelligence (AI) has become a usual component of educational research. This chapter examines the use of AI tools (ChatGPT, ResearchRabbit, Scholarcy, Scite, etc.) in literature reviews, data analysis and academic writing. It uses Technological Pedagogical Content Knowledge (TPACK) framework that focuses on the importance of balance between the content, pedagogy and technology and the Activity Theory that analyses the influence of AI on the relationships between researchers, tools, and systems within the institutions. As real-world applications suggest, AI may help people perform the task quicker and yield more profound insights, but there are still the problems of academic integrity, digital access, and overreliance to tackle. The chapter demands the literacy of AI and the responsible use in such a way that research becomes relevant and universal. Ultimately, AI is to be considered as an assistant and not as a substitute of academic reasoning.

DOI: 10.4018/979-8-3373-2752-5.ch015

INTRODUCTION

Artificial Intelligence (AI) phenomenon is forming a paradigm proverb in the scholarly research, that is completely revolutionizing how researchers create, report and distribute their knowledge. With the ever-changing and evolving technology characterizing an advanced academic institution, the AI has come to take the lead regarding the efficiency, precision, and other procedures that are oriented towards innovation in research creation. Whether it is natural language processing with academic texts to give a summary of them or machine learning to study data, AI technologies are no longer replaceable in the field of active scholars and novice researchers. Even though the mainstream remains technical, the effects of AI do not confine themselves to this area: research in social sciences, education, and humanities is also evolving, which means that it harbors immense opportunities yet happens in parallel to a number of ethical, cognitive, and methodological challenges.

Application of AI technologies in research is complicated. The actual innovation of such a nature as Yewno Discover has turned the process of literature search upside-down as it provides an opportunity to conduct natural, semantic searches of scholarly databases, by reducing the time required to locate a relevant search by orders of magnitude (Michalak, 2024). The models of AI will be able to read up about thousands of articles, identify research trends, and highlight the relevant findings thereby expanding the extent and range of the literature review (Alaa, 2024). A capability to do so can come in handy particularly when identifying the research gaps, or even in formulating research questions. AI provides the researcher with an opportunity to direct more energy and resources into developing the intelligentsia and skills, such as concept designing, critical thinking, and theory-building (Agrawal et al., 2024; Biondi-Zoccai et al., 2025).

Another outstanding role of AI is citation management. The researchers can now manage reference management, bibliography citation and insertion of citations in real-time with greater accuracy and consistency than ever using AI-powered reference management tools, like Zotero, Mendeley, and EndNote (Alaa, 2024; Oyelude, 2024). These platforms tend to integrate well with the generally familiar processors of words, such as Microsoft word and Google documentation with the aim of giving a seamless and natural writing and referencing experience, thereby helping in the iterative optimization of the bibliographic cross sections and advancing the consciousness of the researcher in the domain (Meade et al., 2023; Wahditiya et al., 2023).

Despite all these advantages, there is the hitch to the increased reliance of the scholarly tasks on AI. Especially, the issue of hallucination of citations is among the highest priorities as AI models, such as ChatGPT or Google Gemini, offer references, but in the real sense, they are not but seem real (Watson, 2024). Fake citations may have realistic names of authors, publication years and even journals, and thus they will not be identified easily. They may have a negative outcome when adhered to and not critically analyzed since this may serve to degrade the level of academic integrity as well as lead to misinformation. Even though AI can make the speed of article creation, as it is pointed out in the arguments provided by Akhoon et al. (2024), it has to be within the framework of human control as it has to be vetted in terms of accuracy of facts and scholastic integrity.

In addition, the unquestioning faith in the results of AI is the cause of false science. Both bibliographic and analytical AI suggestions can be taken by the majority of users without any control thus leading to inaccuracy that negatively affects the quality of work (Clelland et al., 2024). This is particularly worrisome when it comes to academic world. In this area, sources must be adequately verified. Overuse of the AI can suppress the abilities of critical thinking and promote thinking shortcuts, compromising the academic rigor in the long term (Zhai et al., 2024).

Academic dishonesty has been one of the playing fields among the widespread use of generative AI. One can be tempted by students and any other kind of researcher (novice) who is going to copy paste/place the results (those words that AI generates which are easy to remember) and consider it his/her own, not even understanding (unconsciously) that he/she has just plagiarized or violated ethical codes of scholars (Kovari, 2025). The problems of authorship and accountability of the work produced by people and AI become even more complicated and complex due to the fluidity of the boundary between them, which requires the development of efficient frameworks of identification and training programs, which would focus on the responsible utilization of AI (Mecca & Shkelzeni, 2023).

The digital divide is also there. Access to a set of innovative AI tools is not equal among the institutions or geographical areas. The new resources of AI may not be used by scientists in the less highly funded universities or in the developing countries as they do not necessarily have the technological infrastructure to make use of it. This kind of gap exacerbates current educational disparities and prevents the representation in the sphere of global academic discourse of an equally broad selection of voices (Mecca & Shkelzeni, 2023; Kovari, 2025; Yaroshenko & Iaroshenko, 2023; Rashidov, 2024).

Moreover, the recent reports have also revealed that over-reliance on AI to accomplish some good processes like reading or writing support can lead to negative impacts on cognitive processes. In an illustrative case scenario, students who were over relying on AI were reported to fail in the critical reading test, which alludes to the threat of the loss of some of the major cognitive skills (Cahyani et al., 2024). In its turn, this led to the growing demand in the solutions which would include teaching critical thinking about AI tools- the educational intervention, which would enable students to keep the skill of the analysis, reasoning, and synthesis even while working with the powerful capabilities of AI (Zhai et al., 2024; Cahyani et al., 2024).

Irrespective of such problems, potential benefits of AI in research are tremendous. Artificial intelligence-based tools may help in delivery of ideas, mapping, and even hypotheses. Applications are presented by ResearchRabbit, Scite, and Litmaps to what might be considered an exciting future, namely to search for a topic of research relevant to one another and trace patterns of citations (Prashar & Chander, 2024; Molopa, 2024). The summarization of heavy literary texts could be accelerated with the help of such tools as Scholarcy, Unriddle, and Avidnote in order to become accessible to researchers and to enable them jump into a massive amount of literature and experience its range successfully (Bui & Bui, 2024; Deshpande, 2023; Kusters et al., 2020).

Furthermore, AI enhances data analysis on both qualitative and quantitative researches. There are such services as MonkeyLearn services, Akkio, or Polymerserch, which analyze and run through complex sets of information in order to highlight pertinent trends and patterns. The AI-based visualization applications, like PowerBI, Flourish, and Julius AI increase the engagement of the researchers since they provide more power to present their findings clearly and in a format that can be understood easily (Abinaya, 2024; Biswas, 2024).

As the advancement of AI becomes entrenched more in the academic setting, it becomes extremely critical that ethical frameworks are presented. Among the challenges that such structures ought to address include information confidentiality, the transparency of algorithms in AI systems and open acknowledgement of work. The academic world can as well initiate an effort of developing AI literacy in the researcher and student departments. It is the awareness of mechanics behind AI-based instruments and constraints they are subjected to and the ability to critically assess consequences AI-based instruments provide (Srivastava, 2024; Shah, 2024; Rashidov & Rashidova, 2024).

Finally, institutional policies and rules should also be established to render the use of AI justifiable in the academic environment. Recent research in the field of AI development should be financially invested into by institutions, the tools available to solve the tasks should be equalized, and discussion of the cross-disciplinary nature about AI morals and approaches to optimization possible should be assisted. One can employ the full potential of the AI as the change making agent of the academic innovation that does not involve or diminish in any respect the integrity and equity of the research process only in the moderated and informed form.

The use of AI tools in the academic management and references research is a possibility and a challenge. The tools increase productivity, offer a detailed analysis, and allow creating explorations. Nevertheless, they do pose a risk of misinformation, academic dishonesty, over-reliance, and unfairness in education as well. Teachers and scientists ought to come to terms with the recognition that they cannot work in a vacuum and there is necessity to take advantages of the opening that Artificial Intelligence offers yet everyone ought to safeguard the very essence of scholarship quality, professionalism and inclusiveness. Chapters, that will be followed, will assist in exploring functions of the AI tools to review literature, analyze data and manage citations and write scholarly works as well as will consider ethical implications and provide certain pieces of strategic advice on the further usage of this practice.

AI TOOLS IN RESEARCH AND EDUCATION

AI tools play great roles in educational research. Basically, an overview of AI will be introduced in this section for offering a good conception of such types tools related to the research. Here it will be disclosed that AI has the power and potentiality to revolutionize data collection, analysis, and interpretation. The section will provide a larger framework for AI's incorporation into educational practices, with an emphasis on research as a critical area of reform. The adoption of Artificial Intelligence (AI) in education has transformed the teaching and learning scenario in different education levels, be it at primary school or at university. AI tools provide a tech individualized training process, improve administrative process optimization, and the ability of teachers to take data-based decisions, thus improving the engagement levels and educational outcomes among the students (Leong et al., 2025; Boumediene & Bouakkaz, 2024). In academia, AI makes adaptive teaching and learning possible and helps university students in their studies by automating duties including literature research, data processing, and writing (Maphalala & Ajani, 2025; Labib & ElSabry, 2024). Such programs as ChatGPT, ResearchRabbit, Scholarcy, and Scite are currently making an impact on the way researchers ask questions, identify research gaps, cite their work, and come up with ideas, thus speeding up the process of academic work and extending its boundaries. As an example, ResearchRabbit and Litmaps help visualize interconnected literature, so possible gaps in the literature review can be found, and Scholarcy and Avidnote allow summarizing large academic documents in concise, yet understandable form. Not only are these applications transforming methodologies, but they are also conforming to the literary models of pedagogy such as TPACK and Activity Theory which focus on balanced inquiry of technology, content area, and pedagogy and the systemic influence of AI on institutional research. Nevertheless, the incorporation of the AI poses some new, urgent concerns, such as hallucinating citations, reduced critical thinking, overdependence, and the ethical concerns of authorship and academic integrity. Digital inequality is amplified by other issues in the field, including algorithmic discrimination and biases, lack of accessibility to AI-based tools, which requires AI-environmental inclusion and controlled ecosystems (Ojha et al., 2024; Boumediene & Bouakkaz, 2024). As the means to alleviate these concerns, the promotion of AI literacy, application of universal design principles, and development of policies of equitable access are necessary. What is more, the COVID-19 pandemic has precipitated the integration of AI in online learning and research environments and has required upgraded digital skills and institutional assistance of both educators and learners (Yadav, 2024; Wangdi, 2024). Notwithstanding its revolutionary possibilities, the successful process of sustainable AI integration depends on the constant professional growth, inter-professional collaboration, and critical thinking concerning its social consequences. With the advancement of this technology, educational stakeholders should conduct an informed debate that would allow employing the positive aspects of AI without compromising the integrity, inclusiveness and ethical conduct of education research and practice (Wangdi, 2024; Ojha et al., 2024).

Table 1. A Concise list of AI Tools Used in Research and Education

AI Tool	Primary Function	Contribution to Research
IBM Watson	Natural language processing and AI analytics platform	Processes large datasets and extracts insights for research decision-making.
Google AI	Machine learning platform by Google for AI model development	Enables training, deployment, and scaling of AI models for research and experimentation.
Research Kick	AI research discovery and literature summarization tool	Accelerates literature reviews by summarizing and recommending relevant research papers.
Concensus	Peer-reviewed semantic search and consensus engine	Synthesizes peer-reviewed results to answer research questions with evidence.
Scispace	AI academic platform for literature search and summarization	Helps scholars find relevant academic papers and summarize key ideas quickly.
ChatGPT	Generative AI for content creation and academic writing	Supports academic content creation, paraphrasing, and question formulation.
ResearchRabbit	Literature discovery and citation network visualization	Identifies scholarly connections and emerging themes through visual citation mapping.
Scite	Citation analysis and context-based classification	Provides citation reliability by analyzing the context and sentiment of citations.
Ref-N-Write	Academic paraphrasing and writing assistant	Improves originality and coherence in academic text writing.
Aveskana	Research topic detection and analysis using AI	Identifies trending research domains and maps knowledge graphs.
Litmaps	Citation-based literature visualization	Assists researchers in identifying and visualizing citation trails and topics.
Connected Papers	Visual exploration of related academic papers	Maps co-citation networks and recommends related academic papers.
Zotero	Reference management system	Manages references, generates citations, and integrates with word processors.
Mendely	Academic reference and collaboration manager	Organizes research references and supports collaboration among researchers.

continued on following page

Table 1. Continued

AI Tool	Primary Function	Contribution to Research
EndNote	Reference and citation manager for researchers	Helps manage and insert citations and bibliographies across research documents.
PaperPal	Academic grammar and writing enhancement tool	Provides language support, grammar correction, and clarity enhancement for academic writing.
Jenni.AI	AI writing assistant for scholarly work	Assists with sentence restructuring, content flow, and academic tone.
PowerBI	Business analytics and data visualization	Visualizes datasets to aid in research reporting and communication.
Flouslrish	Data storytelling and visualization platform	Transforms data into visual stories for research dissemination.
Julius.AI	Data analysis assistant for spreadsheet queries	Answers analytical questions about spreadsheet data for researchers.
PaperPile	Cloud-based reference management tool	Stores and organizes academic references for easy access and citation.
Dimensions	Research metrics and publication analytics platform	Offers metrics and insights about journals, authors, and research impact.
Scholarcy	Academic summarization and study aid tool	Summarizes academic papers to enhance study efficiency and comprehension.
Unriddle	AI-powered reading assistant for comprehension	Assists readers in understanding and retaining information from academic texts.
Avidnote	Digital note-taking and research annotation tool	Enables structured annotation and note organization during literature review.
Gamma	AI presentation and storytelling design tool	Creates AI-assisted presentations that summarize research visually.
Auxi	AI writing assistant for academic writing and editing	Improves research clarity through grammar checks and editing suggestions.
Elicit	Semantic research assistant for literature synthesis	Finds relevant papers, summarizes arguments, and extracts key data.
Akkio	AI-driven data analysis and predictive modeling tool	Generates predictive insights and visualizes complex data patterns.
MonkeyLearn	Text analysis and sentiment classification platform	Performs sentiment and text classification for qualitative research.
Quillbot	Paraphrasing and rewriting assistance	Rewrites content to improve clarity, tone, and academic integrity.
Grammarly	Grammar and academic writing enhancement	Corrects grammar, enhances fluency, and ensures formal academic style.
Turnitin	Plagiarism detection and originality verification	Verifies originality and identifies unintentional content duplication.
Connected Papers	Visual exploration of related academic papers	Maps co-citation networks and recommends related academic papers.
Polymerserch	Scientific paper analysis and visualization engine	Analyzes scientific paper structures and connects related research.

THEORETICAL FRAMEWORK

Technological Pedagogical Content Knowledge (TPACK) Framework – Mishra & Koehler (2006)

The concept of implementing Artificial Intelligence (AI) instruments into academic research described in the chapter has certain harmony with the TPACK framework suggested by Punya Mishra and Matthew J. Koehler (2006). The chatbots, including ChatGPT, ResearchRabbit, Scholarcy, Zotero, and Mendeley, can be considered significant changes in the Technological Knowledge (TK) area because they help researchers to automate literature review, compose research questions, have their citations organized, and even produce structured research ideas. Nevertheless, in order to effectively and ethically employ the said tools in educational research, it is important that there should exist a proportionate inter-relationship between Content Knowledge (CK), Pedagogical Knowledge (PK) and Technoligical knowledge (TK). To give an example, although ChatGPT may be employed in generating an idea, only a researcher that has professionally developed the CK and PK is in a position to ensure that its products are of quality, relevant, and maintain integrity. This is essential in circumventing any form of misuse or excessive use of AI, which the chapter also signifies as a rising issue in the academic practice.

The TPACK framework has the capacity to offer a firm basis of dealing with ethical and pragmatic tensions that have emerged because of adoption of AI. The problems of hallucinated citations, plagiarism and cognitive short takes are symptoms of the misalignment in cases of technology deployed without the proper pedagogical or content foundations. The model introduced by Mishra and Koehler, in turn, challenges educators and researchers to deliberately combine those fields in order to define a responsible and knowledgeable use of AI tools. The focus of the chapter on developing AI literacy, achieving the justice in access to AI, and integrating ethical principles in research practices falls in line with this vision.

Activity Theory – Engestrom (1987), Building on Vygotsky

Yrjo Engestrom (1987) built on the legacy of Lev Vygotsky to elaborate the Activity Theory especially the Expansive Learning Model through which human activities could be comprehended by the use of tools in a complex social system. This framework can be largely applied in the situation of the chapter of the book titled AI in the Research Methodologies. The AI technologies, namely, Scite and the contextual citation analysis, ResearchRabbit and the trend mapping, and Avidnote and the summarization are different mediums that facilitate the research activity system. Such tools alter the interaction between the Subject (the researcher) and the Object (the research aims), and work within a wider Society (institutions of higher learning), which are ruled by the Convention (ethics), and split through the Division of Labor (between educators, researchers and AI developers). The discussion of real-life applications presented in the chapter makes it clear that AI tools are not peripheral but the main elements that transform the process of research.

Activity Theory is also very useful in finding and studying the contradictions in these systems, or rather tensions, which according to the theory are the driving force in change. Such contradictions as the ethical issues surrounding authorship, the digital divide, and excessive dependence on AI-produced products are outlined in the chapter. Such interferences indicate that there is need to adapt general aspects of the systems with what Engestrrom terms as expansive learning-

learning process in which the activity system changes in order to resolve its contradictions. This required reorganization of the research culture can be seen in the demand of the chapter about training in AI ethics, support in institutions, and equal access to tools. In such a way, Activity Theory does not only reveal the comprehension of the work of AI in the context of the existing academic systems, however, is also a philosophy of governing their responsible change.

OPPORTUNITIES OF AI TOOLS IN RESEARCH

AI Tools for Formulating Research Question

Formulating a clear and well-defined research question for article or thesis is an integral part. In this regard, different types of AI are used by the researchers to formulate research questions. These types of tools help to analyze the existing literature, identify trends, and suggest pertinent research problems. AI transforms research methodology by enhancing the identification of research questions and hypothesis development. It offers tools for efficient literature reviews and data analysis, utilizing techniques like natural language processing and expert systems (Srivastava & Shetye, 2024; Kawatra, 2024).

Research Kick: It assists the researchers to come up with research questions by examining past studies that had been conducted in the field of their concern. Research Kick assists a researcher to carry out the required analysis in order that he or she may come to the right research questions of a given topic by reviewing the past studies in his topic of interest. One of such categories of structuring that are provided by this tool and that assist in narrowing down the research questions, in particular, in the context of the clinical and health-based research however can be irrelevant in the context of certain types of studies (Hosseini et al., 2023) what is referred to in the form of the PICO (Population, Intervention, Comparison and Outcome) framework. With the current literature analyzed, it is now possible to find the gaps in the knowledge, the contextual aspects of them which further helps in writing an important and informed research question with Research Kick (Prabakaran, 2023).

Consensus: Main purpose of this software is based on AI which has been developed to help researchers in providing an answer to the research question by synthesizing the outcomes of certain meta-analysis and literature review results. It is based on the artificial intelligence that automates the process of literature retrieval and enhances the quality of the literature synthesis and review process. Not only does it promote efficiency, but it also saves time that is spent to retrieve and analyze huge volumes of scholarly information (Ejjami, 2024; Bolanos et al., 2024). Though AI involvement in such a procedure can definitely be useful, it should be implemented together with a human element, to address some of the probable algorithmic bias, as well as retain the contextual knowledge to draw the sound academic decisions.

Scispace: Based on data analytics and a technique of text mining, the tool helps in developing the research topics. It helps researchers to develop their subjects by use of data insight and text mining where one identifies patterns in un- structured data. Those approaches will assist in the identification of new trends and research interests and guide the researcher to the more targeted and informed questions (Li & Tsui, 2024; Subramani et al., 2024).

ChatGPT: ChatGPT may help brainstorm new research topics using the existing research or data provided to it by a user as an input to come up with ideas about finding a new topic. ChatGPT will also come in handy in academic work at the earlier stages in research when a scholar would require ideas to work on as something built on pre-existing work or simply by directing a prompt to the machine. It can promptly produce a great number of research subjects, which stimulates the imagination and invites to further study (Sok & Heng, 2023; Garrido-Merchán, 2023; Carneros-Prado et al., 2023). Particularly, it contributes to making the research writing easier by forming organized outlines and initial drafts (Sok & Heng, 2023; Bhatia, 2023).

ResearchRabbit: ResearchRabbit is a tool that aids the researchers (AI-based) and assists them to discover scholarly literature, as well as develop potential study inquiries. It also gives recommendations based on the individual interests using the analysis of user curated set of papers (Cole & Boutet, 2023). The platform also displays visual mapping of the studies relationships so that the relationships between the studies are easier to identify, track their tendencies and explore new research areas (Sharma et al., 2022).

Scite: Scite is the other AI powered citation index that aids researchers to determine the authenticity of a scientific research by indexing the context of citation so that the sources support, question and merely mention a fact (Mordaunt et al., n.d.). Its advanced AI allows its users to pose natural language inquiries, receive abridged responses, and heterogeneous sources efficiency. To finish off systematic reviews and compilation of literatures, Scite provides visualized citation mapping and contextual interpretation through its tools, including a web interface and browser extension (deLaubell, 2023).

Ref-N-Write: Although the AI solutions such as Ref-N-Write have acceptable amount of positive impacts, some ethical issues are related to them. Some of the considerations regarding the use of these tools are more related to authorship, originality, and even overuse when it comes to academic integrity and the possibility of plagiarism (Shah, 2024). Moreover, researchers ought to consider the possible inclinations that may lead to algorithms and the need to maintain clarity in the generation and use of AI-improved content as well (Khalifa & Albadawy, 2024).

AI Tools for Generating Research Idea

The genesis of new ideas to conduct any research is one of the most difficult facets in academic research. The topic, approach, and ideas of research are generated in the pattern through varied sources in various fields of academia, and with the given AI-powered technologies, the academic world can assist in resolving the issue of generation of new ideas. Lastly, AI helps the researchers disclose new details and to resolve the complex questions, thereby, turning their research project experiences rigorous and productive (Srivastava & Shetye, 2024).

Aveskana: Aveskana is a research AI assistant that aids in developing new research ideas with a view of performing investigations and finding developing patterns in scholarly works. It helps identify the existing research gaps and popular topics with the help of generative AI models and offers new insights and directions to explore to researchers (Heidt, 2023). Besides ideation, Aveskana also helps scholars finish their studies faster or devote more time to critical thinking and creativity because they do not use time finding information in the literature, developing the manuscripts, and manually referencing a quote (Alaa, 2024). It also contributes to the digitalization of the sphere of higher education, because it provides the mechanisms of creation of the AI tools that may be applied particularly in the academic practice (Aziz et al., 2024).

ChatGPT: ChatGPT offers new ideas in terms of research concepts, hypothesis, and direction of research hence support the brainstorming process. ChatGPT assists scholars to come up with fresh ideas or ideas, hypotheses, and lines of research, and enhances brainstorming. It has already been used to form testable conjectures in materials science (Chen et al., 2024) and to lead to numerous research proposals in the setting of reconstructive plastic surgery by arguing against areas that have received little attention (Farhat et al., 2024). Pedagogically it aids in the research writing and education (Sok & Heng, 2023). Despite all its benefits, it is necessary to make sure that it is not overused and it was utilized so that it helped not only cover the matters of academic integrity and overuse.

Scite: The instrument is an AI-powered one, suggesting the similarity of the topic to be investigated in the future and helping to establish a correlation with the publication on research. Scite is an artificial intelligence-packed citation instrument to enable the researcher to elucidate potential lines of study by estimating the frequency and timing of citation in the academic study. It allows exploring new uncharted areas using intelligent citation mapping and assists in discovering the field of studies that might be related (Islam, 2024; *Unearthing Hidden Research Opportunities*, 2023). The quality of literature reviews could be supported through Scite to guide academic professionals to informative and objective research questions and add to the feasibility of new studies (Ajemba & Arene, 2022; Chand, 2023).

AI Tools for Finding Research Gaps

Research gaps formed an important part as a contributor to the development of advancing academic disciplines. One of the effective allies in this process could be the AI since it could be used to establish the areas in which research is lacking or areas that could be explored due to a proper analysis of academic articles and databases.

Litmaps: Displays the connection between research papers, which guides a researcher in determining the research topic having a gap in information or yet to be explored. Being the visualization tool, Litmaps assists researchers in topic exploration, generating links between academic articles, and identifying the literature gaps. It shows the dynamics of research topics since it creates dynamic citation maps, allowing one to discover unexplored areas, using the research topic of the Litmaps database within a certain time range ("Visual citation navigation of open education resources using Litmaps", 2022; Sulisworo, 2023). The platform boosts the efficiency of research with the help of article import options and facilitates education by stimulating the involvement of students in scholarly materials and common systematic literature review practices (Michalak & Ellixson, 2024).

ResearchRabbit: ResearchRabbit is an artificial intelligence (AI) product that helps researchers trace trends and literature lacunas, hence increasing the effectiveness rate of literature reviews (Prashar & Chander, 2024; Ilegbusi, 2024). An illustration of relations among academic papers can support scholars in identifying unexplored research fields, which eventually leads to raising new research questions and knowledge (Faber et al., 2022; Sharma et al., 2022).

Connected Papers: Connected Papers is an effective program which enables the expert to create his own graph of related publications, revealing the incompleteness of previous studies and the direction in which he should look in more detail (Karampela et al., 2019). It allows advancing communication between studies and, as a result, allows the researcher to understand the literature landscape and identify unexplored areas to investigate more effectively (Behera et al., 2023).

Referencing AI Tools

Managing reference is a significant aspect to organize and handle sources in the academic field. With the aid of AI tools, the tedious task of locating, indexing, and referencing research papers is done with much ease, thus saving researchers a lot of time and effort.

Zotero: Zotero is a reference application that assists researchers to efficiently amass, arrange and reference scholarly materials. It offers an opportunity to create and manage web-based libraries and customize citations in a variety of styles and to create bibliographies quickly (Meade et al., 2023). Academic writing is improved, as well, thanks to attributes such as the incorporated note-taking, storage of the full texts, and connections between related contents (Proske et al., 2023). Zotero has proven to enhance research execution in students when used together with approaches in teaching contexts (Asy Doan et al., 2022; Torres-Salinas, 2024). It has an accessible interface, which is why it is a more popular tool among postgraduate students; preferences towards tools might differ depending on the user or the institution (Yakubu et al., 2025; Meade et al., 2023).

Mendeley: Mendeley is a very robust AI-based reference management system that makes management, annotation, and references in academic literature an easy task. It also provides AI-powered recommendations to related articles and automatically creates bibliographies and makes the management of references efficient and error-free (Fitri et al., 2023; Saidin et al., 2023). The tool will assist researchers in their association by engaging in social networking and make it easier to create manuscripts by connecting with word-processing authors such as Microsoft Word or LaTex (Faturrahman et al., 2023; Wahditiya et al., 2023). It has demonstrated that users can be immensely trained at using Mendeley and can develop their academics well with literacy yet some might learn at a curve during the training and therefore training ought to be continuous so that its full potential is realized in the research setting.

EndNote: EndNote, as well as other reference management tools, are based on artificial intelligence and allow automating the process of generating citations and creating a bibliography, which saves the researcher time and increases the accuracy of citing (Harcourt et al., 2024). These AI-based mechanisms are also reducing research time due to their ease of use in retrieving and analyzing literature and literature retrieval, also facilitated by natural language processing due to tools such as Scite, whereby the natural language of a user is translated into a relevant context of retrieved information (Fraidan, 2024; deLaubell, 2023). On top of that, whether it is voice-controlled commands, it is easier to use, yet further awareness and training are required to maximize the potential of these tools (Alaa, 2024; Fraidan, 2024). Although these advantages cannot be neglected, the issues of over-dependence and possible bias in terms of AI-based citations require much attention on the part of scholars (Alaa, 2024).

Paper Editing AI Tools

Paper editing AI checks the level of academic text by making grammatical edits, provides error-free results and assists academic researchers compile sentences. They are very important to deliver quality research papers.

PaperPal: PaperPal is a generative AI-based editing software, which provides suggestions to improve the clarity, grammar and overall style of an academic manuscript, which makes this tool useful to students and researchers (Romn-Acosta, 2024; Subramanian et al., 2024). The AI in writing does not only automate the text editing but also enhances the coherence and accuracy of text and provides the user with access to develop their writing skills based on personal feedback (Khalifa & Albadawy, 2024).

Jenni.AI: Artificial intelligence (AI) has started to be used as a very useful assistant in the process of writing, particularly in science and academic studies, to increase the readability and continuity of the writings (Giglio & Costa, 2023; Romn-Acosta, 2024). The tools, such as Jenni. AI, assist the researcher to reformat the sentences, repair grammar mistakes, and enhance the readability, which is crucial when a researcher is not fluent in the English language since he or she might find it challenging to grasp the intricacies in the language (Giglio & Costa, 2023; Romn-Acosta, 2024).

Visualization AI Tools

Visual representation of research data may simplify difficult results. Visualization tools are AI-based and assist in transforming data into graphs, compelling charts, and infographics.

PowerBI: AI tools used by Power BI assist in visualizing data based on raw data interpretations and the visualization of trends by enabling researchers to combine data among different sources and present data on graphs (Abinaya, 2024; Tirupati et al., 2024). The platform with sophisticated data modeling, unstructured data analysis with AI, and predictive analysis requires the use of informed decisions (Edge et al., 2018; Tirupati et al., 2024). Active dashboards and the ability to configure reports lead to a better interaction and collaboration (Abinaya, 2024; Xie et al., 2024). Nonetheless, a human element is still needed to smooth the further visualizations to meet particular user requirements (Xie et al., 2024; Deshmukh et al., 2023).

Flourish: Flourish is an AI-powered data visualization app that helps researchers, apply interactivity to their research papers and get more insights out of chaos data sets to make it interesting to their audience. With the implementation of AI, it makes visualizations more personified and offers dynamic data exploration by the use of natural language processing (NLP) and thus the process becomes much more intuitive and efficient. Besides, Flourish is able to operate at scale and runs on very large data sets in real time, shifting the outputs of static visualizations into dynamic ones that facilitate dynamic decision-making (Devineni, 2024; Uddin, 2024).

Julius AI: Julius AI plays a pivotal role in generating visual representations of complex research data, transforming intricate datasets into accessible visuals that enhance understanding and engagement (Biswas, 2024; Hoskinson, 2011). It uses the power of AI to design custom visuals, compile data points across sources, make analogies, and fill the gap between abstract data and the things someone is familiar with and help them understand more (Chen et al., 2024; Biswas, 2024). Such graphics can support cross-disciplinary research, as well as enhance the presentation of research and possibly make them more impactful and cited (Biswas, 2024; Esplugas, 2023).

AI Tools for Literature Review

Literature reviews are time-consuming and critical for understanding the state of research in a specific field. AI tools assist in quickly gathering relevant studies, organizing them, and summarizing key insights. AI tools can enhance the literature review process, though challenges remain in ensuring the accuracy and reliability of AI-generated insights, which may vary depending on the algorithms and datasets used (Pandya, 2023).

PaperPile: PaperPile is an AI-powered reference management tool that enhances the organization and review of research papers, streamlining the citation process and improving academic writing quality (Vijai et al., 2019; Fraidan, 2024). It allows users to efficiently store, organize, and cite references, supporting academic integrity and collaboration (Perkel, 2020). The tool also integrates AI to assist with proofreading and enhance clarity, boosting the chances of publication in prestigious journals (Alalaq, 2024). Despite its benefits, some researchers prefer traditional methods due to concerns about technology reliance and data privacy (Perkel, 2020).

Dimensions: Dimensions is a powerful AI-driven platform that assists researchers in identifying relevant literature by analyzing citation networks and research patterns through advanced bibliometric analysis (Hakkaraki, 2024). It provides valuable insights into publication trends, author contributions, and influential articles, enhancing the research discovery process. For example, a bibliometric study on AI in STEM education demonstrated significant increases in both publications and citations, showcasing Dimensions' ability to track research growth (Jantakun et al., 2024). By employing bibliometric analysis and science mapping techniques, Dimensions uncovers citation patterns and research dynamics, helping researchers understand the intellectual structure of AI research (Mardiani & Iswahyudi, 2023). This facilitates more effective literature discovery and fosters interdisciplinary collaboration, thereby advancing scholarly research.

Summarizing AI Tools

Another significant issue that reflects in carrying out a research is to summarize large bodies of research literatures in order to extract most pertinent facts. In research writings, AI tool can automatically summarize research writings when there is a need to read and evaluate enormous volumes of text. GenAI tools are also enjoying a well-spread and effective implementation level in qualitative and quantitative research methods to streamline the process and create new knowledge (Perkins & Roe, 2024).

Scholarcy: Scholarcy is an empowered technology of artificial intelligence that assists with the optimization of research capacities due to the possibility of summarizing scholarly articles and retrieving their most outstanding results with references. It also pairs well with postgraduate level students since it implies that complicated literature can be discussed in a significantly reduced time frame (Bui & Bui, 2024). The tool assists in highlighting main concepts, organizing the results, and developing citations that could be used immediately, not only when it comes to qualitative studies but also addressing quantitative research (Perkins & Roe, 2024). However, the summarization quality in terms of accuracy and completeness is a topic of concern as well and the loss of more detailed information is of a concern (Bolanos et al., 2024). Scholarcy can, thus, be utilized as a supporting tool as opposed to the alternative to the critical human judgment, which means that the shift toward the AI-blended scholarly work is an incremental process.

Unriddle: Unriddle is a language processing and intelligence tool that is able to convert some complex research results to a small, easy-reading summary, allowing a researcher and student to understand the overview of the massive and challenging academic reports (Deshpande, 2023; Santhoshi et al., 2024). It possesses the following functions as short summarization, read-aloud to increase accessibility, highlight the important words, check the plagiarism, and get the images which saves the time of the research process and provides more comprehension (Rashidov &

Rashidova, 2024; Bui & Bui, 2024). Unriddle allows to simplify the synthesis of literature, thus, enhancing the efficiency of the research and facilitating cross productivity and collaboration across existing boundaries, however, at the same time, the warning is issued that the tool might simplify everything too much and, in such a way, might omit the information that is further crucial, which will demand human input in order not to compromise academic standards (Perkins & Roe, 2024; Srivastava & Shetye, 2024; Sorokina, 2024).

Avidnote: Avidnote is an artificial intelligence powered application that has the objective of enjoying enhanced academic research as it makes it more efficient by summing up and reconstructing scholarly articles in a manner that can be read/understood in a more superior manner than before. Nevertheless, Avidnote provides a high level of summarizing precision, and with the use of transformers-based language models, its F1 was estimated up to 93.5 percent (Radha et al., 2024). This can only be possible by any tools performance potential to offer terse and part-by-part business summary of advanced research articles and helps the user to find the most important information in the shortest period of time. Among the greatest strengths of the software Avidnote, it is possible to mark its ability to change the summarized text into the easily deliverable) slides and such feature allows and encourages to share the knowledge, acquired in the course of academic learning, and to save the time on the preparation stage (Badiani et al., 2023). The tool also promotes inclusivity as the tool is inclusive of audio summaries, which can provide equally accessible use of the tool to the visually impaired and the auditory-learning-preferring users (Deshpande et al., 2023). Such features make the process of literature synthesis much easier, but Avidnote helps to meet other learning and presentation demands and can be a useful application among the scholars willing to explore a significant body of academic materials with more ease and clarity.

Presentation AI Tools

A good presentation is a significant part in reporting research results. AI can help a researcher to come up with visually appealing and interesting presentation to deliver information to a group of audience in a way they could understand.

Gamma: Gamma is an AI that can assist a researcher to create presentations quickly and easily that are more involving, professional and one that is heavy with content. Since the clarity of communication, interaction and effectiveness is the theme of an academic setting, the functionality of the Gamma is an innovative twist in the delivery of highly detailed research facts.

One of the significant pros of Gamma is the simplicity of software interface as it simplifies the process of presentation development and makes the users able to focus on the quality and well-structured content instead of formatting the slides in a manual way (Anas, 2024). This boils down to such usability that would spur its use in other areas particularly education and study of the humanities where we are less likely to see the visual design tools be utilized as best they could. Gamma enables simultaneous creation of presentation content by multiple contributors making them to work in real time without interference. This element of the tool highly improves the efficiency of the staff working in a team-based academic environment, since the feedback and the cycle of academic work become more efficient (Anas, 2024).

Gamma also offers a great variety of design schemes and visual elements in which one can customize his or her presentation and still have something professional to look like provided to whom the intended presentation is too be made. In its turn, its automation does not load the head of researchers as it prepares the information with self-organization and page layouts of the slides that help to shorten production time without losing content (Mansoor et al., 2021).

Auxi: Auxi is an Artificial intelligence inclined tool that is developed to assist the scholars to integrate the smoothing of production of presentation slides and automatic arrangement of material. By applying innovative technologies, Auxi manages to make sure that the visual and communicative levels of academic presentations can be enhanced and, in such a manner, the user will not have to be concerned with the complexity of the presentation and, rather, focus on message development. Under the current scenario in terms of research communication, technologies, like, Auxi, are increasingly beneficial to the researcher who wishes to convey his or her findings in an effective and fairly articulate fashion.

Among the greatest features of Auxi is the provision to generate entirely robotized design suggestions. The tool would give a number of space-maximizing layout choices, hierarchy and aesthetic balance options with the assistance of slide content analysis. This allows a person to create interesting slides within a short period and save time, which would have been spent on the presentation of the slides manually (Maloney et al., 2014). Where large volumes of information must be sent out, there will be automatic layouts that will enable the reading and presentation to listeners or recipients (Lok & Feiner, 2005).

In addition to the layout aids, such systems as Auxi and others enable the retrieval and summarization of the contents. These tools, such as SlideSpawn, are based on learning algorithms and can read scholarly (PDF) material, convert it to a necessary form and summarize it in slide format. Such models can measure the degree of salience in a sentence and whatever appears in a visual is what is most relevant (Singh & Sree, 2024; Kumar & Chowdary, 2024). The use of language models of summarizing methods like BERT also helps in better accuracy of summarization since they bundle the key points in a presentation ready form (Singh & R, 2024).

Auxi is highly focused on the user interaction and customization, thus, the researchers are capable of joining the creative process. The users have the freedom of creating subjects, reorganizing the content flow of the same, and selecting among the templates of the design that would suit the tone and audience of the presentations. Since the given hybrid solution is automated and customizable, it may ensure that the outcome of its implementation will be contextually sufficient and academically exact (Zhang et al., 2017).

Literature Searching AI Tools

The methodology of the research can also be improved through artificial intelligence due to which it becomes more productive in gathering, encapsulation and synthesizing research with the help of the tools which include Consensus, Scispace, and Elicit (Trinh, 2025). It is capable of dealing with data processing and analysis, integration and thus, the research is more efficient and exhaustive (Nashwan & Abukhadijah, 2023). The use of AI will simplify data analysis and make it more effective and lead to the innovation to produce knowledge (Ekundayo et al., 2024). AI research would also be a more precise research framework in the sense that the process of data collection and organization, analysis of groups and meaning would become automated allowing heightening of data reliability studies (Bhushan et al., 2024). It is possible to apply generative AI (GenAI) to the research methodology: in educational research, it makes data collection and analysis more interesting. Data collection will be efficient with the use of web scraping and other related processes that reduce the chances of human error and bias e.g. sentiment analysis (Poornesh, 2025).

***Elicit*:** Elicit is a sophisticated AI-based application, and it will help the researchers to achieve effective and methodical search of the literature. With the entry of a research question, the tool will be in a position to search the database and give a list of all the chosen academic articles to the user (Kung, 2023). This alone is very advantageous in saving time as well as energy consumed in a process of scanning through a large number of papers, which usually happens in the case of empirical studies.

The highest value of high tons of quantitative and qualitative research is the artificial possibility to use the index in a case when professionals desire to recognize the tendencies and make meaningful conclusions within the minimal amount of time possible. According to Kung (2023), AI feature of Elicit enables it to help reduce the amount of time spent on decision-making and helps the researchers to be less concerned with data collection and more concerned with inference and interpretation.

Connected Papers: Connected Papers is a research tool-software that provides a visual platform of the literature search with the formation of network graphs of scholarly articles and knowledge discovery through the network graphs of scholarly articles by way of networks of content similarity as in the form of citation counts. The interface starts by allowing the user to choose a core or a root paper upon which the system would create a graph of the tightly related papers (Behera et al., 2023). An outline of such visualization may help researchers to familiarize itself with the conceptual place of the desired topic and to find out how the research on a traditional subject area is being parceled out, where new emerging research is being apportioned, or what is not being done in the research area.

Focusing on the parallels in terms of methodology and theme, the Connected Papers platform will also allow getting a substantially improved sense of how a particular piece of research can be thought of as part of the larger academic discourse. It is especially useful at the earlier periods of the research when the subject of the tool is compelled to orientate themselves in complex land or follow the path of an academic idea.

ResearchRabbit: The other AI-based product which aids academic studies is the so-called ResearchRabbit that provides interactivity of the literature mapping and evaluation in line with the networks. This site allows making the people using its application more explorative in the name of literature reviews because it allows them to explore related and peripherally related publications that are developed using the dynamic graphs (Sharma et al., 2022; Prashar & Chander, 2024). The scientists will be able to trace collaborations between authors, citation patterns, and evolution of a theme, and it will not be so boring to launch research in the broader and less specific academic networks. ResearchRabbit can particularly use the iterative inquiry. This practice will assist the scholars to customize the configuration of the search process intuitively and get custom-made recommendation, which will limit the cognitive fatigue and increase the concentration levels of the study process (Prashar & Chander, 2024). It facilitates the process of team work and thus to even a greater degree makes the research teams and interdisciplinary activities have a greater productiveness.

Data Analysis AI Tools

Polymerserch: Polymeserch is an artificial intelligence enabled space that can process and provide insights to large scale data in any research scenario. Having been created to work with both quantitative and qualitative information, it uses complex machine learning algorithms to find the relationships, trends, and pattern associations that can be missed with the help of the conventional methods (Wankhade, 2025; Hazarika et al., n.d.).

The most salient power of Polymerserch is the capacity to improve pattern recognition and development of insight. Because of deep integration through deep learning, the tool facilitates the use of the data to make decisions using such techniques as predictive analytics, which is immensely essential in areas like environmental sciences, education, and public health. Torrentira (2024) reports on the multi-functionality of the platform, in which AI approaches found relevance to different datasets, and thus can be appropriate in interdisciplinary studies in which an approach with high-quality analysis scaling is necessary. Polymerserch is extremely efficient while being reliable, and this aspect significantly lowers the amount of manual labor that researchers ever have to do as they can advance into finding a better way to interpret results and use them.

Akkio: Akkio is an intelligent in-place analytics solution, which helps to make the interpretation of non-trivial data in the various fields of research and industry more streamlined. Akkio has made data cleaning, classification, regression, and predictions automated using machine learning algorithms and is especially suitable in handling the hidden connections within a vast amount of data when a researcher wants to find their concealed associations (Hazarika et al., n.d.).

The tool makes the processes accurate and fast by minimizing human error and speeding up procedures. There is quick modeling training and user-friendly interfaces which allow not-so-computer savvy researchers to perform sophisticated data analytics. The real-life uses of Akkio in the fields of finance, marketing, and healthcare also confirm the tool attains its high level of versatility and applicability in deriving actionable information out of the structured data (Hazarika et al., n.d.).

The use during the research enables researchers to be equipped with an effective analytical tool that helps them study the variables, predict the results and give informed suggestions depending on the direction of data trends. Further, its applicability to the various fields of study further demonstrates the increasing significance of AI in the interdisciplinary field of research settings.

MonkeyLearn: MonkeyLearn is a text analysis-focused AI-based platform, which is the reason why it is an extremely good fit in qualitative research. By using natural language processing (NLP), the tool can detect patterns, sort out themes and extract sentiments of an unstructured textual data like interview transcripts, open-ended survey answers, or social media pages (Torrentira, 2024).

Automated thematic analysis is one of the most successful features of MonkeyLearn because it completes a significant part of the process and saves researchers on bias by increasing the objectivity and repeatability of the research results. This tool enables more systematic and transparent interpretation of data given that it changes qualitative input into the form of structured information. According to Torrentira (2024), MonkeyLearn does not only make the analysis faster, but it also increases accuracy because it identifies subtle meanings and frequent topics that can be overlooked in the manual review.

It is also user-friendly and allows tailoring the model-building process with an unruly interface making it approachable to users in other fields such as education, linguistics, and behavioral sciences. MonkeyLearn, therefore, contributes to the rigor and richness of qualitative research due to the promise of an artificial intelligent analysis.

Additional AI Tools

Although generative AI applications (e.g., ChatGPT) and research discovery software (e.g., ResearchRabbit and Scite) are invaluable to the cognitive and reasoning phases of research, there are other AI-enabled products that are instrumental in moving the quality of writing and preventing academic misconduct. The three most useful of them include Quillbot, Grammarly, and Turnitin that should be used by every researcher and academic writer.

Quillbot: Quillbot is a paraphrasing tool that is powered by Artificial Intelligence and assists researchers to rephrase their words, enhance clarity, and originality in their writing. It employs machine learning algorithms to make corrections to proposed alternatives without necessarily altering the original meaning and they are especially relevant in avoiding redundancy and creating coherence in literature reviews and discussions. Researchers usually use Quillbot to polish incomplete drafts, correct style, and format contents to specific dissertation readers. It also allows word processors to help in its integration which results in easy editing at the manuscript preparation stage.

Grammarly: Grammarly is a well-liked AI-based writing tool that provides instant recommendations in terms of grammar, punctuation, style, tone and conciseness. Grammarly improves the explanatory nature and understandability of an academic research, particularly among non-native English scholars. In addition to the rudimentary grammar check, it offers advanced feedback on engagement, delivery, and vocabulary variation the factors critical to producing the polished academic writing. Its artificial intelligence integrated analytics guide the researchers to identify discrepancies and streamline their arguments prior to their publication in peer-reviewed sources.

Turnitin: Turnitin is an advanced plagiarism checker and it has an instrumental role in academic integrity. It searches texts submitted against an enormous library of academic publications, web-based material, and term papers to find similarities and conceivable cases of plagiarism. Turnitin helps researchers, supervisors and institutions to make sure that manuscripts comply with ethical standards of citations and originality. In the setting of AI-aided research writing, Turnitin can act as a mitigation factor, as it can identify the unintentional plagiarism caused by the auto-paraphrase or auto-summarization that the AI tool can provide.

CHALLENGES AND ETHICAL CONSIDERATIONS

Nevertheless, using AI in research can be challenging in spite of its potential. The major issues that will be discussed in this section are the following:

Data Quality and Bias: The algorithms trained in AI are decent as their given data. The danger of AI is that it may generalize possible biases, or errors that exist in the data. The issue of data quality is essential to guaranteeing the proper utilization of AI in research. Algorithmic bias, data privacy, and deterioration of classical research skills identified to be the issues of concern related to the integration of artificial intelligence in the research methodology that would affect the integrity and reliability of an academic research (Muwagunzi et al., 2024; Christou, 2023; Jain, 2023). Awareness on possible bias and limitations AI tools present must be considered by researchers, which might have an impact on the quality and reliability of qualitative research findings (Seals, 2025). The complexity of adopting artificial intelligence in the research process might consist of the reliability and accuracy of the artificial intelligence tools, and the possibility of perversion in the algorithms that will compromise the research results (Vascan, 2024; Khan et al., 2024; Waly, 2024).

Ethical Concerns: The ethical aspects associated with the usage of AI in research are very important. Some of the issues that researchers should address include data privacy, possibility of AI capability of usurping the judgment of human beings and ethical application of AI in decision making. It is significant to establish a symbiosis between the human ingenuity and the capabilities of AI. Although AI can complement human imagination, there are still issues on how to incorporate the artificial intelligence in the conventional approaches to research and encourage collaboration across disciplines (Padakanti et al., 2024). The innovative strategy should not only make the research more efficient but also should help to increase the levels of self-awareness and psychological well-being of teenagers with a better ability to identify emotions and understand their nature (King, 2023).

Equal access and Equity: Significant challenges as regards accessibility and equity of the integration of the AI technologies into the research methods and in the context of the low-resource background do exist. Researchers thoroughly interested in machine development or implementing advanced AI schemes have restrictions in underfunded research facilities or third-world nations where researchers have to face the reality of not being able to spend an infinite amount of funds just to gain access to platforms and infrastructures whose worth can be substantial (Mecca and Shk llzeni, 2023). The existence of such a digital divide may limit access to AI-enhanced studies to an extent that makes some researchers less likely than others to advance their academic activities. On the one hand, Oyelude (2024) emphasizes the fact that the available potential of AI, when it comes to contributing to the academic discourse, is directly growing, both in number and variables; the positive impact of such a project tends to be divided unevenly, hence maintaining the same levels of inequality of research conditions across the globe. Equity is achieved only by making investments in open-access work and sharing tools and collaborative platforms in institutions.

Skill Gaps: The employment of AI in research also entails other new-fangled abilities that are not generally available. According to Contreras and Jaimes (2024), it is important that the researchers also become fluent to communicate with AI systems, understand their outputs, and wield it accordingly. This is a steep learning curve that can be attained where AI usage is in its infancy. Srivastava (2024) further states that the literacy involved in the learning of ethical limits, studying about prompt engineering, choosing of tools has come to be the most essential requisite by a researcher of our day. Nonetheless, even in education, teachers and learners can barely engage in the significant interaction with the AI technologies without well-prepared structures, which limits the utmost solution and application of the technology in students' research.

Case Studies: Real-World Applications of AI in Research

Introduction of Artificial Intelligence (AI) into research practice is not only theoretical; it is currently in active testing and demonstration in the regimes of practical educational activities. As in a prominent instance, the use of IBM Watson in research in education, gave outstanding effectiveness in automated evaluation. According to Campbell et al. (2022), Watson demonstrated ability to assess student short-answer responses, and the results of the categorization process matched those of human moderators of high quality. The application will save a lot of time and bias that accompanies manual grading, but the quality of assessment is not compromised. Besides, Watson can also be applied in early intervention research to forecast academic stress among students. Through the examination of multidimensional data, which would entail behavioral, academic, and emotional data, researchers could construct patterns and risk factor models more successfully and provide prospects of early intervention and improved learning outcomes (Kazmi et al., 2024).

The other important real-life scenario is automated content in literature reviews, where smart tools are used to analyze large academic corpora by using text mining and analyzing sentiments. An example of such tools is Scholarcy, Scite, and Unriddle, which automate extracting key insights and categorizing the intent of citations and produce summaries of long documents. Such features have revolutionized the conventional literature review to be more swift, exhaustive, and not as biased as it was done by researchers. Applications of such nature are particularly beneficial to fields that experience rapid expansion of the literature and allows the researcher to keep up to date and recognize gaps in a more systematic manner.

Acquiring AI literacy and research skills turns out to be another key prerequisite of the contemporary academic process. An inclusion of AI training in research methods, as revealed by Contreras and Jaimes (2024) and Srivastava (2024), imparts the scholars with the necessary adaptations in the areas of document interaction, technological use of generative AI, and data interpretation. Both senior scholars and entry-level scientists need these skills to survive in the progressively AI-mediated world of scientific work. Formal education about such tools as ChatGPT, Dimensions, or Elicit can support not only technical skills but also ethical judgement and scrupulousness, as researchers will acquire the ability to critically judge the results of AI autonomously and to uphold scholarly standards.

When it comes to research that is longitudinal, AI has materialized to be a revolutionary resource in follow-up tracking and analysis of the educational trends over the long-term. Such tools as Akkio and Polymerserch facilitate working with huge and complicated data even during many years of researching so that researchers can track variables like student retention, academic progress, and changes in behaviors with greater accuracy than ever before. The given AI-powered insights guide data-based decision-making and further effective policy interventions. One example is that by identifying trends of student engagement over semesters, schools can be able to rethink their curriculum delivery and student support system to improve results.

All these real-life examples point to the versatile application of AI in contemporary studies: the evaluation, literature search, skills training, and data analysis in the long run. They not only portray the efficiency benefits of AI, but also the relevance of ethical application and competency of the researchers in exploitation of all the duality of AI.

CONCLUSION AND FUTURE RECOMMENDATIONS

Conclusion

Artificial Intelligence (AI) has led to a paradigm shift in the conceptualization, practice and dissemination of academic inquiry. As shown in this chapter, AI has emerged as a powerful tool throughout the research process, including such stages as exploring literature, developing ideas, analyzing data, and writing scholarly texts. ChatGPT, ResearchRabbit, Scite, Scholarcy, Elicit, and so forth, are no longer fringe but ever more central to the everyday practice of researchers. These technologies have transformed efficiency and access allowing greater numbers of researchers to participate substantially in the global knowledge system.

The focus on the aspects of cognitive, technical, and contextual realities of AI tools and ability to understand them through the lenses of some frameworks like Technological Pedagogical Content Knowledge (TPACK) and Activity Theory helps better envision the nature of the discussed relationship between AI tools and researchers. TPACK focuses on the active nature of technology, pedagogy, and content in effective practice whereas Activity Theory provides insights into systemic change and contradictions inducted when AI tools are implemented into research settings. The frames promote the awareness of the fact that the process of integrating AI is not only a technological improvement but a profoundly complicated transformative process that affects epistemological and pedagogical entities.

This analysis creates some important opportunities. The use of AI tools simplifies the literature review procedure by visualizing citations networks, discovering new trends and outlining the gaps within the current body of knowledge. They help narrow down on research questions, structure data and create compatible drafts thereby offloading a considerable burden of cognitive load on researchers. Owing especially in the times of COVID-19 pandemic, the use of AI has facilitated the further transition towards more digital-first research settings that allow adaptable, responsive, and decentralized scholarly practices.

Nevertheless, this technological innovation comes with critical issues. Misinformation problem (e.g. hallucinated citations), failure to critically question the content created through AI, as well as reliance on partial or biased collections of data, ethical issues concerning authorship and novelty are all still largely unsolved. Besides, incorporation of AI may inadvertently create a digital divide favoring persons who can afford the finest equipment and fast broadband services and disadvantaging others. Such difficulties require the creation of strong ethical rules, culturally representative data sets and AI development teams and other ways to avoid bias and guarantee fair access.

Future Recommendations

In order to establish responsible and inclusive AI-enabled research ecosystem, the given recommendations are suggested:

- ***Develop Comprehensive AI Literacy Programs***: Universities are required to provide AI literacy into research training curricula to enable the scholars to become able to critically examine and morally make use of AI products.
- ***Conduct Longitudinal Research***: A longitudinal research ought to be performed in the future to find out how using AI can impact scholarly behaviors in the long term with regards to critical thinking, originality or other aspects of methodological precision.
- ***Encourage Cross-disciplinary Research***: Academic research on AI should be conducted with the input of other disciplines such as technologists, scholars, ethicists and social scientists so that the development of tools is placed in the context of scholarly values and specific needs.

- ***Standardize Ethical Standards***: Bodies of learning and publishing companies ought to make and implement rules on authorship, plagiarism and annotation in conditions where AI tools are utilized in a study.
- ***Provision of Fair Access and Technology***: Government and funding organizations should fund digital infrastructure and open-source AI resources, to accommodate disproportionately marginalized scholarly groups, and thus televise the global technology gap.
- ***Transparency and Explainability of AI Tools***: Artificial Intelligence should emphasize the aspect of transparency by providing the origin of training data, restrictions, and algorithmic decision-making information and/or rules to help researchers make a informed decision.
- ***Institutionalize Human Oversight Mechanisms***: Eligibility requirements to develop the AI-generated research output will require a vigorous review process by a human expert that will support academic integrity and accuracy to various AI outputs.
- ***Promote Responsible innovation***: Institutions and policymakers are required to promote AI innovation and make it based on the principles of inclusivity, fairness, accountability, and sustainability.

To sum up, the potential in the application of AI to change the approach to research is enormous because it promises higher efficiency, creativity, and accessibility. However, it should be temperately inbound; therefore, there should be allegiance to career ethics, active career maintenance, and participatory administration. The academic community as a whole ought to create a collective reflective and thought-provoking policy on AI in research that is more inclusive to all of its duties, as the lines between human and machine work in research continue to diminish. The future of academic labor is not only in the strength of the algorithms, but the wisdom that goes into their use.

REFERENCES

Abinaya, S. (2024). Data visualization using power bi. *International Scientific Journal of Engineering and Management, 03*(04), 1–9. DOI: 10.55041/ISJEM01536

Agrawal, V., Bhardwaj, S., Pathak, N., Dixit, J. K., Agarwal, S., & Momin, M. (2024). *Augmenting Research*. IGI Global., DOI: 10.4018/979-8-3693-1798-3.ch003

Ajemba, M. N., & Arene, E. C.Michael Nnaemeka AjembaEbube Chinwe Arene. (2022). Research gaps for future research and their identification. *World Journal Of Advanced Research and Reviews, 16*(1), 575–579. DOI: 10.30574/wjarr.2022.16.1.1062

Akhoon, I. ul H., Khan, M. Y., & Bhat, T. A. (2024). *Comparative Analysis of AI-Generated Research Content: Evaluating ChatGPT and Google Gemini*. DOI: 10.21203/rs.3.rs-5265799/v1\

Alaa, A. (2024). Harnessing Artificial Intelligence for Enhanced Efficiency in Academic Writing and Research. *Fusion : Practice and Applications, 16*(2), 126–146. DOI: 10.54216/FPA.160209

Alalaq, A. S. (2024). AI tools assisting in the proofreading and scientific review of research papers. *ScienceOpen Preprints*. 2024. DOI: 10.14293/PR2199.001358.v1

Anas, I. (2024). *The Use of the Gamma Application by Teachers in Creating Engaging and Automated Presentations*. DOI: 10.62386/jised.v2i1.52

Badiani, N., Vekaria, S., Bharti, S. K., & Gupta, R. K. (2023). *Summarization of Research Paper into a Presentation* (pp. 755–764). Springer International Publishing. DOI: 10.1007/978-981-99-3315-0_58

Behera, P. K., Jain, S. J., & Kumar, A. (2023). *Visual Exploration of Literature Using Connected Papers: A Practical Approach*. Issues in Science and Technology Librarianship., DOI: 10.29173/istl2760

Bhatia, P. (2023). ChatGPT for academic writing: A game changer or a disruptive tool? *Journal of Anaesthesiology, Clinical Pharmacology, 39*(1), 1–2. DOI: 10.4103/joacp.joacp_84_23

Bhushan, B., Singh, A. P., Sharma, S., Divya, K., Bhimanpallewar, R., & Pareek, R. K. (2024). Utilizing AI to Advance Data Science Research. 1–6. DOI: 10.1109/ICCCNT61001.2024.10724570

Biondi-Zoccai, G., Cazzaro, A., Cobalchin, E., D'Auria, D., Ardizzone, G., Giordano, S., Mirzoyev, U., Seferovic, P., Bajraktari, G., & Muraru, D. (2025). *Artificial Intelligence Tools for Scientific Writing: The Good, The Bad and The Ugly*. Deleted Journal., DOI: 10.62684/BXVS8359

Biswas, S. S. (2024). Seeing Beyond Words: The Revolutionary Role of ChatGPT Vision in Research and Publication. *The Journal of Pediatric Pharmacology and Therapeutics : JPPT : the Official Journal of PPAG, 29*(2), 206–207. DOI: 10.5863/1551-6776-29.2.206

Bolanos, F., Salatino, A. A., Osborne, F., & Motta, E. (2024). Artificial intelligence for literature reviews: Opportunities and challenges. *Artificial Intelligence Review, 57*(9), 259. Advance online publication. DOI: 10.1007/s10462-024-10902-3

Boumediene, H., & Bouakkaz, M. (2024). Artificial Intelligence in Education. *Advances in Educational Technologies and Instructional Design Book Series*, 407–438. DOI: 10.4018/979-8-3693-7220-3.ch014

Bui, T., & Bui, V. H. (2024). Decoding Scholarcy website: A Study on its Research Summarization Efficiency. *Proceedings of the AsiaCALL International Conference, 6*, 71–80. DOI: 10.54855/paic.2465

Cahyani, R. Y. D., Dewi, O. C., & Darmawan, A. (2024). AI AND CRITICAL READING SKILL AMONG UNIVERSITY STUDENTS (The impact of artificial intelligence (AI) on Al-Ghifari University Students' critical reading skills). *The Gist*, *6*(1). Advance online publication. DOI: 10.53675/gist.v6i1.1374

Campbell, J., Ansell, K., & Stelzer, T. (2022). Using IBM's Watson to automatically evaluate student short answer responses. *2017 Physics Education Research Conference Proceedings*. DOI: 10.1119/perc.2022.pr.Campbell

Carneros-Prado, D., Villa, L., Johnson, E., Dobrescu, C. C., Barragán, A., & García-Martínez, B. (2023). Comparative study of large language models as emotion and sentiment analysis systems: A case-specific analysis of GPT vs. IBM Watson. In J. Bravo & G. Urzáiz (Eds.), *Proceedings of the 15th International Conference on Ubiquitous Computing & Ambient Intelligence (UCAmI 2023)* (Vol. 842, pp. 257–268). Springer. DOI: 10.1007/978-3-031-48642-5_22

Chen, C., Maqsood, A., Zhang, Z., Wang, X., Duan, L., Wang, H., Chen, T., Liu, S., Li, Q., Luo, J., & Jacobsson, T. J. (2024). The use of ChatGPT to generate experimentally testable hypotheses for improving the surface passivation of perovskite solar cells. *Cell Reports. Physical Science*, *102058*(7), 102058. Advance online publication. DOI: 10.1016/j.xcrp.2024.102058

Chen, Q., Shuai, W., Zhang, J., Sun, Z., & Cao, N. (2024). Beyond Numbers: Creating Analogies to Enhance Data Comprehension and Communication with Generative AI. *Proceedings of the 2024 CHI Conference on Human Factors in Computing Systems* Article No.: 377, Pages 1 – 14 DOI: 10.1145/3613904.3642480

Christou, P. (2023). How to Use Artificial Intelligence (AI) as a Resource, Methodological and Analysis Tool in Qualitative Research? *The Qualitative Report*. Advance online publication. DOI: 10.46743/2160-3715/2023.6406

Clelland, C. L., Moss, S., & Clelland, J. D. (2024). Warning: Artificial intelligence chatbots can generate inaccurate medical and scientific information and references. DOI: 10.37349/edht.2024.00006

Contreras, M. R., & Jaimes, J. O. P. (2024). Artificial Intelligence Literacy in Research. *2024 IEEE Colombian Conference on Applications of Computational Intelligence (ColCACI)*, 1–6. DOI: 10.1109/ColCACI63187.2024.10666582

Del Giglio, A., & Pereira da Costa, M. U. (2023). The use of artificial intelligence to improve the scientific writing of non-native english speakers. Revista Da Associacao Medica Brasileira, 69. DOI: 10.1590/1806-9282.20230560

deLaubell, L. (2023). Scite. *The Charleston Advisor*, *24*(4), 60–63. DOI: 10.5260/chara.24.4.60

Deshmukh, V., Prithviraj, J., Rautkar, A., Agrawal, R., Dhule, C., & Chavhan, N. (2023)... *Interactive Data Visualization Platform to Present Effective Teacher Performance with Power BI., 1335–1339*, 1335–1339. Advance online publication. DOI: 10.1109/ICAICCIT60255.2023.10466179

Deshpande, D., Unawane, R., Tatiwar, R., Taware, A., Todkar, A., & Munshi, S. (2023). Research article summarizer. In *2023 International Conference for Advancement in Technology (ICONAT)* (pp. 1–4). IEEE. DOI: 10.1109/ICONAT57137.2023.10080317

Devineni, S. K. (2024). AI-Enhanced Data Visualization: Transforming Complex Data into Actionable Insights. Journal of Technology and Systems. DOI: 10.47941/jts.1911

Ejjami, R.Dr. Rachid Ejjami. (2024). Integrative Literature Review 5.0: Leveraging Ai and Emerging Technologies to Redefine Academic Research. *International Journal For Multidisciplinary Research, 6*(5), 28756. Advance online publication. DOI: 10.36948/ijfmr.2024.v06i05.28756

Ekundayo, T., Khan, Z., & Nuzhat, S. (2024). Evaluating the Influence of Artificial Intelligence on Scholarly Research: A Study Focused on Academics. *Human Behavior and Emerging Technologies, 2024*(1), 1–13. DOI: 10.1155/2024/8713718

Engeström, Y. (1987). *Learning by Expanding: An Activity-Theoretical Approach to Developmental Research.* Orienta-Konsultit.

Esplugas, M. (2023). The use of artificial intelligence (AI) to enhance academic communication, education and research: A balanced approach. *The Journal of Hand Surgery, European Volume, 17531934231185746*(8), 819–822. Advance online publication. DOI: 10.1177/17531934231185746

Faber, H. C., Gasparini, A., & Grote, M. G. (2022). Artificial Intelligence-based tools in the context of Open Science. *Septentrio Conference Series, 1*(1). Advance online publication. DOI: 10.7557/5.6636

Farhat, S., de la Fuente Hagopian, A., Hooda, K., Lê, H., & Echo, A. (2024). Chatting Up the Next Big Thing: Generating Novel Ideas for Systematic Reviews in Breast Reconstruction Research Using Chat-GPT. *Cureus.* Advance online publication. DOI: 10.7759/cureus.61955

Faturrahman, M. A., Titin, T., Nusantoro, B. P., Putri, R. R., Novahisa, P., Kusuma Ayu, N. A., & Sandra, K. M. (2023). *Pemanfaatan Aplikasi Mendeley sebagai Sistem Manajemen Referensi untuk Mengoptimalisasi Penulisan Karya Ilmiah Mahasiswa.* Abditeknika., DOI: 10.31294/abditeknika.v3i2.2411

Fitri, I. C., Apriliyanto, R., Jalil, A., & Ananda, P. T. (2023). Peningkatan Kemampuan Mahasiswa Dalam Memanajemen Referensi Ilmiah Melalui Pelatihan Mendeley. DOI: 10.47134/diankes.v1i1.7

Fraidan, A. A. (2024). Enhancing linguistic research through AI-powered reference management: A proposal for a voice-controlled academic assistant. *Edelweiss Applied Science and Technology, 9*(1), 1–9. DOI: 10.55214/25768484.v9i1.2240

Garrido-Merchán, E. C. (2023). Best uses of ChatGPT and Generative AI for computer science research. arXiv.Org, abs/2311.11175. /arxiv.2311.11175DOI: 10.48550

Hakkaraki, V. P. (2024). Exploring the Evolution of Bibliometric Analysis: A Comprehensive Study of Scientific Publications from 1974 to 2024 Using the Dimensions AI Database. *Asian Journal of Information Science and Technology*. DOI: 10.70112/ajist-2024.14.1.3878

Harcourt, E., Loxley, J., & Stanson, B. (2024). Automated Learning of Fine-Grained Citation Patterns in Open Source Large Language Models. DOI: 10.31219/osf.io/xnesr

Heidt, A. (2023). Artificial-intelligence search engines wrangle academic literature. *Nature*, *620*(7973), 456–457. DOI: 10.1038/d41586-023-01907-z

Hoskinson, R. A., Jr. (2011). METHOD AND SYSTEM FOR GENERATING VISUAL REPRESENTATIONS OF DATA (Patent) [Patent]. In *Patent Application Publication*. United States. https://patents.google.com/patent/US20110153683A1/en

Hosseini, M., Jahanshahlou, F., Akbarzadeh, M., Zarei, M., & Vaez-Gharamaleki, Y. (2023). Formulating Research Questions for Evidence-Based Studies. *Journal of Medicine, Surgery, and Public Health, 100046*. Advance online publication. DOI: 10.1016/j.glmedi.2023.100046

Ilegbusi, P. H. (2024). *The integration of Artificial intelligence (AI) in literature review and its potentials to revolutionize scientific knowledge acquisition. AfricArXiv*. DOI: 10.21428/3b2160cd.50b471d6

Islam, R. B.Riyad Bin Islam. (2024). Strategic methods for emerging scholars: Identifying research gaps to enhance scholarly work. *World Journal Of Advanced Research and Reviews*, *23*(3), 679–683. DOI: 10.30574/wjarr.2024.23.3.2711

Jain, M. (2023). Artificial intelligence: A powerful ally in elevating the productivity and quality of research for aspiring scholars. *International Journal of Multidisciplinary Trends, 5*(7), 09–13. DOI: 10.22271/multi.2023.v5.i7a.314

Jantakun, T., Jantakun, K., & Jantakoon, T. (2024). Bibliometric Analysis of Artificial Intelligence in STEM Education. *Higher Education Studies*, *15*(1), 69. DOI: 10.5539/hes.v15n1p69

Karampela, M., Isomursu, M., Porat, T., Maramis, C., Mountford, N., Giunti, G., Chouvarda, I., & Lehocki, F. (2019). The Extent and Coverage of Current Knowledge of Connected Health: Systematic Mapping Study. *Journal of Medical Internet Research*, *21*(9), e14394. Advance online publication. DOI: 10.2196/14394

Kawatra, M. B. (2024). Evolution of AI in Academic Research. In Srivastava, A., & Agarwal, S. (Eds.), *Utilizing AI Tools in Academic Research Writing* (pp. 18–22). IGI Global Scientific Publishing., DOI: 10.4018/979-8-3693-1798-3.ch002

Kazmi, S. M. A., Kazmi, A., & Arava, A. (2024). Adaptability of IBM Watson Cloud Platform to Develop Machine Learning Models for Predicting Students' Academic Stress. DOI: 10.1109/ISEC61299.2024.10664767

Khalifa, M., & Albadawy, M. (2024). Using Artificial Intelligence in Academic Writing and Research: An Essential Productivity Tool. *Computer Methods and Programs in Biomedicine Update*, *5*, 100145. DOI: 10.1016/j.cmpbup.2024.100145

Khan, M., Gai, S., & Yan, H. (2024). Integrating artificial intelligence in research methods: Exploring current platforms. In *Advanced Research Methods for Applied Psychology* (2nd ed., p. 19). Routledge., DOI: 10.4324/9781003362715-6

King, J. (2023). *An Innovative Exploration of Psychological Research Methods Driven by Artificial Intelligence: A Case Study Using Facial Expression Technique to Improve Teenagers' Self Awareness*. International Journal of Education and Humanities., DOI: 10.54097/ijeh.v1li1.13155

Kovari, A. (2025). Ethical use of ChatGPT in education—Best practices to combat AI-induced plagiarism. *Frontiers in Education*, *9*, 1465703. Advance online publication. DOI: 10.3389/feduc.2024.1465703

Kung, J. Y. (2023). Elicit (product review). *The Journal of the Canadian Health Libraries Association*, *44*(1). Advance online publication. DOI: 10.29173/jchla29657

Kusters, R., Misevic, D., Berry, H., Cully, A., Le Cunff, Y., Dandoy, L., Díaz-Rodríguez, N., Ficher, M., Grizou, J., Othmani, A., Palpanas, T., Komorowski, M., Loiseau, P., Moulin Frier, C., Nanini, S., Quercia, D., Sebag, M., Soulié Fogelman, F., Taleb, S., & Wehbi, F. (2020). Interdisciplinary Research in Artificial Intelligence: Challenges and Opportunities. *Frontiers in Big Data*, *3*, 577974. DOI: 10.3389/fdata.2020.577974

Labib, L. N., & ElSabry, E. (2024). Integrating AI Into Higher Education. *Advances in Wireless Technologies and Telecommunication Book Series*, 1–30. DOI: 10.4018/979-8-3373-1132-6.ch001

Leong, W. Y., Leong, Y. Z., & Leong, W. S. (2025). Artificial Intelligence in education. *IET Conference Proceedings.*, 2024(22), 183–184. DOI: 10.1049/icp.2024.4341

Li, S. Y. K., & Tsui, E. (2024). Introduction to data/text mining. In *Handbook on Information Sciences*. Edward Elgar Publishing., DOI: 10.4337/9781035343706.00023

Lok, S., & Feiner, S. (2005). *A Survey of Automated Layout Techniques for Information Presentations*. http://csis.pace.edu/%7Emarchese/CS835/Lec7/lok01survey.pdf

Maloney, C. M., Schilling, J. R., Chung, J., Kunz, A., Pari-Monasch, S., Ko, J., & Onder, O. (2014). *Automatic presentation of slide design suggestions*. https://patents.google.com/patent/US10282075B2/en

Mansoor, M., Chandar, S., & Srinath, R. (2021). AI based Presentation Creator with Customized Audio Content Delivery. *arXiv: Learning*. https://dblp.uni-trier.de/db/journals/corr/corr2106.html#abs-2106-14213

Maphalala, M. C., & Ajani, O. A. (2025). Leveraging artificial intelligence as a learning tool in higher education. *Interdisciplinary Journal of Education Research*, *7*(1), a01. DOI: 10.38140/ijer-2025.vol7.1.01

Mardiani, E., & Iswahyudi, M. S. (2023). Mapping the landscape of artificial intelligence research: A bibliometric approach. *West Science Interdisciplinary Studies*, *01*(08), 587–599. DOI: 10.58812/wsis.v1i08.183

Meade, M., DiCiurcio, W., Radack, T., Michael, M., & Woods, B. R. (2023). Reference Managers. *Clinical Spine Surgery, 37*(2), 77–78. DOI: 10.1097/BSD.0000000000001532

Meça, A., & Shkelzeni, N. (2023). *Academic Integrity in the Face of Generative Language Models.*, DOI: 10.1007/978-3-031-50215-6_5

Michalak, R. (2024). Fostering Undergraduate Academic Research: Rolling out a Tech Stack with AI-Powered Tools in a Library. *Journal of Library Administration, 64*(3), 335–346. Advance online publication. DOI: 10.1080/01930826.2024.2316523

Mishra, P., & Koehler, M. J. (2006). Technological Pedagogical Content Knowledge: A Framework for Teacher Knowledge. *Teachers College Record, 108*(6), 1017–1054. DOI: 10.1111/j.1467-9620.2006.00684.x

Molopa, S. T. (2024). Artificial intelligence-based literature review adaptation. *South African Journal of Library and Information Science*. Advance online publication. DOI: 10.7553/90-1-2390

Mordaunt, M., Lopez, P., Uppala, A., Rosati, D., Rodrigues, N. P., Grabitz, P., & Rife, S. C. (n.d.). scite: a smart citation index that displays the context of citations and classifies their intent using deep.

Muwagunzi, E., Kabuye, R., Ddamulira, C., & Kizza, S. S. (2024). Artificial Intelligence in Academic Research at Bugema University: Transforming Methodologies and Ethical Considerations. *East African Journal of Interdisciplinary Studies, 7*(1), 489–503. DOI: 10.37284/eajis.7.1.2484

Nashwan, A. J., & Abukhadijah, H. (2023). Harnessing Artificial Intelligence for Qualitative and Mixed Methods in Nursing Research. *Cureus*. Advance online publication. DOI: 10.7759/cureus.48570

Ojha, B., Agrawal, A., & Arya, A. (2024). *Artificial Intelligence Integration in Higher Education.* 1–23. DOI: 10.1201/9781003469315-1

Oyelude, A. A. (2024). Artificial intelligence (AI) tools for academic research. *Library Hi Tech News, 41*(8), 18–20. Advance online publication. DOI: 10.1108/LHTN-08-2024-0131

Padakanti, S., Kommidi, V. R., & Kommidi, V. R. (2024). AI in Scientific Research: Empowering Researchers with Intelligent Tools. *International Journal of Scientific Research in Computer Science. Engineering and Information Technology, 10*(5), 416–422. DOI: 10.32628/CSEIT241051012

Pandya, T. P. (2023). Literature Review as Research Methodology: Aid of AI (Artificial Intelligence). *Vidhyayana – An International Multidisciplinary Peer-Reviewed E-Journal, 9*(si1), 123–133. DOI: 10.58213/vidhyayana.v9isi1.1589

Perkel, J. M. (2020). Streamline your writing - and collaborations - with these reference managers. *Nature, 585*(7823), 149–150. DOI: 10.1038/d41586-020-02491-2

Perkins, M., & Roe, J. (2024). Generative AI Tools in Academic Research: Applications and Implications for Qualitative and Quantitative Research Methodologies. /arxiv.2408.06872DOI: 10.48550

Poornesh, M. (2025). Navigating the Future of Educational Research: Leveraging Generative AI for Improved Insights. *The Clearing House: A Journal of Educational Strategies, Issues and Ideas*, •••, 1–8. DOI: 10.1080/00098655.2025.2450435

Prabakaran, S. (2023). *An analytical study on historical research* (pp. 64–70). In *Futuristic Trends in Social Sciences* (pp. 64–66). DOI: 10.58532/V2S2CH8

Prashar, P., & Chander, H. (2024). Role of Research Management Tools for Enhancing Academic Research Efficiency: A Focus on AI-Driven Literature Mapping with Research Rabbit. *Journal of Information and Knowledge*, 313–319. DOI: 10.17821/srels/2024/v61i6/171639

Proske, A., Wenzel, C., & Queitsch, M. B. (2023). *Reference Management Systems*. Springer Nature., DOI: 10.1007/978-3-031-36033-6_14

Radha, N., Swathika, R., Uthayan, K. R., & Krishna B, M. (2024). *AI-Driven Summarization of Academic Literature using Transformer Model. 4*, 359–364. DOI: 10.1109/ICICI62254.2024.00065

Rashid-Abdul Aziz, A., & Nusantara, T. (2024). Key Research Ideas of Artificial Intelligence in Higher Education: Bibliometric Analysis and Information Mapping. *Journal of Higher Education Theory and Practice*, *24*(2). Advance online publication. DOI: 10.33423/jhetp.v24i2.6792

Rashidov, A. (2024). Artificial Intelligence in Scientific Research. *Strategies for Policy in Science and Education, 32*(5s), 35–45. DOI: 10.53656/str2024-5s-3-ald

Rashidov, A., & Rashidova, F. (2024). Challenges and limitations in the use of artificial intelligence in research and some options to overcome them. In *2024 15th International Conference on Computing Communication and Networking Technologies (ICCCNT)* (pp. 1–4). IEEE. DOI: 10.1109/ICCCNT61001.2024.10724588

Saidin, F., Sudirman, A., H, L. O. H., Asriani, , Yusuf, M., Abdullah, A., & Amin, H. (2023). Pemanfaatan Mendeley dan Google Scholar dalam Sitasi Karya Ilmiah. *Kongga*, *1*(1), 24–29. DOI: 10.52423/kongga.v1i1.4

Santhoshi, G., Jyothi, M., Ramya Sri, K., Hasika, G., Varsha, G., & Snigdha, R. (2024). Research paper summarizer using AI. *International Research Journal on Advanced Engineering and Management, 2*(8), 2579–2583. DOI: 10.47392/IRJAEM.2024.0374

Seals, C. (2025). *Using AI for Qualitative Research.* Instats Inc., DOI: 10.61700/Q3YCGXG-D240I91841

Shah, S. (2024). The Role of Artificial Intelligence In Research Writing: A Critical Analysis. *Journal of Universal College of Medical Sciences*, *12*(03), 1–2. DOI: 10.3126/jucms.v12i03.73724

Sharma, R., Gulati, S., Kaur, A., Sinhababu, A., & Chakravarty, R. (2022). Research discovery and visualization using ResearchRabbit: A use case of AI in libraries. *Collnet Journal of Scientometrics and Information Management*, *16*(2), 215–237. DOI: 10.1080/09737766.2022.2106167

Singh, A., & Sree R, U. (2024). Empowering Presentations: Streamlining Content Generation through. *International Journal of Advanced Research in Science. Tongxin Jishu, 5–8*, 5–8. Advance online publication. DOI: 10.48175/IJARSCT-22502

Sok, S., & Heng, K. (2023). ChatGPT for education and research: A review of benefits and risks. *Cambodian Journal of Educational Research, 3*(1), 110–121. DOI: 10.62037/cjer.2023.03.01.06

Sorokina, S. (2024). Exploring Automated Summarization: From Extraction to Abstraction. *Vestnik Volgogradskogo Gosudarstvennogo Universiteta. Seriâ 2. Âzykoznanie, 23*(5), 47–59. DOI: 10.15688/jvolsu2.2024.5.4

Srivastava, A. P. (2024). AI-Powered Data Collection and Analysis. In Srivastava, A., & Agarwal, S. (Eds.), *Utilizing AI Tools in Academic Research Writing* (pp. 114–140). IGI Global Scientific Publishing., DOI: 10.4018/979-8-3693-1798-3.ch008

Srivastava, A. P., & Shetye, S. K. (2024). AI-Enhanced Hypothesis Development and Research Questions. In Srivastava, A., & Agarwal, S. (Eds.), *Utilizing AI Tools in Academic Research Writing* (pp. 88–113). IGI Global Scientific Publishing., DOI: 10.4018/979-8-3693-1798-3.ch007

Subramani, P., Senthamil Selvan, K., Dedgaonkar, S., Vishnoi, M., Rampal, S., & Yadav, D. (2024). Unlocking the Power of Text Mining for Information Understanding. *2024 15th International Conference on Computing Communication and Networking Technologies (ICCCNT)*, Kamand, India, 2024, pp. 1-7. DOI: 10.1109/ICCCNT61001.2024.10724258

Sulisworo, D. (2023). Exploring Research Idea Growth with Litmap: Visualizing Literature Review Graphically. *Bincang Sains Dan Teknologi, 2*(02), 48–54. DOI: 10.56741/bst.v2i02.323

Tirupati, K. K., Joshi, A., Singh, S. P., Chhapola, A., Jain, S. K., & Gupta, A. (2024). Leveraging Power BI for Enhanced Data Visualization and Business Intelligence. *Universal Research Reports, 10*(2), 676–711. DOI: 10.36676/urr.v10.i2.1375

Torrentira, M. C.Jr. (2024). Capabilities and Application of Artificial Intelligence (AI) Models in Qualitative and Quantitative Data Mining, Data Processing and Data Analysis. *European Journal of Education Studies, 74*(3), 198–200. DOI: 10.46827/ejes.v11i9.5521

Torres-Salinas, D. (2024). Curso de escritura académica. Tomar notas con el método Zettelkasten y Zotero. *INFONOMY, 2*(5). Advance online publication. DOI: 10.3145/infonomy.24.055

Trinh, M. A. (2025). AI-Assisted Research Methodology. https://creativecommons.org/licenses/by-nc-sa/4.0/

Uddin, M. K. S. (2024). A review of utilizing natural language processing and ai for advanced data visualization in real-time analytics. *Deleted Journal, 1*(4), 34–49. DOI: 10.62304/ijmisds.v1i04.185

Unearthing Hidden Research Opportunities Through Bibliometric Analysis: A Review. (2023). Asian Journal of Research in Education and Social Sciences. DOI: 10.55057/ajress.2023.5.1.23

Vascan, T. (2024). The Use of Artificial Intelligence in the Research Process. *Acta et Commentationes: tiin e Ale Educa iei, 35*(1), 68–77. DOI: 10.36120/2587-3636.v35i1.68-77

Vijai, C., Natarajan, K., & Elayaraja, M. (2019). Citation Tools and Reference Management Software for Academic Writing. *International Journal of Geographical Information Science, 14*(6), 586–596. DOI: 10.26643/gis.v14i6.14788

Visual citation navigation of open education resources using Litmaps. (2022). Library Hi Tech News, 39(5), 7–11. DOI: 10.1108/LHTN-01-2022-0012

Wahditiya, A. A., Sirajuddin, N., & Zulfadli, Z. (2023). *Pelatihan Penggunaan Aplikasi Mendeley Dalam Mengelola Referensi. Jurnal Pustaka Mitra*. Pusat Akses Kajian Mengabdi Terhadap Masyarakat., DOI: 10.55382/jurnalpustakamitra.v3i5.630

Waly, M. (2024). Artificial Intelligence and Scientific Research. *Sustainability Education Globe*, *2*(1), 1–14. DOI: 10.21608/seg.2024.269596.1001

Wangdi, P. (2024). *Integrating Artificial Intelligence in Education:* DOI: 10.33830/ijrse.v6i2.1722

Wankhade, P. (2025). Data Analysis. *Indian Scientific Journal Of Research In Engineering And Management*, *09*(01), 1–9. DOI: 10.55041/IJSREM40826

Watson, A. (2024). Hallucinated Citation Analysis: Delving into Student-Submitted AI-Generated Sources at the University of Mississippi. *The Serials Librarian*, *85*(5-6), 1–9. DOI: 10.1080/0361526X.2024.2433640

Xie, Y., Luo, Y., Li, G., & Tang, N. (2024). HAIChart: Human and AI Paired Visualization System. *Proceedings of the VLDB Endowment International Conference on Very Large Data Bases*, *17*(11), 3178–3191. DOI: 10.14778/3681954.3681992

Yadav, S. (2024). *Artificial Intelligence (AI) Integration in Higher Education*. 43–59. DOI: 10.1201/9781032644509-4

Yakubu, M., Sain, Z. H., Lawal, U. S., Budiman, S. A., & Permana, D. (2025). Analysis of Online Academic Writing Tools Usage among Postgraduate Students in North-west Nigeria. *Kharisma*, *4*(1), 1–13. DOI: 10.59373/kharisma.v4i1.69

Yaroshenko, T. O., & Iaroshenko, O. I. (2023). Artificial Intelligence (AI) for Research Lifecycle: Challenges and Opportunities. *University Library at a New Stage of Social Communications Development. Conference Proceedings*, *8*, 194–201. DOI: 10.15802/unilib/2023_294639

Zhai, C., Wibowo, S., & Li, L. D. (2024). The effects of over-reliance on AI dialogue systems on students' cognitive abilities: A systematic review. *Smart Learning Environments*, *11*(1), 28. Advance online publication. DOI: 10.1186/s40561-024-00316-7

Zhang, J., Xiao, C., & Watanabe, T. (2017). *A Framework for Presentation Slide Design Support*. 191–196. DOI: 10.1145/3093241.3093261

ADDITIONAL READINGS

Cahyani, H., et al. (2024). *Digital Literacy and AI Competence for University Researchers*. IGI Global Scientific Publishing . DOI: 10.4018/979-8-3693-1973-4.ch004

Kővári, A. (2024). *Generative AI in Higher Education: Opportunities and Challenges in Research Practice*. IGI Global Scientific Publishing. DOI: 10.4018/979-8-3693-1973-4.ch008

Meça, M., & Shkëlzeni, T. (2023). *The Challenges of Using AI Tools in Higher Education Research.* IGI Global Scientific Publishing. DOI: 10.4018/979-8-3693-1973-4.ch006

Oyelude, A. A. (2024). *Academic Libraries and the Application of AI Tools in Research Support.* IGI Global Scientific Publishing. DOI: 10.4018/979-8-3693-1973-4.ch003

Srivastava, A. P., & Agarwal, S. (Eds.). (2024). *Utilizing AI Tools in Academic Research Writing.* IGI Global Scientific Publishing., DOI: 10.4018/979-8-3693-1798-3

KEY TERMS AND DEFINITIONS

AI Literacy: Literacy of how to understand, work with, assess and ethically utilize AI tools in all kinds of research and learning scenarios.

Artificial Intelligence (AI): Modeling of human-like intelligence in computers, whereby, computers can execute processes like reasoning, learning, and problem solving- applies in research to automation and analysis.

Citation Management: Automation of references and documentation structure through AI based tools e.g. Zotero and Mendeley which increase accuracy and efficiency of documentation.

Digital Inequality: This is the breadth between people or organizations that have effective access to the digital resources and those that do not that results in disadvantaged access to taking part in AI-accentuated research.

Ethical AI Use: The method of being transparent, fair and responsible AI concerning the use of AI in research and especially in authorship, detection of bias and managing the data.

Generative AI: It is a branch of AI that generates novel materials like text, images, or code as per the pattern learnt in the already existing materials. One of the examples that can apply in academic writing is chat GPT.

Literature Mapping: A process aided with the usage of AI, during which the tools such as ResearchRabbit allow visualizing how the scholarly articles are connected to each other, allowing the researcher to recognise the trends and gaps.

Multimodal Data Analysis: It is possible to combine and analyze text, images, and sounds, in particular, to study complicated phenomena in education or behavior.

Plagiarism Detection: AIALGORITHMS recognizing COME-up and COME-unless the right touch, such as that which makes sure academic integrity in machine-aided writing research.

Text Summarization: A method used in the application of AI that isolates essential elements of a long text-Scholarcy, and Avidnote are the most popular programs that perform this operation.

Chapter 16
Attribution Theory and AI Misuse in Higher Education:
Implications in Ethically Challenging Environments

Isaac Wasswa Katono
https://orcid.org/0000-0002-6106-3078
Uganda Christian University, Uganda

ABSTRACT

Taking Uganda as an example, the present study seeks to explain how students use attribution theory combined with game and prospect theories to rationalize the misuse of AI in SSA, where the social valuation of online learning processes is at times low. Moral decadence and consumerist tendencies have been on the increase in many parts of SSA, and many examples in Uganda attest to this fact. Further, resource constraints in many academic institutions both private and public, harden the academic environment in SSA. Amid such a terrain, students may seek unethical short cuts in the pursuit of knowledge, such as misuse of AI and then justify their actions based on the happenings in their societies. The collective cultural context in which people subscribe to group norms and values contributes to the rationalization of AI misuse; hence this PRISMA based study, also examines how cultural factors interact to rationalize AI misuse in the academia in SSA. The study advances recommendations that will help to mitigate AI misuse in this region.

1. INTRODUCTION

1.1 The Rise of Artificial Intelligence (AI)

The education sector has undergone unprecedented changes world wide, since the introduction of AI. These changes have transformed the way things are done, the ease of doing them, and the speed and accuracy of doing them, thus ushering in efficiency and effectiveness. For example, AI has revolutionized academia by enabling personalized learning through flexible platforms

DOI: 10.4018/979-8-3373-2752-5.ch016

that facilitate intelligent tutoring, data driven learning tools that can inform curriculum design, inform teaching strategies, and others that address individual learner requirements (Holmes et al., 2023). Categorized based on their core functions and user engagement models, tools like Grok use generative AI to support personalized learning, PenPal enables global peer learning through writing, and Julius which supports data analysis strategies among others. On the other hand, AI has streamlined administrative operations, such as setting of examinations, grading and scheduling, thus improving institutional efficiency (Luckin et al., 2016). Moreover, AI augments inclusivity by supporting translation, text-to-speech, and assistive technologies such as accessibility tools and supportive learning tools (Zawacki-Richter et al., 2019).

However, AI proliferation has introduced problems like incessant misuse among learners (Basha, 2024), such as submitting AI-generated essays or evading plagiarism detection (Skonieczny & Vendramin, 2024). The concern is that such misuse of AI hinders learners from thinking critically, hampering their creativity and academic growth. In light of this anomaly, the present study examines the intersection between the learner's environment and the growing occurrence of unethical behavior manifested in the misuse of AI in the academia. It explores ways in which students rationalize such behavior, often shifting blame onto societal dysfunctions instead of embracing personal accountability and ethical objectivity. To illuminate this problem in the SSA context, the current study focuses on the Ugandan context, and applies attribution theory (Heider, 1958), game theory and prospect theory to explain the concept of AI misuse. This is specifically because Uganda's socio-economic and political characteristics, closely align with those of several neighbouring SSA nations. By situating student behavior within this broader cultural and systemic context, the study seeks to identify the drivers of unethical interactions with AI technologies and possible mitigation measures against them.

According to attribution theory people tend to explain happenings around them, including their responses and behaviors, in terms of either internal causes (dispositional attribution) or external causes (situational attribution). Heider argues that individuals act as "naïve psychologists," seeking to assign causality either to internal dispositions (e.g., ability, effort) or external situations (e.g., luck, task difficulty). This framework was expanded by Rotter (1966) and later by Weiner (1986), who introduced variables such as locus of control, stability, and controllability to explain how attributions influence motivation and, consequently, behavior. In educational environments, attribution theory helps explain how students and educators account for success or failure. Table 1 below presents the various author contributions to attribution theory.

Table 1. Comparative Perspectives on Attribution Theory

Author	Key Contribution	Focus
Fritz Heider (1958)	Introduced the concept of attribution as a way people make sense of behavior.	Differentiated between internal (personal) and external (situational) causes.
Harold Kelley (1967)	Developed the Covariation Model of attribution.	People use consistency, distinctiveness, and consensus to infer causality.
Bernard Weiner (1986)	Extended attribution theory to achievement and motivation.	Proposed three dimensions: locus, stability, and controllability.
Edward Jones & Keith Davis (1965)	Proposed the Correspondent Inference Theory.	Focused on how observers infer intentions and traits from behavior.

continued on following page

Table 1. Continued

Author	Key Contribution	Focus
Julian Rotter (1966)	Developed the Locus of Control concept.	Emphasized internal vs. external control over life events.
Lee Ross (1977)	Identified the Fundamental Attribution Error.	People overemphasize dispositional factors and underestimate situational ones.

1.2 The Social Valuation of AI

Despite the global rise in ICT integration in education, the social valuation of AI and online learning in Uganda remains low, shaped by structural constraints and cultural preferences for face-to-face education (Katono & Kyakulumbye, 2025; Ferretti, 2024). Public skepticism, fuelled by perceptions that online learning prioritizes rote engagement over cognitive development and that AI is overly technical and misaligned with traditional teaching models, limits adoption (Mugizi & Nagasha, 2025; Plantinga et al., 2024; UVCF, 2024). Although the Ugandan government and institutions promote e-learning, uptake in universities, particularly resource-constrained private ones, is hindered by limited faculty digital competence and student access challenges (Mugizi et al., 2023).

This cynicism influences university policies, thus affecting AI integration in curriculum design and academic assessment, hence any misuse of AI worsens the situation. In the sections below, the chapter situates AI misuse within ethically challenging environments, which provide students with an impetus/excuse to rationalize unethical practices due to failures in institutional accountability, consumerist attitudes, weak institutional oversight (Ferretti, 2024), and the social- cultural context.

1.3 Challenges Facing Future AI Development: The Home Environment

Issues of governance, characterized by inadequate policies, oversight, and enforcement play a significant role in shaping AI misuse in the education and others sectors in a country. The dearth of clear ethical guidelines and principles in society and a justice system deemed unfair can translate into AI systems that perpetuate biases, violate privacy, or have other harmful consequences. Uganda has an endemic corruption history and environment, which should have an impact on its youthful population and in particular students: such an environment significantly influences students' cognitive schemas, motivational orientations, and attributional tendencies. This country reportedly loses approximately UGX 20 trillion annually to corruption across sectors such as procurement, taxation, and public service delivery (Inspectorate of Government, 2022). Such persistent fiscal outrages not only undermine institutional trust but also become a powerful negative social example for young people. For those still in educational institutions, this environment influences how they interpret success, failure, diligence, integrity and justice, with blurred lines between merit and manipulation, and fostering external attributions for outcomes within academic and professional realms.

Weiner's attribution theory (1986, 2012) offers a framework for understanding how individuals interpret outcomes in environments marked by systemic dysfunction (see Table 1 above), using three causal dimensions—locus, stability, and control—to explain responsibility for success or failure. In corruption-endemic settings, students often attribute academic or professional success to external, unstable, and uncontrollable factors like corruption, rather than internal qualities such as effort or ability. Many corruption scandals have taken place in Uganda in the last five years (Kaluya & Elliot, 2018).

For example, in 2022, the Inspectorate of Government investigated 1,127 corruption complaints, with Kampala accounting for nearly 20% of cases, reinforcing these perceptions (Inspectorate of Government, 2022). Corruption perceptions indexes further illustrate the depth of the crisis. Uganda scored 26 out of 100, ranking 140th out of 180 countries, with 69% of respondents perceiving an increase in corruption and 46% of public service users admitting to paying bribes (Transparency International, 2024). Such perceptions foster attributional patterns that undermine ethical agency. When students internalize the belief that outcomes are determined by corrupt networks rather than merit, they may disengage from academic pursuits, rationalize unethical behavior, or succumb to apathy. This phenomenon aligns with the concept of learned helplessness, wherein repeated exposure to uncontrollable negative conditions eradicates individuals' belief in their capacity to influence outcomes (Seligman, 1975).

While it is true that the government of Uganda has established commissions of inquiry and investigative panels to address corruption, not much attention has been paid to the resultant reports and recommendations emanating from this effort (Kirya & Sekalala, 2022). Consequently, despite interventions by the Inspectorate of Government (IGG), poor enforcement and limited follow-up have bred a culture of impunity in the country. Unethical practices have permeated various sectors of Ugandan society, with lukewarm responses and persistent regulatory loopholes compounding the issue. This environment permits and tacitly encourages misconduct. Within this context, attribution theory provides a compelling framework for analysing how students rationalize unethical behavior related to artificial intelligence. The European Parliament (2020) underscores the importance of "transparency, accountability, fairness, and regulation" in AI development, which principles are frequently absent in some SSA nations. This study contends that such governance failures send the wrong signals to students, fuel academic dishonesty and intensify the ethical dilemmas associated with AI use in higher education, in transnational economies like Uganda. Thus, society has a duty to rebuild students' attributional frameworks by promoting internal, controllable, prescriptions for success. Such reframing can be operationalized through condemning unethical corrupt tendencies, and punishing of the perpetrators regardless of status. Ethical leadership models that promote resilience against the sinister normalization of corruption require educators and society to actively reshape the interpretive schema through which students construct meaning from their academic and social realities (Weiner, 1985).

1.4 Consumerism, the Cultural Context, Sustainability, and AI Misuse

Katono (2016) provides a vivid account of consumerism in Uganda, offering a compelling exploration of this phenomenon linking it to ethically questionable behavior, particularly among university students. His study reveals that consumerism is not merely a lifestyle choice but is shaped by deeper systemic issues—namely, perceived unfairness and a poor work ethic, both of which are prevalent in contexts with minimal consumer protection. He finds that unethical behavior mediates the relationship between these antecedents and consumerist attitudes, suggesting that material consumption in Uganda is often a response to structural inequities and moral disillusionment.

In the education context, consumerism fosters a transactional mindset where degrees are treated as commodities rather than intellectual achievements (Tomlinson, 2017). This contributes to the problem of AI misuse, since students may prioritize efficiency over mastery, relying on AI tools to bypass traditional learning processes. The chapter asserts that this consumerist attitude erodes academic integrity and promotes the misuse use of AI.

Uganda is a collectivist society, in which the views and values of the group override those of the individual (Hofstede, 1980). This study argues that according to culture conflict theory, there is a relationship between a student's perception of the act of cheating or AI misuse and the immediate organizational subculture or peer group (Curasi, 2013). Hence, a student's overall evaluation of the integrity of the social group will have an impact upon their ethicality in an academic setting. Thus, the more society condones unethical behavior, the more students will engage in academic dishonesty.

Higher education institutions in ethically challenging environments often fail to address sustainability concerns in AI governance (Ferretti, 2024). This study argues that without institutional reforms, AI systems pose societal risks due to misaligned values, including ethical and sustainability concerns. Without robust ethical AI frameworks that consider sustainability, students may use AI irresponsibly, contributing to academic integrity violations and resource overconsumption. This chapter calls for the integration of sustainability principles into AI ethics education and institutional policies.

1.5 Justification and Departure Point

This chapter contributes a distinct perspective to the literature by probing the underexplored intersection of attribution theory, ethically strained academic environments, and AI misuse in higher education particularly as these dynamics unfold within transnational economies. Integrating insights from game and prospect theories, the study offers a detailed account of how and why students rationalize unethical behavior in their interaction with AI in resource constrained contexts. The current study brings new perspectives on AI misuse in four ways.

First, while the focus of prior research has been on examining AI ethics and academic integrity in isolation, this current study examines the ways in which attribution processes interact with contextual pressures in ethically challenging environments to mould student behavior. Second, most scholars that have examined AI misuse focused on the developed countries and emerging markets, but with little attention paid to SSA. The dearth of research that speaks directly to African educational contexts underpins the urgent need to bridge this gap. As Hlongwane et al. (2024) observe, there remains a significant gap in culturally grounded frameworks that reflect the legal, social, and economic realities of AI use across the continent. Third, the impact of the cultural environment on AI misuse has rarely been explored, particularly in a SSA perspective (Hofstede, 1980; Hlongwane, et al., 2024). Fourth, the intersection of attribution, game and prospect theories has not been explored in the study of AI misuse, especially in resource constrained environments.

Given this background, the main objective of this study is to highlight how students may employ attribution theory to justify their misuse of AI in their academic pursuits, with a view to proposing recommendations to mitigate this pervasive problem. The rest of the study is structured as follows: the next section elaborates the theoretical underpinnings of the argument;

while section three presents the methodological approach. Section four examines the drivers of AI misuse and offers mitigation measures. Lastly, section five wraps up the paper, concluding with key insights and future directions.

2. LITERATURE REVIEW

2.1 Theoretical Framework Examining AI Misuse Through Attribution, Game, and Prospect Theories

This study uses a three-pronged approach in order to examine the reasoning behind student misuse of AI in Uganda. This approach examines the intersection of three theories, namely attribution theory, game theory and prospect theory. Their meeting point helps to explore the psychological reasoning, strategic behavior, and risk-related judgments that inform students' engagement in unethical AI practices. By examining the distinctive contributions and interconnections of these theories, the study develops a robust analytical model for diagnosing and addressing AI misuse.

2.2 Attribution Theory as a Foundational Lens

This theory, introduced by Heider (1958) and later refined by Weiner (1972, 1986), and others (see Table 1) provides a firm foundation for examining how individuals interpret the causes of their actions. The theory delineates between internal attributions and external attributions, with the former anchored within the person and making him/her accept responsibility for the outcome of his/her actions, while in the latter, the individual attributes the outcome of her actions to events outside her control, such as institutional shortcomings, socio-cultural conditions, or technological access. Applying this theory to AI misuse in the education context provides us with a strong medium in which to place AI misuse, as students do wrong things, but then attribute the cause not to themselves, but to other issues in the environment, thus preserving their self-image (Weiner 1986, Bandura, 1999). Such tendencies are amplified in contexts where AI governance frameworks are weak or ambiguous, making ethical boundaries appear negotiable or ill-defined.

Such externalization blurs individual accountability and also facilitates moral disengagement (Bandura, 1999). In this process, people cognitively restructure unethical behavior to appear morally acceptable, particularly through mechanisms like diffusion of responsibility and moral justification. This cognitive distancing process enables people to rationalize unethical conduct. This is so especially in systems where corruption or policy laxity is regarded as normal, necessary (for survival) and is generally acceptable to the silent majority. In such a situation, academic dishonesty may be reframed not as a breach of integrity but as a practical coping mechanism within a flawed system (Bandura, 1999).

For instance, a Ugandan undergraduate, may rationalize his AI use by stating: "Our leaders misuse public funds, claim degrees they didn't earn, and nothing happens. Why should I suffer writing ten pages when I can use AI like they use people?" This exemplifies Bandura's concept of "displacement of responsibility," where individuals justify unethical behavior by referencing authority figures who seemingly violate norms with impunity. Thus, AI misuse becomes not a rebellion against rules but a mirror reflecting perceived societal hypocrisy.

Furthermore, the perceived competence of lecturers regarding AI significantly influences students' attributional rationalization. When educators lack the skills to detect, regulate, or ethically model AI use, students may rationalize their misconduct as a logical response to a permissive or incompetent system (Chan & Hu, 2023). This creates a low-risk environment where students might reason, "If my lecturer can't tell, it's not really cheating." Such external attributions reduce cognitive dissonance and further entrench moral disengagement (Bandura, 1999).

2.3 Assessment Design and Attributional Triggers for AI Misuse

Beyond lecturer competence, the design of assessments plays a pivotal role in shaping student behavior around AI. Assessments that emphasize surface-level recall, lack contextual relevance, or fail to reward original thought can inadvertently invite misuse. From an attribution theory standpoint, when students are confronted with superficial tasks, they may rationalize unethical behavior by shifting responsibility outward: "The assignment didn't require my input," or "Anyone could've answered this with AI" (Weiner, 1985). Effective pedagogical design can counteract this logic by reactivating internal attributions and reinforcing academic agency.

A classical example is one of a student who submits a ChatGPT-generated essay for a recycled prompt that lacked a rubric. Her justification, "The question was too broad, and we've done it before. I didn't see the point of writing it again. AI just helped me say what the lecturer wanted," reflects external attribution: the task's lack of novelty and clarity justified her disengagement. This aligns with Biggs's (2003) concept of surface learning, where students focus on task completion rather than conceptual understanding. From a management perspective, this behavior can be analysed through McGregor's (1960) Theory X and Theory Y. A Theory X lens might view the student as inherently lazy, requiring strict oversight, clear rubrics, and punitive measures to enforce original work. Conversely, a Theory Y perspective assumes the student is intrinsically motivated but disengaged due to the task's lack of challenge or relevance. This suggests that fostering deeper engagement through novel, well-structured prompts could encourage authentic learning, reducing reliance on AI tools for superficial compliance.

Empirical studies support this pattern. Cotton et al. (2025) found that generic prompts and fact-based exams are more likely to trigger AI misuse, especially when students feel the task does not require their unique input. Conversely, assessments that emphasize critical thinking, contextual application, and iterative feedback reduce the likelihood of misconduct. The Assessment Design Decisions Framework (Bearman et al., 2016) similarly emphasizes that well-designed tasks promote deeper learning and reduce the appeal of shortcuts. From a game-theoretic perspective, poorly designed assessments lower the "cost" of defection. If students believe that AI can complete the task as well (or better) than they can, the incentive to act ethically diminishes. The system, in effect, rewards strategic disengagement. To counter this, institutions must invest in assessment literacy for faculty. First, assignments should be contextualized to local realities, making generic AI outputs less effective. Second, tasks should also be cognitively demanding, requiring synthesis and evaluation over mere recall. Third, assignments should process-oriented, with checkpoints and feedback loops that track intellectual growth and lastly, assignments should be transparent, with clear expectations and rubrics that delineate ethical AI use. Such reforms not only improve learning outcomes but also shift attribution inward: students begin to see success as a function of effort and insight, not system manipulation.

2.4 Empirical Applications of Attribution Theory in AI Misuse Research

Many studies have been done applying attribution theory, either explicitly or implicitly, to understand AI misuse in academic contexts. Table 2 summarizes key findings from empirical research, highlighting the prevalence of external attributions.

Table 2. Selected Empirical Studies Applying Attribution Theory to AI Misuse

Author	Context	Research Focus	Findings related to attributions
Hua (2023)	Students	AI tool dependence, academic dishonesty, ethical awareness	Students frequently use AI, exhibit limited ethical awareness, and surprisingly, positive attitudes toward academic dishonesty, indicating rationalization.
Perkins et al. (2024)	Students & faculty perspectives on AI in HE	Detection of GPT-4 generated text in higher education	Training faculty to refine their attribution processes could improve detection accuracy, aligning with attribution theory's applications in educational psychology.
Cotton et al. (2025)	Exam/assessment design in HE	Impact of exam design on AI-aided misconduct	Generic prompts and fact-based exams are more likely to trigger AI misuse.
Chan & Hu (2023)	Lecturers' perspectives on AI in HE	Lecturer's AI competence and its impact on personalized learning and ethics	Lecturers lacking AI training are less likely to detect misconduct.
Bearman et.al (2023)	Generative AI in education	Student skills and lecturer roles concerning generative AI	AI adoption by faculty can foster critical thinking but requires facilitative roles, reducing external attributions for AI misuse.

These studies collectively highlight how students' perceptions of institutional gaps, lecturer competence, and assessment design contribute to an external locus of control regarding AI misuse. Findings of these studies imply that addressing these systemic issues is crucial for fostering internal attribution and promoting academic integrity.

2.5 Game Theory and Strategic Adaptation

A combination of Attribution Theory and Game Theory (von Neumann & Morgenstern, 1944) throws light on how students rationalize the misuse of AI. Attribution theory explains how students account for their actions, by rationalizing what they have done or are about to do. On the other hand, Game Theory adds to this explanation by showing the strategic calculations students make within ethically ambiguous academic environments. Just like in a chess game, Game Theory explains how interactions occur among rational agents whose decisions are interdependent: each actor's outcome is driven not solely by their choices but also by the anticipated actions of others.

In higher education context where ethical standards are loosely enforced or are ambiguous, students do not actually act out of sheer ignorance or ill intent. Instead, they function as rational people who weigh the risks and rewards of AI use or misuse within circumstances they face: a shifting landscape of institutional incentives and peer expectations. The Nash equilibrium (where no agents benefit from the change of strategy) becomes particularly relevant here, suggesting that unethical behavior is likely to persist or even become normalized when students believe that others are also engaging in similar practices—and that institutional repercussions are unlikely or inconsistently applied (Caplan, 2011; Şahin & Yüksel, 2021).

This strategic stance underpins a broader systemic issue: academic environments that are ethically frail, may fail to credibly signal consequences of unethical actions, fail to promote ethical consistency, making rational students seek to optimize academic success over integrity. In this way, Game Theory reveals the delicate interdependence between institutional design, student agency, and ethical behavior in the age of AI.

In environments where ethical standards are inconsistently enforced, students often act not out of ignorance or malice, but as rational agents navigating a system of incentives and risks. For instance, a student may weigh the payoff of submitting a ChatGPT-generated essay (high grades with low effort) against the risk of detection (low if oversight is lax), perceiving AI misuse as a dominant strategy in a poorly regulated academic "game."

The Prisoner's Dilemma is particularly instructive in this context (Axelrod, 1984). This model posits a scenario where two individuals must independently decide whether to cooperate (e.g., act ethically, avoid AI misuse) or defect (e.g., use AI unethically). While mutual cooperation yields the best collective outcome (a high-integrity academic environment), individual incentives often lead to mutual defection if trust is low. In Ugandan classrooms, where students suspect that peers are using AI tools undetected—and where lecturers lack the capacity or will to enforce rules (Bearman & Ajjawi, 2023; Perkins et al., 2024) many choose to "defect" pre-emptively. The underlying logic becomes: "If I don't use AI and others do, I'll be disadvantaged," creating a race to the bottom in terms of academic integrity.

This behavior aligns with the Win-Stay, Lose-Shift strategy (Nowak & Sigmund, 1993). As an example, a student who shifted to using AI for lab reports after seeing peers succeed with it may say, "I tried doing it the right way, but my marks were lower than those who used ChatGPT. I'm not stupid—I just don't want to lose." His initial cooperation shifts to defection after experiencing a perceived "loss" (lower grades). This adaptation is strategic, reflecting a response to a system that appears to reward shortcuts and penalize integrity. Similarly, the Tit-for-Tat model applies: students may begin with honest intentions but mirror the behavior of peers or lecturers who appear to misuse AI. If they perceive that others are cheating and succeeding, they reciprocate—not out of defiance, but out of a perceived need for fairness. This conditional morality reflects a reactive ethical stance: "I'll be honest if the system is honest" (Nowak & Sigmund, 1993). These game-theoretic dynamics are significantly exacerbated in environments characterized by low detection probability, where lecturers are unfamiliar with AI tools or lack adequate detection software; high reward for defection, as students can earn better grades with less effort and redirect their energy toward other pursuits; and minimal reputational cost, due to the absence of peer accountability or meaningful institutional consequences for AI misuse.

Moreover, the concept of indirect reciprocity (Nowak & Sigmund, 2005) where individuals act ethically to maintain a good reputation collapses in environments where ethical behavior is not visibly rewarded. If the group norm favours unethical behavior, individuals adapt to survive within that norm. Cultural evolution theory (Henrich, 2015) reinforces this, showing how behaviors are transmitted through social learning. When unethical conduct becomes the group norm, individuals adapt to survive within that moral ecosystem, perpetuating a cycle of normalized misconduct. This creates an "asymmetric information" scenario, where students exploit the knowledge or enforcement gap of lecturers, adopting a defection strategy for short-term gain (Bearman & Luckin, 2023).

2.6 Prospect Theory: Framing Decisions Under Risk

While attribution theory elucidates how individuals justify their behavior and game theory offers strategic lenses, Prospect Theory, advanced by Kahneman and Tversky (1979) illuminates the cognitive biases underlying decision-making under conditions of uncertainty. The key tenet of prospect theory is the concept of loss aversion, which asserts that people tend to experience losses more severely than equivalent gains. This slanted sensitivity results in decision-making that may appear irrational, especially when choices are designed to circumvent loss rather than achieve benefit (Kahneman & Tversky, 1979). In academic settings, this perceived loss leads students to engage in unethical behavior, such as AI misuse, to evade the perceived loss, which can be understood as an attempt to avert perceived threats to academic standing, fairness, or future opportunities; students may believe that those who leverage AI tools have an edge in producing higher-quality work and completing assignments more efficiently (performance outcomes), and when faced with tight deadlines and academic overload, abstaining from AI may feel like sacrificing valuable time-saving resources (time efficiency); furthermore, when classmates normalize AI use (ethical or otherwise) opting out may feel like falling behind or "playing fair in an unfair game" (peer comparison).

Reputational risk: In some environments, not keeping pace technologically can be interpreted as being out of touch or academically weak. These perceptions reframe ethical abstention not as virtuous but as a strategic disadvantage, amplifying the temptation to misuse AI tools. Prospect Theory thus adds depth to the ethical calculus: students are not merely rational actors navigating incentives (as in Game Theory), but emotional decision-makers influenced by fear of relative loss.

Hence, it is the perception of loss that forms the core of the intersection between Prospect Theory and Attribution Theory. Loss aversion may lead students to engage in unethical AI use despite recognizing its implications. Once that decision is made, Attribution Theory helps explain how students justify it: instead of acknowledging personal responsibility, they resort to citing external pressures: peer norms, competitive academic environments, or ambiguous institutional guidelines (Heider, 1958; Weiner, 1986). In this way, students resolve the resulting cognitive dissonance by reframing their actions not as moral transgressions or deviations from ethical norms and values, but as rational or measured responses to systemic constraints: "I had no real choice, the environment compelled me."

Another example of the issue: a student observes classmates effortlessly completing assignments with AI tools. What does he/she do? The fear of falling behind or receiving lower marks (a perceived loss, according to prospect theory) becomes a powerful motivator. To alleviate the internal conflict of engaging in unethical behavior, she tells herself: "The system is broken anyway; lecturers don't provide adequate support, and everyone else is doing it" (an external attribution). In such a case, misconduct becomes both strategically rational (from a game-theoretic perspective of avoiding loss or gaining advantage) and morally excused (through attributional rationalization).

2.7 Summary: Interlinkage and the Integrated Model

The combined application of Attribution Theory, Game Theory, and Prospect Theory provides a comprehensive and nuanced model for understanding AI misuse in ethically compromised higher education environments. Attribution Theory explains the "why": why students externalize blame, engage in moral disengagement, and justify their unethical actions by pointing to systemic corruption, institutional failures, or perceived inadequacies in lecturer competence. It highlights the cognitive mechanisms that allow students to reconcile their behavior with their self-perception.

Game Theory explains the "how": how students strategically adapt their behavior in response to perceived academic and societal norms. It illuminates the dynamics of cooperation versus defection, and how individual choices are shaped by the actions of others, particularly in environments where trust is low and enforcement is weak. The models of Prisoner's Dilemma, Tit-for-Tat, and Win-Stay, Lose-Shift reveal the behavioral strategies adopted to maximize perceived utility within a given "game."

Lastly, Prospect Theory offers insight into the cognitive distortions that influence decision-making when outcomes are uncertain. Central to this framework is the principle of loss aversion: the idea that individuals perceive the pain of losing as more intense than the pleasure of gaining an equivalent amount.

2.8. Institutional Interventions and Attributional Reframing

Attribution Theory suggests that people interpret their actions by attributing causes (either credit or blame) based on perceived control sources (Weiner, 1985). In educational settings, students often externalize blame for misconduct when faced with disorganized, inconsistent, or ethically questionable institutional environments. However, institutions are dynamic and can reshape these attributional patterns through intentional interventions that promote transparency, accountability, and ethical engagement. A particularly effective approach is reframing, which involves shifting the focus of discussions about academic integrity from punitive measures to shared responsibility. Ellis (2018) describes reframing as a way to "get things unstuck" by altering how individuals view their roles and responsibilities. In the context of AI misuse, reframing could involve presenting ethical decision-making not as a mandated rule but as a fundamental academic and professional skill. This change encourages students to internalize responsibility rather than avoid it. Several universities in Uganda have started implementing AI literacy modules within their general education programs. These efforts not only clarify AI technologies but also develop critical skills such as citation ethics, responsible use, and evaluative thinking (see the example of Makerere University 5.1.2).

When students are equipped with both technical knowledge and ethical guidance, the tendency to blame misconduct on ignorance or institutional failure decreases. Faculty-centred interventions further strengthen this ethical environment. Professional development programs can enable lecturers to demonstrate proper AI use, clarify expectations, and redesign assessments with integrity in mind. When institutional messages are reinforced in daily teaching practices, students are more likely to see academic results as a product of their own efforts, thereby reducing moral disengagement and encouraging internal attribution. Additional tools, such as honour codes, AI-use declarations, and peer-led ethics initiatives, can support this cultural transformation. These mechanisms indicate that integrity is not enforced from above but nurtured as a shared value within the academic community. As Ellis (2018) highlights, successful reframing requires alignment across multiple levels: micro (individual behavior), meso (departmental norms), and macro (institutional structures). Ultimately, attributional reframing is not about shifting blame but about restoring student agency. When learners believe their choices are significant, and institutions show a commitment to their ethical development, students are more likely to choose integrity, even when faced with tempting shortcuts enabled by AI.

3. METHODOLOGY

The study employed a systematic review approach (Page et al., 2021) to review the literature on the misuse of AI in education in SSA. Based on a Boolean search, google scholar was used to locate articles, book chapters and books that focused on AI misuse in the developing world. Articles that are of relevance to the study aims and objectives were identified. Focusing on Uganda in particular, government reports from relevant ministries, the IGG, and relevant studies were consulted.

3.1 Search Strategy and Eligibility Criteria

A comprehensive literature search was conducted across multiple academic databases, including Scopus, Web of Science, JSTOR, EBSCOhost, and Google Scholar. Search terms combined thematic keywords such as AI misuse, academic integrity, attribution theory, educational governance, and Sub-Saharan Africa (SSA). Boolean operators and controlled vocabulary (where applicable) were employed to refine results.

Supplementary materials were sourced from reputable institutional platforms, including government education portals, United Nations agency websites, and academic repositories from regional universities. Inclusion criteria prioritized peer-reviewed journal articles, policy papers, and empirical studies published between 2010 and 2024 that addressed AI use in education, ethical implications, or governance structures relevant to SSA contexts. Exclusion criteria included articles lacking theoretical grounding, anecdotal commentary, or studies focused solely on technical AI design without behavioral or institutional analysis.

Keywords and Boolean operators were meticulously combined to ensure a broad yet targeted search, with key terms including ("AI misuse" OR "artificial intelligence misuse" OR "AI academic dishonesty" OR "generative AI misconduct") AND ("attribution theory" OR "game theory" OR "prospect theory" OR "locus of control" OR "moral disengagement") AND ("higher education" OR "university" OR "academic integrity") AND ("Sub-Saharan Africa" OR "Uganda" OR "developing nations" OR "ethically compromised environments"); the eligibility criteria for inclusion were based on study design (qualitative and quantitative studies, theoretical papers, review articles, and grey literature such as reports and policy documents), relevance (focused on AI use/misuse in higher education, directly or implicitly discussing attributional processes, game-theoretic behaviors, or risk perception, especially in relation to ethical environments and cultural contexts), geographical focus (prioritizing SSA and Uganda but also including relevant studies from other global contexts due to the nascent nature of research on AI misuse in SSA), and language (English-only publications).

3.2 Data Extraction and Synthesis

Following the initial broad search, 50 articles were screened based on their titles and abstracts for relevance. 40 full-text articles of potentially relevant studies were then retrieved and reviewed for their contribution to the theoretical framework and contextual understanding. Data extraction focused on identifying core theoretical concepts and their applications, empirical findings related to AI misuse and student rationalizations, insights into the influence of systemic factors such as governance and resources, and cultural dimensions were all examined; proposed interventions and their underlying logic were also considered, and the synthesis of the extracted data involved a conceptual mapping approach that identified recurring themes and interconnections between theoretical constructs (namely attribution theory, game theory, and prospect theory) and their manifestations in the context of AI misuse in Sub-Saharan African universities.

4. FACTORS INFLUENCING AI MISUSE

4.1 AI in Higher Education: Opportunities, Misuse, and Ethical Governance

AI is swiftly reshaping higher education, presenting remarkable opportunities for tailored learning experiences, cutting-edge research, and efficient administration. Tools powered by AI can notably enhance student engagement and problem-solving abilities, as long as students interact with them critically rather than passively accepting AI-generated answers (Zawacki-Richter et al., 2024). However, these advancements have come with significant ethical challenges, especially concerning misuse. The impact of AI on learning: whether it enriches or diminishes it—largely depends on how institutions frame its use, either as a means to foster deeper understanding or as a shortcut that compromises intellectual rigor.

4.2 AI Misuse and Attribution Theory in Learning and Research:

As earlier explained, attribution theory provides a valuable framework for explaining the misuse of AI in the academia: students over depend on AI for academic tasks, they often shift the blame to other external factors such as ambiguous academic guidelines or peer pressure, rather than acknowledging their own weaknesses (Weiner, 1972, 2012). This behavior diminishes critical thinking and promotes superficial reasoning. The same principle applies to academic researchers, who like the students they teach, justify the weakening of methodological quality and rigor by viewing AI tools as passive instruments, instead of addressing their own internal weaknesses (Coeckelbergh, 2020). AI ought to be a supportive tool not a replacement for human cognition, thus enhancing epistemic accountability.

Adding to the complexity is the "many hands problem" in AI-driven research. As automated tools increasingly handle literature reviews, data analysis, and even manuscript writing, accountability for mistakes or biases becomes dispersed (Weiner, 1972, 2012). This dispersion leads to a rise in formulaic papers and reused datasets, often presented without thorough validation (Zhai et al., 2024). The result is a potential decline in originality and methodological depth in scholarly work. AI surfaces as a diagnostic tool: students shift moral responsibility onto the system, citing external pressures to justify internal decisions (Weiner, 1985).

4.3 The Specific Context of Sub-Saharan African (SSA)

Universities in Sub-Saharan Africa encounter a distinct set of challenges that heighten both the allure and the dangers of AI misuse. Persistent deficiencies in research infrastructure, restricted access to current software, and a lack of skilled personnel often lead students and faculty to heavily depend on generative tools. Attribution theory sheds light on this pattern: when researchers view methodological shortcuts as a reaction to systemic inadequacies rather than personal oversight, they might completely abandon rigorous validation (Coeckelbergh, 2020). In these situations, AI misuse becomes less of a deviant behavior and more of a normalized coping mechanism: one that risks sustaining epistemic dependency and undermining research independence.

4.4 Consumerism and AI

A rising consumerist mindset in education (where students perceive themselves as clients and academic achievement as a commodity) has exacerbated the misuse of AI technologies. The rise of student consumerism in higher education fosters an instrumental approach, where students prioritize credentials over deep learning, potentially compromising academic integrity (Naidoo & Jamieson, 2005).

Consequently, students might feel justified in delegating assignments to AI systems, particularly when they rationalize that institutional demands are unclear, overwhelming, or poorly aligned with contemporary learning practices (Hua, 2023). Attribution Theory once again emerges as a tool for diagnosis: students shift moral responsibility onto the system, citing external pressures to justify internal decisions (Weiner, 1985). While many claim to support academic integrity, their actual behavior often diverges: especially when AI misuse seems widespread, low-risk, and undetectable (Hua, 2023). In transnational educational markets like Uganda, where satisfaction metrics and enrolment growth increasingly influence institutional priorities, academic rigor can be sidelined: creating a conducive environment for a culture of ethical evasion (Naidoo & Jamieson, 2005).

4.5 Deepfakes: A Major Example of AI Misuse in SSA Higher Education

Deepfake technology has emerged as a particularly troubling issue within the ethical framework of higher education systems in SSA. Deep fakes refer to digitally fabricated media, created using sophisticated algorithms to imitate individuals or fabricate events; they have evolved from being mere novelties to becoming potential instruments for considerable academic disruption (Westerlund, 2019). Their influence has gone beyond typical concerns like plagiarism or cheating; deepfakes threaten the integrity of institutional records, can undermine authentic work, and jeopardize the reliability of verification systems in environments already challenged by inadequate regulatory structures. In vulnerable academic settings, the unchecked proliferation of this technology could exacerbate misinformation, result in defamation, and even enable false documentation. In SSA academic contexts, deepfakes pose unique and multifaceted risks. These technologies can be weaponized to fabricate academic credentials, impersonate students or faculty, spread disinformation, and ultimately erode institutional credibility (Alanazi & Asif, 2024). The region's accelerated adoption of digital technologies (often outpacing the development of legal, ethical, and technical guardrails) has amplified university-level exposure to such vulnerabilities. As Alanazi and Asif (2024) observe, the potential of deepfakes to distort public trust and destabilize the epistemic legitimacy of educational institutions renders them an urgent focus for policy innovation and institutional reform.

In environments where legal infrastructures and enforcement mechanisms remain underdeveloped, the threat of deepfakes is compounded. Attribution theory (Heider, 1958) offers a critical interpretive lens: students and institutions may rationalize their engagement with or tolerance of deepfake technologies through situational attributions such as:

- **Systemic governance failures**: Inadequate oversight and weak enforcement regimes foster conditions in which unethical uses of AI (including deepfake manipulation) can thrive with minimal consequence (Ferretti, 2024).
- **Digital literacy deficits**: Limited awareness and understanding of AI technologies among students and faculty inhibit critical engagement with the ethical stakes of deepfake production and circulation (European Parliament, 2020).
- **Cultural collectivism**: In contexts where collective harmony and consensus are valorised (Hofstede, 1980), widespread exposure to deepfake content may normalize or diffuse responsibility for unethical behavior, reinforcing collective misattributions and compliance.

Deepfake Incidents in SSA Higher Education

There are many examples of deepfake encounters in SSA. Notable among these is the issue of academic fraud in Nigeria in 2023, where university deep fake AI generated research manuscripts were submitted (Roe& Perkins, 2024). Effoduh (2024) reports cases of AI misuse in Kenya, where deep fake videos were used to discredit candidates in a student election in a university. Similarly, a South African university got image issues when deepfake-generated academic papers were used to obtain admissions and scholarships (Roe & Perkins, 2024).

These cases exemplify the need for urgent governance reforms in the academia cross SSA. There is need to put in place AI-specific legislation in academic institutions, so as to shield them from AI misuse risks that transcend individual transgressions, threatening broader institutional credibility, scholarly legitimacy, and public trust (Roe & Perkins, 2024; Effoduh, 2024).

4.6 Effects of Cognitive Over Dependence of AI in Education

Apart from reputational damage to institutions, the misuse of AI has a profound effect on students. Recent studies show an inverse relationship between frequent AI use and the development of critical thinking abilities (Zhai et al., 2024). Specifically, systematic reviews show that students who often depend on AI systems and tools for academic purposes tend to portray lower decision-making skills and weaker analytical reasoning (Zhai et al., 2024). This over dependence often appears as cognitive offloading (the transfer of intellectual effort to external tools) which may gradually weaken inherent cognitive abilities. This situation illustrates what researchers call the cognitive paradox of AI in education (Crompton & Burke, 2023). According to Zawacki-Richter et al., (2023), while AI improves personalized learning and operational efficiency, it also encourages cognitive dependence, potentially replacing opportunities for active recall, complex problem-solving, and the development of deep conceptual understanding. The consequences of this are many, and include low metacognitive awareness: As AI systems start to influence students' reasoning processes, learners may find it difficult to critically evaluate their own thought patterns, hindering the development of reflective judgment (Weiner, 1972, 2012). Another problem is that of wakened problem-solving skills: continuous use of AI-generated responses can lead to shallow engagement with content, preventing the acquisition of strong analytical and critical thinking skills. Further, persistent over dependence on AI may lead to long-term cognitive trade-offs: Without deliberate pedagogical measures, AI-driven education might prioritize speed and convenience over deep cognitive engagement, weakening the student's role as an active creator of knowledge. These assertions portray the need or a re-evaluation of AI integration strategies within educational institutions, which actively counter cognitive complacency while at the same time promoting resilient intellectual habits.

4.7 Resource Constraints and the Enforcement of Ethical AI Governance in Higher Education

The effective implementation of ethical AI policies in higher education is often obstructed by acute resource limitations, in developing country contexts and SSA is no exception. Below is a presentation of some of these constraints.

Financial Barriers

Many institutions, especially private universities face chronic underfunding that impedes the acquisition and maintenance of infrastructure crucial for ethical AI oversight. In Uganda, many private universities are financially distressed (Nalwoga, 2021), hence limiting the procurement of advanced detection tools for AI-generated content, secure digital platforms, and enabling of equitable access to AI technologies for students and faculty. Further, lack of financial resources constrains the recruitment and retention of professionals with experience in AI ethics and digital forensics; it also curtails faculty development initiatives through training, aimed at embedding AI literacy and misuse detection into pedagogy.

Tensions Between Regulation and Academic Freedom

The enactment and enforcement of AI ethics policies may be viewed as infringement upon academic freedom particularly in instructional design and assessment methodologies. In SSA, this tension is often magnified by institutional narratives or discourses that frame digital investments as externally imposed rather than internally motivated pedagogical initiatives (Heider, 1958). As Zhai et al., (2024) caution, while digital transformation enhances access and operational efficiency, it can simultaneously reduce opportunities for in-person academic engagement: an especially critical dimension for students who rely on physical campus environments for learning and community development.

4.8 Culture and AI Misuse in Sub-Saharan African Higher Education

This study defines culture as "the collective programming of the mind which distinguishes the members of one human group from another" (Hofstede, 1980 p.25). This programming starts at home, and is reinforced by the school, church and state (Hofstede, 1980). Culture is a dynamic process that occurs within a given society, which creates a cognitive map of beliefs, values, meaning, and attitudes that drive perception, thoughts, reasoning, actions, response and interactions (Tung, 1995). Culture influences every thing we do, and in an academic setting, it actively shapes how individuals interpret, justify, and normalize their actions, (Hofstede, 2001). In Sub-Saharan African (SSA) contexts, such as Uganda, cultural orientations significantly influence how students engage with AI technologies, sometimes inadvertently leading to academic misconduct. This section explores how collectivism, power distance, uncertainty avoidance, and short-term orientation intersect with attribution theory to shed light on the socio-cultural logic behind AI-related academic transgressions.

Collectivism and the Diffusion of Responsibility

SSA societies, including Uganda, are predominantly collectivist, hence group norms and values have precedence over individual desires and goals. In such situations, individual identity and moral responsibility are deeply rooted in social networks (Rarick et al., 2013). Hence students in such a context may prioritize group cohesion over strict adherence to abstract academic norms. The misuse of AI is often justified by collective necessity, reducing perceptions of individual liability. This diffusion of responsibility is consistent with attributional patterns that externalize blame and normalize misconduct as a realistic response to communal pressures. The collectivist nature of many SSA societies, coupled with hierarchical power dynamics, often leads students to prioritize social approval over individual ethical standards, thereby increasing AI misuse (Hofstede, 2001; Jobin et al., 2019). Cultural differences, such as collectivist values and hierarchical social structures in many Sub-Saharan African societies, shape ethical perceptions of AI, often prioritizing community norms over individual accountability and rationalizing misuse when it aligns with societal expectations or authority directives (Jobin et al., 2019). Such a cultural context fosters external attributions, where students may justify unethical AI use as a response to societal pressures or lack of enforcement (Weiner, 1986; Bukuluki, 2013).

For example, in a situation where a lecturer assigns a group work. What does a student who is not in agreement with AI misuse do if the group wants to hand in AI generated answers? In such a context, attributional reasoning is not solely psychological but profoundly social. The students may not simply ask, "Is this right?" but rather, "What will others think of me if I refuse to abide by what the group says? Hence this collectivist orientation involuntarily contributes to academic misconduct. In short, in contexts where visible peer behavior and conformity are highly prized, students may feel obliged to use AI tools unethically, not primarily out of personal conviction, but to avoid social exclusion or perceived reputational loss within their close environment.

Bukuluki (2013) argues that in some Ugandan communities, acts typically labelled as corruption (such as misappropriating public funds) can be deemed as acceptable if they demonstrably benefit one's family, clan, or community. This logic regrettably extends into academia: misconduct is not necessarily seen as deviance if it serves perceived collective goals, such as helping a friend pass an exam or maintaining group harmony. In such cases, the attribution of blame becomes diffused across the social unit, and individual responsibility is shredded, leading to ethical detachment (Bandura, 1999).

Power Distance and Strategic Imitation

Woven onto collectivism is the dimension of power distance, which is notably high in many SSA societies, including Uganda (Hofstede, 2001). High power distance signifies an acceptance of unequal distribution of power and authority. In such societies, leaders are often revered, and their actions may set significant moral precedents that are less likely to be questioned. When students observe lecturers manipulating grades, or national leaders acquiring fraudulent credentials without significant consequence, they may internalize the message that power or status exempts one from scrutiny. Misconduct, rather than being seen as shameful, can become aspirational or simply an adaptive tactic in a flawed system, hence this power hierarchy fundamentally reshapes attributional logic.

Thus, students may no longer view cheating or AI misuse as a transgression, but rather as a strategic tactic in a system where rules are applied unevenly. Bandura's (1999) concept of displacement of responsibility is activated here: "If those above me bend the rules and are praised, why shouldn't I?" The result is a psychological drift from personal accountability to strategic imitation. Game theory further underscores this adaptation: in hierarchies where rule enforcement is uneven and outcomes appear to favour defection, students may adopt adaptive cheating strategies not because they are inherently morally bankrupt, but because the system appears to reward misconduct over integrity when misconduct is not only tolerated but sometimes strategically overlooked (Kagaba, 2015). The rational response, then, is to defect rather than be disadvantaged.

Uncertainty Avoidance and the Illusion of Mastery

Uncertainty avoidance is an expression of a society's tolerance for uncertainty and ambiguity, indicating the extent to which a culture programs its members to feel either uncomfortable or comfortable in unstructured situations i.e. different from the usual situation (Inkeles & Levinson, 1969). Uganda is a high uncertainty avoidance society (Hofstede, 2001). In this context, the adoption of AI tools by students can be perceived paradoxically as both a bold leap into modernity and a shortcut to guaranteed success or prestige. Students who embrace AI early may feel they have "arrived" intellectually or technologically, especially when peers and lecturers remain hesitant or uninformed. They may thus misuse AI since they are ahead of others, including their lecturers.

Overconfidence and the Illusion of Mastery in AI Use

Early integration of AI tools in academic settings can create a misleading sense of expertise, leading to overconfidence and potential misuse. Attribution theory provides a good perspective on how students may rationalize such behavior. Instead of viewing their dependence on AI as inappropriate and unethical, students might interpret their performance as a sign of creativity, digital competence, or adaptive intelligence. This shift in attribution often results in thoughts like, "I'm not cheating, I'm just ahead of the curve," or "The system is inefficient; I'm optimizing it" (Weiner, 1985; Bandura, 1999). Such flawed reasoning shifts responsibility away from the individual, especially in institutions with weak oversight and a cultural bias towards certainty. In environments where academic standards are blurred and evaluation criteria are vague, AI tools become more than just aids: they act as psychological havens, providing the illusion of consistent success without the risk of failure or the effort required for genuine learning. This situation creates a refined but dangerous cycle: as students continue to rely on AI for their academic tasks, they start to confuse technical proficiency with true mastery of the subject. This makes them confuse operational skill for intellectual depth, thus bypassing deep learning processes and eroding the value of independent inquiry.

Short-Term Orientation and the Normalization of AI Misuse in Academic Contexts

Long-Term Orientation as opposed to short-term orientation deals with virtue regardless of truth. Values associated with long term orientation are thrift and perseverance, while values associated with short term orientation are respect for tradition, fulfilling social obligations, and protecting one's 'face' (Hofstede, 2001). Short-term orientation affects academic behavior in Uganda because it is a value system that favours immediate rewards over long-term development (Hofstede, 2001). In educational contexts, this often results in a focus on passing exams, achieving high grades, and obtaining credentials, rather than pursuing concrete goals such as critical thinking, intellectual curiosity, and cognitive resilience.

In an environment driven by performance, generative AI tools become appealing as they provide a quick and easy way to produce high-quality work and receive positive evaluations. In contrast, ethical perspectives and genuine scholarly effort are viewed as inefficient or indulgences that detract one from the goal of achieving quick academic success. Such a mindset highlights a deeper institutional issue: when reward systems prioritize superficial achievements over intellectual processes, technological shortcuts not only become tempting but seem logical. Attribution theory provides valuable insight in this instance. When faced with the ethical implications of AI misuse, students often shift responsibility by pointing to institutional shortcomings: "The system only values grades" or "We're never taught how to think critically." These are typical situational attributions (Weiner, 1985), where blame is placed on broader systemic structures. Furthermore, given the socio-economic importance of academic success in SSA (linked to social mobility and family pride plus honour), students may morally justify AI misuse as a way to meet immediate expectations. As Bandura (1999) notes, ethical detachment is more likely when unethical behavior serves a socially accepted goal, such as passing an exam or avoiding loss of face. This short-term focus distorts students' understanding of mastery, reducing education to a transactional activity and eroding its ability to nurture independent, long-term oriented people.

Summary: Cultural intelligence in intervention

The extensive impact of the cultural elements described above requires the enactment of culturally informed institutional approaches. To overcome AI misuse in higher education within SSA, it is imperative that institutions move past individual ethical appeals and instead design systemic changes that recognize and address these entrenched cultural norms. This includes nurturing ethical peer standards, demonstrating integrity by leaders, reducing power imbalances, incentivizing long-term educational pursuits, and integrating AI literacy into culturally relevant contexts and stories. Only through such thorough, culturally agreeable methods can institutions hope to break the ongoing cycle of attributional justification and AI-facilitated academic misconduct, ultimately nurturing a true culture of integrity over time. The three theoretical frameworks discussed (attribution theory, game theory, and prospect theory) unpack the complex issues involved. Attribution theory forms the foundation, illustrating how students rationalize accountability for AI misuse, by externalizing blame to perceived institutional shortcomings, such as unclear AI policies, inconsistent lecturer competence, or poorly designed assessments

(Cotton et al., 2025; Chan & Hu, 2023), thus paving the way for moral disengagement without severe self-reproach (Bandura, 1999).

Game theory provides the behavioral lens, illustrating how students strategically adapt their actions within an academic "game" where ethical standards are inconsistently enforced (Axelrod, 1984; Nowak & Sigmund, 1993). In such environments, "defection" through AI misuse can appear as a rational choice to avoid disadvantage, especially if peers are perceived to be gaining an unfair edge. The dynamics of the Prisoner's Dilemma, Win-Stay, Lose-Shift, and Tit-for-Tat strategies become evident, showcasing how individual choices are shaped by a low-trust environment.

Lastly, *Prospect Theory* (Kahneman & Tversky, 1979) clarifies the decision-making bias, explaining why students are often more sensitive to the perceived "loss" of not using AI (such as lost time or lower grades compared to AI-using peers) than to the long-term cost of engaging in a critical thinking–based education. This loss aversion, coupled with external attributions, creates a powerful incentive for AI misuse.

Crucially, these theoretical dynamics are profoundly shaped by the cultural dimensions prevalent in contexts like Uganda. Collectivism can diffuse individual responsibility within peer groups (Bukuluki, 2013; Rarick et al., 2013), high power distance can lead to the strategic imitation of unethical behavior observed in authority figures (Hofstede, 2001), high uncertainty avoidance can lead to an "illusion of mastery" through AI as a means to guarantee outcomes, and a short-term orientation can prioritize immediate grades over deep learning (Hofstede, 2001). These cultural factors, combined with genuine resource constraints in institutions, contribute to a complex ecosystem where AI becomes a silent accomplice in the erosion of academic integrity.

5. CONCLUSION

Based on a tripartite theoretical model, the current study went out to establish the causes of AI misuse by students in higher institutions of learning in SSA, taking Uganda as an example, and how students rationalize this behavior. *Attribution Theory explains how students externalize blame for AI misuse to societal or institutional factors; Game Theory highlights competitive pressures leading to strategic defection; Prospect Theory accounts for risk- reward trade-offs, where fear of loss drives unethical decisions.*

Disrupting the Cycle of AI Misuse: A Call for Systemic Reform

The study urgues that the pattern of AI misuse is not insurmountable. Instead, it can be mitigated through intentional, comprehensive strategies that reshape both institutional frameworks and individual attribution methods. By investing in educational paradigms that emphasize critical thinking, structured assessments, and personalized learning prompts, deeper engagement can be encouraged, shifting students' focus from blaming external factors to taking responsibility for their academic trajectory (Biggs, 2003; Ulster University, 2024). Additionally, fostering ethical leadership and clear institutional policies (such as well-communicated AI guidelines and digital literacy programs) can enhance accountability and build trust (Ellis, 2018). Importantly, addressing resource constraints through strategic optimization and collaboration between institutions is crucial for enabling universities to both detect and prevent AI-related misconduct. Ultimately, reframing attribution (from systemic blame-shifting to personal and institutional responsibility) is not just a theoretical imperative. It is a practical and ethical necessity. *The future of higher education in SSA depends not only on how institutions regulate AI, but on how they cultivate integrity, responsibility, and resilience in the digital age*

5.1 Recommendations for Mitigating AI Misuse in Higher Education in SSA

Based on insights from the three theoretical perspectives in this study, the study now uses a three-pronged approach to make a case for ethical use of AI in higher institutions. First this section presents two case studies one international and another local, to portray actionable insights about AI. Stanford university demonstrates how the proposed mitigation strategies (rooted in attribution, game, and prospect theories) have been successfully applied, while Makerere University demonstrates how responsible AI use is being promoted in SSA. Second, this section offers some recommendations that can be used to mitigate constraints in AI use, as well as promote ethical behavior in its use. Third, the section makes an attempt to map constraints to AI use to some practical solutions.

5.1.1 The Stanford University

The guidelines for generative AI use in the classroom in this institution offer a robust framework that can be effectively analyzed through the lens of attribution theory. The Stanford GSB policies emphasize clear guidelines for generative AI use in coursework, fostering a culture of internal attribution by promoting responsible engagement with AI tools (Stanford University, 2025; Bearman et al., 2023). Transparency in AI-supported assessment requires clear communication of how AI tools should be used, including their role in decision-making processes and the rationale behind their implementation (Bearman et al., 2023). Educators must establish guidelines that balance the benefits of AI-driven assessments with the need to maintain academic integrity and student trust (Bearman et al., 2023). The policies are designed to dismantle these external excuses and foster a culture of internal attribution, where students take personal responsibility for their academic integrity. One of the most salient measures is the explicit, course-specific guidance. By requiring instructors to state their policy on the syllabus and in class, the university eliminates the excuse of "I didn't know the rules." This clarity shifts the locus of causality from an external, ambiguous policy to a student's personal choice. When a student chooses to misuse AI, they cannot blame the institution's oversight, because the policy was clearly communicated. The practical guidelines further reinforce this internal responsibility. The requirement to cite all AI-generated material forces students to acknowledge their use of the tool, making it a deliberate action they must document. This act of citation is a public declaration of one's methodological choices, directly countering any attempt to externalize blame. Additionally, the policy requires students to fact-check and critically evaluate AI outputs. This measure places the burden of responsibility for the work's accuracy and quality squarely on the student, not the AI tool. A poor grade on a paper with factual errors cannot be blamed on the AI tool; it is a direct consequence of the student's failure to verify the information. Universities in Sub-Saharan Africa (SSA) should emulate these measures, creating a policy environment that promotes ethical use by making it a matter of individual accountability, not outlawing AI. By providing clear guidance and calling for transparency, institutions can nurture an academic culture where students are less likely to justify AI misuse through external attribution and are instead driven to see critical thinking and academic integrity as their own, internally generated responsibilities.

5.1.2 The Makerere University Centre for Artificial Intelligence and Data Science (Mak-CAD)

In a proactive response to the growing influence of artificial intelligence (AI) and the ethical challenges it presents, Makerere University formally established the Centre for Artificial Intelligence and Data Science (Mak-CAD) to drive Africa's technological development through AI innovation (Makerere University, 2025; Hlongwane et al., 2024). Effective AI governance in higher education requires institutional frameworks that prioritize ethical use, stakeholder collaboration, and alignment with sustainable development goals (Hlongwane et al., 2024). Universities in developing regions such as SSA can leverage AI to address local challenges, however success depends on robust policies that ensure equitable access and cultural relevance (Hlongwane et al., 2024). The Makerere initiative was not merely a reaction to academic misconduct, but a strategic move to position the university, and by extension Uganda, at the forefront of the responsible AI revolution in Africa. The Centre was founded with the core mission of harnessing the transformative power of AI to address Africa's most pressing challenges, while simultaneously building a culture of ethical and responsible AI use. Mak-CAD's utility in promoting the good use of AI stems from a multifaceted approach that addresses both the technical and ethical dimensions of the technology. First, the Centre's research and training are based on the principles of responsible AI, ensuring that systems developed are not only effective but also transparent, accountable, and fair. By focusing on these core tenets, Mak-CAD aims to build a new generation of researchers and practitioners who are not only skilled in AI but are also deeply aware of its societal implications. Second, the Centre is positioned as a critical hub for contextualized AI solutions. Instead of adopting generic models from the developed west, Mak-CAD focuses on developing AI applications that are designed to cater for the unique needs and cultural contexts of Africa, particularly in sectors like agriculture, healthcare, and education. This approach promotes a more human-centered and ethical deployment of AI. Finally, by fostering partnerships with global AI hubs and local stakeholders, Mak-CAD reinforces the importance of multi-stakeholder collaboration, ensuring that the development and use of AI are inclusive and benefit all segments of society, thereby directly countering the potential for unchecked, apathetic use of AI. The Centre's work directly aligns with the ethical principles of sustainable development, demonstrating that technological advancement and social responsibility are not mutually exclusive.

5.1.3 General Recommendations

In SSA's context of resource limitations, digital divides, cultural attitudes toward technology, and weak regulatory frameworks, institutions should implement the following strategies.

Governance and Policy

1. **Institutional Transparency:** Institutions need to create, distribute, and regularly update clear and accessible policies regarding the ethical use of AI. Transparent governance processes, particularly concerning AI integration and misconduct resolution, can enhance institutional trust and foster shared accountability.

2. **Strengthening Deepfake Policy Frameworks:** Institutions need to implement strict protocols for identifying and penalizing deepfake-enabled academic fraud. This includes advocating for national regulatory frameworks *that align with global standards while respecting local cultural contexts* (UNESCO, 2024).
3. **Enhance Institutional Oversight and Capacity:** Acquire and maintain advanced tools for identifying AI-generated and manipulated content.

Capacity Building

1. **Digital Literacy Programs:** It is essential for institutions to provide students, faculty, and staff with comprehensive digital skills that go beyond technical proficiency to include AI ethics, data protection, intellectual property, and critical assessment of AI-generated content (Crompton & Burke, 2023). Further, AI literacy programs should be embedded within general education courses and disciplinary-specific curricula. These programs should educate students on the capabilities and limitations of AI, ethical implications of AI use (e.g., data privacy, intellectual property), responsible citation, and critical evaluation of AI-generated content (UNESCO, 2023; Crompton & Burke, 2023).
2. **Open-Source Solutions:** Emphasizing open-source AI tools for detection and ethical governance can decrease reliance on expensive commercial options. *(Zawacki-Richter et al., 2023).*
3. **Strategic Funding Allocation:** Limited resources should be directed towards high-impact areas such as faculty development, ethical policy creation, and essential infrastructure (Deloitte, 2023; Zawacki-Richter et al., 2023).
4. **Faculty Development Programs:** Implement mandatory and ongoing professional development for lecturers and staff to equip them with the ability to model ethical AI use, redesign assessments to be AI-resistant, and manage ethical dilemmas (Cotton et al., 2023; Brown, 2017; Perkins et al., 2024; Chan & Hu, 2023).
5. **Specialized Personnel:** Train academic staff, IT units, and integrity officers in AI ethics, digital forensics, and the operational use of detection software—addressing both human capital and institutional enforcement gaps
6. **Collaborative Initiatives:** Institutions should participate in regional and international collaborations to exchange expertise, tools, and governance models, thereby increasing capacity without incurring redundant costs (Deloitte, 2023; Zawacki-Richter et al., 2023). Collaborative networks and open-source platforms can enhance AI adoption in education by reducing costs and fostering shared expertise across institutions (Zawacki-Richter et al., 2023).
7. **Strategic Funding Allocation:** Limited resources should be directed towards high-impact areas such as faculty development, ethical policy creation, and essential infrastructure (Deloitte, 2023; Zawacki-Richter et al., 2023). The effective integration of AI in higher education requires strategic resource allocation to support infrastructure, training, and equitable access, particularly in under-resourced institutions (Zawacki-Richter et al., 2023).

Pedagogical Innovation

1. **Promote Critical Thinking:** Explicitly foster critical thinking skills to reduce students' blind acceptance of manipulated content, including deepfakes, and to encourage independent problem-solving over passive reliance on AI-generated solutions.
2. **Shift from Recall to Higher-Order Thinking:** Design assignments that emphasize analysis, evaluation, synthesis, and creation—tasks less susceptible to AI automation (Biggs, 2003; Ulster University, 2024).
3. **Contextualized and Personalized Prompts:** Develop prompts that require students to integrate personal experiences, cultural context, or local realities, making it difficult for generic AI outputs to suffice (Patel et al., 2025).
4. **Emphasize Process-Based Evaluation:** Incorporate annotated drafts, oral defences, peer reviews, and other checkpoints that assess intellectual growth and iterative reflection rather than just final products (Brown, 2017).
5. **Enhancing Peer-Review Mechanisms:** To maintain research integrity, peer-review processes must be strengthened—both within academic institutions and scholarly journals—to identify low-quality or AI-generated submissions (Perkins et al. 2024).
6. **Encouraging Collaborative Research Networks:** Promoting data-sharing and cross-institutional research partnerships can reduce overdependence on generative AI tools, while simultaneously improving research quality and originality (Deloitte, 2023 Zawacki-Richter et al., 2023).

Culture and Leadership

1. **Implement Transparency Protocols:** Adopt AI use declaration policies where students explicitly disclose how and when AI tools were used in their assignments. This fosters "ethical metacognition" and encourages accountability (Bearman et al., 2023).
2. **Model Ethical Leadership:** Leaders at all levels—institutional, faculty, and student—must consistently model ethical behavior, transparent decision-making, and responsible AI use (Bandura, 1999).
3. **Challenge Short-Termism:** Realign incentives to reward long-term learning outcomes, critical thinking, and applied skills over mere short-term academic success (Hofstede, 2001).
4. **Foster a Culture of Integrity:** Implement honour codes and peer-led ethics campaigns to reinforce that ethical behavior is a shared responsibility of the academic community, rather than merely enforced from above (Ellis, 2018).

If these multi-layered recommendations are implemented, higher education institutions, particularly in SSA, can strategically address the psychological and systemic drivers of AI misuse. This holistic approach is essential not only for upholding academic integrity but also for ensuring that AI becomes a truly beneficial tool for education and societal development.

5.1.4 Mapping Problems to Solutions

In the table below, the paper presents examples of cases where AI misuse is matched with possible solutions.

Table 3. AI problems and possible solutions

Problem/Driver of AI Misuse	Theoretical Link	Proposed Solution	Expected Outcome
External Attributions (e.g., blaming corruption or weak oversight)	Attribution Theory (Weiner, 1986)	Transparent AI policies and faculty training on ethical modeling	Internal accountability; moral disengagement (Bandura, 1999)
Strategic Defection (e.g., peer AI use leading to "race to the bottom")	Game Theory (Axelrod, 1984)	Assessments with process checkpoints and AI declarations	Cooperation via higher defection costs; fosters Nash equilibrium of integrity
Loss Aversion (e.g., fear of lower grades without AI)	Prospect Theory (Kahneman & Tversky, 1979)	Integrate AI literacy programs; emphasize long-term gains	Ethical use to boost critical thinking
Cultural Factors (e.g., collectivism diffusing responsibility)	Cultural Dimensions (Hofstede, 2001)	Peer-led ethics campaigns and honour codes	Normalizes group integrity norms; counters short-term orientation
Resource Constraints (e.g., financial barriers to detection tools)	Systemic Governance Issues	Collaborative open-source initiatives and prioritized funding	Enhances oversight without high costs; builds institutional trust (Zawacki-Richter et al., 2024).

The table is a well-structured analysis that accurately connects the complex problems of AI misuse to established academic theories. The proposed solutions are practical and directly address the root causes identified.

REFERENCES

Alanazi, S., & Asif, S. (2024). Exploring deepfake technology: Creation, consequences and countermeasures. *Human-Intelligent Systems Integration, 6*(1), 49–60. https://link.springer.com/article/10.1007/s42454-024-00102-6

Axelrod, R. (1984). *The evolution of cooperation.* Basic Books.

Bandura, A. (1999). Moral disengagement in the perpetration of inhumanities. *Personality and Social Psychology Review, 3*(3), 193–209. DOI: 10.1207/s15327957pspr0303_3 PMID: 15661671

Basha, J. Y. (2024). The negative impacts of AI tools on students in academic and real-life performance. *International Journal of Social Sciences and Commerce, 1*(3), 1–16. https://ijssc.org/

Bearman, M., & Ajjawi, R. (2023). Learning to work with the black box: Pedagogy for a world with artificial intelligence. *British Journal of Educational Technology, 54*(5), 1160–1173. DOI: 10.1111/bjet.13337

Bearman, M., Dawson, P., Bennett, S., Hall, M., Molloy, E., Boud, D., & Joughin, G. (2016). How university teachers design assessments: A cross-disciplinary study. *Higher Education, 74*(1), 49–64. DOI: 10.1007/s10734-016-0027-7

Bearman, M., Nieminen, J. H., & Ajjawi, R. (2023). Designing assessment in a digital world: An organising framework. *Assessment & Evaluation in Higher Education, 48*(3), 291–304. DOI: 10.1080/02602938.2022.2069674

Biggs, J. (2003). *Teaching for quality learning at university* (2nd ed.). Society for Research into Higher Education & Open University Press.

Brown, G. T. (2017). *Assessment of student achievement.* Routledge. DOI: 10.4324/9781315162058

Bukuluki, P. (2013). "When I steal, it is for the benefit of me and you": Is collectivism engendering corruption in Uganda? *International Letters of Social and Humanistic Sciences, 5*, 27–44. . DOI: 10.18052/www.scipress.com/ILSHS.5.27

Caplan, B. (2011, October 3). Nash equilibrium in higher education. *Library of Economics and Liberty.* https://www.econlib.org/nash-equilibrium-in-higher-education/

Chan, C. K. Y., & Hu, W. (2023). Students' voices on generative AI: Perceptions, benefits, and challenges in higher education. *International Journal of Educational Technology in Higher Education, 20*(1), 43. DOI: 10.1186/s41239-023-00411-8

Coeckelbergh, M. (2020). *AI ethics.* MIT Press. DOI: 10.7551/mitpress/12549.001.0001

Cotton, D. R., Wyness, L., Jane, B., & Cotton, P. A. (2025). Redefining assessments in the age of AI. In *Teaching and learning in the age of generative AI* (pp. 283–308). Routledge. DOI: 10.4324/9781032688602-18

Crompton, H., & Burke, D. (2023). Artificial intelligence in higher education: The state of the field. *International Journal of Educational Technology in Higher Education, 20*(1), 22. DOI: 10.1186/s41239-023-00392-8

Curasi, C. F. (2013). The relative influences of neutralizing behavior and subcultural values on academic dishonesty. *Journal of Education for Business, 88*(3), 167–175. DOI: 10.1080/08832323.2012.668145

Deloitte. (2023). Artificial intelligence in education: Unlocking new possibilities. https://www2.deloitte.com/us/en/insights/industry/public-sector/ai-in-education.html

Effoduh, J. O. (2024, March 8). The role and potential of artificial intelligence in extremist fuelled election misinformation in Africa. *Global Network on Extremism and Technology.* https://gnet-research.org/2024/03/08/the-role-and-potential-of-artificial-intelligence-in-extremist-fuelled-election-misinformation-in-africa/

Ellis, D. E. (2018). Changing the lens: The role of reframing in educational development. *To Improve the Academy, 37*(1), 142–150. DOI: 10.1002/tia2.20067

European Parliament. (2020). The ethics of artificial intelligence: Issues and initiatives. https://www.europarl.europa.eu/RegData/etudes/STUD/2020/634452/EPRS_STU(2020)634452_EN.pdf

Ferretti, T. (2024). Value alignment without institutional change cannot prevent the societal risks of Artificial Intelligence. *LSE Public Policy Review, 3*(3), 1–12. DOI: 10.31389/lseppr.113

Heider, F. (1958). *The psychology of interpersonal relations.* Wiley. DOI: 10.1037/10628-000

Henrich, J. (2015). *The secret of our success: How culture is driving human evolution, domesticating our species, and making us smarter.* Princeton University Press. DOI: 10.2307/j.ctvc77f0d

Hlongwane, J., Shava, G. N., Mangena, A., & Muzari, T. (2024). Towards the integration of artificial intelligence in higher education, challenges and opportunities: The African context, a case of Zimbabwe. *International Journal of Resource Innovation and Social Sciences, 8*(IIIS, 3S), 417–435. DOI: 10.47772/IJRISS.2024.803028S

Hofstede, G. (1980). Culture's consequences: International differences in work-related values. *Sage (Atlanta, Ga.).*

Hofstede, G. (2001). *Culture's consequences: Comparing values, behaviors, institutions, and organizations across nations* (2nd ed.). Sage.

Holmes, W., Bialik, M., & Fadel, C. (2023). *Artificial intelligence in education: Promises and implications for teaching and learning.* Center for Curriculum Redesign. https://curriculumredesign.org/publications/

Hua, J. H. (2023). Beyond exams: Investigating AI tool impact on student attitudes, ethical awareness, and academic dishonesty in online college assessments. *International Journal of Educational Management and Development Studies, 4*(4), 160–185. https://ijemds.com/. DOI: 10.53378/353030

Inkeles, A., & Levinson, D. J. (1969). National character: The study of modal personality and sociocultural systems. In Lindzey, G., & Aronson, E. (Eds.), *The handbook of social psychology* (Vol. 4, pp. 418–506). Addison-Wesley.

Inspectorate of Government. (2022). *Annual performance report 2021/2022*. Government of Uganda. https://www.igg.go.ug/publications/annual-reports/

Jobin, A., Ienca, M., & Vayena, E. (2019). The global landscape of AI ethics guidelines. *Nature Machine Intelligence*, *1*(9), 389–399. DOI: 10.1038/s42256-019-0088-2

Jones, E. E., & Davis, K. E. (1965). From acts to dispositions: The attribution process in social psychology. *Advances in Experimental Social Psychology*, *2*, 219–266. DOI: 10.1016/S0065-2601(08)60107-0

Kagaba, C. (2015). *Combating real and perceived corruption in Uganda's judiciary*. Anti-Corruption Coalition Uganda. https://www.judiciary.go.ug/files/downloads/Combating%20Real%20and%20Perceived%20Corruption%20by%20Cissy%20Kagaba.pdf

Kahneman, D., & Tversky, A. (1979). Prospect theory: An analysis of decision under risk. *Econometrica*, *47*(2), 263–291. DOI: 10.2307/1914185

Kaluya, M. D., & Elliott, E. W. (2018). Corruption in Uganda: A comparative study of citizens' and public officials' perceptions. *African Social Science Review, 9*(1), 4. https://digitalcommons.kennesaw.edu/assr

Katono, I. W. (2016). Ethically questionable behavior and consumerism in Uganda: A survey of university students. In Gbadamosi, A. (Ed.), *Handbook of research on consumerism and buying behavior in developing nations* (pp. 334–361). IGI Global., DOI: 10.4018/978-1-5225-0282-1.ch015

Katono, I. W., & Kyakulumbye, S. (2025). 12. Constraints to the adoption of blended learning in higher education institutions in an emerging market context: the case of Uganda. *Research Handbook on Information Systems and Technology*, 210-231. DOI: DOI: 10.4337/9781035324583.00019

Kelley, H. H. (1967). Attribution theory in social psychology. In Levine, D. (Ed.), *Nebraska symposium on motivation* (Vol. 15, pp. 192–238). University of Nebraska Press.

Kirya, M. T., & Sekalala, S. (2022). Countering corruption to promote social justice in the Global Fund to Fight AIDS, Tuberculosis and Malaria: The case of Uganda. In Singh, P., & Şule, F. P. (Eds.), *Beyond law and development* (pp. 240–256). Routledge., DOI: 10.4324/9780203745298-15

Luckin, R., Holmes, W., Griffiths, M., & Forcier, L. B. (2016). *Intelligence unleashed: An argument for AI in education*. Pearson. https://www.pearson.com/content/dam/corporate/global/pearson-dot-com/files/innovation/Intelligence-Unleashed-Publication.pdf

Makerere University. (2025). Makerere launches AI and data science centre to drive Africa's technological development. *Makerere University News*. https://news.mak.ac.ug/2025/03/makerere-launches-ai-and-data-science-centre-to-drive-africas-technological-development

McGregor, D. (1960). *The human side of enterprise*. McGraw-Hill.

Mugizi, W., & Nagasha, J. I. (2025). E-Learning. In Bangura, A. K., & Ifedi, J. P. A. (Eds.), *Conceptualizations of Africa: Perspectives from Sciences and Humanities* (pp. 143–163). Springer., DOI: 10.1007/978-3-031-74534-8_8

Mugizi, W., Rwothumio, J., & Kasule, G. W. (2023). Measuring digital teaching competence of academic staff in public universities in Uganda. *African Journal of Education. Science and Technology*, *7*(3), 736–745. DOI: 10.2022/ajest.v7i3.90

Naidoo, R., & Jamieson, I. (2005). Empowering participants or corroding learning? Towards a research agenda on the impact of student consumerism in higher education. *Journal of Education Policy*, *20*(3), 267–281. DOI: 10.1080/02680930500108585

Nalwoga, M. M. (2021). Financial sustainability of private universities in Uganda: A critical perspective. *African Journal of Education, Science and Technology*, *6*(3), 128–139. https://ajest.info/

Nowak, M. A., & Sigmund, K. (1993). A strategy of win-stay, lose-shift that outperforms tit-for-tat in the Prisoner's Dilemma game. *Nature*, *364*(6432), 56–58. DOI: 10.1038/364056a0 PMID: 8316296

Nowak, M. A., & Sigmund, K. (2005). Evolution of indirect reciprocity. *Nature*, *437*(7063), 1291–1298. DOI: 10.1038/nature04131 PMID: 16251955

Page, M. J., McKenzie, J. E., Bossuyt, P. M., Boutron, I., Hoffmann, T. C., Mulrow, C. D., Shamseer, L., Tetzlaff, J. M., Akl, E. A., Brennan, S. E., Chou, R., Glanville, J., Grimshaw, J. M., Hróbjartsson, A., Lalu, M. M., Li, T., Loder, E. W., Mayo-Wilson, E., McDonald, S., & Moher, D. (2021). The PRISMA 2020 statement: An updated guideline for reporting systematic reviews. *BMJ (Clinical Research Ed.)*, *372*(71), n71. Advance online publication. DOI: 10.1136/bmj.n71 PMID: 33782057

Patel, H., Boucher, D., Fallahzadeh, E., Hassan, A. E., & Adams, B. (2025). A state-of-the-practice release-readiness checklist for generative AI-based software products: A gray literature survey. *IEEE Software*, *42*(1), 74–83. DOI: 10.1109/MS.2024.3440190

Perkins, M., Roe, J., Postma, D., McGaughran, J., & Hickerson, D. (2024). Detection of GPT-4 generated text in higher education: Combining academic judgement and software to identify generative AI tool misuse. *Journal of Academic Ethics*, *22*(1), 89–113. DOI: 10.1007/s10805-023-09492-6

Plantinga, P., Shilongo, K., Mudongo, O., Umubyeyi, A., Gastrow, M., & Razzano, G. (2024). Responsible artificial intelligence in Africa: Towards policy learning. *Data & Policy*, *6*, e72. DOI: 10.1017/dap.2024.60

Rarick, C., Winter, G., Barczyk, C., & Merkt, E. (2013). Ugandan culture and its influence on business and leadership practice. *Journal of Global Business Issues*, *7*(2), 37–44. https://franklinpublishing.net/

Roe, J., Perkins, M., & Furze, L. (2024). Deepfakes and higher education: A research agenda and scoping review of synthetic media. *Journal of University Teaching & Learning Practice*, *21*(10), 1–22. DOI: 10.53761/2y2np178

Ross, L. (1977). The intuitive psychologist and his shortcomings: Distortions in the attribution process. In Vol. 10, pp. 173–220). Advances in experimental social psychology. Academic Press. DOI: 10.1016/S0065-2601(08)60357-3

Rotter, J. B. (1966). Generalized expectancies for internal versus external control of reinforcement. *Psychological Monographs: General and Applied, 80* (1, Whole No. 609).

Şahin, F., & Yüksel, İ. (2021). Meaning and uniqueness of ethics and ethical teacher behaviors in the teaching profession. *Inquiry in Education, 13*(2), 2. https://files.eric.ed.gov/fulltext/EJ1338248.pdf

Seligman, M. E. (1975). *Learned helplessness: On depression, development, and death.* W.H. Freeman.

Skonieczny, K., & Vendramin, V. (2024). Academic teachers vs ChatGPT: A comparative study of strategies used by Slovenian and Polish faculties to prevent dishonest use of generative AI tools. *Journal of Contemporary Educational Studies/Sodobna Pedagogika, 75*(4). https://www.sodobnapedagogika.si/en/

Stanford University. (2025). Course policies on generative AI use. *GSB Teaching and Learning Hub.* https://www.gsb.stanford.edu/faculty-research/teaching-learning-hub

Tomlinson, M. (2017). Student perceptions of themselves as 'consumers' of higher education. *British Journal of Sociology of Education, 38*(4), 450–467. DOI: 10.1080/01425692.2015.1113856

Transparency International. (2024). Corruption perceptions index 2024: Uganda. https://www.transparency.org/en/countries/uganda

Tung, R. L. (1995). Strategic management in an era of global alliances: The impact of culture. *Management International Review, 35*(Special Issue 1), 11–31.

Uganda Vice Chancellors' Forum. (2024, October 4). UVCF annual conference 2024: Integrating AI into higher education in Uganda. *Uganda Vice Chancellors' Forum.* https://uvcf.ac.ug/uvcf-annual-conference-2024

Ulster University. (2024). Guidance on AI in assessment design. Retrieved from https://www.ulster.ac.uk/learningenhancement/cqe/strategies/ai

UNESCO. (2023). *Guidance for generative AI in education and research.* United Nations Educational, Scientific and Cultural Organization. https://unesdoc.unesco.org/ark:/48223/pf0000386693

UNESCO. (2024). Six pillars for the digital transformation of education. *United Nations Educational, Scientific and Cultural Organization.* https://unesdoc.unesco.org/ark:/48223/pf0000391299

von Neumann, J., & Morgenstern, O. (1944). *Theory of games and economic behavior.* Princeton University Press.

Weiner, B. (1972). Attribution theory, achievement motivation, and the educational process. *Review of Educational Research, 42*(2), 203–215. DOI: 10.3102/00346543042002203

Weiner, B. (1985). An attributional theory of achievement motivation and emotion. *Psychological Review, 92*(4), 548–573. DOI: 10.1037/0033-295X.92.4.548 PMID: 3903815

Weiner, B. (1986). *An attributional theory of motivation and emotion*. Springer. DOI: 10.1007/978-1-4612-4948-1

Weiner, B. (2012). An attribution theory of motivation. In Van Lange, P. A. M., Kruglanski, A. W., & Higgins, E. T. (Eds.), *Handbook of theories of social psychology* (Vol. 1, pp. 135–155). Sage. DOI: 10.4135/9781446249215.n8

Westerlund, M. (2019). The emergence of deepfake technology: A review. *Technology Innovation Management Review, 9*(11), 39–52. DOI: 10.22215/timreview/1282

Zawacki-Richter, O., Bai, J. Y., Lee, K., Slagter van Tryon, P. J., & Prinsloo, P. (2024). New advances in artificial intelligence applications in higher education? *International Journal of Educational Technology in Higher Education, 21*(1), 32. DOI: 10.1186/s41239-024-00464-3

Zawacki-Richter, O., Marín, V. I., Bond, M., & Gouverneur, F. (2019). Systematic review of research on artificial intelligence applications in higher education – where are the educators? *International Journal of Educational Technology in Higher Education, 16*(1), 39. DOI: 10.1186/s41239-019-0171-0

Zhai, C., Wibowo, S., & Li, L. D. (2024). The effects of over-reliance on AI dialogue systems on students' cognitive abilities: A systematic review. *Smart Learning Environments, 11*(1), 28. DOI: 10.1186/s40561-024-00316-7

Chapter 17
Virtue-Centered AI Learning:
Shaping the Moral Character of Tomorrow

Sooraj Kumar Maurya
https://orcid.org/0000-0002-6974-5508
Zakir Husain Delhi College (Evening), University of Delhi, India

ABSTRACT

This chapter presents the issue of applying virtue ethics to AI-powered education systems, with the main idea deriving that artificial intelligence should promote not only the intellectual but also the moral development. It suggests a virtue-based model based on the postulates of Aristotle about eudaimonia that develops intellectual virtues (i.e., curiosity, critical thinking, perseverance) along with the moral virtues of social responsibility, empathy, and fairness. The chapter shows, through theoretical consideration, how AI can aid ethical interaction, train moral dilemmas, and develop civic-mindedness. It apprehensively discusses the dilemma of value misalignment, biases intensification, and monitoring, promoting the co-development of humans and AI, ethical leadership, and design culture. It ends the chapter with several policy-reforming and design suggestions to guarantee that AI in education does not make students into merely competent citizens, but caring, socially robust ones.

1. INTRODUCTION

1.1 Background and Significance

The educational landscape of the twenty-first century is undergoing a paradigmatic transformation driven by the rapid incorporation of artificial intelligence (AI) technologies. As AI becomes increasingly embedded in pedagogical practices—from personalized learning algorithms to intelligent tutoring systems—it reconfigures not only the mechanisms of instruction but also the conceptual architecture of education itself (Luckin et al., 2016). In the past, educational technologies have been designed to maximize the efficiency of content delivery and enhance

DOI: 10.4018/979-8-3373-2752-5.ch017

performance indicators at the expense of ethical and affective sphere development, representing cognitive performance cognizance predominantly. Nevertheless, the development of AI induces the reconsideration of this instrumentalist journey because it provides possibilities in a new way to promise the development of moral and character. (Ganuthula & Balaraman, 2025)

The advent of artificial intelligence in education should not be interpreted as the agent of accelerating the pace at which knowledge is being transmitted, but rather viewed as a catalyst that possesses the capacity to restructure the normative purposes of education. The incorporation of adaptive learning systems, natural language processing, and affective computing has enabled the development of educational environments that are responsive to students' cognitive and emotional states (Holmes et al., 2019). However, in spite of the success of AI to individualise learning experiences, it is still very quiet on the issue of values: What sort of persons should the students be? What are the possible ways to use technologies to promote empathy, integrity and feelings of justice? These questions highlight a severe gap in the modern discussion, thus the need to recast AI in education as an expressly ethical practice. The renewed interest in moral education is manifested against the background of socio-political polarization, digital misinformation, and technological loneliness. Contemporary educational theorists increasingly argue that the ethical formation of students is not ancillary to academic achievement but is foundational to it. In this parameter AI should never be perceived as value-neutral, but it will be driven in an ideologically colored plane that will influence how it is implemented and its outcomes.

1.2 Defining Virtue-Centered AI

When dealing with such emergent issues, the role of software engineers becomes especially relevant due to consideration of the concept of virtue-centered AI as a pedagogical model linking Aristotelian ethics of virtue to the current trends in the field of artificial intelligence. At its core, virtue ethics is concerned not with rule-following or utilitarian calculus, but with the cultivation of stable character traits—arete—that dispose individuals toward human flourishing (eudaimonia) (Aristotle, Nicomachean Ethics, trans. Irwin, 1999). In contrast to deontological or consequentialist thinking, which focus on principles of action or on consequences respectively, virtue ethics puts its focus on the moral agent, with a view toward the formation of that agent over a lifetime. The emphasis is not to be a giver; it is rather to be good.

This worldview shifts the very concept of educational success with regard to AI-mediated education. Virtue-centered AI systems are predetermined to facilitate the comprehensive formation of intellectual and moral capabilities of students instead of the unhealthy prioritization of relying on technical competencies or standardized scores. This includes fostering intellectual virtues such as curiosity, open-mindedness, and critical thinking, alongside moral virtues such as empathy, fairness, and responsibility (Kristjánsson, 2015). These qualities are not accidental or circumstantial and represent instead the human excellence or social cohesion in ethical ambivalence and technical speed. Thus, AI gains a twofold role in this scheme of things: as a mental crutch and a moral interlocutor. AI can also scaffold individual students, delivering challenges and feedback of a suitable degree depending on the students' level of development, thus allowing an individual student to have their own learning experience and really learn. An ethical interlocutor, AI is able to discuss students in simulated moral dilemmas, ethical reflection and exemplify ethical behavior at the level of pedagogically balanced interactions. Recent advances in affective computing and empathetic interfaces lend further plausibility to this vision, suggesting that machines can, under specific conditions, foster affective and ethical engagement. (Livanis et al., 2024)

Not without philosophical and technical issues, however, such integration exists. The fact that the human virtues can be encoded to operate under the system of machines poses a pretty serious question to the understanding of moral agency, the Utilitarian efficacy of computers and the harmfulness of humanizing algorithms. That brings into focus the need of such human control and for the AI to be considered a supplement, rather than a replacement, to human moral growth. (Fabre et al., 2024) However, the potential of virtue-focused AI presents a favorable avenue toward the resolution of ethical shortcomings by the existing educational paradigms. This can be done through infusing ethics into the process of designing and implementing AI systems such that through such a collaboration, educationists and developers can create learning ecosystems that can foster the realization of all human potentials. This chapter argues that this reconceptualization, besides being desirable, is also necessary so that education can play its role in developing the moral character of future citizens.

2. VIRTUE ETHICS AND THE ETHICAL USE OF AI IN EDUCATION

With AI gaining more and more entrenchment in the educational landscape, including but not limited to customizable learning experiences, auto-graded assignments, and assistive profiling systems, philosophical reflection on the ethical implications of these technologies becomes an ethical imperative. The virtue ethics provide a robust means of meeting this challenge, which is inherently congruent with the objectives of education and particularly suited to situations of human development, moral reasoning, and identity constructions. Unlike rule-based ethical systems of deontological ethics or the utility-maximizing approach of consequentialism, virtuous ethics puts a greater focus on character building and the lifelong path of the moral agent towards eudaimonia, or human flourishing. Such a philosophical inclination fits squarely with the intended meanings of education, especially when the intention of schooling is not viewed strictly as knowledge transmission, but as one that cultivates individuals of integrity, empathy, and wisdom. (Fabre et al., 2024)

The virtue-ethical approach provides a strong alternative to paradigm majorities in ethical design of educational technologies. While deontological theories can be founded in strict, universal rules, which may be transformed into algorithmical constraints, and consequentialist theories may turn decision-making into a matter of calculability, virtue theory is both situationally responsive, agent-centered, and developmentally responsive. The application of virtue ethics to teaching and learning technology would integrate AI not to optimise systems to perform well, but rather to inform it by the telos of moral and intellectual flourishing. Technologies developed based on this model would complement rather than replace developmental teacher-student, student peers, and student-self relationships. These are not the qualities that can be developed only through obedience of regulations or time-efficient work. Instead, they need a learning environment, with augmentation but not overwhelming AI that exemplifies and enables moral investigations, fosters ethical decision-making and honors the developmental process of individuals.

In that sense, virtue ethics can provide the philosophical and practical framework in making AI systems that facilitate growth rather than performance. The development of moral and intellectual virtues could be enhanced through AI provided the systems are developed with pedagogical and ethical intention. Furthermore, putting these systems in place might capture the degree to which real-world-decision-making can be morally convoluted, leaving the learner with a chance to experience and consider moral ambiguity, as opposed to passively being told whether or not their action was correct. Virtue ethics also condemns the growing use of AI systems that replace moral agency of students due to the fact that it is possible to monitor or predict, and over time erode moral agency. Ethical decision-making in educational settings often involves negotiating multiple, competing values. Narrowly-programmed AI systems designed to obey rules or maximise outputs cannot countenance a rich moral life. They can instead result into reliance on external systems of judgment, undermining the ability of the student to make ethical considerations. An AI that is virtuous-oriented would, on the contrary, engage in facilitating the cultivation of phronesis, or practical wisdom that enables learners to determine the proper course of action across a variety of different and complex scenarios. This ability is especially essential at a time when our society is experiencing algorithmic power, cyberspace distraction, and divisive morality talk.

The educational usefulness of virtue ethics is set even further high, when we pay attention to the long-term moral implications of technologically mediated learning. As MacIntyre famously observed, the modern fragmentation of moral discourse has left institutions like schools without coherent visions of the good. Without critically designed AI systems in education, there is a risk that this fragmentation will be increased through prioritizing personalization, prediction, and productivity over character and communal responsibility. Incorporating the virtue ethics into the very foundations of the educational technology design, the institutions will be able to restore a moral telos once again the telos, not merely aimed at bringing forth successful test-takers or efficient problem-solvers, but the telos directed at the creation of wise, just, and compassionate heroes.

This philosophical vision is normatively strong and not only that, but also imperative indeed. With educational establishments around the world implementing AI in the classroom, learning management systems, and even emotional wellbeing tools, educators, designers, and policymakers must question: What type of learner are we engineering with these systems? The virtue ethics forces us to go beyond the spreading of efficiency and personalization and to begin to consider the ethical goal of education itself. It implies that AI as any tool, is to be judged not only in terms of its good performance, but in terms of its contribution to the flourishings of its users in terms of moral and intellectual. (Hagendorff, 2022) An AI-driven education directed by virtue ethics might in the future in which machine judgment would not be frigid agent of improvement, but nuanced ally of the joint human project of being humans.

3. ARTIFICIAL INTELLIGENCE IN EDUCATION: CURRENT LANDSCAPE

The infusion of artificial intelligence (AI) into the educational landscape represents a seismic shift in the methodologies, ideologies, and operational structures of contemporary pedagogy. Although traditional teaching was historically limited by prescriptive curriculum patterns and standard teaching methodologies, the emergence of AI-based technologies provides a potentially highly significant shift: A desire not to merely computerize education content, but to redesign the scaffolding of education that underpins epistemology. Nevertheless, such change, with its potential, is not deprived of philosophical, pedagogical, and ethical issues especially concerning the immoral emptiness of existing AI implementations.

3.1 Personalization and Adaptive Learning

Among the top features, which automatically make AI important in educational intervention, is its ability to be personal. Leveraging machine learning algorithms, data mining, and natural language processing, AI systems can now dynamically tailor instructional content to individual learner profiles, adjusting in real-time to performance data, behavioral indicators, and engagement metrics. The paradigm of adaptive learning implies getting rid of this repetitive pattern that has been notorious with traditional education all along of the one-size-fits-all approach. This capability can be witnessed in the way Knewton and DreamBox Learning adaptive learning platforms enable differentiated pathway through curricular content, which in turn support diverse learning styles, cognitive ability and levels of prior curricular knowledge. (Strielkowski et al., 2024) Such systems operate by continuously analyzing student interactions and adjusting both the content and pacing of instruction, thereby fostering learner autonomy and improving retention outcomes (Pane et al., 2015). Moreover, personalization engenders a more dialogic pedagogical structure. They are involved in a dynamic, adaptive learning process; students are not passive consumers of generic material.

Nevertheless, these systems are noteworthy not merely in the technical sophistication of their design but oftentimes within a stringent epistemological context. The more their focus is on the data and the statistics they will use as the tools of their success, the more likely their contents will be more intellectual rather than ethical, emotional, or social, marginalizing the ethical, emotional, and social aspects of learning. That is, the personalization will increase efficiency, but does not directly promote healthy ethical insight, or character growth in a healthy sense the lack of which ought to become an urgent concern of virtue-focused AI.

3.2 Intelligent Tutoring Systems

A more interactive manifestation of AI in education is found in Intelligent Tutoring Systems (ITSs)—automated platforms designed to simulate the diagnostic, explanatory, and adaptive functions of a human tutor. These systems tend to include a set of AI tools such as chatbots and virtual mentors and recommendation engines in order to provide real time feedback and scaffold student knowledge on a range of topics. For instance, Carnegie Learning's MATHia platform applies cognitive science principles in conjunction with machine learning algorithms to offer context-sensitive guidance, promoting metacognitive reflection and procedural fluency (Koedinger et al., 1997). Similarly, Squirrel AI, a Chinese ed-tech firm, utilizes granular student modeling and reinforcement learning to offer ultra-personalized instruction in core academic disciplines, reportedly adapting to over 10,000 knowledge points.

These systems are especially good at diagnostic analytics which include student misconception identification, performance prediction and scheduled interventions. Moreover, their interfaces increasingly employ affective computing, allowing them to detect emotional states such as frustration or boredom and respond with motivational cues (D'Mello & Graesser, 2015). The ability of the simulated emotional responsiveness provides an illusion of pedagogical presence, and it is a simulation still lacking a true intentional morality. More importantly, ITSs often incorporate recommendation engines, which recommend resources, pathways and peer interactions to learners. These engines use collaborative filtering a content-based algorithms to mimic personalized human recommendation. However, the philosophical neutrality of such algorithms is an illusion; they implicitly encode normative assumptions about what constitutes valuable knowledge, desirable performance, and ideal learner behavior (Selwyn, 2019).

Even though these tools could improve procedural learning and self-regulation, their neutrality in ethical terms is progressively unbearable following their educative force on identity and motivation of students, and belief systems. As a result, scholars have begun to call for a reorientation of ITSs toward virtue-sensitive architectures—systems that are capable not only of diagnosing academic gaps but also of fostering traits such as curiosity, perseverance, and empathy (Vallor, 2016).

3.3 Limitations of Present AI Tools

Although this profound potential of AI in education is at hand, today, its current models are rife with reductionist orientation, i.e., performance-based scoring of the learner as opposed to a learner being a natural, paramount bearer of self-directed, qualitative growth. The principal limitation of current AI tools lies in their instrumental rationality: they are designed primarily to optimize efficiency, accuracy, and content mastery, often at the expense of cultivating moral imagination or socio-emotional intelligence (Biesta, 2010).

The prevalence of the application of learning analytics dashboards is a physical representation of this in that complex processes of human learning are condensed into numbers- click-through rates, time-on-task, assessment scores to form modes of a mechanistic view of education. Under these conditions, knowledge is transformed into a commodity, and morality of students is subordinated to the logic of their performance maximization. The implicit message communicated to learners is that success is measured by speed, correctness, and productivity, rather than by depth, reflection, or ethical engagement (Williamson et al., 2020). There is also a threat of epistemic enclosure posed by algorithmic determinism supporting much of the AI, such as pathways of learning becoming progressively narrow, the result of algorithms that nudge students into limited modalities of learning, controlled by recommender systems based on opaque algorithms that can reinforce current biases or inhibit imaginative thinking. The phenomenon of "automation bias"—where students defer to machine judgments even in the face of error—further exacerbates the erosion of critical autonomy (Goddard et al., 2012).

Moreover, numerous AI tools are created without an inbuilt ethical grammar. They fail to and mostly cannot tell the difference between moral and cognitive righteousness. A student can be successful at solving a mathematical problem or optimizing a code. However, can be ethically inert or even displaced. This mental-moral distinction is a reprise of the Cartesian divide that has haunted Western philosophy of education and has to be questioned when trying to determine how AI can be used to advance the purposes of human flourishing, as opposed to mere technical proficiency.

Thus, there is the risk of being morally disengaged, with technological mediation. When students dwell mainly in a machine-mediated world, they lose much of the chance to learn through the embodied judgment, empathy, and narrative wisdom that they could soak up with human teachers who act like moral apprenticeship masters, exercising judgment and accessing empathy and narrative intelligence, and exposing students to the riches of their discursive repertories. This loss cannot be easily compensated with the help of simulations or fake compassion. It demands a re-situation of AI in virtue-based pedagogies in which moral formation is built in (as opposed to an overlay).

4. DESIGNING VIRTUE-CENTERED AI CURRICULA

Virtue based curriculum design in AI mediated learning setting would require a paradigm shift in the learning paradigm, which tends to explain learning as a passive process of information absorption, to a more holistic paradigm incorporating knowledge building and sharing with the learner together with his intellectual, moral and emotional resolution. This section defines the key virtues to be promoted, the structure of such curricula, and the new technological infrastructure to maintain moral and cognitive development, through the innovative application of AI devices such as gamification, simulation, and ethical nudging.

4.1 Key Intellectual and Moral Virtues to Develop

At the core of virtue-centered education lies the cultivation of both intellectual virtues—traits that govern the pursuit and application of knowledge—and moral virtues—traits that shape the ethical character of the learner. Although intellectual virtues, such as curiosity, critical thinking, and perseverance, promote epistemic excellence, moral virtues, such as empathy, fairness, and social responsibility, support moral agency of the learner in a common social world. Curiosity serves as the engine of intellectual exploration. As Aristotle emphasized in Metaphysics (980a21), "All men by nature desire to know." This innate desire, when properly cultivated, becomes a virtue that leads learners beyond superficial comprehension to deeper, intrinsic engagement with the material. It can be suggested that in AI-assisted education, curiosity can be aroused by personalized content, changing alongside the interests and boundaries of learner inquiry - these boundaries are continuously expanding, without epistemic complacency.

Being an indispensability of the digital age, the informational density and complexity, critical thinking is needed to negotiate it. It involves not merely the logical appraisal of arguments, but the disposition to seek truth with intellectual humility and epistemic courage (Paul & Elder, 2008). It is thereby a distinctly moral practice which requires comparability, transparency and ethically imbued opposition to cognitive partisanship. Critical thinking can be promoted when critical thinking is added to AI curriculums by proposing competing viewpoints, open-ended problem-solving, and dialogues with smart agents. The long-term devotion to the resilience of mental barriers is what is known as perseverance, and it is both a moral and intellectual virtue. It resists the immediate gratification ethos of algorithmic culture and fosters resilience, a trait increasingly associated with academic and psychological well-being (Duckworth et al., 2007). The ability of April systems to scale the difficulty of the tasks, provide non-affective feedback, and positive reinforcement can address the learning capacity of learners to persistently work and behave goal-directed by scaffolding it.

On the moral front empathy, the imaginative and affective ability to identify oneself with the experience of others, is the keystone to ethical citizenship in pluralistic societies. Empathy enables the recognition of moral claims across difference and serves as a bridge between cognitive understanding and ethical action (Hoffman, 2000). Fairness entails an abiding commitment to justice and impartiality in one's interactions, while social responsibility orients learners toward the common good, fostering a sense of accountability to communities both local and global. All these virtues together comprise an ideal of character: the student as an independent morally responsive actor with the ability to act in thoughtful and ethical ways in a technologically mediated world.

4.2 Curriculum Architecture

These virtues must be cultivated effectively using a curriculum architecture that is neither content-nor behaviorally prescriptive but normatively purposeful and epistemically open-ended. A virtue-based curriculum in AI means that lesson plans should not only aim at teaching disciplinary knowledge, but also at prompting and practicing particular virtues during the learning process. This entails the direct incorporation of virtue goals into learning objectives, where the presence, e.g., of competencies in curiosity or fairness is stated together with cognitive goals. To take a possible example, a science module may be designed to achieve the goals of the discipline as well as those of intellectual humility and open-mindedness in testing competing hypotheses. With a cross-cultural and ethical history approach, a historical lesson can seek to provide empathy by viewing events in different ways and with various cultures and moral standpoints. AI-facilitated environments will offer excellent means of developing virtue via project-based learning and inquiry-based learning. These pedagogies encourage learners to pursue sustained, collaborative inquiry into real-world problems, thereby requiring and reinforcing virtues such as perseverance, collaboration, and civic responsibility (Barron & Darling-Hammond, 2008). The support to these pedagogies can be provided by AI systems through provision of personalized scaffolding, resource suggestion, real-time feedback and communication between different groups within various cultural contexts. Additionally, a virtue-sensitive curriculum should enable reflective practices- instants, in time, when learners are critical about their epistemic and moral growth. The development of such reflection can be mediated by AI tools, like digital portfolios or metacognitive prompts, so that the development of virtue can continue to be a primary and unambiguous goal of the educational process.

4.3 Gamification and Simulation

The virtual and augmented reality using a gamified environment and simulations as part of virtue-centered AI curricula can provide the environments that are rich in supporting the embodied practice of ethical reasoning and character-building. When designed with moral intentionality, role-play scenarios, ethical dilemmas, and decision-tree games can simulate complex social and moral contexts in which learners must navigate competing values and ambiguous outcomes. As an example, a simulation can challenge students who need to regulate the ethical consequences of using AI in the context of healthcare, where the efficiency vs. fairness and accuracy vs. inclusivity considerations need to be balanced. The exercises are not testing exercises in critical thinking and problem solving only; they also challenge students to think critically and critically about questions of moral and purpose, and about the actions taken and decisions made. AI systems can track decision-making patterns, offer just-in-time feedback, and highlight moral blind spots—thus transforming ethical reasoning into a skill that is both teachable and assessable.

Moreover, they could also implement moral self-monitoring measures, which are AI-based tools that are aimed at promoting self-control and self-evaluation. These tools may help the learners to analyze the emotional reaction to the stimuli, to determine the ethical consequences of the decisions, and to contrast their self-images with peer or agent responses. (Kristjánsson, 2022) Such tools align with Aristotelian ethics, which emphasizes habituation, moral sensitivity, and continuous self-scrutiny as pathways to virtue. However, these tools must be designed with caution. In the event that gamification is just a means to an end, i.e. acted out without the consideration of reflection, it can corrupt the weightiness of this ethical formation of virtue. Instead, the aim should not be compliance, but transformational change in the dispositions of the learners, who should learn to value the good, not just pick it.

4.4 AI's Feedback Mechanism and Moral Nudging

AI can deliver instant, individually, and contextually tailored judgment, a pedagogical role that is not only applicable to intellectual correction but also to moral nudging very rich affordance in virtue-centered curricula. Sentiment-aware feedback systems, leveraging affective computing and natural language processing, can detect students' emotional states—such as frustration, excitement, or disengagement—and respond with feedback that is emotionally attuned and ethically supportive (D'Mello & Graesser, 2015). Hypothetically, an AI tutor can identify the indicators of ethical discomfort or cognitive dissonance in a dilemma-based simulation and use scaffolded questions in this case to promote more extensive cogitations. Alternatively, the system may nudge learners toward virtues such as kindness or fairness by highlighting the social consequences of their choices or suggesting alternative courses of action that better align with ethical ideals. (Engelen & Nys, 2024)

This moral nudging should be performed ethically transparently and epistemically humbly. Its aim is not to manipulate behavior but to establish an ethical ecology where virtue is made noticeable, desirable, and achievable. Moreover, AI-driven feedback systems can promote collaboration, encouraging students to engage with peers, share perspectives, and negotiate differences—activities that foster interpersonal virtues such as empathy, generosity, and justice (Howard et al., 2021). Yet this power also brings risk. Improperly designed feedback mechanisms have the potential to affirm pre-existing biases, or to humiliate students by failure to be ethical, or to teach artifice instead of working on the authentic virtues. Thus, the architecture of AI nudging systems should be developed with the ethical frameworks and constantly checked and controlled by the human. It is only in the context of such mechanisms that feedback can act not only by being corrective but by being formative, such as the role of feedback is to move learners in the direction of the good in a way which is morally respectful of them as moral particular agents.

5. TECHNOLOGICAL IMPLEMENTATION STRATEGIES

The achievement of virtue-focused AI learning is not only a matter of pedagogical vision but also an equal duty to the ethical development of the technology and its adherence to implementation. The technical construction of AI systems also needs to follow a normative setting, so that ethical principles pursued by algorithms, datasets, user interfaces, and feedback systems are all logically represented. In this part, the author describes three cornerstones of using technology: virtue-aware AI design principles, human-AI co-development, and ethical data considerations.

5.1 Virtue-Aware AI Design Principles

The process to incorporate virtue ethics into AI architectures starts with the design. While conventional machine learning (ML) systems prioritize optimization, efficiency, and predictive accuracy, virtue-aware design reorients these priorities toward moral intentionality, emphasizing the cultivation of epistemic and ethical virtues within the user. To achieve this, AI systems must be engineered with embedded ethical guidelines, manifesting principles such as respect, equity, transparency, and accountability—not as peripheral safeguards, but as core operational functions (Binns, 2018; Moor, 2006). A central principle here is explainability, or the degree to which an AI system can render its decision-making processes intelligible to human users (Doshi-Velez & Kim, 2017). Explainable AI (XAI) is not merely a technical desideratum but an epistemic virtue, fostering intellectual trust, accountability, and moral learning in the user (Lipton, 2018). At the educational level, it can be used to allow learners to question the grounds of AI-based feedback and embrace critical thinking, ethical reflexivity. In comparison, a black-box model is dangerous because it would encourage a culture of epistemic passivity wherein the users take the authority of the algorithm at face value and do not challenge or reflect on it.

Transparency augments explainability by making sure that useful information permeates the objective of a system, design decisions, data provenance, which the users, designers, and regulators of a system all have access to. As Floridi et al. (2018) argue, transparency is essential not only for system auditing but also for cultivating the virtue of institutional honesty, a key component of trustworthiness in educational institutions. The third and more pressing principle is that of bias detection and mitigation. Algorithmic systems—being trained on human-generated data—are susceptible to reproducing and amplifying social biases, including those pertaining to race, gender, class, and cognitive ability (Noble, 2018). In the educational sphere, this can lead to differential treatment of students, distorted assessments, and the perpetuation of epistemic injustice (Fricker, 2007). Therefore, virtue-aware design requires the integration of fairness-aware ML algorithms, periodic bias audits, and redressive feedback systems. In addition, ethical risk assessment must be continuous, not episodic—a process woven into the life-cycle of the AI system from development through deployment and post-use evaluation (Jobin et al., 2019). By integrating virtuous-sensitive design heuristics in the architecture of systems, developers can be sure that AI will serve not only as an effective educational tool, but as a moral teacher, encouraging the moral and cognitive well-being of people using it.

5.2 Human–AI Co-development

Any virtue-based 3 AI system cannot, and perhaps must not, exist as an independent agent in molding student character. Moral development has made the issue a multi-perspectival one, and its roots are not merely technical, but also pedagogic, ethical-theoretical and context-sensitive. As such, the implementation of virtue-centered AI must be conceived as a process of human–AI co-development, involving interdisciplinary collaboration between educators, technologists, philosophers, ethicists, and learners themselves (Rahwan, 2018). Teachers who know classroom dynamics well, have detailed experience with learner diversity, and developmental psychology need to be at the forefront of outlining the outcomes of virtue, the instructional scaffolds, and the assessment plan. The AI system can be relied on to be pedagogically sound and attentive to real learning needs because of their input. Simultaneously, ethics and moral philosophers are necessary to bridge the gap between philosophical concepts relating to virtues and designable requirements in order to prevent moral values becoming more tooled or the promotion of specific ethical models.

Furthermore, student voice must not be marginalized. Participatory design approaches—which involve learners in the design and testing of AI tools—can ensure that virtue-centered systems remain learner-centric, culturally attuned, and responsive to diverse moral sensibilities (Bratteteig & Wagner, 2016). This becomes especially critical due to the danger of moral paternalism, whereby the AI systems incentivize ethical actions with consideration of the ability of the learner to engage in independent moral decisions. The co-development model also implies a reconceptualization of accountability. Instead of diffused or siloed responsibility, co-development fosters shared moral ownership, wherein all stakeholders bear collective responsibility for the system's ethical and educational impact (Calo, 2015). This roughs the current model of technology implementation, which is often more of a obsession with scale than wisdom. The creation of ethics advisory boards, continuous training programs for AI developers in moral education, and the incorporation of values-based design methodologies (such as Value Sensitive Design and Responsible Innovation) are practical pathways to institutionalize co-development in virtue-centered AI education.(Heyder, Passlack, & Posegga, 2023)

5.3 Data Considerations

The nature of datasets on which AI systems are trained deeply defines meaningful epistemic and moral directions of the system. The act of data selection, curation, and representation is not neutral, but normatively loaded and ethically impactful. Therefore, AI based on virtue needs to follow strict data ethics, and diversity, representativeness and fairness are especially important. One of the most pressing risks in this domain is the emergence of moral monoculture—a condition in which training data reflect narrow socio-cultural norms, thereby marginalizing alternative moral frameworks and reinforcing hegemonic values (Greene et al., 2019). To give an illustration, an AI tutor that has been trained only using Eurocentric models of virtue cannot embrace non-Western moral traditions, misserving not only inclusivity but also pedagogical relevance. To address this, the training data should be obtained within the pluralistic educational institutions, which reflects the diversity of cultures, identities, languages, and moral traditions. Data collection must be transparent and subject to ethical review boards to ensure informed consent, privacy protection, and the avoidance of exploitative data practices (Metcalf et al., 2016).

Equally critical is the problem of bias reinforcement. The unbalanced and biased data that AI systems use may lead bias making, e.g., learning that poorer students with disadvantaged backgrounds are less likely to succeed or that they should learn better in a specific way. This does not only amount to infringement of fairness principles, but also dwells upon building of the moral character, by ingraining the forms of inequality in the very mechanisms of education. The bias correction algorithms, the data de-biasing pipelines, and equity-based assessment measures should be introduced on all levels of the AI development pipeline. Additionally, algorithmic impact assessments—similar to environmental impact reports—should be required before any virtue-centered AI system is deployed at scale. Thus, ethical data management is not a side issue but a synthetic factor of virtue-based AI. The training, validating and refining datasets we use to train AI systems should also reflect the virtues we demand them to foster, openness, fairness, diversity and respect.

6. APPLICATIONS

Although the philosophical and technical underpinning of virtue-based AI education provides a strong normative conceptualization, its validity is also justified by the empirical instantiation. It is this part that will explain three case studies to explain how virtue-centered AI curricula are practically possible, ethically deep and pedagogically influential. All cases give an idea about how AI can assist in the development of intellectual and moral virtue across various educational contexts, such as the development of empathy in middle schools or ethical problem-solving through collaborative learning environments.

6.1 Example 1: Middle School Empathy Curriculum via AI

The initial case study is based on an innovative partnership between a group of educational psychologists and AI designers, that were working towards an embedding of an empathy-based curriculum into the interface of a digital learning environment that would be used by American middle school learners. The affective computing solution named the program as EmotionSpace, it strived to recreate the socio-emotional learning situations, in which the students had to communicate, learn, and relate to their virtual classmates, who had different emotional needs, cultural backgrounds, and ethical perspectives. The students were role-playing with AI-driven agents involved in emotional perspective-taking conversations that surround unethical situations: bullying, peer pressure, and intercultural misunderstandings. The AI system utilized natural language processing and sentiment analysis to adapt the interactions in real time based on student inputs, offering nudges and reflective questions to deepen emotional engagement and self-awareness (D'Mello & Graesser, 2015).

The outcomes, as reported in a longitudinal study (Anderson et al., 2022), were striking. Over a 12-week intervention period, students in the AI-mediated empathy curriculum demonstrated statistically significant improvements in prosocial behavior, self-reported empathy scores (using the Interpersonal Reactivity Index), and reduced instances of disciplinary referrals, when compared to control groups receiving traditional social-emotional learning (SEL) instruction. There were increased classroom bonding, and the teachers also noticed students utilizing virtual situations in real life when interacting with their peers. Some of the things learned in EmotionSpace are that culture sensitivity was needed when it comes to building agents because there was a general differentiation in how the students with varied ethnic and linguistic backgrounds react to emotional stimuli. Furthermore, the human facilitation was shown as crucial: as the AI agents were providing the emotionally intelligent comments, having an educator in the picture who would contextualize the experience facilitated advanced reflections about ethics and articulation of morals in students. This case highlights the capacity of AI not only to simulate empathy-inducing experiences but also to function as an empathic co-facilitator, fostering what Hoffman (2000) terms "empathic concern" rather than mere emotional contagion. It highlights the idea that the virtue-sensitive emotionally aware AI can play a significant role in the morality building of students.

6.2 Example 2: Critical Thinking with AI-Augmented Socratic Dialogue

The second example involves the pedagogical practice of the Socratic method and discusses possible enrichment of this method with the help of AI enhancement. An experimental module labeled as DialogosAI was used to scaffold critical thinking and moral reasoning in a philosophy course at one of the secondary schools in Finland. Based on the classical structures of Socratic dialogs, the AI platform presented the students with open ethical questions with a degree of difficulty broadly ranging between climate justice and digital privacy, during which they were asked to engage in recursive inquiry, concept and idea elucidation, and the articulation of a counterargument. The AI agent employed argument mining and discourse analysis algorithms to model the logical structure of student responses, offering follow-up questions designed to elicit cognitive dissonance and dialectical progression (Lawrence & Reed, 2019). It is important to notice that the system was trained not to resort to prescriptive judgments, to be, in effect, a Socratic interlocutor that helped in maintaining a long-term inquiry. Measurable improvement was found in terms of developing critical reasoning skills in students by conducting impact assessments as pre- and post-assessment on the core sections of students in the area of thought-related thinking using the Ennis-Weir Critical Thinking Essay Test. Students also exhibited increased epistemic humility—a disposition to revise one's beliefs in light of new evidence—and more nuanced ethical reasoning, as captured in reflective journals and class debates. Crucially, students described the AI dialogue partner as "demanding but fair," "non-judgmental," and "thought-provoking"—attributes that resonate with Aristotelian notions of phronesis (practical wisdom) and dialectical virtue. Teachers reported that normally reserved students were more willing to engage in conversations with the AI agent, which implies that virtual interlocutors could help to create safe feeling contexts of exploratory reasoning. Yet limitations were also acknowledged. The residual automation bias manifested itself in the fact that some students approached the agent as a source of correct answers in the beginning. This was partially compensated by clear pedagogical pragmatizing in which the teachers explained that the AI was not a function of epistemic authority but rather of dialogical stimulation. The lesson here is that AI should be treated tactfully in an attempt to maintain the non-authoritarian spirit of Socratic inquiry. The model shows how AI can not necessarily serve as a substitute to philosophical instruction but as an amplifier of critical intellectual virtues and empower learners to reason rigorously, transparently, and reflexively.

6.3 Example 3 Collaborative Problem-Solving Projects

The last case presents a discussion on how to use AI to enable virtue-based teamwork and ethical decision-making based on immersive learning simulations. During an interdisciplinary undergraduate course on sustainability and ethics taught at a university level, the participants were involved in a project named UrbanEthica, which is a multi-agent simulation that is driven by reinforcement learning algorithms and is dynamic when it comes to scenario creation. The simulation put students in fictional urban territory to grapple with complicated ethical dilemma: gentrification, resource distribution, environmental deterioration and algorithmic enforcement. Students played the role of stakeholder (urban planner, activist, technologist and policymaker) and had to make a series of inter-related decisions with tradeoffs and solve emergent crises.

The AI system dynamically modified the situation according to the behavior of students and integrated the view of consequences, short-term and long-term effects on different groups of stakeholders. Moral dilemmas were embedded within the simulation's mechanics, requiring students to balance efficiency with fairness, innovation with justice, and individual liberty with collective good.

The achievement of groups of students was not reduced to the effectiveness of the solutions, but also included positive evidence of the moral thinking, empathy, and fair negotiation behavior, as measured by rubrics and reflective post-simulation writings. Findings indicated that students developed a greater appreciation for ethical complexity, increased their capacity for perspective-taking, and reported heightened motivation to address real-world social issues.

Notably, the AI system did not impose any details in its rendition of moral reasoning; it did not tell the right answers but highlighted value-infused outcomes, leaving it to the students to deliberate other decisions and prioritize within the context of their ethical commitments. This aligns with Nussbaum's (2010) conception of education as preparation for democratic citizenship, wherein students are trained to reason morally in pluralistic contexts. The success of the simulation demonstrates the importance of state-of-art ethical complexity mediated by AI, the absence of moralizing or making moral issues more simplistic, the opposite, making moral issues more vivid, more connected, and more personally engaging. (Bertoncini & Serafim, 2023) It shows how AI has a future to create distributed moral agency, where groups come to reason or solve problems of ethical conflict in spite of AI as both a limitation and an accelerator.

7. RISKS, ETHICAL DILEMMAS, AND OVERSIGHT

The aspiration to build virtue-centered artificial intelligence (AI) systems in education, while commendable, is fraught with ethical complexities and ontological ambiguities. AI technologies do not simply reproduce the pedagogical intentions they are transforming the pedagogical values, identities as learners, institutional norms. As such, institutionalizing moral education via AI will have to contend with the inherent peril of instilling incompatibilities of values, bias propagation, excess surveillance, and poorly developed governance rules. In this section, an attempt to discuss these dangers will not be done in order to discredit the virtue-centered paradigm, but to warn against the possibility of virtue unguarded leading to the development of technocratic moralism, a state of affairs in which moral education will fall into the logic of automation and abstraction.

7.1 Value Alignment Problem

The issue of value alignment: how we can make sure that the morality installed into the AI systems aligns with human ethical ideals, pluralistically understood, is the most basic one bedeviling virtue-centered AI. In machine ethics, this issue is often framed as the challenge of aligning AI goals and outputs with human intentions or well-being (Russell et al., 2015). Nevertheless, when the goal changes and becomes not a certain instrumental performance but rather cultivation of virtues, stakes are much higher. The crucial problem is how to frame that question and whether it should be epistemological and normative about who determines what is meant by the notion of the virtue of a given educational setting? When the task of the AI systems is to learn or educate fairness, empathy, or perseverance, whose definitions of these virtues are in play? The Aristotelian tradition, while influential, is not monolithic, and virtue ethics varies across cultures, religions, and epistemic communities (MacIntyre, 1984; Nussbaum, 2001). The absence of a policy of moral pluralism can put AI in hazard of entrenching limited ideals of ethics into the universal code, excluding other moral traditions.

This issue is exacerbated by developer bias. As Noble (2018) and Benjamin (2019) have shown, algorithmic systems often reflect the cultural, racial, and gendered assumptions of their creators. There are dangers of uncritically perpetuating ideologies of power in the context of the pedagogy in educational practice. The AI system developed by a homogenous development team, aiming to maximize the virtue, can potentially implant rather subliminally the hegemonic standards of the politeness, diligence, or respect that may prove alienating or excluding to learners with minoritized backgrounds. So, value alignment cannot be a purely technical project. It must be embedded in a deliberative, participatory, and cross-cultural design process, wherein diverse stakeholders—including students—contribute to defining the ethical goals and boundaries of the system (Floridi et al., 2018).

7.2 Algorithmic Amplification of Bias

In addition to design, the AI systems can be subject to the effect of algorithmic bias amplification centralized on the enhancement of social disparities in the pre-existing data patterns. With educational AI, this is even more insidious since, in addition to evaluating the performance of students, these systems tend to affect the self-attitude of students, their motivation, and their moral notion of themselves. Empirical research has highlighted numerous unintended moral consequences. For instance, facial recognition systems used to detect attention in classrooms have been shown to misread affective cues in students of color, leading to inaccurate feedback and reinforcement of racial stereotypes (Buolamwini & Gebru, 2018). Similarly, predictive analytics tools used to identify "at-risk" students may flag individuals from marginalized socioeconomic backgrounds disproportionately, thereby pathologizing poverty rather than addressing structural inequalities (Eubanks, 2018). These biases are not inert—they shape learner identities. The repeated labels of disengaged and/or poor student performance can make a student who is marginally disengaged and/or poor performer internalize those labels to grow into self-fulfilling prophecies that hamper not only academic performance but also moral agency and self-respect. As Fricker (2007) has argued, such experiences constitute epistemic injustice, wherein individuals are undermined in their capacity to be knowers and moral actors.

In addition, virtue-based systems can unintentionally reward performance of virtue aka any expression of ethical action in the place of genuine moral growth. As an example, students might be taught to manipulate empathy triggers/ fairness measures to obtain positive feedback, without making the moral commitments their own. (Mattioli & Cabitza, 2024) This threatens to turn moral education into a morality theatre game, in which the instrumentally formalized virtue is more a source of right and power. In order to ensure that they do not come to fruition, bias audits, constant dataset rebalancing, and critical pedagogy have to be incorporated into system consideration. The aim is not to do away with any bias whatsoever as this cannot be done but rather to reflexively develop an ethical awareness within the system and its custodians.

7.3 Surveillance vs. Support

Another ethical dilemma in AI-based learning is the nebulous distinction between closely observing and helping. These AI systems usually use massive databases of real-time information eye tracking, keyboard usage, speech analysis to deduce mood and educational requirements. While such data can personalize instruction and foster timely intervention, they also raise serious concerns regarding student privacy, autonomy, and psychological safety (Williamson & Hogan, 2020). The ubiquity of surveillance can have a chilling effect in the readiness of students to experiment, reflect or espouse dissension. In the classroom, it translates into an abandonment of pedagogy as emancipation in favor of pedagogy as behavioral optimization.

Virtue-centered AI systems are particularly vulnerable to this danger. Persistent efforts to track and influence moral action, even with the best intentions, may trespass on moral manipulation where students may be not informed how their choices are being analyzed and influenced. (De Cremer & Narayanan, 2023) The use of sentiment-aware nudging, for example, must be designed with transparency and epistemic humility, lest it devolve into affective coercion rather than moral education. In order to ethically adjust such systems, strict lines should be drawn between guidance and governance. AI can aid, frame, or scaffold an ethical decision, but neither should it preclude deliberation nor deprive learners of the chance of moral error a key ingredient of authentic moral development. Additionally, the consent schemes, data minimalization policies, and the ability to opt out of any AI educational platform should be the norm in any such platform, so that epistemic agency and moral sovereignty are not displaced in a learner.

7.4 Human Oversight as Moral Compass

Since AI systems are characterized by certain dangers and ethical uncertainties, human oversight cannot be viewed as a final resort; instead, it is an essential part of ethical education of AI. Teachers, mentors, and other educational leaders have the role of moral mediators, interpreting, contextualizing, or even disputing the output of AI where applicable. By being present, virtue-centered AI will not be a replacement to human moral formation, being treated as an addition to it instead. The educator fits into several ways in which his or her role is necessary. To begin with, they will be able to put ethical prompts into context so that the students can learn to differentiate between material right thinking and formalistic right thinking. Second, they will be able to contest the results of the algorithms they find ethically suspect and thus avoid being inappropriately labeled or punished. Third, they can provide narrative coherence, linking students' fragmented AI interactions to broader moral narratives of identity, community, and purpose. In addition to classroom, there should be formed ethical institutions of auditing. These groups of ethicists, educators, technologists, and community representatives will be able to assess the virtue-based AI systems with respect to normative standards, detect the arising ills, and uphold accountability. Their role is not merely procedural but epistemic and moral, functioning as stewards of democratic educational values in an increasingly automated world (Calo, 2015). Public consultations, ethical impact assessments and transparency reports should be the norm. Going further, having artificial intelligence utilize moral fail-safes, which are the measures that inform human supervisors that the intelligent systems are functioning beyond the ethical limits, must become an essential element of the educational AI. (Bankins & Formosa, 2023)

8. RECOMMENDATIONS AND ACTIONABLE STRATEGIES

The above-mentioned overview of virtue-centered AI in instruction, including the analysis of ethical theories; the implementation of the same in specific case studies; all comes to the need to focus on integrated, system-level interventions, in order to make sure that artificial intelligence becomes as much an aid to the moral as to the intellectual growth of human beings. Although pedagogical interventions at the individual level or localized experimentation represent interesting evidence of concept, change at scale needs to involve policy, institutional and technical co-alignment. The recommendations here are stated in three levels that are educational policy, institutional infrastructure and developer practices.

8.1 Educational Policy Reforms

On the macro level, national and regional educational policies should mention virtue-centered AI as one of the implicit strategic goals. The existing policy frameworks governing educational technology often emphasize digital literacy, access, and STEM competency but fail to articulate normative visions for the ethical formation of learners in technologically mediated environments. The virtue-based disposition also requires an adjustment of such policies to inculcate the characters of both moral nature, and cognitive quality. First, virtue-centered AI must be integrated into curricular standards. This does not mean adding ethics as an additional topic; it means that ethical reasoning, character education, and emotional intelligence should be regarded as one of the main learning objectives, and the AI is programmed accordingly. Analogous to how environmental sustainability has been mainstreamed across curricula globally, virtue ethics must become a transversal objective, informing assessments, content standards, and teacher evaluation protocols (Kristjánsson, 2015). Second, ethics must be institutionalized within STEM education. Many times science, technology, engineering and mathematics are taught in morally neutral registers as the process of innovation and knowledge production are understood as ideologically unthreatened. Yet, as scholars have long argued, the epistemologies of STEM are entangled with power, politics, and ethical consequence (Harding, 1998; Winner, 1986). Incorporating STEM curricula with the modules that address AI ethics, data justice, and algorithmic fairness, and technology-moral imagination will help the learners engage with the normative aspect of the technological life. In addition, these modules cannot and must not be taught as philosophical thought experiments but in action, and in project-based learning, the students, at the same time, apply and critique AI tools and develop an understanding of their shortcomings on the spot. Ministries of education, curriculum boards, and international educational consortia need to provide policy guidance paperwork, training standards of teachers, and AI ethics incorporation frameworks to allow such reforms. It is easy to see how, without such scaffolding, virtue-centered AI would simply be a dream, instead of an actual system.

8.2 Institutional Strategy

Schools, universities, as well as ed-tech suppliers will be forced to make structural alterations at the institutional level to allow virtue-centered AI. Indeed, the immediate requirement is ethical training of educators. Teachers are the moral stewards of virtue-centered AI systems; their ability to interpret, contextualize, and contest AI outputs is essential to ensuring that these technologies support rather than supplant moral reasoning (Narvaez, 2006). This requires pre-service and in-service module designing in the form of AI literacy, virtue ethics, and the design of pedagogy. This training should not be focused on teaching procedures but should also involve important ethical discussion, only then can educators ask such questions: what are the virtues that should be considered a priority in this learning environment? What are the ways such an AI system can enhance or weaken those virtues? What power dynamics are embedded in algorithmic decision-making? Furthermore, institutes need to invest on virtue-aware AI systems, choosing or designing tools that satisfy the normative design standards. The decision of which procurement should occur should be done on cost-efficiency or technological sophistication, as well as on the behalf of ethical affordances of the system: Can it provide support in moral reflection? Is it transparent and explainable? Does it promote inclusivity and respect for diversity? Universities and especially faculties of education, educational technology and computer science ought to develop interdisciplinary research centers concerned with virtue ethics and educational technology. These centers may serve as the centers of the formation of pedagogical models, the carrying out of impact assessments, and the exchange of information between teachers, ethicists, technologists, and policy-makers. They can also be regarded as incubators of public interest ed-tech, both nurturing the growth of open-source virtue-centered AI tools that can resist being commercialized and contributing to the creation of public interest ed-tech apartments. Finally, institutions must adopt ethical oversight mechanisms. Similar to ethics research boards, AI ethics committees would review proposed deployments, oversee existing practices, and conduct harm inquiry. These bodies should not only consist of institutional actors, but also they should involve civil society and student body, so that it is democratic.

8.3 Developer Guidelines

VCI AI will require an overhaul of the philosophy of designing educational technologies. Developers—often guided by commercial imperatives and computational efficiency—must adopt ethical frameworks that foreground human flourishing, moral pluralism, and pedagogical integrity (Vallor, 2016). To that end, three interrelated strategies are recommended. First, developers must design with virtue ethics principles. This entails translating abstract virtues into functional design elements. To take just two examples, empathy may be implemented in layers of affect-sensitive feedback that encourage the identification of the feelings of others; fairness may be embedded in algorithms that identify and neutralize discriminatory consequences. These translations require careful ethical deliberation and must be context-sensitive, allowing for variation across age groups, cultures, and learning environments. Developers should utilize Value Sensitive Design (VSD) methodologies, which incorporate stakeholder values throughout the design process—from conceptual investigations and empirical stakeholder engagement to technical implementation. (Sadek, Calvo, & Mougenot, 2024)

Second, it has to have an open review and ethical transparency commitment. Educators, ethicists and the general public should have access to question the source code, training sets and decision rules of AI learning tools. This is not only a matter of accountability but also of epistemic justice, allowing communities to contest and reconfigure the tools that shape their moral and intellectual development (Fricker, 2007). Like environmental impact reports, ethical impact assessments should be created before deployment, detailing the compatibility of the system with virtue-based aims as well as any possible harms. These evaluations are to be published and revisited over time into a living library of ethics. Lastly, ethical experimenting is a mindset that developers should adopt: an orientation to concept repetition, ethical humility, and a willingness to listen to and acknowledge feedback. When virtue-centered AI systems are implemented, unforeseen consequences and ethical dilemmas are destined to emerge. The developers are to be open to altering the system parameters, reconnecting with stakeholders, and renewing designs in response to fresh evidence and changing moral standards. To conclude, the programmers need to reject the spirit of technological determinism and adopt the profession of moral design- the art of engineering that integrates ethics and systems thinking along with humanistic sensitivity.

9. CONCLUSION

This chapter has progressed the discussion that the implementation of artificial intelligence technologies in educational settings should break free of the current instrumentalist paradigms which dictate that the focus should be on cognitive efficiency and performance analytics as well as behavioral conformity. Rather, it has offered a virtue-centered conception of AI in learning, a conception, which places the development of moral character and intellectual virtues as central, non-retractable purposes of technologically assisted learning. This is not a fringe addition to digital pedagogy, but an ontological necessity based on a humanistic sense of what it takes to teach in a complex, pluralist and morally messy world.

In its essence, this chapter has justified the idea that AI should become a two-purpose agent: an intellectual development facilitator and an ethical development guide. Drawing upon Aristotelian virtue ethics, the argument has stressed that true education is not merely about transmitting information or optimizing learner outcomes but about nurturing human flourishing (eudaimonia) through the internalization of moral and intellectual virtues. The values of intellectual virtues, including curiosity, critical thinking and perseverance and moral virtues of empathy, fairness and social responsibility help the students to develop the intellectual resources to cope with the 21st century epistemic demands, and the moral aptitudes associated with ethical sensibility and civil engagement respectively.

Notably, this chapter has dismissed the idea that virtue-based AI was a utopic luxury. In the period of emerging algorithmic control, increasing epistemic inequalities, and alienation with technologies, virtue-centered AI is a requirement. The moral neutrality long assumed in the design and deployment of educational technologies is both epistemically naïve and normatively dangerous (Benjamin, 2019; Noble, 2018). It is impossible not to assume that AI systems will reflect moral presuppositions, will construct students as identity, and will develop moral growth, either on purpose or by default. Thus, the key issue is not whether AI in education recognizes ethics, but how willingly and comprehensively it does that. In the future, the ethical issues with AI are only going to get worse as these systems become more advanced, pervasive, and independent. AI will not simply be used by students, but they will dwell in it, educate themselves through it, and in numerous instances, be the object of its decision-making. In such an environment, it is imperative that we prepare learners not only to adapt to AI systems but to critically engage with and shape them in accordance with ethical and democratic values (Floridi et al., 2018; Nussbaum, 2010).

It is time to re-conceptualize human AI collaboration in terms of a morally co-constructive relationship rather than a zero-sum game. When implemented in terms of virtue ethics, AI can be used to scaffold thought about moral problems, it can simulate ethical dilemmas, and it can also help to solve problems collaboratively. It is able to assist students to experience moral complexity in whimsically cognitively demanding and affectively engaging, as well as socially positioned. However, this possibility can only work when AI is introduced into human-centered pedagogies under the leadership and wisdom of educators in the form of moral models and critical interlocutors. Ethical AI in education should also be pluralistic in the future. A paradigm of virtue needs to enable cultural diversity in moral theory, inculcation of epistemological humility in the design of systems, and institutional accountability in the control of systems. No single ethical framework can claim universal authority. Therefore, participatory co-design with educators, students, ethicists, and communities will be essential in shaping AI systems that are both contextually sensitive and normatively robust (Vallor, 2016).

Finally, the potential of virtue-based AI does not necessarily reside in its ability to replicate or substitute human moral capabilities. The potential of virtue-based AI rather resides in supplementing human moral abilities. Thoughtfully constructed AI and ethically utilized AI have the capacity to help build humane, intellectually independent and morally strong citizens who will be ready to face the moral ambiguities of our algorithmic-laden era. That is where the actual future of education lies, in the vision of AI not as technocratic and forced but moral infrastructure.

AI disclosure statement: The author acknowledges the use of AI-based tools for minor language editing or grammatical correction. However, all intellectual contributions, analyses, and conclusions presented in this chapter are entirely the author's own.

REFERENCES

Aristotle, . (1999). *Nicomachean Ethics* (Irwin, T., Trans.). Hackett Publishing.

Bankins, S., & Formosa, P. (2023). The ethical implications of Artificial Intelligence (AI) for meaningful work. *Journal of Business Ethics, 185*, 725–740. https://doi.org/doi:10.1007/s10551-023-05339-7

Biesta, G. (2010). *Good Education in an Age of Measurement: Ethics, Politics, Democracy.* Routledge.

Barron, B., & Darling-Hammond, L. (2008). *Teaching for Meaningful Learning: A Review of Research on Inquiry-Based and Cooperative Learning*. George Lucas Educational Foundation.

Benjamin, R. (2019). *Race After Technology: Abolitionist Tools for the New Jim Code*. Polity Press.

Bertoncini, A. L. C., & Serafim, M. C. (2023). Ethical content in artificial intelligence systems: A demand explained in three critical points. *Frontiers in Psychology, 14*, 1074787. DOI: 10.3389/fpsyg.2023.1074787 PMID: 37063544

Binns, R. (2018). "Fairness in Machine Learning: Lessons from Political Philosophy." *Proceedings of the 2018 Conference on Fairness, Accountability and Transparency*, 149–159.

Bratteteig, T., & Wagner, I. (2016). Unpacking the Notion of Participation in Participatory Design. [CSCW]. *Computer Supported Cooperative Work, 25*(6), 425–475. DOI: 10.1007/s10606-016-9259-4

Buolamwini, J., & Gebru, T. (2018). "Gender Shades: Intersectional Accuracy Disparities in Commercial Gender Classification." *Proceedings of the 1st Conference on Fairness, Accountability and Transparency*, 77–91.

Calo, R. (2015). Robotics and the Lessons of Cyberlaw. *California Law Review, 103*(3), 513–563.

De Cremer, D., & Narayanan, D. (2023). How AI tools can—and cannot—help organizations become more ethical. *Frontiers in Artificial Intelligence, 6*, 1093712. DOI: 10.3389/frai.2023.1093712 PMID: 37426304

Doshi-Velez, F., & Kim, B. (2017). "Towards a Rigorous Science of Interpretable Machine Learning." *arXiv preprint*, arXiv:1702.08608.

. Engelen, B., & Nys, T. R. V. (2024). Pushed for being better: On the possibility and desirability of moral nudging. *Journal of Value Inquiry*. Advance online publication. https://doi.org/ Eubanks, V. (2018). *Automating Inequality: How High-Tech Tools Profile, Police, and Punish the Poor.* St. Martin's Press.DOI: 10.1007/s10790-023-09977-y

Fabre, E. F., Mouratille, D., Bonnemains, V., Palmiotti, G. P., & Causse, M. (2024). Making moral decisions with artificial agents as advisors: A fNIRS study. *Computers in Human Behavior: Artificial Humans, 2*(2), 100096. DOI: 10.1016/j.chbah.2024.100096

Floridi, L., Cowls, J., Beltrametti, M., Chatila, R., Chazerand, P., Dignum, V., Luetge, C., Madelin, R., Pagallo, U., Rossi, F., Schafer, B., Valcke, P., & Vayena, E. (2018). AI4People—An Ethical Framework for a Good AI Society. *Minds and Machines*, *28*(4), 689–707. DOI: 10.1007/s11023-018-9482-5 PMID: 30930541

Fricker, M. (2007). *Epistemic Injustice: Power and the Ethics of Knowing*. Oxford University Press. DOI: 10.1093/acprof:oso/9780198237907.001.0001

Ganuthula, V. R. R., & Balaraman, K. K. (2025). *Beyond digital tools: AI as a psychological catalyst reshaping entrepreneurial self-efficacy in an era of uncertainty. SSRN*. https://ssrn.com/abstract=5247064 or http://dx.doi.org/DOI: 10.2139/ssrn.5247064

Goddard, K., Roudsari, A., & Wyatt, J. C. (2012). Automation bias: A systematic review of frequency, effect mediators, and mitigators. *Journal of the American Medical Informatics Association : JAMIA*, *19*(1), 121–127. DOI: 10.1136/amiajnl-2011-000089 PMID: 21685142

Greene, D., Hoffmann, A. L., & Stark, L. (2019). "Better, Nicer, Clearer, Fairer: A Critical Assessment of the Movement for Ethical Artificial Intelligence and Machine Learning." *Proceedings of the 52nd Hawaii International Conference on System Sciences*. DOI: 10.24251/HICSS.2019.258

Hagendorff, T. (2022). A virtue-based framework to support putting AI ethics into practice. *Philosophy & Technology*, *35*(3), 55. DOI: 10.1007/s13347-022-00553-z

Harding, S. (1998). *Is Science Multicultural? Postcolonialisms, Feminisms, and Epistemologies*. Indiana University Press. DOI: 10.2979/2095.0

Heyder, T., Passlack, N., & Posegga, O. (2023). Ethical management of human-AI interaction: Theory development review. *The Journal of Strategic Information Systems*, *32*(3), 101772. DOI: 10.1016/j.jsis.2023.101772

Hoffman, M. L. (2000). *Empathy and Moral Development: Implications for Caring and Justice*. Cambridge University Press. DOI: 10.1017/CBO9780511805851

Holmes, W., Bialik, M., & Fadel, C. (2019). *Artificial Intelligence in Education: Promises and Implications for Teaching and Learning*. Center for Curriculum Redesign.

Jobin, A., Ienca, M., & Vayena, E. (2019). The Global Landscape of AI Ethics Guidelines. *Nature Machine Intelligence*, *1*(9), 389–399. DOI: 10.1038/s42256-019-0088-2

Kristjánsson, K. (2015). *Aristotelian Character Education*. Routledge. DOI: 10.4324/9781315752747

Kristjánsson, K. (2022). Teaching *phronesis* to aspiring police officers: Some preliminary philosophical, developmental and pedagogical reflections. *International Journal of Ethics Education*, *7*(2), 289–305. DOI: 10.1007/s40889-022-00145-7

Lawrence, J., & Reed, C. (2019). Argument Mining: A Survey. *Computational Linguistics*, *42*(4), 765–818. DOI: 10.1162/coli_a_00364

Lipton, Z. C. (2018). The Mythos of Model Interpretability. *Communications of the ACM*, *61*(10), 36–43. DOI: 10.1145/3233231

Livanis, E., Voultsos, P., Vadikolias, K., Pantazakos, P., & Tsaroucha, A. (2024). Understanding the ethical issues of Brain-Computer Interfaces (BCIs): A blessing or the beginning of a dystopian future? *Cureus, 16*(4), e58243. DOI: 10.7759/cureus.58243 PMID: 38745805

Luckin, R., Holmes, W., Griffiths, M., & Forcier, L. B. (2016). *Intelligence unleashed: An argument for AI in education*. Pearson. https://static.googleusercontent.com/media/edu.google.com/en//pdfs/Intelligence-Unleashed-Publication.pdfMacIntyre, A. (1984). *After Virtue*. University of Notre Dame Press.

Mattioli, M., & Cabitza, F. (2024). Not in my face: Challenges and ethical considerations in automatic face emotion recognition technology. *Machine Learning and Knowledge Extraction, 6*(4), 2201–2231. DOI: 10.3390/make6040109

Metcalf, J., Keller, E., & Boyd, D. (2016). "Perspectives on Big Data, Ethics, and Society." *Council for Big Data, Ethics, and Society White Paper.*

Moor, J. H. (2006). The Nature, Importance, and Difficulty of Machine Ethics. *IEEE Intelligent Systems, 21*(4), 18–21. DOI: 10.1109/MIS.2006.80

Narvaez, D. (2006). Integrative Ethical Education. In Killen, M., & Smetana, J. (Eds.), *Handbook of Moral Development* (pp. 703–733). Lawrence Erlbaum.

Noble, S. U. (2018). *Algorithms of Oppression: How Search Engines Reinforce Racism*. NYU Press. DOI: 10.18574/nyu/9781479833641.001.0001

Nussbaum, M. C. (2001). *Upheavals of Thought: The Intelligence of Emotions*. Cambridge University Press. DOI: 10.1017/CBO9780511840715

Nussbaum, M. C. (2010). *Not for Profit: Why Democracy Needs the Humanities*. Princeton University Press.

Pane, J. F., Steiner, E. D., Baird, M. D., & Hamilton, L. S. (2015). *Continued Progress: Promising Evidence on Personalized Learning*. RAND Corporation. DOI: 10.7249/RR1365

Rahwan, I. (2018). Society-in-the-Loop: Programming the Algorithmic Social Contract. *Ethics and Information Technology, 20*(1), 5–14. DOI: 10.1007/s10676-017-9430-8

Russell, S., Dewey, D., & Tegmark, M. (2015). Research Priorities for Robust and Beneficial Artificial Intelligence. *AI Magazine, 36*(4), 105–114. DOI: 10.1609/aimag.v36i4.2577

Sadek, M., Calvo, R. A., & Mougenot, C. (2024). Designing value-sensitive AI: A critical review and recommendations for socio-technical design processes. *AI and Ethics, 4*(4), 949–967. DOI: 10.1007/s43681-023-00373-7

Selwyn, N. (2019). *Should Robots Replace Teachers? AI and the Future of Education*. Polity Press.

Strielkowski, W., Grebennikova, V., Lisovskiy, A., Rakhimova, G., & Vasileva, T. (2024). AI-driven adaptive learning for sustainable educational transformation. *Sustainable Development*. Advance online publication. DOI: 10.1002/sd.3221

Vallor, S. (2016). *Technology and the Virtues: A Philosophical Guide to a Future Worth Wanting*. Oxford University Press. DOI: 10.1093/acprof:oso/9780190498511.001.0001

Williamson, B., Eynon, R., & Potter, J. (2020). Pandemic Politics, Pedagogies and Practices: Digital Technologies and Distance Education During the Coronavirus Emergency. *Learning, Media and Technology*, *45*(2), 107–114. DOI: 10.1080/17439884.2020.1761641

Winner, L. (1986). *The Whale and the Reactor: A Search for Limits in an Age of High Technology*. University of Chicago Press.

Chapter 18
The Future of A.I. in Education:
Post-Millennial Generations

Mitrajit Biswas
https://orcid.org/0000-0002-0409-867X
O.P. Jindal Global University, India

ABSTRACT

AI's rapid growth is changing education as we know it across the globe. Once a science fiction concept, AI technologies are transforming the methods with which information is created, shared, and consumed. As we advance into the Fourth Industrial Revolution, it is evident that AI is not only enhancing the education sector; it is revolutionizing it, forcing educators, policymakers, and curricular developers to rethink the objectives and frameworks of formal schooling systems. Education powered by AI is no longer a figment of the imagination; it is a practical requirement in an age characterized by digital integration, omnipresent data, and the need for adaptable skills. The development of AI driven solutions from learning and tutoring systems to automated grading and content generation systems highlights the critical need for curriculum futurism, which suggests an alignment of pedagogy to technological advancements while retaining learning as the focal point.

INTRODUCTION

AI's rapid growth is changing education across the globe. Once a science fiction concept, AI technologies are transforming the methods with which information is created, shared, and consumed. As we advance into the Fourth Industrial Revolution, it is evident that AI is not only enhancing the education sector; it is revolutionizing it, forcing educators, policymakers, and curricular developers to rethink the objectives and frameworks of formal schooling systems. Education powered by AI is no longer a figment of the imagination; it is a practical requirement in an age characterized by digital integration, omnipresent data, and the need for adaptable skills. The development of AI driven solutions from learning and tutoring systems to automated grading and content generation systems highlights the critical need for curriculum futurism, which

DOI: 10.4018/979-8-3373-2752-5.ch018

suggests an alignment of pedagogy to technological advancements while retaining learning as the focal point.

AI's rapid growth is no longer just changing education; it is fundamentally reshaping its purpose and practice on a global scale. Once a concept confined to science fiction, AI technologies are now actively transforming how information is created, shared, and consumed. As we advance into the Fourth Industrial Revolution, it is evident that AI is not merely enhancing the education sector but revolutionizing it, forcing educators, policymakers, and curriculum developers to rethink the very objectives and frameworks of formal schooling. (Eubanks, 2018)

However, the current discourse often frames this shift as a matter of technological inevitability rather than pedagogical necessity. The critical gap this chapter addresses is the lack of a cohesive framework that connects AI's potential to the specific learning needs of post-millennial generations (Gen Z and Alpha) while navigating significant ethical and implementation barriers. While global investment in EdTech is projected to surpass $400 billion by 2026, this financial momentum is not always matched by strategic, evidence-based integration. This chapter argues that without a critical, theoretically grounded approach, the integration of AI risks creating technologically advanced but contextually void learning ecosystems.

This transformation is not occurring in a vacuum. It is underscored by major policy initiatives such as UNESCO's "AI and the Futures of Learning" and the European Union's "Digital Education Action Plan," which signal a global consensus on the need for change. The historical progression from early computer-assisted instruction to today's sophisticated generative AI highlights a critical need for curriculum futurism—an approach that aligns pedagogy with technological advancements while keeping human-centric learning at its core.

The development of AI-driven solutions, from adaptive learning systems to automated content generation, makes a compelling case for this shift. Education powered by AI is no longer a distant vision; it is a practical requirement in an age defined by digital integration, omnipresent data, and the demand for adaptable, future-ready skills. (Fullan et al. 2018)

From Passive Learning to Intelligent Personalization

Most contemporary students are digitally savvy and learn best using multimedia resources. This is a challenge with traditional pedagogies that employ a passive approach, based on a fixed syllabus and a singular teaching style. AI fundamentally revolutionizes this by allowing for breaks from traditional learning environments. Advanced analytics enable the implementation of machine learning algorithms that continually monitor a student's performance as they undergo assessments, determining their strengths, gaps, and learning preferences. Content, exercises, and assessments that optimize learning for each student individually can then be provided. Increased personalization leads to higher retention rates and improved levels of anxiety associated with learning and dropout rates (Cuban, 1986). Technology powered by AI that the likes of Century Tech and Squirrel AI in China as well as IBM Watson Education have developed demonstrates the extent to which AI can aid in customized content delivery, pacing, and feedback. These systems are capable of real-time adaptation wherein the level of difficulty or the manner in which a concept is presented is adjusted based on feedback from the learner. These systems ultimately turn a rigid curriculum into a dynamic, responsive framework.

Curriculum as a Service: Generative AI in Content Creation

Creating educational content is easier than ever with generative AI tools such as ChatGPT, DALL·E, and Google Gemini, enabling educators to create lesson plans, quizzes, explanations, visuals, and even videos in minutes. Such tools provide up-to-date information on rapidly changing topics like climate change, digital literacy, and geopolitics, which are inadequately covered by textbooks. Generative AI may explain difficult concepts to learners and create analogies relevant to their cultures. Moreover, historical simulations or scientific phenomena may also be produced in 3D and auditory formats. By democratizing content creation, generative AI reduces the need for centralized publishers and fosters the creation of place-based, interdisciplinary, and inclusive curricula.

Fostering Equity and Inclusion Through AI

It is beyond dispute that AI has the potential to address educational inequities. Students with disabilities and those from different linguistic backgrounds can access learning materials through speech-to-text software, AI sign language avatars, and real-time translators. Programs like Microsoft's Immersive Reader and Google's AI language translation integrate directly with teaching tools so that everyone can access educational materials, regardless of language or cognitive ability . In addition, AI-powered frameworks are able to diagnose patterns of lethargy or academic underperformance within the context of students belonging to underrepresented groups and enable intervention at the right moment. This is how AI acts as an equity multiplier and mitigates the chronic educational disparities that have disadvantaged historically underserved populations.

Data-Driven Insights for Early Intervention

Another important function of AI is predictive analytics. Through examining student behavior and performance, attendance, and participation, AI systems can detect which learners are likely going to fall behind. Educators can then be prepared to take measures that offer prompt intervention, guidance, or modification of instructional materials to more skill-level appropriate levels for the learner. Knewton, DreamBox, and Edgenuity provide data-driven insights that school practitioners can act on and enhance the performance of their students. The derived insights not only assist the learners in question but also aid in curriculum re-design by providing information on what works, what does not, and how the instructional processes have authenticity towards population effectiveness and needs.

Rework of the Burden on Educator Responsibilities and Teacher Duties

The optimization of educational AI systems concerns the automaton of administrative work and evaluative functions at an astounding level AI managed grading, resource attendance, report generation, and even compilation is accurate enough to be dealt with by AI tools. Relieving routine duties from educators allows them more time to do constructive work such as mentoring students, guiding collaborative problem solving, and helping develop critical thinking. Strategic planning and working with information and systems imply that teachers will function as facilitators rather than primary instruction givers; content delivery will, therefore, no longer be their primary role. This paradigm shift will require targeted AI professional development units with strategies training for upskilling which will allow educators to confidently incorporate AI tools into their teaching practices.

Ethics and Implication Hurdles on AI Implementations

All these advancements raise ethical questions regarding design and implementation of AI integrated into curriculum AI bias for instance forces us to ask concepts associated with prejudice, data privacy, or even the digital gap can become sensitive subjects. There is a heightened risk of perpetuating inequity with unrepresentative AI trained systems because of predetermined, opaque datasets putting these AI systems biases' constraints makes equal instructional recommendation illogical. Maintaining trust among students and parents is as crucial as informing them of how the AI makes its decisions—its interpretative reasoning—along with AI explainability. UNESCO's AI Ethics Guidelines and the EU's AI Act law both focus the necessity of human intervention, moral framework, and responsibility in the use of AI in education systems. The collaboration with ethicists, students, and educators make the work towards future curriculum layout a lot more than advanced techniques algorithms—it needs deep moral reasoning.

Equipping Learners with AI Augmentation Skills

The most important focus of curriculum adjusting would be increasing automation, robotics, and AI in the workforce and preparing students for it. Tech-skill inclusion such as STEM competencies and data literacy is critical alongside human abilities like empathy, ethical judgement, reasoning, imagination, and widespread communication. Digital ethics, interdisciplinary problem-solving, AI literacy, and computational thinking must become part of every curriculum. Schools and universities unwilling to adapt to evolving global economies risk creating unqualified learning graduates.

Conclusion to Introduction

As will be demonstrated in the following sections of this chapter, AI presents a game-changing opportunity in smarter and more inclusive education systems as well as readying them for the future. If AI's potential is harnessed in a strategic, thoughtful, and fair manner, curriculum designers would be able to create lifelong learning ecosystems that enable individuals to harness, adapt, innovate and thrive.

In safeguarding curriculum design, it is contextually emphasized that futurist approaches are not end-goals, but more of ongoing endeavors. This proposes embracing AI not as an enemy to traditional education but as a means capable of augmenting humanity's greatest attributes when applied, ethically and optimally.

LITERATURE REVIEW

The application of artificial intelligence (AI) within the context of education has received considerable attention in recent AI-based educational studies. While AI has been increasingly adopted as an innovative teaching technology, using it to modernize curricula has received particular focus in recent times. A comprehensive body of literature spanning computer science, education, informatics, psychology, ethics, and policy studies reveals the complex impact of artificial intelligence on curriculum design.

Key Domains of AI Application in Education

Based on systematic literature reviews, the applications of AI in education have been organized into four primary categories: adaptive learning, personalized instruction, intelligent tutoring systems (ITS), and automated assessment tools. These categories underpin the flexibility of curriculum design and optimization through the evolving focus on pedagogy which is differentiated and data driven. Depending on the learner's interaction and performance, Adaptive Learning Systems (ALS) utilizes machine learning algorithms to modify the content, pace, and complexity of instructions in real-time. Personalized Instruction makes use of prior accomplishment alongside learning styles and other student data to create classwork that maximizes participation and results for individual students. Intelligent Tutoring Systems replicate the role of a tutor by providing complete assistance, motivation, encouragement, and feedback through real-time interaction via chatbots or virtual assistants. Automated Assessment helps educators to grade both formative and summative tasks efficiently, automating tedious administrative tasks and allowing teachers to monitor progress in real time. These technologies are progressing from a rigid, one-dimensional approach to curriculum implementation into a flexible system that accommodates the requirements of learning in the 21st century.

The application of artificial intelligence (AI) within education has generated a vast and multidisciplinary body of research. A comprehensive review of literature spanning computer science, education, psychology, ethics, and policy reveals a complex and often fragmented landscape. This review synthesizes key domains, identifies critical debates, and highlights the theoretical gaps that this chapter aims to address.

Key Domains of AI Application in Education

Systematic reviews (e.g., Zawacki-Richter et al., 2019; Ouyang et al., 2022) typically organize AI applications into four primary categories:

1. Adaptive Learning and Personalized Instruction: Adaptive Learning Systems (ALS) utilize machine learning to modify content, pace, and complexity in real-time based on learner performance. Platforms like CenturyTech and Squirrel AI are frequently cited as exemplars (Chen, 2020). Personalized instruction extends this by tailoring content to learning styles and prior knowledge to maximize engagement.
2. Intelligent Tutoring Systems (ITS): Emulating the role of a human tutor, ITS provides guided assistance, Socratic questioning, and motivational feedback. Research highlights their effectiveness in structured domains like mathematics and programming (Kulik & Fletcher, 2016).
3. Automated Assessment and Feedback: AI tools are increasingly used for grading both formative and summative tasks, from multiple-choice questions to complex essays, freeing up educator time for higher-order tasks.

4. Generative AI in Content Creation: The emergence of Large Language Models (LLMs) like those powering ChatGPT and Elicit has democratized content creation. However, this raises significant questions regarding academic integrity, authorship, and the potential for over-reliance on AI-generated content (Tlili et al., 2023).

Critique and Tensions in the Literature

While the benefits are widely discussed, a critical analysis of the literature reveals significant tensions and debates that are often under-emphasized:

- Teacher Agency vs. Algorithmic Authority: A central debate revolves around the risk of de-professionalizing teachers by ceding pedagogical decisions to opaque algorithms. The literature questions whether AI should augment or automate teaching, highlighting the potential loss of the crucial human element in education (Selwyn, 2019).
- The Promise and Peril of Datafication: AI's efficacy depends on vast amounts of student data, raising profound ethical concerns about privacy, surveillance, and consent (Williamson & Hogan, 2020). Who owns student data, and how is it used beyond the immediate pedagogical context?
- Bias and Inequity: A significant body of research demonstrates that AI systems can perpetuate and even amplify existing societal biases related to race, gender, and socioeconomic status, thereby undermining the goal of educational equity (Noble, 2018; O'Neil, 2016).
- The Digital Divide: The literature consistently points out that the benefits of AI in education are not accessible to all. The digital divide encompasses not only access to hardware and internet but also the digital literacy required to use these tools effectively, creating a new layer of inequity.

The Need for a Guiding Theoretical Framework

The current literature often presents a scattered view of tools and possibilities without a unifying theoretical anchor. The evolution of research from pre-COVID explorations to post-COVID acceleration highlights an urgent need for models that can guide strategic and ethical implementation. This disjointed landscape, full of both promise and peril, demonstrates that simply adopting AI tools is insufficient. A robust theoretical framework is essential to connect technology with pedagogy, navigate ethical challenges, and ensure that AI serves, rather than subverts, the core goals of education. This review points directly to the necessity of integrating established frameworks like TPACK and SAMR with sociocultural and equity-based perspectives to create a holistic model for AI integration.

The Post-Millennial Learner: A New Educational Imperative

A significant gap in the current discourse is the lack of specific analysis of the primary audience for AI-driven education: the post-millennial generations (Gen Z, born 1997-2012, and Gen Alpha, born after 2012). The chapter's focus is incomplete without understanding the unique cognitive and behavioral traits of these digital natives.

- Digital Nativity and Learning Preferences: Unlike previous generations, post-millennials have grown up in a world of ubiquitous connectivity. Their learning preferences are heavily skewed towards immersive, interactive, and gamified experiences. They expect instant feedback and personalized pathways, making traditional, one-size-fits-all curricula feel outdated and disengaging (Twenge, 2017).
- Cognitive Styles: Research suggests that constant exposure to digital media may influence cognitive styles, favoring rapid information processing and multitasking over deep, sustained focus. Educational strategies must account for this, using AI to break down complex topics into manageable, engaging micro-learning modules.
- Social and Collaborative Learning: These generations thrive in social learning environments. AI tools must therefore not only personalize individual learning but also facilitate collaboration, connecting learners in virtual teams and project-based assignments that mirror modern workplace dynamics.

Failing to design AI integration around the specific needs of these learners risks developing solutions that are technologically impressive but pedagogically irrelevant. The "why" of AI in education is intrinsically linked to the "who" it is designed for.

AI With regard to Education: Assisting in Research and Writing

There is a growing body of literature investigating the use of AI tools in assisting academic research and in developing curricula, particularly focusing on higher education. AI tools such as semantic search engines, auto-summarizers, citation managers, and content generators like Elicit, Scite are helping researchers by expediting the synthesis of literature, formulation of hypotheses, and even the initial stages of drafting research papers.

But these advantages come with serious issues. There is some concern that scholars are becoming increasingly reliant upon content produced by AI for deep verification processes. Inquiries pertaining to the authorship, validity, and subjectivity of outputs have become more prominent in the discourse of academic integrity. The literature argues for more institutional policies and the need to instruct students and faculty on digital literacy to understand the ethical boundaries regarding the use of generative AI in dealing with academic work.

Impact and Rigor in AI and Education Research

A review of literature regarding AI tools in the education sector reveals that researchers now focus on incorporating more methodological sternness on the effects of AI in education. A growing body of scoping reviews and literature meta-analyses is putting focus on having specific research questions, efficient search/capture strategies, strong experimental frameworks, detailed reporting, and construct validation to improve replicability and relevance (Benjamin, 2019) . These works also emphasize the importance of mixed methods to gauge the overall impact of AI tools on student performance as well as on changes to their motivation, identity, or engagement. Scholars also contemporaneously argue the need to shift from stage-of-development or proof-of-concept studies towards the longitudinal tracking of AI's curricular impacts, effectiveness measures, and even unused implications associated with classroom adoption of AI technology.

Open Doors: A Decade of AIED Research

Findings highlight both opportunities and challenges from analyzing AIED literature over the past decade. Emerging developments in AI underscore the ability of AI to: Enable non-speakers of the language and other neurodiverse learners to thrive in lessons. Support critical competencies of the digital world such as advanced collaboration, metacognition, and self learning. Disable from learners identifying their needs and altering their content's presentation and instructional sequencing: real time curriculum adaptation.

Addressing these problems presents challenges, such as:

Lack of equitable access to dependable internet services, hardware, and AI powered frameworks represents a form of digital inequity.

Dependency on educational technology such as algorithms to appraise and dictate teaching choices, including workflow processes, indicates the presence of technological over-reliance.

Gap in faculty development reflects the failure of many teachers to utilize AI teaching tools due to lack of proper training, confidence, or skill.

Such challenges imply that effective system-wide curriculum change must be complemented with systemic aid such as teacher support, instructional design frameworks, and strategic planning with ongoing assessment systems.

AI for Automating Systematic Reviews: Emerging Trends

One growing AI sub-domain focuses on leveraging AI technologies to automate certain tasks within systematic literature review processes. AS Review, Research Rabbit, and Connected Papers are examples of applications that attempt to automate evidence synthesis, identification of key literature, and visualization of cross-disciplinary concepts through machine learning and citation networks. While these applications enhance productivity, there are still concerns about their accuracy and lack of clarity with frameworks outside of western academic traditions, including other regional knowledge systems. Caplan, Falk-Krzesinski, and Chalmers argue for the use of these applications as decision support tools, provided their outcomes are assessed alongside expert input.

The Need for a Theory Associated with the Use of AI in Curriculum Development

Calls for integrated models which systematically relate the possibilities offered by AI to pedagogical processes and interaction with curriculum frameworks are becoming frequent in the literature. Adaptations of the TPACK model and SAMR model now exist alongside Bloom's Revised Taxonomy and aim to integrate teaching and learning at AI's levels and with AI's capabilities. Recent advances such as the Human-AI Pedagogical Partnership (HAPP) framework have focused on reciprocal relationships where human teachers co-evolve with AI agents in teaching and learning systems, mutually supporting one another's roles instead of one replacing the other. Such arrangements are important for grounding curriculum design reasoning in a theory and allow for the adoption of AI as more than a mere tool and a pedagogical innovation transforming institution thinking strategically about AI integration.

In concluding this literature review, it has become apparent that there is a lively, multi-directional and multi-faceted field of research on the role AI could, and in some people's view, should play in curriculum design, with stances varying from enthusiastic to careful. There is wide agreement that AI can be effective in personalizing learning, conducting research, and providing equitable opportunities but many wish to control the ethical, quality assurance, and gap issues of such implementations.

Fulfilling the potential of AI-augmented curriculum development relies on future research prioritizing innovation equitably, collaborative governance, and impact assessment by the in longitudinal multi-tenant design. Educators and policymakers can adopt AI meaningfully and construct enduring education frameworks by thoughtfully balancing a 'systems' approach to education.

THEORETICAL FRAMEWORK

The compilation of AI in educational psychology curriculum frameworks requires the integration of multiple theories related to technology that AI interlaces with, as well as sociocultural theories. This approach emphasizes the synthesis of multiple frameworks in order to provide adequate understanding pertaining to how AI technologies can be incorporated in a way to facilitate multi-curricula creation at different levels, while at the same time ensuring such curricula are proactive and responsive to 21st century needs.

Theoretical Framework

To navigate the complexities identified in the literature, this chapter adopts an integrated theoretical framework. This approach synthesizes multiple theories to provide a comprehensive lens for analyzing how AI can be embedded within curricula in a manner that is effective, ethical, and responsive to the needs of 21st-century learners.

1. Constructivist Learning Theory (Bruner, 1966; Vygotsky, 1978): This theory posits that learners actively construct knowledge rather than passively receiving it. AI enhances this process by shifting the focus from information delivery to guided inquiry. AI-driven ITS can use the Socratic method to foster critical thinking, while generative AI can act as a sparring partner for learners to debate issues and co-create knowledge.
2. TPACK Framework (Mishra & Koehler, 2006): This framework highlights the need for knowledge at the intersection of Technology, Pedagogy, and Content. For AI, this evolves into AI-Pedagogical Content Knowledge (AI-PCK)—a deep understanding of how specific AI tools can be used to effectively teach specific content, requiring a fundamental shift in teacher training toward data literacy and AI competencies.
3. SAMR Model (Puentedura, 2006): The SAMR model provides a hierarchy for assessing the transformative potential of AI integration:
    a. Substitution: AI as a direct replacement (e.g., a chatbot for a static FAQ page).
    b. Augmentation: AI as an efficiency tool (e.g., automated grading).

c. Modification: AI enables significant task redesign (e.g., students using generative AI to co-create multimedia projects).
d. Redefinition: AI allows for new tasks previously inconceivable (e.g., using VR simulations with AI-powered characters for medical training). This model challenges educators to move beyond simple efficiency gains toward true pedagogical transformation.

4. Diffusion of Innovations Theory (Rogers, 2003): This theory explains how innovations are adopted within a social system. Understanding the determinants of adoption—relative advantage, compatibility, complexity, trialability, and observability—is crucial for devising strategies that address institutional inertia and faculty resistance.
5. Sociocultural and Equity Perspectives: Grounding the framework in an equity lens is non-negotiable. Critical Pedagogy and Universal Design for Learning (UDL) demand that AI systems be designed to dismantle, not reproduce, systemic inequities. This requires:
   a. Regular audits of algorithms for bias.
   b. Interfaces that are accessible to learners with disabilities.
   c. Content that is culturally and linguistically responsive.

This integrated framework provides a robust model for moving beyond AI as a simple tool and toward its thoughtful integration as a transformative pedagogical partner.

Synthesis

This construct, incorporating the lenses of equity, takes into account the multi-dimensional sociocultural contexts of schooling that of constructionism, technology integration, innovation diffusion aims to provide a comprehensive analysis on AI and curriculum design. It focuses on:

Aligning AI technology integrating with systems of active learning and student engagement.

Transforming educator competencies with relies on the educator's engagement potential to augment AI enable.

Dynamically balanced, multi-focal critical analysis of surface level versus depth of AI integration in a system.

Sociotechnical ethical boundaries within education and governance frameworks of AI the agent within education.

There is a huge difference between using AI as a simple enhancement technology compared to integrating it with an equity-based contextual approach integrated design model for curriculum development. The old model of 'futuristic' education centers on automation needs ongoing research, collaboration of relevant parties, and policies that foster innovative social responsibility.

METHODOLOGY

This chapter employs a qualitative, exploratory research design to investigate the integration of AI into curriculum design. Given that AI adoption is highly context-dependent, a qualitative approach allows for a nuanced understanding of the lived experiences of educators and learners. The methodology triangulates findings from a systematic literature review, in-depth expert interviews, and illustrative case study analysis.

1. Systematic Literature Review: A review was conducted using ERIC, Scopus, and Web of Science (2018-2024) to identify dominant trends, barriers, and theoretical frameworks in AI-in-education research.
2. Expert Interviews: Semi-structured interviews were conducted with a purposive sample (n=18) of curriculum developers, educational technologists, faculty members with AI experience, and policymakers. Thematic analysis was used to identify recurring patterns related to pedagogical strategies, ethical challenges, and implementation hurdles.
3. Case Study Analysis: Multiple case studies were selected to illustrate AI integration in diverse contexts (e.g., a Finnish K-12 school using personalized learning, a South Asian EdTech startup, a US university experimenting with generative AI). This provides practical, real-world examples to ground the theoretical discussion.

The combination of practical theory and blended empirics provides a deep, contextualized understanding of AI in curriculum design. By employing data triangulation and multi-faceted analysis, the evidence-driven insights respond to emerging educational challenges. The insights advance both strategic planning and agile AI-enabled educational innovation that moves from concept to practice.

IMPLEMENTATION CHALLENGES: FROM THEORY TO PRACTICE

While the potential of AI is vast, the path to effective implementation is fraught with practical challenges that the literature often acknowledges but rarely explores in depth. A realistic assessment requires a multi-level analysis of these barriers.

1. Institutional and Systemic Hurdles:
    a. Cost and Sustainability: The licensing, infrastructure, and maintenance costs of sophisticated AI systems are prohibitive for many public institutions, raising questions of financial sustainability.
    b. Infrastructure Gaps: Effective AI relies on robust digital infrastructure, including high-speed internet and modern devices, which remains a major barrier in rural and low-income communities.
    c. Policy and Governance Vacuum: Many institutions lack clear policies for the ethical use of AI, data governance, and academic integrity, leaving faculty and students in a state of uncertainty.
2. Faculty and Pedagogical Barriers:
    a. Teacher Resistance and Training: Many educators lack the confidence, training, or time to integrate AI tools effectively. Without comprehensive professional development that goes beyond basic technical skills, adoption will remain superficial.
    b. Curriculum Rigidity: Traditional, standardized curricula often lack the flexibility to accommodate the personalized, dynamic pathways that AI enables.
    c. Loss of Pedagogical Control: A legitimate fear among educators is that AI will dictate teaching methods, undermining their professional autonomy and judgment.
3. Learner-Centric Challenges:

a. Digital Literacy Gaps: Not all students possess the critical digital literacy skills needed to use AI tools responsibly and effectively, including the ability to evaluate AI-generated information.
b. Data Privacy Risks: Students are often unaware of how their data is being collected, used, and potentially monetized by third-party EdTech vendors.

Addressing these challenges requires a coordinated, system-wide strategy that includes investment in infrastructure, ongoing professional development, and the co-creation of ethical guidelines with all stakeholders.

Evaluation

The implementation of Artificial Intelligence (AI) into educational curriculum planning is profoundly changing teaching methods, school administration, and learner achievements. With the help of evidence, stakeholder input, and several case studies, this analysis synthesizes the most salient AI-related challenges and opportunities in learning and teaching.

Customized Learning Paths

AI algorithms can provide differentiated instruction because of their capability to assess students' learning patterns, prior achievements, and emotional involvement. Platforms like Dream Box and Century Tech are adaptive; they change level, pacing, and content type in real time. Every single student must be challenged, but not to the point where they disengage from learning, fall behind or are outpaced. Personalization of this magnitude, especially in Inclusive settings, greatly aids neurodiverse learners and those from culturally or linguistically diverse backgrounds.

Fulfilling Administrative Duties

Attending tasks such as grading, taking attendance, and scheduling are made easier by automation. As with many technologies nowadays, institutions become more efficient through AI. For instance, Gradescope can automatically grade open-ended assignments in a multiple-choice test format using machine learning. This enhances time previously focused on mundane tasks, allowing for increased time dedicated to lesson planning and student mentorship. Despite these benefits, educators risk losing their invisible guidance role, which can undermine formative assessment approaches devoid of reflective pedagogical frameworks .

Intelligent Content Development

As of now, the teaching process is being streamlined and improves by using AI tools. ScribeSense and Content Technologies Inc. are but two examples of platforms that compose quizzes, modules, and even complete lesson plans. Such tools enable educators to have updated and interesting resources STEM and other quickly changing disciplines, and assist in effortless material creation. However, the reliance on automation raises fears concerning the erosion of content pedagogy and the intentionality behind teaching within an education framework.

Real-Time Analytics and Feedback

AI-powered learning analytics platforms like Knewton or IBM Watson Education provide educators with insights into students' performances, knowledge gaps, and levels of engagement in real-time. Such analytics allow educators to make proactive instructional decisions and for real-time responsive course design. However, data needs to be guided by pedagogy; otherwise, the reliance on numbers will deemphasize more important parts of education like creativity, collaboration, and many other aspects that do not have easily quantifiable metrics.

Adaptive Curriculum Frameworks

Content delivery is no longer the only aspect of curriculum AI is making more agile and responsive; it seeks to adjust how curriculums are designed. Educators are harnessing big data to integrate information on skills and competencies relevant to the labor market. These changes are exemplified in World Economic Forum's "Reskilling Revolution" and UNESCO's "AI and the Futures of Learning" that seek to merge technological advancements with human-centered education.

Optimization of Resources

Through the use of AI, technologies for Predictive Analytics enable the targeted monitoring of potentially vulnerable students, enabling timely guidance. Furthermore, institutions can more accurately "fire" instructional resources through predictive engagement analytics and enrollment forecasts. Unfortunately, data-informed attention does not perpetuate inequermatic contexts and relies upon the decisions made in contextually void learning ecosystems designed for equity in resource-scarce educational settings.

Primary Concern

There is still a lack of ethical, pedagogical, and infrastructural support. Some of these are:

No clarity is offered for the reasoning within algorithms. Explainability is absent. Decision-making is non-transparent.

Fostering inequality—existing bias is augmented.

Shortcomings of the digital base especially with regard to rural and other disadvantaged regions.

Abridged acceptance by teachers citing fear of losing their role or unprepared training.

Suggestion

This corrective analysis aims to add the focus on incorporating Artificial Intelligence (AI) in aiding curriculum development, drawing attention to the underpinnings aiming to ensure that it is utilized with the consideration of pedagogical centers within strategic frameworks.

1. Clarify Goals and Define Key Performance Indicators

Start with identifying cutter through instruction— AI tools advanced including optimization through leaner identification for engagement, agility of the curriculum, or learner and educator performance aides.

2. Pick The Right Tools and Technologies AI Offers

Evaluate tools utilizing framework of educational value like TPACK or SAMR instead of industry buzz.

Conduct pilot trials of technologies within controlled environments and in-person evaluate their usability, accessibility and pedagogical alignment.

Evaluate the possibilities of using open-source software or tools developed by the community in order to enhance transparency and foster personalization.

3. Encourage Stakeholder Participation and Enhance Their Skills

Draft schematic of AI implementation with teachers, students, administrators and IT as active participants, so that buy-in is developed and ownership is created.

Facilitate focused professional development (PD) opportunities such as micro-credentials or workshop-style learning for AI ethics and literacy.

Provide informal collaborative working groups and standing peer mentorships which aid educators in learning to share strategies on AI integration.

4. Focus On Responsible Use and Data Privacy

Create policies of ethical AI use grounded on predominant frameworks like UNESCO AI Ethics Guidelines along with OECD Principles on AI.

Apply data sovereignty and protection, especially for children by anonymizing, encrypting, and storing data through clear opt-in protocols.

Conduct audits of AI tools regularly with external experts to uncover biases, inaccuracies, or unregulated use for independent scrutiny.

5. Put AI To Aid Inclusivity and Fair Opportunities

Subsidize use of digital enabling tools for economically disadvantaged groups and implement principles of UDL in AI-powered curricula.

Adapt teaching materials to local languages and provide them in various formats such as audio, visual, or tactile materials to assist learners of all abilities.

Coordinate with NGOs and governmental programs to assist in closing the gaps in digital infrastructure in disadvantaged areas.

6. Foster Ongoing Review and Adaptation

Form learning loops in which educators and learners evaluate the effectiveness of AI-driven solutions.

Conduct evaluation through mixed methods using quantitative data alongside ethnographically collected data to achieve impact holistic understanding.

Establish internal review committees or innovation labs within organizations for the purpose of developing, refining, and expanding AI strategies.

7. Fostering Teamwork and Interdisciplinary Collaboration

Support collaborative curriculum development that features educators, data scientists, ethicists, and other domain specialists collaborating on a transdisciplinary approach.

Create capstone projects or challenge-based learning where learners solve problems concerning the application of AI in real time.

Encourage international collaborations for sharing innovative practices, particularly those emerging from the Global South, which innovative low-resource solutions may showcase.

To Summarize

AI can be used to transform curriculums because of how efficiently they can be tailored to each learner's unique needs. Though surround AI use in education with careful and ethical intentions. The future of education with AI does not rely solely on automation but rather on augmented intelligence where the educator is empowered, the learner is active, and technology supports instead of supplants. Those institutions that invest strategically in the integration of AI, pedagogical approaches, ethics, and sustainable capacity strengthening will enjoy the benefits of AI in building resilient, future-ready education systems.

Figure 1. The diagram and flow of A.I. Curriculum and its impact on educational outcome

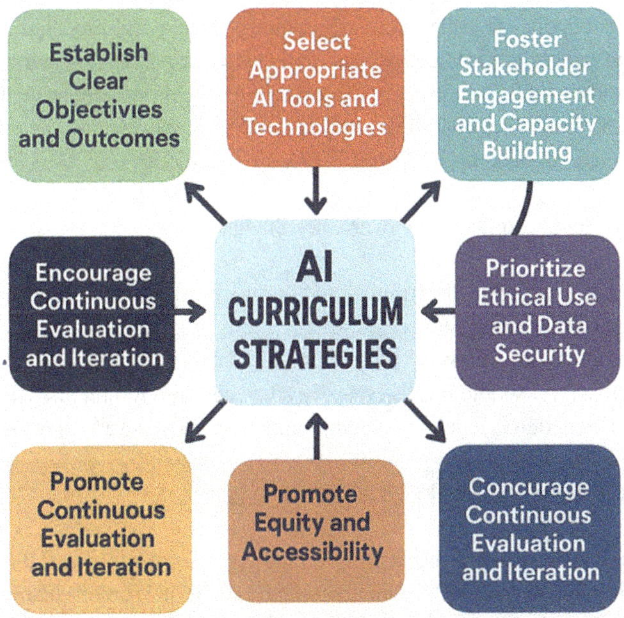

Constraints

The application of artificial intelligence (AI) within the parameters of curriculum development represents more than the adoption of a new technology; it signifies an evolution in system thinking concerning the education model, delivery, learning processes, and overall institutional value. AI technologies present an unprecedented level of opportunity to enhance the personalization, data utilization, inclusivity, and futurism that characterize educational frameworks. Through automating administrative tasks, providing real-time feedback, enhancing content relevance, AI is creating individualized learning frameworks, equipping both learners and educators with skills primed for today's adaptable learning environments.

This chapter has articulated a strategic blueprint designed for strengthening—and in some cases, curing—the 'curriculum' ailment through AI, supplemented by literature, expert testimonials, and case study evidence. It advocates for a balanced approach that includes:

Goal determination balanced with pedagogical-societal frameworks.

Tool selection anchored on usability, scalability, and evidence of effectiveness.

Participation and empowerment by educators to ensure shared ownership.

Guarded ethical and equitable use with protections against data and bias manipulation.

Feedback and evaluation focused on refinement of teaching and educational practices.

Artificial Intelligence (AI) is revolutionizing many industries and the modern education system is no exception. The use of AI enables developing curriculums that ensure students learn to not only participate in an AI driven world, but excel in it. However, integrating AI into curricula requires great attention to being reflective and responsive to emerging social challenges. Integrating AI in curriculum design poses unique challenges, some of them are:

1. Data Confidentiality and Safety.

AI algorithms depend on collecting vast amounts of data and processing it. Schools and institutions are in danger of violating privacy policies when processing learner data devoid of strict governance measures. Data practices from third party AI providers can also pose security risks through undisclosed data handling. Informed consent, encryption, and compliance with data privacy regulations such as GDPR or FERPA are mandatory.

2. Bias in Algorithms and Opaque Governance Shenanigans.

Due to historical systematic discrimination AI trained systems reproduce biases on the basis of gender, nationality, language, or socioeconomic status. For example, learners from the dominating ethnic cultures may be overly represented in adaptive learning systems. Bias diversity in autonomous functions should be systemically advanced through the use of advocacy ethnic frameworks, XAI procedures, regular bias audits, and oversight from educators and technologists.

3. Unresolved Issues of the Socal Digital Divide

Artificial intelligence fosters learning opportunities while assuming that there is prior access to devices, internet, and digital skills (which is not the case in rural or low-income communities).

Accomplishing equity in education requires that policy straddles the use of AI alongside infrastructural frameworks, universal access plans, and offline capability AIs or low-capacity options.

4. Differences in Readiness

Many educators fall under the groups previously mentioned, demonstrating a lack of training, confidence, or time to actively engage AI tools, whereas they are fundamental to the AI adoption process. Institutions should allocate resources toward professional development, peer teaching, and communities of practice. Moreover, educators ought to be active participants in defining the ways AI is, rather passively put, used in education.

5. Cultural and Context Framework Gaps

A majority of AI tools are designed with the Anglophone world or the Global North sections – and don't directly fit into the surrounding taught culture, language, or curriculum. This has a risk of putting in place, 'one-size-fits-all' which contributes to epistemic colonialism. The effective integration of AI tools should approach the area blunders of lack of culture sensitive material accompanied by local language interfaces.

6. Excessive Dependence on Technology

AI efficiency offers great potential, but the overarching risk it brings lies in devaluing judgment, emotional, social interactions, which are actually core to the transformative power in education. Curriculum designers operating within such frameworks must observe a human-in-the-loop philosophy that ensures AI aids rather than takes over teaching.

7. Sustainability and Cost Implications

The use of advanced AI technologies like chatbots require significant expenditures across their life cycle. Public education institutions or small private colleges might face difficulties in affordability and financial sustainability in the long run. Perhaps, open-source tools, collaborative AI purchasing schemes, and public-private partnerships may provide such options.

FINAL REFLECTION

AI applications in curriculum design should be regarded as enhancements rather than replacements. While there is opportunity, this potential will not be realized unless active, intentional, and inclusive custodianship is practiced. Education must continue to be a profoundly human activity, with AI employed to expand—not overshadow—the humanistic values of empathy, imagination, and critical awareness.

DISCUSSION, RECOMMENDATIONS, AND CONCLUSION

The integration of Artificial Intelligence into curriculum design presents a paradigm shift for education. This analysis, supported by literature, expert interviews, and case studies, reveals a field ripe with opportunity but constrained by significant ethical, pedagogical, and infrastructural challenges.

Synthesis of Findings

AI's primary strengths lie in its ability to deliver customized learning paths, automate administrative tasks, and provide real-time analytics. Platforms like DreamBox and Knewton demonstrate the power of personalization, while generative AI tools are revolutionizing content creation. However, these benefits are counterbalanced by the serious risks of algorithmic bias, data privacy violations, teacher de-professionalization, and the exacerbation of the digital divide. The central finding of this chapter is that a "technology-first" approach is destined to fail. Effective integration must be pedagogy-driven, equity-focused, and context-aware.

Recommendations for Strategic Implementation

To harness AI's potential responsibly, a strategic framework is essential:

1. Prioritize Pedagogy Over Technology: Begin with clear learning objectives. Evaluate AI tools using pedagogical frameworks like SAMR and TPACK to ensure they serve educational goals, not just technological novelty.
2. Invest in Human Capacity: Implement sustained, in-depth professional development for educators focused on AI literacy, ethical considerations, and new pedagogical strategies. Create peer mentorship programs to foster collaborative learning.
3. Establish Robust Ethical Governance: Develop clear, transparent policies for data privacy, consent, and the ethical use of AI, based on established frameworks like the UNESCO AI Ethics Guidelines. Conduct regular audits of AI tools for bias and ensure "human-in-the-loop" oversight.
4. Design for Equity and Inclusion: Actively work to close the digital divide through subsidized access and offline-capable tools. Ensure AI-powered curricula adhere to Universal Design for Learning (UDL) principles, with materials adapted for diverse languages, cultures, and abilities.
5. Foster a Culture of Critical Evaluation: Create feedback loops where educators and learners continuously evaluate the effectiveness of AI tools. Use a mixed-methods approach, combining quantitative performance data with qualitative insights into student engagement and well-being.

CONCLUSION: AUGMENTING INTELLIGENCE, NOT REPLACING HUMANITY

AI holds the potential to build more resilient, responsive, and future-ready education systems. However, this potential will only be realized through active, intentional, and inclusive stewardship. The future of education with AI is not one of automation, but of augmented intelligence, where technology empowers educators, engages learners, and supports—rather than supplants—the profoundly human endeavor of teaching and learning. The institutions that invest strategically in pedagogy, ethics, and human capacity will be the ones to truly unlock the transformative power of AI. Education must remain a humanistic enterprise, with AI employed to expand our greatest attributes: curiosity, creativity, critical thinking, and empathy.

REFERENCES

Benjamin, R. (2019). *Race after technology: Abolitionist tools for the new Jim Code*. Polity Press.

Bruner, J. S. (1966). *Toward a theory of instruction*. Belknap Press of Harvard University Press.

Chen, L. (2020). The role of AI in education: A case study of Squirrel AI in China. *International Journal of Information and Education Technology (IJIET), 10*(5), 384–388. DOI: 10.18178/ijiet.2020.10.5.1389

Cuban, L. (1986). *Teachers and machines: The classroom use of technology since 1920*. Teachers College Press.

Eubanks, V. (2018). *Automating inequality: How high-tech tools profile, police, and punish the poor*. St. Martin's Press.

Fullan, M., Quinn, J., & McEachen, J. (2018). *Deep learning: Engage the world change the world*. Corwin.

Kulik, J. A., & Fletcher, J. D. (2016). Effectiveness of intelligent tutoring systems: A meta-analytic review. *Review of Educational Research, 86*(1), 42–78. DOI: 10.3102/0034654315581420

Mishra, P., & Koehler, M. J. (2006). Technological pedagogical content knowledge: A framework for teacher knowledge. *Teachers College Record, 108*(6), 1017–1054. DOI: 10.1111/j.1467-9620.2006.00684.x

Noble, S. U. (2018). *Algorithms of oppression: How search engines reinforce racism*. NYU Press. DOI: 10.18574/nyu/9781479833641.001.0001

O'Neil, C. (2016). *Weapons of math destruction: How big data increases inequality and threatens democracy*. Crown.

Ouyang, F., Zheng, L., & Jiao, P. (2022). Artificial intelligence in online higher education: A systematic review of empirical research from 2011 to 2020. *Education and Information Technologies, 27*(6), 7893–7925. DOI: 10.1007/s10639-022-10925-9

Puentedura, R. R. (2006). *Transformation, technology, and education*. Retrieved from https://hippasus.com/resources/tte/

Rogers, E. M. (2003). *Diffusion of innovations* (5th ed.). Free Press.

Rose, D. H., & Meyer, A. (2002). *Teaching every student in the digital age: Universal design for learning*. ASCD.

Selwyn, N. (2019). *Should robots replace teachers? AI and the future of education*. Polity Press.

Tlili, A., Shehailia, M., Alowayr, A., & Burgos, D. (2023). What if the devil is in the details? A comparative study of ChatGPT-3.5 and ChatGPT-4 for generating literature review papers. *arXiv preprint*. https://arxiv.org/abs/2305.00596

Twenge, J. M. (2017). *iGen: Why today's super-connected kids are growing up less rebellious, more tolerant, less happy—and completely unprepared for adulthood—and what that means for the rest of us*. Atria Books.

UNESCO. (2021). *AI and education: Guidance for policy-makers*. UNESCO Publishing. https://unesdoc.unesco.org/ark:/48223/pf0000376709

Vygotsky, L. S. (1978). *Mind in society: The development of higher psychological processes*. Harvard University Press.

Williamson, B., & Hogan, A. (2020). Commercialisation and privatisation in/of education in the context of COVID-19. *Education International*. https://issuu.com/educationinternational/docs/research_covid-19_en_final

Zawacki-Richter, O., Marín, V. I., Bond, M., & Gouverneur, F. (2019). Systematic review of research on artificial intelligence applications in higher education – where are the educators? *International Journal of Educational Technology in Higher Education*, *16*(1), 39. DOI: 10.1186/s41239-019-0171-0

Chapter 19
Transforming the Future of Management and Medical Education:
AI-Driven Innovations in Curriculum Design

N. Vinodh
https://orcid.org/0009-0002-8662-2646
Saveetha School of Management, Saveetha Institute of Medical and Technical Sciences, Saveetha University, India

A. K. Subramani
https://orcid.org/0000-0003-0783-7113
Saveetha School of Management, Saveetha School of Management, Saveetha Institute of Medical and Technical Sciences, India

R. Vettriselvan
https://orcid.org/0009-0005-1097-0806
Academy of Maritime Education and Training, India

ABSTRACT

AI technologies make fundamental changes to curriculum design thus providing methods to enhance both management and medical education quality. It describes how AI tools modify teaching procedures by creating individualized learning programs and analytics-based institutional management together with flexible spaces. AI systems enable educators to get instant feedback from students through their system which automates repetitive work and shows academic performance data to help teachers maximize their efforts on strategy and creativity. AI in management training produces scenario-based education alongside medical training benefits from AI-based clinical training solutions, diagnostic systems, and patient-oriented educational designs. Implementation of AI technology delivers better learning results while simultaneously training professionals to overcome the complex issues in their active fields. AI can promote educational development through innovation together with solutions for educational gaps as well as create more effective learning structures for management and medical students.

DOI: 10.4018/979-8-3373-2752-5.ch019

INTRODUCTION

Artificial Intelligence (AI) holds one of the most important developments in educational technology throughout the 21st century. Due to its capability to examine big records of data along with pattern detection and autonomous decision ability AI has reshaped traditional operational frameworks across different areas. Artificial Intelligence innovations through AI have started reshaping education especially in management and medical fields to redesign education programs and teaching practices as well as improve learning results (Ali, M. 2025). Education organizations now redefine leadership and healthcare preparation through their updated training approaches that adapt students to sophisticated dynamic worldwide conditions. The established traditional educational institutions face criticisms because their standardized education approach shows inflexibility. The predetermining of educational curricula combined with standardized instruction methods finds limitation in effectively addressing new student population needs and modern-day workforce requirements. Digital transformation at industry levels drives substantial requirements for education institutions to transform their structures (Harris, R. A., & Kazdağlı, H. 2025). The capability of Artificial Intelligence serves as a tool that helps educational transformation by constructing flexible teaching directives drawing from individual learner data. Curriculum design that uses AI lets machine learning algorithms combine with natural language processing to partner with predictive analytics in analyzing learner data thus crafting adaptive learning routes. The systems develop capabilities to detect personal learning characteristics which enables instructors to create individualized study plans based on student requirements. Real-world business scenarios become possible through AI technology in educational management to create simulated situations thus delivering training which closely reflects professional challenges to students. AI-based medical training tools together with diagnosis solutions help students develop their clinical decisions while teaching them safety protocols. These technological advancements produce better student learning results and strengthen their skills needed to practice the profession effectively. AI applications have resulted in three main innovations of intelligent tutoring systems (ITS), automated content generation tools and personalized testing systems. The systems can provide immediate assessments together with detection of missing knowledge and recommendations for additional resource materials. When education staff utilize AI to do administrative tasks they are able to dedicate their time toward interactive mentorship instead of repetitive work. The implementation of AI technology allows educational environments to utilize virtual and augmented reality applications which create immersive collaborative learning situations for students across different fields. Education faces various obstacles during the implementation of Artificial Intelligence systems into learning spaces. Critics raise substantial doubts about both privacy protection of educational data and the impartiality of AI algorithms together with its proper ethical application for determining decisions. Data-driven educational systems encounter fundamental challenges regarding the openness of their operations combined with concerns regarding decisions that determine student educational outcomes because their basis rests on AI models. The availability of AI technological tools presents an urgent challenge because institutions that lack funds or modern infrastructure will risk deepening existing educational gaps between themselves and their learners (J. Lee and J. Cho, 2024). In management education, the use of AI raises ethical considerations about data security and responsible leadership. Both insight and skill regarding ethical challenges during AI implementation need to be included in the proficiency development of upcoming business managers. The medical sector needs an ethical framework to protect patient safety combined with confidentiality and informed consent when using AI for diagnostic tasks as well as treatment planning and patient care decisions. Education benefits from AI implementation only when educators manage innovations through a complete system that protects both human values and ethical practices. The research looks at complete AI-based curriculum creation advancements throughout management education and medical instruction (Akolgo, E., Korda, D. and Dapaah, E. 2024). The foundational elements that guide the implementation of AI in education will be evaluated first. The analysis provides information about constructivist learning concepts and explains the relationship between AI systems and models that support personalized student-learning environments. The discussion moves on to explain essential applications of AI in curriculum development with an analysis of personalized learning platforms alongside virtual simulations and intelligent assessment frameworks and curriculum assessment data analytics. The chapter shows examples of successful implementations but also presents the real obstacles facing the implementation of AI-driven curriculum reforms (Abbasi, B. N., Wu, Y., & Luo, Z. 2025). Artificial Intelligence (AI) is rapidly transforming educational landscapes, yet the integration of AI into curriculum design, particularly in management and medical education, remains inadequately explored despite its potential to revolutionize personalized learning, competency-based training, and data-driven decision-making. While prior research emphasizes AI's capabilities in content automation, predictive analytics, and simulation-based instruction (Ali, 2025; Kayyali, 2025a), there is a notable gap in comprehensive frameworks that align these technologies with pedagogical principles and domain-specific competencies, especially within critical sectors like healthcare and business leadership (Abbasi, Wu, & Luo, 2025). Traditional curricula often fail to meet the adaptive, interdisciplinary demands posed by globalized knowledge economies, as they remain structured around rigid learning models and limited responsiveness to learner variability or labor market dynamics (Harris & Kazdağlı, 2025). Existing scholarship lacks critical synthesis on how AI operationally bridges cognitive models, instructional strategies, and real-time feedback mechanisms to support learner-centered environments. This chapter seeks to address this gap by investigating how AI can be systematically leveraged to enhance curriculum design and delivery in management and medical education through personalized instruction, intelligent assessment, and virtual simulation. Accordingly, the research aims to answer the following questions: (1) How does AI enhance curriculum adaptability and learner engagement in management and medical domains? (2) What technological and pedagogical frameworks support AI-enabled curriculum development? (3) What ethical and infrastructural challenges must be addressed to ensure equitable AI integration across diverse educational contexts?.

CONCEPTUAL FRAMEWORK

The framework that uses AI for curriculum creation operates where technological advances meet modern educational teaching concepts. Artificial intelligence serves as a driving force behind educational development to improve both curriculum planning and teaching delivery methods as well as student participation levels in contemporary times of global adaptation. The framework investigates the process of integrating AI technology into management and medical educational curriculum while focusing on student-specific learning solutions and essential competency development and education effectiveness enhancement. The foundation of AI-driven curriculum design utilizes sophisticated computational resources such as learning algorithms alongside

NLP capabilities and both ITS platforms alongside predictive analytics. The combination of these technologies converts educational programs into flexible systems that focus strongly on learners' needs. AI operates as more than automation technology according to the conceptual framework since it functions as a transformative force that builds realistic interactive learning spaces. Continued learner data analysis enables AI systems to develop customized educational content which responds to students' requirements and learning styles while accounting for their individual preferences. AI application in management education makes possible an easy connection between real-time data analytics and business simulations and complex decision-making models and the curriculum. COVID-19 has generated innovative tools that connect theoretical knowledge to operational situations through business simulations which students utilize to exercise strategic thinking together with leadership abilities. The adaptation in learning platforms provides individualized teaching methods which support different student learning speeds to improve their understanding and knowledge acquisition of management fundamentals. The application of AI tools enables the preparation of soft abilities through virtual role-play systems which evaluate user performance thus developing communication and negotiation capacity. The implementation of AI technology plays essential enhancing functions in the enhancement of traditional medical education instruction techniques. Actual healthcare situations that run on artificial intelligence produce virtual clinical simulations which let medical students perform diagnostic tasks and procedural training without actual patient exposure. Customers using diagnostic AI tools receive clinical case guidance through evidence-based approaches according to Ivanashko et al. (2024). Through its capabilities AI enables educational institutions to establish student-specific learning paths which integrate with their particular medical expertise development directions. The paths support students to gain basic knowledge and advanced clinical skills and expertise. When implementing this conceptual framework educational institutions implement competency-based education (CBE) models at its core. According to CBE students must demonstrate particular measurable abilities instead of simply absorbing information. The methodology gets support from artificial intelligence which provides ongoing evaluation and immediate feedback to allow students to move ahead at their individual speed by proving competence instead of following standard deadlines. The assessment tools based on intelligent systems leverage analytics to detect learning gaps and suggest suitable learning materials and follow student progress throughout the duration (Kayyali, M. 2025a). The data-based procedure helps students achieve necessary professional competency requirements. The theoretical concepts within the framework examine how educational institutions should adopt and implement AI technologies in their operations. The Technology Acceptance Model (TAM) along with other models gives valuable insights which determine why stakeholders would adopt AI in curriculum design. People's acceptance of new technologies is influenced by three main factors: operational benefits which seem useful, using technology without struggle and the way faculty and students feel about technology. Accurate knowledge about implementation factors remains essential for AI success because it directs institutions to develop proper strategies for faculty training programs and physical resource allocations and organizational change management systems. The conceptual framework should include evaluations of all ethical, legal and social ramifications which AI introduces to educational systems. Designing educational curriculum by AI demands that institutions evaluate data protection policies as well as their ability to reveal algorithmic operations and prevent biases that challenge equitable education. A proper system of ethical regulations together with governance mechanisms allows the protection of learner data and promotes fairness between stakeholders while building trust. The proposed framework supports AI utilization that respects student well-being together with maintaining institutional ethical standards. Interdisciplinary teamwork stands out as crucial in the framework for developing AI-driven curricula according to the conceptual framework. Successful curriculum development depends upon contributions from qualified educators as well as AI specialists with instructional designers and policymakers. These stakeholders should unite their efforts to develop educational practices which integrate pedagogical strength with technological austerity and societal and industrial specifications (Kayyali, M. 2025b). Operationalizing this framework also necessitates an understanding of stakeholders' technology adoption behavior. Models such as the Technology Acceptance Model (TAM) elucidate how perceived usefulness, ease of use, and behavioral intention shape faculty and student engagement with AI systems. Furthermore, the implementation of AI must be contextualized within ethical, legal, and institutional frameworks to ensure responsible innovation. Key ethical considerations include algorithmic transparency, data privacy, informed consent, and mitigation of bias in decision-making processes factors especially critical in high-stakes fields such as healthcare and business. Therefore, AI adoption in curriculum design must be embedded in a system of governance that upholds institutional accountability, data protection standards, and learner equity (Kayyali, 2025b). The successful development and deployment of AI-enhanced curricula further require interdisciplinary collaboration among educators, instructional designers, AI engineers, and policy-makers to ensure pedagogical coherence, technical robustness, and industry relevance. This integrative approach ensures that AI is not imposed onto education as an external innovation but is holistically woven into the educational fabric.

THEORETICAL FRAMEWORK

AI-driven curriculum design for management and medical education uses multiple learning theories and current educational concepts as its theoretical basis. AI technologies receive guidance through these educational theories which then helps develop and execute teaching techniques for maximizing student learning outcomes and preserving ethical standards and learner-centric education. Instructors use Constructivist Learning Theory as their leading framework when designing curriculums with AI. According to Constructivism theory students create their knowledge through both experiential interaction and reflective processes instead of receiving information by passive reception (Li, R. and T. Wu 2025). AI systems like intelligent tutoring systems together with adaptive learning platforms help schools employ this teaching method through creation of interactive learning spaces. These systems use individual learning style assessments to modify content as well as previous knowledge and learning speed which enables deep engagement from learners. Both management and medical education adopt constructivist principles by using simulations and problem-based learning and virtual reality scenarios whereby students develop their skills through complex problem-solving while applying theoretical concepts to real-life situations (Osuji, G. E. 2025). Cognitive Load Theory (CLT) addresses how learners should handle information quantities during learning sessions. The three components of cognitive load theory are intrinsic, extraneous and germane loads. AI technology serves as an essential tool to delete superfluous information along with unnecessary tasks that would not benefit educational achievement. AIs accomplish this by providing customized content that divides information into smaller sections while supplying timely evaluations. Intelligent learning systems for medical education ensure medical students follow diagnostic steps correctly when reducing their mental workload and maximizing learning potential. Combining artificial intelligence with case study management enables students to study fewer complex details which allows them to maintain their mission-oriented focus on core decision-making approaches. HCI Theories within the theoretical framework play a key role for understanding how to design usable AI systems that serve educational purposes. HCI theories concentrate on designing interfaces which both seem natural to students and eliminate technological hurdles while building high engagement levels. AI-driven educational tools need to have simple interfaces that students can understand easily since this facilitates learning above system navigation difficulties. An effective design of human-computer interaction improves student participation while motivating learners so they stay actively involved throughout their classroom activities regardless of in-person or virtual learning. The ethical framework together with learning theories make up crucial components when designing curricula with AI automation. AI implementation in education requires us to resolve three main challenges which include privacy issues along with biases and inclusivity considerations (Paul, P.K., Chatterjee, R., Kayyali, M., Das, N. 2025). AI systems receive ethical frameworks to achieve fair practices while maintaining transparent operations with accountable implementation. AI-processed learning content requires special attention to prevent bias from perpetuating since it can harm specific demographic student groups. Data security methods and participant consent protection become essential during medical education because sensitive information is used to construct clinical educational materials. The ethical requirements in management education need to protect intellectual property while making sure that AI applications treat all groups equally. The theoretical framework adopts Equity and Inclusion Paradigms as well as other concepts within education research. Science-based curriculum design systems need to establish equality in learning platforms that benefit students across all social contexts including location and economic status. A solution must actively handle digital accessibility problems while targeting affordability costs and delivering materials that match different cultural backgrounds. The design of AI-curriculums incorporates constructivist learning theory together with cognitive load theory as well as human-computer interaction principles and ethical standards. The collective frameworks create a comprehensive basis to build AI-enhanced curricula which dedicate themselves to students while upholding efficiency and accessibility and upholding ethical standards. The implementation of AI innovations with theoretical foundations enables education institutions to develop inclusive learning programs that improve effectiveness in management and medical education.

REVIEW OF LITERATURE

The use of artificial intelligence (AI) within curriculum development stands as a crucial field of research between management and medical sectors. Educational institutions seek to serve modern learners by implementing AI solutions which allow creation of personalized adaptive learning methods that reflect current professional needs. The present review looks at contemporary AI curriculum design studies and their major advancements while discussing implementation practices and related advantages and problems and pathfinding predictions (Bakthavatchaalam, V., & Sivasankar, K. 2025). Educational institutions embrace AI technology for three main reasons: it strengthens instructional practices and manages paperwork requirements and produces knowledge-based conclusions from educational data. The implementation of AI allows teachers to generate customized educational routes which dynamically change to match students' individual abilities and various learning methods. Student performance data goes through machine learning algorithms which produce recommendations about personalized content along with assignments and assessments. Management education utilizes this capability to add real-time case study elements and decision-making models and simulations to curricular content which provides practical hands-on learning to students. AI helps medical education create virtual clinical scenarios with artificial patients which help students to practice diagnosis methods and medical procedures without safety risks. Research shows that educational institutions currently adopt competency-based education (CBE) as one of their main educational transformation strategies. Artificial Intelligence technologies drive educational transformation by developing continuous evaluation and feedback assessment methods to measure student competency achievement levels (Vettriselvan, R., Velmurugan, P. R., Deepan, A., Jaiswani, G., & Durgarani, M. 2025). When implementing CBE educational models instructors focus on mastering skills with demonstration of learning outcomes rather than spending time in traditional assigned classes. AI platforms powered by AI technology track medical students' clinical ability along with their procedural standard in medical education and management students' protective leadership with their problem-solving capabilities and strategic thinking abilities in management education. Research has shed light on the importance of intelligent tutoring systems (ITS) as an essential subject matter for recent investigations. The AI systems with their knowledge base deliver unique educational pathways and educational assistance that replicates human tutoring experiences. The feedback capacity of ITS allows immediate monitoring of student challenges while providing suitable corrective solutions. The system has achieved promising outcomes in both student participation rates and educational memory retention areas through its use with complicated educational content determinations such as medical diagnosis and managerial analysis. The usage of predictive analytics represents a main component of artificial intelligence systems for curriculum development. Large datasets analyzed by predictive models enable performance forecasting together with risk assessment for students and recommended educational measures to enhance academic success (Velmurugan et al., 2025). Higher education management receives assistance from predictive analytics which enables educators to follow student participation patterns throughout different business scenarios. Through predictive models medical education identifies the ability of students to reason clinically in addition to their susceptibility to committing medical mistakes which enables curriculum modification. Multiple obstacles exist for using AI in curriculum development according to published literature reports. The main concern stems from privacy and security matters in data management (Thurzo, A. 2025). AI systems need to analyze large amounts of data to operate which creates moral uncertainties regarding how student information gets gathered along with its secure storage along with its utilization. The system's ability to maintain prejudice against students remains a major problem because inadequate data inputs can trigger unfair bias-driven results. Research shows that AI-curriculum developers should build transparent systems which promote fairness and inclusivity to avoid magnifying educational inequalities. Faculty members face challenges both in their acceptance and readiness to implement technology based on Artificial Intelligence principles. Successful deployment of AI in curriculum development demands educational staff to possess fundamental familiarity with AI platforms together with their practical uses. The literature shows that faculty professionals need suitable development programs to help them properly use AI tools while teaching according to Farooq M., Ramzan M., and Yen Y. Y. (2025). Institutions need to handle typical employee resistance to change as well as employment replacement fears by using detailed communication and cooperative planning approaches.

The whole development expense along with system maintenance costs of AI-based systems represents an essential factor. Smaller schools operating with limited funding usually find it challenging to establish AI-based solutions because such projects require substantial financial investment. Research indicates that joining forces with technology vendors through collaborative programs presents a possible method to handle financial obstacles in AI implementation. Research demonstrates that accomplished curriculum design using AI requires clear linkage between AI techniques and educational objectives and learning accomplishments (Solanki, R. S., Gautam, K. D., Khan, A. S., Kaur, R., & Bale, A. S. 2024). The absence of pedagogical standards when implementing AI technologies would result in basic technology enhancements instead of fundamental educational transformation. To make AI technology work in curriculum design stakeholders need to implement careful approach and ongoing assessment and involvement of educators to uphold learning quality. The upcoming research predicts various trends which AI will bring to curriculum design frameworks. Immersive technologies like virtual reality (VR) and augmented reality (AR) linked with AI serve to develop more interesting learning spaces (Rauf, A., Nadeem, S., & Tahir, L. 2024). Adaptive learning platforms will advance their capabilities to deliver more customized flexible educational encounters to students. The growing interest in continuous education and micro-certification standards will boost the market need for customizable AI-assisted curriculum programs that adapt to multiple student populations. AI-driven curriculum design for management and medical education shows significant transformative power and that is confirmed by Rosenheck, 2025. While the literature on AI in education is rapidly growing, three key gaps persist. First, there is limited longitudinal research assessing the sustained impact of AI-driven curriculum interventions on student learning outcomes and career readiness. Second, few studies systematically evaluate the interplay between AI systems and ethical/legal compliance mechanisms in diverse cultural or institutional contexts. Third, most current literature is either too techno-centric or pedagogically narrow, lacking integrative models that bridge the technological, ethical, and operational dimensions of AI deployment. This chapter seeks to address these gaps by offering a holistic framework that connects AI capabilities with curriculum elements, grounded in both ethical reflection and implementation feasibility.

RESEARCH METHODOLOGY

The current chapter uses systematic literature review methodology to analyze current research about AI-based curriculum development within management and medical education fields. A systematic review promotes unbiased research through its systematic protocol for discovering relevant studies and evaluation methods. The review investigates artificial intelligence (AI) system integration in curriculum development while assessing their learning outcome effects and discusses upcoming challenges in this field. The research initiation started through the definition of essential research questions together with specific objectives. The research set three key objectives to examine how AI personalizes educational programs and how effective this technology proves for student learning results and what challenges exist regarding both practical and ethical aspects of AI educational deployment. Recent studies from the last five years served as the basis for this review to obtain relevant material about current AI advancements. The research depended on six academic databases that included Scopus, Web of Science, PubMed, IEEE Xplore, Google Scholar, and ERIC. Various knowledge sources including Scopus and Web of Science along with PubMed and IEEE Xplore and ERIC and Google Scholar were selected because they offer extensive peer-reviewed research on education together with technology management and healthcare fields. The research used specific search terms which combined "Artificial Intelligence" with "Curriculum Design" and "Management Education" along with "Medical Education" and "Adaptive Learning" and "Personalized Learning" in order to retrieve pertinent studies. The researchers used combination operators with database-specific components to develop their search parameters which produced only relevant research outcomes. The research used defined criteria for both admitting and eliminating relevant scholarly materials. Research material consisted of peer-reviewed journal articles as well as conference proceedings and white papers and policy reports which studied AI applications in curriculum design for both management education and medical education programs. For admission the investigations needed to appear in English from the recent five-year timeframe while offering either empirical evidence or conceptual frameworks regarding the research focus. The research eliminated published works which did not focus on management and medical domains or failed to support their claims with empirical data. A first step of reviewing titles and abstracts led to full-text assessment for study eligibility confirmation. The researchers obtained relevant information from each article about study objectives with their research design and AI applications together with identified outcomes and challenges. The analysis method relied on thematic breakdown of qualitative information into four main themes including personalized learning pathways combined with intelligent tutoring systems and AI-powered simulations and competency-based education models. The research involved both qualitative synthesis approaches together with quantitative meta-synthesis when applicable to the data. The analysis contained identifying larger patterns by comparing outcomes regarding learning and student participation together with curriculum effectiveness from various studies. A standardized set of criteria evaluated the selected studies for their research design alongside their sample size methodology and was used to review both their technical and ethical standards. Results from studies demonstrated high-quality standards received increased precedence during the analysis. Ethical evaluations were conducted at multiple points during the review stages to maintain both proper research outcomes and academic standards. The methodology displays a rich level of detail although it contains certain limitations. Research papers published in non-English languages could not be considered due to the emphasis on English-language publications. Preventing access to valuable grey literature content including industrial reports and educational case studies became a limitation because the research only included peer-reviewed sources. The systematic method applied in this review enables controllers to establish dependable and reusable methods for studying AI's contribution to curriculum design in management education and medical instruction. Through this structured review method researchers successfully perform a deep examination of AI's impact on curriculum transformation. Amidst the analysis the paper identifies crucial AI technologies which deliver individualized education while producing better student achievements alongside adaptive educational requirements response. Research results derived from this review paper provide fundamental insight into how the subsequent portions of this chapter explore AI curriculum design applications, challenges and ethics and future research directions.

FINDINGS OF THE STUDY

Table 1. **Findings of the Study**

S. No.	Theme	Key Findings	Implications for Curriculum Design
1	Personalization and Adaptivity	AI enables customized learning pathways that enhance student engagement and outcomes.	Develop learner-centric, adaptive curricula that cater to diverse learning needs.
2	Competency-Based Education (CBE)	Continuous AI-based assessments support skill development and mastery of competencies.	Integrate AI tools to track and measure specific competencies.
3	Intelligent Tutoring Systems (ITS)	ITS provide personalized feedback and support, improving knowledge retention and learner autonomy.	Incorporate ITS to enhance individualized learning experiences.
4	Predictive Analytics	Early identification of at-risk students leads to timely academic interventions and support systems.	Use predictive analytics to improve retention and completion rates.
5	Data Privacy and Ethics	Concerns about data security and algorithmic bias require robust ethical frameworks and guidelines.	Ensure ethical compliance in data management and AI applications.
6	Faculty Resistance and Skills Gap	Limited faculty familiarity with AI hinders integration into teaching practices.	Offer professional development and AI literacy programs for educators.
7	Resource and Infrastructure Barriers	High costs of AI implementation restrict adoption in resource-constrained institutions.	Explore partnerships and scalable solutions to reduce costs.
8	Enhanced Learning Outcomes	AI integration leads to improved decision-making, critical thinking, and practical skills in learners.	Design curricula that leverage AI to enhance core learning outcomes.

A distinctive contribution of this study lies in its dual-sector focus integrating both management and medical education domains allowing for cross-pollination of pedagogical strategies and application models. For instance, real-time feedback mechanisms used in medical diagnostics training were observed to enhance leadership simulations in management instruction, suggesting interdisciplinary scalability of AI frameworks. Moreover, the findings highlight gaps in institutional readiness, echoing concerns in Harris and Kazdağlı (2025) about the mismatch between technological capabilities and infrastructure, particularly in under-resourced educational settings. The study adds empirical nuance by documenting how such gaps hinder full-cycle curriculum transformation, reinforcing the need for policy support and ethical oversight. The findings validate many existing assumptions about AI's utility in education while contributing new empirical insights about its sector-specific adaptability and challenges. The literature-grounded categorization in Table 1 provides a clearer lens through which stakeholders can evaluate AI interventions for curricular innovation.

SOLUTIONS AND RECOMMENDATIONS

The effective integration of Artificial Intelligence in curriculum design across management and medical education requires a multi-stakeholder strategy. Solutions must not only address technological deployment but also institutional culture, ethical governance, and pedagogical alignment. The recommendations below are categorized by stakeholder group and prioritized according to high, medium, or low urgency and feasibility.

Table 2. Recommendation for Educators

Recommendation	Priority	Rationale
Provide professional development on AI tools, ITS, and analytics for curriculum design	High	Enhances faculty confidence and adoption; directly improves teaching quality (Ali, 2025)
Encourage co-design of AI-enhanced courses with instructional designers and AI developers	Medium	Promotes pedagogical ownership and ensures relevance to domain-specific learning objectives
Implement formative assessment practices using AI-driven feedback tools	High	Enables personalized support and early intervention; improves learner outcomes (Kayyali, 2025a)
Incorporate ethical discussions on AI use into course content	Medium	Prepares students for real-world AI challenges in business and medicine (J. Lee & J. Cho, 2024)

Table 3. Recommendation for Administrators

Recommendation	Priority	Rationale
Establish infrastructure to support adaptive learning platforms and virtual simulations	High	Prerequisite for AI integration; addresses technological readiness (Harris & Kazdağlı, 2025)
Create internal AI task forces for curriculum planning and data governance	Medium	Ensures institutional alignment, ethical compliance, and long-term scalability
Offer workload adjustments and incentives for faculty engaging in AI curriculum transformation projects	Medium	Motivates faculty participation and innovation
Adopt data protection protocols and transparency guidelines for student analytics	High	Builds trust in AI systems; critical for safeguarding privacy and compliance (Abbasi et al., 2025)

Table 4. Recommendation for Policymakers and Regulators

Recommendation	Priority	Rationale
Provide funding incentives for institutions piloting AI-enhanced curricula, especially in under-resourced settings	High	Addresses digital divide; promotes equitable access to innovation (Akolgo et al., 2024)
Develop national guidelines for ethical use of AI in education, including bias mitigation and algorithmic transparency	High	Ensures legal-ethical alignment and public accountability (J. Lee & J. Cho, 2024)
Support AI literacy initiatives at all education levels	Medium	Prepares future workforce for AI integration in both educational and professional contexts
Promote collaboration between universities, industry, and AI developers for co-creation of domain-specific solutions	Medium	Strengthens ecosystem partnerships and fosters relevance in real-world applications

In the short term, educator training and infrastructure investment are paramount, as they directly influence adoption and performance of AI systems. In the medium term, cross-functional collaboration and governance structures must be built to ensure responsible deployment. In the long term, policy and funding ecosystems should support sustainability and scaling across institutions. These tiered recommendations emphasize that the success of AI-driven curriculum design hinges not only on technological capacity but also on human-centered decision-making, institutional support, and regulatory foresight. Each stakeholder's role must be clearly defined, actively supported, and contextually adapted to ensure inclusive and meaningful educational transformation

FUTURE RESEARCH DIRECTIONS

The evolving landscape of Artificial Intelligence (AI) in curriculum design warrants sustained and focused research to ensure that implementation is effective, ethical, and adaptable. Based on current gaps in scholarly discourse and practical challenges encountered in educational institutions, the following four research directions emerge as critical priorities for future inquiry:

Effectiveness of AI-Driven Pedagogical Models in Competency-Based Education (CBE):

There is a need for longitudinal studies examining how AI-enabled adaptive learning systems influence the development of core competencies in management and medical learners. While current applications show promise in delivering personalized pathways, there is insufficient empirical data comparing outcomes with traditional curriculum models (Kayyali, 2025a). Future research should evaluate whether AI systems genuinely enhance critical thinking, clinical judgment, leadership, and ethical reasoning over time.

Algorithmic Transparency and Bias Mitigation in Educational AI Systems:

As AI continues to influence assessment, feedback, and learning progression, transparency of algorithmic processes and the mitigation of bias become paramount. Investigations should focus on how explainable AI (XAI) techniques can be integrated into educational platforms to ensure that learning recommendations are equitable and interpretable by educators and learners alike (J. Lee & J. Cho, 2024). Ethical implications for diverse student populations especially underrepresented groups must be a central concern.

Scalability and Sustainability of AI Integration in Resource-Constrained Educational Settings:

Although elite institutions may rapidly adopt AI-based curriculum models, resource-limited contexts often face significant infrastructural and policy constraints. Research should examine scalable strategies for equitable AI deployment, particularly in low- and middle-income countries (Akolgo, Korda, & Dapaah, 2024). This includes cost-effective implementation models, open-source AI tools, and partnerships between academia and the private sector.

Human-AI Collaboration Models for Curriculum Co-Design:

There is increasing interest in how AI can augment not replace human expertise in curriculum development. Research should explore models of collaborative curriculum design where educators, instructional designers, and AI systems iteratively co-develop content. Investigating the dynamics of this collaboration will inform how institutions can balance automation with pedagogical judgment and cultural relevance (Abbasi, Wu, & Luo, 2025). These targeted research directions provide a roadmap for scholars and practitioners committed to advancing the field of AI-driven curriculum innovation. A concentrated focus on learning outcomes, ethics, inclusion, and scalability will ensure that future studies contribute to meaningful, systemic transformation in education rather than isolated technological upgrades.

ETHICAL, PEDAGOGICAL, AND TECHNICAL CONSIDERATIONS

The implementation of AI into curriculum development needs detailed evaluation about ethical frameworks and education practices together with technical implementation guidelines. Three main ethical issues within AI-enhanced education involve data privacy breaches alongside algorithmic prejudice against students and differences in accessibility of AI-based assets in education. Institutional education needs to create solid ethical standards for AI deployment which emphasizes clear visibility and fair advantages and barrier-free programs for all users. The use of AI technology should augment educational methods but avoid substituting them with AI-powered educational interactions. AI technology remains unable to match the essential aspects of human educators who accomplish meaningful dialogue and develop critical analysis and give emotional support to students. AI represents an educational tool which enhances teacher capabilities to provide better customized teaching standards. Noiseless AI integration demands that all learners including those who lack resources should access these technologies that feature scalability and reliability. Accelerated adoption of AI in education requires educational institutions to spend on appropriate facilities while setting programs focused on digital competence. These measures equitably enable AI implementation throughout educational activities. Ongoing assessments of AI systems become necessary to maintain their ongoing effectiveness together with their relevance and ethical standards.

COLLABORATION BETWEEN EDUCATORS, POLICYMAKERS, AND TECHNOLOGISTS

AI-driven curriculum integration needs strategic cooperation among teaching professionals together with government regulators and technology experts and academic exploration groups. Educators serve as essential guides for the pedagogical deployment of AI so it communicates with educational targets to deliver better student learning conditions. The authorities who make policies must implement rules which protect both ethical AI practices as well as learner data privacy and establish fair technology access for students. AI developers together with technologists need to develop close partnerships with educators while designing pedagogically sound AI tools which maintain user-friendly interfaces. The educational tools need to provide flexibility for various students while coping with multiple educational settings. Since researchers must assess the influence of AI-based curriculum transformations by collecting evidence which directs best practices as well as innovative development paths.

FUTURE OUTLOOK FOR AI IN MANAGEMENT AND MEDICAL EDUCATION

AI technology evolution will expand its functions in designing curricula which will create fresh opportunities to improve educational delivery and significance. The proper application of AI in management education will create more complicated business simulations as well as predictive analytical tools and decision-making systems that develop student leadership abilities for complex global economic environments. Medical education is expected to benefit from AI development of clinical support systems along with virtual patients and personalized learning formats to enhance diagnostic abilities and procedural Education. Through artificial intelligence-engineered teaching programs educational institutions can generate excellent cross-discipline learning systems. Upcoming academic programs will unite management instruction and medical training so healthcare providers can develop leadership competencies for handling modern healthcare organization challenges. AI technologies help create interdisciplinary curricula through competency analysis and drive community work between different disciplines to develop these programs.

ENSURING EQUITY AND INCLUSIVITY IN AI-ENHANCED EDUCATION

The future challenge for educational technology will be to use artificial intelligence responsibly while fighting against social discrimination in the field. A solution requires educational institutions to deliver required technologies and resources to regions facing digital access challenges. The development of AI tools needs inclusive design principles which enable learners from different backgrounds and with various needs to use the systems effectively. AI systems require proper ethical management to stop the development of biased and discriminatory systems. Transparent decision processes and regular fairness evaluations of AI systems as well as stakeholder involvement must exist for institutions to develop effective AI deployment and development systems. Educational institutions which emphasize ethical factors will create an equally accessible learning environment through their use of AI-driven curriculum development practices.

CONCLUSION

Higher education experiences fundamental change through Artificial Intelligence because it implements new design approaches for management and medical education curriculums. Modern educational systems are evolving because artificial intelligence innovations transform standardized teaching formats into personalized learning experiences. The use of AI technology enables institutions to build customized learning pathways along with curriculum enhancement along with better educational achievements. The educational changes provide emerging professionals with essential capabilities to work effectively in modern technology-oriented professional domains. The examination of AI-driven curriculum design as detailed in this chapter covers all essential theoretical aspects which guide its implementation. The ongoing discussion demonstrates how AI technologies consisting of machine learning algorithms and natural language processing and intelligent tutoring systems and predictive analytics control pedagogical transformation. Modern technological developments allow educators to provide instant feedback based on personalized student learning routes along with interactive practice simulations that connect classroom lessons to practical medical and business skills for digital educational programs. AI technology delivers exceptional potential to develop better evaluation processes while improving student involvement and generating curriculum development solutions that use data-based approaches. The complete achievement of these advantages depends on well-planned implementations of AI technology. Educational institutions should make ethical duty of protecting data privacy combined with bias reduction in artificial intelligence systems and equal access to AI tools a top priority. Strategic measures should simultaneously deal with pedagogical matters regarding human teaching aspects and AI educator augmentation to maintain learning effectiveness. Future adoption of responsible AI depends on various key stakeholders including educators together with policymakers who do research and develop AI technology. The development of ethical safeguards by policymakers requires partnership between technology creators and educators to build AI tools which deliver both pedagogical strength and inclusive characteristics. Research should explore the lasting effects of AI-curriculum adoption on students' educational performance together with their career development as well as their academic opportunities. The implementation of AI-powered curriculum design presents extensive transformative power for managing and medical educational establishments. Educational institutions can create better adaptive inclusive learning environments through responsible strategic implementations of AI technologies. The innovative approaches in education create better student learning conditions which help develop future leaders and medical professionals. AI-enhanced education stands at an initial stage of its development path while promising extensive transformations for educational futures that motivate students.

REFERENCES

Abbasi, B. N., Wu, Y., & Luo, Z. (2025). Exploring the impact of artificial intelligence on curriculum development in global higher education institutions. *Education and Information Technologies*, *30*(1), 547–581. DOI: 10.1007/s10639-024-13113-z

Akolgo, E., Korda, D., & Dapaah, E. (2024). Artificial Intelligence in Healthcare: A Fusion of Technologies. *Journal of Computer and Communications*, *12*(12), 116–133. DOI: 10.4236/jcc.2024.1212008

Ali, M. (2025). The Role of AI in Reshaping Medical Education: Opportunities and Challenges. *The Clinical Teacher*, *22*(2), e70040. DOI: 10.1111/tct.70040 PMID: 39956546

Bakthavatchaalam, V., & Sivasankar, K. (2025). AI in healthcare education: a systematic review of applications in teaching and learning. Transforming Healthcare Sector Through Artificial Intelligence and Environmental Sustainability, 253-274.

Farooq, M., Ramzan, M., & Yen, Y. Y. (2025). Transformative Impact of AI in Education Management.

Harris, R. A., & Kazdağlı, H. (2025). Using TECHnology to predict the future of biomedical education. *FEBS Open Bio*, *15*(1), 48–55. DOI: 10.1002/2211-5463.13953 PMID: 39666874

Ivanashko, O., Kozak, A., Knysh, T., & Honchar, K. (2024). The role of artificial intelligence in shaping the future of education: Opportunities and challenges.

Kayyali, M. (2025a). AI in Higher Education: Revolutionizing Curriculum and Administration. In AI Adoption and Diffusion in Education (pp. 31-62). IGI Global Scientific Publishing.

Lee, J., & Cho, J. (2024). Artificial Intelligence Curriculum Development for Intelligent System Experts in University. *International Journal on Advanced Science, Engineering and Information Technology*, *14*(2), 409–419. DOI: 10.18517/ijaseit.14.2.18860

Li, R., & Wu, T. (2025). Evolution of Artificial Intelligence in Medical Education From 2000 to 2024: Bibliometric Analysis. *Interactive Journal of Medical Research*, *14*(1), e63775. DOI: 10.2196/63775 PMID: 39883926

Osuji, G. E. (2025). AI-Driven Curriculum Development: Navigating Education for a Dynamic Future.

Paul, P. K., Chatterjee, R., Kayyali, M., & Das, N. (2025). Cyber-Physical Systems: Its Foundation, Emergence, Possible Applications, and Issues with Reference to the Education Sector. In Choudhury, A., Kaushik, K., Kumar, V., & Singh, B. K. (Eds.), *Cyber-Physical Systems Security. Studies in Big Data* (Vol. 154). Springer., DOI: 10.1007/978-981-97-5734-3_1

Rauf, A., Nadeem, S., & Tahir, L. (2024). Integrating Artificial Intelligence into Curriculum Design. *Multidisciplinary Journal of Emerging Needs of Curriculum*, *1*(2), 10–19.

Rosenheck, M. (2025). AI in medical education: Challenges and opportunities. *Digital Health*, •••, 27–40.

Solanki, R. S., Gautam, K. D., Khan, A. S., Kaur, R., & Bale, A. S. (2024). AI-Driven Innovations in Higher Education: Key Challenges and Future Prospects. Library of Progress-Library Science, Information Technology & Computer, 44(3).

Thurzo, A. (2025). How is AI Transforming Medical Research, Education and Practice? *Bratislavské Lekárske Listy*, *126*(3), 1–6. DOI: 10.1007/s44411-025-00063-2

Velmurugan, P. R., Catherine, S., & Vettriselvan, R. EP, J., & Rajesh, D. (2025). Innovative Intercultural Communication Training in Translator Education: Cultivating Cultural Competence. In Cutting-Edge Approaches in Translator Education and Pedagogy (pp. 217-244). IGI Global Scientific Publishing.

Vettriselvan, R., Velmurugan, P. R., Deepan, A., Jaiswani, G., & Durgarani, M. (2025). Transforming Virtual Education: Advanced Strategies for Quality Assurance in Online and Distance Learning. In Navigating Quality Assurance and Accreditation in Global Higher Education (pp. 563-580). IGI Global Scientific Publishing.

KEY TERMS AND DEFINITIONS

Adaptive Learning: Adaptive learning refers to educational methods that use technology and AI algorithms to modify the delivery of learning content based on an individual learner's performance, preferences, and needs. These systems continuously assess learner progress and adjust the difficulty level, pace, and content sequence to optimize the learning experience. Adaptive learning enhances personalization, increases learner motivation, and promotes mastery of competencies in both management and healthcare education.

Artificial Intelligence (AI): Artificial Intelligence refers to the simulation of human intelligence processes by machines, particularly computer systems. These processes include learning, reasoning, problem-solving, perception, and language understanding. In education, AI enables the development of intelligent systems that can automate administrative tasks, provide personalized learning experiences, and facilitate data-driven decision-making. AI technologies are transforming traditional educational practices by enhancing instructional design, improving learner engagement, and supporting adaptive learning environments.

Constructivist Learning Theory: Constructivist learning theory posits that learners actively construct their own understanding and knowledge of the world through experience and reflection. AI technologies support constructivist approaches by creating interactive, learner-centered environments that encourage exploration, problem-solving, and collaboration.

Curriculum Mapping: Curriculum mapping is the systematic process of aligning curriculum elements such as learning objectives, instructional content, assessments, and competencies to ensure coherence, consistency, and relevance across a program. AI-driven tools facilitate automated curriculum mapping by identifying gaps, redundancies, and misalignments, supporting curriculum designers in creating responsive and competency-based educational programs.

Ethical AI in Education: Ethical AI in education refers to the application of principles such as fairness, transparency, accountability, privacy, and inclusivity in the design and implementation of AI technologies. Ethical considerations ensure that AI systems do not reinforce biases, protect learner data, and provide equitable access to educational opportunities, fostering trust and acceptance among stakeholders.

Intelligent Tutoring Systems (ITS): Intelligent Tutoring Systems are AI-powered applications designed to simulate one-on-one human tutoring by providing personalized instruction and feedback. These systems analyze learner inputs in real time, adapt content delivery based on individual learning needs, and offer targeted interventions to address knowledge gaps. In management and medical education, ITS can support complex learning scenarios such as business simulations and clinical diagnostic training, improving learner outcomes and engagement.

Predictive Analytics: Predictive analytics involves using statistical techniques, data mining, and machine learning algorithms to analyze historical and current data to predict future outcomes. In the context of education, predictive analytics can identify at-risk students, inform intervention strategies, and support personalized learning pathways. Institutions use predictive analytics to enhance student retention, academic performance, and program effectiveness.

TPACK Model: The Technological Pedagogical Content Knowledge (TPACK) model provides a framework for integrating technology into teaching in a meaningful way. It emphasizes the interplay between three core knowledge areas: content, pedagogy, and technology. In AI-enhanced education, TPACK helps educators design learning experiences that effectively combine these domains to maximize learner engagement and understanding.

Compilation of References

Abbas Khan, M., Khan, H., Omer, M. F., Ullah, I., & Yasir, M. (2025). Impact of artificial intelligence on the global economy and technology advancements. In El Hajjami, S., Kaushik, K., & Khan, I. U. (Eds.), *Artificial general intelligence (AGI) security* (pp. 147–180). Springer Nature Singapore., DOI: 10.1007/978-981-97-3222-7_7

Abbasi, B. N., Wu, Y., & Luo, Z. (2025). Exploring the impact of artificial intelligence on curriculum development in global higher education institutions. *Education and Information Technologies*, *30*(1), 547–581. DOI: 10.1007/s10639-024-13113-z

Abbas, S. G., & Ayaz, N. (2025). EXPLORING THE BENEFITS OF PERSONALIZED LEARNING IN SECONDARY EDUCATION: A DESCRIPTIVE STUDY. *Policy Journal of Social Science Review*, *3*(5), 45–58.

Abinaya, S., Sherly Alphonse, A., Indira, K., & Lavanya, R. (2024). Intelligent tutoring systems. *Adopting Artificial Intelligence Tools in Higher Education*, 226-250. DOI: 10.1201/9781003469315-11

Abinaya, S. (2024). Data visualization using power bi. *International Scientific Journal of Engineering and Management*, *03*(04), 1–9. DOI: 10.55041/ISJEM01536

Abulibdeh, A., Zaidan, E., & Abulibdeh, R (2024). Navigating the confluence of artificial intelligence and education for sustainable development in the era of industry 4.0: Challenges, opportunities, and ethical …. Journal of Cleaner Production. sciencedirect.com

Adetayo, A. J. (2023). Artificial intelligence chatbots in academic libraries: The rise of ChatGPT. *Library Hi Tech News*, *40*(3), 18–21. DOI: 10.1108/LHTN-01-2023-0007

Agius, C. (2022). 6. Social constructivism. *Contemporary Security Studies*, 73-89. DOI: 10.1093/hepl/9780198862192.003.0006

Agrawal, A., Gans, J., & Goldfarb, A. (2019). Economic policy for artificial intelligence. *Innovation Policy and the Economy*, *19*(1), 139–159. DOI: 10.1086/699935

Agrawal, V., Bhardwaj, S., Pathak, N., Dixit, J. K., Agarwal, S., & Momin, M. (2024). *Augmenting Research*. IGI Global., DOI: 10.4018/979-8-3693-1798-3.ch003

Ahmad, W., Rasool, A., Javed, A. R., Baker, T., & Jalil, Z (2021). Cyber security in iot-based cloud computing: A comprehensive survey. Electronics. mdpi.com

AI for Education. (2023, October 11). *Prompt engineering for educators* [Video]. YouTube. https://www.youtube.com/watch?v=NuIKQgX71Fc

Aithal, P. S., Prabhu, S., & Aithal, S. (2024). Future of higher education through technology prediction and forecasting. *Poornaprajna International Journal of Management, Education, and Social Science (PIJMESS), 1*(1), 01-50.

Aithal, P. S., & Maiya, A. K. (2023). Innovations in higher education industry–Shaping the future. [IJCSBE]. *International Journal of Case Studies in Business, IT, and Education, 7*(4), 283–311. DOI: 10.47992/IJCSBE.2581.6942.0321

Ajemba, M. N., & Arene, E. C.Michael Nnaemeka AjembaEbube Chinwe Arene. (2022). Research gaps for future research and their identification. *World Journal Of Advanced Research and Reviews, 16*(1), 575–579. DOI: 10.30574/wjarr.2022.16.1.1062

Akhoon, I. ul H., Khan, M. Y., & Bhat, T. A. (2024). *Comparative Analysis of AI-Generated Research Content: Evaluating ChatGPT and Google Gemini.* DOI: 10.21203/rs.3.rs-5265799/v1\

Akintayo, O. T., Eden, C. A., Ayeni, O. O., & Onyebuchi, N. C.Olateju Temitope Akintayo-Chima Abimbola EdenOyebola Olusola AyeniNneamaka Chisom Onyebuchi. (2024). Inclusive curriculum design: Meeting the diverse needs of students for social improvement. *International Journal of Applied Research in Social Sciences, 6*(5), 770–784. DOI: 10.51594/ijarss.v6i5.1100

Akinwalere, S. N., & Ivanov, V. T. (2022). Artificial intelligence in higher education: Challenges and opportunities. *Border Crossing, 12*(1), 1–15. DOI: 10.33182/bc.v12i1.2015

Akolgo, E., Korda, D., & Dapaah, E. (2024). Artificial Intelligence in Healthcare: A Fusion of Technologies. *Journal of Computer and Communications, 12*(12), 116–133. DOI: 10.4236/jcc.2024.1212008

Akuma, S., & Ndera, T. (2021). Adaptive educational hypermedia system for high school students based on learning styles. [researchgate.net]. *International Journal of Educational and Pedagogical Sciences, 15*(2), 228–234.

Al Hasani, S. H. S., & Husin, N. A. (2021). A review of digital transformation of education in Oman. *Journal of Business Management and Accounting, 11*(2), 41–59. DOI: 10.32890/jbma2021.11.2.3

Alaa, A. (2024). Harnessing Artificial Intelligence for Enhanced Efficiency in Academic Writing and Research. *Fusion : Practice and Applications, 16*(2), 126–146. DOI: 10.54216/FPA.160209

Alalaq, A. S. (2024). AI tools assisting in the proofreading and scientific review of research papers. *ScienceOpen Preprints.* 2024. DOI: 10.14293/PR2199.001358.v1

Alalawi, K., Athauda, R., Chiong, R., & Renner, I. (2025). Evaluating the student performance prediction and action framework through a learning analytics intervention study. *Education and Information Technologies, 30*(3), 2887–2916. DOI: 10.1007/s10639-024-12923-5

Alam, A. (2021, December). Should robots replace teachers? Mobilisation of AI and learning analytics in education. In 2021 International Conference on Advances in Computing, Communication, and Control (ICAC3) (pp. 1-12). IEEE. ssrn.com DOI: 10.1109/ICAC353642.2021.9697300

Alam, A. (2023). Harnessing the Power of AI to Create Intelligent Tutoring Systems for Enhanced Classroom Experience and Improved Learning Outcomes. In Intelligent Communication Technologies and Virtual Mobile Networks (pp. 571-591). Singapore: Springer Nature Singapore. [HTML] DOI: 10.1007/978-981-99-1767-9_42

Alam, A., & Mohanty, A. (2023). Educational technology: Exploring the convergence of technology and pedagogy through mobility, interactivity, AI, and learning tools. Cogent Engineering. tandfonline.com

Alam, A., & Mohanty, A. (2024). Integrated constructive robotics in education (ICRE) model: A paradigmatic framework for transformative learning in educational ecosystem. *Cogent Education, 11*(1), 2324487. DOI: 10.1080/2331186X.2024.2324487

Alamri, H., Lowell, V., Watson, W., & Watson, S. L. (2020). Using personalized learning as an instructional approach to motivate learners in online higher education: Learner self-determination and intrinsic motivation. [academia.edu]. *Journal of Research on Technology in Education, 52*(3), 322–352. DOI: 10.1080/15391523.2020.1728449

Alam, S., Usama, M., Alam, M. M., Jabeen, I., & Ahmad, F. (2023). Artificial intelligence in global world: A case study of Grammarly as e-tool on ESL learners' writing of Darul Uloom Nadwa. *International Journal of Information and Education Technology (IJIET), 13*(11), 1741–1747. DOI: 10.18178/ijiet.2023.13.11.1984

Alanazi, S., & Asif, S. (2024). Exploring deepfake technology: Creation, consequences and countermeasures. *Human-Intelligent Systems Integration, 6*(1), 49–60. https://link.springer.com/article/10.1007/s42454-024-00102-6

Alangari, H. (2024). Disrupting Education: Artificial Intelligence in Higher Education. In *The Evolution of Artificial Intelligence in Higher Education: Challenges, Risks, and Ethical Considerations* (pp. 63-81). Emerald Publishing Limited.

Alawneh, Y. J. J., Sleema, H., Salman, F. N., Alshammat, M. F., & Oteer, R. S., & ALrashidi, N. K. N. (2024). Adaptive Learning Systems: Revolutionizing Higher Education through AI-Driven Curricula. In 2024 International Conference on Knowledge Engineering and Communication Systems (ICKECS) (Vol. 1, pp. 1-5). IEEE. DOI: 10.1109/ICKECS61492.2024.10616675

Aldowah, H., Al-Samarraie, H., & Fauzy, W. M. (2019). Educational data mining and learning analytics for 21st century higher education: A review and synthesis. *Telematics and Informatics, 37*, 13–49. DOI: 10.1016/j.tele.2019.01.007

Alfredo, R., Echeverria, V., Jin, Y., Yan, L., Swiecki, Z., Gašević, D., & Martinez-Maldonado, R. (2024). Human-centred learning analytics and AI in education: A systematic literature review. *Computers and Education: Artificial Intelligence, 6*, 100215. DOI: 10.1016/j.caeai.2024.100215

AlGerafi, M. A. M., Zhou, Y., Oubibi, M., & Wijaya, T. T (2023). Unlocking the potential: A comprehensive evaluation of augmented reality and virtual reality in education. Electronics. mdpi.com

Ali, M. (2025). The Role of AI in Reshaping Medical Education: Opportunities and Challenges. *The Clinical Teacher, 22*(2), e70040. DOI: 10.1111/tct.70040 PMID: 39956546

Ali, O., Murray, P. A., Momin, M., Dwivedi, Y. K., & Malik, T. (2024). The effects of artificial intelligence applications in educational settings: Challenges and strategies. *Technological Forecasting and Social Change*, *199*, 123076. DOI: 10.1016/j.techfore.2023.123076

Ali, Q. I. (2024). Towards more effective summative assessment in OBE: A new framework integrating direct measurements and technology. *Discover Education*, *3*(1), 107. Advance online publication. DOI: 10.1007/s44217-024-00208-5

Ali, S., DiPaola, D., Lee, I., Sindato, V., Kim, G., Blumofe, R., & Breazeal, C. (2021). Children as creators, thinkers, and citizens in an AI-driven future. *Computers and Education: Artificial Intelligence*, *2*, 1–11. DOI: 10.1016/j.caeai.2021.100040

Alkaissi, H., & McFarlane, S. I. (2023). Artificial hallucinations in ChatGPT: Implications in scientific writing. *Cureus*. Advance online publication. DOI: 10.7759/cureus.35179

Allam, H. M., Gyamfi, B., & Alomar, B. (2025). Sustainable innovation: Harnessing AI and living intelligence to transform higher education. *Education Sciences*, *15*(4), 398. DOI: 10.3390/educsci15040398

Alm, A. (2024). Exploring autonomy in the AI wilderness: Learner challenges and choices. *Education Sciences*, *14*(12), 1369. Advance online publication. DOI: 10.3390/educsci14121369

Al-Mansoori, R. S., & Koç, M. (2019). Transformational leadership, systems, and intrinsic motivation impact on innovation in higher education institutes: Faculty perspectives in engineering colleges. *Sustainability (Basel)*, *11*(15), 1–26. DOI: 10.3390/su11154072

Almuhaideb, A. M., & Saeed, S. (2020). Fostering sustainable quality assurance practices in outcome-based education: Lessons learned from ABET accreditation process of computing programs. *Sustainability* [October.]. *Sustainability (Basel)*, *12*(20), 1–26. DOI: 10.3390/su12208380

Almuhanna, M. A. (2024). Teachers' perspectives of integrating AI-powered technologies in K-12 education for creating customized learning materials and resources. *Education and Information Technologies*, *30*(8), 10343–10371. DOI: 10.1007/s10639-024-13257-y

Almutairi, R. T., & Alghammas, A. A. (2025). The effectiveness of using ELSA app on improving Saudi students' English-speaking skills. *International Journal of English Linguistics*, *15*(1), 140–148. DOI: 10.5539/ijel.v15n1p140

Alpaydın, E. (2020). *Introduction to machine learning* (4th ed.). The MIT Press.

Alqahtani, T., Badreldin, H. A., Alrashed, M., Alshaya, A. I., Alghamdi, S. S., bin Saleh, K., Alowais, S. A., Alshaya, O. A., Rahman, I., Al Yami, M. S., & Albekairy, A. M. (2023). The emergent role of artificial intelligence, natural learning processing, and large language models in higher education and research. [sciencedirect.com]. *Research in Social & Administrative Pharmacy*, *19*(8), 1236–1242. DOI: 10.1016/j.sapharm.2023.05.016

Alsaadi, A., & Awashreh, R. (2025). Practical University Training Impact on Job Performance of Translation Graduates in Oman. *Forum for Linguistic Studies*, *7*(2), 786–796. DOI: 10.30564/fls.v7i2.8306

Al-Senaidi, S., Lipsmeyer, L. L., & Poirot, J. (2009). Barriers to adopting technology for teaching and learning in Oman. *Computers & Education, 53*(3), 575–590. DOI: 10.1016/j.compedu.2009.03.015

Altbach, P. G., & Knight, J. (2007). The internationalization of higher education: Motivations and realities. *Journal of Studies in International Education, 11*(3-4), 290–305. DOI: 10.1177/1028315307303542

Al-Zahrani, A. M. (2024). Unveiling the shadows: Beyond the hype of AI in education. *Heliyon, 10*(9), e30696. DOI: 10.1016/j.heliyon.2024.e30696

Alzahrani, F. A. A., Alolaiwi, L., & Alshammari, S. A. (2025). Shaping the future of dental education: A scoping review of artificial intelligence (AI) integration strategies. *Cureus, 17*(5), e84921. DOI: 10.7759/cureus.84921

Amiri, S. M. H. (2025). Digital Transformations in Education: Research Insights for 21st-Century learning. *International Journal of Innovative Science* [IJISET]. *Engineering & Technology, 12*(03), 1–15.

Amiri, S. M. H., Islam, M. M., & Akter, N. (2025). Educating the future: AI's role in shaping next-generation pedagogies. *Available at SSRN* 5234024. DOI: 10.2139/ssrn.5234024

Anas, I. (2024). *The Use of the Gamma Application by Teachers in Creating Engaging and Automated Presentations.* DOI: 10.62386/jised.v2i1.52

Anderson, L. W., & Krathwohl, D. R. (Eds.). (2001). *A taxonomy for learning, teaching, and assessing: A revision of Bloom's taxonomy of educational objectives*. Longman.

Antonopoulou, H., Halkiopoulos, C., Barlou, O., & Beligiannis, G. N. (2021). Transformational leadership and digital skills in higher education institutes: During the COVID-19 pandemic. *Emerging Science Journal, 5*(1), 1–15. DOI: 10.28991/esj-2021-01252

An, X., Shen, X., Bai, J., & Li, Y. (2023). Assessment of intelligent teaching preparation of EFL teachers: Based on two-year data comparison. *International Conference on Computers in Education*. DOI: 10.58459/icce.2023.1377

Anyanwu, A., Olorunsogo, T., Abrahams, T. O., Akindote, O. J., & Reis, O. (2024). Data confidentiality and integrity: A review of accounting and cybersecurity controls in superannuation organizations. [fepbl.com]. *Computer Science & IT Research Journal, 5*(1), 237–253. DOI: 10.51594/csitrj.v5i1.735

Aristotle, . (1999). *Nicomachean Ethics* (Irwin, T., Trans.). Hackett Publishing.

Armony, Y., & Hazzan, O. (2024). *Inevitability of AI technology in education: Futurism perspectives for education for the next two decades*. Springer Nature Switzerland., DOI: 10.1007/978-3-031-72790-0

Arnold, L. (2023). AI and assessment in higher education: Reflections. Retrieved from https://lydiaarnold.net/ai-and-assessment-in-higher-education/

Arumugam, P. P., Todd, V., & Warnakula, A. (2024). Social. In *innovation through disruption in Australasia: the 2024 Contextualising Horizon report* (pp. 2-3). ASCILITE.

Ashrafganjoe, M. (2025). Exploring the role of digital writing tools in enhancing academic writing skills: The case of the Hemingway app in EFL classrooms. *Technology in Language Teaching & Learning*, *7*(1), 102479. DOI: 10.29140/tltl.v7n1.102479

Asri, A. (2024). Utilization of artificial intelligence in improving student achievement. *PARADOKS Jurnal Ilmu Ekonomi*, *7*(4), 451–465. DOI: 10.57178/paradoks.v7i4.990

Asy'ari, M., & Sharov, S. (2024). Transforming Education with ChatGPT: Advancing Personalized Learning, Accessibility, and Ethical AI Integration. *International Journal (Toronto, Ont.)*, *3*(2), 119.

Atlas, S (2023). ChatGPT for higher education and professional development: A guide to conversational AI. uri.edu

Awashreh, R. (2023). Enhancing innovation among business colleges at Omani universities: A theoretical framework. *Seybold Report, 18*(02), 182–196. https://seyboldreport.com

Awashreh, R. (2024 a). Omani private universities: Debates between progress in human development and weak education quality. *The International Journal of Educational Organization and Leadership, 32(1)*, 1-15. Common Ground Research Networks. DOI: 10.18848/2329-1656/CGP/v32i01/1-15

Awashreh, R. (2025 a). Leadership Strategies for Managing Change and Fostering Innovation Over Private Higher Education: Academic Institutions in Oman. In R. Marcão & V. Santos (Eds.), *Evolving Strategies for Organizational Management and Performance Evaluation* (pp. 399-422). IGI Global Scientific Publishing. DOI: 10.4018/979-8-3373-0149-5.ch018

Awashreh, R. (2025 b). Managing business continuity and resilience in higher education institutions without compromising the quality of education. In *Enhancing Resilience in Business Continuity Management*. DOI: 10.4018/979-8-3693-8809-9.ch010

Awashreh, R. (2014b). Be Aware: Navigating Challenges in AI-Driven Higher Education. [Common Ground Research Networks]. *The International Journal of Interdisciplinary Educational Studies*, *20*(1), 203–218. DOI: 10.18848/2327-011X/CGP/v20i01/203-218

Awashreh, R. (2025 c). Navigating Leadership Dynamics: Insights and Strategies Across Domains. In Rahman, M., Koolmon, G., Shaikh, S., & Munna, A. (Eds.), *Optimizing Leadership and Governance in Higher Education* (pp. 203–232). IGI Global., DOI: 10.4018/979-8-3693-3534-5.ch010

Awashreh, R. (2025 d). Omani public governance in the age of artificial intelligence. In *Public Governance Practices in the Age of AI* (pp. 137–166). IGI Global., DOI: 10.4018/979-8-3693-9286-7.ch007

Awashreh, R., & Bremananth, B. (2025). A study on the ethical implementation of AI in collegiate studies using fuzzy implication. *Pakistan Journal of Life and Social Sciences*, *23*(1), 3998–4013. DOI: 10.57239/PJLSS-2025-23.1.00317

Awashreh, R., & Ghunaimi, A. L. (2025a). Bridging Cultural Gaps: Enhancing Student Motivation and Academic Integrity in Oman's Universities. *Forum for Linguistic Studies*, *7*(2), 265–279. DOI: 10.30564/fls.v7i2.8300

Awashreh, R., & Ghunaimi, H. A. L. (2025b). Rethinking the PhD: Aligning higher education with market needs and practical skills. *Frontiers in Learning and Studies*, *7*(2). Advance online publication. DOI: 10.30564/fls.v7i2.7942

Awashreh, R., & Hamid, A. A. (2025). The role of entrepreneurial leadership in driving employee innovation: The mediating effect of knowledge sharing. *Cogent Business & Management*, *12*(1), 2466812. DOI: 10.1080/23311975.2025.2466812

Awashreh, R., & Hassiba, A. (2025). Revolutionizing Education With AI: Personalized Learning, Predictive Analytics, and Gamification. In Ordóñez de Pablos, P., Lytras, M., Alkhaldi, A., & Malik, S. (Eds.), *Insights Into Digital Business, Human Resource Management, and Competitiveness* (pp. 149–170). IGI Global Scientific Publishing., DOI: 10.4018/979-8-3693-9440-3.ch006

Awashreh, R., & Ramachandran, B. (2024). Can artificial intelligence dominate and control human beings? [IRJMS]. *International Research Journal of Multidisciplinary Scope*, *5*(4), 427–438. DOI: 10.47857/irjms.2024.05i04.01569

Axelrod, R. (1984). *The evolution of cooperation*. Basic Books.

Ayeni, O. O., Al Hamad, N. M., Chisom, O. N., Osawaru, B., & Adewusi, O. E. (2024). AI in education: A review of personalized learning and educational technology. *GSC Advanced Research and Reviews*, *18*(2), 261–271. DOI: 10.30574/gscarr.2024.18.2.0062

Badiani, N., Vekaria, S., Bharti, S. K., & Gupta, R. K. (2023). *Summarization of Research Paper into a Presentation* (pp. 755–764). Springer International Publishing. DOI: 10.1007/978-981-99-3315-0_58

Bahroun, Z., Anane, C., Ahmed, V., & Zacca, A. (2023). Transforming education: A comprehensive review of generative artificial intelligence in educational settings through bibliometric and content analysis. *Sustainability (Basel)*, *15*(17), 12983. DOI: 10.3390/su151712983

Baidoo-Anu, D., Gyamerah, K., & Munezhi, M. (2023). Digital divide in higher education in Sub-Saharan Africa: Evidence from online learning during the COVID-19 pandemic. *SN Social Sciences*, *3*(8), 122. Advance online publication. DOI: 10.1007/s43545-023-00717-4

Bakhshi, H., Downing, J. M., Osborne, M. A., & Schneider, P. (2017). *The future of skills: Employment in 2030*. Nesta.

Bakthavatchaalam, V., & Sivasankar, K. (2025). AI in healthcare education: a systematic review of applications in teaching and learning. Transforming Healthcare Sector Through Artificial Intelligence and Environmental Sustainability, 253-274.

Balaban, I., Zlatović, M., & Matus, M. (2024). Using learning analytics dashboards to monitor student progress: The case of a blended computer science university course. *2024 IEEE International Conference on Advanced Learning Technologies (ICALT)*, 72-74. DOI: 10.1109/ICALT61570.2024.00027

Bandura, A. (1999). Moral disengagement in the perpetration of inhumanities. *Personality and Social Psychology Review*, *3*(3), 193–209. DOI: 10.1207/s15327957pspr0303_3 PMID: 15661671

Bandura, A. (2023). Cultivate self-efficacy for personal and organizational effectiveness. In Locke, E., & Pearce, C. (Eds.), *Principles of organizational behavior* (pp. 113–135). Wiley., DOI: 10.1002/9781394320769.ch6

Bankins, S., & Formosa, P. (2023). The ethical implications of Artificial Intelligence (AI) for meaningful work. *Journal of Business Ethics*, *185*, 725–740. https://doi.org/doi:10.1007/s10551-023-05339-7

Ban, T., & Heng, K. (2023). Improving the quality of Cambodian higher education: Key challenges and suggestions. *Cambodian Journal of Educational Research*, *3*(2), 35–61. DOI: 10.62037/cjer.2023.03.02.03

Barlow, J. H., Ellard, D. R., Hainsworth, J. M., Jones, F. R., & Fisher, A. (2005). A review of self-management interventions for panic disorders, phobias, and obsessive-compulsive disorders. *Acta Psychiatrica Scandinavica*, *111*(4), 272–285. DOI: 10.1111/j.1600-0447.2005.00499.x

Barron, B., & Darling-Hammond, L. (2008). *Teaching for Meaningful Learning: A Review of Research on Inquiry-Based and Cooperative Learning*. George Lucas Educational Foundation.

Barrows, H. S. (1986). A taxonomy of problem-based learning methods. *Medical Education*, *20*(6), 481–486. DOI: 10.1111/j.1365-2923.1986.tb01386.x

Basha, J. Y. (2024). The negative impacts of AI tools on students in academic and real-life performance. *International Journal of Social Sciences and Commerce*, *1*(3), 1–16. https://ijssc.org/

Bates, T., Cobo, C., Mariño, O., & Wheeler, S. (2020). Can artificial intelligence transform higher education? *International Journal of Educational Technology in Higher Education*, *17*(1), 42. DOI: 10.1186/s41239-020-00218-x

Bayly-Castaneda, K., Ramirez-Montoya, M. S., & Morita-Alexander, A. (2024, August). Crafting personalized learning paths with AI for lifelong learning: a systematic literature review. In *Frontiers in Education* (Vol. 9, p. 1424386). Frontiers., DOI: 10.3389/feduc.2024.1424386

Bearman, M., & Ajjawi, R. (2023). Learning to work with the black box: Pedagogy for a world with artificial intelligence. *British Journal of Educational Technology*, *54*(5), 1160–1173. DOI: 10.1111/bjet.13337

Bearman, M., Dawson, P., Bennett, S., Hall, M., Molloy, E., Boud, D., & Joughin, G. (2016). How university teachers design assessments: A cross-disciplinary study. *Higher Education*, *74*(1), 49–64. DOI: 10.1007/s10734-016-0027-7

Bearman, M., Nieminen, J. H., & Ajjawi, R. (2023). Designing assessment in a digital world: An organising framework. *Assessment & Evaluation in Higher Education*, *48*(3), 291–304. DOI: 10.1080/02602938.2022.2069674

Becker, K., & Park, K. (2011). Effects of integrative approaches among science, technology, engineering, and mathematics (STEM) subjects on students' learning. *Journal of STEM Education: Innovations and Research*.

Begamudra Rangavittal, P. (2024). Transforming higher education with artificial intelligence - Benefits, challenges, and future directions. [IJSR]. *International Journal of Science and Research (Raipur, India)*, *13*(5), 1635–1642. DOI: 10.21275/SR24525214415

Behera, P. K., Jain, S. J., & Kumar, A. (2023). *Visual Exploration of Literature Using Connected Papers: A Practical Approach.* Issues in Science and Technology Librarianship., DOI: 10.29173/istl2760

Bellhäuser, H., Dignath, C., & Theobald, M. (2023). Daily automated feedback enhances self-regulated learning: A longitudinal randomized field experiment. *Frontiers in Psychology, 14,* 1125873. DOI: 10.3389/fpsyg.2023.1125873

Bellini, V., Semeraro, F., Montomoli, J., Cascella, M., & Bignami, E. (2024). Between human and AI: Assessing the reliability of AI text detection tools. *Current Medical Research and Opinion, 40*(4), 353–358. DOI: 10.1080/03007995.2024.2310086

Benjamin, R. (2019). *Race after technology: Abolitionist tools for the new Jim Code.* Polity Press.

Benjamin, R. (2019). *Race After Technology: Abolitionist Tools for the New Jim Code.* Polity Press.

Bennett, E. E., & McWhorter, R. R. (2021). Virtual HRD's role in crisis and the post-COVID-19 professional lifeworld: Accelerating skills for digital transformation. *Advances in Developing Human Resources, 23*(1), 5–25. DOI: 10.1177/1523422320973288

Bentley, S. V., Naughtin, C. K., McGrath, M. J., Irons, J. L., & Cooper, P. S. (2024). The digital divide in action: How experiences of digital technology shape future relationships with artificial intelligence. *AI and Ethics, 4*(4), 901–915. DOI: 10.1007/s43681-024-00452-3

Bertoncini, A. L. C., & Serafim, M. C. (2023). Ethical content in artificial intelligence systems: A demand explained in three critical points. *Frontiers in Psychology, 14,* 1074787. DOI: 10.3389/fpsyg.2023.1074787 PMID: 37063544

Bevan Jones, R., Stallard, P., Agha, S. S., Rice, S., Werner-Seidler, A., Stasiak, K., Kahn, J., Simpson, S. A., Alvarez-Jimenez, M., Rice, F., Evans, R., & Merry, S. (2020). Practitioner review: Co-design of digital mental health technologies with children and young people. [wiley.com]. *Journal of Child Psychology and Psychiatry, and Allied Disciplines, 61*(8), 928–940. DOI: 10.1111/jcpp.13258

Bhandari, P. (2024). Ethical considerations in research: Types & examples. Scribbr. https://www.scribbr.com/methodology/research-ethics/

Bharat, V. (2024). Futuristic higher education landscape: Skill-building for a Viksit Bharat workforce. *University News, 62,* 201.

Bhatia, A., Bhatia, P., & Sood, D. (2024). Leveraging AI to transform online higher education: Focusing on personalized learning, assessment, and student engagement. International Journal of Management and Humanities (IJMH) Volume-11 Issue-1.

Bhatia, P. (2023). ChatGPT for academic writing: A game changer or a disruptive tool? *Journal of Anaesthesiology, Clinical Pharmacology, 39*(1), 1–2. DOI: 10.4103/joacp.joacp_84_23

Bhosle, A. (2024). Real-time analytics and AI transforming data engineering for sustainable learning in cloud environments. In *Smart Education and Sustainable Learning Environments in Smart Cities* (pp. 347–364). IGI Global., DOI: 10.4018/979-8-3693-7723-9.ch021

Bhushan, B., Singh, A. P., Sharma, S., Divya, K., Bhimanpallewar, R., & Pareek, R. K. (2024). Utilizing AI to Advance Data Science Research. 1–6. DOI: 10.1109/ICCCNT61001.2024.10724570

Bhutoria, A (2022). Personalized education and artificial intelligence in the United States, China, and India: A systematic review using a human-in-the-loop model. Computers and Education: Artificial Intelligence. sciencedirect.com

Bhutoria, A. (2022). Personalized education and Artificial Intelligence in the United States, China, and India: A systematic review using a Human-In-The-Loop model. *Computers & Education: Artificial Intelligence, 3*, 100068. DOI: 10.1016/j.caeai.2022.100068

Bicknell, K., Brust, C., & Settles, B. (2023). How Duolingo's AI Learns what you Need to Learn: The language-learning app tries to emulate a great human tutor. *IEEE Spectrum, 60*(3), 28–33. DOI: 10.1109/MSPEC.2023.10061631

Biesta, G. (2010). *Good Education in an Age of Measurement: Ethics, Politics, Democracy.* Routledge.

Biggs, J. (2003). *Teaching for quality learning at university* (2nd ed.). Society for Research into Higher Education & Open University Press.

Bi, M., Struyven, K., & Zhu, C. (2023). Variables that influence teachers' practice of differentiated instruction in Chinese classrooms: A study from teachers' perspectives. *Frontiers in Psychology, 14*, 1124259. DOI: 10.3389/fpsyg.2023.1124259

Binns, R. (2018). "Fairness in Machine Learning: Lessons from Political Philosophy." *Proceedings of the 2018 Conference on Fairness, Accountability and Transparency*, 149–159.

Binns, R., Van Kleek, M., Veale, M., Lyngs, U., Zhao, J., & Shadbolt, N. (2018). 'It's Reducing a Human Being to a Percentage' Perceptions of Justice in Algorithmic Decisions. In *Proceedings of the 2018 Chi conference on human factors in computing systems* (pp. 1-14). DOI: 10.31235/osf.io/9wqxr

Biondi-Zoccai, G., Cazzaro, A., Cobalchin, E., D'Auria, D., Ardizzone, G., Giordano, S., Mirzoyev, U., Seferovic, P., Bajraktari, G., & Muraru, D. (2025). *Artificial Intelligence Tools for Scientific Writing: The Good, The Bad and The Ugly.* Deleted Journal., DOI: 10.62684/BXVS8359

Biswas, S. S. (2024). Seeing Beyond Words: The Revolutionary Role of ChatGPT Vision in Research and Publication. *The Journal of Pediatric Pharmacology and Therapeutics : JPPT : the Official Journal of PPAG, 29*(2), 206–207. DOI: 10.5863/1551-6776-29.2.206

Black, P., & Wiliam, D. (1998). Assessment and classroom learning. *Assessment in Education: Principles, Policy & Practice, 5*(1), 7–74. DOI: 10.1080/0969595980050102

Blignaut, H., Erasmus, E., & Du Toit-Brits, C. (2023). *Joyful learning: Advocating for self-directed learning through authentic, playful problem-based learning.* NWU Self-Directed Learning Series., DOI: 10.4102/aosis.2023.BK409.04

Bloom, B. S., & Krathwohl, D. R. (1956). *Taxonomy of Educational Objectives longmans.* Green & Co.

Bognár, L., Ágoston, G., Bacsa-Bán, A., Fauszt, T., Gubán, G., Joós, A., Juhász, L. Z., Kocsó, E., Kovács, E., Maczó, E., Mihálovicsné Kollár, A. I., & Strauber, G. (2024). Re-evaluating components of classical educational theories in AI-enhanced learning: An empirical study on student engagement. *Education Sciences*, *14*(9), 974. Advance online publication. DOI: 10.3390/educsci14090974

Bognár, L., & Khine, M. S. (2025). The shifting landscape of student engagement: A pre-post semester analysis in AI-enhanced classrooms. *Computers and Education: Artificial Intelligence*, *8*, 100395. DOI: 10.1016/j.caeai.2025.100395

Bolanos, F., Salatino, A. A., Osborne, F., & Motta, E. (2024). Artificial intelligence for literature reviews: Opportunities and challenges. *Artificial Intelligence Review*, *57*(9), 259. Advance online publication. DOI: 10.1007/s10462-024-10902-3

Bond, M., Bedenlier, S., Marín, V. I., & Händel, M. (2021). Emergency remote teaching in higher education: Mapping the first global online semester. *International Journal of Educational Technology in Higher Education*, *18*(1), 50. DOI: 10.1186/s41239-021-00282-x

Booyse, D., & Scheepers, C. B. (2024). Barriers to adopting automated organisational decision-making through the use of artificial intelligence. *Management Research Review*, *47*(1), 64–85. DOI: 10.1108/MRR-09-2021-0701

Borges do Nascimento, I. J., Marcolino, M. S., Abdulazeem, H. M., Weerasekara, I., Azzopardi-Muscat, N., Gonçalves, M. A., & Novillo-Ortiz, D. (2021). Impact of big data analytics on people's health: Overview of systematic reviews and recommendations for future studies. *Journal of Medical Internet Research*, *23*(4), e27275. DOI: 10.2196/27275

Borromeo, A. S., Manaloto, A. M., Delos Santos, M. J. M., Antonio, R. P., Soyosa, M. D., & Wide, W. (2025). Harnessing generative AI in nursing education: A bibliometric review. *Teaching and Learning in Nursing*, *20*(3), e1002–e1011. DOI: 10.1016/j.teln.2025.04.014

Botelho, A., Baral, S., Erickson, J. A., Benachamardi, P., & Heffernan, N. T. (2023). Leveraging natural language processing to support automated assessment and feedback for student open responses in mathematics. *Journal of Computer Assisted Learning*, *39*(3), 823–840. DOI: 10.1111/jcal.12793

Boud, D., & Falchikov, N. (2007). *Rethinking assessment in higher education: Learning for the longer term*. Routledge. DOI: 10.4324/9780203964309

Boumediene, H., & Bouakkaz, M. (2024). Artificial Intelligence in Education. *Advances in Educational Technologies and Instructional Design Book Series*, 407–438. DOI: 10.4018/979-8-3693-7220-3.ch014

Boussakuk, M., Bouchboua, A., El Ghazi, M., Fattah, M., & El Bekkali, M (2020). A fully individualized adaptive and intelligent educational hypermedia system: Details of cleveruniversity. International Journal, 8(5). researchgate.net

Bozkurt, A. (2023). ChatGPT, Üretken yapay zeka ve algoritmik paradigma değişikliği. *Alanyazın*, *4*(1), 63–72. DOI: 10.59320/alanyazin.1283282

Bozkurt, A., Karadeniz, A., Baneres, D., Guerrero-Roldán, A. E., & Rodríguez, M. E. (2021). Artificial intelligence and reflections from educational landscape: A review of AI studies in half a century. *Sustainability (Basel), 13*(2), 800. Advance online publication. DOI: 10.3390/su13020800

Brass, J. & Lynch, T. L (2020). Personalized learning: A history of the present. Journal of curriculum theorizing. jctonline.org

Bratteteig, T., & Wagner, I. (2016). Unpacking the Notion of Participation in Participatory Design. [CSCW]. *Computer Supported Cooperative Work, 25*(6), 425–475. DOI: 10.1007/s10606-016-9259-4

Brcic, M. & Yampolskiy, R. V (2023). Impossibility Results in AI: a survey. Acm computing surveys. acm.org

Breazeal, C., Moore, K. S., Ali, S., Perret, B., Zhou, X., Zhang, H., & Lee, I. (2023). Make-a-Thon for middle school AI educators. In *SIGCSE 2023: Proceedings of the 54th ACM Technical Symposium on Computer Science Education, 1*, 305–311. DOI: 10.1145/3545945.3569743

Brits, C. D., & Blignaut, J. H. (2023). Recognizing the importance of educator behavior in SDL. *Advances in Higher Education and Professional Development*, •••, 95–119. DOI: 10.4018/978-1-6684-6772-5.ch006

Brod, G., Kucirkova, N., Shepherd, J., Jolles, D., & Molenaar, I. (2023). Agency in educational technology: Interdisciplinary perspectives and implications for learning design. *Educational Psychology Review, 35*(1), 25. DOI: 10.1007/s10648-023-09749-x

Brookhart, S. M. (2008). *How to Give Effective Feedback to Your Students*. Association for Supervision and Curriculum Development.

Browner, E. (2023, July 5). AI proves time-saving potential for teachers, but are they ready? *Clever Blog*. https://www.clever.com/blog/2023/07/artificial-intelligence-teachers-K12

Brown, G. T. (2017). *Assessment of student achievement*. Routledge. DOI: 10.4324/9781315162058

Bruner, J. S. (1966). *Toward a theory of instruction*. Belknap Press of Harvard University Press.

Bui, T., & Bui, V. H. (2024). Decoding Scholarcy website: A Study on its Research Summarization Efficiency. *Proceedings of the AsiaCALL International Conference, 6*, 71–80. DOI: 10.54855/paic.2465

Bukuluki, P. (2013). "When I steal, it is for the benefit of me and you": Is collectivism engendering corruption in Uganda? *International Letters of Social and Humanistic Sciences, 5*, 27–44. . DOI: 10.18052/www.scipress.com/ILSHS.5.27

Buolamwini, J., & Gebru, T. (2018). "Gender Shades: Intersectional Accuracy Disparities in Commercial Gender Classification." *Proceedings of the 1st Conference on Fairness, Accountability and Transparency*, 77–91.

Cahyani, R. Y. D., Dewi, O. C., & Darmawan, A. (2024). AI AND CRITICAL READING SKILL AMONG UNIVERSITY STUDENTS (The impact of artificial intelligence (AI) on Al-Ghifari University Students' critical reading skills). *The Gist, 6*(1). Advance online publication. DOI: 10.53675/gist.v6i1.1374

Calo, R. (2015). Robotics and the Lessons of Cyberlaw. *California Law Review, 103*(3), 513–563.

Campbell, J., Ansell, K., & Stelzer, T. (2022). Using IBM's Watson to automatically evaluate student short answer responses. *2017 Physics Education Research Conference Proceedings.* DOI: 10.1119/perc.2022.pr.Campbell

Caplan, B. (2011, October 3). Nash equilibrium in higher education. *Library of Economics and Liberty.* https://www.econlib.org/nash-equilibrium-in-higher-education/

Carneros-Prado, D., Villa, L., Johnson, E., Dobrescu, C. C., Barragán, A., & García-Martínez, B. (2023). Comparative study of large language models as emotion and sentiment analysis systems: A case-specific analysis of GPT vs. IBM Watson. In J. Bravo & G. Urzáiz (Eds.), *Proceedings of the 15th International Conference on Ubiquitous Computing & Ambient Intelligence (UCAmI 2023)* (Vol. 842, pp. 257–268). Springer. DOI: 10.1007/978-3-031-48642-5_22

CASP14. (2025). https://predictioncenter.org/casp14

Catherin, T. C., Vettriselvan, R., Mathur, S., Regins, J. C., & Velmurugan, P. R. R. (2025). Integrating AI and Learning Analytics in Distance Learning: Strategies for Educators and Institutions. In AI and Learning Analytics in Distance Learning (pp. 207-228). IGI Global.

Cau, R., Pisu, F., Suri, J. S., & Saba, L. (2025). Addressing hidden risks: Systematic review of artificial intelligence biases across racial and ethnic groups in cardiovascular diseases. *European Journal of Radiology, 183,* 111867. Advance online publication. DOI: 10.1016/j.ejrad.2024.111867

Cazzaniga, M., Jaumotte, F., Li, L., Melina, G., Panton, A, J., Pizzinelli, C., Rockall, E. J., & Tavares, M. M. (2024). Gen-AI: artificial intelligence and the future of work. *Staff Discussion Notes* No. 2024/001, DOI: DOI: 10.5089/9798400262548.006

Celik, B., Yildiz, Y., & Kara, S. (2025). Using ChatGPT as a virtual speaking tutor to boost EFL learners' speaking self-efficacy. *Australian Journal of Applied Linguistics.* DOI: 10.29140/ajal.v8n1.102418

Celik, I., Gedrimiene, E., Silvola, A., & Muukkonen, H. (2023). Response of learning analytics to the online education challenges during the pandemic: Opportunities and key examples in higher education. *Policy Futures in Education, 21*(4), 387–404. DOI: 10.1177/14782103221078401

Cengiz, S., & Peker, A. (2025). Generative artificial intelligence acceptance and artificial intelligence anxiety among university students: The sequential mediating role of attitudes toward artificial intelligence and literacy. *Current Psychology (New Brunswick, N.J.), 44*(9), 7991–8000. Advance online publication. DOI: 10.1007/s12144-025-07433-7

Chan, C. K. Y. (2023). A comprehensive AI policy education framework for university teaching and learning. *International Journal of Educational Technology in Higher Education, 20*(1), 38. DOI: 10.1186/s41239-023-00408-3

Chan, C. K. Y., & Hu, W. (2023). Students' voices on generative AI: Perceptions, benefits, and challenges in higher education. *International Journal of Educational Technology in Higher Education, 20*(1), 43. DOI: 10.1186/s41239-023-00411-8

Chang, D. H., Lin, M. P. C., Hajian, S., & Wang, Q. Q. (2023). Educational design principles of using AI chatbot that supports self-regulated learning in education: Goal setting, feedback, and personalization. *Sustainability (Basel), 15*(22), 16345. DOI: 10.3390/su151712921

Chassignol, M., Khoroshavin, A., Klimova, A., & Bilyatdinova, A. (2018). Artificial Intelligence trends in education: A narrative overview. *Procedia Computer Science, 136*, 16–24. DOI: 10.1016/j.procs.2018.08.233

Chaudhry, M. A., Cukurova, M., & Luckin, R. (2022, July). A transparency index framework for AI in education. In *International Conference on Artificial Intelligence in Education* (pp. 195-198). Cham: Springer International Publishing. https://doi.org/DOI: 10.1007/978-3-031-11647-6_33

Chawla, M. (2022), COMPAS Case Study: Investigating Algorithmic Fairness of Predictive Policing, Human stories & ideas.

Chen, X., Zou, D., Xie, H., Cheng, G., & Liu, C. (2022). Two decades of artificial intelligence in education. Educational Technology & Society. ln.edu.hk

Chen, C., Maqsood, A., Zhang, Z., Wang, X., Duan, L., Wang, H., Chen, T., Liu, S., Li, Q., Luo, J., & Jacobsson, T. J. (2024). The use of ChatGPT to generate experimentally testable hypotheses for improving the surface passivation of perovskite solar cells. *Cell Reports. Physical Science, 102058*(7), 102058. Advance online publication. DOI: 10.1016/j.xcrp.2024.102058

Chen, C., Sok, P., & Sok, K. (2007). Benchmarking potential factors leading to education quality: A study of Cambodian higher education. *Quality Assurance in Education, 15*(2), 128–148. DOI: 10.1108/09684880710748901

Chen, L. (2020). The role of AI in education: A case study of Squirrel AI in China. *International Journal of Information and Education Technology (IJIET), 10*(5), 384–388. DOI: 10.18178/ijiet.2020.10.5.1389

Chen, L., Chen, P., & Lin, Z. (2020). Artificial intelligence in education: A review. *IEEE Access : Practical Innovations, Open Solutions, 8*, 75264–75278. https://ieeexplore.ieee.org/abstract/document/9069875. DOI: 10.1109/ACCESS.2020.2988510

Chen, Q., Shuai, W., Zhang, J., Sun, Z., & Cao, N. (2024). Beyond Numbers: Creating Analogies to Enhance Data Comprehension and Communication with Generative AI. *Proceedings of the 2024 CHI Conference on Human Factors in Computing Systems* Article No.: 377, Pages 1 – 14 DOI: 10.1145/3613904.3642480

Chen, X., Zou, D., Xie, H., Cheng, G., & Liu, C. (2022). Two decades of artificial intelligence in education. *Journal of Educational Technology & Society, 25*(1), 28–47.

Chen, X., Zou, D., Xie, H., Cheng, G., & Liu, C. (2022). Two Decades of Artificial Intelligence in Education: Contributors, Collaborations, Research Topics, Challenges, and Future Directions. *Journal of Educational Technology & Society, 25*(1), 28–47. https://www.jstor.org/stable/48647028

Chigbu, B. I., Umejesi, I., & Makapela, S. L. (2024). Adaptive intelligence revolutionizing learning and sustainability in higher education: enhancing learning and sustainability with AI. In *Implementing interactive learning strategies in higher education* (pp. 151–176). IGI Global. DOI: 10.4018/979-8-3693-3559-8.ch006

Chiu, T. K. (2024). Future research recommendations for transforming higher education with generative AI. *Computers and Education: Artificial Intelligence*, *6*, 100197. DOI: 10.1016/j.caeai.2023.100197

Chiu, T. K. F., & Chai, C.-S. (2020). Sustainable curriculum planning for artificial intelligence education: A self-determination theory perspective. *Sustainability (Basel)*, *12*(14), 5568. DOI: 10.3390/su12145568

Chomsky, N., & Skinner, B. F. (1959). A Review of B. F. Skinner's verbal behavior. *Language*, *35*(1), 26–58. DOI: 10.2307/411334

Chowdhury, S., & Das, D. K. (2024). Academic performance analysis of the students with feature retraction using machine learning algorithms. *2024 4th International Conference on Sustainable Expert Systems (ICSES)*, 1060-1064. DOI: 10.1109/ICSES63445.2024.10763310

Christou, P. (2023). How to Use Artificial Intelligence (AI) as a Resource, Methodological and Analysis Tool in Qualitative Research? *The Qualitative Report*. Advance online publication. DOI: 10.46743/2160-3715/2023.6406

Chu, T. S., & Ashraf, M. (2025). Artificial intelligence in curriculum design: A data-driven approach to higher education innovation. *Preprints*.

Clark, H. (2023). *The AI infused classroom: Inspiring ideas to shift teaching and maximize meaningful learning in the world of AI*. Elevate Books EDU.

Claude, J., & Borbalan, R. (2025). The transformative impact of artificial intelligence on Higher Education: A critical reflection on current trends and Futures Directions -. https://journals.sagepub.com/doi/10.1177/2212585X251319364

Clelland, C. L., Moss, S., & Clelland, J. D. (2024). Warning: Artificial intelligence chatbots can generate inaccurate medical and scientific information and references. DOI: 10.37349/edht.2024.00006

Cody, R. A., Boldt, G. T., & Gubbins, E. J. (2023). How Teachers Make Decisions in Response to Professional Learning: A Study on Grade 3 Differentiation in Mathematics. *Journal of Advanced Academics*, *35*(1), 156–185. DOI: 10.1177/1932202X231221143

Coeckelbergh, M. (2020). *AI ethics*. MIT Press. DOI: 10.7551/mitpress/12549.001.0001

Conati, C., Barral, O., Putnam, V., & Rieger, L. (2021). Toward personalized XAI: A case study in intelligent tutoring systems. [PDF]. *Artificial Intelligence*, *298*, 103503. DOI: 10.1016/j.artint.2021.103503

Conradie, P. W. (2014). Supporting self-directed learning by connectivism and personal learning environments. *International Journal of Information and Education Technology (IJIET)*, *4*(3), 254–259. DOI: 10.7763/IJIET.2014.V4.408

Contreras, M. R., & Jaimes, J. O. P. (2024). Artificial Intelligence Literacy in Research. *2024 IEEE Colombian Conference on Applications of Computational Intelligence (ColCACI)*, 1–6. DOI: 10.1109/ColCACI63187.2024.10666582

Contrino, M. F., Reyes-Millán, M., Vázquez-Villegas, P., & Membrillo-Hernández, J. (2024). Using an adaptive learning tool to improve student performance and satisfaction in online and face-to-face education for a more personalized approach. *Smart Learning Environments, 11*(1), 6. DOI: 10.1186/s40561-024-00292-y

Cotton, D. R., Wyness, L., Jane, B., & Cotton, P. A. (2025). Redefining assessments in the age of AI. In *Teaching and learning in the age of generative AI* (pp. 283–308). Routledge. DOI: 10.4324/9781032688602-18

Cowin, J. (2023, November 6). *Targeted prompts for EFL teachers using AI* [Virtual presentation] [Slide show; Presentation]. Dr. J's Education Blog. https://drcowinj.files.wordpress.com/2023/11/targeted-prompting-for-efl-educators-using-ai-morocco-workshop-ppt.pdf

Crompton, H., & Burke, D. (2023). Artificial intelligence in higher education: The state of the field. *International Journal of Educational Technology in Higher Education, 20*(1), 22. DOI: 10.1186/s41239-023-00392-8

Cuban, L. (1986). *Teachers and machines: The classroom use of technology since 1920*. Teachers College Press.

Curasi, C. F. (2013). The relative influences of neutralizing behavior and subcultural values on academic dishonesty. *Journal of Education for Business, 88*(3), 167–175. DOI: 10.1080/08832323.2012.668145

Czerkawski, B. C. (2024). Designing language learning experiences with generative AI tools. *Advances in Educational Technologies and Instructional Design*, •••, 324–341. DOI: 10.4018/979-8-3693-0872-1.ch015

Daepp, M. I., & Counts, S. (2025, June). The Emerging Generative Artificial Intelligence Divide in the United States. In *Proceedings of the International AAAI Conference on Web and Social Media* (Vol. 19, pp. 443-456). https://doi.org/DOI: 10.1609/icwsm.v19i1.35825

Dai, C. P., & Ke, F. (2022). Educational applications of artificial intelligence in simulation-based learning: A systematic mapping review. *Computers and Education: Artificial Intelligence, 3*, 100087.

Darvishi, A., Khosravi, H., Sadiq, S., & Gašević, D. (2022). Incorporating AI and learning analytics to build trustworthy peer assessment systems. *British Journal of Educational Technology, 53*(4), 844–875. DOI: 10.1111/bjet.13233

Das, S., Mutsuddi, I., & Ray, N. (2025). Artificial Intelligence in Adaptive Education: A Transformative Approach. In Advancing Adaptive Education: Technological Innovations for Disability Support (pp. 21-50). IGI Global.

Daugherty, P. R., Wilson, H. J., & Chowdhury, R. (2020). Using artificial intelligence to promote diversity. *How AI Is Transforming the Organization*, 15-22. DOI: 10.7551/mitpress/12588.003.0006

Davis, F. D. (1989). Perceived usefulness, perceived ease of use, and user acceptance of information technology. *Management Information Systems Quarterly, 13*(3), 319–340. DOI: 10.2307/249008

De Cremer, D., & Narayanan, D. (2023). How AI tools can—and cannot—help organizations become more ethical. *Frontiers in Artificial Intelligence*, *6*, 1093712. DOI: 10.3389/frai.2023.1093712 PMID: 37426304

De La Haye, D. C., Daniels, S. R., & Simmons, A. L. (2023). Working after incarceration: An integrative framework of pre- and post-hire experiences of formerly incarcerated individuals. *Human Resource Management Review*, *33*(3), 100966. DOI: 10.1016/j.hrmr.2023.100966

Deardorff, D. K. (2006). Identification and assessment of intercultural competence as a student outcome of internationalization. *Journal of Studies in International Education*, *10*(3), 241–266. DOI: 10.1177/1028315306287002

Dede, C. (2020). The role of digital technologies in deeper learning. In OECD (Ed.), *Teaching, learning and assessment for adults: Improving foundation skills* (pp. 153–174). OECD Publishing.

Degni, F. (2024). AI in education: The impact of artificial intelligence on education. *ResearchGate*. DOI: 10.13140/RG.2.2.21373.99048

Degni, F. (2024). The impact of artificial intelligence on education. *Advances in Educational Technologies and Instructional Design*, •••, 55–94. DOI: 10.4018/979-8-3693-6170-2.ch003

Del Giglio, A., & Pereira da Costa, M. U. (2023). The use of artificial intelligence to improve the scientific writing of non-native english speakers. Revista Da Associacao Medica Brasileira, 69. DOI: 10.1590/1806-9282.20230560

Del Pilar Gonzalez, N. A., & Chiappe, A. (2024). Learning analytics and personalization of learning: a review. *Ensaio Avaliação E Políticas Públicas Em Educação, 32*(122). https://doi.org/DOI: 10.1590/s0104-40362024003204234

deLaubell, L. (2023). Scite. *The Charleston Advisor*, *24*(4), 60–63. DOI: 10.5260/chara.24.4.60

Delello, J. A., Sung, W., Mokhtari, K., Hebert, J., Bronson, A., & De Giuseppe, T. (2025). AI in the classroom: Insights from educators on usage, challenges, and mental health. *Education Sciences*, *15*(2), 113. DOI: 10.3390/educsci15020113

Deloitte. (2023). Artificial intelligence in education: Unlocking new possibilities. https://www2.deloitte.com/us/en/insights/industry/public-sector/ai-in-education.html

Demaidi, M. N. (2023). Artificial intelligence national strategy in a developing country. *AI & Society*. Advance online publication. DOI: 10.1007/s00146-023-01779-x

Demirören, M., Turan, S., & Taşdelen Teker, G. (2020). Determinants of self-regulated learning skills: The roles of tutors and students. [physiology.org]. *Advances in Physiology Education*, *44*(1), 93–98. DOI: 10.1152/advan.00121.2019

Deri, M. N., Singh, A., Zaazie, P., & Anandene, D. (2024). Leveraging Artificial Intelligence in Higher Educational Institutions: A Comprehensive Overview. *Revista de Educación y Derecho*, (30).

Deshmukh, V., Prithviraj, J., Rautkar, A., Agrawal, R., Dhule, C., & Chavhan, N. (2023)... *Interactive Data Visualization Platform to Present Effective Teacher Performance with Power BI.*, *1335–1339*, 1335–1339. Advance online publication. DOI: 10.1109/ICAICCIT60255.2023.10466179

Deshpande, D., Unawane, R., Tatiwar, R., Taware, A., Todkar, A., & Munshi, S. (2023). Research article summarizer. In *2023 International Conference for Advancement in Technology (ICONAT)* (pp. 1–4). IEEE. DOI: 10.1109/ICONAT57137.2023.10080317

Dever, D. A., Sonnenfeld, N. A., Wiedbusch, M. D., Schmorrow, S. G., Amon, M. J., & Azevedo, R. (2023). A complex systems approach to analyzing pedagogical agents' scaffolding of self-regulated learning within an intelligent tutoring system. *Metacognition and Learning*, *18*(3), 659–691. DOI: 10.1007/s11409-023-09346-x

Devillers, L., Fogelman-Soulié, F., & Baeza-Yates, R. (2021). AI & human values: Inequalities, biases, fairness, nudge, and feedback loops. In Braunschweig, B., & Ghallab, M. (Eds.), *Reflections on Artificial Intelligence for Humanity* (pp. 76–89). Springer International Publishing., DOI: 10.1007/978-3-030-69128-8_6

Devineni, S. K. (2024). AI-Enhanced Data Visualization: Transforming Complex Data into Actionable Insights. Journal of Technology and Systems. DOI: 10.47941/jts.1911

Diep, M. C., & Dang, M. H. (2025). Exploring factors influencing the adoption of ChatGPT as a supportive tool in EFL Lesson Creation. *AsiaCALL Online Journal*, *16*(1), 111–139. DOI: 10.54855/acoj.251616

Dignum, V. (2019). *Responsible artificial intelligence: how to develop and use AI in a responsible way* (Vol. 2156). Springer., DOI: 10.1007/978-3-030-30371-6

Ding, A.-C. E., Shi, L., Yang, H., & Choi, I. (2024). Enhancing teacher AI literacy and integration through different types of cases in teacher professional development. *Computers and Education Open*, *6*, 100178. DOI: 10.1016/j.caeo.2024.100178

Doeur, B. (2022a). Promoting higher education reforms in Cambodia: Challenges and the way forward. *Cambodian Journal of Educational Research*, *2*(2), 116–128. DOI: 10.62037/cjer.2022.02.02.07

Doeur, B. (2022b). Promoting teachers' continuous professional development in Cambodian higher education: Issues and recommendations. *Cambodian Journal of Educational Research*, *2*(1), 119–134. DOI: 10.62037/cjer.2022.02.01.07

Dong, C. (2024). Educational concepts and methodologies in the AI era: Challenges and responses. *Frontiers of Digital Education*, *1*(1), 69–77. DOI: 10.1007/s44366-024-0022-y

Doroudi, S. (2023). The intertwined histories of artificial intelligence and education. [springer.com]. *International Journal of Artificial Intelligence in Education*, *33*(4), 885–928. DOI: 10.1007/s40593-022-00313-2

Doshi-Velez, F., & Kim, B. (2017). "Towards a Rigorous Science of Interpretable Machine Learning." *arXiv preprint*, arXiv:1702.08608.

Drushchak, N., Tyshchenko, V., & Polyakovska, N. (2025, April). Towards Responsible AI in Education: Hybrid Recommendation System for K-12 Students Case Study. In *2025 IEEE/ACM International Workshop on Responsible AI Engineering (RAIE)* (pp. 61-68). IEEE. DOI: DOI: 10.1109/RAIE66699.2025.00015

Duffourc, M. N., Gerke, S., & Kollnig, K. (2023). Privacy of personal data in generative AI data lifecycle. *NYU J. Intell. Prop. & Ent. L., 13*, 219.

Dulundu, A. (2024). AI in education: Benefits and concerns. *Next Generation Journal for The Young Researchers, 8*(1), 81. DOI: 10.62802/3fr4f412

Dziubaniuk, O., Ivanova-Gongne, M., & Nyholm, M. (2023). Learning and teaching sustainable business in the Digital Era: A connectivism theory approach. *International Journal of Educational Technology in Higher Education, 20*(1), 20. Advance online publication. DOI: 10.1186/s41239-023-00390-w

Eau, G., Judah, K., & Shahid, H. (2019). How can adaptive platforms improve student learning outcomes? A case study of open educational resources and adaptive learning platforms. SSRN *Electronic Journal*. DOI: 10.2139/ssrn.3478134

Eden, C. A., Chisom, O. N., & Adeniyi, I. S. (2024). Integrating AI in education: opportunities, challenges, and ethical considerations. *Magna Scientia Advanced Research and Reviews, 10*, 006-013. DOI: 10.30574/msarr.2024.10.2.0039

Edmett, A., Ichaporia, N., Crompton, H., & Crichton, R. (2024). *Artificial intelligence and English language teaching: Preparing for the future* (Version Second edition). British Council. DOI: 10.57884/78EA-3C69

Education Week. (2023, June 21). *ChatGPT & education: 8 ways AI improves student outcomes*. https://www.edweek.org/events/webinar/chatgpt-education-8-ways-ai-improves-student-outcomes

Edwards, R. A., White, B. A. A., & Findyartini, A. (2025). Innovations in teaching and learning for health professions educators. *Frontiers in Medicine*, •••, 12.

Effoduh, J. O. (2024, March 8). The role and potential of artificial intelligence in extremist fuelled election misinformation in Africa. *Global Network on Extremism and Technology*. https://gnet-research.org/2024/03/08/the-role-and-potential-of-artificial-intelligence-in-extremist-fuelled-election-misinformation-in-africa/

Eger, S., Cao, Y., D'Souza, J., Geiger, A., Greisinger, C., Gross, S., Hou, Y., Krenn, B., Lauscher, A., Li, Y., Lin, C., Moosavi, N. S., Zhao, W., & Miller, T. (2025). Transforming science with large language models: A survey on AI-assisted scientific discovery, experimentation, content generation, and evaluation. *arXiv preprint*, arXiv:2502.05151.

Ehsan, U., Wintersberger, P., Liao, Q. V., Watkins, E. A., Manger, C., Daumé Iii, H., Riener, A., & Riedl, M. O. (2022). Human-xentered explainable AI (HCXAI): Beyond opening the black-box of AI. *CHI Conference on Human Factors in Computing Systems Extended Abstracts*, 1–7. DOI: 10.1145/3491101.3503727

Ejjami, R.Dr. Rachid Ejjami. (2024). Integrative Literature Review 5.0: Leveraging Ai and Emerging Technologies to Redefine Academic Research. *International Journal For Multidisciplinary Research, 6*(5), 28756. Advance online publication. DOI: 10.36948/ijfmr.2024.v06i05.28756

Ekundayo, T., Khan, Z., & Nuzhat, S. (2024). Evaluating the Influence of Artificial Intelligence on Scholarly Research: A Study Focused on Academics. *Human Behavior and Emerging Technologies, 2024*(1), 1–13. DOI: 10.1155/2024/8713718

Elearning Industry. (2023). Revolutionizing education with AI-driven assessments. https://elearningindustry.com/revolutionizing-education-with-ai-driven-assessments

Elibox, W., Khan, K., Khan, A., Smart, S., & Cockburn, B. N. (2025). The INSPIRE framework for transformative and inclusive education: A case study of the science faculty at a Commonwealth university. *Quality Assurance in Education, 33*(4), 585–602. DOI: 10.1108/QAE-02-2025-0037

Elkhatat, A. M., Elsaid, K., & Almeer, S. (2023). Evaluating the efficacy of AI content detection tools in differentiating between human and AI-generated text. *International Journal for Educational Integrity, 19*(1), 17. DOI: 10.1007/s40979-023-00140-5

Ellikkal, A., & Rajamohan, **S.** (2024). AI-enabled personalized learning: Empowering management students for improving engagement and academic performance. *Vilakshan - XIMB Journal of Management, ahead-of-print.* DOI: 10.1108/XJM-02-2024-0023

Ellis, D. E. (2018). Changing the lens: The role of reframing in educational development. *To Improve the Academy, 37*(1), 142–150. DOI: 10.1002/tia2.20067

El-Sabagh, H. A. (2021). Adaptive e-learning environment based on learning styles and its impact on development students' engagement. [springer.com]. *International Journal of Educational Technology in Higher Education, 18*(1), 53. DOI: 10.1186/s41239-021-00289-4

Em, S. (2025). *Effectiveness of school directors' transformational leadership on teachers' self-efficacy and job performance in Cambodia* [The University of Cambodia]. CJESS Online Library. https://ejournal.educationalfields.com/index.php/CJESSOL/article/view/63

Em, S., Chin, P., & Pen, D. (2024). COVID-19 and school closures: Transformation of shadow education in the Cambodian context. In Md. B. Alam (Ed.), *Shadow education in Asia: Policies and practices* (pp. 136-159). IGI Global Scientific Publishing. DOI: 10.4018/979-8-3693-2952-8.ch009

Embl, N. D. (2025). European Molecular Biology Laboratory.EMB L.org.https://www.embl.org

Em, S., & Khampirat, B. (2025a). Facilitating scholarly pursuits in higher education: Cambodia's endeavors toward research advancement. In Mdikana, A. A. (Ed.), *Enhancing research output in higher education: Research proposals, profiles, and publishing* (pp. 39–66). IGI Global Scientific Publishing., DOI: 10.4018/979-8-3373-0806-7.ch002

Em, S., & Khampirat, B. (2025b). Cooperative education for sustainability: AI in learning opportunities, challenges, and future directions. In Tariq, M. U., & Sergio, R. P. (Eds.), *Convergence of AI, education, and business for sustainability* (pp. 75–92). IGI Global Scientific Publishing., DOI: 10.4018/979-8-3373-1917-9.ch004

Engeness, I., & Gamlem, S. M. (2025). Exploring AI-driven feedback as a cultural tool: A cultural-historical perspective on design of AI environments to support students' writing process. *Integrative Psychological & Behavioral Science, 59*(1), 23. Advance online publication. DOI: 10.1007/s12124-025-09894-8

Engeness, I., Nohr, M., & Fossland, T. (2025). Investigating AI Chatbots' Role in Online Learning and Digital Agency Development. *Education Sciences, 15*(6), 674. DOI: 10.3390/educsci15060674

Engeström, Y. (1987). *Learning by Expanding: An Activity-Theoretical Approach to Developmental Research*. Orienta-Konsultit.

Englmeier, K., & Contreras, P. (2024). How AI can help learners to develop conceptual knowledge in digital learning environments. *2024 IEEE 12th International Conference on Intelligent Systems (IS)*, 1-6. DOI: 10.1109/IS61756.2024.10705253

Ercan, S. I. A., & Akin, O. (2024). International insights on AI risk: Comparative analysis of international organizations. In *2024 8th International Artificial Intelligence and Data Processing Symposium (IDAP)*, 1-8.

Esplugas, M. (2023). The use of artificial intelligence (AI) to enhance academic communication, education and research: A balanced approach. *The Journal of Hand Surgery, European Volume*, *17531934231185746*(8), 819–822. Advance online publication. DOI: 10.1177/17531934231185746

Essa, S. G., Celik, T., & Human-Hendricks, N. E. (2023). Personalized adaptive learning technologies based on machine learning techniques to identify learning styles: A systematic literature review. *IEEE Access : Practical Innovations, Open Solutions*, *11*, 48392–48409. https://ieeexplore.ieee.org/abstract/document/10124747. DOI: 10.1109/ACCESS.2023.3276439

Eubanks, V. (2018). *Automating inequality: How high-tech tools profile, police, and punish the poor*. St. Martin's Press.

European Commission, High-Level Expert Group on Artificial Intelligence. (2019, April 8). *Ethics guidelines for trustworthy AI*. European Commission. https://digital-strategy.ec.europa.eu/en/library/ethics-guidelines-trustworthy-ai

European Commission. (2020). *European Skills Agenda for Sustainable Competitiveness*. Social Fairness and Resilience.

European Data Protection Board (EDPB). (2025). Guidelines 01/2025 on Pseudonymisation. Retrieved from: https://www.edpb.europa.eu/system/files/202501/edpb_guidelines_202501_pseudonymisation_en.pdf

European Parliament. (2020). The ethics of artificial intelligence: Issues and initiatives. https://www.europarl.europa.eu/RegData/etudes/STUD/2020/634452/EPRS_STU(2020)634452_EN.pdf

Evangelista, E. D. L. (2025). Ensuring academic integrity in the age of ChatGPT: Rethinking exam design, assessment strategies, and ethical AI policies in higher education. *Contemporary Educational Technology*, *17*(1), 1–19. DOI: 10.30935/cedtech/15775

Faber, H. C., Gasparini, A., & Grote, M. G. (2022). Artificial Intelligence-based tools in the context of Open Science. *Septentrio Conference Series*, *1*(1). Advance online publication. DOI: 10.7557/5.6636

Fabre, E. F., Mouratille, D., Bonnemains, V., Palmiotti, G. P., & Causse, M. (2024). Making moral decisions with artificial agents as advisors: A fNIRS study. *Computers in Human Behavior: Artificial Humans*, *2*(2), 100096. DOI: 10.1016/j.chbah.2024.100096

Fam, D., Neuhauser, L., & Gibbs, P. (2020). *Transdisciplinary theory, practice and education: The art of collaborative research and collective learning*. Springer.

Fan, Y., Matcha, W., Uzir, N. A. A., Wang, Q., & Gašević, D. (2021). Learning analytics to reveal links between learning design and self-regulated learning. *International Journal of Artificial Intelligence in Education, 31*(4), 980–1021. DOI: 10.1007/s40593-021-00249-z

Farhat, S., de la Fuente Hagopian, A., Hooda, K., Lê, H., & Echo, A. (2024). Chatting Up the Next Big Thing: Generating Novel Ideas for Systematic Reviews in Breast Reconstruction Research Using Chat-GPT. *Cureus.* Advance online publication. DOI: 10.7759/cureus.61955

Farooq, M., Ramzan, M., & Yen, Y. Y. (2025). Transformative Impact of AI in Education Management.

Faturrahman, M. A., Titin, T., Nusantoro, B. P., Putri, R. R., Novahisa, P., Kusuma Ayu, N. A., & Sandra, K. M. (2023). *Pemanfaatan Aplikasi Mendeley sebagai Sistem Manajemen Referensi untuk Mengoptimalisasi Penulisan Karya Ilmiah Mahasiswa.* Abditeknika., DOI: 10.31294/abditeknika.v3i2.2411

Feldman-Maggor, Y., Cukurova, M., Kent, C., & Alexandron, G. (2025). The Impact of Explainable AI on Teachers' Trust and Acceptance of AI EdTech Recommendations: The Power of Domain-specific Explanations. *International Journal of Artificial Intelligence in Education, 35*(5), 1–34. DOI: 10.1007/s40593-025-00486-6

Fenu, G., Galici, R., & Marras, M. (2022, July). Experts' view on challenges and needs for fairness in artificial intelligence for education. In *International Conference on Artificial Intelligence in Education* (pp. 243-255). Cham: Springer International Publishing. [PDF] DOI: 10.1007/978-3-031-11644-5_20

Ferretti, T. (2024). Value alignment without institutional change cannot prevent the societal risks of Artificial Intelligence. *LSE Public Policy Review, 3*(3), 1–12. DOI: 10.31389/lseppr.113

Ferster, B. (2022). *Intelligent tutoring systems.* Intelligent Tutoring Systems., DOI: 10.4324/9781138609877-REE6-1

Finley, K. (2015). *Using Satellites to Stop Deforestation Before It Happens.* Wired.

Fitri, I. C., Apriliyanto, R., Jalil, A., & Ananda, P. T. (2023). Peningkatan Kemampuan Mahasiswa Dalam Memanajemen Referensi Ilmiah Melalui Pelatihan Mendeley. DOI: 10.47134/diankes.v1i1.7

Fletcher, A. K. (2024). Self-assessment as a student-agentic zone of proximate competence development. *Educational Review, 76*(4), 956–978. DOI: 10.1080/00131911.2022.2103520

Floridi, L., & Cowls, J. (2019). A unified framework of five principles for AI in society. *Harvard Data Science Review.* Advance online publication. DOI: 10.1162/99608f92.8cd550d1

Floridi, L., Cowls, J., Beltrametti, M., Chatila, R., Chazerand, P., Dignum, V., Luetge, C., Madelin, R., Pagallo, U., Rossi, F., Schafer, B., Valcke, P., & Vayena, E. (2018). AI4People—An Ethical Framework for a Good AI Society. *Minds and Machines, 28*(4), 689–707. DOI: 10.1007/s11023-018-9482-5 PMID: 30930541

Forbes, A., & Powling, M. (2023, March 5). *Artificial Intelligence (AI) education for teachers.* Coursera. https://www.coursera.org/learn/artificial-intelligence-education-for-teachers

Fraidan, A. A. (2024). Enhancing linguistic research through AI-powered reference management: A proposal for a voice-controlled academic assistant. *Edelweiss Applied Science and Technology*, *9*(1), 1–9. DOI: 10.55214/25768484.v9i1.2240

Francisco, R., & Silva, F. (2022). A recommendation module based on reinforcement learning to an intelligent tutoring system for software maintenance. *Proceedings of the 14th International Conference on Computer Supported Education.* DOI: 10.5220/0011083900003182

Francisco, R., & Silva, F. (2022). Intelligent tutoring system for computer science education and the use of artificial intelligence: A literature Review. In *Proceedings of the 14th International Conference on Computer Supported Education*, 338–345. DOI: 10.5220/0011084400003182

Fricker, M. (2007). *Epistemic Injustice: Power and the Ethics of Knowing.* Oxford University Press. DOI: 10.1093/acprof:oso/9780198237907.001.0001

Fui-Hoon Nah, F., Zheng, R., Cai, J., Siau, K., & Chen, L. (2023). Generative AI and ChatGPT: Applications, challenges, and AI-human collaboration. *Journal of Information Technology Case and Application Research*, *25*(3), 277–304. DOI: 10.1080/15228053.2023.2233814

Fullan, M., Quinn, J., & McEachen, J. (2018). *Deep learning: Engage the world change the world.* Corwin.

Funa, A. A., & Gabay, R. A. E. (2025). Policy guidelines and recommendations on AI use in teaching and learning: A meta-synthesis study. *Social Sciences & Humanities Open*, *11*, 101221. DOI: 10.1016/j.ssaho.2024.101221

Gan, W., Sun, Y., & Sun, Y. (2020, November). Knowledge interaction enhanced knowledge tracing for learner performance prediction. In 2020 7th international conference on behavioural and social computing (BESC) (pp. 1-6). IEEE. researchgate.net DOI: 10.1109/BESC51023.2020.9348285

Gandhi, P., & Singh, N. (2023). *From healthcare canary to a failed prodigy a case study in the "AI age" for business schools for decades.* IPM Watson.

Ganiyu, T. O. (2025). *Academic integrity in the AI era: Battling cheating with innovation.* AI and Ethics, Academic Integrity and the Future of Quality Assurance in Higher Education.

Gannar, S., & Kilani, C. (2025). Contextualized learning and social constructivism: Implementing a project-based approach in information systems development education. *Journal of Science Learning*, *8*(1), 15–24. DOI: 10.17509/jsl.v8i1.72667

Ganuthula, V. R. R., & Balaraman, K. K. (2025). *Beyond digital tools: AI as a psychological catalyst reshaping entrepreneurial self-efficacy in an era of uncertainty. SSRN.* https://ssrn.com/abstract=5247064 or http://dx.doi.org/DOI: 10.2139/ssrn.5247064

García-López, I. M., González González, C. S., Ramírez-Montoya, M.-S., & Molina-Espinosa, J.-M. (2025). Challenges of implementing ChatGPT on education: Systematic literature review. *International Journal of Educational Research Open*, *8*, 100401. DOI: 10.1016/j.ijedro.2024.100401

Gardner, J., O'Leary, M., & Yuan, L. (2021). Artificial intelligence in educational assessment: 'Breakthrough? Or buncombe and ballyhoo?'. *Journal of Computer Assisted Learning*, *37*(5), 1207–1216. DOI: 10.1111/jcal.12577

Gautam, D. (2024). Revolutionizing Education through Innovative Technological Solutions. As the editors of Transforming Learning. *Power and Education*, •••, 60.

George, A. S. (2024). Reimagining India's engineering education for an AI-driven future. *Partners Universal International Research Journal*, *3*(3), 1–20.

Georgia Institute of Technology. (2025). *Jill Watson: The virtual teaching assistant*. Design & Intelligence Lab. https://dilab.gatech.edu/jill-watson/

Gering, Z., Feher, K., Harmat, V., & Tamassy, R. (2025). Strategic organisational responses to generative AI-driven digital transformation in leading higher education institutions. *The International Journal of Organizational Analysis*, *33*(12), 132–152. DOI: 10.1108/IJOA-09-2024-4850

Ghimire, A., & Edwards, J. (2024, July). From guidelines to governance: A study of AI policies in education. In *International Conference on Artificial Intelligence in Education* (pp. 299-307). Cham: Springer Nature Switzerland. https://doi.org/DOI: 10.1007/978-3-031-64312-5_36

Ghosh, D. (2024). Using AI for student success: Early warning, performance analytics, and automated grading in education cyber-physical systems. In Dutta, P. K., Raj, P., Sundaravadivazhagan, B., & Selvan, C. P. (Eds.), *Artificial intelligence solutions for cyber-physical systems* (pp. 236–243). Auerbach Publications., DOI: 10.1201/9781032694375-13

Ghoson, N. H., Meyrueis, V., Benfriha, K., Guiltat, T., & Loubere, S. (2025). A review on the static and dynamic risk assessment methods for OT cybersecurity in Industry 4.0. *Computers & Security*, *150*, 104295. Advance online publication. DOI: 10.1016/j.cose.2024.104295

Giannakos, M., & Cukurova, M. (2023). The role of learning theory in multimodal learning analytics. *British Journal of Educational Technology*, *54*(5), 1246–1267. DOI: 10.1111/bjet.13320

Gikandi, J. W., Morrow, D., & Davis, N. E. (2011). Online formative assessment in higher education: A review of the literature. *Computers & Education*, *57*(4), 2333 2351. DOI: 10.1016/j.compedu.2011.06.004

Gladwin, O. (2024). *Integrating AI into education: Designing pedagogies to enhance critical thinking and analytical skills*. Unpublished. DOI: 10.13140/RG.2.2.28378.56007

Gligorea, I., Cioca, M., Oancea, R., Gorski, A.-T., Gorski, H., & Tudorache, P. (2023). Adaptive learning using artificial intelligence in e-learning: A literature review. *Education Sciences*, *13*(12), 1216. DOI: 10.3390/educsci13121216

Goddard, K., Roudsari, A., & Wyatt, J. C. (2012). Automation bias: A systematic review of frequency, effect mediators, and mitigators. *Journal of the American Medical Informatics Association : JAMIA*, *19*(1), 121–127. DOI: 10.1136/amiajnl-2011-000089 PMID: 21685142

Goel, A. K., & Polepeddi, L. (2018). Jill Watson: A virtual teaching assistant for online education. In *Learning engineering for online education* (pp. 120-143). Routledge.

Goh, K. M., Mansor, M., Fuad, D. R. S. M., & Juharyanto, J. (2024). Designing Future-Ready Education: Criteria for AI Learning Tool Selection and AI Learning Design. *Semarak International Journal of Innovation in Learning and Education*, *4*(1), 1–12. DOI: 10.37934/sijile.4.1.112a

Goh, T. T. (2025). Learning management system log analytics: The role of persistence and consistency of engagement behaviour on academic success. *Journal of Computers in Education*, •••, 1–24. DOI: 10.1007/s40692-025-00358-x

Goldsteen, A., Ezov, G., Shmelkin, R., Moffie, M., & Farkash, A. (2022). Data minimization for GDPR compliance in machine learning models. *AI and Ethics*, *2*(3), 477–491. DOI: 10.1007/s43681-021-00095-8

Gomez, M. J., Armada Sanchez, A., Albaladejo-González, M., Garcia Clemente, F. J., & Ruipérez-Valiente, J. A. (2024, April). Utilizing explainable AI to enhance real-time student performance prediction in educational serious games. In *Proceedings of the 39th ACM/SIGAPP Symposium on Applied Computing* (pp. 93-94). https://doi.org/DOI: 10.1145/3605098.3636109

Gonzalez-DeHass, A. R. (2019). Self-regulated learning. *Parent Involvement for Motivated Learners*, 83-103. DOI: 10.4324/9781351021906-5

Gonzalez-Nucamendi, A., Noguez, J., Neri, L., Robledo-Rella, V., & García-Castelán, R. M. G. (2023, October). Predictive analytics study to determine undergraduate students at risk of dropout. *In Frontiers in Education (Vol. 8*, p. 1244686). Frontiers Media SA. https://doi.org/DOI: 10.3389/feduc.2023.1244686

Grajeda, A., Burgos, J., Cordova Olivera, P., & Sanjines, A. (2023). Assessing student-perceived impact of using artificial intelligence tools: Construction of a synthetic index of application in higher education. *Cogent Education*, *11*(1), 2287917. Advance online publication. DOI: 10.1080/2331186X.2023.2287917

Greene, D., Hoffmann, A. L., & Stark, L. (2019). "Better, Nicer, Clearer, Fairer: A Critical Assessment of the Movement for Ethical Artificial Intelligence and Machine Learning." *Proceedings of the 52nd Hawaii International Conference on System Sciences*. DOI: 10.24251/HICSS.2019.258

Green-Eneix, C., & Kohnke, L. (2025). GenAI and chatbots: Insights into AI and language teaching and learning, 240-260.

Gross, S., Mokbel, B., Hammer, B., & Pinkwart, N. (2015). Learning Feedback in Intelligent Tutoring Systems: Report of the FIT Project, Conducted from December 2011 to March 2015. *Kunstliche Intelligenz*, *29*(4), 413–418. DOI: 10.1007/s13218-015-0367-y

Grubaugh, S., & Levitt, G. (2024). Debate Centered Civics Education: Using AI to Teach Future Ready Skills and Better Prepare Students for College, Careers, and Civic Life. *Technium Social Sciences Journal*, *70*, 165–170. DOI: 10.47577/tssj.v70i1.12635

Grubov, V. V., Khramova, M. V., Goman, S., Badarin, A. A., Kurkin, S. A., Andrikov, D. A., Pitsik, E., Antipov, V., Petushok, E., Brusinskii, N., Bukina, T., Fedorov, A. A., & Hramov, A. E. (2024). Open-loop neuroadaptive system for enhancing student's cognitive abilities in learning. *IEEE Access : Practical Innovations, Open Solutions*, *12*, 49034–49049. DOI: 10.1109/ACCESS.2024.3383847

Guan, C., Mou, J., & Jiang, Z. (2020). Artificial intelligence innovation in education: A twenty-year data-driven historical analysis. *International Journal of Innovation Studies*, *4*(4), 134–147. DOI: 10.1016/j.ijis.2020.09.001

Gujjula, R., & Sanghera, K. (2023). Ethical considerations and data privacy in AI education. *Journal of Student-Scientists' Research, 5*. https://doi.org/DOI: 10.13021/jssr2023.3958

Gulikers, J. T. M., Bastiaens, T. J., & Kirschner, P. A. (2004). A five-dimensional framework for authentic assessment. *Educational Technology Research and Development, 52*(3), 67–86. DOI: 10.1007/BF02504676

Gunasekara, S., & Saarela, M. (2025). Explainable AI in Education: Techniques and Qualitative Assessment. *Applied Sciences (Basel, Switzerland), 15*(3), 1239. DOI: 10.3390/app15031239

Guo, H., Yi, W., & Liu, K. (2024). Enhancing constructivist learning: The role of generative AI in personalised learning experiences. *Proceedings of the 26th International Conference on Enterprise Information Systems*, 767-770. DOI: 10.5220/0012688700003690

Guo, K., & Li, D. (2024). Understanding EFL students' use of self-made AI chatbots as personalized writing assistance tools: A mixed methods study. *System, 124*, 103362. DOI: 10.1016/j.system.2024.103362

Gupta, T. (2024). Adaptive learning systems: Harnessing AI to personalize educational outcomes. *International Journal for Research in Applied Science and Engineering Technology, 12*(11), 458–464. DOI: 10.22214/ijraset.2024.65088

Gusrianto, E. & Iswahyuni. (2025). Exploring learning experience with ELSA speak for independent learning: A case study. In M. I. Sukardi, D. Ardhian, T. R. Indhiarti, V. A. Dwigantara, & T. B. Widagdo (Eds.), *Proceedings of the International Conference on Advances in Humanities, Education and Language (ICEL 2024)* (Vol. 913, pp. 219–229). Atlantis Press SARL. DOI: 10.2991/978-2-38476-388-7_20

H.R. 6791 - 118th Congress (2023): Artificial intelligence literacy act of 2023. (2023, December 15). https://www.congress.gov/bill/118th-congress/house-bill/6791

Hagendorff, T. (2022). A virtue-based framework to support putting AI ethics into practice. *Philosophy & Technology, 35*(3), 55. DOI: 10.1007/s13347-022-00553-z

Haji, S. A. (2020). Exploring the frequent use of the learning management systems (LMS) features and learners' interactions in higher education / Explorer L'UTILISATION FRÉQUENTE des FONCTIONNALITÉS des SYSTÈMES de GESTION de L'APPRENTISSAGE (LMS) et des interactions avec Les APPRENANTS dans L'ENSEIGNEMENT SUPÉRIEUR. *European Journal of Open Education and E-learning Studies, 5*(2). Advance online publication. DOI: 10.46827/ejoe.v5i2.3477

Hakkaraki, V. P. (2024). Exploring the Evolution of Bibliometric Analysis: A Comprehensive Study of Scientific Publications from 1974 to 2024 Using the Dimensions AI Database. *Asian Journal of Information Science and Technology*. DOI: 10.70112/ajist-2024.14.1.3878

Han, L., Du, B., Sun, L., Fu, Y., Lv, Y., & Xiong, H. (2021, August). Dynamic and multi-faceted spatio-temporal deep learning for traffic speed forecasting. In Proceedings of the 27th ACM SIGKDD conference on knowledge discovery & data mining (pp. 547-555). [HTML] DOI: 10.1145/3447548.3467275

Hanafi, A. M., Ahmed, M. S., Almansi, M. M., & Al-Sharif, O. A. (2025). Generative AI in academia: A comprehensive review of applications and implications for the research process. *International Journal of Engineering and Applied Sciences - October 6 University, 2*(1), 91–110.

Han, S. (2015). Book review: The Handbook of Automated Essay Evaluation: Current Applications and New Directions. *Language Testing, 32*(4), 543–545. DOI: 10.1177/0265532215576839

Hansson, T., & Berg, M. (2022). *Making better programmers: The impact of automated feedback on students.* DIVA. https://www.diva-portal.org/smash/record.jsf?pid=diva2%3A1703320&dswid=-2092

Hao, M., Wang, Y., & Peng, J. (2024). Empirical research on AI technology-supported precision teaching in high school science subjects. *Applied Sciences (Basel, Switzerland), 14*(17), 7544. DOI: 10.3390/app14177544

Harb, A., Khliefat, A., Alazaizeh, M. M., & Eyoun, K. (2024). Do personality traits predict students' interest and intentions toward working in the tourism and hospitality industry? Evidence from a developing country. [researchgate.net]. *Journal of Hospitality & Tourism Education, 36*(2), 165–181. DOI: 10.1080/10963758.2023.2175690

Harcourt, E., Loxley, J., & Stanson, B. (2024). Automated Learning of Fine-Grained Citation Patterns in Open Source Large Language Models. DOI: 10.31219/osf.io/xnesr

Harding, S. (1998). *Is Science Multicultural? Postcolonialisms, Feminisms, and Epistemologies.* Indiana University Press. DOI: 10.2979/2095.0

Harris, R. A., & Kazdağlı, H. (2025). Using TECHnology to predict the future of biomedical education. *FEBS Open Bio, 15*(1), 48–55. DOI: 10.1002/2211-5463.13953 PMID: 39666874

Hasan, M. A., Noor, N. F. M., Rahman, S. S. B. A., & Rahman, M. M. (2020). The transition from intelligent to affective tutoring system: A review and open issues. [ieee.org]. *IEEE Access : Practical Innovations, Open Solutions, 8*, 204612–204638. DOI: 10.1109/ACCESS.2020.3036990

Hatim Kagalwala. (2020). Personalized learning algorithms: Enhancing student engagement through AI-driven tools. *GLOBAL PERSPECTIVES: CROSS-DISCIPLINARY CONTRIBUTIONS TO MULTIDISCIPLINARY RESEARCH.* DOI: 10.25215/8198391754.29

Hattie, J., & Timperley, H. (2007). The power of feedback. *Review of Educational Research, 77*(1), 81–112. DOI: 10.3102/003465430298487

Haug, B. S., & Mork, S. M. (2021). Taking 21st century skills from vision to classroom: what teachers highlight as supportive professional development in the light of new demands from educational reforms. DOI: 10.1016/j.tate.2021.103286

Hayat, A. A., Keshavarzi, M. H., Zare, S., Bazrafcan, L., Rezaee, R., Faghihi, S. A., Amini, M., & Kojuri, J. (2021). Challenges and opportunities from the COVID-19 pandemic in medical education: A qualitative study. *BMC Medical Education, 21*(1), 247. DOI: 10.1186/s12909-021-02682-z

Hazzan-Bishara, A., Kol, O., & Levy, S. (2025). The factors affecting teachers' adoption of AI technologies: A unified model of external and internal determinants. *Education and Information Technologies, 30*(11), 15043–15069. Advance online publication. DOI: 10.1007/s10639-025-13393-z

He, X., & Kang, M. S. (2025). The application of ChatGPT in Chinese MTI students' autonomous learning. *Arab World English Journal (AWEJ) Special Issue on Artificial Intelligence, 17.*

Heffernan, N. T., & Heffernan, C. L. (2014). The ASSISTments Ecosystem: Building a Platform that Brings Scientists and Teachers Together for Minimally Invasive Research on Human Learning and Teaching. *International Journal of Artificial Intelligence in Education, 24*(4), 470–497. DOI: 10.1007/s40593-014-0024-x

Heider, F. (1958). *The psychology of interpersonal relations.* Wiley. DOI: 10.1037/10628-000

Heidt, A. (2023). Artificial-intelligence search engines wrangle academic literature. *Nature, 620*(7973), 456–457. DOI: 10.1038/d41586-023-01907-z

Hemachandran, K., Verma, P., Pareek, P., Arora, N., Rajesh Kumar, K. V., Ahanger, T. A., Pise, A. A., & Ratna, R. (2022). Artificial intelligence: A universal virtual tool to augment tutoring in higher education. *Computational Intelligence and Neuroscience, 2022*, 1410448. Advance online publication. DOI: 10.1155/2022/1410448

Hendijani, Z. D. (2025). Learning English through online platforms: An analysis of language learning methods via websites and educational platforms like coursera and edx compared to traditional teaching met. *TMP Universal Journal of Research and Review Archives, 4*(1). Advance online publication. DOI: 10.69557/ujrra.v4i1.151

Heng, K. (2024). Understanding Cambodian provincial university students' perspectives on Cambodia's vision to become a knowledge-based society. *SAGE Open, 14*(2), 1–14. DOI: 10.1177/21582440241242197

Heng, K., & Doeur, B. (2024). Cambodia's aspirations to become a knowledge-based society: Challenges and recommendations. *Policy Futures in Education, 22*(8), 1647–1661. DOI: 10.1177/14782103241234408

Heng, K., & Sol, K. (2022). Education: Key to making Cambodia great again. *Cambodian Journal of Educational Research, 4*(3), 1–18. https://kimkongheng.wordpress.com/2022/08/04/education-key-to-making-cambodia-great-again/. DOI: 10.62037/cjer.2022.02.02.01

Heng, K., Sol, K., & Em, S. (2023). COVID-19 and digital transformation of Cambodian higher education: Opportunities, challenges, and the way forward. In de Pablos, P. O., Zhang, X., & Almunawar, M. N. (Eds.), *Handbook of research on education institutions, skills, and jobs in the digital era* (pp. 307–327). IGI Global Scientific Publishing., DOI: 10.4018/978-1-6684-5914-0.ch018

Henrich, J. (2015). *The secret of our success: How culture is driving human evolution, domesticating our species, and making us smarter.* Princeton University Press. DOI: 10.2307/j.ctvc77f0d

Herath, H. M. S. S., Herath, H. M. K. K. M. B., Madhusanka, B. G. D. A., & Guruge, L. G. P. K. (2024). Data protection challenges in the processing of sensitive data. In *Data Protection: The Wake of AI and Machine Learning* (pp. 155–179). Springer Nature Switzerland., DOI: 10.1007/978-3-031-76473-8_8

Herminawati, S., & Ramli, M. (2024). Implementation of a problem-based learning model with the assistance of AI to improve students' critical thinking abilities and creativity. *Journal of Educational Innovation Research, 14*(2). https://www.researchgate.net/publication/389071816

Hernández-de-Menéndez, M., Morales-Menendez, R., Escobar, C. A., & Ramírez Mendoza, R. A. (2022). Learning analytics: State of the art. *International Journal on Interactive Design and Manufacturing*, *16*(3), 1209–1230. DOI: 10.1007/s12008-022-00930-0

Heyder, T., Passlack, N., & Posegga, O. (2023). Ethical management of human-AI interaction: Theory development review. *The Journal of Strategic Information Systems*, *32*(3), 101772. DOI: 10.1016/j.jsis.2023.101772

Hilali, K., Chergui, M., & Ammoumou, A. (2023). *Adaptive learning systems: A comprehensive overview and identification of challenges. Operations and Decisions*. ICTMOD.

Hillier, W., & Blog, W. (2023). The best guide to Predictive vs. prescriptive analytics. Career Foundry. https://careerfoundry.com/en/blog/data-analytics/predictive-vs-prescriptive-analytics/ Home[eXtyles2.1] -

Hlongwane, J., Shava, G. N., Mangena, A., & Muzari, T. (2024). Towards the integration of artificial intelligence in higher education, challenges and opportunities: The African context, a case of Zimbabwe. *International Journal of Resource Innovation and Social Sciences*, *8*(IIIS, 3S), 417–435. DOI: 10.47772/IJRISS.2024.803028S

Hmelo-Silver, C. E. (2004). Problem-based learning: What and how do students learn? *Educational Psychology Review*, *16*(3), 235–266. DOI: 10.1023/B:EDPR.0000034022.16470.f3

Hoffman, M. L. (2000). *Empathy and Moral Development: Implications for Caring and Justice*. Cambridge University Press. DOI: 10.1017/CBO9780511805851

Hofstede, G. (1980). Culture's consequences: International differences in work-related values. *Sage (Atlanta, Ga.)*.

Hofstede, G. (2001). *Culture's consequences: Comparing values, behaviors, institutions, and organizations across nations* (2nd ed.). Sage.

Hoke, T. (2025). Education for 21st Century Learners. In *Proceedings of the ICSDI 2024* Volume 2*: Proceedings of the 2nd International Conference on Sustainability: Developments and Innovations* (Vol. 2, p. 458). Springer Nature.

Holmes, W., Bialik, M., & Fadel, C. (2019). Artificial intelligence in education promises and implications for teaching and learning. Center for Curriculum Redesign. https://discovery.ucl.ac.uk/id/eprint/10139722

Holmes, W., Bialik, M., & Fadel, C. (2022). Artificial Intelligence in Education: Promises and Implications for Teaching and Learning.

Holmes, W., Bialik, M., & Fadel, C. (2023). Artificial intelligence in education. In *Data ethics: Building trust: How digital technologies can serve humanity*, 621-653. DOI: 10.58863/20.500.12424/4276068

Holmes, W., Bialik, M., & Fadel, C. (2023). *Artificial intelligence in education: Promises and implications for teaching and learning*. Center for Curriculum Redesign. https://curriculumredesign.org/publications/

Holmes, W., Bialik, M., & Fadel, C. (2019). *Artificial intelligence in education promises and implications for teaching and learning*. Center for Curriculum Redesign.

Holmes, W., Bialik, M., & Fadel, C. (2019). *Artificial intelligence in education: Promise and implications for teaching and learning*. Center for Curriculum Redesign.

Holmes, W., Bialik, M., & Fadel, C. (2019). *Artificial Intelligence in Education: Promises and Implications for Teaching and Learning*. Center for Curriculum Redesign.

Honson, V., Vu, T., Tran, T. P., & Tejada Estay, W. (2024). Using learning analytics to alleviate course and student support administrative load for large classes: A case study. *Journal of Work-Applied Management*, *16*(2), 303–315. DOI: 10.1108/JWAM-11-2023-0121

Hooda, M., Rana, C., Dahiya, O., Rizwan, A., & Hossain, M. S. (2022). Artificial intelligence for assessment and feedback to enhance student success in higher education. [wiley.com]. *Mathematical Problems in Engineering*, *2022*(1), 5215722. DOI: 10.1155/2022/5215722

Hooshyar, D., Weng, X., Sillat, P. J., Tammets, K., Wang, M., & Hämäläinen, R. (2024). The effectiveness of personalized technology-enhanced learning in higher education: A meta-analysis with association rule mining. *Computers & Education*, *223*, 105169. DOI: 10.1016/j.compedu.2024.105169

Hörmann, F. (2024), Generative artificial intelligence takes Siemens' predictive maintenance solution to the next level, press.siemens.com

Hoskinson, R. A., Jr. (2011). METHOD AND SYSTEM FOR GENERATING VISUAL REPRESENTATIONS OF DATA (Patent) [Patent]. In *Patent Application Publication*. United States. https://patents.google.com/patent/US20110153683A1/en

Hosseini, M., Jahanshahlou, F., Akbarzadeh, M., Zarei, M., & Vaez-Gharamaleki, Y. (2023). Formulating Research Questions for Evidence-Based Studies. *Journal of Medicine, Surgery, and Public Health*, *100046*. Advance online publication. DOI: 10.1016/j.glmedi.2023.100046

Howard, J. J., Rabbitt, L. R., & Sirotin, Y. B (2020). Human-algorithm teaming in face recognition: How algorithm outcomes cognitively bias human decision-making. Plos one. plos.org

Hua, J. H. (2023). Beyond exams: Investigating AI tool impact on student attitudes, ethical awareness, and academic dishonesty in online college assessments. *International Journal of Educational Management and Development Studies*, *4*(4), 160–185. https://ijemds.com/. DOI: 10.53378/353030

Huang, L. (2023). Ethics of artificial intelligence in education: Student privacy and data protection. *Science Insights Education Frontiers*, *16*(2), 2577–2587. DOI: 10.15354/sief.23.re202

Hur, J. W. (2024). Fostering AI literacy: Overcoming concerns and nurturing confidence among preservice teachers. *Information and Learning Science*. Advance online publication. DOI: 10.1108/ILS-11-2023-0170

Hussong, J., Mattheus, H., Wachs, S., Equit, M., & von Gontard, A. (2021). Evaluation of a bladder and bowel training program for therapy-resistant children with incontinence. [HTML]. *Journal of Pediatric Urology*, *17*(3), 302–e1. DOI: 10.1016/j.jpurol.2021.01.042

Huwer, J., Huwer, J., Irion, T., & Schaal, S. (2023). From TPACK to DPACK: The "Digitality-related pedagogical and content knowledge"-model in STEM-education. *Education Sciences, 13*(8), 769. DOI: 10.3390/educsci13080769

Hyperspace. (2023). AI-powered cross-cultural team simulations in virtual spaces. *Hyperspace News*. https://hyperspace.mv/ai-powered-cross-cultural-team-simulations-in-virtual-spaces/

Ibrahim, K. A. A. A., Kassem, M. A. M., & Lami, D (2024). … Assisted Language Assessment (ICALA) in philosophy-based language instruction: unraveling the effects on critical thinking, self-evaluation, academic resilience, and …. Language Testing in Asia. springer.com

Idowu, J. A. (2024). Debiasing education algorithms. *International Journal of Artificial Intelligence in Education, 34*(4), 1510–1540. DOI: 10.1007/s40593-023-00389-4

Ifenthaler, D., & Yau, J. Y.-K. (2020). Utilising learning analytics to support study success in higher education: A systematic review. *Educational Technology Research and Development, 68*(4), 1961–1990. DOI: 10.1007/s11423-020-09788-z

Ilegbusi, P. H. (2024). *The integration of Artificial intelligence (AI) in literature review and its potentials to revolutionize scientific knowledge acquisition. AfricArXiv*. DOI: 10.21428/3b2160cd.50b471d6

Ilić, M. P., Păun, D., Popović Šević, N., Hadžić, A., & Jianu, A. (2021). Needs and performance analysis for changes in higher education and implementation of artificial intelligence, machine learning, and extended reality. *Education Sciences, 11*(10), 1–21. DOI: 10.3390/educsci11100568

Ilić, M., Mikić, V., Kopanja, L., & Vesin, B. (2023). Intelligent techniques in e-learning: A literature review. *Artificial Intelligence Review, 56*(12), 14907–14953. DOI: 10.1007/s10462-023-10508-1

Indumathy, I., & Mujra, P. (2025). Sustainable Learning. *Smart Education and Sustainable Learning Environments in Smart Cities*, 381.

Inkeles, A., & Levinson, D. J. (1969). National character: The study of modal personality and sociocultural systems. In Lindzey, G., & Aronson, E. (Eds.), *The handbook of social psychology* (Vol. 4, pp. 418–506). Addison-Wesley.

Inspectorate of Government. (2022). *Annual performance report 2021/2022*. Government of Uganda. https://www.igg.go.ug/publications/annual-reports/

International Baccalaureate. (2025, March 6). *Artificial intelligence (AI) in learning, teaching, and assessment*. https://www.ibo.org/programmes/artificial-intelligence-ai-in-learning-teaching-and-assessment/

Iqbal, Q., & Ahmad, N. H. (2021). Sustainable development: The colors of sustainable leadership in a learning organization. *Sustainable Development (Bradford), 29*(1), 108–119. DOI: 10.1002/sd.2135

Irmert, N., Franco, C., & Isaksson, S. (2024). *The effects of generative AI on learning*. AEA Randomized Controlled Trials., DOI: 10.1257/rct.14930-1.0

Irons, A., & Elkington, S. (2021). Enhancing learning through formative assessment and feedback. sunderland.ac.uk

Ishrat, M., Khan, W., Faisal, S. M., Ansari, M. S. H., & Ahmad, F. (2025). Future Trends and Challenges for AI and Sustainability in TVET. *Integrating AI and Sustainability in Technical and Vocational Education and Training (TVET)*, 1-32.

Islam, R. B.Riyad Bin Islam. (2024). Strategic methods for emerging scholars: Identifying research gaps to enhance scholarly work. *World Journal Of Advanced Research and Reviews, 23*(3), 679–683. DOI: 10.30574/wjarr.2024.23.3.2711

Ismail, I. A., & Aloshi, J. M. (2024). Data privacy in AI-driven education: An in-depth exploration into the data privacy concerns and potential solutions. In Keeley, K. L. (Ed.), *AI applications and strategies in teacher education* (pp. 223–252). IGI Global Scientific Publishing., DOI: 10.4018/979-8-3693-5443-8.ch008

ITU. (2023). Measuring Digital Development: Facts and Figures.

Ivanashko, O., Kozak, A., Knysh, T., & Honchar, K. (2024). The role of artificial intelligence in shaping the future of education: Opportunities and challenges.

Jackson, D., & Michelson, G. (2022). Showcasing employability skills in higher education: A review of key frameworks and practices. *Higher Education Research & Development, 41*(2), 401–416.

Jackson, K. M., & Papa, R. (2024). Understanding artificial intelligence in education. In Jackson, K. M., & Papa, R. (Eds.), *AI changing the arc of educational leadership* (pp. 7–31). Springer., DOI: 10.1007/978-3-031-71415-3_2

Jafari, D., & Yazdi, Z. S. (2024). Transforming Education with AI: The Development of a Personalized Learning Algorithm for Individual Learning Styles. *Journal of Algorithms and Computation, 56*(2), 135–150.

Jagals, D. (2025). Metacognition: The cognitive and affective architecture of self-directed learning. *NWU Self-Directed Learning Series*, 1-19. DOI: 10.4102/aosis.2024.BK484.01

Jain, M. (2023). Artificial intelligence: A powerful ally in elevating the productivity and quality of research for aspiring scholars. *International Journal of Multidisciplinary Trends, 5*(7), 09–13. DOI: 10.22271/multi.2023.v5.i7a.314

Jaiswal, A., & Arun, C. J. (2021). Potential of Artificial Intelligence for transformation of the education system in India. [ed.gov]. *International Journal of Education and Development Using Information and Communication Technology, 17*(1), 142–158.

Jantakun, T., Jantakun, K., & Jantakoon, T. (2024). Bibliometric Analysis of Artificial Intelligence in STEM Education. *Higher Education Studies, 15*(1), 69. DOI: 10.5539/hes.v15n1p69

Jauhiainen, J. S., & Garagorry Guerra, A. (2024, November). Generative AI and education: dynamic personalization of pupils' school learning material with ChatGPT. *In Frontiers in Education (Vol. 9,* p. 1288723). Frontiers Media SA. https://doi.org/DOI: 10.3389/feduc.2024.1288723

Jeon, J. H. (2021). Chatbot-assisted dynamic assessment (CA-DA) for L2 vocabulary learning and diagnosis. *Computer Assisted Language Learning, 36*(7), 1338–1364. DOI: 10.1080/09588221.2021.1987272

Jia, F., Sun, D., Qian, M., & Looi, C. (2022). Developing an AI-based learning system for L2 learners' authentic and ubiquitous learning in English language. *Sustainability (Basel), 14*(23), 15527. DOI: 10.3390/su142315527

Jiang, N., Liu, X., Liu, H., Lim, E. T. K., Tan, C.-W., & Gu, J. (2023). Beyond AI-powered context-aware services: The role of human–AI collaboration. *Industrial Management & Data Systems, 123*(11), 2771–2802. DOI: 10.1108/IMDS-03-2022-0152

Jin, S. (2022). The effects of self-directed learning through an AI speaking application in an EFL speaking class on learners' self-directed learning ability and speaking skills. *Studies in English Education, 27*(3), 381–414. DOI: 10.22275/SEE.27.3.07

Jobin, A., Ienca, M., & Vayena, E. (2019). The global landscape of AI ethics guidelines. *Nature Machine Intelligence, 1*(9), 389–399. DOI: 10.1038/s42256-019-0088-2

Johannes, C., & Haase, A. (2022). The impact of feedback mode on learning gain and self-efficacy: A quasi-experimental study. *Active Learning in Higher Education, 25*(3), 391–407. DOI: 10.1177/14697874221131970

Jomaa, N. J., Attamimi, R., & Al Mahri, M. (2025). The use of artificial intelligence (AI) in teaching English vocabulary in Oman: Perspectives, teaching practices, and challenges. *World Journal of English Language, 15*(3), 1–13. DOI: 10.5430/wjel.v15n3p1

Jonassen, D., Spector, M. J., Driscoll, M., Merrill, M. D., Van Merrienboer, J., & Driscoll, M. P. (2008). *Handbook of research on educational communications and technology*. Routledge., DOI: 10.4324/9780203880869

Jones, E. E., & Davis, K. E. (1965). From acts to dispositions: The attribution process in social psychology. *Advances in Experimental Social Psychology, 2*, 219–266. DOI: 10.1016/S0065-2601(08)60107-0

Jones, K. M. (2019). Learning analytics and higher education: A proposed model for establishing informed consent mechanisms to promote student privacy and autonomy. *International Journal of Educational Technology in Higher Education, 16*(1), 1–22. DOI: 10.1186/s41239-019-0155-0

Jonker, A., & Rogers, J. (2025). What is algorithmic bias? IBM. https://www.ibm.com/think/topics/algorithmic-bias#:~:text=Algorithmic%20bias%20occurs%20when%20systematic,produce%20unfair%20or%20discriminatory%20outcomes

Jopp, D. S., & Cohen, M. (2023). Developing reflective AI learners through ePortfolios: Evidence from interdisciplinary coursework. *International Journal of Educational Technology in Higher Education, 20*(1). Advance online publication. DOI: 10.1186/s41239-023-00378-7

Jordan, M. I., & Mitchell, T. M. (2015). Machine learning: Trends, perspectives, and prospects. *Science, 349*(6245), 255–260. DOI: 10.1126/science.aaa8415

Jose, D. (2024). Data privacy and security concerns in AI-integrated educational platforms. *Recent trends in Management and Commerce, 5*(2), 87-91. DOI: 10.46632/rmc/5/2/19

Jowallah, R. J. (2023). Integrating artificial intelligence (AI) into the curriculum. *Advances in Educational Technologies and Instructional Design*, •••, 355–368. DOI: 10.4018/979-8-3693-0074-9.ch015

Jung, C. (2017). The effects of a self-directed learning-enhancement program on nursing students' self-directed learning abilities, self-efficacy, empowerment, and clinical practice competency. *Asia-pacific Journal of Multimedia services convergent with Art. Humanity & Society*, *7*(10), 319–329. DOI: 10.14257/AJMAHS.2017.10.47

Jurado-Castro, J. M., Vargas-Molina, S., Gomez-Urquiza, J. L., & Benitez-Porres, J. (2023). Effectiveness of real-time classroom interactive competition on academic performance: A systematic review and meta-analysis. *PeerJ. Computer Science*, *9*, e1310. DOI: 10.7717/peerj-cs.1310

Kagaba, C. (2015). *Combating real and perceived corruption in Uganda's judiciary.* Anti-Corruption Coalition Uganda. https://www.judiciary.go.ug/files/downloads/Combating%20Real%20and%20Perceived%20Corruption%20by%20Cissy%20Kagaba.pdf

Kahmann, R., Droop, M., & Lazonder, A. W. (2022). Meta-analysis of professional development programs in differentiated instruction. *International Journal of Educational Research*, *116*, 102072. DOI: 10.1016/j.ijer.2022.102072

Kahneman, D., & Tversky, A. (1979). Prospect theory: An analysis of decision under risk. *Econometrica*, *47*(2), 263–291. DOI: 10.2307/1914185

Kaluya, M. D., & Elliott, E. W. (2018). Corruption in Uganda: A comparative study of citizens' and public officials' perceptions. *African Social Science Review*, *9*(1), 4. https://digitalcommons.kennesaw.edu/assr

Kamalov, F., Santandreu Calonge, D., & Gurrib, I. (2023). New era of artificial intelligence in education: Towards a sustainable multifaceted revolution. *Sustainability (Basel)*, *15*(16), 12451. DOI: 10.3390/su151612451

Karaman, Z. T. (2022). An understanding of inter and transcisciplìary aspects of urman resilience. https://www.scirp.org/journal/paperinformation?paperid=116576

Karampela, M., Isomursu, M., Porat, T., Maramis, C., Mountford, N., Giunti, G., Chouvarda, I., & Lehocki, F. (2019). The Extent and Coverage of Current Knowledge of Connected Health: Systematic Mapping Study. *Journal of Medical Internet Research*, *21*(9), e14394. Advance online publication. DOI: 10.2196/14394

Karataş, F., & Aksu Ataç, B. (2025). When TPACK meets artificial intelligence: Analyzing TPACK and AI-TPACK components through structural equation modelling. *Education and Information Technologies*, *30*(7), 8979–9004. DOI: 10.1007/s10639-024-13164-2

Kartik, M., & Follow. (2025). Machine learning algorithms. Geeks forGeeks. https://www.geeksforgeeks.org/machine-learning-algorithms/

Kasthuri, H., Kamreddy, A., & Mandadi, S. (2025). Reimagine Education. *Available at SSRN* 5176532.

Kaswan, K. S., Dhatterwal, J. S., & Ojha, R. P. (2024). AI in personalized learning. In *Advances in technological innovations in higher education* (pp. 103–117). CRC Press. DOI: 10.1201/9781003376699-9

Kasztelnik, K. (2024). Artificial intelligence-assisted curriculum development: Innovations in designing educational content for the 21st century learner. *Journal of Higher Education Theory and Practice*, *24*(11). Advance online publication. DOI: 10.33423/jhetp.v24i11.7367

Katchapakirin, K., Anutariya, C., & Supnithi, T. (2022). ScratchThAI: A conversation-based learning support framework for computational thinking development. [springer.com]. *Education and Information Technologies*, *27*(6), 8533–8560. DOI: 10.1007/s10639-021-10870-z

Katona, J., & Gyonyoru, K. I. K. (2025). AI-based Adaptive Programming Education for Socially Disadvantaged Students: Bridging the Digital Divide. *TechTrends*, *69*(5), 1–18. DOI: 10.1007/s11528-025-01088-8

Katono, I. W., & Kyakulumbye, S. (2025). 12. Constraints to the adoption of blended learning in higher education institutions in an emerging market context: the case of Uganda. *Research Handbook on Information Systems and Technology*, 210-231. DOI: DOI: 10.4337/9781035324583.00019

Katono, I. W. (2016). Ethically questionable behavior and consumerism in Uganda: A survey of university students. In Gbadamosi, A. (Ed.), *Handbook of research on consumerism and buying behavior in developing nations* (pp. 334–361). IGI Global., DOI: 10.4018/978-1-5225-0282-1.ch015

Kawatra, M. B. (2024). Evolution of AI in Academic Research. In Srivastava, A., & Agarwal, S. (Eds.), *Utilizing AI Tools in Academic Research Writing* (pp. 18–22). IGI Global Scientific Publishing., DOI: 10.4018/979-8-3693-1798-3.ch002

Kayyali, M. (2025). AI in Higher Education: Revolutionizing Curriculum and Administration. In *AI Adoption and Diffusion in Education* (pp. 31-62). IGI Global Scientific Publishing.

Kayyali, M. (2025). AI in Higher Education: Revolutionizing Curriculum and Administration. In AI Adoption and Diffusion in Education (pp. 31-62). IGI Global.

Kayyali, M. (2025a). AI in Higher Education: Revolutionizing Curriculum and Administration. In AI Adoption and Diffusion in Education (pp. 31-62). IGI Global Scientific Publishing.

Kazin, C. (2022). Fostering Learner Agency Through Intentional Learning Design: Six Principles. In A. Brower & R. Specht-Boardman (Eds.), *New Models of Higher Education: Unbundled, Rebundled, Customized,* and DIY (pp. 1-16). IGI Global Scientific Publishing. DOI: 10.4018/978-1-6684-3809-1.ch001

Kaziya, K. (2025). Adopting Differentiated Instruction in High School Mathematics Classrooms: Challenges and Successes in Kalomo District, Zambia. *International Journal of Research and Innovation in Social Science*, *9*(4), 5479–5506. DOI: 10.47772/IJRISS.2025.90400391

Kazmi, S. M. A., Kazmi, A., & Arava, A. (2024). Adaptability of IBM Watson Cloud Platform to Develop Machine Learning Models for Predicting Students' Academic Stress. DOI: 10.1109/ISEC61299.2024.10664767

Kelley, H. H. (1967). Attribution theory in social psychology. In Levine, D. (Ed.), *Nebraska symposium on motivation* (Vol. 15, pp. 192–238). University of Nebraska Press.

Kem, D. (2022). Personalised and adaptive learning: Emerging learning platforms in the era of digital and smart learning. [researchgate.net]. *International Journal of Social Science and Human Research, 5*(2), 385–391. DOI: 10.47191/ijsshr/v5-i2-02

Kennedy, K. J., & Sundberg, D. (2020). Teachers and curriculum change: Emerging responses to new professional responsibilities. *Journal of Curriculum Studies, 52*(3), 261–275. DOI: 10.1080/00220272.2020.1734667

Kennedy, T. J., & Sundberg, C. W. (2020). 21st Century Skills. In Akpan, B., & Kennedy, T. J. (Eds.), *Science Education in Theory and Practice. Springer Texts in Education.* Springer., DOI: 10.1007/978-3-030-43620-9_32

Ke, Y. (2024). ASEAN Four's middle-income trap dilemma: Evidence of the middle technology trap. *Asian Review of Political Economy, 3*(1), 1–29. DOI: 10.1007/s44216-024-00033-5

Khairullah, S. A., Harris, S., Hadi, H., Sandhu, R. A., Ahmad, N., & Alshara, M. (2025). Implementing artificial intelligence in academic and administrative processes through responsible strategic leadership in the higher education institutions. *Frontiers in Education, 10*, 1548104. DOI: 10.3389/feduc.2025.1548104

Khalifa, M., & Albadawy, M. (2024). Using Artificial Intelligence in Academic Writing and Research: An Essential Productivity Tool. *Computer Methods and Programs in Biomedicine Update, 5*, 100145. DOI: 10.1016/j.cmpbup.2024.100145

Khan Academy. (2023, March 14). *Khan Academy announces GPT-4 powered learning guide* [Video]. YouTube. https://www.youtube.com/watch?v=yEgHrxvLsz0

Khan, A. A., & Iqbal, M. (2024). Integrating PBL and AI tools in biomedical engineering education: A case study approach. arXiv Preprint. https://arxiv.org/abs/2503.16558

Khan, A., Ayega, D., Aguilar, I., & Baker, R. (2020). *The digital tutor and student engagement techniques: An intelligent way to engage students in ITS.* Innovate Learning Summit. [HTML]

Khan, M., Gai, S., & Yan, H. (2024). Integrating artificial intelligence in research methods: Exploring current platforms. In *Advanced Research Methods for Applied Psychology* (2nd ed., p. 19). Routledge., DOI: 10.4324/9781003362715-6

Khatun, M., Islam, R., Kumar, S., Hossain, R., & Mani, L. (2024). The impact of artificial intelligence on educational transformation: Trends and future directions. Journal of information systems and informatics, 6(4), 2347-2373. DOI: DOI: 10.51519/journalisi.v6i4.879

Khieng, S., Madhur, S., & Chhem, R. (Eds.). (2015). *Cambodia education 2015: Employment and empowerment.* Cambodia Development Resource Institute.

Khine, M. S. (2024). AI in teaching and learning and intelligent tutoring systems. *Artificial Intelligence in Education*, 467-570. DOI: 10.1007/978-981-97-9350-1_4

Khine, M. S. (2024). Ethics, and the Future of Education in an AI-Driven World. In *Artificial Intelligence in Education: A Machine-Generated Literature Overview* (pp. 629–735). Springer Nature Singapore. DOI: 10.1007/978-981-97-9350-1_6

Khor, E. T., & K, M. (2024). A Systematic Review of the Role of Learning Analytics in Supporting Personalized Learning. *Education Sciences, 14*(1), 51. DOI: 10.3390/educsci14010051

King, J. (2023). *An Innovative Exploration of Psychological Research Methods Driven by Artificial Intelligence: A Case Study Using Facial Expression Technique to Improve Teenagers' Self Awareness*. International Journal of Education and Humanities., DOI: 10.54097/ijeh.v11i1.13155

Kirya, M. T., & Sekalala, S. (2022). Countering corruption to promote social justice in the Global Fund to Fight AIDS, Tuberculosis and Malaria: The case of Uganda. In Singh, P., & Şule, F. P. (Eds.), *Beyond law and development* (pp. 240–256). Routledge., DOI: 10.4324/9780203745298-15

Kitamura, Y. (2016). Higher education in Cambodia: Challenges to promote greater access and higher quality. In Collins, C. S., Lee, M. N. N., Hawkins, J. N., & Neubauer, D. E. (Eds.), *The Palgrave handbook of Asia Pacific higher education* (pp. 365–380)., DOI: 10.1057/978-1-137-48739-1_24

Klein, J. T. (2019). Beyond interdisciplinarity: Transforming the curriculum in higher education. *The Journal of General Education, 68*(1–2), 102–120. DOI: 10.5325/jgeneeduc.68.1-2.0102

Knight, J. (2013). *The changing landscape of higher education internationalisation – for better or worse? Perspectives*. Policy and Practice in Higher Education.

Koedinger, K. R., D'Mello, S., McLaughlin, E. A., Pardos, Z. A., & Rosé, C. P. (2015). Data mining and education. *Wiley Interdisciplinary Reviews: Cognitive Science, 6*(4), 333–353. DOI: 10.1002/wcs.1350

Koehler, M. J., Mishra, P., & Cain, W. (2013). What is technological pedagogical content knowledge (TPACK)? *Journal of Education, 193*(3), 13–19. DOI: 10.1177/002205741319300303

Kohnke, L., & Zou, D. (2025). The role of ChatGPT in enhancing English teaching: A paradigm shift in lesson planning and instructional practices. *Journal of Educational Technology & Society, 28*(3), 4–20.

Kolchenko, V. (2018). Can modern AI replace teachers? Not so fast! Artificial intelligence and adaptive learning: Personalized education in the AI age. *HAPS Educator, 22*(3), 249–252. DOI: 10.21692/haps.2018.032

Kolluru, V., Mungara, S., & Chintakunta, A. N. (2018). Adaptive learning systems: Harnessing AI for customized educational experiences. *International Journal of Computer Science and Information Technologies, 6*(3), 13–26. DOI: 10.5121/ijcsity.2018.6302

Komljenovic, J (2022). The future of value in digitalised higher education: why data privacy should not be our biggest concern. Higher Education. springer.com

Kooli, C (2023). Chatbots in education and research: A critical examination of ethical implications and solutions. Sustainability. mdpi.com

Korucu-Kış, S. (2024). Zone of proximal creativity: An empirical study on EFL teachers' use of ChatGPT for enhanced practice. *Thinking Skills and Creativity, 54*, 101639. DOI: 10.1016/j.tsc.2024.101639

Kosinski, M. (2025), What is black box AI and how does it work? IBM. https://www.ibm.com/think/topics/black-box-ai

Kovari, A. (2025). Ethical use of ChatGPT in education—Best practices to combat AI-induced plagiarism. *Frontiers in Education*, *9*, 1465703. Advance online publication. DOI: 10.3389/feduc.2024.1465703

Krahnke, K. J., & Krashen, S. D. (1983). Principles and practice in second language acquisition. *TESOL Quarterly*, *17*(2), 300. DOI: 10.2307/3586656

Krauss, C., Streicher, A., Poxleitner, E., Altun, D., Müller, J., An, T. S., & Müller, C. (2023, June). Best-of-breed: Service-oriented integration of artificial intelligence in interoperable educational ecosystems. In *International Workshop on Learning Technology for Education Challenges* (pp. 267–283). Cham: Springer Nature Switzerland. https://doi.org/DOI: 10.1007/978-3-031-34754-2_22

Kristjánsson, K. (2015). *Aristotelian Character Education*. Routledge. DOI: 10.4324/9781315752747

Kristjánsson, K. (2022). Teaching *phronesis* to aspiring police officers: Some preliminary philosophical, developmental and pedagogical reflections. *International Journal of Ethics Education*, *7*(2), 289–305. DOI: 10.1007/s40889-022-00145-7

Krstić, L., Aleksić, V., & Krstić, M. (2022). Artificial intelligence in education. *RE:view*, 223–228. Advance online publication. DOI: 10.46793/TIE22.223K

Kuhail, M. A., Alturki, N., Alramlawi, S., & Alhejori, K. (2023). Interacting with educational chatbots: A systematic review. *Education and Information Technologies*, *28*(1), 973–1018. DOI: 10.1007/s10639-022-11177-3

Kuleto, V., Ilić, M., Dumangiu, M., Ranković, M., Martins, O. M. D., Păun, D., & Mihoreanu, L. (2021). Exploring opportunities and challenges of artificial intelligence and machine learning in higher education institutions. *Sustainability (Basel)*, *13*(18), 1–16. DOI: 10.3390/su131810424

Kulik, J. A., & Fletcher, J. D. (2016). Effectiveness of intelligent tutoring systems: A meta-analytic review. *Review of Educational Research*, *86*(1), 42–78. DOI: 10.3102/0034654315581420

Kumar, A., Kumar, A., Bhoyar, S., & Mishra, A. K. (2024). Does ChatGPT foster academic misconduct in the future? *Public Administration and Policy*, *27*(2), 140–153. DOI: 10.1108/PAP-05-2023-0061

Kung, J. Y. (2023). Elicit (product review). *The Journal of the Canadian Health Libraries Association*, *44*(1). Advance online publication. DOI: 10.29173/jchla29657

Kurt, V. (2017). Intelligent tutoring systems for continuous, embedded assessment. *The Future of Assessment*, 113-138. DOI: 10.4324/9781315086545-5

Kush, J. C. (2025). Integrating sensor technologies with conversational AI: Enhancing context-sensitive interaction through real-time data fusion. *Sensors (Basel)*, *25*(1), 249. DOI: 10.3390/s25010249

Kussmaul, C., & Pirmann, T. (2021). Guided inquiry learning with technology: Investigations to support social constructivism. *Proceedings of the 13th International Conference on Computer Supported Education*, 483-490. DOI: 10.5220/0010458104830490

Kusters, R., Misevic, D., Berry, H., Cully, A., Le Cunff, Y., Dandoy, L., Díaz-Rodríguez, N., Ficher, M., Grizou, J., Othmani, A., Palpanas, T., Komorowski, M., Loiseau, P., Moulin Frier, C., Nanini, S., Quercia, D., Sebag, M., Soulié Fogelman, F., Taleb, S., & Wehbi, F. (2020). Interdisciplinary Research in Artificial Intelligence: Challenges and Opportunities. *Frontiers in Big Data*, *3*, 577974. DOI: 10.3389/fdata.2020.577974

Kuzhabekova, A., Moldashev, K., Baigazina, A., & Chanchem, V. (2024). Readjustment of returning scholars: Experiences of Cambodian researchers. *Minerva*, *62*(3), 457–479. DOI: 10.1007/s11024-024-09522-6

Kyambade, M., & Namatovu, A. (2025). Health-care leaders' perspectives on AI implementation in Uganda: Overcoming barriers, driving innovation and strategic considerations. *Leadership in Health Services*, *38*(2), 299–317. DOI: 10.1108/LHS-06-2024-0052

Kyza, E. A., & Georgiou, Y. (2025). Curriculum Redesign to Increase Equity and Promote Active Citizenship in Science Education. *Education Sciences*, *15*(3), 319. DOI: 10.3390/educsci15030319

Labib, L. N., & ElSabry, E. (2024). Integrating AI Into Higher Education. *Advances in Wireless Technologies and Telecommunication Book Series*, 1–30. DOI: 10.4018/979-8-3373-1132-6.ch001

Lai, W. Y. W., & Lee, J. S. (2024). A systematic review of conversational AI tools in ELT: Publication trends, tools, research methods, learning outcomes, and antecedents. *Computers and Education: Artificial Intelligence*, *6*, 100291. DOI: 10.1016/j.caeai.2024.100291

Larsen, V. G., Tollin, N., Sattrup, P. A., Birkved, M., & Holmboe, T. (2022). What are the challenges in assessing circular economy for the built environment? A literature review on integrating LCA, LCC and S-LCA in life cycle sustainability assessment (LCSA). *Journal of Building Engineering*, *50*, 104203. DOI: 10.1016/j.jobe.2022.104203

Latifi, S., & Gierl, M. (2021). Automated scoring of junior and senior high essays using Coh-Metrix features: Implications for large-scale language testing. *Language Testing*, *38*(1), 62–85. DOI: 10.1177/0265532220929918

Lau, S., & Perez, J. (2024). Global virtual teams projects and developing AI literacy: A mixed-methods study on preparing students for the international technology-infused workplace. *International Journal of Educational Technology and Global Learning*. https://www.researchgate.net/publication/388222830

Lawrence, J., & Reed, C. (2019). Argument Mining: A Survey. *Computational Linguistics*, *42*(4), 765–818. DOI: 10.1162/coli_a_00364

Lawrence, S. S., Othmani, S., & Dalwai, T. (2024). Toward a knowledge-based economy: Empowering higher education in Oman with AI for Vision 2040 achievement. In El-Masri, M. A., & Madbouly, A. (Eds.), *Finance and law in the metaverse world* (pp. 133–142). Springer., DOI: 10.1007/978-3-031-67547-8_12

Leask, B. (2015). *Internationalizing the Curriculum*. Routledge. DOI: 10.4324/9781315716954

Lee, J., & Cho, J. (2024). Artificial Intelligence Curriculum Development for Intelligent System Experts in University. *International Journal on Advanced Science, Engineering and Information Technology*, *14*(2), 409–419. DOI: 10.18517/ijaseit.14.2.18860

Leguisamo, M., Posada, G. J., Pilco-Chambilla, F. W., & Mena, M. I. (2025). Personalization of Learning through Artificial Intelligence: An Analysis of Adaptive Models in Digital Education. *Journal of Information Systems Engineering & Management*, *10*(30s), 836–846. Advance online publication. DOI: 10.52783/jisem.v10i30s.4922

Leong, W. Y., Leong, Y. Z., & Leong, W. S. (2025). Artificial Intelligence in education. *IET Conference Proceedings.*, 2024(22), 183–184. DOI: 10.1049/icp.2024.4341

Leu, D. J., Kinzer, C. K., Coiro, J., Castek, J., & Henry, L. A. (2017). New literacies: A dual-level theory of the changing nature of literacy, instruction, and assessment. *Journal of Education*, *197*(2), 1–18. DOI: 10.1177/002205741719700202

Li, S. (2023). Personalized tutoring and support. *Learning Analytics Enhanced Online Learning Support*, 144-175. DOI: 10.4324/9781032637044-5

Liang, W., To, J., & Lo, Y. Y. (2024). A journey towards teacher empowerment in differentiated Instruction: Implications for a Sustainable Teacher Professional Development Model. *Asia Pacific Education Review*, ●●●, 1–13. DOI: 10.1007/s12564-024-09977-y

Li, L., Chen, C. P., Wang, L., Liang, K., & Bao, W. (2023). Exploring artificial intelligence in smart education: Real-time classroom behavior analysis with embedded devices. *Sustainability (Basel)*, *15*(10), 7940. Advance online publication. DOI: 10.3390/su15107940

Lin, C. C., Huang, A. Y. Q., & Lu, O. H. T (2023). Artificial intelligence in intelligent tutoring systems toward sustainable education: a systematic review. Smart Learning Environments. springer.com

Lindsay, E. D., Johri, A., & Bjerva, J. (2025). A framework for responsible development of automated student feedback with generative AI. In *Proceedings of the IEEE Global Engineering Education Conference (EDUCON 2025): Special Session: Generative AI and Ethical Integration in Higher Education* (pp. ...). IEEE Press. https://doi.org/DOI: 10.1109/EDUCON62633.2025.11016572

Lin, J., Singh, S., Sha, L., Tan, W., Lang, D., Gašević, D., & Chen, G. (2022). Is it a good move? Mining effective tutoring strategies from human–human tutorial dialogues. [github.io]. *Future Generation Computer Systems*, *127*, 194–207. DOI: 10.1016/j.future.2021.09.001

Lin, M. P.-C., Liu, A. L., Poitras, E., Chang, M., & Chang, D. H. (2024). An Exploratory Study on the Efficacy and Inclusivity of AI Technologies in Diverse Learning Environments. *Sustainability (Basel)*, *16*(20), 8992. DOI: 10.3390/su16208992

Lippert, A., Shubeck, K., Morgan, B., Hampton, A., & Graesser, A. (2020). Multiple agent designs in conversational intelligent tutoring systems. Technology [ed.gov]. *Knowledge and Learning*, *25*(3), 443–463. DOI: 10.1007/s10758-019-09431-8

Lipton, Z. C. (2018). The Mythos of Model Interpretability. *Communications of the ACM*, *61*(10), 36–43. DOI: 10.1145/3233231

Li, R., & Wu, T. (2025). Evolution of Artificial Intelligence in Medical Education From 2000 to 2024: Bibliometric Analysis. *Interactive Journal of Medical Research, 14*(1), e63775. DOI: 10.2196/63775 PMID: 39883926

Li, S. Y. K., & Tsui, E. (2024). Introduction to data/text mining. In *Handbook on Information Sciences*. Edward Elgar Publishing., DOI: 10.4337/9781035343706.00023

Liu, B., Zhang, J., Lin, F., Jia, X., & Peng, M. (2025, May). One size doesn't fit all: A personalized conversational tutoring agent for mathematics instruction. In *Companion Proceedings of the ACM on Web Conference 2025* (pp. 2401-2410). https://doi.org/DOI: 10.1145/3701716.3717527

Liu, Y. (2024). Using AI technology to create an inclusive environment for diverse online learners. In Kyei-Blankson, L., Keengwe, J., & Ntuli, E. (Eds.), *Designing Equitable and Accessible Online Learning Environments*. IGI Global., DOI: 10.4018/979-8-3693-0268-2.ch006

Liu, Y. (2025). Voiceless Algorithms: Examining equity implications of AI-driven educational reforms from student lens. In Taukeni, S. G., & Mollaoğlu, M. (Eds.), *Integrating the Biopsychosocial Model in Education*. IGI Global., DOI: 10.4018/979-8-3693-3707-3

Liu, Y., & Curtin, J. (2025). Sustainability in Higher Education - Integrating Leadership, Policy, and Teaching Practices for a Brighter Future. In Taukeni, S. G., & Mollaoğlu, M. (Eds.), *Higher Education and Quality Assurance Practices*. IGI Global., DOI: 10.4018/979-8-3693-6765-0

Livanis, E., Voultsos, P., Vadikolias, K., Pantazakos, P., & Tsaroucha, A. (2024). Understanding the ethical issues of Brain-Computer Interfaces (BCIs): A blessing or the beginning of a dystopian future? *Cureus, 16*(4), e58243. DOI: 10.7759/cureus.58243 PMID: 38745805

Li, Z., Wang, C., & Bonk, C. J. (2024). Exploring the utility of ChatGPT for self-directed online language learning. *Online Learning : the Official Journal of the Online Learning Consortium, 28*(3). Advance online publication. DOI: 10.24059/olj.v28i3.4497

Lok, S., & Feiner, S. (2005). *A Survey of Automated Layout Techniques for Information Presentations*. http://csis.pace.edu/%7Emarchese/CS835/Lec7/lok01survey.pdf

London School of International Business. (2025). *Professional Certificate in AI-Infused Curriculum Design*. https://www.lsib.co.uk/2022/course-details.aspx?CourseTitle=Professional+Certificate+in+AIInfused+Curriculum+Design

Looi, C. K., & Jia, F. (2025). Personalization capabilities of current technology chatbots in a learning environment: An analysis of student-tutor bot interactions. *Education and Information Technologies, 30*(10), 1–31. DOI: 10.1007/s10639-025-13369-z

Lopez-Huertas, M. (2013). Reflexions on multidimensional knowledge: Its influence on the foundation of knowledge organization. *Knowledge Organization, 40*(6), 400–407. DOI: 10.5771/0943-7444-2013-6-400

Lorenz, U., & Romeike, R. (2023). What Is AI-PACK? – Outline of AI competencies for teaching with DPACK. In J.-P. Pellet & G. Parriaux (Eds.), *Informatics in Schools. Beyond bits and bytes: Nurturing informatics intelligence in education* (Vol. 14296, pp. 13–25). Springer Nature Switzerland. DOI: 10.1007/978-3-031-44900-0_2

Lu, K., Hao, L., Wang, I. J., & Liu, A. (2024, July). Eighth Graders and a Math Intelligent Tutoring System: A Deep Neural Network Analysis. In *International Conference on Artificial Intelligence in Education* (pp. 38-46). Cham: Springer Nature Switzerland. https://doi.org/DOI: 10.1007/978-3-031-64312-5_5

Luan, H., Geczy, P., Lai, H., Gobert, J., Yang, S. J. H., Ogata, H., Baltes, J., Guerra, R., Li, P., & Tsai, C.-C. (2020). Challenges and future directions of big data and artificial intelligence in education. *Frontiers in Psychology*, *11*, 1–10. DOI: 10.3389/fpsyg.2020.580820

Luckin, R. (2017). Towards artificial intelligence-based assessment systems. *Nature Human Behaviour, 1*, 0028.

Luckin, R., & Holmes, W. (2016). *Intelligence Unleashed: An argument for AI in Education.* Pearson. https://static.googleusercontent.com/media/edu.google.com/en/pdfs/Intelligence-Unleashed-Publication.pdf

Luckin, R., & Holmes, W. (2016). Intelligence unleashed: An argument for AI in education. URI: https://discovery.ucl.ac.uk/id/eprint/1475756

Luckin, R., Holmes, W., Griffiths, M., & Forcier, L. B. (2016). Intelligence Unleashed: An Argument for AI in Education. Pearson. https://static.googleusercontent.com/media/edu.google.com/en//pdfs/Intelligence-Unleashed-Publication.pdf

Luckin, R., Holmes, W., Griffiths, M., & Forcier, L. B. (2016). *Intelligence unleashed: An argument for AI in education*. Pearson. https://static.googleusercontent.com/media/edu.google.com/en//pdfs/Intelligence-Unleashed-Publication.pdfMacIntyre, A. (1984). *After Virtue*. University of Notre Dame Press.

Luckin, R., Holmes, W., Griffiths, M., & Forcier, L. B. (2016). *Intelligence unleashed: An argument for AI in education.* Pearson. https://www.pearson.com/content/dam/corporate/global/pearson-dot-com/files/innovation/Intelligence-Unleashed-Publication.pdf

Luckin, R., Holmes, W., Griffiths, M., & Forcier, L. B. (2016). *Intelligence Unleashed: An Argument for AI in Education.* Pearson.

Lytras, M. D., Serban, A. C., Alkhaldi, A., Aldosemani, T., & Malik, S. (2024). Digital transformation in higher education in times of artificial intelligence: Setting the emerging landscape. In Lytras, M. D., Serban, A. C., Alkhaldi, A., Malik, S., & Aldosemani, T. (Eds.), *Digital Transformation in Higher Education, Part A* (pp. 1–22). Emerald Publishing Limited., DOI: 10.1108/978-1-83549-480-620241001

MacLellan, C. J., & Koedinger, K. R. (2022). Domain-general tutor authoring with apprentice learner models. [springer.com]. *International Journal of Artificial Intelligence in Education, 32*(1), 76–117. DOI: 10.1007/s40593-020-00214-2

Madni, A. M. (2007). Transdisciplinarity: Reaching beyond disciplines to find connections. *Journal of Integrated Design & Process Science*, *11*(1), 1–11. DOI: 10.3233/JID-2007-11101

Mageira, K., Pittou, D., Papasalouros, A., Kotis, K., Zangogianni, P., & Daradoumis, A. (2022). Educational AI chatbots for content and language integrated learning. *Applied Sciences (Basel, Switzerland)*, *12*(7), 3239. DOI: 10.3390/app12073239

Maghsudi, S., Lan, A., Xu, J., & van Der Schaar, M. (2021). Personalized education in the artificial intelligence era: What to expect next. [PDF]. *IEEE Signal Processing Magazine*, *38*(3), 37–50. DOI: 10.1109/MSP.2021.3055032

Mahajan, P. (2025). What is Ethical: AIHED Driving Humans or Human-Driven AIHED? A Conceptual Framework enabling the Ethos of AI-driven Higher education. *arXiv preprint arXiv:2503.04751*.

Majumder, A. (2025). Rise & impact of AI agents in digital landscape. *American Journal of Intelligent Systems*, *14*(1), 10–17.

Makerere University. (2025). Makerere launches AI and data science centre to drive Africa's technological development. *Makerere University News*. https://news.mak.ac.ug/2025/03/makerere-launches-ai-and-data-science-centre-to-drive-africas-technological-development

Makinde, A. I., Adeleye, S. A., Oronti, A. O., & Jimoh, I. T. (2024). Revolutionizing education. Artificial Intelligence for Wireless Communication Systems: Technology and Applications, 103.

Malmi, L., Sheard, J., Kinnunen, P., Simon, , & Sinclair, J. (2020). Computing education theories: What are they and how are they used? *ACM Inroads*, *11*(1), 54–64. DOI: 10.1145/3381889

Maloney, C. M., Schilling, J. R., Chung, J., Kunz, A., Pari-Monasch, S., Ko, J., & Onder, O. (2014). *Automatic presentation of slide design suggestions*. https://patents.google.com/patent/US10282075B2/en

Mampota, S., Mokhets'engoane, S. J., & Kurata, L. (2023). Connectivism theory: Exploring its relevance in informing Lesotho's integrated curriculum for effective learning in the digital age. *European Journal of Education and Pedagogy*, *4*(4), 6–12. DOI: 10.24018/ejedu.2023.4.4.705

Mamun, M. A. A. (2022). Fostering self-regulation and engaged exploration during the learner–content interaction process: The role of scaffolding in the online inquiry-based learning environment. *Interactive Technology and Smart Education*, *19*(4), 482–509. DOI: 10.1108/ITSE-11-2021-0195

Mane, P. A., & Jagtap, S. (2024). AI-enhanced educational platform for personalized learning paths, automated grading, and real-time feedback. *International Journal of Scientific Research in Engineering and Management*, *08*(12), 1–7. DOI: 10.55041/IJSREM39921

Mangal, M., & Pardos, Z. A. (2024). Implementing equitable and intersectionality-aware machine learning in education: A practical guide. *British Journal of Educational Technology*, *55*(5), 2003–2038. DOI: 10.1111/bjet.13484

Mansoor, M., Chandar, S., & Srinath, R. (2021). AI based Presentation Creator with Customized Audio Content Delivery. *arXiv: Learning*. https://dblp.uni-trier.de/db/journals/corr/corr2106.html#abs-2106-14213

Maphalala, M. C., & Ajani, O. A. (2025). Leveraging artificial intelligence as a learning tool in higher education. *Interdisciplinary Journal of Education Research*, *7*(1), a01. DOI: 10.38140/ijer-2025.vol7.1.01

Mardiani, E., & Iswahyudi, M. S. (2023). Mapping the landscape of artificial intelligence research: A bibliometric approach. *West Science Interdisciplinary Studies*, *01*(08), 587–599. DOI: 10.58812/wsis.v1i08.183

Mariyono, D., & Abror, M. (2024). AI in enhancing cultural sensitivity. *Jurnal EDUCATIO: Jurnal Pendidikan Indonesia, 10*(2), 296. DOI: 10.29210/1202424847

Markauskaite, L., Marrone, R., Poquet, O., Knight, S., Martinez-Maldonado, R., Howard, S., Tondeur, J., De Laat, M., Buckingham Shum, S., Gašević, D., & Siemens, G. (2022). Rethinking the entwinement between artificial intelligence and human learning: What capabilities do learners need for a world with AI? *Computers and Education: Artificial Intelligence, 3*, 1–16. DOI: 10.1016/j.caeai.2022.100056

Martindale, J. (2023, May 2). *Here are 11 things that ChatGPT will refuse to do.* Digital Trends. https://www.digitaltrends.com/computing/everything-chatgpt-refuses-to-do/

Martinez-Maldonado, R., Van Leeuwen, A., & Swiecki, Z. (2023). Artificial intelligence techniques for supporting face-to-face and online collaborative learning. *Handbook of Artificial Intelligence in Education*, 422-439. DOI: 10.4337/9781800375413.00031

Martin, F., Chen, Y., Moore, R. L., & Westine, C. D. (2020). Systematic review of adaptive learning research designs, context, strategies, and technologies from 2009 to 2018. [odu.edu]. *Educational Technology Research and Development, 68*(4), 1903–1929. DOI: 10.1007/s11423-020-09793-2

Mattioli, M., & Cabitza, F. (2024). Not in my face: Challenges and ethical considerations in automatic face emotion recognition technology. *Machine Learning and Knowledge Extraction, 6*(4), 2201–2231. DOI: 10.3390/make6040109

Matz, S. C., Bukow, C. S., Peters, H., Deacons, C., Dinu, A., & Stachl, C. (2023). Using machine learning to predict student retention from socio-demographic characteristics and app-based engagement metrics. *Scientific Reports, 13*(1), 5705. DOI: 10.1038/s41598-023-32484-w

McCarthy, J. (2007). From here to human-level AI. *Artificial Intelligence, 171*(18), 1174–1182. DOI: 10.1016/j.artint.2007.10.009

McGregor, D. (1960). *The human side of enterprise*. McGraw-Hill.

McKinsey Global Institute. (2017). Jobs lost, jobs gained: Workforce transitions in a time of automation. McKinsey & Company. https://www.mckinsey.com/featured-insights/future-of-work/jobs-lost-jobs-gained-what-the-future-of-work-will-mean-for-jobs-skills-and-wages

Meade, M., DiCiurcio, W., Radack, T., Michael, M., & Woods, B. R. (2023). Reference Managers. *Clinical Spine Surgery, 37*(2), 77–78. DOI: 10.1097/BSD.0000000000001532

Mean, U., & Flores, E. (2024). Digital transformation in Cambodian higher education and its impact on teaching and learning outcomes. *Journal of Accounting, Finance, Economics, and Social Sciences, 9*(1), 23–34. DOI: 10.62458/jafess9(1)3

Meça, A., & Shkelzeni, N. (2023). *Academic Integrity in the Face of Generative Language Models.*, DOI: 10.1007/978-3-031-50215-6_5

Melo-López, V.-A., Basantes-Andrade, A., Gudiño-Mejía, C.-B., & Hernández-Martínez, E. (2025). The Impact of Artificial Intelligence on Inclusive Education: A Systematic Review. *Education Sciences, 15*(5), 539. DOI: 10.3390/educsci15050539

Memarian, B., & Doleck, T. (2024). Human-in-the-loop in artificial intelligence in education: A review and entity-relationship (ER) analysis. *Computers in Human Behavior: Artificial Humans, 2*(1), 100053. DOI: 10.1016/j.chbah.2024.100053

Metcalf, J., Keller, E., & Boyd, D. (2016). "Perspectives on Big Data, Ethics, and Society." *Council for Big Data, Ethics, and Society White Paper.*

Mhasawade, V., Zhao, Y., & Chunara, R (2021). Machine learning and algorithmic fairness in public and population health. Nature Machine Intelligence. nature.com

Miangah, T. M., & Nezarat, A. (2012). Mobile-assisted language learning. *International Journal of Distributed and Parallel Systems, 3*(1), 309–319. DOI: 10.5121/ijdps.2012.3126

Miao, F., Holmes, W., Huang, R., & Zhang, H. (2021). *AI and education: Guidance for policy-makers.* UNESCO, 45.

Michalak, R. (2024). Fostering Undergraduate Academic Research: Rolling out a Tech Stack with AI-Powered Tools in a Library. *Journal of Library Administration, 64*(3), 335–346. Advance online publication. DOI: 10.1080/01930826.2024.2316523

Michel-Villarreal, R., Vilalta-Perdomo, E., Salinas-Navarro, D. E., Thierry-Aguilera, R., & Gerardou, F. S. (2023). Challenges and opportunities of generative AI for higher education as explained by ChatGPT. *Education Sciences, 13*(9), 856. DOI: 10.3390/educsci13090856

Microsoft. (n.d.). *Generative AI for beginners: 12 lessons to get started building with generative AI* [GitHub repository]. GitHub. https://microsoft.github.io/generative-ai-for-beginners/

Microsoft. (n.d.-b). *Prompts for educators.* GitHub. https://github.com/microsoft/prompts-for-edu/blob/main/Educators/README.MD

Mijan, A.-A., Hasan, M. R., & Hasan, M. (2025). AI and academia: Navigating the adoption of artificial intelligence in universities. *International Journal of Technology in Education and Science, 9*(1), 54–65. DOI: 10.46328/ijtes.602

Mikton, J. (2023, October 16). *Integrating AI with the IB learner profile.* IB Community Blog. https://beyonddigital.org/2023/10/19/integrating-ai-with-the-ib-learner-profile/

Min, Y., & Andaya, M. (2024). Enhancing student writing skills through Gamification: Evaluating the effectiveness of Textopia, an AI-driven platform for personalized writing prompts and feedback. *Advanced Natural Language Processing*, 225-234. DOI: 10.5121/csit.2024.141020

Mirea, C.-M., Bologa, R., Toma, A., Clim, A., Plăcintă, D.-D., & Bobocea, A. (2025). Transforming Learning with Generative AI: From Student Perceptions to the Design of an Educational Solution. *Applied Sciences (Basel, Switzerland), 15*(10), 5785. DOI: 10.3390/app15105785

Mishra, D., Mishra, R. K., & Agarwal, R. (2025). Impacts of artificial intelligence on society. *Journal of Science Research International, 11*(1).

Mishra, P. (2024). Revolutionizing education with AI and ML. In Ouaissa, M., Ouaissa, M., Lamaazi, H., Hamlaoui, M. E., & Reddy, K. K. (Eds.), *Internet of behavior-based computational intelligence for smart education systems* (pp. 53–94). IGI Global Scientific Publishing., DOI: 10.4018/979-8-3693-8151-9.ch003

Mishra, P., & Koehler, M. J. (2006). Technological pedagogical content knowledge: A new framework for teacher knowledge. *Teachers College Record*, *108*(6), 1017–1054. DOI: 10.1111/j.1467-9620.2006.00684.x

Mislevy, R. J. (2024). Sociocognitive and argumentation perspectives on psychometric modeling in educational assessment. *Psychometrika*, *89*(1), 64–83. DOI: 10.1007/s11336-024-09966-5

Mohamed Riyath, M. I., & Muhammed Rijah, U. L. (2022). Adoption of a learning management system among educators of advanced technological institutes in Sri Lanka. *Asian Association of Open Universities Journal*, *17*(2), 161–177. DOI: 10.1108/AAOUJ-03-2022-0032

Mohammed, S. J., & Khalid, M. W. (2025). Under the world of AI-generated feedback on writing: Mirroring motivation, foreign language peace of mind, trait emotional intelligence, and writing development. *Language Testing in Asia*, *15*(1), 7. Advance online publication. DOI: 10.1186/s40468-025-00343-2

Molopa, S. T. (2024). Artificial intelligence-based literature review adaptation. *South African Journal of Library and Information Science*. Advance online publication. DOI: 10.7553/90-1-2390

Moor, J. H. (2006). The Nature, Importance, and Difficulty of Machine Ethics. *IEEE Intelligent Systems*, *21*(4), 18–21. DOI: 10.1109/MIS.2006.80

Mordaunt, M., Lopez, P., Uppala, A., Rosati, D., Rodrigues, N. P., Grabitz, P., & Rife, S. C. (n.d.). scite: a smart citation index that displays the context of citations and classifies their intent using deep.

Morley, J., Floridi, L., Kinsey, L., & Elhalal, A. (2019). *From What to How: An Initial Review of Publicly Available AI Ethics Tools, Methods and Research to Translate Principles into Practices*. arXiv.org. https://arxiv.org/abs/1905.06876

Mourya, A., Jobanputra, B., & Pai, R. (2024). AI-powered clinical trials and the imperative for regulatory transparency and accountability. *Health and Technology*, *14*(1), 1071–1081. DOI: 10.1007/s12553-024-00904-0

Mousavinasab, E., Zarifsanaiey, N., & Niakan Kalhori, R., S., Rakhshan, M., Keikha, L., & Ghazi Saeedi, M. (. (2021). Intelligent tutoring systems: A systematic review of characteristics, applications, and evaluation methods. [academia.edu]. *Interactive Learning Environments*, *29*(1), 142–163. DOI: 10.1080/10494820.2018.1558257

Mouta, A., Sánchez, E. T., & Llorente, A. M. P. (2020). Sense of agency in times of automation: A teachers' professional development proposal on the ethical challenges of AI applied to education. In Bittencourt, I. I., Cukurova, M., Muldner, K., Luckin, R., & Millán, E. (Eds.), *Artificial Intelligence in Education* (Vol. 12164, pp. 405–408). Springer International Publishing., DOI: 10.1007/978-3-030-52240-7_73

Mueller, J. (2018). Authentic assessment toolbox. http://jfmueller.faculty.noctrl.edu/toolbox

Mugizi, W., & Nagasha, J. I. (2025). E-Learning. In Bangura, A. K., & Ifedi, J. P. A. (Eds.), *Conceptualizations of Africa: Perspectives from Sciences and Humanities* (pp. 143–163). Springer., DOI: 10.1007/978-3-031-74534-8_8

Mugizi, W., Rwothumio, J., & Kasule, G. W. (2023). Measuring digital teaching competence of academic staff in public universities in Uganda. *African Journal of Education. Science and Technology*, *7*(3), 736–745. DOI: 10.2022/ajest.v7i3.90

Mukhamediev, R. I., Popova, Y., Kuchin, Y., Zaitseva, E., Kalimoldayev, A., Symagulov, A., Levashenko, V., Abdoldina, F., Gopejenko, V., Yakunin, K., Muhamedijeva, E., & Yelis, M. (2022). Review of artificial intelligence and machine learning technologies: Classification, restrictions, opportunities, and challenges. *Mathematics*, *10*(15), 1–25. DOI: 10.3390/math10152552

Murdan, A. P., & Halkhoree, R. (2024). Integration of artificial intelligence for educational excellence and innovation in higher education institutions. *2024 1st International Conference on Smart Energy Systems and Artificial Intelligence (SESAI)*, 1-6. DOI: 10.1109/SESAI61023.2024.10599402

Murtaza, M., Ahmed, Y., Shamsi, J. A., Sherwani, F., & Usman, M. (2022). AI-based personalized e-learning systems: Issues, challenges, and solutions. *IEEE Access : Practical Innovations, Open Solutions*, *10*, 81323–81342.

Muwagunzi, E., Kabuye, R., Ddamulira, C., & Kizza, S. S. (2024). Artificial Intelligence in Academic Research at Bugema University: Transforming Methodologies and Ethical Considerations. *East African Journal of Interdisciplinary Studies*, *7*(1), 489–503. DOI: 10.37284/eajis.7.1.2484

My Speaking Score. (n.d.). *My speaking score.* https://www.myspeakingscore.com/

N. L., ... & Shimada, A. (2024). Evaluating algorithmic bias in models for predicting academic performance of Filipino students. *arXiv preprint arXiv:2405.09821*. DOI DOI: 10.5281/zenodo.12729935

Naeem, M., Rizvi, S. T. H., & Coronato, A (2020). A gentle introduction to reinforcement learning and its application in different fields. IEEE access. ieee.org

Nagahisarchoghaei, M., Nur, N., Cummins, L., Nur, N., Karimi, M. M., Nandanwar, S., Bhattacharyya, S., & Rahimi, S. (2023). An empirical survey on explainable AI technologies: Recent trends, use-cases, and categories from technical and application perspectives. *Electronics (Basel)*, *12*(5), 1–59. DOI: 10.3390/electronics12051092

Naidoo, R., & Jamieson, I. (2005). Empowering participants or corroding learning? Towards a research agenda on the impact of student consumerism in higher education. *Journal of Education Policy*, *20*(3), 267–281. DOI: 10.1080/02680930500108585

Nalwoga, M. M. (2021). Financial sustainability of private universities in Uganda: A critical perspective. *African Journal of Education, Science and Technology*, *6*(3), 128–139. https://ajest.info/

Naqvi, W. M., Ganjoo, R., Rowe, M., Pashine, A. A., & Mishra, G. (2025). Critical thinking in the age of generative AI: Implications for health sciences education. *Frontiers in Artificial Intelligence*, *8*, 8. DOI: 10.3389/frai.2025.1571527

Narvaez, D. (2006). Integrative Ethical Education. In Killen, M., & Smetana, J. (Eds.), *Handbook of Moral Development* (pp. 703–733). Lawrence Erlbaum.

Naseer, F., & Khawaja, S. (2025). Mitigating conceptual learning gaps in mixed-ability classrooms: A learning analytics-based evaluation of AI-driven adaptive feedback for struggling learners. *Applied Sciences (Basel, Switzerland)*, *15*(8), 4473. Advance online publication. DOI: 10.3390/app15084473

Nashwan, A. J., & Abukhadijah, H. (2023). Harnessing Artificial Intelligence for Qualitative and Mixed Methods in Nursing Research. *Cureus*. Advance online publication. DOI: 10.7759/cureus.48570

National Education policy (2020). Government of India, Ministry of Education. https://www.education.gov.in/nep/about-nep

National Student Clearinghouse Research Center. (2024). Undergraduate enrollment showing signs of second straight year of growth. https://www.studentclearinghouse.org/news/undergraduate-enrollment-showing-signs-of-second-straight-year-of-growth/#:~:text=Graduate%20programs%20are%20also%20seeing,key%20findings%20in%20the%20report: Nicolescu, B. (2010). Transdisciplinarity: The hidden third, between the subject and the object. *Human and Social Studies, 1(2), 13-28.*

Nazaretsky, T., Ariely, M., Cukurova, M., & Alexandron, G. (2022). Teachers' trust in AI-powered educational technology and a professional development program to improve it. *British Journal of Educational Technology*, *53*(4), 914–931. DOI: 10.1111/bjet.13232

Ng, A. (2023). *AI for everyone*. DeepLearning AI. https://www.deeplearning.ai/courses/ai-for-everyone/

Ng, D. T. K., Leung, J. K. L., Chu, S. K. W., & Qiao, M. S. (2021). Conceptualizing AI literacy: An exploratory review. *Computers and Education: Artificial Intelligence*, *2*, 100041. DOI: 10.1016/j.caeai.2021.100041

Nguyen, A., Ngo, H. N., Hong, Y., Dang, B., & Nguyen, B.-P. T. (2023). Ethical principles for artificial intelligence in education. *Education and Information Technologies*, *28*(4), 4221–4241. DOI: 10.1007/s10639-022-11316-w

Nguyen, L. T., & Tuamsuk, K. (2022). Digital learning ecosystem at educational institutions: A content analysis of scholarly discourse. *Cogent Education*, *9*(1), 2111033. DOI: 10.1080/2331186X.2022.2111033

Nicola-Gavrilă, L. (2023). Education and technology in a data driven society: Turning data into education intelligence. In *Digital Future in Education: Paradoxes, Hopes and Realities* (pp. 12–33). RITHA Publishing. https://doi.org/DOI: 10.57017/SERITHA.2023.DFE.ch1

Nicol, D., & Macfarlane-Dick, D. (2006). Formative Assessment and Self-Regulated Learning: A Model and Seven Principles of Good Feedback Practice. *Studies in Higher Education*, *31*(2), 199–218. DOI: 10.1080/03075070600572090

Nikhil, V. (2024). A comprehensive study on AI-enhanced personalized learning in STEM courses. *Adopting Artificial Intelligence Tools in Higher Education*, 149-170. DOI: 10.1201/9781003469315-7

Nissenbaum, H (2020). Protecting privacy in an information age: The problem of privacy in public. The ethics of information technologies. cpeterson.org

Noble, S. U. (2018). *Algorithms of Oppression: How Search Engines Reinforce Racism*. NYU Press. DOI: 10.18574/nyu/9781479833641.001.0001

Nowak, M. A., & Sigmund, K. (1993). A strategy of win-stay, lose-shift that outperforms tit-for-tat in the Prisoner's Dilemma game. *Nature*, *364*(6432), 56–58. DOI: 10.1038/364056a0 PMID: 8316296

Nowak, M. A., & Sigmund, K. (2005). Evolution of indirect reciprocity. *Nature*, *437*(7063), 1291–1298. DOI: 10.1038/nature04131 PMID: 16251955

Ntjamba, F. C., & Ashipala, D. O. (2025a). Association between learning styles and academic success in nursing and midwifery education. *Motivating Engagement, Belonging, and Success in Higher Education Student Experience*, 245-268. DOI: 10.4018/979-8-3693-8089-5.ch009

Ntjamba, F. C., & Ashipala, D. O. (2025b). Ethical dimensions of AI in the Metaverse. *Advances in Computational Intelligence and Robotics*, •••, 195–212. DOI: 10.4018/979-8-3373-0340-6.ch010

Ntjamba, F. C., & Ashipala, D. O. (2025c). Beyond reality: Integrating AI and Metaverse technologies for enhanced scientific collaboration. *Advances in Computational Intelligence and Robotics*, •••, 99–118. DOI: 10.4018/979-8-3373-0340-6.ch005

Ntjamba, F. C., & Ashipala, D. O. (2025d). Innovative pathways: AI and the Metaverse in interdisciplinary research and knowledge discovery. *Advances in Computational Intelligence and Robotics*, •••, 119–138. DOI: 10.4018/979-8-3373-0340-6.ch006

Nuong Deri, M., Singh, A., Zaazie, P., & Anandene, D. (2024). Leveraging Artificial Intelligence in Higher Educational Institutions: A Comprehensive Overview. Education & Law Review/ Revista de Educaci6n y Derecho, (30).

Nur Fitria, T. (2021, December 20). *Artificial intelligence (AI) in education: Using AI tools for the teaching and learning process*.

Nurjanah, D. (2016). Good and similar learners' recommendation in adaptive learning systems. *Proceedings of the 8th International Conference on Computer Supported Education*, 434-440. DOI: 10.5220/0005864304340440

Nussbaum, M. C. (2001). *Upheavals of Thought: The Intelligence of Emotions*. Cambridge University Press. DOI: 10.1017/CBO9780511840715

Nussbaum, M. C. (2010). *Not for Profit: Why Democracy Needs the Humanities*. Princeton University Press.

Nwana, H. S. (1990). Intelligent tutoring systems: An overview. *Artificial Intelligence Review*, *4*(4). Advance online publication. DOI: 10.1007/BF00168958

O'Neil, C. (2016). *Weapons of math destruction: How big data increases inequality and threatens democracy*. Crown.

Octavio, M., González Argüello, M. V., & Pujolà, J.-T. (2024). ChatGPT as an AI L2 teaching support: A case study of an EFL teacher. *Technology in Language Teaching & Learning*, *6*(1), 1142. DOI: 10.29140/tltl.v6n1.1142

Odri, G.-A., & Yoon, D. J. Y. (2023). Detecting generative artificial intelligence in scientific articles: Evasion techniques and implications for scientific integrity. *Orthopaedics & Traumatology: Surgery & Research*, *109*(8), 103706. DOI: 10.1016/j.otsr.2023.103706

OECD. (2018). Preparing our youth for an inclusive and sustainable world: The OECD PISA global competence framework.

OECD. (2021). AI and the Future of Skills, Volume 1: Capabilities and Assessments. OECD Publishing. https://doi.org/DOI: 10.1787/5f65ff73-en

OECD. (2021). *AI and the future of skills: Education and training for the digital age*. OECD Publishing., DOI: 10.1787/5f65ff73-

OECD. (2021). Future of education and skills 2030: Curriculum analysis. OECD Publishing. https://www.oecd.org/education/2030-project/

OECD. (2023). *OECD Digital Education Outlook 2023: Towards an Effective Digital Education Ecosystem*. OECD Publishing., DOI: 10.1787/c74f03de-

OECD. (2024). *Recommendation of the council on artificial intelligence*. OECD Legal Instruments. https://legalinstruments.oecd.org/en/instruments/OECD-LEGAL-0449

Oganetse, D. K. (2025). Personalized learning for incarcerated students. *Mitigating Learner Disadvantages in Teaching and Learning*, 359-396. DOI: 10.4018/979-8-3693-8623-1.ch013

Ojha, B., Agrawal, A., & Arya, A. (2024). *Artificial Intelligence Integration in Higher Education*. 1–23. DOI: 10.1201/9781003469315-1

Oladele Jegede, O. (2024). Artificial intelligence and English language learning: Exploring the roles of AI-driven tools in personalizing learning and providing instant feedback. *Universal Library of Languages and Literatures, 01*(02), 06-19. DOI: 10.70315/uloap.ullli.2024.0102002

Olari, V., & Romeike, R. (2021). Addressing AI and data literacy in teacher education: A review of existing educational frameworks. *In the proceedings of The 16th Workshop in Primary and Secondary Computing Education, 17*, 1–2. DOI: 10.1145/3481312.3481351

Oliveira, G., Grenha Teixeira, J., Torres, A., & Morais, C. (2021). An exploratory study on the emergency remote education experience of higher education students and teachers during the COVID-19 pandemic. [nih.gov]. *British Journal of Educational Technology*, *52*(4), 1357–1376. DOI: 10.1111/bjet.13112

Onyebuchi, N. C., Unachukwu, C. C., & Osawaru, B. (2024). Review of AI in education: Transforming learning environments in Africa. *International Journal of Applied Research in Social Sciences*, *5*(10), 637–654. DOI: 10.51594/ijarss.v5i10.725

Open, A. I. (2025a). *ChatGPT release notes*. https://openai.com/research/chatgpt

Open, A. I. (2025b). *How can educators respond to students presenting AI-generated content as their own?* https://help.openai.com/en/articles/8313351-how-can-educators-respond-to-students-presenting-ai-generated-content-as-their-own

Oraif, I. (2023). Natural language processing (NLP) and EFL learning: A case study based on deep learning. *Journal of Language Teaching and Research, 15*(1), 201–208. DOI: 10.17507/jltr.1501.22

Oregon State University Ecampus. (n.d.). *Advancing meaningful learning in the age of AI: artificial intelligence tools – Faculty support.* Oregon State Ecampus. Oregon State Ecampus. https://ecampus.oregonstate.edu/faculty/artificial-intelligence-tools/meaningful-learning/

Ortiz, E. A., Vergara, N. C., Pabón, T. F., Gambi, G. D. N., Giambruno, C., Alfaro, M. P., & Segura, D. R. (2025). AI and Education: Building the Future Through Digital Transformation.

Osuji, G. E. (2025). AI-Driven Curriculum Development: Navigating Education for a Dynamic Future.

Ou, C. (2024). Artificial intelligence and student engagement. *Designing Socially Dynamic Digital Learning*, 151-173. DOI: 10.4324/9781003368076-18

Ouyang, F., Zheng, L., & Jiao, P. (2022). Artificial intelligence in online higher education: A systematic review of empirical research from 2011 to 2020. *Education and Information Technologies, 27*(6), 7893–7925. DOI: 10.1007/s10639-022-10925-9

Owoseni, A., Kolade, O., & Egbetokun, A. (2024). Generative AI and its implications for higher education students and educators. *Generative AI in Higher Education*, 1-25. DOI: 10.1007/978-3-031-60179-8_1

Oyebode, O., Fowles, J., Steeves, D., & Orji, R. (2023). Machine learning techniques in adaptive and personalized systems for health and wellness. *International Journal of Human-Computer Interaction, 39*(9), 1938–1962. DOI: 10.1080/10447318.2022.2089085

Oyelude, A. A. (2024). Artificial intelligence (AI) tools for academic research. *Library Hi Tech News, 41*(8), 18–20. Advance online publication. DOI: 10.1108/LHTN-08-2024-0131

Ozer, M., Kose, Y., Kucukkaya, G., Mukasheva, A., & Ciris, K. (2025). Adapting to the AI disruption: Reshaping the IT landscape and educational paradigms. In Arabnia, H. R., Deligiannidis, L., Amirian, S., Ghareh Mohammadi, F., & Shenavarmasouleh, F. (Eds.), *Foundations of computer science and frontiers in education: Computer science and computer engineering* (pp. 366–374). Springer Nature Switzerland., DOI: 10.1007/978-3-031-85930-4_33

Padakanti, S., Kommidi, V. R., & Kommidi, V. R. (2024). AI in Scientific Research: Empowering Researchers with Intelligent Tools. *International Journal of Scientific Research in Computer Science. Engineering and Information Technology, 10*(5), 416–422. DOI: 10.32628/CSEIT241051012

Padovano, A., & Cardamone, M. (2024). Towards human-AI collaboration in the competency-based curriculum development process: The case of industrial engineering and management education. *Computers and Education: Artificial Intelligence, 7*, 100256. DOI: 10.1016/j.caeai.2024.100256

Page, M. J., McKenzie, J. E., Bossuyt, P. M., Boutron, I., Hoffmann, T. C., Mulrow, C. D., Shamseer, L., Tetzlaff, J. M., Akl, E. A., Brennan, S. E., Chou, R., Glanville, J., Grimshaw, J. M., Hróbjartsson, A., Lalu, M. M., Li, T., Loder, E. W., Mayo-Wilson, E., McDonald, S., & Moher, D. (2021). The PRISMA 2020 statement: An updated guideline for reporting systematic reviews. *BMJ (Clinical Research Ed.), 372*(71), n71. Advance online publication. DOI: 10.1136/bmj.n71 PMID: 33782057

Pandya, T. P. (2023). Literature Review as Research Methodology: Aid of AI (Artificial Intelligence). *Vidhyayana – An International Multidisciplinary Peer-Reviewed E-Journal, 9*(si1), 123–133. DOI: 10.58213/vidhyayana.v9isi1.1589

Pane, J. F., Steiner, E. D., Baird, M. D., Hamilton, L. S., & Pane, J. D. (2017). *Informing Progress: Insights on personalized learning implementation and effects*. RAND. https://www.rand.org/pubs/research_reports/RR2042.html

Pane, J. F., Griffin, B. A., McCaffrey, D. F., & Karam, R. (2013). Effectiveness of Cognitive Tutor Algebra I at scale. *Educational Evaluation and Policy Analysis, 36*(2), 127–144. DOI: 10.3102/0162373713507480

Pane, J. F., Steiner, E. D., Baird, M. D., & Hamilton, L. S. (2015). *Continued Progress: Promising Evidence on Personalized Learning*. RAND Corporation. DOI: 10.7249/RR1365

Pan, L., Luo, H., & Gu, Q. (2025). Incorporating AI literacy and AI anxiety into TAM: Unraveling Chinese scholars' behavioral intentions toward adopting AI-assisted literature reading. *IEEE Access : Practical Innovations, Open Solutions, 13*, 38952–38963. DOI: 10.1109/ACCESS.2025.3546572

Pan, M., Guo, K., & Lai, C. (2025). Using artificial intelligence chatbots to support English as a Foreign language students' self-regulated reading. *RELC Journal, 56*(3), 781–793. DOI: 10.1177/00336882241264030

Pardos, Z. A., Tang, M., Anastasopoulos, I., Sheel, S. K., & Zhang, E. (2023, April). Oatutor: An open-source adaptive tutoring system and curated content library for learning sciences research. In Proceedings of the 2023 chi conference on human factors in computing systems (pp. 1-17). acm.org DOI: 10.1145/3544548.3581574

Park, E. (2021). Understanding how students control their learning in adaptive learning environments. *Proceedings of the 2021 AERA Annual Meeting*. DOI: 10.3102/1687712

Park, J. (2019). An AI-based English grammar checker vs. human raters in evaluating EFL learners' writing. *Multimedia-Assisted Language Learning, 22*(1), 112–131. DOI: 10.15702/MALL.2019.22.1.112

Patel, N. S., & Lim, J. T. H. (2024). Critical design futures thinking and GenerativeAI: a Foresight 3.0 approach in higher education to design preferred futures for the industry. *foresight*.

Patel, H., Boucher, D., Fallahzadeh, E., Hassan, A. E., & Adams, B. (2025). A state-of-the-practice release-readiness checklist for generative AI-based software products: A gray literature survey. *IEEE Software, 42*(1), 74–83. DOI: 10.1109/MS.2024.3440190

Paul, P. K., Chatterjee, R., Kayyali, M., & Das, N. (2025). Cyber-Physical Systems: Its Foundation, Emergence, Possible Applications, and Issues with Reference to the Education Sector. In Choudhury, A., Kaushik, K., Kumar, V., & Singh, B. K. (Eds.), *Cyber-Physical Systems Security. Studies in Big Data* (Vol. 154). Springer., DOI: 10.1007/978-981-97-5734-3_1

Paulsen, L., & Lindsay, E. (2024). Learning analytics dashboards are increasingly becoming about learning and not just analytics: A systematic review. *Education and Information Technologies, 29*(11), 14279–14308. Advance online publication. DOI: 10.1007/s10639-023-12401-4

Pedro, F., Subosa, M., Rivas, A., & Valverde, P. (2019). Artificial intelligence in education: Challenges and opportunities for sustainable development. https://repositorio.minedu.gob.pe/handle/20.500.12799/6533

Pemberton, C., & Mynard, J. (2023). Promoting and evaluating students' development of self-directed language learning and reflective abilities. *Promoting Reflection on Language Learning*, 150-166. DOI: 10.2307/jj.22679696.15

Pentina, I., Hancock, T., & Xie, T (2023). Exploring relationship development with social chatbots: A mixed-method study of replika. Computers in Human Behavior. researchgate.net

Perkel, J. M. (2020). Streamline your writing - and collaborations - with these reference managers. *Nature, 585*(7823), 149–150. DOI: 10.1038/d41586-020-02491-2

Perkins, M. (2023). Academic integrity considerations of AI large language models in the post-pandemic era: ChatGPT and beyond. *Journal of University Teaching & Learning Practice, 20*(2). Advance online publication. DOI: 10.53761/1.20.02.07

Perkins, M., Roe, J., Postma, D., McGaughran, J., & Hickerson, D. (2024). Detection of GPT-4 generated text in higher education: Combining academic judgement and software to identify generative AI tool misuse. *Journal of Academic Ethics, 22*(1), 89–113. DOI: 10.1007/s10805-023-09492-6

Petersen, R., Weisse, M., Lewandowski, E., Swartz, T., & Wang, L. (2018), Artificial Intelligence Helps Distinguish the Forest from the Trees: Part 1, Global Forest Watch, globalforestwatch.org.

Petraki, E., & Khat, K. (2022). Challenges and constraints in the design of an ESP course in Cambodia: Implications for higher education institutions. *Asia Pacific Journal of Education, 42*(2), 260–275. DOI: 10.1080/02188791.2020.1798738

Phan, S. (2015). Envisioning a higher education system for the 21st century: Cambodia [University of British Columbia]. DOI: 10.14288/1.0166746

Piaget, J. (1972). The epistemology of interdisciplinary relationships. In *Centre for Educational Research and Innovation (CERI), Interdisciplinarity: Problems of teaching and research in uni versities* (pp. 127–139). Organization for Economic Co-operation and Development.

Plantinga, P., Shilongo, K., Mudongo, O., Umubyeyi, A., Gastrow, M., & Razzano, G. (2024). Responsible artificial intelligence in Africa: Towards policy learning. *Data & Policy, 6*, e72. DOI: 10.1017/dap.2024.60

Pohn, B., Mehnen, L., Fitzek, S., Choi, K.-E., Braun, R. J., & Hatamikia, S. (2025). Integrating artificial intelligence into pre-clinical medical education: Challenges, opportunities, and recommendations. *Frontiers in Education, 10*, 1570389. DOI: 10.3389/feduc.2025.1570389

Pokrivcakova, S. (2019). Preparing teachers for the application of AI-powered technologies in foreign language education. *Journal of Language and Cultural Education*, *7*(3), 135–153. DOI: 10.2478/jolace-2019-0025

Poole, N., & Leslie, S. (2020). Enhancing the student experience. *Flexibility and Pedagogy in Higher Education*, 53-64. DOI: 10.1163/9789004438118_005

Poornesh, M. (2025). Navigating the Future of Educational Research: Leveraging Generative AI for Improved Insights. *The Clearing House: A Journal of Educational Strategies, Issues and Ideas*, •••, 1–8. DOI: 10.1080/00098655.2025.2450435

Portuguez-Castro, M. (2024). Reimagining the future of business education through educational innovation. *International Journal of Markets and Business Systems*, *5*(2), 192–208. DOI: 10.1504/IJMABS.2024.10069258

Prabakaran, S. (2023). *An analytical study on historical research* (pp. 64–70). In *Futuristic Trends in Social Sciences* (pp. 64–66). DOI: 10.58532/V2S2CH8

Prabhu, M., & Premraj, J. A. (2025). Artificial consciousness in AI: A posthuman fallacy. *AI & Society*, *40*(4), 2995–3008. DOI: 10.1007/s00146-024-02061-4

Prashar, P., & Chander, H. (2024). Role of Research Management Tools for Enhancing Academic Research Efficiency: A Focus on AI-Driven Literature Mapping with Research Rabbit. *Journal of Information and Knowledge*, 313–319. DOI: 10.17821/srels/2024/v61i6/171639

Pratama, M. P., Sampelolo, R., & Lura, H (2023). Revolutionizing education: harnessing the power of artificial intelligence for personalized learning. Klasikal: Journal of education, language teaching and science, 5(2), 350-357. journalfkipuniversitasbosowa.org

Pratama, M. P., Sampelolo, R., & Lura, H. (2023). Revolutionizing education: harnessing the power of artificial intelligence for personalized learning. Klasikal: Journal of education, language teaching and science, 5(2), 350-357.

Prompt Library — AI for education. (2024, January 5). *Prompt library*. AI For Education. https://www.aiforeducation.io/prompt-library

Proske, A., Wenzel, C., & Queitsch, M. B. (2023). *Reference Management Systems*. Springer Nature., DOI: 10.1007/978-3-031-36033-6_14

Prothero, A. (2023, November 16). *What educators know about artificial intelligence, in 3 charts*. Education Week. https://www.edweek.org/technology/what-educators-know-about-artificial-intelligence-in-3-charts/2023/07

Puentedura, R. R. (2006). *Transformation, technology, and education*. Retrieved from https://hippasus.com/resources/tte/

Qodad, A., Benyoussef, A., El Kenz, A., & Elyadari, M. (2020). Toward an adaptive educational hypermedia system (AEHS-JS) based on the overlay modeling and felder and silverman's learning styles model for job seekers. [iJET]. *International Journal of Emerging Technologies in Learning, 15*(8), 235–254. DOI: 10.3991/ijet.v15i08.10574

Qushem, U. B., Christopoulos, A., Oyelere, S. S., Ogata, H., & Laakso, M. J. (2021). Multimodal technologies in precision education: Providing new opportunities or adding more challenges? [mdpi.com]. *Education Sciences, 11*(7), 338. DOI: 10.3390/educsci11070338

Quy, V. K., Thanh, B. T., Chehri, A., Linh, D. M., & Tuan, D. A. (2023). AI and Digital Transformation in Higher Education: Vision and Approach of a Specific University in Vietnam. *Sustainability (Basel), 15*(14), 11093. DOI: 10.3390/su151411093

Radha, N., Swathika, R., Uthayan, K. R., & Krishna B, M. (2024). *AI-Driven Summarization of Academic Literature using Transformer Model. 4*, 359–364. DOI: 10.1109/ICICI62254.2024.00065

Rahman, N. A., Zulkornain, L. H., Mat, A. C., & Kustati, M. (2023). Assessing writing abilities using AI-powered writing evaluations. *Journal of ASIAN Behavioural Studies, 8*(24), 1–17. DOI: 10.21834/jabs.v8i24.420

Rahwan, I. (2018). Society-in-the-Loop: Programming the Algorithmic Social Contract. *Ethics and Information Technology, 20*(1), 5–14. DOI: 10.1007/s10676-017-9430-8

Rai, T. (2025). Ethical aspects in machine learning: An agnostic approach. *AI and Ethics, 5*(6), 5691–5703. DOI: 10.1007/s43681-025-00704-w

Rajput, R. (2025). Use of artificial intelligence to solve problems in the classroom. *New Technological Applications in the Flipped Learning Model*, 32.

Ramesh, D., & Sanampudi, S. K. (2022). An automated essay scoring systems: A systematic literature review. *Artificial Intelligence Review, 55*(3), 2495–2527. DOI: 10.1007/s10462-021-10068-2

Ramezani, A., Bijani, H., & Oroji, M. R. (2025). Comparative analysis of AI vs. human feedback effects on IELTS candidates' writing performance. *Journal of Foreign Language Teaching and Translation Studies, 10*(1), 17–40.

Ramnani, S. (2024). Exploring Ethical Considerations of Artificial Intelligence in Educational Settings: An Examination of Bias, Privacy, and Accountability. [IJNRD]. *International Journal of Novel Research and Development, 9*(2), 2456–4184. http://doi.one/10.1729/Journal.37869

Ramspek, C. L., Jager, K. J., Dekker, F. W., Zoccali, C., & van Diepen, M. (2021). External validation of prognostic models: What, why, how, when and where? [oup.com]. *Clinical Kidney Journal, 14*(1), 49–58. DOI: 10.1093/ckj/sfaa188

Rane, N., Choudhary, S., & Rane, J. (2023). Education 4.0 and 5.0: Integrating artificial intelligence (AI) for personalized and adaptive learning.

Raposa, E. B., Bartolotta, K., Forbes, N., Monjaras-Gaytan, L. Y., Garcia, Y., Ulerio, G., & Salusky, I. (2024). Emotional distress and access to mental healthcare among first-generation college students during the onset of the COVID-19 pandemic. [HTML]. *The Journal of Higher Education*, •••, 1–29.

Rarick, C., Winter, G., Barczyk, C., & Merkt, E. (2013). Ugandan culture and its influence on business and leadership practice. *Journal of Global Business Issues, 7*(2), 37–44. https://franklinpublishing.net/

Rashid, A. B., & Kausik, M. A. K. (2024). AI revolutionizing industries worldwide: A comprehensive overview of its diverse applications. *Hybrid Advances, 7*, 1–34. DOI: 10.1016/j.hybadv.2024.100277

Rashid-Abdul Aziz, A., & Nusantara, T. (2024). Key Research Ideas of Artificial Intelligence in Higher Education: Bibliometric Analysis and Information Mapping. *Journal of Higher Education Theory and Practice, 24*(2). Advance online publication. DOI: 10.33423/jhetp.v24i2.6792

Rashidov, A., & Rashidova, F. (2024). Challenges and limitations in the use of artificial intelligence in research and some options to overcome them. In *2024 15th International Conference on Computing Communication and Networking Technologies (ICCCNT)* (pp. 1–4). IEEE. DOI: 10.1109/ICCCNT61001.2024.10724588

Rashidov, A. (2024). Artificial Intelligence in Scientific Research. *Strategies for Policy in Science and Education, 32*(5s), 35–45. DOI: 10.53656/str2024-5s-3-ald

Rauf, A., Nadeem, S., & Tahir, L. (2024). Integrating Artificial Intelligence into Curriculum Design. *Multidisciplinary Journal of Emerging Needs of Curriculum, 1*(2), 10–19.

Reich, J., & Ruipérez-Valiente, J. A. (2019). The MOOC pivot. *Science, 363*(6423), 130–131. DOI: 10.1126/science.aav7958

Rekha, K., Gopal, K., Satheeskumar, D., Anand, U. A., Doss, D. S. S., & Elayaperumal, S. (2024, May). AI-powered personalized learning system design: Student engagement and performance tracking system. In *2024 4th International Conference on Advance Computing and Innovative Technologies in Engineering (ICACITE)* (pp. 1125–1130). IEEE. https://doi.org/DOI: 10.1109/ICACITE60783.2024.10617155

Reyes, R., Mariñas, J. M., Tacang, J. R., Asis, L. J., Sayman, J. M., Flores, C. C., Palima, Z., & Sumatra, K. (2024, October). The relationship between attitude towards AI and AI literacy of university students. *International Journal of Multidisciplinary Studies in Higher Education, 1*(1), 37–46. DOI: 10.70847/587958

Rincon-Flores, E. G., Castano, L., Guerrero Solis, S. L., Olmos Lopez, O., Rodríguez Hernández, C. F., Castillo Lara, L. A., & Aldape Valdés, L. P. (2024). Improving the learning-teaching process through adaptive learning strategy. *Smart Learning Environments, 11*(1), 27. DOI: 10.1186/s40561-024-00314-9

Rizi, M. H. P., & Seno, S. A. H. (2022). A systematic review of technologies and solutions to improve security and privacy protection of citizens in the smart city. [HTML]. *Internet of Things : Engineering Cyber Physical Human Systems.*

Rizvi, I., Bose, C., & Tripathi, N. (2025). Transforming Education: Adaptive Learning, AI, and Online Platforms for Personalization. In *Technology for Societal Transformation: Exploring the Intersection of Information Technology and Societal Development* (pp. 45–62). Springer Nature Singapore. DOI: 10.1007/978-981-96-1721-0_4

Rizvi, S., Rienties, B., Rogaten, J., & Kizilcec, R. F. (2024). Are MOOC learning designs culturally inclusive (enough)? *Journal of Computer Assisted Learning*, *40*(6), 2496–2512. DOI: 10.1111/jcal.12883

Roe, J., Perkins, M., & Furze, L. (2024). Deepfakes and higher education: A research agenda and scoping review of synthetic media. *Journal of University Teaching & Learning Practice*, *21*(10), 1–22. DOI: 10.53761/2y2np178

Rogers, E. M. (2003). *Diffusion of innovations* (5th ed.). Free Press.

Roscoe, R. D. (2014). *Developing pedagogically-guided algorithms for intelligent writing feedback | International Journal of Learning Technology*. International Journal of Learning Technology. https://www.inderscienceonline.com/doi/abs/10.1504/IJLT.2013.059131

Rose, D. H., & Meyer, A. (2002). *Teaching every student in the digital age: Universal design for learning*. ASCD.

Rosenheck, M. (2025). AI in medical education: Challenges and opportunities. *Digital Health*, •••, 27–40.

Roshanaei, M., Olivares, H., & Lopez, R. R. (2023). Harnessing AI to foster equity in education: Opportunities, challenges, and emerging strategies. *Journal of Intelligent Learning Systems and Applications*, *15*(04), 123–143. DOI: 10.4236/jilsa.2023.154009

Ross, L. (1977). The intuitive psychologist and his shortcomings: Distortions in the attribution process. In Vol. 10, pp. 173–220). Advances in experimental social psychology. Academic Press. DOI: 10.1016/S0065-2601(08)60357-3

Rotter, J. B. (1966). Generalized expectancies for internal versus external control of reinforcement. *Psychological Monographs: General and Applied, 80* (1, Whole No. 609).

Rusk, N. (2016). Deep learning. *Nature Methods*, *13*(1), 35–35. DOI: 10.1038/nmeth.3707

Russell, S. J., & Norvig, P. (2016). *Artificial intelligence: a modern approach*. pearson.

Russell, S., & Norvig, P. (2020). Pearson. A foundational text in AI that covers key algorithms and techniques. A Modern Approach (4th ed.).

Russell, S. J., & Norvig, P. (2020). *Artificial intelligence: A modern approach* (4th ed.). Pearson.

Russell, S., Dewey, D., & Tegmark, M. (2015). Research Priorities for Robust and Beneficial Artificial Intelligence. *AI Magazine*, *36*(4), 105–114. DOI: 10.1609/aimag.v36i4.2577

Sachdeva, R. (2024). *Transforming Skill-Based Education: Development and Evaluation of an AI-Assisted.* Modular Platform Enabling Non-Technical Stakeholders to Create and Deliver Scalable, Standardized E-Learning Courses.

Sadek, M., Calvo, R. A., & Mougenot, C. (2024). Designing value-sensitive AI: A critical review and recommendations for socio-technical design processes. *AI and Ethics*, *4*(4), 949–967. DOI: 10.1007/s43681-023-00373-7

Sadigzade, Z. (2025). AI-powered feedback in ESL writing classes: Pedagogical opportunities and ethical concerns. *Journal of Azerbaijan Language and Education Studies*, *2*(4), 5–17. DOI: 10.69760/jales.2025004000

Sadler, D. R. (2008). Indeterminacy in the use of preset criteria for assessment and grading. *Assessment & Evaluation in Higher Education*, *34*(2), 159–179. DOI: 10.1080/02602930801956059

Sætra, H. S. (2025). Scaffolding human champions: AI as a more competent other. *Human Arenas*, *8*(1), 56–78. DOI: 10.1007/s42087-022-00304-8

Safonova, N., & Mykhailenko, V. (2025). Implementation of artificial intelligence for personalization education tracks in tertiary education. *Innovate Pedagogy*, *2*(80), 142–148. DOI: 10.32782/2663-6085/2025/80.2.29

Şahin, F., & Yüksel, İ. (2021). Meaning and uniqueness of ethics and ethical teacher behaviors in the teaching profession. *Inquiry in Education*, *13*(2), 2. https://files.eric.ed.gov/fulltext/EJ1338248.pdf

Saidin, F., Sudirman, A., H, L. O. H., Asriani, , Yusuf, M., Abdullah, A., & Amin, H. (2023). Pemanfaatan Mendeley dan Google Scholar dalam Sitasi Karya Ilmiah. *Kongga*, *1*(1), 24–29. DOI: 10.52423/kongga.v1i1.4

Saini, N. (2023, August 28). *The impact of ChatGPT on language learning*. Linkedin. https://www.linkedin.com/pulse/impact-chatgpt-language-learning-dr-nitin-saini/

Saiyad, S., Bhagat, P., Virk, A., Mahajan, R., & Singh, T. (2021). Changing assessment scenarios: Lessons for changing practice. *International Journal of Applied & Basic Medical Research*, *11*(4), 206–213. DOI: 10.4103/ijabmr.IJABMR_334_21

Sajja, R., Sermet, Y., Cikmaz, M., Cwiertny, D., & Demir, I (2024). Artificial intelligence-enabled intelligent assistant for personalized and adaptive learning in higher education. Information. mdpi.com

Sajja, R., Sermet, Y., Cwiertny, D., & Demir, I. (2023). Integrating AI and learning analytics for data-driven pedagogical decisions and personalized interventions in education. *arXiv*. /arXiv.2312.09548DOI: 10.48550

Sajja, R., Sermet, Y., Cikmaz, M., Cwiertny, D., & Demir, I. (2024). Artificial intelligence-enabled intelligent assistant for personalized and adaptive learning in higher education. *Information (Basel)*, *15*(10), 596. DOI: 10.3390/info15100596

Salas-Pilco, S. Z., Xiao, K., & Oshima, J. (2022). Artificial intelligence and new technologies in inclusive education for minority students: A systematic review. *Sustainability (Basel)*, *14*(18), 11789. Advance online publication. DOI: 10.3390/su142013572

Salendab, F. A., Tago, K. L., Cogo, D. A., & Demafeliz, R. E. (2026). Transforming Higher Education: Theoretical Foundations and Innovative Pedagogies for Holistic Student Development. In *Higher Education Classrooms as Places for Inquiry: Stories and Methods from Practitioner Researchers* (pp. 207-236). IGI Global Scientific Publishing. DOI: DOI: 10.4018/979-8-3373-0305-5.ch007

Salim, S. (2024). *Artificial intelligence (AI) and teaching learning*. In P. Agarwal & N. Khan (Eds.), *The digital classroom: Integrating technology for effective learning* (pp. [insert page range if known]). Archives Publishing. https://doi.org/DOI: 10.25215/9358793864.22

Salman, H. A., Aliif, M., Ibrahim, R., & Mahmood, J. (2025). Systematic analysis of generative AI tools integration in academic research and peer review. *Online Journal of Communication and Media Technologies, 15*(1), e202502. DOI: 10.30935/ojcmt/15832

Sälzer, C., & Roczen, N. (2018). Global competence in the age of artificial intelligence. OECD Education Working Papers.

Sam, R.,, , Zain, A. N. M., & Jamil, H. (2012). Cambodia's higher education development in historical perspectives (1863-2012). *International Journal of Learning and Development, 2*(2), 224–240. DOI: 10.5296/ijld.v2i2.1670

Samadhiya, A., Kumar, A., Mulat-Weldemeskel, E., Luthra, S., Garza-Reyes, J. A., & Yadav, S. (2025). Next-gen quality learning: How can AI technologies shape education 4.0 and 5.0 towards the SDGs from multiple stakeholders' perspective? *The TQM Journal*. Advance online publication. DOI: 10.1108/TQM-11-2024-0441

Sam, C., & Dahles, H. (2017). Stakeholder involvement in the higher education sector in Cambodia. *Studies in Higher Education, 42*(9), 1764–1784. DOI: 10.1080/03075079.2015.1124851

Saniyah, S. M.Sari Mahibatus Saniyah. (2023). Duolingo and learner autonomy: Investigating the role of personalization and gamification in promoting self-directed language learning. *ENJEL: English Journal of Education and Literature, 2*(2), 141–147. DOI: 10.30599/enjel.v2i02.529

Santhoshi, G., Jyothi, M., Ramya Sri, K., Hasika, G., Varsha, G., & Snigdha, R. (2024). Research paper summarizer using AI. *International Research Journal on Advanced Engineering and Management, 2*(8), 2579–2583. DOI: 10.47392/IRJAEM.2024.0374

Santiago, P., & Cerna, L. (2020). Promoting inclusive education for diverse societies: A conceptual framework. OECD Education Working Papers, No. 260. OECD Publishing. DOI: 10.1787/19939019

Saputra, I., Kurniawan, A., Yanita, M., Putri, E. Y., & Mahniza, M. (2024). The evolution of educational assessment: How artificial intelligence is shaping the trends and future of learning evaluation. *Indonesian Journal of Computer Science, 13*(6). Advance online publication. DOI: 10.33022/ijcs.v13i6.4465

Saraswati, G., Farida, A., & Yuliati, Y. (2023). Implementing AI Replika in higher education speaking classes: Benefits and challenges. *ELT Forum: Journal of English Language Teaching, 12*(3), 207-215. DOI: 10.15294/elt.v12i3.76525

Sari, I. F., Yulia, Y., Hidayat, A. R., & Irwanto, I. M. R. (2025). Implementation of artificial intelligence in teachers' technological pedagogical and content knowledge in EFL context. *Pertanika Proceeding, 1*(2). Advance online publication. DOI: 10.47836/pp.1.2.010

Săseanu, A. S., Gogonea, R. M., & Ghi ă, S. I. (2024). The social impact of using artificial intelligence in education. *Amfiteatru Economic, 26*(65), 89–105. DOI: 10.24818/EA/2024/65/89

Sbardella, T., & Pakula, A. (2024). Investigating the transformative power of AI-driven intelligent tutoring systems in online language learning environments. *INTED Proceedings, 1*, 3557–3562. DOI: 10.21125/inted.2024.0940

Scavarelli, A., Arya, A., & Teather, R. J (2021). Virtual reality and augmented reality in social learning spaces: a literature review. Virtual Reality. carleton.ca

Schiavo, G., Businaro, S., & Zancanaro, M. (2024). Comprehension, apprehension, and acceptance: Understanding the influence of literacy and anxiety on acceptance of artificial Intelligence. *Technology in Society*, *77*, 102537. DOI: 10.1016/j.techsoc.2024.102537

Schiff, D. (2022). Education for AI, not AI for education: The role of education and ethics in national AI policy strategies. *International Journal of Artificial Intelligence in Education*, *32*(3), 527–563. DOI: 10.1007/s40593-021-00270-2

Schmid, R., Pauli, C., & Petko, D. (2022). Examining the use of digital technology in schools with a school-wide approach to personalized learning. *Educational Technology Research and Development*, *70*(1), 1–20. DOI: 10.1007/s11423-022-10167-z

Schultz, M., Young, K., Gunning, T. K., & Harvey, M. L. (2022). Defining and measuring authentic assessment: A case study in the context of tertiary science. *Assessment & Evaluation in Higher Education*, *47*(1), 77–94. DOI: 10.1080/02602938.2021.1887811

Schützeneder, J., Michael, G., Porlezza, C., & Mazzoni, P (2024). AI and automation. A key task for the present and future, DOI: .DOI: 10.4324/9781032630410-13

Schwartz, O. (2024). In 2016, Microsoft's racist Chatbots revealed the dangers of online conversation. IEEE Spectrum. https://spectrum.ieee.org/in-2016-microsofts-racist-chatbot-revealed-the-dangers-of-online-conversation

Seals, C. (2025). *Using AI for Qualitative Research*. Instats Inc., DOI: 10.61700/Q3YCGXG-D240I91841

Sedrakyan, G., Malmberg, J., Verbert, K., Järvelä, S., & Kirschner, P. A. (2020). Linking learning behavior analytics and learning science concepts: Designing a learning analytics dashboard for feedback to support learning regulation. [ou.nl]. *Computers in Human Behavior*, *107*, 105512. DOI: 10.1016/j.chb.2018.05.004

Selbst, A. D (2021). An institutional view of algorithmic impact assessments. Harv. JL & Tech.. harvard.edu

Seligman, M. E. (1975). *Learned helplessness: On depression, development, and death*. W.H. Freeman.

Selim, A. S. M. (2024). The transformative impact of AI-powered tools on academic writing: Perspectives of EFL university students. *International Journal of English Linguistics*, *14*(1), 14. DOI: 10.5539/ijel.v14n1p14

Selwyn, N. (2019). *Should robots replace teachers? AI and the future of education* (1st ed.). Polity Press.

Selwyn, N. (2019). *Should Robots Replace Teachers? AI and the Future of Education*. Polity Press.

Sengul, C., Neykova, R., & Destefanis, G. (2024). Software engineering education in the era of conversational AI: Current trends and future directions. *Frontiers in Artificial Intelligence*, *7*, 1–23. DOI: 10.3389/frai.2024.1436350

Seo, K., Tang, J., Roll, I., Fels, S., & Yoon, D. (2021). The impact of artificial intelligence on learner–instructor interaction in online learning. *International Journal of Educational Technology in Higher Education, 18*(1), 1–23. DOI: 10.1186/s41239-021-00292-9

Sethi, S., & Singh, M. (2024). *Blended Learning and AI in Higher Education: Adapt, Evolve, Thrive*. Cambridge Scholars Publishing.

Settles, B., & Meeder, B. (2016). *A trainable spaced repetition model for language learning*. https://www.semanticscholar.org/paper/A-Trainable-Spaced-Repetition-Model-for-Language-Settles-Meeder/cb836d2b8e126dc31ded5e674d73021604dcc6e0

Setyaningsih, E., Asrori, M., Ngadiso, , Sumardi, , Zainnuri, H., & Hariyanti, Y. (2024). Exploring high school EFL teachers' experiences with MagicSchool AI in lesson planning: Benefits and insights. *Voices of English Language Education Society, 8*(3), 685–700. DOI: 10.29408/veles.v8i3.27700

Shadbolt, N., O'Hara, K., De Roure, D., & Hall, W. (2019). Privacy, trust and ethical issues. In *Lecture notes in social networks* (pp. 149–200). Springer., DOI: 10.1007/978-3-030-10889-2_4

Shah, S. (2024). The Role of Artificial Intelligence In Research Writing: A Critical Analysis. *Journal of Universal College of Medical Sciences, 12*(03), 1–2. DOI: 10.3126/jucms.v12i03.73724

Shaik, T., Tao, X., Li, Y., Dann, C., McDonald, J., Redmond, P., & Galligan, L. (2022). A review of the trends and challenges in adopting natural language processing methods for education feedback analysis. [ieee.org]. *IEEE Access : Practical Innovations, Open Solutions, 10*, 56720–56739. DOI: 10.1109/ACCESS.2022.3177752

Sharma, R., Gulati, S., Kaur, A., Sinhababu, A., & Chakravarty, R. (2022). Research discovery and visualization using ResearchRabbit: A use case of AI in libraries. *Collnet Journal of Scientometrics and Information Management, 16*(2), 215–237. DOI: 10.1080/09737766.2022.2106167

Shaznay, N. (2025). Bridging the Industry-Higher Education Gap with Critical Design Futures Thinking and GenAI for Innovation. In *The Rise of Intelligent Machines* (pp. 268–288). Chapman and Hall/CRC.

Shoukat, B., & Adnan, M. S. (2025). TECHNOLOGY FEEDBACK AND STUDENT MOTIVATION IN TECHNOLOGY-ENHANCED LEARNING ENVIRONMENTS: A CORRELATIONAL STUDY. *Policy Research Journal, 3*(1), 838–854. Retrieved from https://policyresearchjournal.com/index.php/1/article/view/347

Shrestha, A. K., & Joshi, S. (2025, January). Toward ethical AI: A qualitative analysis of stakeholder perspectives. In *2025 IEEE 15th Annual Computing and Communication Workshop and Conference (CCWC)* (pp. 00022-00029). IEEE. https://doi.org/DOI: 10.1109/CCWC62904.2025.10903879

Shrestha, A. K., Barthwal, A., Campbell, M., Shouli, A., Syed, S., Joshi, S., & Vassileva, J. (2024). Navigating AI to unpack youth privacy concerns: An in-depth exploration and systematic review. *arXiv preprint arXiv:2412.16369*. https://doi.org//arXiv.2412.16369DOI: 10.1109/IEMCON62851.2024.11093125

Shute, V. J. (2008). Focus on formative feedback. *Review of Educational Research, 78*(1), 153–189. DOI: 10.3102/0034654307313795

Shwedeh, F., Salloum, S. A., Aburayya, A., Fatin, B., Elbadawi, M., Alghurabli, Z., & Al-Dabbagh, T. (2024). AI adoption and educational sustainability in higher education in the UAE. In Al-Marzouqi, A., Salloum, S. A., Al-Saidat, M., Aburayya, A., & Gupta, B. (Eds.), *Artificial intelligence in education: The power and dangers of ChatGPT in the classroom* (pp. 201–229). Springer., DOI: 10.1007/978-3-031-52280-2_14

Silalahi, R. M. (2019). Understanding Vygotsky's zone of proximal development for learning. *Polyglot: Jurnal Ilmiah, 15*(2), 169. DOI: 10.19166/pji.v15i2.1544

Simamora, R. M. (2020). The Challenges of online learning during the COVID-19 pandemic: An essay analysis of performing arts education students. *Studies in Learning and Teaching, 1*(2), 86–103.

Singh, N., Gunjan, V. K., & Nasralla, M. M (2022). A parametrized comparative analysis of performance between proposed adaptive and personalized tutoring system "seis tutor" with existing online tutoring system. IEEE Access. ieee.org

Singh, A., & Sree R, U. (2024). Empowering Presentations: Streamlining Content Generation through. *International Journal of Advanced Research in Science. Tongxin Jishu, 5–8*, 5–8. Advance online publication. DOI: 10.48175/IJARSCT-22502

Singleton, C. (2001). Computer-based assessment in education. *Educational and Child Psychology, 18*(3), 58–74. DOI: 10.53841/bpsecp.2001.18.3.58

Singun, A. (2025). Unveiling the barriers to digital transformation in higher education institutions: A systematic literature review. *Discover Education, 4*(1), 37. DOI: 10.1007/s44217-025-00430-9

Sinha, R. (2025). *Cultural biases in AI: How your prompts might be making things worse*. PsyChatWork. https://psychatwork.substack.com/p/cultural-biases-in-ai-how-your-prompts

Sivasubramanian, K., Jaheer Mukthar, K. P., Raju, V., & Srinivas, K. (2022). The impact of digital learning management system on students of higher education institutions during COVID-19 pandemic. In *Technologies, Artificial Intelligence and the Future of Learning Post-COVID-19: The Crucial Role of International Accreditation* (pp. 657–678). Springer International Publishing., DOI: 10.1007/978-3-030-93921-2_34

Skonieczny, K., & Vendramin, V. (2024). Academic teachers vs ChatGPT: A comparative study of strategies used by Slovenian and Polish faculties to prevent dishonest use of generative AI tools. *Journal of Contemporary Educational Studies/Sodobna Pedagogika, 75*(4). https://www.sodobnapedagogika.si/en/

Slade, S., & Prinsloo, P. (2013). Learning Analytics. *The American Behavioral Scientist, 57*(10), 1510–1529. DOI: 10.1177/0002764213479366

Smith, I., Cherma, S., & Adebayo, H. (2025). AI and blockchain in education: Secure and personalized learning experiences.

Sokhanvar, Z., Salehi, K., & Sokhanvar, F. (2021). Advantages of authentic assessment for improving the learning experience and employability skills of higher education students: A systematic literature review. *Studies in Educational Evaluation, 70*, 101030. Advance online publication. DOI: 10.1016/j.stueduc.2021.101030

Sok, S., & Bunry, R. (2021). Internationalization of higher education in Cambodia: Toward an agenda for higher education development. *International Journal of Comparative Education and Development, 23*(3), 193–211. DOI: 10.1108/IJCED-08-2020-0049

Sok, S., & Heng, K. (2023). ChatGPT for education and research: A review of benefits and risks. *Cambodian Journal of Educational Research, 3*(1), 110–121. DOI: 10.62037/cjer.2023.03.01.06

Solanki, R. S., Gautam, K. D., Khan, A. S., Kaur, R., & Bale, A. S. (2024). AI-Driven Innovations in Higher Education: Key Challenges and Future Prospects. Library of Progress-Library Science, Information Technology & Computer, 44(3).

Solis Trujillo, B. P., Velarde-Camaqui, D., Gonzales Nuñez, C. A., Castillo Silva, E. V., & Gonzalez Said de la Oliva, M. D. P. (2025, May). The current landscape of formative assessment and feedback in graduate studies: a systematic literature review. In *Frontiers in Education (Vol. 10,* p. 1509983). Frontiers Media SA. https://doi.org/DOI: 10.3389/feduc.2025.1509983

Song, C., Shin, S.-Y., & Shin, K.-S. (2024). Implementing the Dynamic Feedback-Driven Learning Optimization Framework: A machine learning approach to personalize educational pathways. *Applied Sciences (Basel, Switzerland), 14*(2), 916. DOI: 10.3390/app14020916

Song, Y., Weisberg, L. R., Zhang, S., Tian, X., Boyer, K. E., & Israel, M. (2024). A framework for inclusive AI learning design for diverse learners. *Computers and Education: Artificial Intelligence, 6*, 100212. DOI: 10.1016/j.caeai.2024.100212

Sorokina, S. (2024). Exploring Automated Summarization: From Extraction to Abstraction. *Vestnik Volgogradskogo Gosudarstvennogo Universiteta. Seriâ 2. Âzykoznanie, 23*(5), 47–59. DOI: 10.15688/jvolsu2.2024.5.4

Southworth, J., Migliaccio, K., Glover, J., Glover, J., Reed, D., McCarty, C., Brendemuhl, J., & Thomas, A. (2023). Developing a model for AI Across the curriculum: Transforming the higher education landscape via innovation in AI literacy. *Computers and Education: Artificial Intelligence, 4*, 1–10. DOI: 10.1016/j.caeai.2023.100127

Sperling, K., Stenberg, C.-J., McGrath, C., Åkerfeldt, A., Heintz, F., & Stenliden, L. (2024). In search of artificial intelligence (AI) literacy in teacher education: A scoping review. *Computers and Education Open, 6*, 100169. DOI: 10.1016/j.caeo.2024.100169

Spitzer, M. W. H., & Moeller, K. (2024). Performance increases in mathematics within an intelligent tutoring system during COVID-19-related school closures: A large-scale longitudinal evaluation. *Computers and Education Open, 6*, 100162. DOI: 10.1016/j.caeo.2024.100162

Srinivasa, K. G., Kurni, M., & Saritha, K. (2022). Harnessing the power of AI in education. In K. G. Srinivasa, M. Kurni, & K. Saritha, *Learning, teaching, and assessment methods for contemporary learners* (pp. 311–342). Springer Nature Singapore. DOI: 10.1007/978-981-19-6734-4_13

Sriram, A., Ramachandran, K., & Krishnamoorthy, S. (2025). Artificial intelligence in medical education: Transforming learning and practice. *Cureus, 17*(3), e80852. DOI: 10.7759/cureus.80852

Staake, J. (2023, July 22). *20 Ways teachers can use ChatGPT to make their lives easier.* We Are Teachers. https://www.weareteachers.com/chatgpt-for-teachers/

Stanford University. (2025). Course policies on generative AI use. *GSB Teaching and Learning Hub*. https://www.gsb.stanford.edu/faculty-research/teaching-learning-hub

Stein, D. J., Shoptaw, S. J., Vigo, D. V., Lund, C., Cuijpers, P., Bantjes, J., Sartorius, N., & Maj, M. (2022). Psychiatric diagnosis and treatment in the 21st century: Paradigm shifts versus incremental integration. *World Psychiatry; Official Journal of the World Psychiatric Association (WPA)*, *21*(3), 393–414. DOI: 10.1002/wps.20998

Strielkowski, W., Grebennikova, V., Lisovskiy, A., & Rakhimova, G. (2024). AI-driven adaptive learning for sustainable educational transformation. *Sustainable Development*. Advance online publication. DOI: 10.1002/sd.3221

Su, J. & Zhong, Y (2022). Artificial Intelligence (AI) in early childhood education: Curriculum design and future directions. Computers and Education: Artificial Intelligence. sciencedirect.com

Subramani, P., Senthamil Selvan, K., Dedgaonkar, S., Vishnoi, M., Rampal, S., & Yadav, D. (2024). Unlocking the Power of Text Mining for Information Understanding. *2024 15th International Conference on Computing Communication and Networking Technologies (ICCCNT)*, Kamand, India, 2024, pp. 1-7. DOI: 10.1109/ICCCNT61001.2024.10724258

Su, J., Ng, D. T. K., & Chu, S. K. W. (2023). Artificial intelligence (AI) literacy in early childhood education: The challenges and opportunities. *Computers & Education: Artificial Intelligence*, *4*, 100124. DOI: 10.1016/j.caeai.2023.100124

Su, J., & Zhong, Y. (2022). Artificial intelligence (AI) in early childhood education: Curriculum design and future directions. *Computers and Education: Artificial Intelligence*, *3*, 1–12. DOI: 10.1016/j.caeai.2022.100072

Sulisworo, D. (2023). Exploring Research Idea Growth with Litmap: Visualizing Literature Review Graphically. *Bincang Sains Dan Teknologi*, *2*(02), 48–54. DOI: 10.56741/bst.v2i02.323

Sumagang, S. J., & Balano, N. L. (2025). Embracing Diversity: General Education Teachers' Lived Experiences in Teaching Learners with Special Needs in an Inclusive Setting. *International Journal of Innovation and Scientific Research*, *12*(6), 729–739. DOI: 10.51244/IJRSI.2025.12060059

Sumathy, V., & Navamani, G. (2024). AI-Driven Personalized Learning: Enhancing Student Success through Adaptive Technologies. Library of Progress-Library Science, Information Technology & Computer, 44(3).

Sundari, M. S., Penthala, H. R., & Nayyar, A. (2024). Transforming Education through AI-Enhanced Content Creation and Personalized Learning Experiences. In *Impact of Artificial Intelligence on Society* (pp. 98–118). Chapman and Hall/CRC. [HTML] DOI: 10.1201/9781032644509-7

Sun, X., Yang, Y., & Du, Q. (2025). Advancing total quality management in higher education through AI and big data analytics. *Total Quality Management & Business Excellence*, *36*(9-10), 1–23. DOI: 10.1080/14783363.2025.2495103

Sural, I., & Yazici, M. (2021). Learner performance and satisfaction level in personalized learning environments. *Research Anthology on Developing Effective Online Learning Courses*, 1386-1410. DOI: 10.4018/978-1-7998-8047-9.ch069

Suskie, L. (2009). *Assessing student learning: A common sense guide* (2nd ed.). Jossey-Bass.

Sutrisno, D., Inawati, I., & Hermanto, H. (2023). Enhancing student learning autonomously: Exploring the global impact of artificial intelligence. [ELTEJ]. *English Language Teaching Educational Journal*, *6*(2), 137–150. DOI: 10.12928/eltej.v6i2.9100

Švábenský, V., Verger, M., Rodrigo, M. M. T., Monterozo, C. J. G., Baker, R. S., Saavedra, M. Z. N. L., . . . Shimada, A. (2024). Evaluating algorithmic bias in models for predicting academic performance of filipino students. arXiv preprint arXiv:2405.09821.

Swamy, V., Du, S., Marras, M., & Kaser, T. (2023, March). Trusting the explainers: teacher validation of explainable artificial intelligence for course design. In LAK23: *13th International Learning Analytics and Knowledge Conference* (pp. 345-356). https://doi.org/DOI: 10.1145/3576050.3576147

Sweeney, E., (2024), Siemens' AI tools are harnessing 'human-machine collaboration' to help workers solve maintenance problems, Business insider.

Takaoka, K., Yamazaki, K., Sakurai, E., Yamashita, K., & Motomura, Y. (2019). Development of an integrated AI platform and an ecosystem for daily life, business, and social problems. In Ahram, T. Z. (Ed.), *Advances in artificial intelligence, software and systems engineering* (pp. 300–309). Springer International Publishing., DOI: 10.1007/978-3-319-94229-2_29

Talaghzi, J., Bennane, A., Himmi, M. M., Bellafkih, M., & Benomar, A. (2020, September). Online adaptive learning: A review of literature. In *Proceedings of the 13th International Conference on Intelligent Systems: Theories and Applications* (pp. 1-6). https://doi.org/DOI: 10.1145/3419604.3419759

Tani, V. C. D. (2025). The rise of AI-Powered economies: how artificial intelligence is reshaping global business and governance. https://www.linkedin.com/pulse/rise-ai-powered-economies-how-artificial-intelligence-bentenbi-rkajc/

Tapalova, O. & Zhiyenbayeva, N (2022). Artificial intelligence in education: AIEd for personalised learning pathways. Electronic Journal of e-Learning. ed.gov

Tariq, M. U. (2025). AI and Work-Life Balance: Transforming Employee Wellbeing in the Modern Workplace. In Ahmed, E., Babar, A., Samad, A., Ahmed, R., & Beydoun, G. (Eds.), *Strengthening Human Relations in Organizations With AI* (pp. 85–110). IGI Global Scientific Publishing., DOI: 10.4018/979-8-3693-6507-6.ch004

Tariq, M. U. (2025). *AI-Driven Learning and Engagement in Higher Education.* IGI Global., DOI: 10.4018/979-8-3693-4074-5

Tariq, M. U. (2025). Bridging Cultures and Languages: Innovative Literacy Strategies for Inclusive and Engaged Classrooms. In Tussey, J., & Haas, L. (Eds.), *Supporting Cultural Differences Through Literacy Education* (pp. 257–282). IGI Global Scientific Publishing., DOI: 10.4018/979-8-3693-9271-3.ch010

Tariq, M. U. (2025). Revitalizing Pedagogy: Integrating Indigenous Knowledge and Practices Into Higher Education Disciplines. In Kgari-Masondo, M. (Ed.), *Indigenous Teaching Disciplines and Perspectives for Higher Education* (pp. 379–400). IGI Global Scientific Publishing., DOI: 10.4018/979-8-3693-9296-6.ch018

Tasdelen, O., & Bodemer, D. (2025). Generative AI in the Classroom: Effects of Context-Personalized Learning Material and Tasks on Motivation and Performance. *International Journal of Artificial Intelligence in Education, 35*(5), 1–22. DOI: 10.1007/s40593-025-00491-9

Taub, M., Azevedo, R., Rajendran, R., Cloude, E. B., Biswas, G., & Price, M. J. (2021). How are students' emotions related to the accuracy of cognitive and metacognitive processes during learning with an intelligent tutoring system? [nsf.gov]. *Learning and Instruction, 72*, 101200. DOI: 10.1016/j.learninstruc.2019.04.001

TED. (2023, May 1). *How AI could Save (not destroy) education | Sal Khan | TED* [Video]. YouTube. https://www.youtube.com/watch?v=hJP5GqnTrNo

Temper, M., Tjoa, S., & David, L. (2025). Higher Education Act for AI (HEAT-AI): A framework to regulate the usage of AI in higher education institutions. *Frontiers in Education, 10*, 1–13. DOI: 10.3389/feduc.2025.1505370

Tetzlaff, L., Hartmann, U., Dumont, H., & Brod, G. (2022). Assessing individualized instruction in the classroom: Comparing teacher, student, and observer perspectives. *Learning and Instruction, 82*, 101655. DOI: 10.1016/j.learninstruc.2022.101655

Texas Distance Learning Association (TxDLA). (2023). AI intelligence in career education: Aligning assessment with workforce readiness. https://www.txdla.org/ai-intelligence-in-career-educaiton/

Thanh, N. N. (2024). The opportunities and challenges of public policy communication in the context of digital transformation in Vietnam. *Journal of Strategy and Management, 31*(12), 13–21. DOI: 10.59394/JSM.18

Thiem, K. C. & Dasgupta, N (2022). From precollege to career: Barriers facing historically marginalized students and evidence-based solutions. Social Issues and Policy Review. researchgate.net

Thurzo, A. (2025). How is AI Transforming Medical Research, Education and Practice? *Bratislavské Lekárske Listy, 126*(3), 1–6. DOI: 10.1007/s44411-025-00063-2

Timbs, A. (2025). The cognitive convergence of AI and human learning: How learning theories illuminate artificial intelligence. DOI: 10.2139/ssrn.5182286

Tirupati, K. K., Joshi, A., Singh, S. P., Chhapola, A., Jain, S. K., & Gupta, A. (2024). Leveraging Power BI for Enhanced Data Visualization and Business Intelligence. *Universal Research Reports, 10*(2), 676–711. DOI: 10.36676/urr.v10.i2.1375

Tlili, A., Shehailia, M., Alowayr, A., & Burgos, D. (2023). What if the devil is in the details? A comparative study of ChatGPT-3.5 and ChatGPT-4 for generating literature review papers. *arXiv preprint*. https://arxiv.org/abs/2305.00596

Tomlinson, M. (2017). Student perceptions of themselves as 'consumers' of higher education. *British Journal of Sociology of Education, 38*(4), 450–467. DOI: 10.1080/01425692.2015.1113856

Topali, P., Chounta, I. A., Martínez-Monés, A., & Dimitriadis, Y. (2023). Delving into instructor-led feedback interventions informed by learning analytics in massive open online courses. *Journal of Computer Assisted Learning, 39*(4), 1039–1060. DOI: 10.1111/jcal.12799

Torrentira, M. C.Jr. (2024). Capabilities and Application of Artificial Intelligence (AI) Models in Qualitative and Quantitative Data Mining, Data Processing and Data Analysis. *European Journal of Education Studies, 74*(3), 198–200. DOI: 10.46827/ejes.v11i9.5521

Torres-Salinas, D. (2024). Curso de escritura académica. Tomar notas con el método Zettelkasten y Zotero. *INFONOMY, 2*(5). Advance online publication. DOI: 10.3145/infonomy.24.055

Trajkovski, G., & Hayes, H. (2025). AI-Assisted formative assessment and feedback. In *AI-Assisted Assessment in Education: Transforming Assessment and Measuring Learning* (pp. 283–312). Cham: Springer Nature Switzerland. https://doi.org/DOI: 10.1007/978-3-031-88252-4_7

Trajkovski, G., & Hayes, H. (2025). The Future of AI in Educational Assessment. In *AI-Assisted Assessment in Education: Transforming Assessment and Measuring Learning* (pp. 347–380). Springer Nature Switzerland. DOI: 10.1007/978-3-031-88252-4_9

Transparency International. (2024). Corruption perceptions index 2024: Uganda. https://www.transparency.org/en/countries/uganda

Tri, N. M., & Hoang, P. D. (2023). The Impact of Digital Transformation in Higher Education: The Case Study from Vietnam. *Journal of Higher Education Theory and Practice, 23*(5). Advance online publication. DOI: 10.33423/jhetp.v23i5.5922

Trinh, M. A. (2025). AI-Assisted Research Methodology. https://creativecommons.org/licenses/by-nc-sa/4.0/

Troussas, C., Krouska, A., Alepis, E., & Virvou, M. (2020). Intelligent and adaptive tutoring through a social network for higher education. [HTML]. *New Review of Hypermedia and Multimedia, 26*(3-4), 138–167. DOI: 10.1080/13614568.2021.1908436

Tung, R. L. (1995). Strategic management in an era of global alliances: The impact of culture. *Management International Review, 35*(Special Issue 1), 11–31.

Tuomi, I. (2018). *The Impact of Artificial Intelligence on Learning, Teaching, and Education: Policies for the Future*. European Commission.

Twabu, K., & Nakene-Mginqi, M. (2024). Developing a design thinking artificial intelligence driven auto-marking/grading system for assessments to reduce the workload of lecturers at a higher learning institution in South Africa. *Frontiers in Education, 9*, 1512569. Advance online publication. DOI: 10.3389/feduc.2024.1512569

Twenge, J. M. (2017). *iGen: Why today's super-connected kids are growing up less rebellious, more tolerant, less happy—and completely unprepared for adulthood—and what that means for the rest of us*. Atria Books.

Tyagi, S., Gupta, V., & Mehndiratta, V. (2024). Building Smart Campuses: Integrating AI in Higher Education. In *Recent Trends in Artificial Intelligence Towards a Smart World: Applications in Industries and Sectors* (pp. 399–431). Springer Nature Singapore. DOI: 10.1007/978-981-97-6790-8_15

Tzenios, N. (2020). Clustering students for personalized health education based on learning styles. [sagescience.org]. *Sage Science Review of Educational Technology, 3*(1), 22–36.

Tzuriel, D. (2021). The socio-cultural theory of Vygotsky. *Social Interaction in Learning and Development*, 53-66. DOI: 10.1007/978-3-030-75692-5_3

Uche-Anya, E., Anyane-Yeboa, A., Berzin, T. M., Ghassemi, M., & May, F. P. (2022). Artificial intelligence in gastroenterology and hepatology: How to advance clinical practice while ensuring health equity. [nih.gov]. *Gut*, *71*(9), 1909–1915. DOI: 10.1136/gutjnl-2021-326271

Uddin, M. K. S. (2024). A review of utilizing natural language processing and ai for advanced data visualization in real-time analytics. *Deleted Journal*, *1*(4), 34–49. DOI: 10.62304/ijmisds.v1i04.185

Udeh, C. G.Chinemelum Goodness Udeh. (2025). The role of generative AI in personalized learning for higher education. *World Journal of Advanced Engineering Technology and Sciences*, *14*(2), 205–207. DOI: 10.30574/wjaets.2025.14.2.0077

Uganda Vice Chancellors' Forum. (2024, October 4). UVCF annual conference 2024: Integrating AI into higher education in Uganda. *Uganda Vice Chancellors' Forum*. https://uvcf.ac.ug/uvcf-annual-conference-2024

Ulster University. (2024). Guidance on AI in assessment design. Retrieved from https://www.ulster.ac.uk/learningenhancement/cqe/strategies/ai

Unearthing Hidden Research Opportunities Through Bibliometric Analysis: A Review. (2023). Asian Journal of Research in Education and Social Sciences. DOI: 10.55057/ajress.2023.5.1.23

UNESCO. (2019). *ICT Competency Framework for Teachers*. ICT-CFT.

UNESCO. (2021). *AI and education: Guidance for policy-makers*. UNESCO Publishing. https://unesdoc.unesco.org/ark:/48223/pf0000376709

UNESCO. (2021). *Recommendation on the ethics of artificial intelligence*. https://unesdoc.unesco.org/ark:/48223/pf0000381137

UNESCO. (2021). Reimagining our futures together: A new social contract for education.

UNESCO. (2022). Guidance for generative AI in education and research. United Nations Educational, Scientific and Cultural Organization. https://unesdoc.unesco.org/ark:/48223/pf0000386125

UNESCO. (2023). *Guidance for generative AI in education and research*. United Nations Educational, Scientific and Cultural Organization. https://unesdoc.unesco.org/ark:/48223/pf0000386693

UNESCO. (2023, December 4). *AI competency frameworks for school students and teachers*. https://www.unesco.org/en/digital-education/ai-future-learning/competency-frameworks

UNESCO. (2024). Six pillars for the digital transformation of education. *United Nations Educational, Scientific and Cultural Organization*. https://unesdoc.unesco.org/ark:/48223/pf0000391299

UNESCO. (2024, August 8). *AI competency framework for teachers*. DOI: 10.54675/ZJTE2084

UNSW. (2020). Ethical and responsible use of Artificial Intelligence in UNSW. https://www.student.unsw.edu.au/notices/2024/05/ethical-and-responsible-use-artificial-intelligence-unsw

Unterhalter, E. (2021). Education and the capability approach: Taking stock. *Cambridge Journal of Education*, *51*(1), 27–43.

Uzun, Y., Suraworachet, W., Zhou, Q., Gauthier, A., & Cukurova, M. (2025). Engagement with analytics feedback and its relationship to self-regulated learning competence and course performance. *International Journal of Educational Technology in Higher Education, 22*(1), 17. DOI: 10.1186/s41239-025-00515-3

Vadisetty, R., & Polamarasetti, A. (2024, December). AI-Augmented Skill Development Roadmaps: Tailoring 12-Month Learning Paths for Future-Ready Careers in Education 4.0 and Industry 4.0. In *2024 13th International Conference on System Modeling & Advancement in Research Trends (SMART)* (pp. 655-661). IEEE.

Valle, N., Antonenko, P., Valle, D., Sommer, M., Huggins-Manley, A. C., Dawson, K., Kim, D., & Baiser, B. (2021). Predict or describe? How learning analytics dashboard design influences motivation and statistics anxiety in an online statistics course. [springer.com]. *Educational Technology Research and Development, 69*(3), 1405–1431. DOI: 10.1007/s11423-021-09998-z

Vallor, S. (2016). *Technology and the Virtues: A Philosophical Guide to a Future Worth Wanting*. Oxford University Press. DOI: 10.1093/acprof:oso/9780190498511.001.0001

Valtonen, T., López-Pernas, S., Saqr, M., Vartiainen, H., Sointu, E. T., & Tedre, M. (2022). The nature and building blocks of educational technology research. [sciencedirect.com]. *Computers in Human Behavior, 128*, 107123. DOI: 10.1016/j.chb.2021.107123

Van Zyl, H. M., Burger, Y., & Carsten, L. (2020). Curriculum design as an enabler of student involvement and success in Higher Education. *South African Journal of Higher Education, 34*(5), 177–191. DOI: 10.20853/34-5-4267

Vascan, T. (2024). The Use of Artificial Intelligence in the Research Process. *Acta et Commentationes: tiin e Ale Educa iei, 35*(1), 68–77. DOI: 10.36120/2587-3636.v35i1.68-77

Vashishth, T. K., Sharma, V., Sharma, K. K., Kumar, B., Panwar, R., & Chaudhary, S. (2024). AI-driven learning analytics for personalized feedback and assessment in higher education. In *Using Traditional Design Methods to Enhance AI-Driven Decision Making* (pp. 206–230). IGI Global., DOI: 10.4018/979-8-3693-0639-0.ch009

Velmurugan, P. R., Catherine, S., & Vettriselvan, R. EP, J., & Rajesh, D. (2025). Innovative Intercultural Communication Training in Translator Education: Cultivating Cultural Competence. In Cutting-Edge Approaches in Translator Education and Pedagogy (pp. 217-244). IGI Global Scientific Publishing.

Vesna, L., Sawale, P. S., Kaul, P., Pal, S., & Murthy, B. S. N. V. R. (2025). Digital divide in AI-powered education: Challenges and solutions for equitable learning. *Journal of Information Systems Engineering & Management, 10*(21), 1–9. DOI: 10.52783/jisem.v10i21s.3327

Vettriselvan, R., & Ramya, R. (2025). Sustainable Curriculum Design and Development: A Comprehensive Approach. In Smart Education and Sustainable Learning Environments in Smart Cities (pp. 471-486). IGI Global.

Vettriselvan, R., Deepan, A., Garg, P. K., Suresh, N. V., & Velmurugan, P. R. (2025). Advanced Text Analysis, Simplification, Classification, and Synthesis Techniques: Leveraging AI for Enhanced Medical Education. In Using AI Tools in Text Analysis, Simplification, Classification, and Synthesis (pp. 37-66). IGI Global Scientific Publishing.

Vettriselvan, R., Velmurugan, P. R., Deepan, A., Jaiswani, G., & Durgarani, M. (2025). Transforming Virtual Education: Advanced Strategies for Quality Assurance in Online and Distance Learning. In Navigating Quality Assurance and Accreditation in Global Higher Education (pp. 563-580). IGI Global Scientific Publishing.

Viberg, O., Kizilcec, R. F., Wise, A. F., Jivet, I., & Nixon, N. (2024). Advancing equity and inclusion in educational practices with AI-powered educational decision support systems (AI-EDSS). *British Journal of Educational Technology*, *55*(5), 1974–1981. DOI: 10.1111/bjet.13507

Vieriu, A. M., & Petrea, G. (2025). The impact of artificial intelligence (AI) on students' academic development. *Education Sciences*, *15*(3), 343. DOI: 10.3390/educsci15030343

Vijai, C., Natarajan, K., & Elayaraja, M. (2019). Citation Tools and Reference Management Software for Academic Writing. *International Journal of Geographical Information Science*, *14*(6), 586–596. DOI: 10.26643/gis.v14i6.14788

Villegas-Ch, W., Buenano-Fernandez, D., Navarro, A. M., & Mera-Navarrete, A. (2025). Adaptive intelligent tutoring systems for STEM education: Analysis of the learning impact and effectiveness of personalized feedback. *Smart Learning Environments*, *12*(1), 1–31. DOI: 10.1186/s40561-025-00389-y

Vishwanath, A. L. S., Seng, N., Goh, P., Lee, S., Khader, M., Ong, G., & Chin, J. (2020). Cyber hygiene. The concept, its measure, and its initial tests, Decision Support Systems, Volume 128, 2020, 113160, ISSN 0167-9236.

Visual citation navigation of open education resources using Litmaps. (2022). Library Hi Tech News, 39(5), 7–11. DOI: 10.1108/LHTN-01-2022-0012

von Neumann, J., & Morgenstern, O. (1944). *Theory of games and economic behavior*. Princeton University Press.

Voogt, J., Erstad, O., Dede, C., & Mishra, P. (2013). Challenges to learning and schooling in the digital networked world of the 21st century. *Journal of Computer Assisted Learning*, *29*(5), 403–413. DOI: 10.1111/jcal.12029

Vygotsky, L. S. (1978). *Mind in society. The development of higher psychological processes*. Harvard University., https://www.scirp.org/reference/referencespapers?referenceid=803661

Vygotsky, L. S. (1978). *Mind in society: The development of higher psychological processes*. Harvard University Press.

Wadhwani, M. K., & Mirza, M. I. (2025). AI-POWERED GIG EDUCATION: TRANSFORMING WORKFORCE RESILIENCE AND ECONOMIC RECOVERY IN THE DIGITAL AGE.

Wagner, G., Lukyanenko, R., & Paré, G. (2021). Artificial intelligence and the conduct of literature reviews. *Journal of Information Technology*, *37*(2), 209–226. DOI: 10.1177/02683962211048201

Wahditiya, A. A., Sirajuddin, N., & Zulfadli, Z. (2023). *Pelatihan Penggunaan Aplikasi Mendeley Dalam Mengelola Referensi. Jurnal Pustaka Mitra*. Pusat Akses Kajian Mengabdi Terhadap Masyarakat., DOI: 10.55382/jurnalpustakamitra.v3i5.630

Waladi, C., & Lamarti, M. S. (2024). Adaptive AI-driven assessment for competency-based learning scenarios. In *Innovative Instructional Design Methods and Tools for Improved Teaching* (pp. 215–226). IGI Global Scientific Publishing., DOI: 10.4018/979-8-3693-3128-6.ch010

Waladi, C., Lamarti, M. S., & Khaldi, M. (2025). AI-driven personalized learning pathways customizing education for every student. *Advances in Educational Technologies and Instructional Design*, •••, 63–78. DOI: 10.4018/979-8-3693-8965-2.ch004

Walkington, C., & Bernacki, M. L. (2020). Appraising research on personalized learning: Definitions, theoretical alignment, advancements, and future directions. [tandfonline.com]. *Journal of Research on Technology in Education*, *52*(3), 235–252. DOI: 10.1080/15391523.2020.1747757

Walter, Y. (2024). Embracing the future of artificial intelligence in the classroom: The relevance of AI literacy, prompt engineering, and critical thinking in modern education.

Walter, Y. (2024, February 26). Embracing the future of Artificial Intelligence in the classroom: The relevance of AI literacy, prompt engineering, and critical thinking in modern education. *International Journal of Educational Technology in Higher Education*, *21*(1), 15. DOI: 10.1186/s41239-024-00448-3

Waly, M. (2024). Artificial Intelligence and Scientific Research. *Sustainability Education Globe*, *2*(1), 1–14. DOI: 10.21608/seg.2024.269596.1001

Wang, J. (2025). Revolutionizing Education for Sustainable Development Through Adaptive Learning and Artificial Intelligence. In Rethinking the Pedagogy of Sustainable Development in the AI Era (pp. 63-92). IGI Global. DOI: 10.4018/979-8-3693-9062-7.ch004

Wang, J., Xiao, R., Hou, X., Li, H., Tseng, Y. J., Stamper, J., & Koedinger, K. (2025, July). LLMs to Support K–12 Teachers in Culturally Relevant Pedagogy: An AI Literacy Example. In *International Conference on Artificial Intelligence in Education* (pp. 152-160). Cham: Springer Nature Switzerland. https://doi.org/DOI: 10.1007/978-3-031-99264-3_19

Wangdi, P. (2024). *Integrating Artificial Intelligence in Education:* DOI: 10.33830/ijrse.v6i2.1722

Wang, Q., Woo, H. L., & Quek, C. L. (2021). Enhancing AI literacy through student-centered design. *Interactive Learning Environments.*

Wang, S., Wang, F., Zhu, Z., Wang, J., Tran, T., & Du, Z. (2024). Artificial intelligence in education: A systematic literature review. *Expert Systems with Applications*, *252*, 124167. DOI: 10.1016/j.eswa.2024.124167

Wang, Z. (2025). The Impact of Teacher Feedback on Student Motivation in Online Learning Environments: A Study Based on Self-Determination Theory. *Journal of Education, Humanities, and Social Research*, *2*(2), 13–27. DOI: 10.71222/syf4kg35

Wang, Z., & Feng, J. (2023). Teaching quality evaluation based on student's zone of proximal development (ZPD) prediction. *Journal of Education and Educational Research*, *6*(1), 44–48. DOI: 10.54097/jeer.v6i1.14157

Wankhade, P. (2025). Data Analysis. *Indian Scientific Journal Of Research In Engineering And Management*, *09*(01), 1–9. DOI: 10.55041/IJSREM40826

Warschauer, M., & Healey, D. (1998). Computers and language learning: An overview. *Language Teaching*, *31*(2), 57–71. DOI: 10.1017/S0261444800012970

Watson, A. (2024). Hallucinated Citation Analysis: Delving into Student-Submitted AI-Generated Sources at the University of Mississippi. *The Serials Librarian*, *85*(5-6), 1–9. DOI: 10.1080/0361526X.2024.2433640

Watters, A (2023). Teaching machines: The history of personalized learning. [HTML]

Weber-Wulff, D., Anohina-Naumeca, A., Bjelobaba, S., Foltýnek, T., Guerrero-Dib, J., Popoola, O., Šigut, P., & Waddington, L. (2023). Testing of detection tools for AI-generated text. *International Journal for Educational Integrity*, *19*(1), 26. DOI: 10.1007/s40979-023-00146-z

Weiner, B. (1972). Attribution theory, achievement motivation, and the educational process. *Review of Educational Research*, *42*(2), 203–215. DOI: 10.3102/00346543042002203

Weiner, B. (1985). An attributional theory of achievement motivation and emotion. *Psychological Review*, *92*(4), 548–573. DOI: 10.1037/0033-295X.92.4.548 PMID: 3903815

Weiner, B. (1986). *An attributional theory of motivation and emotion*. Springer. DOI: 10.1007/978-1-4612-4948-1

Weiner, B. (2012). An attribution theory of motivation. In Van Lange, P. A. M., Kruglanski, A. W., & Higgins, E. T. (Eds.), *Handbook of theories of social psychology* (Vol. 1, pp. 135–155). Sage. DOI: 10.4135/9781446249215.n8

Weiss, D. J. (1982). Improving Measurement Quality and Efficiency with Adaptive Testing. *Applied Psychological Measurement*, *6*(4), 473–492. DOI: 10.1177/014662168200600408

West, S. M., Whittaker, M., & Crawford, K. (2019) Discriminating Systems Gender, Race and Power in AI. AI Now Institute. - References - *Scientific Research Publishing*. https://www.scirp.org/reference/referencespapers?referenceid=3758256

Westerlund, M. (2019). The emergence of deepfake technology: A review. *Technology Innovation Management Review*, *9*(11), 39–52. DOI: 10.22215/timreview/1282

Wiggins, G. (1998). Educative Assessment: Designing Assessments to Inform and Improve Student Performance.

Williams, B. (2025). AI tools for transcribing and coding field interviews - insight7 - AI tool for Interview Analysis & Market Research. Insight7. https://insight7.io/ai-tools-for-transcribing-and-coding-field-interviews/

Williamson, B., & Hogan, A. (2020). Commercialisation and privatisation in/of education in the context of COVID-19. *Education International*. https://issuu.com/educationinternational/docs/research_covid-19_en_final

Williamson, B., & Eynon, R. (2020). Historical threads, missing links, and future directions in AI in education. *Learning, Media and Technology*, *45*(3), 223–235. DOI: 10.1080/17439884.2020.1798995

Williamson, B., Eynon, R., & Potter, J. (2020). Pandemic Politics, Pedagogies and Practices: Digital Technologies and Distance Education During the Coronavirus Emergency. *Learning, Media and Technology*, *45*(2), 107–114. DOI: 10.1080/17439884.2020.1761641

Winner, L. (1986). *The Whale and the Reactor: A Search for Limits in an Age of High Technology*. University of Chicago Press.

Winstone, N. E., & Boud, D. (2022). The need to disentangle assessment and feedback in higher education. *Studies in Higher Education*, *47*(3), 656–667. DOI: 10.1080/03075079.2020.1779687

Wise, A. F. (2018). Learning analytics: Using data-informed decision-making to improve teaching and learning. *Contemporary Technologies in Education*, 119-143. DOI: 10.1007/978-3-319-89680-9_7

Wong, G. K. W., Ma, X., Dillenbourg, P., & Huan, J (2020). Broadening artificial intelligence education in K-12: Where to start?. ACM inroads. epfl.ch

Woolf, B. P. (2010). *Building intelligent interactive tutors: Student-centered strategies for revolutionizing e-learning*. Morgan Kaufmann.

World Economic Forum. (2020). The future of jobs report 2020.

World Economic Forum. (2025). The Future of Jobs Report 2025. https://www.weforum.org/publications/the-future-of-jobs-report-2025/

Write & Improve with Cambridge. (n.d.). https://writeandimprove.com/workbooks#/wi-workbooks

Xiao, H., Liu, C., Hou, F., & Liu, H. (2024). Impact of subsidy on the new type of forestry operating entity's input: Moderating effect of the rising labor cost. *Natural Resources Forum, 1477*. Advance online publication. DOI: 10.1111/1477-8947.12530

Xiao, Y., & Zhi, Y. (2023). An exploratory study of EFL learners' use of ChatGPT for language learning tasks: Experience and perceptions. *Languages (Basel, Switzerland)*, *8*(3), 212. DOI: 10.3390/languages8030212

Xie, B., Tian, Y., & Lee, M. J. (2024). Collaborative curricular co-design for AI education: Lessons from humanities and STEM teachers. Proceedings of the AAAI Conference on Artificial Intelligence and Education. https://www.benjixie.com/publication/eaai-2024/

Xie, Y., Luo, Y., Li, G., & Tang, N. (2024). HAIChart: Human and AI Paired Visualization System. *Proceedings of the VLDB Endowment International Conference on Very Large Data Bases*, *17*(11), 3178–3191. DOI: 10.14778/3681954.3681992

Xin, J. J. (2024). Investigating EFL teachers' use of generative AI to develop reading materials: A practice and perception study. *Language Teaching Research*, 13621688241303321. Advance online publication. DOI: 10.1177/13621688241303321

Xi, X., Higgins, D., Zechner, K., & Williamson, D. M. (2008). Automated scoring of spontaneous speech using speechrater v1.0. *ETS Research Report Series*, *2008*(2), i-102. DOI: 10.1002/j.2333-8504.2008.tb02148.x

Xu, S., Su, Y., & Liu, K. (2025). Investigating student engagement with AI-driven feedback in translation revision: A mixed-methods study. *Education and Information Technologies*, *30*(12), 16969–16995. Advance online publication. DOI: 10.1007/s10639-025-13457-0

Xu, Z. (2024). AI in education: Enhancing learning experiences and student outcomes. *Applied and Computational Engineering*, *51*(1), 104–111. DOI: 10.54254/2755-2721/51/20241187

Yadav, S. (2024). *Artificial Intelligence (AI) Integration in Higher Education*. 43–59. DOI: 10.1201/9781032644509-4

Yahchouchi, G., & Rotabi, S. (2025). AI and Education: Preparing the MENA's Workforce for the Future. In *AI in the Middle East for Growth and Business: A Transformative Force* (pp. 27–41). Springer Nature Switzerland. DOI: 10.1007/978-3-031-75589-7_3

Yakubu, M., Sain, Z. H., Lawal, U. S., Budiman, S. A., & Permana, D. (2025). Analysis of Online Academic Writing Tools Usage among Postgraduate Students in North-west Nigeria. *Kharisma*, *4*(1), 1–13. DOI: 10.59373/kharisma.v4i1.69

Yan, J., Tian, H., Sun, X., & Song, L. (2025, April). Role of artificial intelligence in enhancing competency assessment and transforming curriculum in higher vocational education. In *Frontiers in Education (Vol. 10*, p. 1551596). Frontiers Media SA. https://doi.org/DOI: 10.3389/feduc.2025.1551596

Yang, W. (2022). Artificial intelligence education for young children: Why, what, and how in curriculum design and implementation. *Computers and Education: Artificial Intelligence*, *3*, 100061. Advance online publication. DOI: 10.1016/j.caeai.2022.100061

Yaroshenko, T. O., & Iaroshenko, O. I. (2023). Artificial Intelligence (AI) for Research Lifecycle: Challenges and Opportunities. *University Library at a New Stage of Social Communications Development. Conference Proceedings*, *8*, 194–201. DOI: 10.15802/unilib/2023_294639

Yaseen, H., Mohammad, A. S., Ashal, N., Abusaimeh, H., Ali, A., & Sharabati, A.-A. A. (2025). The Impact of Adaptive Learning Technologies, Personalized Feedback, and Interactive AI Tools on Student Engagement: The Moderating Role of Digital Literacy. *Sustainability (Basel)*, *17*(3), 1133. DOI: 10.3390/su17031133

Yesilyurt, Y. E. (2023). AI-enabled assessment and feedback mechanisms for language learning: Transforming pedagogy and learner experience. In Kartal, G. (Ed.), *Transforming the language teaching experience in the age of AI* (pp. 25–43). IGI Global., DOI: 10.4018/978-1-6684-9893-4.ch002

Yilmaz, O (2021). Augmented Reality in Science Education: An Application in Higher Education. Shanlax International Journal of Education. ed.gov

Yilmaz, B. (2017). *Effects of adaptive learning technologies on math achievement: A quantitative study of ALEKS math software*. University of Missouri-Kansas City.

Yilmaz, R., Yurdugül, H., Yilmaz, F. G. K., Şahín, M., Sulak, S., Aydin, F., & Ömer, O. R. A. L. (2022). Smart MOOC integrated with intelligent tutoring: A system architecture and framework model proposal. [sciencedirect.com]. *Computers and Education: Artificial Intelligence*, *3*, 100092. DOI: 10.1016/j.caeai.2022.100092

Younas, M., El-Dakhs, D. A. S., & Jiang, Y. (2025). A comprehensive systematic review of AI-driven approaches to self-directed learning. *IEEE Access : Practical Innovations, Open Solutions, 13*, 38387–38403. DOI: 10.1109/ACCESS.2025.3546319

Yousef, M., Deeb, S., & Hashlamon, K. (2025). AI usage among medical students in Palestine and AI's capability in conducting the research itself: A cross-sectional study. *ResearchSquare*, 1–19.

Yuan[1], L., Hou[1], B., Feng, D., & Rahman[1], S. S. A. (2025, June). Predictive Analytics in Education: Leveraging AI for Personalizing Student Learning Trajectories. In *Proceedings of the 2nd International Conference on Educational Development and Social Sciences (EDSS 2025)* (Vol. 924, p. 309). Springer Nature. DOI:DOI: 10.2991/978-2-38476-400-6_38

Yuan, M., & Recker, M. (2020). The role of digital badges in motivating learning and documenting skills in higher education. *Journal of Learning Analytics*, *7*(1), 83–96.

Yusuf, S. O., Abubakar, J. E., Durodola, R., Ocran, G., Hadassah, A., & Yusuf, P. O. (2024). Impact of AI on continuous learning and skill development in the workplace: A comparative study with traditional methods. *World Journal of Advanced Research and Reviews*, *23*(2), 1129–1140. DOI: 10.30574/wjarr.2024.23.2.2439

Zary, A., & Zary, N. (2025). Artificial intelligence in technical and vocational education and training: Empirical evidence, implementation challenges, and future directions. *Preprints.*

Zawacki-Richter, O., Bai, J. Y., Lee, K., Slagter van Tryon, P. J., & Prinsloo, P. (2024). New advances in artificial intelligence applications in higher education? *International Journal of Educational Technology in Higher Education*, *21*(1), 32. DOI: 10.1186/s41239-024-00464-3

Zawacki-Richter, O., Marín, V. I., & Bond, M. (2023). Delphi study on artificial intelligence in higher education: Trends, opportunities, and institutional readiness. *International Journal of Educational Technology in Higher Education, 20*, 6. Advance online publication. DOI: 10.1186/s41239-023-00377-6

Zawacki-Richter, O., Marín, V. I., Bond, M., & Gouverneur, F. (2019). Systematic review of research on artificial intelligence applications in higher education – where are the educators? *Educational Research Review*, *28*, 100290. DOI: 10.1016/j.edurev.2018.11.001

Zawacki-Richter, O., Marín, V. I., Bond, M., & Gouverneur, F. (2019). Systematic review of research on artificial intelligence applications in higher education – Where are the educators? *International Journal of Educational Technology in Higher Education*, *16*(1), 1–27. DOI: 10.1186/s41239-019-0171-0

Zhai, C., Wibowo, S., & Li, L. D. (2024). The effects of over-reliance on AI dialogue systems on students' cognitive abilities: A systematic review. *Smart Learning Environments*, *11*(1), 28. Advance online publication. DOI: 10.1186/s40561-024-00316-7

Zhang, J., Xiao, C., & Watanabe, T. (2017). *A Framework for Presentation Slide Design Support.* 191–196. DOI: 10.1145/3093241.3093261

Zhang, H., Lee, I., Ali, S., DiPaola, D., Cheng, Y., & Breazeal, C. (2023). Integrating ethics and career futures with technical learning to promote AI literacy for middle school students: An exploratory study. [springer.com]. *International Journal of Artificial Intelligence in Education, 33*(2), 290–324. DOI: 10.1007/s40593-022-00293-3

Zhang, L., Basham, J. D., & Yang, S. (2020). Understanding the implementation of personalized learning: A research synthesis. [HTML]. *Educational Research Review, 31*, 100339. DOI: 10.1016/j.edurev.2020.100339

Zheng, B., Wang, Y., & Zhang, Y. (2022). Capstone experiences and project-based learning in AI education: Measuring student readiness and application skills. *Education and Information Technologies, 27*, 6543–6560.

Zhou, C. (2023). Integration of modern technologies in higher education, with the example of artificial intelligence use. *Education and Information Technologies, 28*(4), 3893–3910. DOI: 10.1007/s10639-022-11309-9

Zhou, X., & Schofield, L. (2024). Using social learning theories to explore the role of generative artificial intelligence (AI) in collaborative learning. *Journal of Learning Development in Higher Education,* (30). Advance online publication. DOI: 10.47408/jldhe.vi30.1031

Zou, J. Y., & Schiebinger, L. (2018). AI can be sexist and racist — It's time to make it fair. *Nature, 559*(7714), 324–326. DOI: 10.1038/d41586-018-05707-8 PMID: 30018439

Zulianti, H., Hastuti, H., Nurchurifiani, E., Hastomo, T., Maximilian, A., & Ajeng, G. D. (2024). Enhancing novice EFL teachers' competency in AI-powered tools through a TPACK-based professional development program. *World Journal of English Language, 15*(3), 117. DOI: 10.5430/wjel.v15n3p117

Zulu, E., Haupt, T., & Tramontin, V. (2018). Cognitive loading due to self-directed learning, complex questions and tasks in the zone of proximal development of students. *Problems of Education in the 21st Century, 76*(6), 864-880. DOI: 10.33225/pec/18.76.864

About the Contributors

Reda M. S. Abdelaal (registered member of the Egyptian Syndicate for Professional Engineers) received a B.S. in Mechanical Engineering from Helwan University, Cairo, Egypt, in 1979; an M.Eng. degree in Operations Research from the same university in 1982; and a Ph.D. degree in Industrial Engineering from the School of Industrial Technology, Bradford University, England, in 1986. Since 1986, he has worked as an Assistant Professor, Associate Professor, and Full Professor with the Department of Production Engineering, College of Engineering, Helwan University, Cairo, Egypt. His bibliography is included in Marquis Who's Who in the World (14th ed., 1997). In 2000, he joined King Abdulaziz University (KAU) as a Full Professor with the Department of Industrial Engineering, College of Engineering. He was the Director of the College Academic Accreditation Unit (AAU) from 2004 to 2007 and an active member of the College Accreditation Support Unit from May 2007 to 2021. He was the manager of the Strategic Planning Unit at the Vice-Presidency for Business and Knowledge Creativity from 2017 to 2021. He also held the position of Distinguished Adjunct Professor at King Abdulaziz University from August 2021 to December 2023. He has been recognized as an IDEAL Scholar by the Accreditation Board for Engineering and Technology (ABET, USA) and earned 21 professional development hours from ABET. Dr. Abdelaal has participated in constructing and implementing strategic planning for several public and private organizations, and he has been involved in more than 30 training programs both inside and outside Egypt, including in Arab and foreign countries. He has served as an investigator/co-investigator for more than 35 funded projects and has received over 20 appreciation certificates from different sectors. Dr. Abdelaal was a Distinguished Adjunct Professor at AlMaarefa University from July 2023 to June 2024 and currently serves as an independent researcher based in Egypt. In 2025, he contributed a book chapter titled "The Strategic Transformation Journey of AlMaarefa University: Navigating New Horizons" as part of the book "Navigating Quality Assurance and Accreditation in Global Higher Education," published by IGI Global. His research interests and publications cover areas such as operations research, system analysis and design, strategic planning, industrial scheduling models, engineering education, multi-criteria decision-making, assessment, and accreditation subjects.

Mustafa Kayyali, Ph.D. is an ardent advocate for excellence in higher education, driven by a relentless pursuit of quality, recognition, and innovation. As the Manager of HE Higher Education Ranking, he leads initiatives that play a crucial role in shaping the landscape of academia. Having earned a Master's in Quality Management and Evaluation in Higher Education from Universitat

Oberta de Catalunya, followed by a Ph.D. in Quality Management from Azteca University, his academic pursuits have laid a strong foundation for his expertise in Accreditation, Quality Assurance, and Higher Education Rankings. Dr. Kayyali has made significant contributions to academic literature, boasting more than 50 published papers and 20 book chapters. Additionally, he takes pride in his role as a translator, having translated 5 books, thus bridging language gaps and promoting knowledge exchange on a global scale. In recognition of his expertise, Dr. Kayyali holds key affiliations with esteemed institutions. He is privileged to be a part of the British Accreditation Council's Accreditation Committee, the Slovenian Quality Assurance Agency as an International Expert, and the Agency for Control and Quality Assurance of Higher Education AKOKVO as an Accreditation Expert. His international engagements also include being an expert for the Kosovo Accreditation Agency KAA and the ECBE - European Council for Business Education, as well as serving as a Lead Auditor at the Centre of Assessments for Excellence (COAE). Dr. Kayyali has also submitted a patent to USPTO about rankings entitled Holistic & Multidimensional Ranking Methodology for Universities. As an entrepreneur, researcher, translator, and publisher, Dr. Kayyali is deeply involved in various facets of the academic world. His diverse interests encompass Management, Translation, Interpretation, and Academic Consulting, contributing to a well-rounded understanding of the industry.

***

Iftikhar Alam received MS and PhD in Computer Science from the Department of Computer Science, University of Peshawar, Pakistan. He is currently working as an associate professor of computer science at City University of Science and Information Technology, Peshawar, Pakistan. His PhD research is user/group modelling on smart TV for enhancing personalization services in general and recommendations in specific. His research interest also includes software engineering, recommender systems, user modelling, group modelling, smart TV, ubiquitous computing, web mining, search engines, augmented reality, and mobile-based systems for People with special needs. He published several articles in international journals and conferences.

Zulfiqar Ali was born in Pakistan. He received his Master Degree Localization and Internationalization, Deep learning, and Machine Learningfrom Kohat University of Science and Technology (KUST), and Ph.D. degree from Graz University of Technology, Austria. Currently, he is an Assistant Professor at City University of Science & Information Technology, Pakistan. His main area of research interest is related to software engineering, mobile applications and testing,

Daniel Opotamutale Ashipala (PhD) is a senior lecturer and Head of Department for the School of nursing and Public Health (SoNPH), General Nursing Science department in the Faculty of Health Sciences and Veterinary Medicine (FHSVM) at the University of Namibia, Namibia. His research interests include Primary health Care, Health care services and Nursing education, and Mental health. He has published a quite number of peer reviewed articles on the delivery of teaching and learning in higher education studies. He completed his PhD at Stellenbosch University in Cape Town, South Africa. His doctoral work focused on developing a framework to facilitate the implementation of a task shifting approach for nurses in the Namibia PHC services.

Andi Asrifan, S.Pd., M.Pd. is a senior lecturer in the Doctoral Program in English Language Education at the Graduate School of Universitas Negeri Makassar (UNM), Indonesia. With a Doctor of Education in English Language Education, he has demonstrated a consistent commitment to advancing research in English as a Foreign Language (EFL), digital pedagogy, and the integration of artificial intelligence (AI) in language instruction. Dr. Asrifan previously served as Head of the Institute for Cooperation and International Affairs at Universitas Muhammadiyah Sidenreng Rappang and continues to collaborate across academic institutions, both nationally and internationally, actively. Over the past two years, Dr. Asrifan has led several research initiatives focused on AI-driven curriculum development, bilingual education in Southeast Asia, and digital parenting in urban Indonesia. He is frequently invited as a keynote speaker at international conferences and serves as a reviewer and editorial board member for various Scopus-indexed journals. His publications have appeared in high-impact outlets and span the disciplines of education, linguistics, and cultural studies.

Raed Awashreh, a Professor of Management and Public Administration, has over 25 years of experience in academia and industry across NGOs, government, and the private sector. He has taught undergraduate and postgraduate students in the UAE, Oman, and the West Bank, supervised theses, and served as a postgraduate examiner and journal reviewer. He has published extensively on human capital, governance, education, management, policy, leadership, and AI applications. Beyond academia, he consults on strategy, governance, and organizational development. He holds a Doctorate from Flinders University, Australia, and a Master's from the Middlebury Institute, USA.

Rashmia S. Baraguir is a Licensed Professional Teacher and researcher specializing in Mathematics education. She is currently an Instructor I at Sultan Kudarat State University. She holds a Master of Arts in Education major in Mathematics from Notre Dame of Marbel University and a Bachelor of Secondary Education in Mathematics from Notre Dame of Salaman College. With extensive teaching experience at both secondary and tertiary levels, she has also served as Student Advisory Council Moderator from 2017 to 2018. Her academic and research interests focus on advancing mathematics instruction and student development. Skilled in documentation, facilitation, and computer applications, she communicates effectively in English, Filipino, Iranun, and Maguindanaon.

Donald A. Cogo is an Assistant Professor at Sultan Kudarat State University - Kalamansig Campus, specializing in Filipino language and literature. He has completed the academic requirements for a Doctor of Philosophy in Education, major in Filipino, at the University of Southern Mindanao. He also holds a Master of Arts in Education, major in Filipino, from St. Michael's College, Iligan City, and a Bachelor of Secondary Education, major in Filipino, from Sultan Kudarat State University. A licensed professional teacher, Cogo is also a literary writer whose works have been featured in various journals, including Kusina ng Talinhaga, Dreamers publishing services, and Pinagpala Publishing services. His research and literary contributions have been recognized and registered with the Intellectual Property Office of the Philippines (IPOPHIL) as author and co-author. Beyond academia, he serves as the provincial coordinator of Samahan ng mga Guro at Iba Pang Propesyonal sa Wika Inc. (SAGIP-WIKA). Passionate about preserving and promoting Filipino literature, he actively engages in community initiatives, conducting workshops for aspiring writers and delivering lectures on the significance of Filipino cultural narratives.

Dao Chanh Thuc Professional Title: Lecturer in Sports Science Affiliation: An Giang University - Vietnam National University, Ho Chi Minh City, Vietnam Education: Dr. Dao Chanh Thuc completed his doctoral program in Sports Science at the University of Sports and Physical Education, Ho Chi Minh City, Vietnam. His prominent research focused on the fields of physical education, sports training, and athletic performance. Career and Contributions: - Dr. Dao Chanh Thuc is a dedicated lecturer and researcher in the field of Sports Science. He is a faculty member at An Giang University - Vietnam National University, Ho Chi Minh City, where he has made significant contributions to the development of the sports science curriculum and research initiatives. - His expertise includes physical education, sports training, sports biomechanics, and the physiological aspects of athletic performance. - Dr. Dao Chanh Thuc has conducted numerous studies aimed at improving the physical fitness and performance of students and athletes. His work often emphasizes the importance of tailored training programs and the integration of modern scientific methods in sports training.

|Hamdo Ebrahim - Contributing Author|Dr.Hamdo Ebrahim, I very pleased to inform you that I hold a PhD in Mechanical Engineering, specialized in Composite Materials, from Idlib University, Syria, a Master's degree in Aeronautical Engineering from, and BA in Mechanical Engineering, specialized in Nuclear Energy, from Aleppo University. I have experience in academic teaching in various fields (Applied Mechanics - Production) during my journeys at the Universities that corresponded to my bachelor, master, and PhD degrees, The subjected that are in the circle of my interests are (thermal sciences, structural design, materials properties, and Artificial intelligence). Furthermore, I am currently working in Al Maaref University of Applied sciences as Dean of Mechatronics engineering, looking forwards for more and more academic contributions and having a wide knowledge in Mechatronics applications.

Sereyrath Em is a Cambodian government teacher of English with a higher education degree, a university lecturer, and an educational researcher with 18 years of experience in teaching, instructing, and lecturing. He holds three doctoral degrees: PhD in Educational Science, PhD in Educational Administration, and PhD in Cooperative Education. He currently serves as an Editor at the Cambodian Journal of Educational Research (CJER) and is the Founder and Editor-in-Chief of the Cambodian Journal of Educational and Social Sciences (CJESS). He also serves as a reviewer for many well-known journals and publishers such as IGI Global, Cogent Education, Frontiers, MDPI, Taylor & Francis, and Palgrave Macmillan, among other Scopus-indexed outlets. So far, he has published around 100 scholarly pieces in highly reputable journals and publishers.

Saddam Hossain is a doctoral researcher in English Linguistics at Khulna University, Bangladesh, where his PhD focuses on "Exploring the Synergy between Co-Curricular Activities and EFL Proficiencies in Shaping Holistic Development of the Students: A Study at Secondary Level in Bangladesh". His work critically engages with applied linguistics, English language teaching (ELT), and the intersections of co-curricular innovation, digital technologies, and adolescent development. Alongside his academic research, he holds the position of District Child Affairs Officer at the Bangladesh Shishu Academy under the Ministry of Women and Children

Affairs, where he contributes to the planning and monitoring of child-centered educational and developmental programs. Hossain holds advanced degrees in English Literature and ELT and has authored peer-reviewed journal articles and a book chapter exploring artificial intelligence in education, pedagogy, and applied linguistics. He has presented at national and international conferences and was awarded the Prime Minister's Education Assistance Trust Fellowship in recognition of his doctoral research. His academic interests include technology-enhanced learning, socio-emotional development, and sustainable pedagogy.

Andi Syarifah Irmadani, S.ST., M.Keb, is a lecturer and professional midwife at the Institute of Health Sciences Pelamonia Makassar, Indonesia. She earned her Master's degree in Midwifery from Universitas Hasanuddin and holds a Diploma IV in Midwifery Education from Universitas Mega Rezky Makassar, along with a Diploma III from the Pelamonia Midwifery Academy under Kodam VII/Wirabuana. With over nine years of experience in maternal health and midwifery education, she began her career at Puskesmas Segeri in Pangkep Regency (2015–2016) and later served as a program manager at the Aisyah Midwifery Academy (2017–2018). Since 2021, she has been actively involved in academic teaching, research, and community service at the undergraduate midwifery program of Pelamonia Institute. Her scholarly interests include antenatal care, maternal nutrition, pregnancy risk detection, and technology-based health education. She has authored several scientific articles, including works on family planning, anemia, chronic energy deficiency, and the use of digital media in maternal health education. As an advocate for evidence-based midwifery practice and digital innovation in maternal care, she continues to contribute to improving women's health outcomes and advancing midwifery education in Indonesia.

Juvrianto Chrissunday Jakob is a dedicated English lecturer at the Civil Engineering Department of Ambon State Polytechnic, Indonesia. With a strong academic background and a passion for education, his areas of expertise encompass Teaching English as a Foreign Language (TEFL), integrating Technology in Language Learning, Discourse Analysis, and English for Specific Purposes (ESP). These fields reflect his commitment to equipping students with language skills tailored to their professional and academic needs. Juvrianto holds a master's degree in English Education from Universitas Negeri Makassar, Indonesia, where he honed his skills in pedagogy and research. His scholarly pursuits focus on exploring innovative teaching methodologies and the application of modern tools in language instruction, ensuring his teaching methods align with the evolving demands of education in the digital era. Beyond his role as a lecturer, Juvrianto is an active contributor to academic communities. He serves as a tutor and language instructor, helping learners enhance their English proficiency. His dedication to academic excellence is further evident in his role as a reviewer for several local and international journals, where he evaluates and supports the dissemination of research in his field. Juvrianto's professional journey is driven by his belief in lifelong learning and his desire to foster effective communication skills in students and professionals alike. His contributions to the intersection of language, technology, and education underscore his impact as an educator and scholar.

K. Gayathri, working as Associate Professor in the Department of Physics, Academy of Maritime Education and Training, Chennai

Md. Shahjahan Kabir is a professor and head of the English Discipline at Khulna University. With a strong passion for teaching English language, linguistics, and literature, he excels in motivating diverse students. His research interests include ELT, linguistics, CALT, CALL, TALT, MALT, MALL, curriculum, poetry, and drama.

Youmei Liu received her Doctor of Education in Curriculum and Instruction focusing on instructional technology in 2003 from the College of Education at the University of Houston (UH). She has been serving as a Director of Assessment and Accreditation Services since 2011. Before assuming this position, she worked as an educational production specialist and an instructional designer. She is also an adjunct faculty at the Jack J. Valenti School of Communications at UH, and has been teaching Information and Communication Technology course for over 20 years. Dr. Liu functioned as a conference chair for the Society of International Chinese Educational Technology (SICET) and the Chinese American Educational Research and Development Association (CAERDA) in the US. She has rich research experience and has numerous publications in the areas of quality course design, innovative use of educational technology, distance education and mobile learning, cross-cultural communication, and social capital development in e-learning and social media platforms.

Bitan Kumar Mandal is an Additional Deputy Commissioner (Senior Assistant Secretary) at the Office of the Deputy Commissioner, Khulna, Bangladesh. He is engaged in public administration, local governance, and development coordination, with experience supporting multi-sectoral initiatives related to community resilience, disaster management, social protection, and service delivery. His professional work includes facilitating government–community partnerships, supervising field-level program implementation, and strengthening institutional processes for effective public service.

Sooraj Kumar Maurya is a distinguished scholar and Assistant Professor in the Department of Philosophy at Zakir Husain Delhi College (Evening), University of Delhi. He completed his B.A., M.A., and D.Phil. in Philosophy from the University of Allahabad, where his doctoral research examined the ethical discourse on affirmative action in Western philosophical traditions. With a deep grounding in classical and contemporary philosophy, Dr. Maurya brings a critical lens to questions of justice, rights, and socio-political transformation. Dr. Maurya's academic oeuvre comprises over 35 peer-reviewed publications, including articles in Scopus-indexed journals and UGC-CARE-listed platforms, covering a wide spectrum of themes in normative ethics, political philosophy, feminist theory, philosophy of law, and applied ethics. He has authored and co-edited books on topics ranging from digital education to socio-economic challenges, and has contributed chapters to prestigious international volumes published by Springer, Routledge, and Wiley. His forthcoming monograph, The Ethics of Affirmative Action: Balancing Equality and Fairness (Apple Academic Press, CRC Press, Taylor & Francis Group, 2026), critically engages with contemporary debates on equality and public reasoning in democratic societies. Beyond his publications, Dr. Maurya has served as Managing Editor of the International Journal of Applied Ethics and actively participates in national and international seminars, editorial boards, curriculum development, and faculty training programs. His scholarship stands at the intersection of philosophy and public policy, offering normative clarity on issues such as justice, equity, and rights in a complex and evolving world.

Musdalifah is a dedicated educator and researcher specializing in English language teaching, academic writing, and assessment in ELT. She obtained her Bachelor's, Master's, and Doctoral degrees in English Education from Universitas Negeri Makassar, Indonesia. Her academic journey is complemented by extensive teaching experience, particularly in English for Specific Purposes (ESP) and English for General Purposes (EGP), across various institutions. She has actively participated in numerous international conferences and workshops, including the 15th Asia TEFL Conference and the International Seminar on Motivation and Motivating Practices in Teaching and Learning in collaboration with the University of Leeds. She has also been a speaker at several academic events, presenting research on English language pedagogy, learning strategies, and ESP curriculum development. Musdalifah is a prolific researcher with publications in Scopus-indexed and nationally accredited journals. Her notable works include studies on the implementation of Number Heads Together (NHT) to enhance vocabulary learning and ESP curriculum development for nursing students based on needs analysis. She is an active member of TEFLIN and Asia TEFL, contributing to the advancement of English language education. Her current research focuses on integrating Artificial Intelligence in ESP curriculum and bilingual approaches to English for Educational Technology.

Vinodh N is currently pursuing his PhD as a Research Scholar at Saveetha School of Management, SIMATS, Saveetha University, Chennai. Concurrently, he serves as an Assistant Professor in the MBA Department at St. Joseph College of Engineering, Chennai, Tamil Nadu, India. He earned his Master of Philosophy (M.Phil) degree from Sri Venkateshwara University, Tirupati, and holds an MBA from Madras University, Chennai. With over Seventeen years of teaching experience across various esteemed educational institutions in Chennai, Mr. He exemplifies a strong commitment to academia and scholarly research. His contributions to the field are underscored by his publications in SCOPUS indexed journals

Fransisco Chindongo Ntjamba is a registered nurse holding a Bachelor of Nursing Science Clinical, (Honors') from the University of Namibia, School of Nursing and Public Health, General Nursing Department in the Faculty of Health Sciences and Veterinary Medicine (FHSVM). He is a NIMART-trained & a Provider Initiated Testing and Counseling (PITC NURSE), specializing in sexual reproductive health and focusing on HIV testing, prevention, treatment initiation, and ongoing care. In addition to his qualifications, Fransisco is an academic researcher who has published research studies in nursing education, mental health, and interdisciplinary innovations, including Artificial Intelligence on human healthcare. His career is defined by a commitment to advancing healthcare through both direct patient care and research, with key interests in Primary Health Care, healthcare services, nursing education, and mental health. He is dedicated to improving healthcare through evidence-based practices and community outreach initiatives, particularly in HIV prevention and treatment.

Rachel Anne S. Nuñez, LPT, PhD, is a faculty member of the Teacher Education Department at Notre Dame University, where she also serves as a research coordinator. She earned her Bachelor of Secondary Education major in English from Notre Dame University, and later completed her Master of Arts in Education major in English and Doctor of Philosophy in Educational Administration at Cotabato State University. With over a decade of teaching experience in senior high school and tertiary levels, she has likewise extended her expertise internationally by teaching English as a Second Language to Japanese learners. She previously served as Program Head of the Bachelor of Arts in Communication and the General Education Department at STI Cotabato, and actively contributed as research coordinator, school coordinator of STI Tagisan ng Talino, and adviser of Speaktacle Campus Connection, the institution's digital news outlet. She was awarded a research grant from International Alert Philippines and the Notre Dame University Research Center and Publication Center. She has presented her studies in various academic conferences, including the Hybrid Second Annual International Conference on Religion, Culture, Peace, and Education held at Payap University in Chiang Mai, Thailand in 2023, and the 1st Madayaw International Multidisciplinary Research Conference at San Pedro College, Davao City in 2018. Her scholarly work has also been published in the Global Scientific Journals (GSJ Publisher).

Dina Pen, head of the library and an assistant professor of the Faculty of Social Science, Faculty of Arts, Humanities, and Foreign Language of Svay Rieng University, Svay Rieng, Cambodia. He is also the Head of the Advisory Board of the Cambodia Journal of Educational and Social Sciences (CJESS). His main research interests in higher education include job satisfaction and motivation, quality assurance, qualification framework and public administration, political science, gender equity, women in politics, and policy. He has not only published extensively in international journals and book chapters on education but also reviewer

R. Swadhi working as Additional Coordinator, Academic and Examination Cell, Saraswathi Institute of Medical Sciences, Hapur, Uttar Pradesh. She Comleted her Ph.D. in the Department of Physics, AMET University, Chennai.

R. Vettriselvan, an Associate Professor, AMET University, specialized in HRM and Marketing. He is acting as Mentor, Saraswathi Institute of Medical Sciences, Hapur. He served as Review Board member, National Council for Higher Education, Malawi, Head of the Department, School of Commerce and Management Studies, St. Eugene University, Zambia, and Director, Research and Publication, St. John the Baptist University, Malawi. He has published 28 books and 86 articles in peer reviewed journals and edited book chapters. Under his guidance two have completed and five are pursuing their PhD.

Rismawati Sudirman is a distinguished academic and consultant with a robust focus on sustainability reporting. She currently holds the position of lecturer and Head of the Quality Assurance Institute at Universitas Muhammadiyah Palopo, where she has been pivotal in ensuring the quality of university processes and outputs since February 2020. Additionally, she serves as an Assurer for Sustainability Reporting at the National Center for Sustainability Reporting in Jakarta, specializing in the evaluation of sustainability reports for mining companies across Indonesia. Her academic qualifications are extensive, comprising a Bachelor's degree in Economics and Accounting, a Master's degree in Accounting Science, and a Doctorate in Accounting from Universitas Brawijaya, Malang. Rismawati is also a certified specialist in sustainability reporting, risk management, and tax planning, holding several prestigious certifications including Certified Sustainability Reporting Specialist (CSRS) and Certified Risk Management Practitioner (CRMP). In her professional capacity, she has provided consultancy services in financial management and tax compliance for companies such as PT. Reski Barito Timur and PT. Helay Raya. Furthermore, she has authored multiple publications on taxation and management, contributing significantly to the academic community. Her interests in reading, writing, and travel reflect her commitment to lifelong learning and professional growth in her field.

S. Kumaresh, Working as Assistant Professor in School of Management, Hindustan Institute of Technology and Science, Padur, Chennai. Having 13 years of teaching experience in India and 5 yrs of Research Experience. Published 15 research papers in various reputed international refereed Journals, 4 papers in Scopus, 4 papers in UGC Care, bestowed Best Paper Award in various International Conferences. He is Certified Soft Skill Trainer and Training to given various stream of students to enhance their soft skills

Gopukumar S. T is working as an Research Associate Professor in the Department of General Surgery, Saveetha medical college and Hospital, Saveetha University, chennai. He have more than 15 years of experience in academics and have published more than 100 publications. He has sound knowledge in Bioinformatics, Homoeopathy and Nanotechnology.

Fahad Salendab is a scholar and leader in the field of higher education, holding a Ph.D. in Educational Administration. As a Licensed Professional Teacher and Associate Professor, he has dedicated his career to advancing the quality of education through research, teaching, and leadership. A multi-awarded faculty member, Dr. Salendab is recognized for his outstanding contributions to education, research, and institutional development. He is a registered author with the National Book Development Board (NBDB). His commitment to research is further reflected in his role as Regular Member of the DOST-National Research Council of the Philippines, where he collaborates on initiatives that address critical issues in education and development. As an active participant in accreditation processes, Dr. Salendab ensures the continuous improvement of academic programs, demonstrating his dedication to quality assurance and institutional growth.

Rany Sam is the Vice-Rector of the National University of Battambang (NUBB), a public university in northwest Cambodia, which he joined in 2008. He has been the Cambodian Director of the Confucius Institute at the National University of Battambang since 2019. He is a member of the Southeast Asia Research Academy (SEARA) and a country director of the Society of Transnational Academic Researchers (STAR) Scholars. He received his PhD in Education from the School of Educational Studies at the University of Science Malaysia (USM) in 2016. In 2017 and 2022, he graduated from the Royal School of Administration in Cambodia with diplomas in public administration, leadership, and innovation programs. He graduated with a Bachelor's and Master's Degrees in Law (LL.B & LL.M) at the Royal University of Law and Economics (RULE), Cambodia, in 2004 and 2007, respectively. For his key achievement, he has published 80 academic papers and book chapters; he is also a project coordinator and member in various projects, including 10 Erasmus+ Capacity Building in Higher Education, 1 Korean ODA, 1 USAID, and 1 World Bank-funded Higher Education Improvement Project (HEIP). His email address is samrany82@gmail.com/sam.rany@nubb.edu.kh, and his mobile phone number is +855 (92) 646-680.

Mardy Serey is an associate professor at Svay Rieng University, Cambodia.

Amrik Singh is an assistant professor in CUHP. he is an academician from last 4 years. he has 15 patents and ample of book chapters and research paper.

A. K. Subramani holds a Ph.D. in Business Administration from Manonmaniam Sundaranar University, Tirunelveli, India, and has over 19 years of teaching experience. He has published 80 research articles in international journals, including two in the ABDC-A category, ten in ABDC-B, two in ABDC-C, 38 in Scopus-indexed journals, and ten in Web of Science-indexed journals. He has also presented papers at various national and international conferences. He has completed more than 35 courses through the Swayam online platform in human resource management, business analytics, and intellectual property rights. He has earned several NPTEL Star recognitions, including Evangelist, Motivated Learner, Enthusiast, and Discipline Star. He serves as a peer reviewer for reputable journals published by Inderscience and Emerald. His research interests include human resource management and organisational behaviour. He has been honoured with the Teaching and Research Excellence Award and the Distinguished Teacher Award – Management.

Muhammad Usman Tariq has more than 16+ year's experience in industry and academia. He has authored more than 200+ research articles, 110+ case studies, 150+ book chapters and several books other than 4 patents. He is founder and CEO of The Case HQ, a unique repository for courses, narrative and video case studies. Additionally, he is President of Gulf Higher Education (Gulf HE) focused on advancing academic practice. He has been working as a consultant and trainer for industries representing six sigma, quality, health and safety, environmental systems, project management, and information security standards. His work has encompassed sectors in aviation, manufacturing, food, hospitality, education, finance, research, software and transportation. He has diverse and significant experience working with accreditation agencies of ABET, ACBSP, AACSB, WASC, CAA, EFQM and NCEAC. He is a Principal Fellow of Advance HE UK, Senior Fellow of SEDA UK, and Chartered Fellow of CIPD UK other than Senior Member IEEE.

Farhana Yeasmin has been a faculty member in the Department of English at Jashore University of Science and Technology since 2017. She holds a PhD in English from Khulna University, specializing in Technology-Assisted English Language Testing. Her research interests include language teaching, testing, policy, curriculum design, and world literature.

Index

A

C

D

E

F

G

H

I

L

M

V

www.ingramcontent.com/pod-product-compliance
Lightning Source LLC
LaVergne TN
LVHW061533290926
849162LV00004B/777